Abortion in the Developing World

Abortion in the Developing World

editors

Axel I. Mundigo
Cynthia Indriso

World Health Organization

Zed Books
London • New York

Abortion in the Developing World
is published in South Asia by Vistaar Publications (A division of Sage Publications India Pvt Ltd), Post Box 4215, New Delhi – 110 048, India, and in the rest of the world by Zed Books Ltd, 7 Cynthia Street, London N1 9JF, UK, and Room 400, 175 Fifth Avenue, New York, NY 10010, USA, in 1999.

Distributed in the USA exclusively by St. Martin's Press, Inc., 175 Fifth Avenue, New York, NY 10010, USA.

A catalogue record for this book is available from the British Library.

US cataloging-in-publication data has been applied for from the Library of Congress.

ISBN: 1 85649 649 X (Hb)
ISBN: 1 85649 650 3 (Pb)

Cover design by Bharati Mirchandani.

To
the women, all over the world,
who unselfishly agreed to be interviewed
and discuss a highly sensitive personal issue

Axel I. Mundigo

Contents

List of Tables

List of Figures

Foreword

I can never forget an encounter in my early professional practice, more than 35 years ago. I was on clinical duty in the emergency room, when a young woman was admitted in extreme distress and agony. On pelvic examination, it was with a sense of shock that I found her intestines in the vagina. It turned out that she had had a botched abortion, during which the uterus was perforated and the intestines were mistaken for the products of conception and pulled down into the vagina. Her life was saved by emergency surgery but her uterus had to be removed. When she recovered, I ventured very gently to ask her why she did that to herself. I still recall hearing her weak voice answering with another question: Do you doctors understand what it means to a woman to have an unwanted pregnancy? It was only recently that we began trying to understand.

The abortion issue has been the subject of intensive debate among men: legal scholars, moralists, men of religion and politicians. The voices of women have been drowned in this loud debate despite the fact that it is women whose bodies, psyche, health and life are directly concerned. Everyday, hundreds of women lose their lives in the process of trying to terminate an unwanted pregnancy under unsafe circumstances. Few studies have ventured to explore why women are pushed to take this dangerous course.

It took conviction and courage to consider an international initiative to improve our understanding about the problem of unsafe abortion, its underlying causes and its consequences in women's lives. The World Health Organization was best suited to take this initiative, with its assets of objectivity, concern about health and the trust of member states. The Social Science Research Unit of the Special Programme of Research, Development and Research Training in Human Reproduction had the professional expertise and the reputation for research excellence essential for the success of such a major research initiative.

The initiative was announced in 1989. What came as a pleasant surprise to many of us at the time was the vigorous response of the international scientific community, and the positive attitude of member states across all cultures. The Unit was overwhelmed by good research proposals from all regions of the developing world.

The debate in the Cairo International Conference on Population and Development in 1994 and in the Beijing Fourth World Conference on Women in 1995 finally highlighted the need 'to recognize and deal with the health impact of unsafe abortion as a major public health concern'. The debate was not easy. Some people seem to think that if you move yourself away from a problem that you dislike, shut your ears to the sounds of pain, and close your eyes to the sights of sufferings, the problem will no longer exist.

For someone concerned about women's health, and as a former director of the Special Programme, it is gratifying to see the outcome of these case studies on abortion enter into the public domain. I hope it will improve the understanding, particularly among policy makers, about the plight of women faced with difficult reproductive health choices, when they are not empowered to make decisions that respect their dignity and save their lives and their health.

MAHMOUD F. FATHALLA
Senior Advisor, Biomedical and Reproductive Health Research
The Rockefeller Foundation; and
Former Director of the UNDP/UNFPA/WHO/World Bank Special Programme of Research, Development and Research Training in Human Reproduction, World Health Organization

Preface

Unsafe induced abortion, particularly in countries where the practice is illegal, is an important contributor to reproductive ill-health and to maternal deaths, all events that are fully preventable. In developing countries where abortion is legal, the services are often concentrated in urban centres and unsafe abortion continues to exist in rural and remote areas. For women who have access to legal abortion services, induced abortion is often used as a back-up for contraceptive failure or as an alternative to effective contraception, even when family planning is readily available. In other countries where family planning access is limited and health service infrastructure generally poor, induced abortion may be the only alternative for women who want to space their pregnancies or do not wish to have another child. The reasons for resorting to abortion vary from one context to another across developing as well as developed countries.

The WHO Special Programme of Research, Development and Research Training in Human Reproduction, aware that induced abortion was a major reproductive health problem and the cause of untold suffering for many women around the world decided, early in 1989, to undertake a pioneering effort to understand the determinants or reasons why women resort to abortion in various cultural, social and service availability contexts. Another aspect of induced abortion for which information was lacking concerned the consequences of unsafe induced abortion for women, especially for their health status and emotional wellbeing. To this effect, through its Task Force for Social Science Research on Reproductive Health, the Special Programme announced a research initiative on the determinants and consequences of induced abortion aimed at developing countries.

The Special Programme of Research in Human Reproduction was in a particularly strong position to undertake research on such a sensitive issue— being an integral part of WHO lent the right health profile to the initiative and being a scientific research programme of worldwide renown made it possible to deal with induced abortion above the usual controversies caused by religious and political ideology. In fact, when the plans for the research initiative were presented to the World Health Assembly, in May 1989, not a single country opposed it.

The announcement of the research initiative on induced abortion coincided with an External Evaluation of the Special Programme which among other recommendations stated that 'reproductive health research must be placed in its social, cultural and behavioural context' noting also that 'these aspects must be given greater attention in the future'. These recommendations further endorsed the importance of the initiative whose objectives were precisely to understand women's reproductive health behaviour within their own social and cultural context and, especially, to gain a better insight into the relationship between abortion and contraceptive behaviour.

Acknowledgements

This book would not have been possible without the cooperation of women all over the world who volunteered to answer questions about one of the most intimate dilemmas of their reproductive lives—the decision and circumstances under which they opted to end a pregnancy. Our thanks go to them as well as to the researchers, in particular those who wrote the chapters for this book, and their committed interviewers who often worked under extremely difficult field circumstances, asking questions that required tact and patience, devotion and understanding. Our thanks go also to the Special Programme of Research, Development and Research Training in Human Reproduction of the World Health Organization that provided the financial and technical means to carry out the research, analyze the data, and write up the results. The Colegio de Mexico, a leading graduate training and research centre in Mexico City was host to the first Workshop on Research on Induced Abortion, held from 13 to 17 November 1989, that marked the beginning of the research initiative by congregating the principal investigators of the winning projects to discuss issues of research planning and methodology pertaining to their forthcoming work. We are very grateful to the authorities of the Colegio de Mexico who provided us with an ideal academic environment and the necessary support to hold a very successful workshop. Similarly, at the conclusion of the research, the Universidad Externado de Colombia hosted a major conference, from 15 to 18 November 1994, that allowed the Latin American researchers to present their results in an international forum and share their experience with representative policy makers. We would like to express our gratitude to the rector and staff of the university for their unfailing support.

While it would be difficult to name all the persons who at various stages contributed to this research initiative, it would be appropriate to name the technical advisors that participated in the Colegio de Mexico workshop and provided excellent lectures and research guidance to the participants: Dr Lourdes Arizpe, Colegio de Mexico, Mexico; Dr Wendy Baldwin, National Institute of Child Health and Human Development, Washington, D.C., USA; Mrs Margaret Bone, Office of Population and Surveys, London, England; Lic Gustavo Cabrera, Colegio de Mexico, Mexico; Dr Mercedes Concepcion,

University of the Philippines, Manila, Philippines; Dr Tomas Frejka, then Population Council, Mexico; Dr Sylvia Hartman, Pan American Health Organization, Mexico; Dr Lorenzo Moreno, Office of Population Research, Princeton University, USA; Dr Yolanda Palma, Ministry of Health and Social Assistance, Mexico; Dr Thomas Pullum, University of Texas, Austin, USA; and Dr Erica Taucher, National Institute of Nutrition, Santiago, Chile.

Special thanks go also to Dr Iqbal Shah, Special Programme of Research in Human Reproduction, Geneva, Switzerland, who not only attended the Mexico workshop but also provided substantive advice over the several years of the initiative's progress and supervised the last details leading to the publication of this book. Mr Jitendra Khanna who dealt directly with the publishers and followed up the process of publication also deserves special thanks. Ms Maud Keizer, the secretary of the Special Programme's Social Science Research Unit, who typed the manuscript and many difficult tables, also deserves our gratitude.

THE EDITORS

1

Introduction

Cynthia Indriso and Axel I. Mundigo

Abortion-Related Morbidity and Mortality: The Global Picture

Induced abortion is an ancient practice, experienced by women of all backgrounds in every part of the world. Among the issues related to reproductive health, none has more controversial connotations than abortion nor carries a heavier burden of stigmatization, including moral and religious condemnation. Its exact incidence, therefore, as well as that of abortion-related mortality and morbidity is still difficult to establish.

Nonetheless, the data that are available demonstrate that induced abortion is very prevalent in the developing world, despite the fact that contraceptive prevalence rates have increased dramatically in the last 30 years. Although the frequency and distribution of abortion vary, there is no country where abortions do not occur. Recent estimates for developing world regions provide an overall figure of around 30 million induced abortions annually, broken down as follows: 3.4 million in Africa (high range estimate); 11.9 million in East Asia; between 5.2 and 12.5 million in South and South-East Asia; and between 4.4 and 6.2 million in Latin America. This means that of all births averted by either contraception or abortion, up to one-third are averted by induced abortion in Africa; up to 22 per cent in East Asia; between 11–23 per cent in South and South-East Asia; and between 21–28 per cent in Latin America (Frejka, 1993).

Many estimate that the incidence of induced abortion is increasing worldwide. Reasons for this increase are attributed to a variety of changing trends worldwide, including a desire for smaller families, shifts from rural to urban residence, and the increase in non-marital sexual activity (Coeytaux et al., 1993).

The Need for Safe Abortion

In many countries in the developing world, induced abortion is illegal and therefore, largely unsafe. Of the 20 million unsafe abortions that occur each year in the world, some 70,000 result in death, representing a case fatality of 0.4 per 100 unsafe interventions. The highest levels of case fatality are in Africa (0.6) and Asia (0.4), with a much lower rate in Latin America (0.1). Similarly, the risk of dying from an unsafe abortion is much higher in the developing world, 1 in 250 procedures, than in the developed world, where the figure is only 1 in 3,700 procedures. In fact, most of the unsafe abortions that occur in the world today, close to 90 per cent, occur in developing countries (WHO, 1994). Death is not the only tragic cost of unsafe abortion. Many more women survive the experience, only to suffer lifelong consequences of serious complications. Sepsis, haemorrhage, uterine perforation, and cervical trauma often lead to problems of infertility, permanent physical impairment and chronic morbidity.

Even in countries where abortion is permitted by law, safe services are not available to all women. In the former USSR and India, for example, where abortion is allowed, many procedures are still performed outside the legal and formal health system, resulting in high numbers of unsafe abortions. Out of all illegal abortions, it is estimated that about 25 per cent occur in Latin America, 25 per cent in the former USSR, 13 per cent in India, and 10 per cent in Sub-Saharan Africa (Dixon-Mueller, 1990; Henshaw and Morrow, 1990; WHO, 1991).

When restrictions on abortion are lessened, the number of abortion-related deaths and mortality decrease, owing to the greater availability of safe procedures performed by trained health professionals. In the United States, for example, death rates due to abortion fell by 85 per cent in the five years following legalization (Tietze, 1981). In the example of Romania, the abortion law was made more restrictive in 1966, and by 1984, the number of abortion-related deaths had increased by 600 per cent. When abortion became legally available once again in 1990, abortion mortality fell by 67 per cent in the first year (Romania Ministry of Health, 1991). Experience from other countries also confirms that legalization of abortion does not result in increased abortion rates, it only changes the conditions under which abortions are performed.

Despite the evidence that allowing abortion on liberal grounds reduces morbidity and mortality risks from induced abortion, only 22 per cent of the 190 countries in the world have abortion laws allowing it on request. Even countries such as Finland and the United Kingdom only offer abortion when it is justifiable for health as well as economic and social reasons. And the gap between developed and developing countries is very marked when we observe the reasons under which abortion can be legally performed. In over 80 per cent of the developed countries, for example, abortion is permitted not only to save the life of the woman, but also to preserve the physical health of the woman, to preserve her mental health, in the case of rape or incest, and when there is foetal impairment. Yet in developing countries, these reasons are much less accepted by the legal system; for example, only 26 per cent of these countries allow abortion in the case of rape or incest and only 23 per cent allow it in the case of foetal impairment. Only 6 per cent of the world's developing countries allow abortion on demand, among them Albania, China, Cuba, the Democratic Republic of Korea, Tunisia, Vietnam and most of the new countries emerging from the former USSR. But for the most part, in entire regions of the developing world abortion remains outside the law. In Africa, for example, safe abortion is not an option for most women. And it is the poorest women in all countries who bear the brunt of this unequal access to safe abortion services (United Nations, 1994).

It must also be emphasized that legalization of abortion is a necessary, but not sufficient, condition for reducing the number of unsafe abortions. The many descriptions in this volume of women who resort to self-induced abortion or abortion performed by unskilled providers, even when it is permitted by law, attest to the need to make safe abortion services much more accessible. Health care systems must learn how to respond to liberal laws with the appropriate administrative and structural support.

The HRP Research Initiative

In consideration of the fact that induced abortion continues to result in needless deaths and serious illness to the poorer women in the developing world, the Task Force for Social Science Research on Reproductive Health of the Special Programme of Research, Development and Research Training in Human Reproduction (HRP) launched a major research initiative in 1989 on the determinants and consequences of induced abortion, with a focus on developing countries. Emphasis was given to projects from countries where abortion laws were restrictive, although some studies were supported in countries where abortion was legal, but services were not always accessible nor of good quality.

The primary goal was to increase the knowledge base on the reasons why women seek abortion, even in contexts where family planning services are widely available and where abortion is punishable by law. Given the known difficulties of conducting large-scale surveys to assess induced abortion incidence, the Task Force also decided to support projects that offered new methodological insights and appeared to be feasible for application to large communities (e.g., the study in Colombia by Zamudio). Attention to the relationship between abortion and contraceptive behaviour, as well as to the consequences of induced abortion for the wellbeing of women were also important criteria for project selection.

The decision to launch this research initiative was made during a critical time, following the 1984 Mexico World Population Conference, where abortion had taken centre stage in an ideologically charged public debate. Eventually, the HRP proposal received strong and full endorsement from its donors as well as from the World Health Assembly. More recently, the 1994 United Nations International Conference on Population and Development in Cairo and the Beijing Platform for Action endorsed at the UN Fourth World Conference for Women in September 1995 has recognized unsafe abortion as 'a major threat to the health and lives of women' and called for the promotion of 'research to understand and better address the determinants and consequences of induced abortion, including its effects on subsequent fertility, reproductive and mental health and contraceptive practice as well as research on treatment of complications of abortions and post-abortion care' (United Nations, 1995: para 110[i]).

It is hoped that these research studies undertaken in different political, economic, social and cultural contexts will assist in meeting these goals and provide information useful for policy makers and for strengthening the public dialogue in countries where women's health advocates are working towards legal reform and normative change in the health codes to de-penalize abortion.

Part I: Between Abortion and Contraception

The complexity of the relationship between contraceptive needs and behaviour and the use of induced abortion remains, for the most part, unexplored territory in reproductive health research. For most women in the developing world, where abortion is usually illegal and unsafe, contraception would seem to offer a better fertility regulation option. Yet the research findings in this book bring to light the extensive use of induced abortion in many developing countries, even in those thought to have good family planning programmes, such as Mauritius, Mexico and Colombia.

All the studies in this section link induced abortion to a sizeable gap between effective contraceptive use and childbearing intentions. In the Nepal study, unplanned pregnancy accounted for 95 per cent of induced abortion among women, but the majority of them were not using contraception. In the Dominican Republic, scarcely 25 per cent of women were using a contraceptive method when they became pregnant unintentionally. In the Colombia study, 79 per cent of unwanted pregnancy was due to the non-use of contraception. Even in China, where contraception is easily and widely accessible, both Gui and Luo Lin et al., in their studies, find that non-use of contraception is a primary reason for unwanted pregnancy and abortion. The other studies paint a similar picture.

These studies also point to the serious unmet need for safe and effective ways to limit or space births not only among non-users of methods, but also among women who are using some form of contraception. High rates of contraceptive failure, for example, were found in places where contraception has been legally and widely available for decades. In the China study by Gui, IUD in situ is the overriding reason for contraceptive failure; this is in a country where IUD users constitute 85 per cent of total users of reversible methods (Ping, 1995). Similarly, the study in China by Luo Lin et al. demonstrated a high method failure rate of 37 per cent; of these, an astonishing 65 per cent were IUD users. In the Cuba study by Alvarez, it was found that three out of every four women who had an abortion in the last 12 months were using a modern method of contraception. High failure rates are also reported in the Colombia and Dominican Republic studies.

Also emphasized is the fact that non-married women, not just married women, have an unmet need for family planning. And as we will discuss in detail in Part III, the unmet need for contraception among adolescent girls is a serious reproductive health problem that is on the rise.

In their search for explanations, the researchers in this volume challenge us to look more closely at how reproductive decisions are made and how such decisions are influenced by equally relevant, but less-researched aspects of contraceptive behaviour, such as women's and men's expressed views and concerns regarding contraceptive methods and services that are offered to them, gender relations, and the economic and cultural forces associated with sexual activity and pregnancy.

Exploring the Gap Between Contraceptive Need and Use

Although contraceptives have become more widely available in recent decades, a sizeable proportion of people who want to manage their fertility are not able to do so freely, effectively, and in a way that they consider safe. It is now widely recognized that an emphasis on demographic objectives during the early phases in the development of many family planning programmes worldwide, without adequate consideration of the conditions that encourage people's use of them, has helped create the existing gap between contraceptive need and use. There is a growing body of literature that documents the failure of many family planning programmes to deliver user-friendly services, free of coercion and pressure, and respectful of the informational needs and personal preferences of the people who need to use them (Ross and Frankenberg, 1993).

Information Giving

The enormous gulf between what services consider the appropriate information to be given to clients and what women and men feel they need to know in order to select the right method for their particular needs and to use it effectively is a major contributing factor to the existing gap between contraceptive need and use. As well illustrated by these studies, most women and men surveyed had not been educated about methods in a way that respects their right, as well as their capacity, to choose a contraceptive method themselves.

Many of these studies show that the notion of method 'knowledge' commonly applied in national surveys seems to be a poor indicator of whether women actually know how to use a method. Typically, the respondent is reputed to 'know' a method merely if she or he can state it or recognize it when it is mentioned. In fact, no or insufficient information on how to actually use a method seemed characteristic of most women's experiences in these studies.

In the Dominican Republic study, reported method 'knowledge' among the women is sometimes higher than that of the general population. There was also a considerable degree of prior use as well as current use of methods among the women in the sample; in fact, they had more contraceptive experience, on an average, than the general population of women in the country. The author concludes, however, that one of the major determinants of unwanted pregnancy is a lack of knowledge among women and men about human reproduction and about the characteristics, correct use and possible side effects of methods. The study found, for example, that only 25 per cent of the women who have used the pill know how to use it correctly. The author points out that about 60 per cent of pill users nationwide buy their supply over the counter in pharmacies, although the study group experience indicates that obtaining the pills in a clinic or public hospital does not ensure that a woman will get appropriate medical screening, counselling and follow-up either.

This same gap between so-called knowledge and information was found in the Turkey study by Akin. Here, authors concluded that the use of withdrawal is a primary determinant of abortion, which they attribute to, among other factors, poor knowledge of other methods of contraception. It was found that men and women rely mostly on friends and relatives for information about methods rather than on health personnel. The Colombia study also concludes that lack of information about more effective methods and how to use them contributes to the practice of induced abortion.

Similarly, the Cuba study concludes that contraceptive failure results, in part, from the fact that women's understanding of how methods actually work is much lower than their more general knowledge of methods. In a country with such an extensive network of health services, the author discovered that the main source of method knowledge was a female friend; a woman's informal social network played a much more decisive role in the way she understood how the various methods work. The reason for repeat abortion among the women in the Nepal study was that they were unaware of the risk of conception following abortion.

In Gui's study in China, among users, reasons for failure included wrong calculation of the safe period and wrong use of pills. The large majority of these Chinese women who experienced contraceptive failure said that health personnel in their local family planning units were not well-qualified and should share the responsibility for what happened; they said they received poor guidance from them on how to master the use of various methods. Three out of every four women whose unwanted pregnancy was due to non-use of contraception declared that family planning workers in their places of residence knew nothing about their contraceptive status, or were indifferent, or did not provide any guidance. The study in China by Luo Lin et al. also attributed contraceptive failure and non-use to misinformation and lack of information.

User Views on Method Safety and Effectiveness

Studies about method acceptability increasingly point out the need to consider women's and men's perceptions and concerns about method side effects and safety. The studies in this section help illustrate the importance of this. In Nepal, for example, reasons for non-use among women who aborted because they did not want more children included a fear of side effects, which was found to apply to all hormonal methods available, including Depo-Provera, Norplant, the pill and the IUD. Women preferred either to expose themselves to unwanted pregnancy (a risk they were largely unaware of) or to wait for a convenient time to undergo sterilization. The Dominican Republic study also revealed that side effects and health concerns are associated with the low and ineffective use of the pill as well as its discontinuation. The main reason given by women for non-use of methods in the China study by Gui was that 'contraception is troublesome'. In Turkey, Akin found that strong fears about the side effects of modern methods was a principle reason for their non-use.

These studies also reveal that even though the great majority of women who seek abortion can also be very motivated to regulate their fertility, and have a high level of method knowledge and experience, their perception of the effectiveness of the method offered to them is not always in harmony with the definition of effectiveness that researchers, programme planners, and policy makers alike apply to methods. The widespread use of withdrawal in many countries is a good example of this fundamental difference in perspective. Its use is completely confidential, not requiring a physical examination or contact with a clinic or pharmacy and it has no economic costs. It has the added advantage of not being associated with any proven health concern or serious side effects, particularly impairment of fertility. It also provides a flexibility—an immediate reversibility—that many couples seem to value highly. These are all factors that contribute to the method being 'effective' in the minds of many of the men and women who use it, while many family planning professionals tend to view this method as ineffective and therefore discourage its use.

Method effectiveness in the minds of users is also seen to be weighed against socioculturally and politically acceptable reproductive behaviour and norms. In the Dominican Republic study, for example, method use is shown to be based on the expectation of ending the reproductive cycle, often at an early age, by means of sterilization once the desired family size has been reached. In fact, 88 per cent of the women in the sample did not initiate contraceptive use until after the birth of their first child. Women's contraceptive practices in China reflect limitations imposed on them by the government's policy to control family size. As a result, women's choice of a method is primarily restricted to provider-controlled methods, mainly the IUD after first birth and sterilization after the second (Ping, 1995). As Luo Lin et al. note, not all contraceptive use is truly voluntary; some women would like to have a larger family and this feeling naturally affects use effectiveness. The Turkey study by Akin showed that ignoring women's culturally based preferences for female providers to perform IUD insertion, and for more accessible services, was found to contribute to the use of less effective methods.

Resolving the disharmony between viewpoints about method effectiveness may lie in a greater recognition of the fact that fertility regulation is not a timeless strategy. These studies help to emphasize that the use of contraception is not a single decision that is made only once, by women alone, usually at the beginning of their reproductive life—or worse, only at the start of married life—with only small adjustments made after that. The seeming mind-changing and ambiguity in fertility regulation behaviour in the form of 'discontinuation' and 'switching' is actually evidence of how strongly motivated women and men are to adapt the existing reality of available contraceptive options to their real-life fertility regulation needs and preferences. In many cases, for example, women in these studies whose more traditional fertility regulation practices failed to meet their needs shifted to the use of modern methods. Many women whose first method was a modern one were seen shifting to a more traditional one when side effects were too problematic. Many women worldwide use more than one method; and they may mix or alternate methods, sometimes within short periods of time. Withdrawal, in particular, has been found to be commonly used with other methods (Rogow and Horowitz, 1995).

Unfortunately, women's and men's changing contraceptive needs, mixed with incomplete information about available methods and intermittent or poor quality contraceptive supplies, bring about unwanted pregnancy. The experience of abortion following method ineffectiveness or failure subsequently pushed many women towards the use of modern, longer-acting, and even permanent methods of fertility control. This decision was often made in spite of any preference they had for more short-term or traditional methods of fertility regulation, especially in the early part of their reproductive lives.

Equally distressing is that many women, when left only with the choice between uncomfortable side effects or method failure, can become pessimistic about the usefulness of contraception and simply stop using any method at all. In the Mauritius study, in a country noted for its good family planning services, the author concludes that the low use of reliable methods and non-use reflects the women's 'lack of confidence in all family planning methods'. Gui concludes in his study on China that women's perception of contraception as 'troublesome' also reflects their lack of confidence in the methods available and how they work. Similarly, in the Dominican Republic study, the low-income women's experience led the authors to feel that only surgical steriliza-tion and celibacy provide any real assurances against unwanted pregnancy; modern methods may work, but they are always a risky proposition.

Gender Dynamics

Until recently, studies of contraceptive behaviour and needs largely ignored gender dynamics in sexual relations and reproduction. Some of the studies in this section illustrate that the choice and acceptability of a fertility regulation method is strongly influenced by the preferences and pressures of other peo-ple in a woman's life, particularly her sexual partner.

A primary reason for non-use of contraception in the Nepal study was opposition from a woman's husband. This study also revealed that many women were under pressure from their husbands and in-laws to get pregnant in spite of what they themselves wanted to do; they explained that their mar-riage was unstable and that their husband would bring a second wife to the household if they did not produce a child. This threat had even compelled some women to have a subsequent pregnancy immediately after a spontane-ous abortion. In Mauritius, a number of women resorted to abortion because of their husband's refusal to use a family planning method. In short, women lacked decision-making power vis-à-vis their fertility regulation behaviour.

Method discontinuation was partly attributed to the husband's disapproval in the Dominican Republic study. The author notes that the three most popu-lar methods—withdrawal, periodic abstinence and condoms—demand a degree of bargaining power vis-à-vis their male partners that very few Domin-ican women possess. Information from the study sample showed that low-income men are reluctant to take on direct responsibility for the choice of a modern method or its use—such a role runs contrary to prevailing male atti-tudes in this culture.

The use of withdrawal in Turkey was thought by the researchers to be a reflection of the preference, among both women and men, for men to domi-nate in decisions about the choice of fertility regulation methods (including abortion); and men had a clear preference for withdrawal. Men's knowledge of contraception, particularly modern methods, was also found to be lower than women's. Moreover, male dominance in the fertility decision-making process was linked to a woman's self-esteem. For example, women who thought that men are generally more intelligent than women, that men have a right to beat their wives, and other views that indicated low self-image tended to use effective contraception less, have fewer induced abortions, and have a higher than average fertility than women who did not agree with such views.

When women worked for wages outside the home, they used more modern methods and had fewer pregnancies, in both the urban and rural samples of women. The author concludes that a woman's greater control over economic resources seemed to outweigh the influence of traditional cultural values that place men in a more dominant decision-making role within the household.

Several studies elsewhere have shown that social support from husbands is important for continued contraceptive use (PATH, 1989). Studies conducted in African and Islamic countries have shown that programmes involving husbands contribute to the successful use of modern contraceptives (cited in Trottier et al., 1994: 289). In a study of first-time use of DMPA (Depotmedroxyprogesterone) among rural women in Bangladesh, those whose husbands approved of family planning had significantly longer use durations than those whose husbands disapproved (Riley et al., 1994).

In another example of gender relations analysis, the China study by Gui in this section considered the influence of sexual satisfaction between a couple on the non-use of contraception. Women and men who discussed their sexual life with one another 'often' and were mutually satisfied, had a lower level of non-use of contraception. Non-use was highest among women and men who 'never' discussed issues relating to their sex lives. Similarly, non-use of contraception was nearly twice as high among women and men who 'never' discussed contraception with one another compared to those couples who 'often' talked about the use of methods. The author also concludes that the correct use of more traditional methods, such as rhythm, seemed to be based on the quality of inter-spousal communication about sexual and contraceptive behaviour. For example, couples who 'sometimes' or 'never' engaged in 'discussion of how to use contraceptives' had the highest proportion of 'wrong calculation of the safe period'.

Do Women Rely on Abortion as a Contraceptive Method?

The fear that women tend to replace contraception by abortion and that the availability of abortion results in decreased motivation to use contraception has been expressed by a number of researchers and policy makers as well as by opponents of more liberal abortion laws. It is a belief that often serves as an obstacle to more widespread de-penalization of abortion in many places.

Several of the studies in this volume provide some evidence that the reason women seek abortion is not their preference for abortion over contraception, but rather the poor quality and accessibility of suitable contraceptive methods and services. Again, we see that it is actually a strong desire to control fertility using available contraception that actually lies behind so much method switching, discontinuation, and even apparent non-use of methods among women who experience unwanted pregnancy and then seek abortion.

In the Slovenia study, for example, which looked closely at the possible relationship between available and safe abortion services and the use of 'less effective' methods, nearly all the women who had an abortion had used contraception either steadily or during a limited period of time prior to conception and at conception. The sample was divided almost evenly between women who used a more effective method and women who used a less effective method or no method at all. The women in this latter group, however, did not realize that they were exposing themselves to a high risk of getting pregnant at the time. This is supported by the fact that they had above average contraceptive use and half of them reported that they thought the method they were using was an effective protection against pregnancy. The author suggests that easy accessibility of abortion did not reduce a woman's motivation to use contraception; abortion was used as an emergency measure when contraception had failed.

The Cuba study also emphasizes that women choose abortion with reservation, even where it is legally and easily available on demand. The author found that the predominant attitude of women, regardless of whether or not they have abortion experience, is that of ambivalence. This is in contrast to their attitude towards contraception, which is highly positive.

The often agonizing moral and ethical dilemmas that women face in deciding how to handle an unwanted pregnancy are described throughout this volume, and attest to the general reluctance of women to have an abortion, regardless of whether it is legal or not. In fact, sterilization is often the preferable solution of many women in these studies to any further risk of unwanted pregnancy and abortion, especially among older women.

Conclusions

Whatever the complexities of the relationship between contraceptive realities and abortion behaviour, all the studies call for general improvement in the quality of reproductive health services as a way to reduce the need for abortion. In the Colombia study alone, the findings suggest that one-fifth of all abortions could be avoided by improving access to higher quality contraceptive information and services.

The importance of individual and ethical counselling that respects women's and men's reproductive rights, including their ability to make their own decisions about which method to use and when, their sexual practices, and their concerns about side effects and health risks, cannot be underestimated. There is also an urgent need to make available a wider range of methods to allow users greater freedom to choose what suits their needs best.

More fundamentally, these studies illustrate that services need to be reoriented in a way that recognizes that women and men are responsible actors and decision makers, very much involved in their reproductive destinies. Fertility regulation also needs to be recognized as a dynamic process.

Research Gaps

In order to facilitate such a change and create reproductive health services that truly respond to people's fertility regulation needs, the following areas of research need to be explored and considered more carefully.

Gender

We are nowhere near a comprehensive understanding of how gender shapes reproduction in different cultural contexts and at different moments in a woman's reproductive life. Much more gender research is needed. It is a powerful tool for exploring the influence of male–female differences and disparities in the area of fertility behaviour. Such an approach recognizes the importance of power and negotiation within the sexual relationship, answering critical questions such as who has input into contraceptive decision-making and how the differences in women's and men's access to and control over resources influence fertility behaviour.

Method Acceptability

There is a need to identify more precisely the qualities that are believed to determine whether a contraceptive is acceptable, including both modern and traditional methods. More method-specific information is needed on what are perceived as method side effects by women and men and what constitute their health concerns within different social and cultural contexts. What do they consider a safe and effective method, for example? It is also important in research to differentiate between the fear and anxiety felt by users, which is possibly due to a lack of clear and complete information, and their actual experience with methods.

Both men and women need to be included in this research, which should focus on user views, particularly as they relate to the temporal structure of their reproductive behaviour and needs. To what degree the quality and modes of service delivery influence method acceptability must also be part of the process of identifying women and men with unmet needs.

Emergency Contraception

Recently there has been a surge of interest in adding 'emergency contraception', defined as methods used immediately after unprotected intercourse to prevent unwanted pregnancy, to the list of fertility regulation options. The technology used, such as the Yuzpe regimen (combined estrogen–progestogen therapy) and postcoital insertion of an IUD, has been available for about 30 years, and both these techniques can be made easily available as part of routine services (van Look and von Hertzen, 1993). More recently, the use of mifepristone as a method of emergency contraception is being studied (Klitsch, 1991).

The results of these studies would seem to support making such an approach more widely available, given the high rates of method failure and ineffectiveness. It is essential, however, that researchers, programme planners, and policy makers all keep a firm distinction in their minds between emergency contraception and early medical abortion. A distinct moral and ethical difference in women's minds can be found between preventing unwanted pregnancy and terminating a pregnancy that has been confirmed, which should be respected. Other considerations, particularly the biomedical ones, are certainly beyond the scope of this chapter.

Part II: The Quality of Abortion Care

Evidence shows that the quality of reproductive health care services is a key factor in an individual's or couple's ability to initiate and sustain the use of fertility regulation methods and the essential elements of high quality care are now widely recognized (Bruce, 1990; WHO, 1995b). High-quality care is also about accessibility: the largest number of people must be able to benefit from it, which means that they must understand how to obtain it.

In the case of abortion, the quality of care received often means the difference between life and death. In a context where abortion is restricted, the thin line between the two is drawn at the point of treatment for life-threatening complications. Unfortunately, most medical facilities in developing countries are unprepared to deal with cases of botched abortion and those that are equipped are also usually overburdened. Many women get referred, without receiving any treatment from providers, to other hospitals a great distance away. Elu draws the conclusion that most of the Mexican women in her study could have received better care if the health providers had been more compassionate and well-trained and the facilities better equipped, regardless of whether women had 'institutional rights' to them. Elu's study in Mexico also emphasizes that 'access' to abortion cannot be resolved by physical proximity. It means an approach to the situation that answers women's own perceived reproductive health care needs in a way that is consistent with their values and way of life, with an understanding of the complex cultural values that support its existence.

These studies highlight the need to focus more directly on the needs and preferences of the women who seek abortion as well as on the attitudes and skills of the providers of abortion services, in order to improve the quality of abortion care. All women who seek abortion, no matter how poor or uneducated, deserve to have their concerns and situations as individuals addressed with care and compassion. Similarly, the concerns and perceptions of providers must also be explored and understood, particularly in situations where abortion is illegal and the law does not distinguish between treatment of an incomplete abortion and actually performing one.

What is especially unique about this group of studies is that they illustrate that the quality of abortion care needs to be addressed, regardless of the policy context. Certain fundamental elements of abortion care that profoundly affect women continue to be widely neglected, even in places where safe abortion is widely available.

Women's Experiences of Abortion

In a broad sense, the studies included in this section, like the studies in Part I, reinforce the failure of family planning programmes to effectively respond to women's needs and desire to control their fertility. Non-use of contraception among these women was high, as was contraceptive failure. In the China study by Zhou, for example, a number of women felt angry and betrayed because modern methods of contraception had failed them, particularly the IUD. Gender relations appears again as a significant contributing factor to explain unmet need. In Elu's study in Mexico, for example, some women never used contraception, stopped using contraception, or got pregnant at the request of their male partners, who later changed their minds or refused to take responsibility for the pregnancy. Other women became pregnant without their male partner's knowledge in the hope of strengthening an unstable relationship, but later had to abort because the man did not want the child.

Understanding of Abortion Safety and Risk

A characteristic that marginalizes women who seek abortion, particularly those who resort to clandestine procedures, is their apparent lack of concern or awareness of the risks involved in the procedure. Some information was revealed about the ways in which women who confront an abortion actually understand and define the notion of safety. To what degree, if any, did their perception of safety influence their decision to abort?

In the countries where abortion is legal and more accessible, as in China and Turkey (and Cuba, studied in Part I of this book), medical safety and the risk of the abortion procedure emerges as an expressed concern of the women. Women wanted, and expected, the provider to be competent. It is important to note how women define competency; in Turkey, women judged a provider to be skillful if the procedure was quick and painless for them. In contrast, where abortion is restricted, a concern for safety seemed a luxury that most women literally could not afford. These women had a more fatalistic attitude towards the situation, accepting that without economic resources to pay the high price for a safe procedure, they could do nothing but submit to a clandestine procedure while praying for 'luck' to be on their side.

The link between the quality of abortion care and the economic situation of women is particularly well illustrated by Elu in Mexico. The stories of the desperate attempts at self-induced abortion by married women, who risked leaving several children and a husband behind, are particularly powerful. The use of misoprostol (also known as cytotec, a drug used to treat ulcers) by two-thirds of the women in the Brazil study by Misago is described as a cheap way for poor women to circumvent the tight restriction on legal abortion. Fortunately, most of the women sought hospital care soon after bleeding started, which resulted in a lower rate of complications than those found among women in previous studies.

The Nepal study (Part I) found a positive relationship between the educational level and occupational status of a woman's male partner and her use of safe abortion services. Women whose male partners had a higher educational level and higher paying jobs visited private clinics more for safer abortions, which are more expensive, than women whose partners had lower educational and occupational status.

Actual knowledge of different medical abortion techniques and their possible risks was low to nonexistent among almost all the women, including among those who had a safe and legal procedure. The China study by Zhou, for example, revealed widespread myths among women about whether the procedure was harmful to subsequent reproductive health and its effect on future pregnancy. In the Turkey study by Bulut, most women were unsure about which method had been used for their abortion. And in the Cuba study (Part I), again in a context where safe abortion is legal and accessible, nearly 40 per cent of the women had only a vague idea or did not know what the actual procedure for abortion was. Also, a high proportion of women expressed a fear of becoming infertile; and one in 10 women worried that an abortion might lead to death.

Abortion Information and Counselling

In its simplest form, counselling is the provision of information about the abortion procedure, to help a woman feel more relaxed beforehand. At its best, abortion counselling recognizes that the experience belongs to a continuum of events that are inextricably linked to a woman's sense of identity as a sexual being, her self-esteem and her future. As a source of in-depth psychological and emotional support, such counselling helps a woman to confront her situation and her feelings about her sexual life in order to 'break the cycle of reproductive risk-taking behaviour' (Londoño, 1989). As Elu illustrates in her study of poor women in Mexico, the concept of unwanted pregnancy is not as simple as it would appear. The 'desire' for a pregnancy is not necessarily conscious or rational and it is rarely contemplated in advance. Counsellors must have compassion and respect for the internal and external conflicts the experience of deciding to abort an unwanted pregnancy creates in most women's lives.

Neither simple counselling nor more empowering and in-depth support was offered to the great majority of the women in the studies throughout this volume. Women in the Turkey study by Bulut described a lack of individual attention from providers and said they felt 'rushed'. Several women pointed out the need for pre-abortion counselling services, such as screening for health problems, discussion of how and why the pregnancy occurred, and information on what to expect during the abortion procedure, including information about the type of method being used. Some women also expressed a desire to have a choice of abortion technique.

Pain Management

Whether and to what degree women who undergo abortion experience pain is usually not a priority among abortion care providers, particularly in a context where the procedure is usually unsafe to begin with. In almost all the studies in this volume, concern about serious morbidity and mortality from unsafe procedures easily outweighed all other concerns among women, researchers and providers alike. Nonetheless, pain has been shown to rank high on the list of women's concerns when they confront the prospect of an abortion. It is also an aspect of abortion that can have profound implications for a woman's future sexual wellbeing.

Both these points are well illustrated in the China study by Zhou, where abortion has been legal and accessible to all women for decades and therefore the complication rate from the procedure is shown to be minimal. (See also the two studies by Luo Lin et al. in this volume). But the degree of pain women experienced was, by their own accounts, overwhelming. One woman even chose to carry a subsequent unwanted pregnancy to term to avoid the pain of another abortion. Many women also mentioned that they experienced subsequent and serious psychological anxiety towards coitus as a result of the experience. Similarly, a very high percentage of women surveyed in both hospital settings in the Turkey study by Bulut also experienced pain and found the procedure 'difficult', even though other medical complications, such as bleeding, were found to be minimal.

Post-Abortion Family Planning Counselling and Services

Women who have just had an abortion need information that facilitates informed choices about how to control their fertility, as all the studies in Part I illustrate. The urgent need to establish closer links between family planning and abortion information and services is also reflected in these studies, where post-abortion counselling was rarely offered to women to help them avoid another unwanted pregnancy.

In the China study by Zhou, all the women who had an abortion, especially those with a history of abortion, very much longed for safer and more effective contraceptive methods. In the Turkey study by Akin (Part I), only one-third of the women who had an abortion received counselling or information about family planning methods, irrespective of whether the procedure had been performed in a public hospital or by a private doctor. In the Nepal study (Part I), none of the 1,241 women who had just had an abortion were aware that they could soon be at risk of conception when they were discharged from the hospital/clinic. The study team noticed that clinicians made no effort to provide post-abortion family planning counselling.

The women who sought abortion in the study in Turkey by Bulut expressed their strong desire to learn more about family planning methods; and the majority rated post-abortion family planning counselling as poor. An interesting finding with important service implications is that the more educated women in this study were more successful at 'extracting' information from their providers than less educated women. It appeared that a woman had to ask for and insist on information, which takes a certain amount of self- confidence. The use of modern methods six months after the abortion was shown to be much higher, 80 per cent, where family planning and abortion services were more integrated, compared to women who had abortions at the health facility where the two services were completely separate, at 36 per cent. The women's rating of overall quality of care they received, while generally low in both hospitals studied, was ranked significantly higher in the hospital where abortion and family planning services were linked.

Unfortunately, an established connection between abortion services and family planning services, including systematic referral, were lacking in all the other studies, whether abortion was legal or not. There also seemed to be some hints of provider bias in the provision of methods to women who have just had an abortion and also some provider disagreement about the timing of post-abortion contraceptive use. Although none of the research focused on specific problems encountered, it is clear that the gap between contraceptive need and use was not addressed in any effective way during this critical time in a woman's reproductive life. Other important studies have also found a serious neglect of post-abortion contraceptive services (Benson et al., 1992; Neamatalla and Verme, 1995).

Provider Beliefs, Attitudes and Technical Competence

Provider–client interaction, in addition to the technical competence of the providers, is now widely recognized as an essential component of quality care. What has been less well considered is that this same element must also be present to achieve quality abortion care. Moreover, there is an important sociocultural dimension to this interaction.

While other studies in this volume also highlight the importance of provider skill and views in abortion care (see, for example, Elu on Mexico and Zhou on China), the unique contribution of this group of studies is that they call particular attention to the way that the beliefs and attitudes of health care providers are brought to bear on the care and treatment of a woman with an unwanted pregnancy. They also remind us of the simple fact that health care workers in all parts of the world, regardless of legal and social sanctions, are frequently called upon to provide care for women undergoing, or who have undergone, abortion.

As with the studies about women's experiences of abortion, the influence of abortion policy on the quality of services and on the health of women is evident in these research projects, where abortion was a criminal act or severely restricted in each of the settings studied. In fact, almost all providers in each of the studies noted that unsafe abortion is a major health problem in their country.

Belief versus Action

To what degree, if any, do the personal views and religious beliefs of providers affect their treatment of women who need abortion care? A possible negative impact on the health of women is suggested by the study in Sri Lanka by Hewage, where it was found that a conservative attitude on the part of the providers—61 per cent disapproved of contraception for non-married women—could be contributing to the occurrence of unwanted pregnancy. Similarly, 41 per cent of these providers said that abortion was on the increase in their country because women were 'ignoring social values'. Clearly, for some of these health providers, a more humane approach to abortion presented an ethical and moral conflict between their personal beliefs and their clients' rights and wishes. (It should be noted that these providers worked in government facilities, mainly hospitals—not the so-called 'private sector', where most illegal abortions are performed.) Similarly, other research has demonstrated that some providers have a harsh and punishing attitude towards women who have multiple abortions (Neamatalla and Verme, 1995).

In the other three studies in this group, however, personal belief and behaviour on the part of the providers were not so easily harmonized. In fact, stated opinion was often contrary to action. Here, it is important to note that all three study samples comprised or included providers from the nonformal sector, such as traditional birth attendants (TBAs), who have the closest contact with women in the communities and therefore more likely to come face-to-face with requests for abortion as well as the life-threatening complications of self-induced or unsafe, illegal procedures. The research conducted by Cadelina in the Philippines shows that in spite of the fact that the great majority of TBAs said they did not approve of abortion, primarily for religious reasons, and laws were restrictive, a significant number of them admitted that they gave women information on abortion methods and on how to locate abortionists; some admitted to performing abortions themselves. Similarly, in the Indonesia study by Djohan, where attitudes of both formal and nonformal sector providers generally seem opposed to abortion, again because of religious beliefs and restrictive laws, some midwives said they assisted ob-gyn doctors who performed abortions; and half of the midwives said they would actually perform an abortion. Also, some TBAs accompanied women to a clinic for abortion. In Mexico, Pick shows that although market herb vendors had more stated negative views towards women who wanted an abortion than pharmacists, they were more likely to provide an abortifacient.

What makes so many of these providers act contrary to strong personal beliefs and/or risk criminal punishment? In Indonesia, the willingness of qualified health care providers to finally assist a woman who requests an abortion seemed ultimately practical. It is better to help a woman than to have her go to an untrained person. In Mexico, Pick explains that provider beliefs about abortion do not have a predictable impact on their actions because the issue is surrounded by a tremendous amount of guilt, which causes a lot of ambiguity in speech and action. Offering abortifacients to women is also an important source of income for these vendors. In the Philippines, some of the vocal opposition to abortion expressed by the TBAs is attributed not to their actual personal opinion but to their growing reputation as abortionists, which diminishes their social standing in the community.

Conclusions

The obvious starting point for quality abortion care is to ensure that all women have access to a safe procedure. These studies also clearly point to the need to re-think how women who seek an abortion should be treated and the kind of information they need to be given in order to truly address their reproductive health needs, both physical and emotional ones.

Individual, personal attention to each woman who seeks an abortion is essential. Counselling that explains the details of the abortion procedure can help reduce anxiety considerably and is a key factor in women's overall satisfaction with abortion services. Efforts should be made to do whatever is possible to minimize the level of pain women may experience during an abortion. As Luo Lin shows in her larger study (Part I), pre-abortion counselling can significantly lower stress and depression levels among women who have an abortion; and other studies have shown that pre-abortion psychological counselling and a sensitive and compassionate staff can greatly minimize the need for analgesic and anaesthetic drugs (Nasser, 1989; Stubblefield, 1989). As Zhou suggests in his study, the availability and use of appropriate anaesthetic techniques and skills of application should be improved in China. Bulut suggests that women in Turkey be given a choice of anaesthetic techniques. A choice of abortion techniques should also be offered wherever feasible.

Post-abortion contraceptive counselling is also a critical factor to women's overall satisfaction with services. In Turkey, the study by Bulut concluded that contraceptive counselling before the procedure is also helpful. Such information and services must be provided in a responsible and ethical way. As Bulut points out, while IUD insertion immediately after abortion may be the easiest method for providers to offer, it must be accompanied by appropriate counselling. Follow-up is also essential.

Integrate Services

It is essential that abortion care be linked to family planning services in order to reduce the need for abortion, particularly where it is illegal or not easily accessible. In these situations, women are unlikely to get family planning services from clandestine providers and thus remain vulnerable to additional unwanted pregnancies and repeat unsafe abortion.

In general, maternity hospitals or clinics that offer care to women with abortion complications resulting from unsafe procedures should also have facilities that provide these women with post-abortion family planning services. If that is not possible, upon discharge, women should be referred to family planning services where they should receive special attention. Better referral systems that alert family planning providers to the case situation should be tested and implemented, but always with the priority of preserving the privacy and anonymity of the woman. Similarly, closer attention should be paid to the provider side, including their training, attitudes and understanding of the problem. For example, family planning and abortion providers should be trained together and work collaboratively. Research has found that their training is often different, with the result that abortion providers are not necessarily well-informed about contraceptive methods and advances; and conversely, family planning providers may know little about abortion techniques and the appropriate conditions for immediate post-abortion contraception (Neamatalla and Verme, 1995).

The unique study in Chile by Molina and his colleagues gives an example of what can be accomplished when services are well-integrated. When women determined to be at high risk for abortion had individual discussions in private and in their homes about their contraceptive needs and preferences with a supportive counsellor, their use of contraception increased noticeably and abortions in the community declined. In the control study community where no intervention had taken place, abortion ratios increased by 30 per cent.

Provide Wider Access to Safe Medical Abortion

The obvious need for safe, accessible and affordable methods of pregnancy termination requires a closer study of the different possible approaches to safe medical abortion by biomedical scientists. In some of these studies, the suggestion for easier access to medical abortion was made by the women themselves.

The use of mifepristone for medical abortion was raised often as a topic of discussion among both the women and providers in the study by Zhou in China and suggested as a way to avoid the psychological harm of too much pain and reduce the possible medical risks associated with surgical procedures, such as dilatation and curettage (D&C).

In the Mauritius study, where abortion is ruled a criminal act, the use of misoprostol (cytotec) to induce abortion was reported by 36 per cent of women, as high as the use of crude methods such as inserting bicycle spokes, jumping from heights, massage and herbs. The author cites this as an example of how Mauritian women will quickly adopt a new method of pregnancy termination that promises to be safer and more effective than other available methods. The widespread and illegal use of cytotec was also reported in the Brazil study by Misago, where again, abortion is tightly restricted and a safe procedure is too expensive for most women. The author also notes, albeit cautiously, that the use of cytotec reduced the complications of induced abortion found in other studies. Another recent study on the use of cytotec in Brazil confirms that its main advantage for women is that it is relatively inexpensive compared with other available methods. Women in this study also felt that it made the abortion experience less traumatic because it reduced the often agonizing delay between the decision to abort and the event itself, with administration possible in private without a trip to the clinic. The drug's influence in reducing the complications of unsafe abortion found in other studies was also confirmed (Barbosa and Arilha, 1993). Another recent study has found a combination of methotrexate and misoprostol to be a safe and effective alternative to invasive methods for the termination of early pregnancy (Hausknecht, 1995).

Interesting research on women's views on the experience of medical abortion in Stockholm revealed that nearly half the women commented spontaneously on the relief they felt when they realized that they were going to have a medical abortion, rather than a surgical one (Holmgren, 1994). As the author describes: 'To them a surgical procedure meant that someone would operate inside very fragile parts of their bodies, which they found threatening.' This same study also found that women described an 'ethics of care'; it was important that their abortion be performed as early as possible.

Improve the Provider Dimension

These studies present a strong case for letting family planning workers and abortion providers at the primary care level play a role in efforts aimed at reducing the practice of unsafe abortion. In the Philippine study, for example, traditional practitioners, despite their use of unsafe methods, are more popular than medical doctors throughout the country, mostly because they are less expensive and women are assured of complete confidentiality. It is suggested that their role be utilized in reducing unsafe abortion; for example, by improving their skills in counselling women about sexuality and contraception. In the Indonesian study, the role of the nonformal health sector providers (TBAs and PLKBs) remains central in caring for the women that the formal sector does not help. Educating and training these health workers could be an effective way to reduce levels of unsafe abortion. In the Sri Lanka study, 78 per cent of the respondents recommended the family health worker (FHW), a woman who visits households regularly, as the best person to handle a sex education programme at primary and secondary school levels. Pick suggests educational programmes for pharmacists and market herb vendors in Mexico, preferably as part of wider training on reproductive health and family planning. Such training could encourage providers to treat women more humanely, discourage the ineffective use of widely prescribed metrigen and the dangerous use of quinine, and emphasize the importance of providing clients with accurate information about family planning methods so that repeat abortion is prevented.

While these studies highlight the role of nonformal health personnel, doctors in the formal health sector, particularly obstetricians–gynaecologists, also need to take part in ensuring that safe abortion services are readily available. Training in the management of botched abortion must also be a part of their responsibilities. It cannot be assumed that obstetricians–gynaecologists know how to perform a safe abortion. In many countries, including developed ones such as the United States, many obstetrician–gynaecologists are not trained in the application of modern abortion techniques, let alone in the management of incomplete abortion (Pick, this volume; Rosenfield, 1994).

Regarding technique, the older method of D&C is more commonly used in developing country settings, although it has a higher complication rate and requires more modern and costly surgical facilities, which further limit the availability of abortion services (Sundstrom, 1993). In fact, replacing D&C with vacuum aspiration (VA) and manual vacuum aspiration (MVA) has been shown by several studies to be an easy and immediate way to make abortion and the treatment of incomplete abortion safer and much more accessible (Baird et al., 1995; Coeytaux et al., 1993). Other studies have also demonstrated that the technique of MVA early in gestation (also referred to as menstrual regulation), can be used by specially trained paramedicals and is effective, inexpensive and accepted by women in rural areas (Sundstrom, 1993). Bulut concludes that her study in Turkey supports women's preference for menstrual regulation, with its advantages of provision by non-medical personnel and no need for anaesthesia. No matter which technique is used, provider training on how to lower psychological stress before the procedure must also be given.

As these studies make clear, provider attitudes are powerful determinants of women's experience of abortion and their acceptance of post-abortion contraception. It is important to find ways to ensure that the general attitude of health personnel at all levels be sensitive to women's needs and empowerment, regardless of the personal attitudes towards abortion of the providers themselves.

Research Gaps

Generally, little attention has been given to what makes women comfortable, both physically and psychologically, as they go through the experience of induced abortion. Women's views and provider skills regarding different abortion techniques and types of pain management need to be studied in various settings, particularly the use of menstrual regulation. As just mentioned, safe methods of medical abortion should be thoroughly explored by biomedical experts.

The appropriateness and content of post-abortion family planning counselling and services need to be defined more carefully. Is counselling more useful to women before or after the abortion? When is it appropriate for women to start various methods of contraception following abortion? More method-specific information needs to be gathered, with close scrutiny of how the provider dimension is affecting the situation: Which methods are more commonly offered in different settings and why? Does post-abortion counselling consider a woman's recent contraceptive experience leading up to the unwanted pregnancy? What is her attitude towards resuming sexual activity? Careful attention to provider–client interaction is needed, particularly the way that providers may be influencing a woman's right to free and informed choice about contraception post-abortion. Provider bias and coercion tends to be a particular problem in cases where women have had a repeat abortion.

Part III: Adolescent Sexuality and Abortion

About one-fifth of the people of the world, more than one billion, are adolescent, usually defined as those aged 10–19 years (WHO, 1995c). It is estimated that more than 50 per cent of the world's population is below the age of 25, of whom more than 80 per cent live in the developing world (United Nations, 1993). With respect to sexuality, the lower age is normally defined by puberty, while the upper age is more a sociocultural boundary than a physiological one, with marriage traditionally signalling entry into adulthood.

Yet it has only been relatively recently that the health of adolescents and young people has been recognized as an important focus of attention. This has come about largely as a result of mounting evidence that they are increasingly sexually active and the trend for unwanted pregnancy among them is also on the rise (Fathalla et al., 1990; Senanayake and Ladjali, 1994).

It is not difficult to understand why adolescent sexual activity often leads to unwanted pregnancy. Their access to sex education and family planning information and services is the exception rather than the rule in most parts of the world, and as a result, the majority lack knowledge about the basic reproductive functioning of their bodies and about the power and meaning of their emerging sexuality. As revealed by Ehrenfeld's qualitative study in Mexico, 'the vagina seemed not to exist' for many of the girls who had recently aborted. They were completely ignorant about female anatomy and physiology. They had little or no knowledge of contraception and most had become pregnant just after becoming sexually active. In Mpangile's study in Tanzania, a total of 89 per cent of the women, aged 17 years or less, knew nothing about either modern or traditional methods of contraception. As the author points out, this is undoubtedly related to the fact that contraceptive use by students is prohibited by school regulations and single women and adolescents are not welcome in family planning clinics in Tanzania. These findings are supported by larger studies of contraceptive use among adolescents (United Nations, 1989). Adolescents face obstacles to obtaining contraceptives such as parental or spousal consent, specified minimum age, and the requirement of marriage—reflecting religious and cultural concerns that seek to prevent premarital sexual activity.

The study in Korea by Kwon provides an example of how the interplay of gender relations and self-image, and sociocultural norms and expectations influences adolescent sexual behaviour as well. Although 79 per cent of the girls interviewed said they knew about contraception, more than 80 per cent of them had not used any contraception during their first sexual experience. Most had worried about getting pregnant at the time, but hesitated to use any contraception because they feared their male partner would label them a 'bad quality girl'. In fact, the non-married girls who regarded themselves as 'virtuous' were those least likely to use contraception, not because they were ignorant, but because to do so would have contradicted their moral self-image. Another example is found in the Mexico study. All the girls, except one, said they had first intercourse at their boyfriend's request, and 98 per cent had not used contraception at the time. As one girl explained: 'It is not something you think about, for who can think at that moment? Love is what counts.' Also significant is the finding in this study that formal unions were established as a consequence of a girl becoming pregnant, and not from an expressed desire to formalize a relationship.

The influence of sociocultural norms and expectations is also shown clearly in the China study by Luo Lin et al. Although contraceptives are freely or inexpensively available over the counter in China, 93 per cent of the unmarried sample of young women seeking abortion said that neither they nor their partners had used contraception at the time the woman got pregnant. These non-married women reported that they felt too embarrassed to seek contraception at a pharmacy or at the local family planning clinic, illustrating how a strong social stigma against premarital sexual activity can effectively prevent the use of contraception.

Young girls who decide to carry their unplanned pregnancy to term usually face insurmountable difficulties, particularly shame and social isolation from their family and peers, interruption of employment or careers, increased economic hardship, and a diminished opportunity for a later marriage. Not surprisingly, the most common solution to an unwanted pregnancy for a non-married girl in most parts of the world is an abortion. In the China study, for example, the main reason given by 93 per cent of the girls for having an abortion was the fact that they were not married. In the Korea study, the conclusion is drawn that abortion is relied on as a strategy for dealing with unwanted, out-of-wedlock pregnancy. Indeed, all the premarital pregnancies in this sample had ended in abortion. Although precise figures are unavailable, adolescents aged 15–19 account for at least 10 per cent of the induced abortions that occur each year throughout the world (Senanayake and Ladjali, 1994).

Moreover, the studies in this section as well as information from many other sources also illustrate that it is unsafe abortion, either self-induced or performed by an unqualified abortionist, that non-married adolescent girls most often seek—whether or not abortion is legal in their country (Fathalla et al., 1990; WHO, 1995c). In the Tanzania study, nearly a third of the victims of unsafe abortion were teenagers, of whom almost half were 17 years of age or younger; about one in every four were students in primary or secondary school. Incomplete abortion was diagnosed for 72 per cent of them and post-abortion sepsis was the most common complication; almost 53 per cent of all the women also had signs of trauma to their genitals. In the Korea study, in virtually every in-depth interview and focus group session, unsafe or unhygienic abortions were reported to be widespread. Some girls said they had tried to self-induce abortion before going to a provider. The authors point out that a safe procedure is very expensive and thus unaffordable for most non-married young women in Tanzania. In the Mexico study, the wish to end the unwanted pregnancy was very clear in the minds of most of the girls, overriding all other considerations, even the life-threatening risks of the inevitable illegal, unsafe procedure. Even a high proportion of the Mexican girls who ended up carrying their pregnancy to term had actually wanted to abort the pregnancy. As in Korea, they did not have the money to obtain a safe abortion and most had tried unsuccessfully to self-induce an abortion using methods such as drug injections, herbal infusions, quinine tablets, or violent physical exercise—in combination or repeatedly.

The exception to the common experience of physical and emotional trauma from an unsafe abortion was found in the study in China, where abortion has been legal and accessible to all women for decades. All the non-married women in the sample had easy access to abortion by qualified providers under safe conditions. As a result, the medical complication rate from the procedure was minimal compared to the other studies in this section.

Adding to the trend to seek unsafe abortion is the fact that adolescents often present themselves too late for abortion, when the procedure carries the greatest risk. Even where abortion is legal, it is not easy for a young non-married girl without support or finances to seek an abortion early enough. Reasons include denial, feelings of shame and guilt, inability to seek medical care without discovery, or simple ignorance about the consequences of delayed treatment. Again, an exception to this general trend was found in the China study, where the majority of young women, 64 per cent, had their abortion when gestation was between 41–60 days. This illustrates that widespread dissemination of health information and safe services that include young non-married women can reduce their risk of mortality and morbidity from abortion.

It is significant that the topic of sexually transmitted diseases (STDs) and HIV infection surfaced more clearly in the adolescent studies of abortion than in any of the other abortion studies in this volume. Among sexually active young people, STDs are most frequent in those who are youngest, and appear to be increasing throughout the world, although diagnosis and reporting is poor (WHO, 1989). In many countries, 60 per cent of all new HIV infections are among 15–24-year olds, with a female to male ratio of 2:1. The largest number of these infections is in Sub-Saharan Africa, but the biggest recent increase has been in Latin America and South and South-East Asia (WHO, 1995c). Information from other sources shows that many young people have heard about these diseases, but as with knowledge about contraception, having this information does not seem to affect their reproductive behaviour. The reasons relate to the same sociocultural factors just discussed.

However, it must be emphasized that young girls are especially vulnerable to STDs and HIV/AIDS, because they tend to marry, or have intercourse, with men who have had more sexual exposure. In the Tanzania study, for example, one-third of the girls aged 14–17 years said they had been made pregnant by men who were 45 years of age or older. Added to this is an already existing biomedical risk of infection among young girls because they have an immature cervix and limited vaginal secretions, which provide less of a barrier to infection. Forced first intercourse, which is not uncommon among young girls and was reported in all the studies in this section, leads to genital trauma and cuts and thus increases the risk of infection (WHO, 1995c). Naturally, young girls engaged as sex workers are the most vulnerable to infection. They are likely to be patronized by men who in most societies have many more sexual partners than the women and thus are more likely to infect their 'clients'. In the Korea study, 14 per cent of the young women interviewed said they had gotten an STD as a result of their first sexual experience.

Conclusions

The Beijing Platform for Action, approved at the UN Fourth World Conference on Women in September 1995, emphasized the problems for adolescents just discussed, stating:

> Counselling and access to sexual and reproductive health information and services for adolescents are still inadequate or lacking completely, and a young woman's right to privacy, confidentiality, respect, and informed consent is often not considered.... The trend toward early sexual experience, combined with a lack of information and services, increases the risk of unwanted and too early pregnancy, HIV infection and other STDs, as well as unsafe abortion (United Nations, 1995: para 95).

The actions it recommended included the implementation of education and information programmes on sexual and reproductive health issues and on STDs, including HIV/AIDS, in school curricula from the primary level; and full attention to meeting the service needs of adolescents to enable them to deal in a positive and responsible way with their sexuality (United Nations, 1995: para 108).

When considering the best approaches to meeting the reproductive health needs of adolescents, it must be kept in mind that they do not comprise a homogeneous group; there is wide variation in their characteristics, such as age, cultural views of sexuality and marriage, basic education, employment opportunities and access to reproductive health information. This makes the provision of contraceptive services difficult at best. In the absence of an ideal method of contraception for adolescents, it is important to make available as wide a range of suitable methods as possible with good quality counselling services. In cases of abortion, including treatment of abortion complications, counselling both before and after the procedure is especially important—indeed, critical, for psychological wellbeing.

The encouragement of sexual responsibility among boys and young men should be a priority when setting up sex education programmes. It is young girls, and not their male partners, who suffer the consequences when premarital sex results in unwanted pregnancy and there is therefore an urgent need to make boys aware of the consequences of their sexual actions for their female partners.

Research Gaps

Adolescent sexual behaviour and its determinants is very much an under-researched area. A closer look at the gap between contraceptive knowledge and behaviour, following the examples of the studies in Part I is needed. Keeping in mind the possible influence of peers and parents, adolescents' own views and perceptions about their sexuality and sexual practices, contraception, partner relationships, and goals for their future must be studied and understood. A critical dimension to this kind of research is gender relations, particularly the study of the attitudes and role of male partners, concerning contraception, sexual responsibility and decision-making. Profiles of the boys and 'sugar daddies' who took part in the sexual relations or fathered a child are conspicuously absent from the studies presented in this section.

The way that adolescents are reacting to the threat of HIV/AIDs and other STDs is also an important topic for research on adolescent reproductive health. Here again, a gender-based approach is crucial, not least because of a sexual double standard in most cultures that allows men, but not women, to have multiple sexual partners. Such inequality in sexual power and control often leaves young girls helpless to protect themselves against infection as well as unwanted pregnancy. In this context, understanding the sexual attitudes and behaviour of the male partner becomes essential to any effort aimed at reducing HIV/AIDs transmission (WHO, 1995d)

Another emerging area for research is the role that coercion and sexual abuse play in the scenario of adolescent reproductive health. Each of the studies in this section revealed cases of forced sex, in the form of rape, incest, or coercion by an employer. (Other studies in this volume also reveal that rape is not uncommon, especially among young girls; see, e.g., the study in Mexico by Elu.) Other available data indicate high rates of childhood and adolescent sexual abuse in many parts of the world, which has been shown to increase a young girl's risk of getting pregnant as well as contracting infection, for a variety of psychosocial reasons (Heise, 1994; Heise et al., 1994).

Final Comments

In all the studies in this volume, abortion clearly emerges as a prevalent and persistent threat for many women of reproductive age, regardless of their particular socioeconomic and cultural background, and the policy context of the country in which they live.

The sections and chapters that follow illustrate simply and undeniably that women will adopt strategies to manage their reproductive life using whatever resources are available to them, even if such approaches mean risking their life and challenging or opposing oppressive social and legal systems that limit their reproductive rights. The evidence in this volume shows that when contraceptive methods are not available or acceptable, or fail, people take other steps to regulate their fertility. Women are not passive agents in their reproductive destinies.

The lengths women will go to in order to end an unwanted pregnancy and the social networks and methods they use to solve such a critical reproductive health problem become important clues to understanding what people's true fertility regulation motivations, needs and preferences are. More research needs to be done along these lines.

These studies also point the way towards creating more responsive reproductive health services that help women and men manage their fertility more effectively. Wider access to safe abortion and the essential elements of high quality abortion care have also been clearly outlined. Even where the actual provision of safe abortion is restricted or prohibited, there is an urgent need for essential abortion-related services of high quality, such as effective and compassionate treatment of women suffering from complications of unsafe procedures and post-abortion counselling to prevent repeat abortion. An essential conclusion is that family planning and abortion services should be better linked through effective referral systems, to ensure that women who have an abortion also receive competent support to help them manage their fertility.

For these improvements in the quality of care offered by reproductive health and abortion services to be successfully implemented, it is necessary to solicit and obtain the full cooperation and participation of the health care providers who have daily contact with women and their families. These studies also challenge the ethics of withholding the simple medical technology and knowledge required to perform a safe abortion from these providers, who are faced with the demand for abortions and the life-threatening complications of unsafe procedures every day.

The Beijing Platform for Action fully endorses these conclusions, urging 'all governments and relevant intergovernmental and nongovernmental organizations to strengthen their commitment to women's health, to deal with the health impact of unsafe abortion as a major public health concern and to reduce the recourse to abortion through expanded and improved family planning services...' (United Nations, 1995: para 12.17). It calls for ready access to reliable information and compassionate counselling to women who have an unwanted pregnancy, as well as the prompt offering of post-abortion counselling, education and family planning services. It also calls for a review of laws that contain punitive measures against women who have undergone illegal abortions (United Nations, 1995: para 107[k]).

None of the researchers in this volume nor the thousands of women interviewed in these studies have advocated abortion as a method of family planning. No one has questioned that contraception remains a better alternative to abortion. But there is no perfect method and no perfect delivery system, and there is not likely to be one anytime soon. There will always be failures, whatever the reason. And millions of women will resolve these failures with the use of abortion. They should not be condemned. They should not be coerced into motherhood. And they should certainly not be forced to suffer or to die if the alternative is a relatively simple, inexpensive procedure that poses essentially no risk to their health when performed under safe conditions by adequately trained health personnel.

† References

Baird, T.L., R.E. Gringle and F.C. Greenslade. 1995. *MVA in the treatment of incomplete abortion: Clinical and programmatic experiences.* Carrboro, North Carolina: IPAS.

Barbosa, R.M. and M. Arilha. 1993. The Brazilian experience with cytotec. *Studies in Family Planning* 24 (4): 236–40.

Benson, J., A.H. Leonard, J. Winkler, M. Wolf and K.E. McLaurin. 1992. *Meeting women's needs for post-abortion family planning: Framing the questions.* Issues in Abortion Care 2. Carrboro, North Carolina: IPAS.

Bruce, J. 1990. Fundamental elements of the quality of care: A simple framework. *Studies in Family Planning* 21 (2): 61–91.

Coeytaux, F.M., A.H. Leonard and C.M. Bloomer. 1993. Abortion. In: M. Koblinsky, J. Timyany and J. Gay (eds), *Women: A global perspective.* Boulder, Co.: Westview Press, pp. 133–46.

Dixon–Mueller, R. 1990. Abortion policy and women's health in developing countries. *International Journal of Health Services* 20: 297–314.

Fathalla, M., A. Rosenfield and C. Indriso (eds). 1990. Reproductive health: Global issues, Vol. 3, Chapter 6. In: *The FIGO manual of human reproduction, 1990.* United Kingdom: Parthenon Publishing.

Frejka, T. 1993. The role of induced abortion in contemporary fertility regulation. Proceedings of the International Population Conference of the International Union for the Scientific Study of Population, Montreal, Canada, Chapter 5, pp. 209–14.

Hausknecht, R.U. 1995. Methotrexate and misoprostol to terminate early pregnancy. *The New England Journal of Medicine* 333 (9): 537–40.

Heise, L. 1994. Gender-based violence and women's reproductive health. *International Journal of Gynecology and Obstetrics* 46 (2): 221–29.

Heise, L.L. with J. Pitanguy and A. Germain. 1994. *Violence against women: The hidden health burden.* Washington, D.C.: World Bank.

Henshaw, S.K. and E. Morrow. 1990. *Induced abortion: A world review, 1990 Supplement.* New York: The Alan Guttmacher Institute.

Holmgren, K. 1994. *Legal abortion during very early pregnancy: Women's experiences and ethical conflicts.* Stockholm: Karolinska Institute.

Klitsch, M. 1991. Antiprogestins and the abortion controversy: A progress report. *Family Planning Perspectives* 23 (6): 275–82.

Londoño E., M.L. 1989. Abortion counselling: Attention to the whole woman. *International Journal of Gynecology and Obstetrics* (Suppl. 3): 169–74.

Nasser, J. 1989. Commentary on pain management during abortion from a Latin American physician's perspective. *International Journal of Gynecology and Obstetrics* (Suppl. 3): 141–43.

Neamatalla, G.S. and C.S. Verme. 1995. Postabortion women: Factors influencing their family planning options. AVSC Working Paper (9): 1–11. New York: AVSC (Access to Voluntary and Safe Contraception).

PATH (Program for Appropriate Technology in Health). 1989. Summary of Findings from Oral Contraceptives Focus Group Discussions: Report to USAID/Cairo. Washington, D.C.: PATH.

Ping, Tu. 1995. IUD discontinuation patterns and correlates in four counties in North China. *Studies in Family Planning* 26 (3): 169–79.

Riley, A.P., M.K. Stewart and J. Chakraborty. 1994. Program- and method-related determinants of first DMPA use duration in rural Bangladesh. *Studies in Family Planning* 25 (5): 255–67.

Rogow, D. and S. Horowitz. 1995. Withdrawal: A review of the literature and an agenda for research. *Studies in Family Planning* 26 (3): 140–53.

Romania Ministry of Health. 1991. Mortalitatea materna. (Unpublished document.) Bucharest: Directorate for MCH.

Rosenfield, A. 1994. Abortion and women's reproductive health. *International Journal of Gynecology and Obstetrics* 46: 173–79.

Ross, J.A. and E. Frankenberg. 1993. Findings from two decades of family planning research. New York: The Population Council.

Senanayake, P. and M. Ladjali. 1994. Adolescent health: Changing needs. In: World report on women's health. *International Journal of Gynecology and Obstetrics* 46 (2): 137–43.

Stubblefield, P.G. 1989. Control of pain for women undergoing abortion. *International Journal of Gynecology and Obstetrics* (Suppl. 3): 131–40

Sundstrom, K. 1993. Abortion: A reproductive health issue. Washington, D.C.: Population, Health, and Nutrition Department, The World Bank.

Tietze, C. 1981. *Induced abortion: A world review.* 4th Edition. New York: The Population Council.

Trottier, D.A., L.S. Potter, B.A. Taylor and L.H. Glover. 1994. User characteristics and oral contraceptive compliance in Egypt. *Studies in Family Planning.* 25 (5): 284–92.

United Nations. 1989. *Adolescent reproductive behavior: Evidence from developing countries.* Vol. II. New York: Department of Economic and Social Affairs.

———. 1993. Distribution of the world populations, 1992 Revision. New York: Dept. of Economic and Social Development, United Nations (ST/ESA/SER.A/134).

———. 1994. *World abortion policies.* New York: Department for Economic and Social Information and Policy Analysis, Population Division.

———. 1995. *Beijing declaration and platform for action.* Fourth world conference on women: Action for equality, development and peace. Beijing, China, 4–15 September 1995.

van Look, P.V. and H. von Hertzen. 1993. Emergency contraception. *British Medical Bulletin* 49 (1): 158–70.

WHO. 1989. *The health of youth: Facts for action: Youth and STDs.* Geneva, Switzerland: WHO.

———. 1991. *Maternal mortality: A global factbook.* Geneva, Switzerland: WHO.

———. 1994. *Abortion: A tabulation of available data on the frequency and mortality of unsafe abortion.* 2nd Edition. Geneva, Switzerland: WHO (WHO/FHE/MSM/93.13).

———. 1995a. *Complications of abortion: Technical and managerial guidelines for prevention and treatment.* Geneva, Switzerland: WHO.

———. 1995b. Quality of care: Doing things the right way. *Safe Motherhood Newsletter* 17 (March–June): 4–6. Geneva, Switzerland: WHO.

———. 1995c. Adolescent health and development: The key to the future. Geneva, Switzerland: WHO (WHO/ADH/94.3 Rev.1).

———. 1995d. Partners in health: Men's role in women's reproductive health. A working paper prepared for the 11th Commonwealth Health Minister's Conference, Cape Town, South Africa, December 1995.

PART I

The Relationship between Abortion and Contraception

2

Prevention of Pregnancy in High-Risk Women: Community Intervention in Chile

Ramiro Molina, Cristian Pereda, Francisco Cumsille,
Luis Martinez Oliva, Eduardo Miranda
and Temistocles Molina

Introduction

Maternal mortality due to unsafe, illegal induced abortion is a major reproductive health problem affecting developing countries. When abortion is practised clandestinely, the real number of abortions that take place is difficult to estimate. This is the case in most of Latin America where, with the exception of Cuba, Guyana and Barbados and Belize in the English-speaking Caribbean, abortion is not permitted (Paxman et al., 1993).

Recent estimates for Latin American countries reveal that there are from three to four clandestine abortions for every 10 births in Brazil and Colombia and two for every 10 births in Peru (Singh and Wulf, 1991). For metropolitan Santiago, Chile, estimates based on a fertility survey show that the abortion ratio is about four per 10 livebirths—all of them performed clandestinely (APROFA/CERC, 1990; Requena, 1990).

In general, the objective of health authorities everywhere should be to lower abortion by increasing effective contraceptive use among couples who are sexually active and do not desire a pregnancy. In some countries where abortion is illegal, including Chile, effective family planning programmes have successfully increased the prevalence of contraceptive use, followed by a decrease in hospital reporting of abortion complications and a marked decrease in maternal mortality due to induced abortion (Molina et al., 1990).

These decreases in abortion-related maternal mortality can sometimes be linked to improved access to services, including availability of intensive-care units, and better medical techniques to treat septic shock and other complications. Similarly, another reason for such a decline may be the increased 'professionalism' of private clandestine abortion services that have displaced the traditional backstreet abortionists. Offering women a safer abortion in hygienic clinical environments, although still illegal, has contributed to reducing infection, septic shock and other complications that traditionally account for deaths due to illegal abortion (Singh and Wulf, 1993).

Another factor that may explain the decline of deaths due to induced abortion complications, however, is simply improper hospital recording of cases of induced abortion. This occurs when the law is very restrictive, with patients as well as hospital staff punishable by law. In such instances, it is more likely that personnel will write a different diagnosis in the file, most commonly 'spontaneous abortion'.

The clandestine nature of induced abortion in many developing countries makes it a difficult subject for research. Case identification is a common problem. Moreover, it is difficult to undertake studies with cases and controls that allow a better assessment of the relationship between contraception and induced abortion. Equally difficult is to clearly demonstrate the preventive effect of family planning in lowering unsafe abortions. Studies of this nature could be very useful in strengthening family planning programmes and in developing more effective strategies for the prevention of clandestine abortion (World Bank, 1993).

Research in the area of maternal and child health, including maternal mortality, has led to the identification of risk indicators that permit health staff to detect women who need special care to prevent the negative outcomes associated with high-risk pregnancy, such as high parity, history of perinatal or early infant mortality, pregnancy at a young age or over 35 years. The application of a risk criteria in maternal care has made it possible to concentrate health actions and apply scarce resources to specific groups, with great success (PAHO, 1986).

Similarly, studies on induced abortion have shown that there are identifiable groups of women in a population that consistently choose abortion to regulate their fertility, among them women with poor knowledge of sexual and reproductive functions, and women who are strongly opposed to using modern contraception for a variety of reasons (Weisner, 1990). Moreover, findings from fertility surveys and descriptive epidemiological studies have identified certain variables associated with induced abortion risk. But it is very difficult to apply a predictive risk criteria to individual cases during routine service work, such as primary health care visits. Data from these abortion risk studies, moreover, have not been used to identify the underlying risk factors that could help predict abortion behaviour. This is because most study designs do not include case controls, or survey data based on reproductive histories are affected by memory recall problems that make past events unreliable for predicting future behaviour (Barreto et al., 1992).

Another approach, although more difficult, is to assess abortion risk among women of fertile age, according to information about previous unwanted pregnancies. This is based on the view that abortion behaviour is directly related to negative attitudes towards a pregnancy. Moreover, the decision of going ahead with pregnancy termination will depend on various factors, one of them being the availability and accessibility of abortion services. In countries where abortion is illegal, for example, often the woman has no other recourse but to accept her unwanted pregnancy and have the child (Viel and Pereda, 1991). In such situations, general information on previous unwanted pregnancies is not a good enough predictor of abortion; what is needed is information on previous unwanted pregnancies that were voluntarily interrupted. This is a more appropriate indicator of future abortion risk, as behaviours tend to repeat themselves over a lifetime.

In summary, a preventive strategy that concentrates on early detection of abortion risk, within a specified population known for its high incidence of induced abortion, would seem an appropriate, albeit difficult, means to lower abortion. We believe that such a strategy is worth pursuing, particularly if applied to such populations of low socioeconomic level and in countries where abortion is illegal and unsafe. This project set out to do exactly that.

Study Objectives

The main objective of this study is based on the hypothesis that by improving family planning services, and by focusing them on women identified as having a high risk of induced abortion, it is possible to achieve a significant reduction in abortion rates in areas known for their high abortion incidence. We would test this hypothesis in low-income urban communities where we knew induced abortion rates to be high.

The basic study design consisted of a 'before' survey to identify high-risk women, followed by an intervention. The intervention we were planning included improved services in two communities; and in one of these two, an additional effort to visit women, identified as having a high risk of abortion, in their homes. A third community would serve as a control area. An 'after' measurement would follow to verify whether we had succeeded or not. In general, our aim was to determine the preventive effect of a sustained family planning intervention on women previously identified as having a high risk of abortion. We were also interested in comparing women who were exposed to different levels of abortion risk, and observing their behaviour when they had been subjected to different degrees of intervention intensity.

One of the main challenges arising from our research objectives was precisely how to identify women with high abortion risk. Therefore, our first requirement was to develop a simple predictive instrument that would permit us to assess such risks. Next, we had to apply the instrument to all women of fertile age in the communities selected for the intervention to identify those with high risk of abortion. To achieve this initial goal, it was first necessary to undertake a detailed retrospective survey that would provide us with the necessary information on their reproductive histories, including abortion, to build the predictive instrument.

Research Methodology

To meet our stated objectives, we selected for our study the three communities of Pincoya, Cortijo and Quinta Bella, all situated in the northern sector of Santiago, the capital of Chile. The three communities had comparable characteristics, including: low socioeconomic level; similar population profiles; equal access to public means of transportation; similar primary health care facilities provided by the Ministry of Health; and sufficient geographic separation to prevent contamination of the intervention effect across communities, either through personal communication or by seeking health care services in a neighbouring community.

We realized from the start that this would be a long project, taking several years, and would require careful planning for its various stages. We divided the project activities into five clearly distinct phases, which we explain next and which correspond, approximately, to the structure of this chapter.

Phase I included the planning of the project, the selection of the three communities to be included, and the development of questionnaires and sampling designs for the retrospective survey, the first field activity. This phase included carrying out the 'before' retrospective survey that was necessary to document the existing abortion and fertility patterns of these communities.

Phase II consisted of developing a predictive instrument to detect abortion risk based on the information obtained from the retrospective survey. The predictive instrument was tested and then applied to all three communities. As a result, women were classified into two groups: those with high risk of abortion (HRA); and those with low risk of abortion (LRA).

During Phase III, we designed the intervention and selected the two communities where it would be applied, and the third that would be the control area. To facilitate the identification of women with different abortion risks, an epidemiological map was prepared that included all households in these communities.

Phase IV was devoted to the implementation of the intervention in the two selected communities. The intervention period lasted 18 months.

Finally, Phase V assessed the impact of the 18-month intervention by means of a post-intervention, or 'after' survey. This second survey covered the same women that were surveyed originally in all three communities. The study concluded with the analysis of a vast amount of information.

Phase I: The First Survey

Our first activity was to develop and test the survey questionnaire, which was developed following a detailed analysis of previous survey interviews utilized in abortion studies conducted in Chile. During this phase, we paid particular attention to items directly related to abortion issues (Armijo and Monreal, 1986; Faúndes et al., 1968; Pereda, 1986; Requena, 1965).

The study questionnaire was tested three times by trained staff, both in a community and in a hospital context, with women who did or did not have a clinically confirmed abortion. Our first draft took 45 minutes to apply. Tests using double blind approaches were conducted in one community with women who had a known background of abortion, but with the interviewers unaware of what the abortion status of the woman was. The information obtained in this test matched very closely the hospital data and we considered the results very reassuring. The final survey questionnaire was greatly improved as a result.

Once the field data collection phase started, the completed questionnaires were entered into computers immediately following the field interview and supervisor verification. This procedure facilitated the correction of information. Errors were thus easily rectified when detected by the data codifiers or during the process of data cleaning, because it was easy to return to the original case, if necessary, to clarify the error. We used trained interviewers, mostly nurse-midwives, who worked intensely to complete the fieldwork in the shortest possible time. One decision we took was to interview on Saturdays and Sundays, which helped to complete the survey in a shorter time. On weekends it was also easier to contact women who were absent from the household during the week. Two coders entered the information into computers and they were, in turn, supervised by a data manager. One of the innovative aspects we included during the fieldwork was a mobile office that was parked near the blocks where the interviewers were deployed. This 'office' was an old school bus we rented from the university for the duration of the fieldwork. It allowed us to achieve substantial reductions in the field costs of the project. The field supervisors used this office to do the first data checking and to assess on the spot the progress of the fieldwork.

Sampling

From the start we decided to conduct the study in a lower-income area of Northern Santiago where clear physical demarcations, such as a large cemetery, separate specific communities within this large urban area. The three communities of Pincoya, Cortijo and Quinta Bella were randomly selected.

To calculate the sample size needed for the initial survey, an incidence of 70 induced abortions per 1,000 women of reproductive age (WRA) was estimated for the previous two years in the general area where we planned to conduct the study. This figure was estimated on the basis of discharges due to abortion complications from two hospitals that cover the area. A decreasing assumption, to 55 abortions per 1,000 WRA, was estimated for the second survey, which represented the change we expected after 18 months of intervention. The result was a sample size of 2,000 women to be interviewed in each community, or a total sample of 6,000 women. To our surprise, the initial survey found a rate of 98 abortions per 1,000 WRA, based on abortions reported for the previous two years before the interview.

To select 2,000 women in each community, local area information derived from the 1982 Census and made available by the National Institute of Statistics (INE) was used. The census tract data included detailed maps for each of the three communities we had selected. Although the existing maps were helpful, we had to redraw them with updated information that permitted us to identify every house in these communities.

Within each community, the blocks were randomly selected, then the houses in each block were equally selected, until 2,000 households were obtained; thus providing us with the necessary total to interview 6,000 women of reproductive age. To avoid problems of information exchange within households, we decided to interview only one woman per household. To replace households without a woman of fertile age, we made a second, and even a third selection of households from blocks not included in the original sample, following the same random procedure.

With these successive rounds, a total of 6,020 households were selected and 5,842 women were actually interviewed. Thus we arrived at 97.6 per cent of our intended total sample. From this group we eliminated 12 women who provided incomplete information and 828 women who were not sexually active (had never engaged in sexual intercourse) and had as a consequence no abortion risk. Therefore, we ended up with a study sample of 5,014 women.

The Interview Process

The woman to be interviewed in each household was identified following a procedure recommended by the Survey Research Center of the United States. A page listing each woman in the household, in descending order of age, was attached to each interview questionnaire. In each case, the woman to be interviewed was pre-selected from the household list utilizing a table of random numbers. A different random numbers series was used for each household. This procedure prevented the interviewer from choosing who to interview or from applying other selection criteria. A further advantage was that it did not over-enumerate women who stayed at home during the day: women who worked outside the home were left a message in writing with a specific time and date when the interviewer would return.

Forty interviewers participated in the field phase. All were female and most of them were midwives, except for two social workers and three high school teachers. They received a 10-day training course from the principal investigator and five field supervisors, all of whom had ample survey experience. The same team conducted the second survey.

Some Results from the First Survey

Some of the sample characteristics for each community are shown in Table 2.1. One of the important findings of the first survey was that women did report their abortion experience. When they were asked what type of abortion they had, however, most women, 72 per cent, reported their abortions as spontaneous. This proportion was more than twice the highest proportion reported in the literature for a population (Singh and Wulf, 1993). This meant that there was a clear under-reporting of induced abortion, most probably due to fear of punitive action. As noted earlier, a similar declaration happens in hospitals for the very same reason.

Table 2.1: Sample Characteristics for Each Community

Variables	Pincoya	Cortijo	Quinta Bella
Average age (in years)	32	33	33
Marital status:			
% legally married	67	74	69
% cohabiting	18	12	14
Marital duration:			
> 10 years	38	39	39
Years of schooling (average)	8	9	9
Residence in Santiago:			
10 years or more (%)	95	95	95
Housing:			
House or apartment (%)	81	91	84
Rooms, dilapidated (%)	19	9	16
Living children	2.5	2.3	2.2
Total number of women	1,613	1,620	1,674

We had expected this situation, because abortion is a criminal act in Chile. Therefore, our decision of first asking if the woman had ever experienced an abortion, and then for the type, seemed the correct method of inquiry. Since it was obvious that most reported abortions were not or could not be spontaneous, we simply decided to put all reported abortions into one category—'abortion'—without attempting to separate events that could not be identified one way or another.

Phase II: Developing the Predictive Instrument

During this phase of our study, we set out to develop a predictive instrument that would be sensitive to abortion risk. The first criteria was to analyze the abortion history of the women interviewed during the first survey. We had to use the past as the best predictor of future behaviour and, therefore, try to identify which variables or factors were closely associated with any previous abortion. As noted, the data were biased towards abortions reported as spontaneous, although this was a systematic bias that applied equally to all three communities.

For women with or without abortion history, key independent variables were compared. To establish a better basis for comparison with the results of the second survey, which was to take place two years later, we decided on a second criteria: to consider a two-year reference period for abortion for both surveys. This made sense since the intervention that would follow the first survey was expected to last two years. In this way the 5,014 women selected for inclusion in our analysis during the first survey were divided into three groups: (a) Those without history of abortion—3,492; (b) Those with history of abortion two years or more before the survey (before 1987)—1,270; (c) Those with history of abortion during the two years preceding the survey (1987–88)—252.

The classification into these three subgroups allowed us to learn about abortion during two reference periods: (1) abortion that occurred in the more distant past, that is, before 1987; and (2) more recent abortions, during 1987 and 1988. We wanted to see whether background variables (e.g., age, marital status, etc.) for these subgroups exhibited different trends given that the predictive risk could be differentially affected by time or changes since the occurrence of the last reported abortion.

We found that the variables analyzed for each group showed the same effects over time. Nevertheless, the associative tendencies of the statistically significant variables were more evident in the group with more recent abortion. Given these results, a third criteria for the analysis was adopted; the 5,014 women were separated into two groups: (a) Women with history of induced, spontaneous or non-specified abortion in the past two years—252; (b) Women without history of abortion in the past two years (includes women with longer history of abortion in the past)—4,762.

A comparative univariate analysis was performed on these two subgroups to find the significant variables that were later included in the multivariate analysis necessary for the development of the predictive instrument.

Multivariate Analysis

A first selection of significant variables associated to abortion risk was made. Almost all the variables in the questionnaire were first considered, each of them independently, and some in combination, in order to analyze the differences between the women in group (*a*) and group (*b*), as defined earlier.

The odds ratio (OR) of the most significant variables was calculated with limits of confidence of 95 per cent. To select the significant variables a value of p smaller or equal to 0.05 was accepted. After this initial step, a logistic regression was performed.

The logistic regression including 4,907 women was performed using SAS software. The regression model selected the variables that were closely associated with the risk of abortion, with a p value of less than 0.10. We eliminated 107 cases because of incomplete information on some variables required by the regression model.

The logistic regression showed that when nine variables from those selected in the previous analysis were sequentially introduced into the model, they fulfilled the conditions of increasing, in a significant way, the association with abortion in the last two years. These variables and their categories were: age, below 35 years; marital status, cohabiting; union duration, less than 10 years; previous unions, several; sterilization, not contemplating; contraception, used mostly traditional methods; use of IUD, never used; housing, living in single rooms, or shared or dilapidated houses; fertility, three or more children, the last under five years of age (see Table 2.2).

Table 2.2: Abortion Risk Factors

Variable	Item	Beta Coefficient	Variable Number
Age	Under 35	0.05**	1
Partner relations	Cohabiting	1.40**	2
Sterilization	No	1.36**	3
Previous use of methods	Some spacing***	0.40*	4
Marriage duration	10 years or less	1.18**	5
Previous marital cohabitation	Yes	0.58**	6
Previous IUD use	No	0.42*	7
Housing type	Poor, dilapidated	0.31*	8
Fertility level	3–10 children alive, last born under 5 years	0.32*	9

* significant at the 0.05 level.
** significant at the 0.001 level.
*** methods include monthly injectables, rhythm, condom, withdrawal and vaginal douche.

With these nine variables, we then had the elements of a predictive instrument which, with the assistance of a regression model, allowed us to sort out the women in the sample according to their abortion risk. The category that included women with high risk of abortion (HRA), included those cases whose probability of having an abortion was higher than average for the sample, which was found to be 5.03 per cent. As a result, 1,911 women were classified as being in the high-risk category and 3,056 fell into the low-risk category

Table 2.3: Actual and Predicted Abortion Values

	Abortion Status	Predictive Value		
		High Abortion Risk	Low Abortion Risk	Total
Actual Value	With abortion experience*	184	63	247
	No abortion experience	1,727	2,993	4,720
	Total	1,911	3,056	4,967

Note: The predictive value was obtained by the application of the nine variables shown in Table 2.2.
  * Refers to abortion experience during the previous two years.

(Table 2.3). For all three communities we now had an estimate of which women had a high or a low risk of induced abortion.

The women at high risk of abortion were distributed according to their community of residence as follows: 36 per cent of the high risk women (681) lived in Pincoya, where they represented 42 per cent of the total sample of all women of reproductive age in that community; another 30 per cent (581) lived in Cortijo, where they represented 36 per cent of the total sample of women of reproductive age in that community; and 34 per cent (649) lived in Quinta Bella, where they represented 39 per cent of the sample of women of reproductive age in that community. High-risk women living in Pincoya were selected to receive 'full' intervention; those in Cortijo, 'partial' intervention; and those in Quinta Bella, the control community, nothing at all.

Phases III and IV: The Intervention

The Planning Phase

During the third phase of the study we planned the intervention and selected Pincoya and Cortijo as the communities to be intervened utilizing a random procedure. Both communities were provided with additional staff resources for their clinics, including a part-time physician, a midwife and an auxiliary nurse, the latter two full-time. In addition to improvements in service quality, a wider choice of contraceptive methods was made available. The only difference between the two communities was that the 'full' intervention in Pincoya was designed so that all women classified as having a high abortion risk were visited in their homes by a specially trained social worker to discuss their family planning and related reproductive health needs. As already noted, in Quinta Bella, the 'control' community, there was no intervention at all.

The Implementation Phase

The 'full' and 'partial' interventions in Pincoya and Cortijo, respectively, were initiated in September 1989 and lasted 18 months, ending in February 1991. The actual intervention constituted the fourth phase of our project.

In Pincoya, each woman classified as having a high risk of abortion was identified by name and address from a confidential list obtained from the computer listings. A social worker visited each one to see if they wished to discuss any reproductive health needs, such as information and services to regulate their fertility. (Women who did not work at home were visited on Saturdays and Sundays.) The women were also informed of the improved family planning services being made available in the community clinic. The social worker focused on motivation and basic education on contraception, and arranged for appointments at the local family planning clinic, if requested. The midwife assigned by the project to the Pincoya clinic registered compliance with all appointments arranged by the social worker. The social worker and midwife worked closely together.

The service improvement in the second community, Cortijo, was implemented as in Pincoya, but no special effort was made to advertise it. Word of mouth was expected to be sufficient for the purposes of the study.

Phase V: The Second Survey

The second, or 'after', survey was carried out 24 months following the completion of the first survey and it marked the final, or fifth phase, of the study. Interviewers were able to locate 73 per cent of the women included in the first survey: 3,588 women out of the 4,967 in the first survey, for all three communities.

The loss to follow-up in the three communities was: 16.9 per cent in Pincoya; 32.3 per cent in Cortijo; and 31.2 per cent in Quinta Bella. Most of the loss was due to change of address, as many people in these communities are migrants and tend to move around in the various communities in the periphery of Santiago. Additionally, the presence of 'allegados', or people who do not have a stable home and come to live temporarily with relatives or friends, added to the problem. There was a rather high proportion of such cases by the time of the second survey. Also, the population in these communities is young and prone to fluctuation.

While 3,588 women were interviewed in the second survey, the analysis included only 2,991 women because we excluded 597 women due to incomplete information (284) or due to absence of sexual intercourse between surveys (313). Moreover, to observe the change in behaviour among women who were true potential users of contraception between the first and second surveys, we had to create a sub-sample that eliminated an additional 735 women who had been sterilized at the time of the first survey or who had become sterilized or pregnant by the time of the second survey. This resulting sub-sample of women 'exposed' to pregnancy and abortion was considerably reduced to 2,256.

In each of the communities, the breakdown for the various analysis groups was: in Pincoya, we interviewed 1,086 women, eliminated 233 who were either sterilized or pregnant; and of the remaining 853 'exposed' women, 43 per cent (366) were found to have a high risk of abortion. In Cortijo, we interviewed 936 women, eliminated 276, and of the remaining 660 'exposed' women, 35 per cent (233) were in the high-risk category. Lastly, in Quinta Bella, we interviewed 969 women, eliminated 226, and of the 743 'exposed' women, 38 per cent (285) were found to have a 'high risk' of abortion.

The criteria used for the classification of women with high risk of abortion in the second survey was exactly the same used in the first survey (women identified as having high risk of abortion in the first survey maintained that classification in the second). However, we felt this approach could introduce a bias in our analysis. To assess the potential for such bias, the profile of the nine main abortion risk factors of the women lost to follow-up (1,916) was compared with that of the women we were able to re-interview (2,991). The factors that behaved differently were: age, previous contraceptive use, marriage lasting less than 10 years and fertility level. These differences, although marked, were not significant, except for the fertility variable, which did show a significant difference. Later, we used these factors to adjust abortion rates in the before–after comparisons, and thus reduced the possibility of any bias (Table 2.4).

In the main analysis itself, for each risk factor, a significant difference could be observed among the three communities. However, differences are much smaller between women included and excluded from re-interview in the second survey, within each community. As a result, we feel that

Table 2.4: Abortion Risk Factors: Women Included in the Second Survey Compared with Women Excluded from the Analysis● ˙

Variable*	Pincoya			Cortijo			Quinta Bella		
	Inclu-ded	Exclu-ded	P Value	Inclu-ded	Exclu-ded	P Value	Inclu-ded	Exclu-ded	P Value
Age	57.1	67.6	0.0	53.1	61.1	0.001	57.4	64.0	0.01
Partner	17.9	18.0	0.93	11.3	12.6	0.44	12.5	16.7	0.01
Sterilization	90.8	89.9	0.58	84.2	89.9	0.00	87.7	90.4	0.09
Previous use	42.2	43.3	0.89	46.3	47.4	0.65	47.4	45.2	0.39
Marriage: > 10 years	26.6	32.1	0.02	29.7	35.4	0.01	29.9	31.6	0.45
Cohabitation	16.3	16.9	0.76	11.0	12.0	0.33	10.8	13.3	0.11
No IUD	27.1	33.0	0.01	27.7	36.8	0.00	29.9	34.2	0.06
Housing	17.5	22.6	0.01	9.4	8.5	0.52	14.2	17.7	0.05
Fertility	19.4	19.2	0.89	18.1	14.0	0.03	17.3	18.6	0.51
Total	1,086	527	–	936	684	–	969	705	–

Note: 'Included' women are those re-interviewed in the second survey; 'excluded' women are lost to follow-up cases for whom background characteristics data were available from the first survey.

* For details on variable names and the meaning of each item selected as risk factor please refer to Table 2.2.

comparisons between the first and the second survey are valid even though some of the women interviewed in the first survey could not be included in the second.

Evaluating the Intervention

Before and After Effects

Our second, or 'after' survey was designed as a comparison of the fertility history of women two years 'before' the first survey (1987–88) to that of two years 'after' the first survey (1989–90). The 18-month intervention period itself fell within this second two-year period.

For example, the proportions of abortions in the three communities in the survey 'before' the intervention were compared to the proportions 'after' the intervention, adjusted by the differences in risk factors in the model. Each woman was considered as an observation unit, and these data were entered in an adjusted logistic regression model that considered as dependent variable 'Y' the pregnancies during the previous 24 months. Two 'dummy' variables to represent the three communities were created, and then added as independent variables together with the nine core variables from the original model. Analysis of the interaction of the model was excluded because our interest was to study, by controlling other variables, the relationship between the women's behaviours in each community.

The comparison of the proportion of abortions in the three communities found in the second 'after' survey was done in the same way as the comparison between proportions found in the first and second surveys, but with a modification: the responses obtained in the first survey were included as a control variable. That is to say, the dependent variable that was used in the 'before' analysis was now included as an independent variable in the 'after' analysis.

Contraceptive Use

In the first survey, women were asked about current use of contraception at the time of the interview. In the second or 'after' survey, current use included use of contraception during the entire period of observation, that is, during the two-year period between the first and the second survey. Given this change in the reference period, we anticipated an increase in contraceptive users in the second survey.

Table 2.5 shows a decrease in women using temporary methods in the full-intervention community of Pincoya, from 66.9 per cent to 60.3 per cent, but a marked increase in women using permanent methods, from 2.2 per cent to 13.6 per cent during the two-year period between surveys. Described another way, at the time of the first survey, 7.6 per cent of the women in

Table 2.5: Changes in Contraceptive Use and Pregnancy Status between the First and Second Surveys, by Community

Community and Contraceptive Status	Status at First Survey		Second Survey: Contraceptive and Pregnancy Status of Women Classified According to Status in the First Survey							
First Survey	Total		Users		Non-Users		Sterilized		Pregnant	
	No.	(%)	No.	(%)	No.	(%)	No.	(%)	No.	(%)
Pincoya:										
Users	727	(66.9)	537	73.9	89	12.2	84	11.6	17	2.3
Non-users	253	(23.3)	86	34.0	141	55.7	18	7.1	8	3.2
Sterilized	24	(2.2)	–	–	–	–	24	100	–	–
Pregnant	82	(7.6)	32	39.0	22	26.8	22	26.8	6	7.4
All women	1,086	(100)	655	60.3	252	23.2	148	13.6	31	2.9
Cortijo:										
Users	648	(69.2)	427	66.0	85	13.1	115	17.7	21	3.2
Non-users	171	(18.3)	49	28.7	99	57.9	15	8.8	8	4.6
Sterilized	50	(5.3)	–	–	1	2.0	49	98.0	–	–
Pregnant	67	(7.2)	50	74.6	16	23.9	–	–	1	1.5
All women	936	(100)	526	56.2	201	21.5	179	19.1	30	3.2
Quinta Bella:										
Users	665	(68.6)	470	70.7	99	14.9	78	11.7	18	2.7
Non-users	191	(19.7)	52	27.2	122	63.9	10	5.2	7	3.7
Sterilized	55	(5.7)	–	–	–	–	55	100	–	–
Pregnant	58	(6.0)	31	53.3	22	37.9	4	6.9	1	1.7
All women	969	(100)	553	57.1	243	25.0	147	15.2	26	2.7

Pincoya were pregnant; at the time of the second survey 26.8 per cent of these same women had chosen sterilization.

The most dramatic change, in all three communities, in the period between surveys, was the increase in the number of women who opted for female sterilization. For all three communities, it jumped from 4.3 per cent to 15.8 per cent in this short period. As a result, there were fewer women pregnant in the second than in the first survey, in all three communities.

Total contraceptive prevalence, both the use of permanent as well as other methods, increased from 69.1 to 73.9 per cent in Pincoya; and from 74.5 to 75.3 per cent in Cortijo. It decreased, however, from 74.3 to 72.3 per cent in Quinta Bella, the control community, despite the strong increase in female sterilization in that community during the same period. Although Pincoya showed the largest increase in contraceptive use, it was, to a large extent, because of a switch to sterilization.

Abortion Rates and Ratios for Women of Reproductive Age

Abortion rates and ratios are presented for the total sample and for high-risk women in all three communities, in Tables 2.6 and 2.7.

Table 2.6: Abortion Rates: All Women and High-Risk Women, Before and After the Intervention

Community	Abortion Rates, per 1,000 Women, 15–49 Years				
	Before		After		
All Women	Abortions	Rate	Abortions	Rate	% Change
Pincoya	64	58.9	26	23.4	− 59.4
Cortijo	43	45.9	21	22.4	− 51.2
Quinta Bella	54	55.7	37	38.2	− 31.4
Total (All)	161	53.8	84	28.1	− 47.7
High-Risk Women					
Pincoya	50	112.6	14	31.5	− 72.0
Cortijo	28	93.6	9	30.1	− 67.8
Quinta Bella	41	119.9	20	58.5	− 51.2
Total (HRW)	119	109.6	43	39.6	− 63.9

Table 2.7: Abortion Ratios: All Women and High-Risk Women, Before and After the Intervention

Community	Abortion Ratios, per 1,000 Pregnancies		
	Before	After	
All Women	Ratio	Ratio	% Change
Pincoya	135.9	130.0	− 4.3
Cortijo	115.9	128.8	+11.2
Quinta Bella	134.0	207.9	+55.0
Total (All)	154.8	155.3	+0.3
High-Risk Women			
Pincoya	165.0	109.4	− 33.7
Cortijo	140.7	97.8	− 30.4
Quinta Bella	172.2	200.0	+16.1
Total (HRW)	193.8	134.4	− 30.7

Abortion rates decreased by 59 per cent in Pincoya, the community with full intervention. In Cortijo, where the intervention was only partial, the rates also decreased by 51 per cent. And in the control area of Quinta Bella, rates decreased by 31 per cent. These decreases in abortion rates are in line with our initial expectations and support our study hypothesis (Table 2.6).

With respect to abortion ratios, shown in Table 2.7, the impact of the intervention is even more evident. Abortion ratios decreased by 4 per cent in Pincoya; but increased by 11 per cent in Cortijo and by 55 per cent in Quinta Bella. The increase in the abortion ratio in Cortijo, however, is simply a reflection of a larger relative decline in pregnancies than in abortions, although both experienced a decline. As already noted (Table 2.5), in all three communities the number of pregnancies declined substantially during the period of the intervention, probably due, at least in part, to the population of women becoming older. The decrease in Pincoya was 58 per cent; in the other two communities, 56 per cent.

Tests of significance show that differences between the community with full intervention and the control community are significant, as are the differences between the community with partial intervention and the control area. However, the differences between the communities with full and partial intervention are not statistically significant. The implication of these findings is important for policy, because it shows that the added cost of individual home visits, while effective, may not be justified.

Abortion Rates and Ratios for High-Risk Women

For each of the three communities, we also looked at the women we had classified as having a high risk of abortion. The lower half of Tables 2.6 and 2.7 show the abortion rates and ratios for these women. In Pincoya, abortion rates decreased by 72 per cent; in Cortijo, by 68 per cent; and in Quinta Bella, by 51 per cent. Abortion ratios decreased by 34 per cent in Pincoya and by 30 per cent in Cortijo, but increased 16 per cent in Quinta Bella. As in the group comprising all women of reproductive age, the truly significant differences were between the two communities that received the intervention and the one that did not, but not between the two intervened communities.

Abortion Risk and Contraception

Our final analysis aims at documenting the complex inter-relationship between abortion, abortion risk, and contraceptive use by level of intervention in each of the three communities. This is perhaps the most important step in the analysis of our data, as it provides the most direct answer to the central hypothesis of our study regarding the impact of family planning on abortion.

To fully understand the effects of the intervention in terms of behavioural outcomes, we had to consider the different levels of abortion risk among women of reproductive age as well as their contraceptive status. To this effect, as noted before, we eliminated from the analysis pregnant women whose pregnancy was advanced, or who had been sterilized or had a hysterectomy in both the first and second surveys. The purpose was to have a population truly exposed to the risk of pregnancy and abortion, even though this substantially reduced our study sample.

The women who received the full intervention of home visits and services in Pincoya, and who, as a consequence, adopted effective methods of contraception, showed the largest decrease in abortion rates, 83 per cent, and in abortion ratios, 52 per cent (Tables 2.8 and 2.9). In contrast, women in

Table 2.8: Abortion Rates among High-Risk Women, by Contraceptive Status: Before and After the Intervention

Communities	Using Contraception			Not Using Contraception		
	Women	Abortions	Rate	Women	Abortions	Rate
Pincoya:						
Before	278	28	100.7	88	10	113.6
After	286	5	17.5	80	6	75.0
% change			−82.6			−34.0
Cortijo:						
Before	196	14	71.4	37	7	189.2
After	186	4	21.5	47	4	85.1
% change			−69.9			−55.0
Quinta Bella:						
Before	226	21	92.9	59	14	237.3
After	227	10	44.1	58	7	120.7
% change			−52.5			−49.1

Note: Rates are per 1,000 women of reproductive age.

Table 2.9: Abortion Ratios among High-Risk Women, by Contraceptive Status: Before and After the Intervention

Communities	Using Contraception			Not Using Contraception		
	Women	Abortions	Rate	Women	Abortions	Rate
Pincoya:						
Before	170	28	164.7	42	10	238.1
After	63	5	79.4	23	6	260.9
% change			−51.8			+9.6
Cortijo:						
Before	114	14	122.8	20	7	350.0
After	42	4	95.2	15	4	266.7
% change			−22.5			−23.8
Quinta Bella:						
Before	158	21	141.9	32	14	437.5
After	52	10	192.3	17	7	411.8
% change			+35.5			−5.9

Note: Ratios are per 1,000 pregnancies.

Pincoya who received the full intervention, but who did not change their contraceptive behaviour, had a significantly lower decrease in abortion rates of 34 per cent; and an increase in abortion ratios of 10 per cent. The abortion rate decreases are statistically significant when either Pincoya or Cortijo, the intervened areas, are compared with the control area, Quinta Bella.

When comparing the 'before/after' behavioural changes in each group, the most significant effect was the shift to more effective contraceptive use in the two intervened communities. Among non-users of contraception there was also a clear decrease in abortion risk in these communities, although not as pronounced as among women using contraception. In Pincoya, there is a greater difference between the decrease in abortion rates between women using and not using contraception than in the other communities (Table 2.8). The pattern of change in abortion ratios among users of contraception matches that of the abortion rates, although among non-users, the pattern is less clear (Table 2.9).

When considering relative risk, we found a greater increase in the risk of abortion among non-users of contraception in the community with full intervention. The increase in risk is particularly high among women who were classified as having a 'high risk' of abortion, but who did not adopt effective contraception. The increase in relative risk appears to be lower in the partially intervened and control communities, which may be explained by the fact that we did not search out and visit the women with high risk of abortion in these areas as we did in the fully intervened community where such risk applied to just a few women. These findings generally confirm that women who do not use contraception have a higher risk of abortion.

Discussion and Policy Implications

Abortion, regardless of its legal status, is a reality for many women facing unwanted pregnancy. Despite the increased outreach of family planning programmes, abortion continues to exist and has played an important role in fertility declines. Nevertheless, the relationship between abortion and contraception continues to be poorly understood.

Our study, starting with the development of an instrument to identify and predict abortion risk, followed by an intervention designed to apply the instrument in three low-income communities, including a control group, has demonstrated that increasing the prevalence of contraceptive use among women identified as having a high abortion risk does reduce its incidence.

The predictive instrument developed to identify abortion risk is perhaps the most innovative aspect of our study. It is easily applicable by health staff with basic training in primary health care and community work. Its application allows concentrated efforts within segments of a population where primary prevention is needed the most, such as among women of low socioeconomic level in developing countries where abortion is illegal and its incidence is high.

Because of the difficulties in obtaining totally reliable data on induced abortion, we decided on the alternative strategy of classifying all types of abortion, including both spontaneous and induced, under a single category. The levels of spontaneous abortion reported were far too high to be realistic anyway. And by placing all abortions into a single category, we did not under-enumerate the level of induced abortion, which would have risked a major bias.

Although we were aware that improved methods for measuring induced abortion prevalence have been suggested, such methods require greater anonymity than was possible in our intervention study, which necessitated home visits to high-risk women. We felt this was true even though we were not contacting them about their past abortion behaviour but rather trying to help them prevent repeat abortion.

Our results show that more personalized family planning services, in association with risk detection, can succeed in lowering abortion. Definitely the population who received the benefit of the full intervention and who subsequently increased their use of effective contraception showed the clearest decline in abortion rates. These behavioural changes could be observed, even in a relatively short period of time, which had been one of our main concerns when we planned the study. It is possible, therefore, to suggest that such approaches be incorporated in discussions concerning family planning strategy, particularly when the goal is to lower abortion. A risk approach can be more effective than a more typical clinic-based family planning programme in contexts such as those of the communities studied.

In experimental situations involving human populations there is always the danger of external interference that can introduce unexpected biases as a result of changes in the larger national or local context. Such changes are often beyond the control of the project staff. We were lucky that there were no major changes in the family planning policy of the Ministry of Health of Chile during the intervention period between September 1989 and February 1991. Although the project did coincide with the discussion of an amendment to eliminate an article in the national health legislation that allowed pregnancy interruption for therapeutic reasons. The amendment was passed but it is doubtful that this became an issue for discussion among the women in the communities we studied.

Another factor that facilitated the study was the important and constant institutional and professional support provided by the health area director in charge of the clinics servicing the communities that were intervened. We were also fortunate that there were no changes in local health service policies during the period in any of the clinics serving the three communities studied.

There was one possibility of an external source introducing unexpected bias, however. One of our own project staff, the social worker assigned to home visits in Pincoya, was a highly motivated woman. She was able to make an average of three visits to each woman classified as having a high risk of induced abortion and she was able to establish a very close relationship with most of them. As the intervention continued, she became an influential person in the community and encouraged pregnant women to continue their pregnancies, which eventually resulted in an increase in live births. She also promoted contraception very strongly. Local women may have decided against a clandestine abortion to avoid feeling ashamed in front of this very friendly, yet strong, community worker. Was there also a fear that she might denounce them to the authorities if she found out that they had an illegal abortion? This could be a possibility, but it does not seem probable under the circumstances. However, this potential bias cannot be verified. In Cortijo, the partially intervened community, there was no social worker to undertake personal motivation or community work and the outcome of the intervention was, as we have already noted, less successful in terms of reducing the abortion rate and ratio. In short, the personal dimension in intervention work is important, albeit difficult to measure.

In conclusion, we believe our study has shown that an effective intervention, of improved family planning services with personalized inputs, directed at women with high risk of abortion, can be successful in lowering abortion incidence in populations of low socioeconomic status, especially in contexts where abortion is illegal.

We may also suggest that by applying a risk strategy in communities with high incidence of illegal induced abortion, it may be possible to lower maternal mortality due to complications of unsafe abortion (Sotelo, 1993). The cost of implementing a programme of this type more widely could be recovered from savings obtained from eliminating hospitalizations due to abortion complications.

After this initial experimental experience, we recommend that our intervention model be tested in other settings. The application of the predictive instrument to identify abortion risk in communities different from those studied in Chile might validate further our results and permit this approach to be extended to primary health care services in other countries where abortion is illegal, particularly in the Americas.

✝ References

APROFA/CERC. 1990. Encuesta de fecundidad en area metropolitana de Santiago, Final Report, unpublished, Santiago: Chile.

Armijo, R. and **T. Monreal.** 1968. Epidemiología del aborto en Chile. Communication presented to the Chilean Health Society, unpublished, Santiago, Chile.

Barreto, T., O.M. Campbell, L. Davies, V. Faveau, V. Filippi, W. Graham, M. Mamdami, C. Rooney and **N.F. Toubia.** 1992. Investigating induced abortion in developing countries: Methods and problems. *Studies in Family Planning* 23: 159–70.

Faúndes, A., G. Rodríguez and **O. Avendaño.** 1968. The San Gregorio experimental family planning program: Changes observed in fertility and abortion rates. *Demography* 5 (2): 836–45.

Maramatsu, M. 1988. Japan, In: Paul Sachdev. *International Handbook on Abortion.* New York: Greenwood Press, pp. 293–301.

Molina, R., C. Pereda, F. Cumsille et al. 1990. Prevención el embarazo en mujeres con alto riesgo de aborto. In: M. Requena (ed.). *Aborto inducido en Chile.* Santiago de Chile: Edición Sociedad Chilena de Salud Pública, Impresora CRECES Ltda.

Panamerican Health Organization (PAHO). 1986. Manual sobre enfoque de riesgo en la atención materno-infantil. PALTEX: Para ejecutores de programas de Salud, No. 7.

Paxman, J.M., A. Rizo, L. Brown and **J. Benson.** 1993. La epidemia clandestina: La práctica del aborto ilegal en América Latina. *Perpectivas Internacionales en Planificación Familiar. Número Especial,* pp. 9–15.

Pereda, C. 1986. Factors and predictors of discontinuation of oral contraceptives and IUDs in public health clinics of Santiago, metropolitan area, Final Report to WHO/HRP, Santiago, Chile.

Requena, B,M. 1965. Social and economic correlates of induced abortion in Santiago, Chile. *Demography* 2:2.

———. 1990. *Aborto inducido en Chile*. Santiago, Chile: Sociedad Chilena de salud pública, Impresora CRECES Ltda.

Singh, S. and **D. Wulf.** 1991. Cálculo de los niveles de aborto en el Brasil Colombia y Perú a base de datos hospitalarios y de encuestas de fecundidad. *Perspectivas Internacionales en Planificación Familiar. Número Especial*, pp. 14–23.

———. 1993. The likelihood of induced abortion among women hospitalized for abortion complication in four Latin American countries. *International Family Planning Perspectives* 19(4). December: 134–41.

Sotelo, M. 1993. El enfoque de riesgo y la mortalidad materna: Una perspectiva latinoamericana (informe especial). *Boletín de la Oficina Panamericana de la Salud*. 114 (4): 289–301.

Viel, B. and **C. Pereda.** 1991. El embarazo no deseado. Resultados de un proyecto apoyado por HRP/OMS, (82046). *Boletín de la Asociación Chilena de Protección de la Familia* No. 1/12 Enero Diciembre.

Weisner, H.M. 1990. Comportamiento reproductivo y aborto inducido en mujeres Chilenas de sectores populares. Una perspectiva antropológica. In: M. Requena (ed.). *Aborto inducido en Chile*. Santiago, Chile: Edición Sociedad Chilena de Salud Pública, Impresora CRECES Ltda.

World Bank. 1993. Inversión en salud. USA: Oxford University Press.

3

Factors Affecting Induced Abortion Behaviour Among Married Women in Shanghai, China

Gui Shi-xun

Introduction

The family planning programme implemented by the government of China in the late 1970s and then strengthened during the 1980s has been very success-ful in Shanghai in at least one sense: the total fertility rate in 1990 reached the very low level of 1.23 children per woman. Moreover, in 1993, Shanghai expe-rienced negative growth, with a birth rate of 6.5 per thousand, and a mortality rate of 7.3 per thousand, which resulted in a rate of natural increase of –0.8 per thousand (for the population with de jure household registration). Pro-jections for the next century show a continuing negative rate of natural increase for Shanghai (Gui Shi-xun et al., 1994).

Despite the high use of contraception in Shanghai, the municipality has traditionally had a higher rate of induced abortion than reported for other parts of China. According to results from the First In-depth Fertility Survey of China (State Statistical Bureau, 1986), the abortion rate for Shanghai Municipality in 1983 was 119.5 per thousand women, a much higher rate than Hebei (50.9 per thousand) and Shaanxi (38.3 per thousand), the other two provinces included in the survey (see also: Gao Er-sheng et al., 1988). While there has been a decline in the induced abortion rate for women in Shanghai in recent years, its level still remains fairly high: 68 per thousand in 1991 (Research Team on Induced Abortion, 1994).

Undoubtedly, the extensive use of induced abortion, which is legal in China, plays an important role in maintaining such a low level of fertility. This would indicate that there is some urgency for the family planning authorities to lower the rates of induced abortion and the number of unwanted pregnancies.

Objectives

The main purpose of our study was to identify the factors that affect the decision to have an induced abortion among married women in both the urban and surrounding rural areas of Shanghai. We also wanted to identify approaches that could lead to a reduction of the induced abortion rate, especially repeat abortions, to protect women's health. To this effect a survey of social, psychological and demographic factors affecting unwanted pregnancy among married women was carried out in Shanghai in 1991. This chapter presents a preliminary analysis of the findings of this survey.

Research Methodology

The survey of 10 sites started on 22 April 1991. Six sites in the urban area of Shanghai included: the International Peace Maternal and Child Hospital; the No. 1 Maternal and Child Hospital of Shanghai; the No. 1 People's Hospital of Shanghai; and the Maternal and Child Hospital in Luwang, Changlin and Putuo districts. The survey also included four sites in rural areas: the Maternal and Child Hospital in Jiading County, in Chuangsha County and in Songjian County; and the Center Hospital of Fengxian County. All these hospitals were selected as part of a plan laid out in collaboration with the Chinese Family Planning Technology Center.

A simple random sampling procedure was used to select the women for the survey. The potential subjects were all women who registered at any of the hospitals selected requesting an induced abortion. Women had to have de jure household registration in Shanghai, that is, legal residence in the municipality. Based on the statistical data on the estimates of total induced abortions for married women in Shanghai in 1990, we arrived at a sample size of 2,806 women ($\alpha = 0.05$). The ratio between urban and rural areas was 65.6/34.4, which determined how the sample size was divided.

The final study population was reduced to 2,765 women, representing a 98 per cent response rate; 2,760 men were also interviewed. For these subjects, 2,644 women, or 95.6 per cent, were cases with gestations of 'equal to or less than 90 days' (first trimester); and for 121 women, or 4.4 per cent, gestations were 'equal to or more than 91 days' (second trimester).

All field personnel, including supervisors and interviewers, were female medical workers who received training in how to conduct face-to-face interviews. Subjects were interviewed just before and after the induced abortion. In order to guarantee confidentiality and to ensure the quality of the interviews, a list of married women who had registered for abortion was used to identify the addresses of the study subjects. As a result, in the actual questionnaire used for the survey, the name and address of the subjects was not recorded, which ensured complete anonymity.

Study Results

Abortion Incidence Among Married Women

Abortion by Age

Women aged 25–29 years represented the largest proportion, nearly a third, among the 2,765 married women who had an induced abortion, followed by the 30–34 age group. These two age groups represented 61 per cent of the women in the sample (Table 3.1). Given that we knew exactly the proportion that our sample represented of all the women who had an abortion in Shanghai, we decided to estimate abortion rates by age for the total Shanghai Municipality. One problem was the lack of information on married women, by age, according to de jure household registration of Shanghai, in mid-1991. In order to circumvent this problem, the proportion of the 20–49-year-old female population on 1 July 1990, derived from the fourth census of Shanghai, was used. The census data on the number of married women was used to calculate the denominator; the induced abortion rate for all married women with de jure household registration in 1991 was used to obtain the total number of induced abortions in 1991. This total was 70.32 times larger than the sample size. Next, we took the number of women in each age group in our sample, all of whom had an abortion, and expanded each group 70.32 times. This approach gave us the total abortions by age. Then that number was divided by the number of married women for each age group and the results were estimated age-specific abortion rates for married women in Shanghai in 1991.

The resulting age-specific rates are shown in Table 3.1. They reveal that while abortions are proportionally higher in the 25–34-year age group, the actual abortion rate is much higher for the very young women. The total abortion rate, that is, the average number of abortions a woman would have if she experienced the abortion pattern of these women over her lifetime, would be 2.3 abortions.

Table 3.1: Married Women by Age, Shanghai, 1991*

Age Group	20–24	25–29	30–34	35–39	40–44	45–49	Total
Proportion	17.5	32.1	29.4	16.1	4.8	0.1	100.0
Rates	195.7	114.7	75.3	47.9	21.1	1.0	**2.3

* Women who had an abortion (N = 2,765).
** Total abortion rate.

Abortion and Education

The sample of women was highly educated. The majority, 80.8 per cent, had completed junior and senior middle school; only 10 per cent had finished primary school or less. Another 10 per cent had completed training school, college or a higher level. Utilizing a similar procedure as for age-specific rates, we used data from the fourth census of Shanghai to estimate abortion rates for these educational categories (Table 3.2). It is clear from these data that the higher the educational level, the more likely a woman is to end an unplanned pregnancy by abortion.

Table 3.2: Married Women by Education, Shanghai, 1991*

Education Level	Illiterate	Near Illiterate	Primary	Senior H. School	Junior H. School	Training School	College or More	Total
Proportion (%)	0.8	3.0	6.3	40.0	40.8	6.2	2.9	100.0
Rates	–	44.2**	25.2	62.6	95.5	134.4	122.2	

* Women who had an abortion (N = 2,765).
** Includes illiterate women.

Abortion and Occupation

The women who had the highest proportion of induced abortion were production and transportation workers; the second highest were technicians; and the third highest were service workers. We also estimated induced abortion rates by occupation, which are shown in Table 3.3. What this reveals is that there is a high correlation with our findings by educational level: women in higher level occupations, such as technical, business, office and service jobs, have the highest rates of abortion.

Table 3.3: Married Women by Occupation, Shanghai, 1991*

Occupation	Technician	Manager	Office Worker	Businessman	Attendant	Agriculture Worker	Production	Other Worker	Not Working	Total
Proportion (%)	15.6	1.0	8.7	8.6	9.7	3.0	45.5	0.1	7.8	100.0
Rates	79.4	53.6	149.2	92.5	64.1	19.8	62.2	292.6	345.6	

* Women who had an abortion (N = 2,765).

Abortion and Residence

The proportion of women with established urban residence (registered) among our sample of 2,765 married women was 72.3 per cent. Those with rural registration amounted to 27.7 per cent. The corresponding abortion rates for these groups are 77.8 per thousand and 51.2 per thousand, respectively. In short, in Shanghai, married urban women have higher abortion rates than married rural women.

Abortion and Health

Induced abortion, especially repeated induced abortions, may impact negatively on health and have long-term adverse effects. Of the 1,446 married women who had experienced one previous induced abortion, 11.8 per cent believed the operation had been harmful to their health, and among this group one-third claimed the harm was serious. Of 350 women who had experienced two previous induced abortions, 16.1 per cent responded that their operation had been harmful; and among them, a half claimed the harm was serious. Similar responses were given by women with three or more previous abortions, yet, despite this concern they returned for still another abortion as a result of their current unwanted pregnancy.

Reasons for Abortion

Reasons for Abortion in the Past

A large majority of induced abortions are the result of women's wishes to terminate unwanted pregnancies resulting either from contraceptive failure or from non-use of contraception, which accounted for 96.3 per cent of all abortions in our study sample. The rest were for health or other personal reasons.

Among the 2,765 women in our sample, nearly half were requesting an abortion for the first time, 47.7 per cent. The other half of the sample, 1,446 women, had experienced one or more abortions in the past. Among these women, the distribution of these earlier abortions was: 69.4 per cent had experienced one previous abortion; 24.2 per cent had two; 4.9 per cent had three; 1.0 per cent had four; and 0.5 per cent had five or more. One woman had experienced seven induced abortions in the past.

Among the 1,004 women who had one previous abortion, the main reason for the unwanted pregnancy was non-use of contraceptive methods (54.8 per cent). As the number of previous abortions increases, however, contraceptive failure becomes the dominant reason for seeking abortion. Women with more abortion experience tend to be older and less likely to continue risking unwanted pregnancy; however, given the poor quality of methods available, their use of contraception does not always prevent an unwanted pregnancy (Table 3.4).

Reasons for the Current Abortion

Of the 2,765 pregnant women requesting abortion at the time of the study, 24.7 per cent had not used contraception at the time of conception. A very large proportion, 75.3 per cent, reported that contraceptive failure had led them to seek an abortion. This led us to explore the reasons for not using

Table 3.4: Reasons for Pregnancy Termination in the Past (%)*

Causes	Induced Abortions						
	1	*2*	*3*	*4*	*5*	*6*	*7*
(N)	*(1,004)*	*(350)*	*(71)*	*(14)*	*(5)*	*(1)*	*(1)*
Not using	54.8	28.1	14.1	10.0	16.6	0	0
Failure	45.1	71.7	84.8	85.0	66.7	100.0	100.0
No answer	0.1	0.2	1.1	5.0	16.7	0	0
Total	100.0	100.0	100.0	100.0	100.0	100.0	100.0

* Women who had one or more previous abortions (N =1,446).

contraception in a city such as Shanghai, where services are widely available. We also looked at possible explanations for such a high rate of contraceptive failure.

Reasons for Not Using Contraception

To understand why one-fourth of the couples were not using contraception at the time they became pregnant, we decided to see what factors may have had an effect on their behaviour. We included in our analysis the background characteristics of the women and their husbands, such as their economic and social position, sexual behaviour, and general living and working environment.

Overall, we selected 29 variables, which were grouped into five main factors for analysis. The first factor was personal background and included the age of the women and their husbands. The second factor measured economic circumstances and included the occupation of each woman and her husband, within the six months before the current pregnancy, as well as the average net household income during the previous year. The third factor reflected social conditions and included the women and men's educational level, de jure residence registration, leisure time during the week of conception, duration of marriage, fertility history, induced abortion history, and knowledge of contraception. The fourth factor reflected the women and men's contraceptive and sexual behaviour, and included: whether the couple discussed the choice of contraceptive methods; mutual sexual satisfaction; the frequency of sexual intercourse per week during the six months before the current pregnancy; and who initiated sexual intercourse during the period of conception. The fifth factor defined the living/working environment and included: their area of residence within the six months prior to the current pregnancy; the type of work unit; attitude of neighbours towards abortion; attitudes of colleagues towards abortion; and whether the family planning programme staff in the woman's district and work unit knew about their contraceptive status before the current pregnancy.

The results showed that the proportion of women who became pregnant due to non-use of contraception varied significantly by each of the five main factors described above. For example, except for women aged 45–49 years and men aged 50 years or more (a relatively small group), the younger the subjects, the higher the proportion who became pregnant due to non-use of contraception (Table 3.5).

Table 3.5: Main Reasons for Pregnancy Termination, by Age (%)*

Contraception		20–24	25–29	30–34	35–39	40–44	45–49	50+
Women	Non-use	49.0	25.7	18.3	11.9	11.4	25.0	–
	Failure	51.0	74.3	81.7	88.1	88.6	75.0	–
	Total	100.0	100.0	100.0	100.0	100.0	100.0	–
Men	Non-use	67.6	31.1	19.3	16.2	11.1	16.7	25.0
	Failure	32.4	68.9	80.7	83.8	88.9	83.3	75.0
	Total	100.0	100.0	100.0	100.0	100.0	100.0	100.0

* Women who had an abortion (N = 2,765) and the men concerned (N = 2,760).

It is also quite interesting that in almost all age groups, men tend to report higher proportions of non-use than the women. This difference was particularly noticeable among the younger age groups. Does this mean that younger men are less aware of their wives' contraceptive choices and use? We do not have the answer to this question, but it seems from our data that as couples get older, they tend to discuss their contraceptive decisions and choices more openly with each other.

Women with only primary education were the most likely to fall into the non-use category. In fact, the proportion of women who became pregnant due to non-use of contraception was highest in the middle or lower levels of the educational scale. Moreover, except for the illiterate group, the lower the men's educational level, the higher the percentage of women not using contraception. Contraceptive failure, on the other hand, seemed to be more common among the illiterate or the more highly educated women (Table 3.6).

Table 3.6: Main Reasons for Pregnancy Termination, by Education (%)*

Education		Illiterate	Near Illiterate	Primary	Junior	Senior	Under College	College or More	No Answer
Women	Non-use	21.7	28.0	35.3	27.5	22.9	10.5	17.3	0
	Failure	78.3	72.0	64.7	72.5	77.1	89.5	82.7	0
	Total	100.0	100.0	100.0	100.0	100.0	100.0	100.0	0
Men	Non-use	0	38.2	29.7	28.4	24.4	13.9	13.8	0
	Failure	100.0	61.8	70.3	71.6	75.6	86.1	86.2	100.0
	Total	100.0	100.0	100.0	100.0	100.0	100.0	100.0	100.0

* Women who had an abortion (N = 2,765) and the men concerned (N = 2,750).

The educational level of the men seems to have an important influence on contraceptive behaviour; among the more educated men the proportions of 'non-use' as a reason for the pregnancy termination of their wives are very low.

The proportion of women who became pregnant due to non-use of contraception was higher when they and the men had rural de jure household registration; 33.3 per cent and 32.4 per cent, respectively. The proportions were lower among women and men with urban de jure household registration; 21.4 per cent and 22.1 per cent, respectively.

Women and men who were not working during the six months prior to the pregnancy were the highest proportions not using contraception: 47.9 per cent and 37.5 per cent, respectively. Among specific occupational groups, women engaged in agriculture, forestry, animal husbandry and fishery were the highest proportions not using, at 27.4 per cent; for the men, the percentage was 27.9 per cent. These proportions were above average, perhaps indicative of their rural, more traditional habits and values. Second among non-users was the group of women and men in productive activities and transportation; at 25.7 per cent and 27.1 per cent, respectively. It is clear that the relationship between non-use and occupation is a close one and that non-use as a reason for pregnancy termination is lower among men and women with higher paying jobs, such as those in technical or office positions. At the same time, men and women in these kinds of jobs use more efficient methods but also experience higher rates of contraceptive failure. They seek abortions because they fear that their job situation could be negatively affected by a pregnancy that is not permitted by the one-child policy (Table 3.7).

The patterns of non-use by type of work unit are shown in Table 3.8. As already noted, the proportions not using contraception were particularly high among non-working women and men and also for men and women working in individual or private working units, where they do not have to report to family planning field supervisors often. Such units are small-scale and have emerged as a result of a more open market oriented policy in China. Women and men working in state enterprises or in collective units had lower non-use levels, probably because of better family planning surveillance by local cadres. This was confirmed when we explored the degree of family planning inputs in relation to the use of contraception. We found that the proportion of women not using contraception was higher where supervision by the family planning programme staff was lower. Of the 683 women not using contraceptive methods, 71.7 per cent said the family planning programme monitors did not know they were 'not using'. Another 12.4 per cent who were not using methods said the family planning workers knew it, but were indifferent. The remaining 15.9 per cent of non-users explained that the family planning workers were opposed to their not using contraception, but did not offer them any guidance.

Interestingly, the more leisure time the women and men had during the month before the pregnancy, the higher the percentage of non-use of

Table 3.7: Main Reasons for Pregnancy Termination, by Occupation (%)*

Occupation		Technician	Manager	Office Worker	Businessman	Attendant	Agriculture Worker	Production	Other Worker	No Job	No Answer
Women	Non-use	17.6	25.0	17.0	23.6	20.1	27.4	25.7	0	47.9	0
	Failure	82.4	75.0	83.0	76.4	79.9	72.6	74.3	100.0	52.1	100.0
	Total	100.0	100.0	100.0	100.0	100.0	100.0	100.0	100.0	100.0	100.0
Men	Non-use	16.3	19.4	17.8	30.0	26.2	27.9	27.1	100.0	37.5	30.0
	Failure	83.7	80.6	82.2	70.0	73.8	72.1	72.9	0	62.5	70.0
	Total	100.0	100.0	100.0	100.0	100.0	100.0	100.0	100.0	100.0	100.0

* Women who had an abortion (N = 2,764) and the men concerned (N = 2,730). (Occupations for one woman and 20 men were 'not clear'.)

Table 3.8: Current Pregnancy Causes, by Type of Working Unit (%)*

Type of Working Units		State	Collective	Individual	Private	Joint Ventures	Other	No Employment	Not Clear
Women	Non-use	18.5	27.3	40.0	40.0	26.8	20.8	47.9	0
	Failure	81.5	72.7	60.0	60.0	73.2	79.2	52.1	100.0
	Total	100.0	100.0	100.0	100.0	100.0	100.0	100.0	100.0
Men	Non-use	20.6	31.4	35.8	41.7	21.7	29.5	37.5	16.7
	Failure	79.4	68.6	64.2	58.3	78.3	70.5	62.5	83.3
	Total	100.0	100.0	100.0	100.0	100.0	100.0	100.0	100.0

* Women who had an abortion (N = 2,762) and the men concerned (N = 2,744). (Types of working unit for three women and six men were 'not clear'.)

contraception. This percentage was higher for the women and men who had an average leisure time of 36–42 hours every week, 42.0 per cent and 45.8 per cent, respectively (Table 3.9). This indicates, as in previous tables, that men and women who are not working tend to have a greater tendency not to use contraception. It seems also that people with 36 or more hours of 'leisure time' may actually be 'unemployed'.

Table 3.9: Main Reasons for Pregnancy Termination, by Couples' Leisure Time (%)*

Leisure Time (Hours per Week)		0	1–7	8–14	15–21	22–28	29–35	36–42	43+	Not Clear
Women	Non-use	18.0	18.5	20.7	26.0	34.0	33.3	42.0	41.1	75.0
	Failure	82.0	81.5	79.3	74.0	66.0	66.7	58.0	58.9	25.0
	Total	100.0	100.0	100.0	100.0	100.0	100.0	100.0	100.0	100.0
Men	Non-use	26.4	20.9	21.1	25.0	28.2	29.7	45.8	40.9	16.7
	Failure	73.6	79.1	78.9	75.0	71.8	70.3	54.2	59.1	83.3
	Total	100.0	100.0	100.0	100.0	100.0	100.0	100.0	100.0	100.0

* Women who had an abortion (N = 2,761) and the men concerned (N = 2,732). (The leisure time of four subjects and 18 husbands was 'not clear'.)

As expected, the proportion not using contraception was higher (50.6 per cent) among childless women than among women who had children (22.2 per cent).

The less knowledge of contraceptive methods women had, the higher the rate of non-use. The result showed that among 2,082 women who experienced contraceptive failure, the average number of methods known was 4.8. Among 683 women not using contraception, the same average was much lower: 3.6 methods.

Similarly, women and men who talked more frequently about their choice of contraceptive methods were the least likely to report non-use as the reason for an abortion. The proportions not using any contraceptive method were: 15.9 per cent for couples who 'often' talked about the use of methods; 22 per cent for couples who 'sometimes' talked about this; 24.8 per cent for couples who 'seldom' talked; and 29.9 per cent for couples who 'never' discussed contraception.

The frequency of sexual intercourse was directly correlated with non-use of contraception. Couples who had sex more frequently had a higher proportion of women not using contraceptives. The actual proportions not using were: 22.9 per cent for couples who had sexual relations 'once a week'; 24.2 per cent, for 'twice a week'; 26.6 per cent, for '3 times a week'; 28.0 per cent, for '4 times a week'; 63.6 per cent, for '5 times a week'; and 69.2 per cent for '6 times a week'. This finding is interesting in that it runs contrary to expectations; one would assume that couples who are more sexually active would be most worried about pregnancy protection.

Women and men who declared to have lower levels of sexual satisfaction were more likely to be non-users of contraception. Those who discussed their sexual life 'often' and were mutually satisfied, had a lower level of non-use, 20.4 per cent (measured during the six months prior to pregnancy). Women and men who responded 'seldom' and 'sometimes' to their frequency of discussion about sexual life had somewhat higher levels of non-use, 22.5 per cent and 23.7 per cent, respectively. Among women and men who 'never' discussed issues relating to their sex lives, non-use was highest (30.4 per cent).

A Closer Look at Contraceptive Non-Use

We wanted to explore whether not using contraception at the time the pregnancy occurred was part of an established behavioural pattern or a one-time occurrence. For this line of inquiry, we decided to look into the main reasons for not using contraceptive methods in the two years prior to the current pregnancy.

We presented 15 possible reasons to 793 women (a sub-set of our main sample) who had a previous abortion and who had not used contraception to avoid that earlier pregnancy, provided the pregnancy occurred within the two years preceding the interview. We asked these women to rank each reason according to its applicability. The reasons included: (*a*) desire to have a child according to the family planning policy; (*b*) desire to have a birth even though it is not permitted by the family planning policy; (*c*) lactation makes pregnancy impossible; (*d*) not aware of contraceptive methods; (*e*) no confidence in contraceptive methods; (*f*) husband not cooperative; (*g*) contraception may impair health; (*h*) contraception may affect sexual ability; (*i*) contraceptive use interferes with sexual enjoyment; (*j*) contraception is troublesome; (*k*) induced abortion is not harmful to health; (*l*) after induced abortion women can be taken care of by the government or work units; (*m*) no contraception available; (*n*) unmarried; (*o*) other reasons.

The results showed that for these women with previous abortion experience and who, for the last two years, had not used contraception, the three major reasons for non-use were: 'unmarried' (32.5 per cent); 'protected by lactation' (24.8 per cent); 'did not know any methods' (17.3 per cent). For 124 women who had two previous induced abortions, the two main reasons were the same: 'unmarried' (23.4 per cent); 'protected by lactation' (19.4 per cent). The other main reasons for this second group were 'desire to have a birth according to the family planning policy' and 'method seen as troublesome' (16.9 per cent). For 13 women who had three previous abortions, the first major reason was the same as for the other two groups: 'unmarried' (23.1 per cent). The other primary reasons were 'desire to have a birth according to the family planning policy' and 'consider that contraception may impair health' (15.4 per cent, each). Of two women who had experienced four induced abortions, one was unmarried and another did not know of contraceptive methods. Lastly, one subject had experienced five induced abortions, because she had no confidence in any contraceptive method. What is striking here is that so many women had sought abortion because they were unmarried. This is clearly an indication that efforts should be made to provide family planning information to unmarried women, even within the context of large, metropolitan areas such as Shanghai. Similarly, the large number of pregnancies due to poor understanding of the protective effect of breastfeeding could be corrected by improving counselling to post-partum women.

For the 683 women now seeking abortion and who had not used contraception during the immediate time preceding the current pregnancy, the three major reasons for non-use were: believing that 'contraception is troublesome' (24.9 per cent); that a woman is protected 'during lactation period' (21.7 per cent); and 'desire to have a birth permitted by family planning policy' (13.6 per cent) (Table 3.10).

Table 3.10: The 10 Major Reasons for Not Using Contraception at the Time of the Current Pregnancy

Ranking of Reasons	The Concrete Reasons	%*
1st	contraception is troublesome	24.9
2nd	protected during lactation period	21.7
3rd	wanted a child within policy	13.6
4th	contraceptives not available	9.7
5th	other reasons	9.7
6th	did not know contraceptive methods	8.9
7th	methods impair health	4.0
8th	no confidence in contraception	3.5
9th	husband not cooperative	2.5
10th	wanted a child outside policy	1.5

* N = 683 women.

Considering the demographic, economic, social characteristics, sexual behaviour and environmental factors affecting the women and men's non-use, the first five factors shown in Table 3.10 were selected for a cross-sectional analysis. We found that the proportions of those who believed they were 'protected during lactation' and who 'desired to have a birth according to the family planning policy' were higher among younger women and men. For both the women and men, the proportions who believed that they were protected by lactation is quite high and in all cases higher among the men. The distribution for women who believed that 'contraception is troublesome' by age group was lower at both extremes and higher for the middle age groups.

It is also important to note that the proportion of women saying that there were 'no contraceptives available during sexual intercourse' increased with age; going from 8.0 per cent in the 20–24 age group, to 10.5 per cent in the 25–29 age group, to 10.7 per cent in the 30–34 age group, and to 13.2 per cent in the 35–39 age group. Among 66 women who said that contraceptives were not available, the reasons were also interesting: 34.8 per cent of these women did not get the contraceptives because they found the method troublesome; and 21.2 per cent responded that it was inconvenient to get them. Similarly, the proportion of women with no confidence in contraceptive methods increased with age; going from 2.1 per cent in the 20–24 age group, to 2.6 per cent in the 25–29 age group, to 4.7 per cent in the 30–34 age group, to 7.5 per cent in 35–39 age group, and to 13.3 per cent in the 40–44 age group.

Among men and women who tended to have better communication on issues regarding contraception, particularly those who discussed it 'often', or 'sometimes' in the six months preceding the current pregnancy, the proportion of women and men not using contraception due to feeling protected 'during the lactation period' was highest (23.3 per cent and 25.2 per cent, respectively. In the same group, those who believed that contraceptives are 'troublesome' were 16.7 per cent for women and 23.3 per cent for men. In contrast, among women and men who 'seldom' or 'never' discussed contraception, the first reason given for not using contraceptives was that they were 'troublesome' (32.2 per cent and 21.2 per cent, respectively). The issue of perceiving methods of contraception as 'troublesome' reappears constantly and should be interpreted as a feeling of distrust and fear of the available choices, which are restricted to IUD or sterilization for couples seeking long-term contraception.

The Effect of Quality of Services

An important factor influencing the use of contraception, particularly the elimination of doubts and fears of methods, is the quality of services and follow-up offered by the staff of the family planning programme. Among women whose contraceptive status was unknown by the family planning workers who resided in the same district, the proportion of women who believed that contraceptives were 'troublesome' was 27.7 per cent, and among similar women where the family planning workers were in the same unit, the corresponding proportion was 32.0 per cent. In short, about a third of the women who had little or no contact with the family planning workers, either where they resided or worked, were worried about using contraception. But even among women whose non-use of contraception before the pregnancy was known by the local family planning workers, the proportion of women who said they had not used a method during sexual intercourse due to 'nonavailability of contraceptives' was similarly high, at 24.2 per cent. This is indicative of inadequacies in the local personalized supervisory systems that have been set up to help couples to use contraception effectively. Undoubtedly, the family planning programme had a major influence in determining whether or not couples were using effective contraceptives. A challenge to the programme is to change negative attitudes, particularly among women and men who believe that contraceptives are troublesome, by improving counselling, logistics, and the quality of care being provided by the existing services.

Contraceptive Failure

In addition to non-use of contraception as a reason for unwanted pregnancy and abortion, the other main reason for abortion among our sample of married women was contraceptive failure. To better understand the dynamics of this situation, first we explored the reasons why contraceptives had failed previously. We asked respondents to give scores to 15 possible reasons why they thought their method had failed: (*a*) pregnancy with IUD in situ; (*b*) IUD expulsion; (*c*) IUD overdue for removal; (*d*) oral pills taken improperly; (*e*) oral pills in deteriorated condition; (*f*) improper use of injectables; (*g*) condom breakage; (*h*) improper use of condoms; (*i*) wrong calculation of the safe period; (*j*) withdrawal failure; (*k*) new contraceptive failure; (*l*) male sterilization failure; (*m*) female sterilization failure; (*n*) other reasons; and (*o*) not clear. The next step was to explore contraceptive failure at the time of the current pregnancy.

Failure Before the Current Pregnancy

We first looked at information for 652 women who had experienced one previous induced abortion due to method failure. Among these women the most important reasons for failure were: 'IUD in situ' (23.2 per cent); 'wrong calculation of the safe period' (18.6 per cent); and 'oral pills taken improperly' (13.8 per cent). For another 317 women who had experienced two previous induced abortions, the three major reasons were: 'IUD in situ' (27.8 per cent); 'expulsion of IUD' (15.8 per cent); and 'wrong calculation of the safe period' (13.2 per cent). For 78 women who had experienced three previous induced abortions, the three major reasons were: 'IUD in situ' (37.2 per cent); 'wrong calculation of the safe period' (15.4 per cent); 'oral pills taken improperly' (12.8 per cent).

These data show clearly that IUD in situ is a major reason given for contraceptive failure, regardless of the number of previous abortions these women had. The data also point to the high failure of traditional methods, indicated by the high proportion of women who did not calculate the 'safe period' correctly.

Failure at the Time of the Current Pregnancy

Among the 2,082 women requesting an induced abortion for contraceptive failure—the cause of the current unwanted pregnancy—the three major reasons given were: 'IUD in situ' (25.0 per cent); 'wrong calculation of the safe

Table 3.11: The 10 Major Reasons for Contraceptive Failure for the Current Pregnancy

The Order	The Concrete Reasons	Proportion (%)*
1st	IUD in situ	25.0
2nd	wrongly calculated safe period	22.6
3rd	IUD expulsion	11.1
4th	improperly using condoms	10.1
5th	condom breakage	9.2
6th	oral pills taken improperly	7.9
7th	uncontrolled ejaculation	5.5
8th	other reasons	3.8
9th	reason not clear	2.7
10th	oral pills deteriorated	2.1

* N = 2,082.

period' (22.6 per cent), and 'IUD expulsion' (11.1 per cent) (Table 3.11). Considering the couples' personal background, their economic and social characteristics, sexual behaviour and environmental effects, 25 key variables were selected for a cross-sectional analysis to better understand these reasons for contraceptive failure.

The results regarding age showed that the younger the women, the higher the proportion of pregnancies due to 'IUD expulsion' and the lower the proportion of pregnancies due to 'improper use of condom'. The older the men, the higher the proportion of pregnancies due to 'wrong calculation of the safe period'.

For both women and men (excluding illiterate respondents), the lower the educational level, the higher the proportion of pregnancies due to 'IUD in situ' and 'oral pills taken improperly'. Illiterate women had the highest proportion of pregnancies due to 'oral pills deteriorated' (11.1 per cent).

It is quite interesting to note that contraceptive failure due to 'wrong calculation of the safe period' increases with the age of the man, but more noticeably with the level of education of both men and women.

Women and men in non-manual occupations such as 'technical', 'manager', 'office worker', had the highest proportion of unwanted pregnancy due to 'wrong calculation of the safe period'; ranging from 30–34 per cent among the women, and between 27–36 per cent for the men. Conversely, for people in manual occupations, such as 'agriculture, forestry, animal husbandry and fishery', the 'attendant' group, and the 'producer and transportation' group, 'IUD in situ' was the most important reason; ranging between 30–39 per cent for the women and between 28–42 per cent for the men.

As expected, among women with poorer knowledge of contraception, the proportion of 'oral pills taken improperly' was higher. For 164 pregnant women due to pill failure, the methods they knew averaged 4.0, which was lower than the average for all groups. However, women using less reliable methods, including withdrawal, tended to know more methods. For example, among the 471 women pregnant due to 'wrong calculation of the safe period', the average knowledge was 5.6 methods; 114 women pregnant due to 'uncontrolled ejaculation' (withdrawal) knew 5.4 methods; 211 women pregnant due to 'improper use of condoms' knew 5.1 methods; and 199 women pregnant due to 'condom breakage' knew 5.3 methods, higher than the average of all groups.

The explanation for these seemingly contradictory data about women's knowledge and actual use perhaps can be found in the data on gender relations. Correct use of the rhythm method seemed to be based on the quality of inter-spousal communication on matters dealing with sexual and contraceptive behaviour. To illustrate this point, we found that couples who 'sometimes' or 'never' engaged in 'discussion of how to use contraceptives' within six months before the current pregnancy, had the highest proportion of 'wrong calculation of the safe period' (29.2 per cent for women and 25.6 per cent for men).

Because effective use of the rhythm method, and any other method of contraception, also requires more education and motivation by couples, we decided to look into the work situation of these couples. We found that for couples working in a 'state work unit', or in a 'joint ventures unit', the main reason for contraceptive failure was 'wrong calculation of the safe period'. For these two work situations, the proportions were 31.0 per cent and 36.7 per cent for the women, and 29.0 per cent and 36.2 per cent for men, respectively. By contrast, among couples working in a 'collective unit' (or in an 'individual unit'), the main reason for contraceptive failure was 'IUD in situ' (33 per cent for women and 35–38 per cent for men). It would seem that couples working in collective units would have closer monitoring and easier access to correct information and services, therefore their use of the more modern methods, such as the IUD, is more extensive and failure more common, compared to the use of the more traditional methods, for example, withdrawal.

It was not surprising, therefore, that from the women's own personal perspectives, regardless of the actual method itself, 34.0 per cent considered that their contraceptive failure was attributed to low 'contraceptive quality'. Poor method quality was reflected in the high proportions attributing their current pregnancy to the following method-related problems: 'IUD in situ', 'IUD expulsion', 'oral pills deterioration', and 'condom breakage' (81.3 per cent, 62.5 per cent, 44.4 per cent and 40.3 per cent, respectively).

The Effect of Quality of Services

A large proportion of women who experienced contraceptive failure, 71.7 per cent, considered that their family planning unit should share the responsibility for their contraceptive failure.

Among these 1,493 women, 50.5 per cent felt that contraceptive operatives (personnel) in their local family planning units were not well-qualified; another 24.9 per cent felt that the proper use of the method had not been explained well to them; 8.4 per cent said that they had not been given effective contraceptive methods; 3.3 per cent complained that effective contraceptives could not be purchased from the medical units; and 2.4 per cent considered the services after performing contraceptive insertion were not good enough. The rest, 10.5 per cent, gave a variety of other negative opinions about the support they had received.

Further criticism of the family planning services was expressed by most women who thought their contraceptive failure was due to 'IUD in situ', 'IUD expulsion', or 'failure of male sterilization'; they said it was the result of performing 'not qualified procedures'. The proportions of women who felt that their family planning units should bear this responsibility, by each type of method failure, were 70.4 per cent, 75.2 per cent, and 100 per cent, respectively.

Similarly, failure of methods that depend on the user for effectiveness, such as 'oral pills taken improperly', 'oral pills deteriorated', 'wrong calculation of the safe period', 'improper use of condom', and 'withdrawal failure', was attributed in large part to the poor guidance provided by the family planning workers on how to master the use of these methods. These views were held with regard to each of the above reasons for method failure by 85.7 per cent, 71.4 per cent, 64.3 per cent, 61.9 per cent and 41.7 per cent, respectively. In the case of condoms, particularly in situations where condom breakage was the cause of the pregnancy, a large proportion of women and men attributed the problem to poor contraceptive quality. Overall, substantial proportions felt that the family planning sections (including the health section) were responsible for not sending the effective contraceptives to users in time or for not assisting users in the proper utilization of methods.

Discussion

Our study of 2,765 married women requesting abortion in Shanghai and 2,760 men, mostly husbands of these women, shows clearly that unwanted pregnancy results from either not using contraception or from contraceptive failure, both of which are related to the poor quality of family planning services, particularly monitoring and counselling.

The fundamental recommendation that emerges as a result of these findings is that Shanghai municipal authorities and family planning programme personnel should shift the focus of their work from a preoccupation with the declining birth rate, which is now very low, to reducing the level of unwanted pregnancy among women of childbearing age. This strategy should be based on an effort to improve the overall reproductive health of women, which includes improvements in the quality of contraceptives and informational and support services. In these efforts, it is imperative to take into consideration women's expressed reproductive health needs and preferences.

For example, all women of childbearing age should be allowed to select contraceptive methods freely based, on their own preferences and choices. This would necessitate a wider range of available methods and a higher level of quality, particularly of IUDs, whose failure rate constitutes the major cause of unwanted pregnancy experienced by the women in our study. Among IUD users who experienced failure the usual reason given was: 'IUD in situ' or 'IUD expulsion'. In fact, these were the first and the third reasons for contraceptive failure given by the sample as a whole, together representing 36.1 per cent of all causes of unwanted pregnancy. The high level of IUD failure indicates that there are serious problems with the manufacturing of IUDs being dispensed to women, particularly in the quality of IUD insertion and post-insertion follow-up services.

Other reasons for contraceptive failure, such as 'wrong calculation of the safe period', even among married women with above-average education and knowledge of contraception, could be avoided by providing better information and individual guidance to users of contraception.

We found that although a large number of married women had access to contraceptive services, they chose not to use any contraception at all. Often they said the methods were troublesome; in other cases, they felt protected by lactation. These were the two main reasons given for not using contraception before the current pregnancy. Together, they represent 46.0 per cent of the reason for non-use. The perception of contraceptive methods as 'troublesome' reflects the women's lack of confidence in the methods available and how they work. There is also the fact that a large proportion of women seeking abortion as a result of not using contraception at the time the pregnancy occurred were unmarried, indicating the need to improve information to single women.

Similarly, the quality of local reproductive health care and staff services was also seen as a major factor in unwanted pregnancy as a result of non-use of contraception. Three out of every four women whose abortion was due to non-use of contraception declared that family planning workers in their places of residence knew nothing about their contraceptive status, or were indifferent or did not provide any guidance. There would seem to be a serious problem in the quality of care given in the reproductive health services being offered to women in Shanghai. To lower induced abortion among women who experience unwanted pregnancy, it is necessary to strengthen the technical training and capacity of family planning workers at all levels in the system. At the same time, the distribution system should be updated so that women can more conveniently get their contraceptives. From the women's own perspectives, three suggestions emerge for ways to reduce induced abortions in Shanghai, all related to reproductive health and family planning education: (*a*) emphasize that induced abortion, particularly when repeated, can be harmful to women's health; (*b*) greatly improve information on the correct use of contraceptive methods; (*c*) provide women with better information and guidance on methods when they experience contraceptive failure.

Lastly, the study showed clearly that the causes and reasons for unwanted pregnancy varied according to demographic, economic, social and behavioural factors, as well as service care and quality. We suggest targeting particular groups of women who are at highest risk of abortion and repeat abortion for improved reproductive health services and education with the purpose of preventing unwanted pregnancy and therefore lowering induced abortion. These recommendations are addressed to family planning officials and heads of service units in Shanghai. They include the following groups: (*a*) Younger married women of childbearing age (in their 20s) of higher educational and occupational level, as well as those who are not presently working (urban de jure household registration); (*b*) Married women in their 20s with lower education and working in rural areas especially in farming occupations; (*c*) Married women, particularly those in their 30s and whose education is below average, and who often hold 'troubled' attitudes towards contraception, and have little or no contact with their local family planning unit; (*d*) Single women, particularly younger women who are employed; and (*e*) Older, more educated women in higher occupational levels who are sexually active and use less effective methods.

In this chapter we have explored the main causes why women in Shanghai have induced abortions. We have tried to single out groups of women exposed to the risk of unnecessary abortion and made some suggestions on how to improve their contraceptive knowledge and use. We hope that these findings are helpful to the family planning authorities of China.

✝ References

Gao Er-sheng, Wu Zhuo-chun, Zhang Ming-dong. 1988. The analysis of induced abortion in Shaanxi Province, Hebei Province and Shanghai city. *Population—Studies and reports* 4.

Gui Shi-xun et al. 1994. The study on the measure of the population administration under the negative natural increase of population in Shanghai. Shanghai: East Normal University.

Research Team on Induced Abortion. 1994. The status of induced abortion and measures to reduce induced abortion in Shanghai. *Population Information* 3.

State Statistical Bureau, Department of Population Statistics. 1986. Principal report, China in-depth fertility survey. Vol. 1. Beijing.

4

First-Trimester Induced Abortion: A Study of Sichuan Province, China

Luo Lin, Wu Shi-zhong, Chen Xiao-qing
and Li Min-xiang

Introduction

Induced abortion is one of the oldest methods of fertility regulation and one of the most widely used. It is practised in remote rural societies as well as in large modern urban centres, even when it carries great health risks and economic costs. Its use is particularly prevalent in developing countries that are in the initial stages of their fertility transition. Indeed, the World Health Organization reports that between 40 and 60 million abortions take place around the world every year (WHO, 1990), making the procedure one of the most frequently performed health interventions in the world. It is a social and medical reality of such worldwide significance that it can no more be legislated out of existence than the controversy surrounding it can be stilled. And no matter how effective family planning services and practices become, there will always be a need for access to safe abortion services (David, 1992).

Access to modern contraception and safe induced abortion has been available in China since 1953, when the government approved the first population act. Drafted by the Ministry of Health and approved by the State Council, the document specifically eased the requirements that needed to be met for women to have a legal abortion. The procedure was fully legalized in 1956, and shortly thereafter, the necessary social and service conditions were instituted.

However, a much greater effort to strengthen abortion services took place as a result of national family planning policies instituted in the late 1970s and during the 1980s to reduce fertility. This official birth control campaign began in 1971, and was vigorously promoted throughout China as one of the 'Four Modernizations', along with industrial development, agrarian change and education. Known as *wan xi shao*, or 'later-longer-fewer', this voluntary programme included strong material incentives for limiting family size.

Less than a decade after this campaign began, the government renewed its efforts to sharply limit fertility. A new legislation, known as the one-child-family policy, was announced in 1979, because Chinese leaders feared that if the reproductive patterns stimulated by the anarchism of the Cultural Revolution continued unabated, the situation would completely exhaust all the country's resources and ultimately lead to disaster. At this time, the average number of children per couple had already declined to just below three children.

This policy-driven fertility transition was facilitated by the legalization and availability of modern contraceptive methods to married couples, which had begun in the 1950s. Contraceptive use then declined in the 1960s, but access to family planning was greatly expanded again during the 1970s. By 1988, 71 per cent of 206 million married Chinese women of reproductive age were using a modern method of contraception (State Family Planning Commission of China, 1992). And in 1993, China announced to the world that its fertility rate had fallen to below replacement level and that it now stood at about 1.7 children per family.

The fertility decline was also helped along by the availability of induced abortion. Its legalization in 1956 had permitted its use on request and on broad grounds; to save the life of the woman, to preserve her physical or mental health, in cases of rape or incest, where there is foetal impairment, and for economic or social reasons. Then in 1987, the Sichuan Family Planning Law was approved by the Sixth Sichuan Province People's Representative Council and its 15th item added that induced abortion must be performed by a doctor who had a certification given by the Medical and Family Planning Department and that it must take place in an approved health facility, such as a hospital or clinic. As a result, in Sichuan Province, as elsewhere in China, legal abortion has proved to be a very safe procedure; the abortion-related mortality rates are much lower than those associated with childbearing in other parts of the world. This situation provides a stark contrast to countries where induced abortion is illegal and unsafe, and therefore often responsible for a large proportion of maternal mortality.

Because the controversy over the strategy used to produce China's rapid fertility decline was so widely publicized and often misunderstood, some comment is offered here, although an in-depth discussion is beyond the scope of this paper. It is true that failure to comply with the rigorous one-child policy means that food coupons are denied, housing and school benefits removed, and heavy fines imposed on the household. While some of the more extreme cases reported in the international press are indeed true, they are by no means the intention of the government nor a generalized practice.

Moreover, the Chinese official position regarding the use of abortion has always been that use of contraception is the best way to control fertility;

and that induced abortion should not be relied upon as a method of contraception. It is a procedure considered to be primarily a back-up method when contraceptive failure occurs (Ge Quanging et al., 1982).

Objectives of the Study

The present study, conducted in six rural counties of Sichuan Province, China, has had a twofold objective. The first has been to understand the generally most important determinants of induced abortion among a rural population of women, which, in the case of China, has meant focusing on contraceptive behaviour. The second, and more significant objective has been to evaluate the quality of first-trimester abortion services and the physiological and psychological sequelae of the procedure among a rural population of women.

We were particularly interested in the safety of the procedure and in any possible complications experienced, particularly those of a psychological nature. We anticipated that responses to psychological questions would be the most difficult to obtain and interpret as David (1992) has noted. Although a substantial literature exists on psychological sequelae, conclusions among the different studies are often contradictory. Interpretation of psychological data has always been problematic and diversity is generally due to the limitations inherent in the research methods used, political influences, and value judgements. As a point of reference, although based only on a review of the literature, it appears that psychological distress is generally greatest before the abortion. This general conclusion was found in all the studies, even though the quality of their research designs varied widely. The finding was particularly clear in studies conducted in the United States.

The analysis of our study data placed particular emphasis on the general background of the women in the sample, including age, parity, contraceptive method used before and after the abortion, general behaviour patterns and reports of gynaecological sequelae. Given our awareness of the challenge involved in evaluating the psychological dimension of induced abortion, depressive symptomatology was assessed by the application of CES-D and SCL-90 scales. We found that depressive symptoms were higher before the abortion, declining with time following the abortion. This then corroborated findings from other studies.

Research Methodology

Sichuan is China's most populous province, where approximately 9.6 per cent of the country's estimated 1.1 billion people live. Our study was conducted in six rural counties of this province with different geography, income and health facilities, including capability to perform induced abortion. Changxi and Jiang-go are in remote mountainous regions far away from Chengdu, the capital city of Sichuan Province; Guanxin and Pengxin are in distant hilly and plain areas; and Guanghan and Xinngdu are in the rice-growing plain areas much closer to Chengdu City. We chose these different and geographically widespread counties to ensure that abortion was observed in a diverse context. The basic data on population in the six counties is shown in Table 4.1.

Table 4.1: Population of the Six Counties, 1991

County	Population	Women Aged 15–49
Guanghan	537,692	128,792
Xinngdu	538,843	128,792
Pengxin	742,733	173,528
Guanxin	549,212	166,259
Changxi	765,309	170,841
Jaing-go	644,215	130,096

Source: Data provided by the Sichuan Population Information and Research Center, Chengdu, China.

General Design

Gathering the sample of women for this prospective clinical follow-up study required access to family planning clinic and hospital records as well as interviews with clinic patients. All consecutive cases admitted for first-trimester induced abortion, with a pregnancy test to confirm pregnancy, in clinics or hospitals in the six counties selected were eligible to participate in the study. After this initial screening, we verified that each woman selected was participating voluntarily.

The fieldwork was conducted locally in the six counties over a period of one year, between July 1990 and June 1991. More than 100 gynaecologists, psychologists and providers from county or region hospitals and family planning clinics joined the fieldwork phase of the study. Local doctors were recruited as interviewers because fertility regulation is such a sensitive issue in China. We hoped their participation would help the women to feel at ease and to respond to the questions more openly and honestly during the face-to-face interviewing process. These doctors participated in a one-week pre-survey training course, which was held in Chengdu, at the Sichuan Family Planning Research Institute. The participants who passed the course examination were selected as interviewers.

Individual interviews with 4,000 women, aged 18–40, who underwent first-trimester abortion at hospitals and family planning clinics took place. A pre-abortion assessment and baseline interview was held two days before the abortion procedure. Then during the six-month period following the event, interviews took place at set time intervals of 15, 90 and 180 days after the procedure. At the time of every interview, a physical examination was also conducted to identify any possible medical problems arising from the abortion.

Pre-Abortion Assessment

Women scheduled to undergo first-trimester abortion, either by vacuum aspiration, aspiration and curettage, or curettage only, were seen first by trained gynaecologists and psychologists two days before the procedure. This initial meeting had four purposes: (*a*) to confirm first-trimester pregnancy with the necessary medical tests (laboratory or ultrasound); (*b*) to assess the woman's request to terminate her pregnancy and to perform a physical examination (including laboratory tests, if needed); (*c*) to make sure she would participate voluntarily in the study; (*d*) to initiate the collection of baseline background and psychological data.

During this assessment, a series of questions were asked about the woman's personal background, reproductive history, contraceptive use, feelings about this pregnancy, and the reasons for deciding to have an abortion. The physical examination provided the following information: temperature, blood pressure, and an estimate of the gestational period, including configuration of the uterus. Laboratory tests included: urine (pregnancy) test, blood test (white blood cells, haemoglobin), bleeding time, clotting time and routine urinalysis. Standardized tests were also given to assess psychological distress. After completing this initial interview, the woman returned home if she lived nearby the clinic or hospital.

On the day of their intervention, the interviewer again met each woman to explain the procedure and the requirements of the research, to obtain their consent, and to introduce the follow-up questionnaires.

Collection of Post-Abortion Data

Two days after the pre-abortion assessment, the woman underwent induced abortion. Post-operative clinical data were collected in the recovery room shortly after the abortion procedure was completed, usually within 15–20 minutes. This questionnaire gathered detailed information about the abortion procedure and the woman's feelings about it, including: technique used, volume of blood, reaction during and after the operation, trauma, course of operation, duration of the operation and blood pressure. Similarly, some questions were asked from the operating doctor, such as, what his training and experience was in performing induced abortions.

In the face-to-face interviews scheduled at set time intervals following the procedure, detailed information was gathered on: post-abortion care (job, nutrition, rest, health care); any short-term medical consequences of the induced abortion, such as bleeding, pelvic infection, retained tissue, cervical or uterine trauma, uterine perforation; and psychosocial outcomes, as assessed by standardized tests of SCL-90 and CES-D. Data were also collected on demographic and medical characteristics by means of structured interview forms. The follow-up rate for each scheduled visit at 15, 90 and 180 days after the procedure, was 99.83 per cent, 99.28 per cent and 98.70 per cent, respectively, indicating a high rate of compliance and cooperation.

Psychosocial Assessment

The 90-item Symptoms Checklist (SCL-90), which is a self-rating questionnaire, and the 'Depression Scale' (CES-D) of the Center for Epidemiologic Studies were used to evaluate psychological distress levels. To test for stability of factors across time, these evaluations were performed at baseline (two days before operation), and on day(s) 15, 90 and 180 after the abortion was performed.

The Scales

The SCL-90 is a multi-dimensional symptom, self-reporting inventory comprising 90 items, each rated on a five-point scale of distress (0 to 4) from 'not-at all' to 'extremely' distressing. As a research instrument, it is well-suited for use in protocols where the major criterion of interest involves assessment of an outpatient symptomatic configuration (Derogatis et al., 1976). During the interview survey, the SCL-90 instrument was completed by the patient. When the patient could not complete the inventory, it was administered by a trained doctor.

The other instrument used, the CES-D, was developed by the United States National Institute of Mental Health in 1977. It has been widely used in epidemiological research and to assess the degree of seriousness of depression manifested by patients after clinical examination. The CES-D has a demonstrated capacity to identify clinically abnormal populations. Respondents use a four-point system scale, ranging from 'rarely, never' (less than one day a week) to 'often' (at least five to seven days a week), to indicate the frequency with which they experienced each of the 20 symptoms of depression during the past week. The total score of CES-D is divided into three grades; a score of 16 or greater on the CES-D is an indicator of depressive symptomatology (Radloff, 1977).

During the interview survey, we paid particular attention to the prevention of response bias, such as the tendency of an individual to answer all questions in the same direction (positive or negative). Since the 1980s, SCL-90 and CES-D have been used in Chinese populations as psychiatric measurement instruments (Jin Hua et al., 1986; Lin Xinchen et al., 1990).

Statistical Analysis

To accomplish the goal of reaching a better understanding of the consequences of induced abortion in terms of health and psychosocial outcomes, we used the T-test, analysis of variance, and multiple linear regression analyses in this study. All the statistical analyses were performed using version 6.07 of SAS (on MicroVAX-II) in the Computer Center of the Sichuan Family Planning Research Institute. The additional analyses were done using the SPSS statistical package at the Population Research Center of The University of Texas at Austin, in the United States. In this chapter we refer to the main patterns emerging from the regression analyses, but we have not included the detailed statistical tables.

Sociodemographic Characteristics of the Women

As shown in Table 4.2, the incidence of abortion among this sample of 4,000 women is concentrated among the younger age groups: Three out of every four abortions took place among women less than 30 years of age. The average age of the study subjects was 25 years.

Table 4.2: Age Distribution of a Study Sample

Age (years)	Women	
	Number	%
< 20	148	3.7
20–24	1,567	39.1
25–29	1,319	33.0
30–34	524	13.1
35–39	427	10.7
40–44	15	0.4
Total	4,000	100.0

The study population was mostly rural, 84.7 per cent, while 15.3 per cent lived in urban areas. Gestational age of less than 40 days was true for 5.5 per cent of the women; less than 60 days for 69.5 per cent; and less than 90 days for 25 per cent. Over their lifetime, the women had from one to eight births, although the mean number of births was quite low, as expected: 1.57 births. Pregnancies ranged from one to 10, but again, the average was low: 1.37 pregnancies.

Most of the women were married (88.6 per cent); another 11.4 per cent were single. Ten per cent had no education; 39 per cent had completed primary school; 42.8 per cent had completed middle school; and the rest had completed high school or higher education. Most of the women were in farming occupations, 77.4 per cent; another 10.4 per cent were working mostly in factories; 6.6 per cent were housewives; and 2.4 per cent were in other occupations, such as teacher, cadre or doctor.

Except for 14 per cent of the women who had been pregnant before but who had no prior abortions, the rest of the women—a very large majority—had previous abortion experience. One-third had one prior abortion;

and 52 per cent had two or more prior abortions. For this current abortion, vacuum aspiration accounted for 47.8 per cent of the procedures; vacuum aspiration and curettage, 3.7 per cent; and curettage only, 48.4 per cent.

Study Results and Discussion

The Main Determinants of Induced Abortion

Our results indicate that the main reasons why these women sought an abortion are related to having an unintended pregnancy, which, in large part, is due to ineffective contraceptive practice or non-use of contraception. It is important to note that 37 per cent of the women declared that their contraceptive method had failed. Being unmarried was also a strong determinant of induced abortion. Together, these factors affect the present-day fertility profile in China (Table 4.3).

Table 4.3: Reasons to Request Induced Abortion

	Women	
Reasons	Number	%
Unintended pregnancy	1,995	49.9
Contraceptive failure	1,471	36.8
Being unmarried	424	10.6
Economic problem	38	1.0
Health condition	34	0.8
Family problem	13	0.3
Foetal condition	25	0.6
Total	4,000	100.0

Contraceptive Behaviour

In Sichuan Province, most couples using contraception are using IUDs, vasectomy or tubal ligation. The IUD is more popular among younger women and sterilization is more popular among older women. The pill, condom and other contraceptive methods also are used, but their use is more problematic, because it requires an efficient and steady supply of contraceptives.

At least three factors can affect contraceptive practice in China. The first is that although most couples use contraception voluntarily, not all contraceptive use is truly voluntary. Some women would naturally like to have a larger family than the current law permits and this feeling would naturally affect use effectiveness. Furthermore, contraception can be ineffective even when reliable methods are used, due to user inefficiency (poor knowledge of the method) or because the quality of the contraceptive supply is not very good. The consequence of low motivation to use, incorrect use, or poor quality of a method is a high risk of pregnancy.

The extent of method failure in our study group was significant: 36.8 per cent of the 4,000 women interviewed chose to abort because their contraceptive method had failed. Among these 1,471 women, 65.5 per cent were using an IUD; 6.1 per cent were using pills; 6.8 per cent were using a condom, and 21.6 were using other methods (Table 4.4). Another large proportion, about half of the total sample, declared that they were seeking abortion because of an 'unintended pregnancy'. Among these 1,995 women, 87 per cent were not using any method. The other 13 per cent in this group may have experienced method failure of some kind, since they all reported that they were using a method, primarily the IUD.

Table 4.4: Women Who Experienced Contraceptive Failure, by Method

Method Used	Number	%
IUD	964	65.5
Pills	90	6.1
Condom	100	6.8
Various others	317	21.6
Total	1,471	100.0

In many Western industrialized countries, abortion rates are highest among young, unmarried women and lowest in women over the age of 35. The decline is due to the widespread use of surgical sterilization among women in these older age groups (Tietze and Henshaw, 1986). In China, a similar trend can be deduced.

Marital Status

To end the Chinese custom of early marriage, particularly the practice of betrothing children in or before their teens, in 1950 the Chinese law set the age for marriage at 18 for women and 20 for men. Then again in 1980, this time primarily to reduce the country's overall fertility rate, the Chinese marriage law reset the minimum age for marriage higher, at 20 for women and 22 for men.

Such a law has great influence in a country like China, where premarital sexual relations and fertility have been socially and publicly forbidden for centuries. Indeed, in our study population, 10.6 per cent of the women requested abortion simply because they were unmarried (Table 4.3). Nearly all of these 424 unmarried women, 94.8 per cent, were less than 24 years of age, and a similar proportion had not been using contraception when the pregnancy occurred.

Our findings show that sexual relations and fertility continues to exist among women in rural areas who are younger than the legal age for marriage.

Unfortunately, the custom of earlier sexual union between these couples continues without them being able to learn about or have access to contraception, because the social and political stigma against premarital relations also continues to be strong. The result is that they choose to have abortions. (The situation of unmarried women in rural China is discussed in a later section of this book on adolescence.)

The Quality of Abortion Services

Among the 4,000 women interviewed, the division was nearly equal among those who underwent vacuum aspiration (47.8 per cent), and those who underwent curettage (48.3 per cent). The balance, 3.9 per cent, had a combined aspiration and curettage.

Provider Training

Most abortions were performed by doctors who graduated from medical college, medical vocational school, and who learned family planning techniques from specialized training programmes. The majority had more than three years of experience in the use of abortion techniques. The high degree of appropriate training was not surprising given the 1987 Sichuan Province Family Planning Law, which requires that induced abortion be performed by a doctor who has certification by the Medical and Family Planning Department and that it must take place in an approved health facility, such as a hospital or family planning clinic.

Medical Complications

Abortion in China appears to be a very safe procedure. None of the 4,000 women reported serious medical complications such as pelvic infection, retained tissue, cervical or uterine trauma, or uterine perforation. Bleeding and fever, shown in Tables 4.5, 4.6 and 4.7, indicated normal levels. Almost no post-operative fever was reported and nearly half of the women reported

Table 4.5: **Blood Loss During Operation**

	Women	
Volume (ml)	*Number*	*%*
< 50	2,744	68.6
50–100	1,044	26.1
101–200	166	4.2
201–300	28	0.7
> 300	14	0.3
Unknown	4	0.1
Total	4,000	100.0

Table 4.6: State of Bleeding < 15 Days Post-Operation

Amount of Bleeding	Number of Cases	%
No bleeding	1,951	48.9
Spotting	1,740	43.6
Same as menses	274	6.9
More than menses	28	0.7
Total	3,993	100.0

Table 4.7: Short-Term Fever 15 Days After Abortion

Fever	Number of Cases	%
No	3,830	95.9
Yes	139	3.5
Unknown	24	0.6
Total	3,993	100.0

minor bleeding or spotting episodes following the abortion. In short, induced abortion provided by medically trained personnel and performed in appropriate health facilities in hospitals or clinics have proven to be safer than childbirth.

Psychological Sequelae: Assessment by CES-D

The CES-D was designed for use in general population surveys and is, therefore, a short, structured, self-reporting instrument to measure depression levels. The scale contains 20 symptoms that a person may have experienced over a period of time, for example, during the past week. As Radloff (1977) explains, the CES-D list was 'designed to measure current level of depressive symptomatology, with emphasis on the affective component: depressed mood'.

It is clear that the 20 items of the CES-D instrument are all symptoms related to depression. For epidemiologic research, a simple total score is recommended as an estimate of the degree of depressive symptomatology (Radloff, 1977).

The results of the CES-D assessments before and after induced abortion showed a significant decrease in the total mean score: from 6.83 (S.D. = 6.37) at the time of the first contact, before the induced abortion took place, to a much lower mean score of 2.77 (S.D. = 3.68) 180 days after the abortion (Table 4.8). These scores decreased as the time from the intervention increased, indicating a significant reduction in the general level of depression as time passed after the abortion. Similarly, the proportion of women suffering from actual depressive symptoms showed a significant decrease 180 days following the abortion. At the time of first contact, 4.7 per cent of the women were suffering from depression to 0.9 per cent after the abortion (Table 4.9).

Both these measures indicate that there is a greater level of psychosomatic infirmity before the abortion, which tends to disappear with time, becoming negligible six months later.

Table 4.8: Total Score by CES-D at Admission and at Time Intervals After Abortion

Time Interval	Women Interviewed	Total Score	
		Mean	S.D.
Before	4,000	6.83	6.37
Day 15 after	3,993	4.93	4.95
Day 90 after	3,971	3.13	4.05
Day 180 after	3,948	2.77	3.68

$F = 4.07, p < 0.00001$.

Table 4.9: Percentages of Depression Before and After Induced Abortion

Time Interval	Depressive Symptoms		
	Women Interviewed	Number of Cases	%
Before	4,000	189	4.7
Day 15 after	3,993	71	1.8
Day 90 after	3,971	51	1.3*
Day 180 after	3,948	35	0.9*

* $p < 0.000001$, compared with the baseline (data before abortion).

Analysis of Component Factors

The 20 items included in the CES-D scale can be reduced to four principal component factors which are indicative of mood or disposition at the time of or just before the abortion:

1. Depressed affect (blues, depressed mood, lonely, crying, sad)
2. Positive affect (good, hopeful, happy, enjoying life)
3. Somatic and retarded activity (irritable, loss of appetite, low energy, poor sleep, low initiative)
4. Interpersonal (unfriendly, dislike of people)

We present the negative, or depressive, states derived from the component factor scales of CES-D in Tables 4.10 and 4.11. Of the 4,000 women interviewed two days before their induced abortion, 1,457 women, representing 36 per cent of the total, had felt depressed for at least three–four days during the past week (not feeling good, hopeful, happy or enjoying life). Another 787 women, or 20 per cent, reported that they had felt this way for five–seven days; that is, they showed a significant absence of the positive affect. Six months later, these levels of depression or negative feelings had decreased substantially: 1,096 women, representing 27.4 per cent, had felt depressed for three–four days during the past week; while 152 women, representing 4 per cent, had felt this way for most of the week preceding the interview. The number of women experiencing loss of appetite or tiredness also decreased substantially over time, from 691 women two days before the abortion to 39 women six months later (Tables 4.10 and 4.11).

Table 4.10: Factor Scale Obtained Two Days Before Abortion

| | Feeling this Way During the Past Week for: | | | |
| | 3–4 Days | | 5–7 Days | |
Mood	No.	%	No.	%
Not feeling good	301	7.5	291	7.3
Not feeling hopeful	387	9.7	185	4.6
Not feeling happy	429	10.7	178	4.5
Not enjoying life	340	8.5	133	3.3
Poor appetite	510	12.8	103	2.6
Low energy	181	4.5	34	0.9

Table 4.11: Factor Scale Obtained 180 Days After Abortion

| | Feeling this Way During the Past Week for: | | | |
| | 3–4 Days | | 5–7 Days | |
Mood	No.	%	No.	%
Not feeling good	202	5.1	106	2.7
Not feeling hopeful	334	8.5	10	0.3
Not feeling happy	331	8.4	18	0.5
Not enjoying life	229	5.8	18	0.5
Poor appetite	26	0.7	1	0.0
Low energy	13	0.3	2	0.1

We have used the term 'depression' as it refers to the syndrome of behaviours that have been identified in descriptive studies of depressed individuals (for example, Grinker et al., 1961). It includes verbal statements of dysphoria, self-depreciation, guilt, material burden, social isolation, somatic complaints and a reduced rate of many behaviours. Klein (1974) suggested that severely depressed patients are characterized by absence of positive affect as well as presence of strong negative affect. Garrison et al. (1991) suggested that in general, findings of studies that include adults indicate that although the CES-D can be useful in screening depressed persons, the group selected as 'probable cases' will also include a substantial number of individuals with other diagnoses or with no diagnoses at all.

The sensitivity, and specificity, of the CES-D score may vary due to different cultures and behaviours. So the distribution of CES-D scores may be different in the special communities we studied, which were essentially rural. Also, this research concentrated on induced abortion among Chinese women. It may be important that 'optimal cutting points', along with their corresponding sensitivities, specificities, and positive predictive values, may vary among adults with different cultural characteristics. In fact, the authors' findings, and those of Zhang Minyuan et al. (1987), suggest that if the goal of a screening measure is to detect cases of major depression rather than overall psychiatric impairment, then cutting points in the score may be different among a Chinese adult population than, for example, a similar American group.

Also, it should be noted that there are no reports on CES-D and SCL-90 scores obtained from a population of Chinese pregnant women. Therefore, we do not compare our results of the distribution of CES-D scores with other research results. In this study, we have mainly used the CES-D scales for purposes of comparing depressive symptoms before and after induced abortion.

Multivariate Analysis

We asked ourselves the question, what differences might exist in the social or behavioural manifestations between women who were particularly resistant to suffering from depression and those who were prone to depression? In other words, what were the risk factors associated with depression? A multiple regression analysis was performed using the total score of CES-D as the dependent variable, and background characteristics of the 4,000 cases as independent variables. The latter included: occupation, education, age, number of previous abortions, number of pregnancies, children's situation, subject's feeling when learning about this pregnancy, reasons to seek an induced abortion, and provider's training and level of education.

The results showed that the factors associated with a depressive state were different before and after the abortion. Before the abortion, the factors that explained a higher level of depression, when fitted simultaneously into the regression were: younger age, greater number of previous pregnancies, not being married, unhappy when learning about the pregnancy and higher education. After the abortion, the factors more closely associated with depression changed to: previous number of abortions, non-manual occupation, urban residence, a more advanced pregnancy, pre-existing health problems, lower perception of provider training and higher frequency of coitus.

These findings support some fairly natural explanations about why some women experience a depressed psychological state when faced with an unwanted pregnancy and subsequent abortion. Before the abortion, for example, younger women would be particularly susceptible to a negative state of mind, because the 20–24-year age group is a period of life generally known to be especially sensitive to depression; their lives are usually more unsettled and uncertain than the lives of older women. A greater number of previous pregnancies would also contribute to a depressed state of mind, as there is a greater possibility of previous abortion experience, which possibly carries with it a painful memory of physical and/or psychological harm. Unmarried women would find the prospect of an abortion particularly depressing, because they might have wished to carry the pregnancy to term if they had been married.

After an abortion, the memory of the experience would naturally just add to any feelings of pain or sadness from previous abortions. Women would tend to respond in the same manner to another experience with the same stressful stimuli. Women with non-manual jobs usually have more intellectually demanding responsibilities; so they would tend to experience greater psychological pressure from an unexpected pregnancy and induced abortion, which would cause them to be more emotionally upset about the unexpected event. A more advanced pregnancy indicates greater ambivalence about the decision to abort; so that any feelings of regret afterward would tend to be stronger for these women. Naturally, all these circumstances cause even more depression when a woman suffers from pre-existing health problems.

Provider training is another important factor, both technically and psychologically, because it can ease the anxiety related to the abortion experience. This factor is particularly influential and has a positive effect when providers talk to a woman beforehand and discuss her thoughts and feelings concerning the situation. Our findings also show that providers with less experience, and undoubtedly younger, were more concerned and helpful with their patients than the more experienced doctors. This dimension of provider care requires further exploration.

Psychological Sequelae: Assessment by SCL-90

Another approach we chose for measuring the psychological sequelae of induced abortion was the application of the SCL-90 scale, which measures the intensity of psychological distress experienced by the women themselves. The SCL-90 scale was developed by Derogatis on the basis of Hopkin's Checklist (Derogatis et al., 1976) and is intended for clinical use. It consists of 90 items that cover a wide range of problems or symptoms of psychological distress. Each item is graded with a five-score system, in which '0' represents 'No, I do not have such a problem or symptom', and '4' means 'Yes, I have the problem or symptom and it is very serious'.

The results of these self-reporting measurements before and after induced abortion also revealed a significant decrease in the total score after induced abortion (Figure 4.1), thus confirming once more our findings that stress and depression tend to disappear after the abortion but are highest just before it takes place.

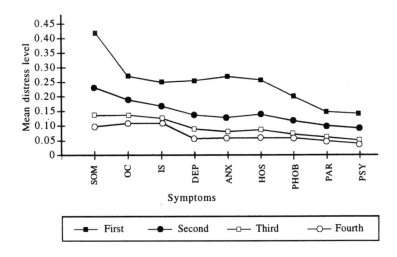

Figure 4.1: Mean Level of SCL-90 Symptomatic Profile

Factor Score

The 90 items of SCL-90 scale are usually divided into nine main components or factors: Factor 1 (SOM) or somatization, made up of 12 items, mainly the complaints of subjective somatic discomforts; Factor 2 (OC), obsessive-compulsive, 10 items; Factor 3 (IS), interpersonal sensitivity, nine items; Factor 4 (DEP), depression, 13 items; Factor 5 (ANX) anxiety, 10 items; Factor 6 (HOS) hostility, six items; Factor 7 (PHOB) phobic anxiety, seven items; Factor 8 (PAR) paranoid ideation, six items; and Factor 9 (PSY), psychoticism, 10 items (see Figure 4.1). The factor score equals the summary score of the items embraced by the factor divided by the number of items embraced by the factor.

The profile of factor scores by SCL-90 before abortion (black squares) and after (the three other lines shown, with the lowest line representing the scores six months after the intervention) illustrate the much higher level in all these factors before the intervention and then their subsequent decrease, reaching very low levels six months later. Of the nine factor scores, the highest level before the abortion is somatization and associated behaviours, followed by anxiety and hostility. Somatization reflects distress arising from perceptions of bodily dysfunction, such as complaints focused on cardiovascular, gastrointestinal, respiratory and other systems with strong autonomic mediation. It also includes headaches, backaches, pain and discomfort localized in the gross musculature as are other somatic equivalents of anxiety. The factors for which we observed the highest scores are all associated with psychological distress. Depression is also among these higher scores.

Comparing the relatively high level in the total scores of CES-D and SCL-90 before induced abortion and their reduction following induced abortion implies that the impact of an unexpected pregnancy and the impending abortion upon women is an extremely stressful event that involves mental and psychological tension, particularly anxiety and depression. These symptoms subside after the abortion.

Summary and Conclusions

We have studied the socioeconomic background of a large sample of women who requested abortion in rural areas of Sichuan Province, China. We have paid particular attention to the identification of the physiological and psychological factors that affect the sequelae of abortion, with follow-up for up to six months to verify any changes in attitude and behaviour among the women. Three main conclusions emerge from our analyses.

First, induced abortion provided by medically trained personnel and performed in appropriate health facilities, either in hospitals or family planning clinics, is a safe and harmless procedure in rural China. This conclusion is based on the findings that there was no pelvic infection, retained tissue, cervical or uterine trauma, uterine perforation or serious bleeding complications after induced abortion among the women studied. A small proportion, 1.8 per cent of the 4,000 women in the study, had retained tissue and underwent dilatation and curettage again. Another 51.14 per cent of patients reported some vaginal bleeding on day 15 following the abortion. However, the general picture that emerges is a very safe one.

Unwanted pregnancies put women in many other parts of the developing world at risk of morbidity and mortality associated with pregnancy and childbearing, mostly as a result of laws that restrict access to a safe procedure. Our results show that if abortions are performed under safe medical condition, there is a lower risk of morbidity and mortality than for pregnancy and childbirth.

Our second main conclusion, demonstrated from the results of our application of psychological tests to women before and after they obtained legal abortions, is that distress and depression levels were highest before the abortion and significantly lower six months later. High depression and distress were associated with non-manual occupations, number of previous abortions, number of previous deliveries, and provider training. We also found that pre-abortion individual counselling can significantly lower stress and depression levels and is therefore very important. A strong recommendation is that the provider's training level should be continually improved, with emphasis placed on learning techniques to lower the psychological stress of women before they have an abortion procedure.

Third, we found that the main determinants of abortion among this study sample were related to contraceptive behaviour (contraceptive failure, and/or non-use of methods due to either misinformation, lack of information, or low motivation) and unmarried status. Most of the 4,000 women were aged less than 30 years, which also supports this conclusion.

So while it is true that over the last several decades the Chinese government has successfully reduced the birth rate of its large population, the results of this study reveal that efforts are still needed to improve the quality of family planning services, particularly information given to users, in order to reduce contraceptive failure. The main barriers to improving systematic use by the population include the inconvenience of the necessary procedures and the persistent problems of supply, cost and quality.

Another factor related to contraceptive failure in China particularly is that the Chinese national family planning policy encourages the insertion of IUDs after the birth of the first child. Some studies comparing IUD failure (reflected by pregnancy) and expulsion rates of various IUDs made in China have shown that IUDS made in China had higher failure and expulsion rates (State Family Planning Commission of China, 1985; Gao Ji et al., 1986; Second Clinical Group of National IUD Research, 1987). Although this study did not intend to measure contraceptive failure, it clearly showed that 65.5 per cent of the 1,471 women whose main reason to seek an abortion was contraceptive failure, were using an IUD. We found the large contribution of IUD failure to abortion astonishing.

To eliminate these barriers, a major effort to reduce unwanted pregnancy and abortion through improved family planning services should be undertaken. We suggest more widespread promotion of effective contraception methods and improved information about them, especially to high-risk groups. Moreover, our findings reinforce the need to introduce a better IUD with lower failure rates, especially in poorer communities in China. This would be a more effective way to prevent unintended pregnancy and its outcome. In fact, since this study took place, the government of China has announced its decision to convert from the stainless steel ring to the copper TCu-220C and TCu-380A devices for all new insertions from the beginning of 1993.

For those women who must have an abortion, we suggest that the technical training and capacity of clinic and hospital staff be continually monitored and improved, in order to reduce the volume of blood loss and other physical effects during induced abortion as well as to diminish the psychological impact on the subjects before and after abortion.

When modern contraception is widely available and used effectively, abortion can be reduced. It is our hope that the survey results reported here will be useful in evolving the development of population policy in China and other countries, especially to help reduce the number of abortions worldwide.

✟ References

David, H.P. 1992. Abortion: Psychosocial trends. Prepared for presentation at the annual meeting of the Population Association of America, Denver, CO, 30 April 1992.

Derogatis, L.R., K. Rickles and A.F. Rock, 1976. The SCL-90 and the MMPI: A step in the validation of a new self-report scale. *British Journal of Psychiatry* 128: 280–89.

Gao Ji, Shen He, Zheng Su, Fan Huimin, Wu Minghui, Han Lihui and Yao Guongzhen. 1986. A randomized comparative clinical evaluation of the steel ring, V Cu-200 and TCu-220C. *Surgical Contraception* 33 (5): 443–54.

Garrison, C.Z., C.L. Addy, K.L. Jackson, R.E. McKeown and J.L. Waller. 1991. The CES-D as a screen for depression and other psychiatric disorders in adolescents. *Journal of the American Academy of Child Adolescent Psychiatry* 30 (4): 636–40.

Ge Quanging et al. 1982. *Medical encyclopedia of China*. Shanghai: Shanghai Science and Technology Press, p. 64.

Grinker, R.R., J. Miller, M. Sabshin, R.J. Nunn and J.C. Nunnally. 1961. *The phenomenon of depression*. New York: Harper & Row.

Jin Hua, Wu Wenyuan, Zhang Minyuan. 1986. Analytic of averment on results among normal Chinese by using SCL-90. *Journal of Psychosis and Neurology of China* 2: 260–62.

Klein, D.F. 1974. Endogonomophic depression. *Archives of General Psychiatry* 31: 447–54.

Lin Xinchen, Li Lin, Wu Tiejian, Chao Heijie, Zhou Fongron. 1990. Investigation and analysis of depression symptoms among teachers in middle schools. *Social Medicine in China* 4: 36–37.

Radloff, L.S. 1977. The CES-D scale: A self-report depression scale for research in the general population. *Applied Psychological Measurement* 1: 385.

Second Clinical Group of National IUD Research. 1987. A randomized multicentre comparative study of three types of IUDs (two-year follow-up). *Reproduction and Contraception* 7 (3): 39–47.

Sichuan Population Information and Research Center. 1991. Chengdu, China.

State Family Planning Commission of China. 1985. A clinical trial of three commonly used IUDs. In: State Family Planning Commission of China. *A condensed summary of family planning scientific research during the sixth five-year plan*. Beijing: State Family Planning Commission of China, pp. 19–21.

———. 1992. Data from the two-per-thousand national fertility survey. Presentation to the Rockefeller Foundation, Beijing, China, May.

Tietze, C. and S.K. Henshaw. 1986. *Induced abortion: A world review 1986*. 6th Edition. New York: The Alan Guttmacher Institute.

World Health Organization (WHO). 1990. *Abortion: A tabulation of available information on the frequency and mortality of unsafe abortion*. Geneva: WHO.

Zhang Minyuan, Ren Fumin, Fun Bin, Wang Zhinyu. 1987. Investigation of depression symptoms among normal people and application of CES-D. *Journal of Psychosis and Neurology of China* 20: 67–69.

5

Abortion Practice in a Municipality of Havana, Cuba

Luisa Alvarez, Caridad Teresa Garcia, Sonia Catasus,
Maria Elena Benitez and Maria Teresa Martinez

Introduction

Cuba is the only country in Latin America where abortions are legally performed in large numbers within the framework of the official health services. The liberalization of the Social Defense Code by the Cuban government in 1964 permitted a broader interpretation of earlier codes that had made abortion more restricted. Since then, abortion has become increasingly common, particularly as contraceptive choice is limited and the methods are not always available.

Abortion is freely available on request in hospitals up to 12 weeks gestation. It is performed by means of manual vacuum aspiration with Karman syringe, without anaesthesia, up to 45 days of amenorrhoea. (This same technique is used for menstrual regulation.) For a first-trimester abortion, a woman has lab tests to determine whether there are indications of STDs/HIV. She is also required to bring a urine specimen on the day of the procedure for the extraction of corionic gonadotropin. Women who request an abortion at more than 12 weeks gestation must have their case reviewed by a special medical committee of the hospital if their reason is a medical one and by a social worker if their reason is a socioeconomic one. All women who have an abortion receive a medical examination, although it is not required by law. Nor is parental consent required for women less than 16 years of age. All that is necessary is that the clinic register the name and address of the woman.

Research supports the conclusion that abortion in Cuba plays an important role in fertility regulation. At least two studies attribute the rapid decline of fertility in Cuba from 3.7 children per woman in 1972 to 1.81 in 1990 to abortion, together with contraception and nuptiality (Hollerbach and Díaz-Brisquet,

1983; Alvarez, 1987). Another study that compared fertility trends during the last 20 years with abortion rate profiles, concluded that abortion has had a dominant influence on fertility, particularly in urban areas (Alvarez, 1985).

More than 140,000 pregnancy interruptions are performed every year; in 1990, the number of abortions reached 147,530. The number of live births in this same year was 186,658, creating a relationship of eight abortions per 10 live births (MINSAP1, 1990). Since 1968, when estimates of abortion were first reported, the figures have progressively increased from 37.9 abortions per 1,000 women of reproductive age in 1968, to 59.4 in 1990. This latter rate includes abortions as well as menstrual regulations (MINSAP2, 1990).

Data from 1987–88 show that the abortion rate among women less than 20 years of age was almost the same as for women aged 25–29. Moreover, the age distribution of the abortion rate has shifted; it is higher now among younger women. The contribution of women students to the overall abortion rate is almost twice as high as that of working women: 852.0 per 1,000 women students compared to 448.3 per 1,000 working women in 1987–88 (MINSAP2, 1990).

To begin to understand the practice of abortion in Cuba, however, it is important to realize that contraceptive use is also high in this country, about 75 per cent. This raises the obvious question: Why does abortion continue to play a major role in fertility regulation among Cuban women? This question compelled us to begin the search for the factors that influence abortion practice in order to provide a scientific basis for incidence-reducing strategies. We wanted to identify the determinants of abortion practice, rather than to study abortion as one of the proximate determinants of fertility as most previous studies have done.

Ours is the first research on abortion in Cuba in which the relationship between abortion practice and contraceptive use and the important overall influence of socioeconomic and psychological factors are all considered simultaneously to fully understand why women seek abortion (García, 1987; García and González, 1991; Kerlinger, 1988).

Research Methodology

Our abortion study was conducted in Havana City in the municipality called '10 de Octubre', which has the second largest population in the country. In July 1990, this area had an estimated 239,703 inhabitants (CEE, 1990). As in the rest of the country, the birth rate here has been decreasing since the mid-1960s; in 1990, it reached a level of 13.7 live births per 1,000 inhabitants.

The female population of Havana City Province has typically resorted to abortion to control fertility. In fact, this province has the highest levels of abortion per live births; in 1988, 53.5 abortions per 100 live births were reported here, compared to other provinces where abortions did not exceed 49.5 per 100 live births (MINSAP2, 1990).

We based our study on a cross-sectional sample, which was selected by utilizing a random cluster approach. The sample was larger than required with a total of 2,197 women in 27 clusters (registered family doctors' offices), which were selected through a systematic random selection procedure. In the end, we interviewed 1,965 sexually active women, aged 13–34 (Table 5.1). We chose women residing in areas covered only by the primary health care system. This means that each woman has been assigned to a specific family doctor's office under the 'System of Family Doctor Care Services' of the municipality. In April 1989, this system consisted of 227 service units, which together cover more than 70 per cent of the area's population. These smaller units are part of the poli-clinics, which are at the core of the primary health care system of Cuba.

Table 5.1: **Summary of the Main Characteristics of the Population Studied**

	Number	*Percentage*
Age (years)		
Under 20	184	9.4
20–24	503	25.6
25–29	756	38.5
30–34	522	26.5
Education		
Primary/technical	107	5.4
Secondary	554	28.2
Pre-university	945	48.1
University	359	18.3
Occupation		
Working	1,292	65.8
Not working	673	34.2
Marital Status		
Married	883	44.9
Consensual union	586	29.8
Single	184	9.4
Divorced/separated	312	15.9
Abortion Experience		
None	894	46
Recent abortion*	198	10
Previous abortion	873	44
Contraceptive Use		
Currently using	1,351	69
Not using	614	31

* In the last 12 months.

We decided that it was necessary to include all voluntary pregnancy interruptions, whether by standard abortion techniques or by menstrual regulation. We obtained a list of women who fulfilled the requirements for the study from information registered by the selected family doctors' offices.

Prior to the study, all instruments were tested and the participating personnel received theoretical and practical training. The collection of all information was carried out by groups of four to six interviewers under the guidance of a supervisor, who in addition, was responsible for reviewing the information before its submission to the control office.

In home visits to the women selected, household information was obtained from a member of the family over 13 years of age who was capable of answering the questions. Private interviews were held with each woman individually to obtain personal data. To obtain the psychological data, two questionnaires were self-administered following the personal interview in a sub-sample of women. To evaluate the psychological data, two Likert-type scales were used, one for abortion and the other for contraception.

Response Rate

Of the 2,197 women selected, 1,965 were interviewed, creating a response rate of 90.1 per cent. Of the women interviewed, 94.1 per cent showed a level of cooperation considered good or excellent. From the sub-sample of 613 women selected to answer the two self-administered questionnaires, 585 responded to the one on abortion and 567 responded to the one on contraception.

Main Results

A Discussion of Abortion, Pregnancy and Fertility Rates by Selected Socioeconomic Variables

Generally, we found that among the 1,965 women who participated in our survey, 9.7 per cent aged 13–34 years had an abortion in the previous 12 months (in 1990), and 54 per cent had at least one abortion during their lifetime. More than one-third of the women explained that their abortion had been a menstrual regulation. In the following sections we discuss some of the most compelling findings from our research.

Age

The abortion rate (expressed per 100 women) is highest among younger women, especially those under 20 years of age; among them, more than two abortions were performed per each live birth in the year prior to the survey. With increasing age, there is an increase in the proportion of women with abortion experience, although the actual abortion rate goes down (Table 5.2). Similarly, the proportion of women who had at least two abortions increases among older women; for example, among women over 30, one out of every three stated that they had experienced at least two pregnancy interruptions.

Table 5.2: Age-Specific Fertility and Abortion Rates*

Age (years)	Pregnancy	Fertility	Abortions	Abortion Ratio
< 20	34.2	9.8	20.7	211.2
20–24	29.7	11.4	12.0	105.3
25–29	24.1	9.8	8.2	83.7
> 30	16.7	5.6	6.7	119.6

* Rates are per 100 women; the events (pregnancy, live birth, abortion)
are for the 12 months preceding the interview.

The pregnancy rate is twice as high in women under 20 years of age than in those over 30 years of age. Fertility rates by age reach a maximum value in the group aged 20–24 years; while in the under-20 age group, they are similar to those among women aged 25–29 years.

The abortion ratio, defined as the number of abortions per live births (a proxy for number of pregnancies), is a useful measure in that it is independent of other factors unrelated to reproduction. Moreover, unlike the abortion rate, the abortion ratio reflects views about family size and availability and access to contraceptive services. In Cuba, as in other countries, the ratio is particularly high for adolescents. In the study population, the abortion ratio is 211 abortions per 100 live births for women under 20; the next highest ratio is for older women, 30–35, for whom the ratio is 120 abortions per 100 live births. These are the age groups for whom an unwanted pregnancy poses the greatest difficulty.

Education

For each level of education, when the influence of age is eliminated (using age-standardized rates), pregnancy, fertility and abortion rates showed significant variation; for example, all rates were lower among more educated women (Table 5.3). This shows that education influences fertility behaviour regardless of the age of the woman. Moreover, we found no variation in contraceptive use to explain this relationship. (We discuss this in more detail in a later section.)

Employment Status

Abortion and pregnancy rates are significantly higher among unemployed than employed women, which is expected. However, once employment status was controlled by age, these rates narrowed significantly. Something similar occurred with these rates when we looked at specific occupational categories. There was significant variation until we controlled by age, with one exception: Abortion rates for manual labourers remained somewhat higher than

Table 5.3: Age-Standardized Fertility and Abortion Rates by Education, Occupation, Marital Status and Origin of the Partner

	Pregnancy	Fertility	Abortion
Education			
Primary	19.3	3.2	11.1
Technical	25.6	10.4	11.0
Secondary	34.5	12.6	14.5
Pre-university	24.9	9.4	9.3
University	23.4	8.7	9.5
Occupation			
Professional/technical	22.8	9.1	5.7
Managerial	35.7	17.9	11.9
Administrative	21.1	7.5	9.2
Manual worker	24.7	8.3	15.6
Service worker	24.3	6.5	10.9
Other workers	36.6	11.8	10.1
Students	20.8	1.9	11.2
Marital status			
Married	28.2	13.7	8.1
Consensual union	25.8	6.6	12.3
Single	12.5	0.1	11.5
Divorced/separated	18.9	7.3	9.3
Origin of the partner			
City	25.7	9.4	10.8
Town	25.7	11.2	8.0
Countryside	38.6	20.3	7.2

for other occupational categories. Here we see that age has a greater effect on fertility behaviour than either employment status or type of occupation. In examining these findings, however, we have to consider the uniqueness of Cuba's centrally planned economy, with universal employment and a highly specialized labour force.

Marital Status

For this analysis, we created three main marital categories that conform to the Cuban situation in particular, and to the larger Caribbean pattern of sexual unions in general. These were, namely: married women; women in consensual unions, which are often of long duration and relatively stable but non-formalized; and single women. In addition, we created a separate category for divorced, separated and widowed women.

Marital status was significantly different for abortion, pregnancy and fertility rates, which is to be expected. These differences remained after the rates were standardized by age (Table 5.3). Age-standardized marital rates show that abortion is highest among women in consensual unions (12.3 per cent), and nearly as high among single women (11.5 per cent). However, pregnancy rates are much lower among single women, than among women in consensual unions (12.5 per cent compared to 25.8 per cent). The highest pregnancy rate was among married women (28.2 per cent), who also had the lowest abortion rate of 8 per cent. For all women, except married women, there were more pregnancies ending in an abortion than in a live birth.

Partner Characteristics

Women who regularly lived with their partner had higher pregnancy rates and lower age-standardized abortion rates (8.4 per cent) than women who did not live with their partner (13.5 per cent). Similarly, the abortion ratio was very high for women not living with their sexual partner (275 abortions per 100 live births), while those living together showed a much lower abortion ratio (63 abortions per 100 live births).

Of the variables related to the sexual partner, the strongest statistical significance was found in abortion rates by origin of the partner. That is to say, the highest abortion rates were observed when the male partner was born or had resided for a long time in the municipality (10.8 per cent) as compared to if he was born in the countryside (7.2 per cent). This relationship became stronger when we looked at the abortion ratio: 149 abortions per 100 live births for women whose partner is of urban origin, which is twice as high as for women whose partner is of rural origin. Interestingly, when we looked at the same characteristic for the women themselves, the relationship was weaker; although the abortion ratio was still slightly higher for urban-raised women than for those of rural origin. None of the other partner-related variables in the study seem to have as clear-cut a relationship to the rate of abortion.

Household Structure

We decided to look next at the gender of the head of the household, one of the attributes most frequently examined in family studies (Benítez, 1990). A majority of the women in the study, 58 per cent, lived in female-headed households, where the highest pregnancy and abortion rates were found. There were 130 abortions per 100 live births in female-headed households, compared to 81.2 abortions per 100 live births in male-headed households.

We then differentiated households according to whether they were nuclear or extended. These had different fertility profiles, with women in nuclear households having much smaller families. Both types of households had similar abortion rates (around 10 per cent). The abortion ratio, however, was twice as high among women living in nuclear households (182 abortions per 100 live births). This probably indicates that nuclear families have a much higher motivation for maintaining lower family size in the face of difficulties in obtaining appropriate housing and the child care support normally provided by an extended household.

Family Income

Pregnancy and abortion rates were found to differ significantly according to income level. Households with the lowest and highest per capita income had the lowest abortion rates. Going up the income ladder, the second income group from the bottom ($25.00 to $74.00 in national currency) had the highest abortion rate. The abortion ratio was almost twice as high for the highest income families (123 abortions per 100 live births), compared to the lowest income families. There was an inverse relationship between income level and fertility rate.

Multivariate Analysis

From the preceding discussion, we can conclude that being young, residing in a female-headed household, living in an extended household, being single, and having a low income are all factors that increased the risk of abortion among the women in our study. However, all these factors may not have had the same amount of influence on abortion practice.

Understanding the relative risk of having an abortion required a different type of analysis. A logistic regression was run with previous abortion experience (during the 12 months prior to our study) as the dependent variable. The logistic regression model showed significant results for several factors. Among household-related variables, an unmarried head of household had an abortion risk 50 per cent higher than a married head of household; low-income ($25–$74) groups had an abortion risk 61 per cent higher than other income groups. Among personal characteristic variables, women under 25 years of age had an abortion risk 66 per cent higher than women over 25 years of age; women in a consensual union had an abortion risk 46 per cent higher than single or married women. With respect to partner characteristics, a higher abortion risk of 60 per cent or more was found for women not cohabiting with their sexual partner and for women whose partners were urban-raised.

The model also included variables related to contraception. Two variables were significant: contraceptive use and knowledge of intrauterine devices. For the first of these, the abortion risk was 47 per cent higher among users than non-users. For the second, the ratio was less than one, which indicates that IUD knowledge was a factor of protection. This finding seems to suggest that users of contraception had a higher risk of abortion than non-users at the time of the interview.

Abortion Versus Menstrual Regulation

Knowledge

Regardless of whether there had been a previous experience of abortion, 40 per cent of the women in our study had only a vague idea or did not know what the actual procedure for abortion was. Among women who had more than one abortion, knowledge of the abortion procedure improved somewhat. Our findings were similar regarding knowledge of menstrual regulation, although the overall level of knowledge was much lower. It is only the women who had more than one abortion who had a fairly high level of knowledge of menstrual regulation (56 per cent). In short, women knew more about standard abortion procedures than they did about menstrual regulation techniques, regardless of actual experience.

Preference and Perceived Risks

All women in the study were asked which technique they preferred, abortion or menstrual regulation. There was no real expression of preference; most women said that they resorted to abortion because they were not aware of the reliability of modern contraception.

Regarding the more standard abortion techniques, a high proportion of women expressed a fear of becoming infertile (59 per cent among those who never had an abortion and somewhat less for those with abortion experience). The second greatest concern was that the procedure would have adverse effects on their health. In addition, one out of every 10 women worried that an abortion might lead to death.

Conversely, most women perceived menstrual regulation as a very simple procedure. Negative attitudes towards it were less well-defined than those towards the more standard abortion procedures, with women saying that it might have negative health consequences. A fairly large number of women confessed that they could not offer an opinion about menstrual regulation because they did not know enough about it.

Contraceptive Knowledge and Use

Contraceptive knowledge in the population surveyed is high for the IUD, oral contraception, and the condom, which reached 98.8, 87.8 and 72.2 per cent, respectively. However, in this study we wanted to try to determine the extent of knowledge about actual use rather than just having heard about a method. The vast majority of women had fairly good actual knowledge about condoms and IUDs; that is, 80.3 and 78.8 per cent, respectively. But actual knowledge about oral contraceptives and sterilization was much lower; about 50.3 and 55.6 per cent, respectively. Actual knowledge about other methods was low or elementary (see Table 5.4).

Table 5.4: Contraceptive Knowledge

Method	Knowledge*	
	Had Ever Heard	Actual
Pill	87.8	50.3
IUD	98.8	78.8
Diaphragm	59.0	33.5
Condom	72.2	80.3
Female sterilization	11.2	55.6
Vasectomy	5.8	5.1
Rhythm	8.8	11.4
Withdrawal	6.5	36.8

* Knowledge is defined by two categories: an intuitive, spontaneous response; or knowledge of how to actually use the method.

In a country with such an extensive network of health services, it was surprising to discover that the main source of knowledge was a female friend for five of the nine methods examined. Health institutions were recognized as the main source of information for IUDs (40.1 per cent), but even in this case, a female friend was still a relevant source. Only vasectomy and chemical products were associated with information derived from the mass media; 33.2 per cent and 23.4 per cent, respectively. There is no doubt that the informal network plays a much more decisive role on the way women understand how the various methods work. Contraceptive use correlated with the standard socioeconomic variables of education, employment, occupation, and whether or not the woman had a sexual partner. Employed women used or were using contraceptive methods slightly more than those who were unemployed. Students showed the highest percentage of contraceptive use (76.4 per cent), followed by women employed in administration (73.1 per cent), and service activities (72.3 per cent).

Seventy per cent of women with a sexual partner were using some form of contraception. Remarkably, 58.5 per cent of women without a sexual partner were still using a method: 13.0 per cent were taking oral contraceptives; 38.9 per cent had an IUD. In addition, 5 per cent were sterilized.

Overall, the data on contraceptive knowledge and use shows that most women are aware of the existence of modern contraceptive methods. However, their understanding of how these methods work and how to use them is much lower, because the source of information is inadequate and the choice of methods is limited.

Abortion and Contraception

Personal Experience

There are no significant differences in patterns of contraceptive use between women who never had an abortion and women who have a previous history of abortion. For both these groups, contraceptive prevalence is about 68 per cent (see Table 5.5). Among women who had a recent abortion (within the past year), contraceptive use was somewhat higher (75 per cent), as one would expect. For all three groups (no abortion, previous or recent), the pattern of method use is different. Women who never had an abortion tend to have a more diversified pattern of use that includes both traditional and modern methods. Women with a history of abortion have a much higher use of IUDs. However, pill use is lower among these women and highest for women who have never had an abortion. Sterilization increases among women with a previous history of abortion as compared to the other groups.

Table 5.5: Contraceptive Use by Abortion Practice

Contraceptive Use	Abortion Practice (%)		
	Recent	Previous	Never
Using	75.0	68.5	67.6
Method			
Pill	15.1	10.0	16.6
IUD	51.6	48.9	39.8
Condom	2.6	1.5	2.8
Sterilization	2.1	7.1	5.5
Rhythm	0.5	0.7	1.3
Withdrawal	0.5	0.1	0.9
Others	2.6	0.2	0.7
None	25.0	31.5	32.4
Total number of women	(198)	(873)	(894)

Reversing the coin by looking now at the study population divided into three different groups—women who have never used contraception, ever-users, and current users—the pattern of abortion experience that emerges is interesting. Three out of four women who never used contraception had not had an abortion. Among the two groups of contraceptive users, nearly half had had a previous abortion and another 10 per cent had an abortion in the 12 months preceding the interview (Table 5.6). This would seem to indicate that having an abortion is part of the path of initiating or sustaining contraceptive use.

Table 5.6: Abortion Experience by Contraceptive Use Status

Abortion Experience	Contraceptive Use		
	Using	Ever-Used	Never-Used
Recent	10.7	8.5	4.6
Previous	45.2	50.7	22.0
Never	44.1	40.8	73.4
Total number of women	(1,351)	(505)	(109)

Personal Opinion

There were important differences in the views expressed by the women about abortion and contraception. Three different attitudes emerged: positive support for abortion or contraception; negative view of abortion or contraception; or ambivalence towards these issues.

Among the women who had been pregnant at least once, the majority (68 per cent) felt ambivalent about abortion. Thirty per cent were opposed to it, and a small minority expressed a positive opinion about it. These same women expressed a very different view about contraception: A large majority (81 per cent) were in favour of it; ambivalence was much lower (15 per cent); and opposition was truly negligible.

Among the women who had actually experienced an abortion, the attitude towards abortion continued to be highly ambivalent (78 per cent); only a few more women expressed a more positive view. Similarly, a positive attitude towards contraception increased slightly among these women, to 83 per cent.

None of the women who carried their pregnancy to term expressed a positive attitude towards abortion; 65 per cent were ambivalent; and 35 per cent opposed it.

Conclusions and Recommendations

Cuban women have a very high level of awareness of contraceptive methods. Despite this awareness of contraception, however, detailed knowledge of how methods actually work or are used is, at best, elementary. This is probably because the main source of information is the informal network of family and friends. Contraceptive use is also high. The most commonly used methods are IUDs and oral contraceptives.

Therefore, it was remarkable to discover that three out of every four women who had an abortion in the past 12 months were using a method of contraception. Looking for clues to explain this contradictory situation leads to the inescapable conclusion that there is a high level of method failure, discontinuation or inconsistent use. There seems to be also a fair amount of method switching, perhaps as a result of intermittent contraceptive supplies. If not done correctly, this behaviour exposes women to the risk of unwanted pregnancy when they think they are protected. As a result, abortion continues to play a critical role in fertility regulation. Women who are single, under 25 years of age, raised in an urban context, with higher than primary education, unemployed or employed as manual workers have a higher risk of abortion. Having a partner but not cohabiting with him, or having a partner of urban origin, adds to this risk.

Equally importantly, we found that regardless of the fact that abortion is available on demand in Cuba, it is practised with reservation. It is only among women with multiple abortions that opposition to it decreases; and even among these women, the predominant attitude is ambivalence. For a population whose reproductive behaviour is characterized by such high rates of induced abortion, it is critical to note that frank approval of this approach to fertility regulation is minimal. Moreover, this study shows that this attitude is true for all women, regardless of whether or not they have experienced an abortion. This is in contrast to their attitude towards contraception, which is highly positive.

Based on these results, it seems clear that what is needed in Cuba is a major change in family planning services. Women should be able to approach fertility regulation in a way that allows a more rational and effective use of contraception. Moreover, future studies should attempt to understand the factors that affect contraceptive compliance and continuation. This would contribute to reducing their apparent and unwilling reliance on induced abortion.

While this study explored the situation in only one municipality of Havana, the findings indicate that they may, at least in part, reflect the determinants that explain the high incidence of induced abortion among women throughout Cuba.

✝ References

Alvarez, L. 1985. *La Fecundidad en Cuba*. La Habana: Editorial Ciencias Sociales.

———. 1987. Determinantes próximos de la fecundidad en Cuba. Modelo de Bongaarts. *Revista Cubana de Administración de la Salud*. 13(4) October–December.

Benítez, M.E. 1990. *El hogar y la familia cubana: Una caracterización sociodemográfica*. La Habana: CEDEM.

CEE. 1990. Boletín Demográfico. Publication No. 20. La Habana.

García, C.T. 1987. Contracepción y aborto: Características de las mujeres que solicitan estos servicios. *Programa y resumen del 21 Congreso Interamericano de Psicología*. 29 June–3 July 1987, La Habana, p. 208.

García, C.T. and P. González. 1991. Factores relacionados con la selección entre el aborto y la continuidad del embarazo en adolescentes de Ciudad de La Habana. *Programa y resumen de la Jornada de temas terminados INEN*. February, La Habana.

Hollerbach, P. and S. Díaz-Brizquet. 1983. Fertility determinants in Cuba. Committee on Population and Demography. Report No. 26. Washington, D.C.: National Academy Press.

Kerlinger, F.N. 1988. Foundations of behavioral research. 3rd Edition. Hong Kong: HRW International Edition.

MINSAP1. 1990. Informe Anual 90. La Habana: Estadísticas del Ministerio de Salud Pública.

MINSAP2. 1990. El Aborto en Cuba. La Habana: Resumen de Publicaciones. Dirección de Estadística.

6

Social Determinants of Induced Abortion in the Dominican Republic

Denise Paiewonsky

Introduction

A number of social, economic and demographic factors relative to illegal abortion practices in the Dominican Republic are discussed in this chapter, with special emphasis on contraceptive behaviour. This presentation is based on the results of a larger study, entitled 'Social Determinants and Consequences of Induced Abortion in the Dominican Republic' conducted in 1992, which was an exploratory and descriptive study of the social determinants of abortion, including the methods used, the role of religious beliefs and the decision-making process.

The Dominican Penal Code, Article 317, which was first adopted in the mid-nineteenth century, punishes voluntary induced abortion in all cases. No exception is made for therapeutic indications nor for rape or incest. Nevertheless, legal actions on this matter are extremely rare and, when they do take place, they are initiated against the abortionist by relatives of women who have died because of poorly performed procedures, and only rarely by the state. The strictness of the law ensures that clandestine abortion services remain underground, unsafe and expensive. Moreover, the non-enforcement of the law contributes to the country's high abortion rate. By the end of the 1980s, the number of abortions was estimated at about 65,000 annually, or roughly one abortion for every three births (Paiewonsky, 1988). A new study published in 1994 by the Alan Guttmacher Institute (AGI) estimates that the number of abortions had risen to 82,500 annually by the early 1990s (AGI, 1994).

The 'invisible' maternal morbidity and mortality resulting from the illegal nature of the procedure creates a major contradiction within the national public health system, given that close to 10 per cent of its maternal beds—and an even larger share of its medical resources—regularly go to the treatment of abortion complications resulting from unsafe procedures (Paiewonsky, 1988).

Although official statistics rank illegal abortion among the main causes of maternal morbidity and mortality in this country (SESPAS, 1992), national studies on the subject are scarce and limited and include only Calventi (1975), UNPHU (1975), and Paiewonsky (1988), AGI (1994).

Objectives

The project's first general objective therefore was to provide the medical, research and public health communities with reliable information concerning some aspects of the abortion situation in the Dominican Republic. A second general objective was to encourage the implementation of specialized prevention and/or maternal health care programmes. This is particularly relevant given that the country's public health policies do not explicitly cover abortion prevention or post-abortion medical attention.

The more specific objective of this research was to explore the possible impact of some basic social determinants on certain factors related to the decision-making process connected with abortion. The social determinants selected were age, education, marital status, household situation and the occupational status of both the woman and her husband. The decision-making factors included the nature and stability of the marital union, parity, childbearing intentions, access to abortion services, risk perception and others.

These objectives and the selection of variables were based on the main premise that social determinants act on decision-making factors, which in turn result in behaviour related to the practice of both contraception and abortion. Contraceptive use is therefore seen as a major intermediate variable between the effect of social determinants and the decision to terminate a pregnancy. This chapter, therefore, concentrates on the social and behavioural determinants of pregnancy termination, with special emphasis on the role of contraceptive behaviour.

Research Methodology

The study was conducted in two large maternity hospitals in Santo Domingo, the capital of the Dominican Republic, between March and May of 1992. The data were collected through structured interviews with 352 abortion patients seeking services, mostly for post-abortion complications, at these hospitals. Three hundred and nine women were interviewed at the country's largest maternity hospital, the Maternidad Nuestra Señora de la Altagracia (MNSA), which is a public health institution. Another 43 women were interviewed at the Santo Domingo Maternal and Child Clinic, which belongs to the Instituto

Dominicano de Seguros Sociales (IDSS), a semi-public social security institution. The former provides services to the most impoverished social sectors; the latter covers mainly a wage-earning, working class population.

The procedure for conducting fieldwork was to interview all abortion cases being admitted with abortion complications at both institutions, beginning on a set date, until the projected sample size of 350 was attained. The IDSS Clinic was chosen to provide a control sample so that populations with different socioeconomic profiles could be compared. Before the interviews started, the interviewers received an intensive training course.

The hospital data was supplemented with detailed qualitative information derived from in-depth interviews with 19 lower-class and 13 middle-class women who had previously obtained abortions. These in-depth interviews were carried out once the fieldwork at the hospitals was completed and included a different sample of women. The middle-class women were included not only for comparison purposes, but also to counter the lower- class bias of most hospital-based abortion research in the region.

Some Methodological Problems

As is usually the case with research on induced abortion, two methodological problems arose that could affect the interpretation of the hospital data. The first was the respondent's reluctance to acknowledge the voluntary nature of her abortion, which is perfectly understandable in a country where abortion is illegal, punishable by law, and severely condemned by religious and social mores. The second problem was the negative impact the hospital surroundings had on the interview process; the crowded, noisy, impersonal environment without a secure place for privacy was detrimental to building the trust necessary for discussion of such a sensitive issue. Public or semi-public hospitals (such as the IDSS) provide the only feasible location for a project of this nature in the Dominican Republic, but their intrinsic characteristics are far from ideal for this kind of interview.

We also observed a very negative attitude on the part of the hospital staff towards women who arrived with abortion complications, which was not conducive to the interview process. Despite repeated appeals by the project's personnel, MNSA physicians and other staff frequently threatened to report the abortion patients to the police, mocked them in their faces or questioned their sexual morality.

Interview Questionnaire

The questionnaire was devised with the anticipation that respondents would be reluctant to discuss the topic of abortion. Thus, the first four sections were designed to gather information on socioeconomic and demographic characteristics, reproductive history and contraceptive behaviour. This information was essential for the analysis of determinants, allowing us to have a unit for analysis even if the respondent refused to answer the abortion questions, all of which were in the last section. This also meant that if the patient refused to acknowledge a voluntary termination of pregnancy or even to discuss the subject altogether, this would affect mainly the psychosocial and health data, and have little bearing on the quality of the data discussed in this chapter, except in one important respect: This design made it impossible to distinguish between spontaneous abortions and induced abortions.

Induced Versus Spontaneous Abortions

Given the absence of infallible, or even merely reliable, medical criteria to differentiate between these two types of events, this project treated all cases as if they were induced.

Barreto et al. (1992) present just one recent example in the long list of studies detailing the difficulties of separating spontaneous from induced abortions in hospital settings. In this context, the classification criteria proposed by WHO in the 1980s provide a starting point, although it falls short of resolving the issue. According to a recent study that applied this classification to hospital data from four South American countries (Singh and Wulf, 1993), the percentage of possible induced abortions amounts to 67 per cent of the cases reviewed. Several Dominican experts who were consulted on this matter all felt that the proportion of voluntary terminations among abortion cases treated in public hospitals in the Dominican Republic is probably higher, amounting to 75 per cent of all patients, perhaps more.

In light of these uncertainties, the decision to treat all abortions as voluntary inductions creates an unavoidable bias in the statistical analysis, which must be taken into account when the hospital data are considered.

Characteristics of the Study Population

As shown in Table 6.1, the hospital sample is made up mostly of relatively young women, of low socioeconomic status, who emigrated to the Santo Domingo metropolitan area from the provinces. This is, generally speaking, the typical patient profile for public maternity hospitals in the Dominican Republic. However, when comparing the age structure of respondents to that of the general population of women giving birth at the MNSA hospital during the study period, we found the abortion sample to be slightly older. In particular, while teenagers account for 25 per cent of all women giving birth at the MNSA, they make up 18 per cent of all abortion patients.

As expected, the biggest difference between IDSS and MNSA hospital patients is in their educational level. Among MNSA patients, 70 per cent had only primary schooling—almost half of which had not advanced beyond the fourth grade—while 60 per cent of IDSS patients had some secondary or

Table 6.1: Characteristics of the Study Population

| Selected Characteristics | Number of Abortion Cases | | | | | |
| | MNSA Hospital | | IDSS Hospital | | Total | |
	(N)	%	(N)	%	(N)	%
Age (years)						
Less than 15	1	0.3	0	0.0	1	0.3
15–19	54	17.5	3	7.0	57	16.2
20–24	103	33.3	12	27.9	115	32.7
25–29	73	23.6	16	37.2	89	25.3
30–34	44	14.2	8	18.6	52	14.8
35–39	17	5.5	4	9.3	21	6.0
40–44	15	4.9	0	0.0	15	4.3
45 and over	2	0.7	0	0.0	2	0.5
Birthplace						
D.N. urban*	88	28.5	11	25.6	99	28.1
D.N. rural	19	6.1	1	2.3	20	5.7
Interior urban	76	24.6	16	37.2	92	26.1
Interior rural	124	40.1	15	34.9	139	39.5
No information	2	0.7	0	0.0	2	0.6
Residence						
D.N. urban	239	77.4	31	72.1	270	76.7
D.N. rural	45	14.6	7	16.3	52	14.8
Interior urban	6	1.9	2	4.7	8	2.2
Interior rural	18	5.8	3	7.0	21	6.0
No information	1	0.3	0	0.0	1	0.3
Education level						
No education	25	8.1	0	0.0	25	7.1
Primary (1–4)	68	22.0	3	7.0	71	20.2
Primary (5–8)	121	39.1	14	32.6	135	38.4
Secondary	83	26.9	20	46.5	103	29.3
University	12	3.9	6	14.0	18	5.0
Marital status						
Single	10	3.2	1	2.3	11	3.1
Union	210	68.0	23	53.5	233	66.2
Legal marriage	33	10.7	12	27.9	45	12.8
Separated	27	8.7	4	9.3	31	8.8
Widow/divorced	1	0.3	0	0.0	1	0.3
Married/union but living alone	28	9.1	3	7.00	31	8.8
Total	309	100.0	43	100.0	352	100.0

* D.N. refers to the urban area of Santo Domingo and outlying areas, a few of which are still rural in some of their characteristics.

university education. These educational disparities have their largest impact on the type of economic activity these women are engaged in. But they do not appear to influence other variables where important effects were anticipated, such as contraceptive behaviour and parity.

As has been shown for both the Dominican Republic (UNPHU, 1975) and for most Third World countries generally (Henshaw and Morrow, 1990), women who obtain abortions are typically married with children. This was the case for our hospital sample, where about 80 per cent of respondents said they were presently in a marital union, and only 3 per cent described themselves as never-married singles. The only significant difference between the two hospital populations in this regard was the type of marital union. At the MNSA hospital, 68 per cent of the women declared to be in a sexual union and 11 per cent said they were legally married. At the IDSS social security hospital, the proportion of women legally married was substantially higher, 28 per cent; and the proportion cohabiting was a somewhat lower 54 per cent. Two out of three women in marital unions had been in their present relationship for three or more years; and 40 per cent, for five or more years.

The women in the sample initiated marriage and childbirth at a relatively early age, as is generally the case with Dominican women: The respondents' mean age at first marriage was 17.9 years, and their mean age at first pregnancy was 19.2 years. This is nearly exactly the same figure for the median age at first birth nationwide, which is 19.2 years (DHS, 1991). At the time of the interview, 84 per cent of the women had had children, with a mean of 1.8 live children per women, albeit only one-third of the sample had concluded childbearing.

Forty-two per cent of the 272 women with living children in the sample had a child under two years of age. This is worth noting because the in-depth interviews show repeat pregnancies are a frequent motive for abortion. As for childbearing intentions, 65 per cent of the total sample (352 respondents) wanted more children, as opposed to 34 per cent who did not. (See Table 6.7, which includes these data.) However, two-thirds of those wanting more children stated they would like to wait at least a year before their next pregnancy, and only one-fifth said they would like a pregnancy immediately or in less than a year. Adding the respondents who did not want more children to those wishing to wait at least a year before their next pregnancy, we concluded that three out of four women did not want the pregnancy that just ended in abortion.

Main Results

In the following section, we discuss the relationship of key personal background factors to the social and behavioural determinants of abortion.

Paid Employment

Paid employment was proposed as a major variable affecting the sample's reproductive, contraceptive and abortion behaviours. Thus several of the study's main hypotheses refer to occupational status and type of work. Starting from the assumption that women who work outside the home would be more motivated to regulate their fertility, and taking into consideration Tietze and Henshaw's (1986) account of the positive correlation between contraceptive use and abortion experience, we anticipated: first, a higher proportion of women with some contraceptive experience among those working outside the home; and, second, that the proportion of economically active women would be higher in the abortion sample than in the general population of women.

Although some interesting correlations were found, for the most part, the data did not support these hypotheses nor did they reveal significant correlations between occupational status or type of work (paid domestic, formal sector, informal sector) and the reproductive, contraceptive or abortion behaviour of the respondents.

Only 17 per cent of the women had never worked, 45 per cent were not working, and 38 per cent were working at the time of the interview. Of these, three out of four reported regular work—whether in the formal or informal sectors—and the rest reported occasional work. These percentages are virtually identical to those of a subsample of women taken from the general population sample of the National Demographic and Health Survey of the Dominican Republic (DHS, 1991), which was matched to the socioeconomic profile of the hospital sample.

Although parity did not show significant variation according to occupational status and type of work, contraceptive practice did show some variance. As shown in Table 6.2, women currently working had greater contraceptive experience than unemployed and never-employed women, although the difference was not very significant.

The age of the youngest child was the only variable that strongly predicted occupational status, so that the percentage of presently employed women

Table 6.2: Percentage Distribution of the Study Sample by Work Status, Type of Work and Contraceptive Experience

Characteristics of Contraceptive Use	Work Status				
	Not Working	Formal Sector Work	Informal Sector Work	Never Worked	Total
Has not used	28.9	18.9	20.0	25.0	24.7
Has used	71.1	81.1	80.0	75.0	75.3
Modern method	29.6	32.1	33.8	43.3	33.2
Traditional method	12.6	15.1	7.4	16.7	12.5
Both kinds of methods	28.9	34.0	38.8	15.0	29.6
Total	100.0	100.0	100.0	100.0	100.0
Number of women	159	53	80	60	352
Percentages	45.2	15.1	22.7	17.1	100.0

increased steadily from 30 per cent among those with a child under six months, to 50 per cent among those whose youngest child is seven years or older. When considering the relative significance of paid employment in the women's decision to postpone pregnancy, one must take into account the fact that 18 per cent of women who have ever worked left their last employment due to childcare demands. This percentage rises to 30 per cent when other domestic and family causes are included.

Contraceptive Knowledge and Practice

Contraception emerged as the study's most significant variable, and most of the major hospital findings refer to it. The data show, first of all, a huge gap between the respondent's current contraceptive practices and their child-bearing intentions. These women seem very committed to regulating their fertility, and they have considerable contraceptive experience, but their contraceptive practices are very ineffective. The data was analyzed in light of the culturally prevalent contraceptive patterns, characterized by a late start in contraceptive adoption and inconsistent method use. This approach to fertility regulation is, ultimately, based on the expectation of ending the reproductive cycle by means of surgical sterilization, often at an early age, once desired family size has been reached.

Contraceptive Knowledge

Despite the sample's generally low educational level, their rates of so-called method knowledge are similar—and sometimes higher—than those of the general population of women aged 15–44 (DHS, 1991). One hundred per cent know about female sterilization, 99.4 per cent about the pill, 96 per cent about the IUD, and 78.4 per cent about implants. These percentages must be regarded with considerable scepticism, however, given the notion of method 'knowledge' commonly applied in surveys. The respondent is reputed to 'know' the method merely if she can state it or recognize it when it is mentioned to her. In fact, the study findings show that one of the major determinants of unwanted pregnancy and abortion is precisely a lack of adequate information and comprehension of the characteristics, correct use, side effects, and other elements about contraceptive methods.

Prior Contraceptive Use and Prevalence

Table 6.3 reveals a considerable degree of prior use as well as current use of contraceptive methods in our study group. Three out of four women in our sample had used a contraceptive method at some point in their lives, and 25 per cent reported using contraception around the time of their last pregnancy (the one that ended in abortion).

Table 6.3: Percentage Distribution of the Sample According to Selected Indicators of Contraceptive Use

Indicators	MNSA Hospital		IDSS Hospital		Total	
	(N)	%	(N)	(%)	(N)	%
General use						
Has used	233	75.4	32	74.4	265	75.3
Never used	76	24.6	11	25.6	87	24.7
Use at time of last pregnancy						
Used method	74	24.0	13	30.2	87	24.7
Didn't use method	139	45.0	18	41.9	157	44.6
No information	20	6.4	1	2.3	21	6.0
Never used method	76	24.6	11	25.6	87	24.7
Immediate intention to use						
Thought to use	240	77.7	28	65.1	268	76.1
Didn't think to use	66	21.3	15	34.9	81	23.0
No information	3	1.0	0	0.0	3	0.9
Had children when use began						
Yes	169	54.7	23	53.5	192	54.5
No	62	20.0	9	20.9	71	20.2
No Information	2	0.7	0	0.0	2	0.6
Never used	76	24.6	11	25.6	87	24.7
Number of women	309	100.0	43	100.0	352	100.0

By comparison, the latest Demographic and Health Survey reports national contraceptive prevalence rates of 37 per cent for all women of reproductive age, and 56 per cent for all married women of reproductive age, although these figures go down to 11.5 and 18 per cent, respectively, when sterilized women are excluded (DHS, 1991). The DHS also shows that 55 per cent of women aged 15–44 and 78 per cent of married women had used contraceptives, although almost half of these ever-users nationwide are actually sterilized, with 34 per cent of them never having used a contraceptive method (either modern or traditional) prior to sterilization. If sterilization users are excluded, the figures go down to 46.8 and 65.4 per cent, respectively, for all women and married women. The women in our sample, therefore, appear to have significantly more contraceptive experience than the general population of women.

Interestingly, Table 6.3 shows that when comparing the two hospital populations in our study, no significant differences were found in any of the variables related to contraception. In particular, the proportion of ever-users and the proportion who initiated contraception before their first birth are virtually identical among MNSA and IDSS respondents. This would indicate that, despite the differences in educational attainment, both groups of women have similar contraceptive behaviour and similar problems in the use of methods.

The in-depth interviews reveal that the time during the women's reproductive cycle when contraception is initiated and abortion is decided upon, are the variables that are most sensitive to social class differentials. Ninety-two per cent of the middle-class women interviewed started contraception before the birth of the first child, in contrast to only 18 per cent of low-income women. Likewise, 76.5 per cent of the low-income women had children prior to their first abortion, as compared to 31 per cent of the middle-class women.

Most of the women in our sample, 88 per cent, did not initiate contraceptive use until after the birth of their first child. This fits the long-held traditional pattern of family formation, where union is followed very quickly by pregnancy and childbirth. This pattern may be changing, however, especially among younger women. We found that while the proportion of women over 30 years of age who started contraception prior to childbirth is insignificant, the proportion increases progressively among the younger age groups, exceeding 20 per cent among the teenagers. As a result, half of the non-mothers in our sample have had some contraceptive experience, a figure that stands in sharp contrast to the corresponding figure of 19 per cent in the general population.

Method Choice

One-quarter of our respondents (87 women) reported the use of some method of contraception at the time the last pregnancy occurred, which raises the question of why these women experienced such high rates of contraceptive failure. The reason apparently lies in their choice of methods. One-fifth were using periodic abstinence and a full third were using withdrawal, which indicates that more than half of the study sample relied on the so-called traditional methods of least efficacy. It is also interesting that 16 per cent, a fairly substantial proportion, said they were using the pill at the time they became pregnant. The condom also had a high failure rate, since 10 per cent of the women declared that their partner had used one at the time they became pregnant. In all these cases, it would appear that it is not a case of method failure, but rather a case of poor use of the method itself. These findings have important relevance for national family planning efforts: Women, particularly when they adopt user-controlled methods, must be given enough information and in a way that enables them to fully understand their use, including how to deal with possible or expected side effects, which is particularly important for 'modern' methods such as oral contraception and IUDs.

Contraceptive Use Redefined

In the interest of obtaining a more precise assessment of the contraceptive experience of our study group, a new variable was created. We labelled this 'total time-use'. This variable represents the total length of time of every segment of contraceptive use by each respondent during her lifetime, regardless of the specific method used. As shown in Table 6.4, 38.5 per cent of all ever-users in the sample had a total lifetime-use under six months for all methods combined; and almost half of them (48.7 per cent) did not exceed 12 months. Only a quarter of ever-users reached a total lifetime-use of more than two years. The duration of use increased with age.

Table 6.4: Age-Specific Percentage Distribution of Women Who Had Used Methods, by Total Time Use and Methods Used

Age (years)	Total Time Use of Methods Used								
	0–1 Months	*2–6 Months*	*7–11 Months*	*1–2 Years*	*3–4 Years*	*5 Years and Over*	*Never-Used*	*No Information*	*Total* (N)
<15	0.0	0.0	0.0	0.0	0.0	0.0	1.2	0	1
15–19	24.1	17.8	22.2	5.1	5.7	0.0	29.9	0	57
20–24	44.8	41.1	48.2	40.7	22.9	16.2	21.8	2	115
25–29	13.8	20.6	22.2	28.8	45.7	27.0	21.8	2	89
30–34	6.9	12.3	3.7	15.3	8.6	37.9	14.9	1	52
35–39	6.9	2.7	3.7	3.4	14.3	8.1	6.9	0	21
40–44	3.5	2.7	0.0	6.8	2.9	10.8	3.5	0	15
45 and over	0.0	2.8	0.0	0.0	0.0	0.0	0.0	0	2
Total	100.0	100.0	100.0	100.0	100.0	100.0	100.0		
Number of women (N)	29	73	27	59	35	37	87	5	352

* The total number of women is 260 when never-users and no information cases are excluded.

When total time-use for specific methods was estimated, we found that 86 per cent of condom users, 75 per cent of withdrawal and vaginal tablets users, and 53 per cent of pill users reported employing their method for less than six months. It is interesting to note that the largest number of ever-users in our sample had used the pill (67.5 per cent) and withdrawal (42.3 per cent).

For the most part, the data reveal a pattern of inconsistent and incorrect use of these methods, with a high rate of early discontinuation, often without replacement of another method. Although about 75 per cent of the sample reported having used at least one modern method, the percentage of users who used a second method drops to 42 per cent, and, as noted before, only 25 per cent were using a method around the time of their last conception (Table 6.5).

Significantly, method preference among users varied according to previous contraceptive experience. As shown in Table 6.5, the method of choice for women using contraception for the first time was the pill, amounting to over half of first-time users; while withdrawal and the condom followed far behind. Women who used a second method also favoured the pill, the condom and withdrawal, but there was a dramatic decrease in pill-use and a doubling in the percentage using withdrawal. The decrease in pill-use was even greater

Table 6.5: Percentages of Ever-Users of Contraceptives by First Method Used, Second Method Used and Method Used at the Time of Last Pregnancy, by Specific Methods

Method	First Method	Second Method	Method at Last Pregnancy
Pill	54.8	21.6	16.1
IUD	6.4	8.7	3.4
Implant	0.8	2.7	0.0
Injection	0.4	0.7	0.0
Vaginal foam/tablets	1.5	6.0	2.3
Condom	12.6	16.6	10.3
Periodic abstinence	6.4	8.7	20.6
Withdrawal	15.5	29.5	33.3
Other	1.6	5.5	8.3
Folkloric method	0.0	0.0	5.7
Total	100.0	100.0	100.0
Number of women (N)	265	149	87

among those using a method at the time of the last pregnancy, while the percentages using withdrawal and periodic abstinence had more than doubled. Women seem to begin to regulate their fertility using a modern method, but for some reason their experience is not satisfactory and they switch to traditional methods that are much less effective. It is at this point in time that the risk of unwanted pregnancy and abortion increases dramatically.

The very infrequent use of IUDs, injectables and vaginal methods is not peculiar to these women but rather reflects the norm for the general population. In fact, the respondent's percentage distribution by individual methods is quite similar to that for Dominican women in general, except for withdrawal, which occurs twice-as-often among the women in our hospital sample (DHS, 1991).

Contraceptive Discontinuation and Method Switching

Why is it that women give up their original choice of method, often a more effective one, to use a method that reduces their autonomy and places them at a greater risk of unwanted pregnancy and abortion?

Oral contraception revisited: When considering the enormous shift from pill use to the methods of withdrawal and periodic abstinence shown in Table 6.5, one must take into account the reasons for discontinuing the first and second methods presented in Table 6.6. One should also keep in mind the characteristics of pill-use in the Dominican Republic, where only one in five women of reproductive age, and one in four who have ever used the pill, know how to use it correctly (DHS, 1991). Development Associates (1991) also found very high levels of misinformation on correct pill usage, and Moreno and Goldman (1991) rank the Dominican Republic number one in failure rates among pill users in their country sample.

Table 6.6: Percentage Distribution of Women Who Have Used More Than One Method, According to Reasons for Discontinuation of Both First and Second Methods Used

Reason for Discontinuation of Method	First Method		Second Method	
	(N)	%	(N)	%
Got pregnant while using	30	11.3	31	20.8
Wanted to get pregnant	41	15.5	17	11.4
Husband disapproved	26	9.8	31	20.8
Side effect	81	30.6	26	17.5
Health concerns	24	9.1	0	0.0
Wanted more effective method	7	2.6	6	4.0
Uncomfortable to use	7	2.6	6	4.0
Infrequent sexual relations	5	1.9	0	0.0
End of marriage/union	8	3.0	5	3.4
Carelessness	7	2.6	0	0.0
Other	28	10.6	25	16.8
No information	1	0.4	2	1.3
Number of women (N)	265	100.0	149	100.0

The starting point for understanding the difficulties with oral contraceptives is the fact that 61 per cent of pill users nationwide buy their pill over the counter in pharmacies (DHS, 1991). This means that—probably in the overwhelming majority of cases—the user does not receive adequate information or follow-up. Among the low-income women interviewed in-depth, incorrect use and/or premature discontinuation of the pill were a major cause of unwanted pregnancy. Our study group experience indicates that obtaining the pill in a clinic or public hospital does not insure that a woman will get appropriate medical screening, counselling and follow-up either.

The reasons for discontinuation shown in Table 6.6 fit the information in Table 6.5 quite neatly. Excluding the women who quit the method because they wanted to get pregnant, the leading cause for discontinuation of the first method is method side effects, which together with health concerns, account for 40 per cent of all cases.

The in-depth interviews also suggest that both these factors—method side effects and health concerns—are closely associated with the low and ineffective use of the pill found in the Dominican context. When the reasons for discontinuation of the first and second methods are compared, the proportion of side effects/health concerns responses drops dramatically, while the proportion of women who became pregnant using the method and whose husbands oppose the method double. Both of these factors are compatible with periodic abstinence and especially, withdrawal, which shows the biggest increase.

Gender relations: When looking at the methods most commonly used by respondents, and the order of use, one must take into account that—except for the pill—the three most popular methods (withdrawal, periodic abstinence and condoms) require not only men's consent but also their active participation in contraceptive decision-making and practice. The information provided by the in-depth interviews, however, showed that low-income men seldom become involved in family planning decision-making, and are extremely reluctant to take on direct responsibility for method choice or use. Such a role of greater responsibility in the fertility regulation process runs contrary to the prevailing male attitudes and degree of interest in reproductive matters in this culture. Moreover, the use of these methods demands a degree of bargaining power vis-à-vis their male partners that very few Dominican women possess.

Contraceptive Intentions and Childbearing Aspirations

The sample's distribution by childbearing aspirations, according to contraceptive behaviour and contraceptive intentions, is shown in Table 6.7. Among the women who did not want more children—who made up 34 per cent of the sample—16 per cent had never used contraception and 47 per cent were not using a method around the time of their last conception. This means that 63 per cent of the women who had completed childbearing were not using any method of contraception at the time of their last pregnancy. Immediately after the abortion, however, 90 per cent of them stated their intention to start practising effective contraception. This points to a serious need for hospital-based postpartum family planning services that would give women appropriate services and advice about suitable contraceptive choices and options.

Table 6.7: **Percentage Distribution of the Sample's Desire to Have More Children, According to Use of Contraception at the Time of Last Pregnancy and Intention to Use Contraception**

Contraception	Desire to Have More Children	No Desire	No Information
Actual use			
Used	21.9	30.8	0.0
Didn't use	43.0	47.5	50.0
No information	5.7	5.8	25.0
Never used	29.4	15.9	25.0
Intention to use			
Thought to use	68.4	90.0	100.0
Didn't think	31.1	8.3	0.0
No information	0.5	1.7	0.0
Number (N)	228	120	4
Percentage (%)	64.8	34.1	1.1

Among the women who still wanted more children, 68 per cent stated they now intended to use contraception—a percentage three times higher than the proportion of users among them at the time of their last pregnancy. These figures point to the extent of the unmet need for family planning services in the country, although they probably also reflect the fact that women are especially receptive to contraception immediately after abortion.

Discussion: The Determinants of Induced Abortion

The following profile of abortion patients who arrived at two maternity hospitals in Santo Domingo for treatment of abortion complications has emerged: They are mostly young, married women with children, who have completed childbearing and have at some time worked outside the home. Their occupational status shows no significant association with their reproductive behaviour, and—surprisingly—neither does their educational level.

Without recourse to a strictly comparable population of women who have not had abortions, it is methodologically impossible to propose correlations or comparisons with a more general population or with control cases to ascertain variation in behaviour. The same applies to the analysis of the data on contraception, the variable that provides the most suggestive findings. Nonetheless, the findings allow for a more thorough exploration of the ways in which contraceptive behaviour acts as a determinant of abortion, beyond the rudimentary association between inefficient or non-existent contraception, unwanted pregnancy and induced abortion. So, in spite of the methodological limitations inherent in a hospital sample, the following analysis is proposed by way of hypotheses for further research and verification.

First we suggest that the contraceptive behaviour of the sample be understood within the broader context of the sociocultural patterns that characterize the reproductive and contraceptive behaviours of Dominican women generally. Although the national contraceptive prevalence rate is relatively high—56 per cent of all married women are using a method—the fact that 38.5 per cent of all married women have been surgically sterilized must be taken into account. In fact, surgical sterilization is the method used by two out of every three current users of contraception in the Dominican Republic. Mean age at the time of sterilization has been falling steadily, so that one in four women underwent the procedure before the age of 25, and six out of 10 before the age of 30 (DHS, 1991). The small proportion of women using reversible methods indicates that large population groups do not employ contraception as a means of postponing or spacing childbirth, but rather resort to sterilization to terminate childbearing once the desired parity has been achieved. The minority that do adopt modern contraception to postpone or space their pregnancies usually resort to the pill, whose use is characteristically inefficient and of short duration (Báez, 1992). As noted in the previous section, there is a curious pattern of moving away from a potentially effective method—the pill—to less effective, but less troubling traditional methods, such as withdrawal and periodic abstinence. The low effectiveness of these methods, combined with a high motivation to limit family size, increases the risk of induced abortion.

The decline in the total fertility rate from 7.5 births in the mid-1960s to 3.3 births per woman in the 1988–91 period took place for the most part without any substantial transformation in traditional reproductive patterns. That is, many women continue to begin childbearing at an early age and to have their pregnancies close together; the lower mean number of births is explained by the choice of surgical sterilization at increasingly younger ages, whereby women put a final stop to childbearing (Báez, 1992).

Many of the factors in this country that tend to favour surgical sterilization over methods that space births have been described elsewhere: widespread ignorance of human biology and the reproductive cycle (Development Associates, 1991; DHS, 1991); widespread lack of information on correct use of the pill (DHS, 1991) and all other contraceptive methods (Development Associates, 1991); issues of quality in family planning services, relating to user satisfaction and method discontinuation (Hardy et al., 1991). Báez and Cordero (1991) examined supply factors that historically favoured the recourse to female sterilization, and Molina et al. (1989) describe shortcomings in service provision and unmet needs. According to DHS (1991), 17 per cent of married women nationwide have unmet contraceptive needs, and the percentage rises to 30 per cent among uneducated women.

Together with the shortcomings in service provision and contraceptive choice, the lack of information and counselling poses additional problems for women. The result is often an inappropriate contraceptive choice, leading to method failure or premature discontinuation (Dixon-Mueller, 1990). Method discontinuation is strongly associated with the availability and quality of contraceptive counselling, particularly in relation to side effects and health concerns. Cotten et al. (1992) show that discontinuation rates in two African countries were two to four times higher among those women who said they had not received appropriate counselling, than among those who were satisfied with the counselling they had received.

Although our study questionnaire did not attempt to gauge contraceptive knowledge, correct use, or method and counselling availability, the sample's contraceptive data are quite consistent with severe deficiencies in all the above-mentioned factors. Our data show, for example, that respondents did not base their contraceptive decisions on their short-term childbearing intentions; 75 per cent of them did not want to get pregnant at the time of their last conception, although only 25 per cent were trying to prevent pregnancy.

Moreover, our in-depth interviews, in addition to revealing an extreme lack of contraceptive information and very inefficient practices, disclosed a fatalistic outlook on the ultimate inevitability of pregnancy and childbirth among the low-income women. Unlike middle-class women, who regard fertility control as both feasible and desirable, these women often expressed the feeling that pregnancy is ultimately unavoidable, even if contraception can help prevent it at a given time. From this point of view, only surgical steriliza-tion and celibacy provide any real assurances; modern effective contra-ception may work, but it is always a risky proposition.

The outcome of these factors is that low-income women in particular are placed at highest risk of induced abortion. They begin their reproductive lives in a sociocultural environment that fosters childbirth immediately after early marriage, short pregnancy intervals and surgical sterilization at an early age. But the day-to-day reality of their lives—economic difficulties, marital prob-lems, the demands of a small child—clash with more abstract cultural values and expectations when an unwanted pregnancy occurs. At the crossroads where real life, abstract cultural expectations, and inefficient or nonexistent contraception meet, abortion becomes the only way out for those women who realize that they cannot carry an unwanted or unplanned pregnancy to term.

The question of why the women in our hospital sample decided to end their pregnancies and not carry them to term is of particular interest given the fact that an impressive number of Dominican women carry unwanted or unplanned pregnancies to term each year. According to ENDESA-91, 40 per cent of all births in the previous five years were unintended (24 per cent were unplanned and 16 per cent unwanted).

The answer is revealed most clearly in their contraceptive histories, which indicate that this population was particularly motivated to regulate their fer-tility. And we already know that in populations where both abortion and con-traception are available, and where a significant number of women/couples wish to regulate their fertility, women with some contraceptive experience are more likely to terminate a pregnancy than those with no contraceptive experience (Tietze and Henshaw, 1986; Llovet and Ramos, 1988). This is so because women/couples with contraceptive experience are precisely the ones who have the strongest motivation to regulate their fertility, and are there-fore more likely than their non-contracepting counterparts to resort to abortion.

Despite being mostly poor and uneducated, the women in our study had more contraceptive experience, on average, than the general population of women in the country (DHS, 1991). However, their contraceptive practices were particularly ineffective, even though most of them had attempted to space births rather than conform to the prevailing sociocultural pattern. A perfect example is the fact that, of the 25 per cent of women in our study who were using some form of contraception at the time of last conception, and only one in three was using a modern method. Similarly, although 75 per cent of respondents had used at least one method, only 42 per cent had ever used a second one. Moreover, the discontinuation rates for specific methods were very high: during the first six months of use, 86 per cent discontinued the con-dom; 75 per cent, withdrawal and vaginal methods; 53 per cent, the pill; and 48 per cent, periodic abstinence. The total time of use for all methods combined was also very low: 38.5 per cent of women used them less than six months; and 48.7 per cent, for less than a year.

In summary, our analysis suggests that, although the majority of women in our sample appeared to be strongly motivated to regulate their fertility, their contraceptive practices were especially inefficient. It is precisely this discrepancy between a high degree of contraceptive intention and motivation, on the one hand, and very ineffective contraceptive practice, on the other, which created the conditions for unwanted pregnancy and subsequent abortion.

Conclusion and Policy Considerations

Although the majority of women in the Dominican Republic deliver their babies in public hospitals and clinics, contraceptive services have become increasingly scarce in these settings. A decade ago, the public health sector was, by far, the main provider of contraceptive services; it now covers less than a third of all users, having been replaced by private clinics and pharmacies (DHS, 1991). This means that the number of women obtaining family planning services as part of their overall maternal–child health care has dropped dramatically, and thus the chance has been lost for integrated health services covering postpartum and post-abortion care, a time when both the demand for and the receptivity of women to contraception is at its peak.

This general lack of contraceptive services became evident during our fieldwork at the two hospitals included in our study. At the MNSA there are no post-abortion family planning services whatsoever; while IDSS patients get an occasional pamphlet and short speech on the subject. One of the more problematic aspects of the disarticulation of maternal care and family planning services is the high number of pill users who obtain them in pharmacies without prescription and counselling on their use. This is particularly troublesome given the fact that only one in four women who have ever utilized the pill know its correct use. The pill is the country's most commonly used reversible method and, by far, the method of choice among first-time users in our sample. But under these conditions it is not surprising that over half of the women discontinued their use or became accidentally pregnant within six months. As with the general female population, the respondents seldom use IUDs, implants, injectables or vaginal methods.

The contraceptive behaviour of the women in our sample must be placed in a context where early surgical sterilization has become the norm; where women (and men) have very little knowledge of human reproduction and of the way contraceptives work; where contraceptive supply is not sufficiently varied nor accessible; where the state has increasingly relinquished its duty of providing women/couples with the means to regulate their fertility; and where men are reluctant to accept responsibility for contraceptive practice. Given this context, it is apparent that no matter how inefficient or precarious the respondents' contraceptive behaviour may appear, they are actually interested in family planning. This interest, however, is often thwarted by the many difficulties and obstacles they must overcome in their attempts to gain control over their fertility.

The study findings demonstrate an urgent need for the implementation of a national abortion prevention programme, focused primarily on two goals: (a) providing women/couples with the knowledge they need in order to make well-informed—and thus appropriate—contraceptive choices; and, (b) providing integral, timely, varied and widely accessible contraceptive services to everyone who needs them. The incorporation of a vastly improved family planning programme to the maternal health services offered by public institutions is an essential condition for the attainment of these goals.

If, as Pinotti and Faúndes (1989: 97) say, every unwanted pregnancy symbolizes society's failure to provide the woman with the means to avoid that pregnancy, then the abortion situation provides a severe yardstick for judging the nature and extent of family planning in the Dominican Republic.

✝ References

Alan Guttmacher Institute (AGI). 1994. *Aborto clandestino: Una realidad latinoamericana*. New York: The Alan Guttmacher Institute.

Báez, Clara. 1992. República Dominicana: La esterilización como opción única. ¿Una solución?. Document prepared for the workshop 'Planificación familiar: Necesidades actuales y perspectivas futuras', organized by Demographic and Health Surveys and the Centro Latinamericano de Demografía. Santiago de Chile: DHS/CELADE. (Unpublished document).

Báez, Clara and **Carmela de Cordero.** 1991. Factores que inciden en la demanda de anticoncepción quirúrgica voluntaria en la República Dominicana. Santo Domingo: Instituto de Estudios de Población y Desarrollo, PROFAMILIA. (Unpublished document).

Barreto, Thalia, D.M. Campbell, L. Davies, V. Faveau, V. Filippi, W. Graham, M. Mamdami, C. Rooney and **N.F. Toubia.** 1992. Investigating induced abortion in developing countries: Methods and problems. *Studies in Family Planning* 23 (3): 159–70.

Calventi, Vinicio. 1975. El aborto provocado como problema médico-social. Posibles soluciones en una sociedad en proceso de cambios. In: *Seminario Sobre Problemas de Población en la República Dominicana*. Santo Domingo: Universidad Autónoma de Santo Domingo, Consejo Nacional de Población y Familia, PROFAMILIA.

Cotten, Niki, J. Stanback, H. Maidouka, J.T. Thomas Taylor and **T. Turk.** 1992. Early discontinuation of contraceptive use in Niger and The Gambia. *International Family Planning Perspectives*, 18 (4): 145–49.

Development Associates. 1991. Mitos, creencias motivaciones, razones y/o experiencias negativas sobre los métodos anticonceptivos. Final Project Report, Denise A. Ureña (Consultant). Santo Domingo: Development Associates, Inc.

Demographic and Health Survey (DHS). 1991. Encuesta de Salud-ENDESA. Santo Domingo, Dominican Republic.

Dixon-Mueller, Ruth. 1990. Abortion policy and women's health in developing countries. *International Journal of Health Services*, 20 (2): 297–314.

Hardy, E., C. Baez, A. Faundes, C. Mora, T. Rodriguez, F. Alvarez and **V. Brache.** 1991. Obstáculos para la consulta de planificación familiar desde el punto de vista de las mujeres atendidas. *Población y Desarrollo*, No. 1, 1990. Santo Domingo: Asociación Dominicana Pro Bienestar de la Familia.

Henshaw, Stanley and Evelyn Morrow. 1990. *Induced abortion. A world review 1990 supplement.* New York: The Alan Guttmacher Institute.

Llovet, Juan J. and Silvina Ramos. 1988. La práctica del aborto en las mujeres de sectores populares de Buenos Aires, *Documento CEDES/4.* Buenos Aires: Centro de Estudios de Estado y Sociedad.

Molina, Maritza, P. Tactuk, C. Baez and N. Ramirez. 1989. Estudio de demanda no satisfecha y oferta de servicios de planificación familiar en la República Dominicana. Santo Domingo: Instituto de Estudios de Población y Desarrollo—PROFAMILIA (Final Project Report— Unpublished Document).

Moreno, Lorenzo and Noreen Goldman. 1991. Tasas de falla de anticonceptivos en países en desarrollo: evidencia de las Encuestas de Demografía y Salud. *Perspectivas Internacionales de Planificación Familiar,* Special 1991 Issue: 2–7.

Paiewonsky, Denise. 1988. *El aborto en la República Dominicana.* Santo Domingo: Centro de Investigación para la Acción Femenina (CIPAF).

Pinotti, José A. and Aníbal Faúndes. 1989. Unwanted pregnancy: Challenges for health policy. *International Journal of Gynecology and Obstetrics,* Suppl. 3: 97–102.

Secretaría de Estado de Salud Pública y Asistencia Social (SESPAS). *Memorias Anuales, 1982–92.* Santo Domingo: Departamento de Cómputos, SESPAS.

Singh, Susheela and Deirdre Wulf. 1993. The likelihood of induced abortion among women hospitalized for abortion complications in four Latin American countries. *International Family Planning Perspectives,* 19 (4): 134–41.

Tietze, Christopher and Stanley K. Henshaw. 1986. *Induced abortion: A world review 1986.* New York: The Alan Guttmacher Institute.

Universidad Nacional Pedro Henríquez Ureña (UNPHU), Centro de Investigaciones—Unidad de Estudios Sociales. 1975. *Estudio del Aborto en 200 Mujeres de la República Dominicana.* Santo Domingo.

✝

7

The Use of Induced Abortion in Mauritius: An Alternative to Fertility Regulation or an Emergency Procedure?

Geeta Oodit and Uma Bhowon

Introduction

Every year between 40 and 60 million women worldwide seek termination of an unwanted pregnancy, often under unsafe conditions. Induced abortion is the oldest and still one of the most widely used methods of fertility control. Yet for religious and moral reasons, few countries have been able to look dispassionately at the effects of unsafe abortion on women's health.

Mauritius is an island nation of just over one million people, situated 2,000 kilometres off the east coast of Africa and 900 kilometres from Madagascar. The country has a multi-ethnic population and one of the highest population densities in the world, with over 570 people per square kilometre. Mauritians trace their origins to the three continents of Europe, Asia and Africa. The largest ethnic group is that of the Indo-Mauritians, comprising Hindus and Muslims and constituting about 70 per cent of the population. The 'general population' of mostly Catholics comprises Creoles, Franco-Mauritians and Chinese, who constitute the remaining 30 per cent of the population.

As in many countries, abortion in Mauritius is illegal. The law does not permit it on any grounds, stating that: 'Any physician, surgeon, or any pharmacologist who shall point out or administer such means of miscarriage, shall, in every case where miscarriage shall have ensued, be condemned to Penal Servitude.'

Despite these legal restrictions, the practice of induced abortion is very much a part of the reproductive health picture in Mauritius. It is estimated that about 2,500 women receive hospital treatment for post-abortion complications. These hospital admissions are merely the tip of the iceberg in many African countries as well as in Mauritius, where it is calculated that there are about as many abortions as live births.

At the same time, Mauritius is known as one of the most successful countries in the world with regard to contraceptive prevalence and fertility control. It has had one of the most successful family planning programmes, which was introduced in 1957. This is due to a broad-based health infrastructure, where family planning services are provided through a network of primary health care (PHC) centres, community centres, industries and the Mauritius Family Planning Association (MFPA) clinics; natural family planning is provided by a Catholic-run organization known as Action Familiale.

So why has induced abortion continued to play such a significant role in the reproductive life of women of Mauritius? With the rise of per capita income in the country, there has been a concomitant increase in the cost of living. One response to this has been the rapid entry of a large number of women into the workforce, but without the social infrastructure to support them. As a result, the two-child family norm is now well-established, which means that women need a reliable means of fertility control for 15–20 years of their reproductive life. Unfortunately, sterilization is illegal in Mauritius so that couples who have reached their ideal family size have no recourse but to continue to use reversible means of birth control.

Another contributing factor is that the average age at marriage is now 24.7 years for women in Mauritius, a rise that has meant an increase in premarital sexual activity. But family planning services in Mauritius are still mainly geared to married couples; and the younger unmarried people 'do not perceive that family planning is for them'.

Objectives

The government of Mauritius is increasingly aware of the serious negative health consequences of backstreet abortion on maternal health and on the health resources of the country. It is not able on its own, however, to stimulate a debate on the issue given the sensitivity and controversy surrounding abortion in a multi-racial country like Mauritius. Moreover, for a debate to be effective, there must be adequate information on the antecedents, methods and consequences of abortion.

MFPA therefore undertook a study on the use of induced abortion in Mauritius with the aim of assisting policy makers in the formulation of policies and programmes for the elimination of unsafe abortion and for more effective utilization of family planning services.

Research Methodology

We envisioned a two-stage process in the formulation of our study design. The first would be a preliminary survey focused on interviews with women admitted to hospitals with complications due to abortion. The second would be a community-based survey of knowledge, attitudes, behaviour, and practices (KAP) of women in their childbearing years. This report is the outcome of the first stage, which provides a baseline for the second stage.

The study was conducted using a combination of quantitative and qualitative data collection techniques. First, in-depth unstructured interviews were held with clinic staff of the participating hospitals and with a purposive sample of women who were admitted to the hospitals with complications due to abortion. The interview for medical personnel included items on views regarding legal status of abortion, consequences for women having recourse to abortion, and the nature of complications.

Next we conducted structured interviews with 475 women in their reproductive years, both married and unmarried, who had been hospitalized for treatment of post-abortion complications. These women comprised the main study sample. The instrument contained variables that could have a bearing on a woman's abortion experience and was divided into five main sections: demographic variables; reproductive history; abortion experience; knowledge, attitudes, behaviour and practices of contraception and abortion; and accessibility of FP services.

The study was conducted at three large government hospitals. Initially, two urban-based hospitals were selected for the study, but during the course of fieldwork, we found that the number of admissions of abortion cases with complications were fewer in these urban-based hospitals than in a rural-based hospital. We therefore decided to include admissions to this third hospital in the study, which would give us more cases and also provide representation of women from the more rural areas. The women were selected on the basis of admission to all three hospitals during a period of four months. Field researchers visited each of the three hospitals each day to identify women admitted with abortion complications.

The selection and training of the field research team was an important phase of the study, because induced abortion is such a sensitive topic. They had to be acquainted with the local context and to feel comfortable with the issue themselves, because abortion for many women in Mauritius is a secret act clouded with shame and culturally taboo.

For the in-depth interviews, 30 women were randomly selected from among those already interviewed. As for key informants, 10 doctors and five nurses constituted the sample.

In the discussion of the results in the next section, we contrast the data we obtained to those of the 1991 Contraceptive Prevalence Survey (CPS), which measured the level of contraceptive prevalence, method mix and source of contraception. While the results reported for the CPS can be considered representative of Mauritius, the results reported from the sample of 475 women in our study can be considered representative of only those women admitted to hospitals with abortion complications and not of the totality of women who had abortions during the study period.

Study Results

Sociodemographic Profile of the Study Sample

It is important to place our study sample within the context of the general population by comparing their sociodemographic characteristics to those of the CPS. While the CPS sample looked only at women in 'unions' between the ages of 13 and 44, our study, in contrast, included all women being treated for abortion complications regardless of their age or marital status. Among these 475 women of our study, 25 were not in union (5.5 per cent) and 23 were under the age of 19. The mean age of our respondents was 28.3 years, which is younger than the CPS sample.

The highest proportions of induced abortion cases was in the 20–24-year-old age group and the smallest was in the 40–44-year-old age group; 26 and 24 per cent, respectively. The pattern of distribution of women by number of children suggests that abortion was occurring mainly among women who had children. The ethnic distribution showed that the creole segment of the population was significantly over-represented and the Hindu population under-represented. Almost three-quarters of the women, 72.6 per cent, had completed primary level education and 27.4 per cent had received secondary education. The women were equally representative of urban and rural residence (49.5 per cent and 50.5 per cent, respectively), although it is usually difficult to differentiate between rural and urban areas in Mauritius because of massive urbanization. In short, the women in the sample were younger, less well-educated, and more of creole origin than the women in the CPS sample.

The Process of Abortion

In order to understand the abortion process, questions were asked about the method used to abort, the length of gestation at the time of the abortion, and the main reasons for the abortion.

Methods Used

When women were asked how their recent abortion was performed, their responses were organized first according to the method they had used to abort. Many women reported the use of a combination of methods, some used sequentially, until one worked. The crude procedures (used in 35.5 per cent of the cases) were mostly self-induced or performed by practitioners in unhygienic conditions. The women described the methods used in the following ways:

- Bicycle spokes or umbrella ribs were inserted into the vagina until bleeding started.
- Heavy loads, such as buckets of water, were carried on the head, sides, and/or stomach to put pressure on the body, especially on the uterus, until it started to bleed.
- Jumping from heights, such as tables, to induce bleeding.
- A child was made to jump on the stomach of the women until she felt pain or bleeding started.
- Massage by 'femme sage (traditional mid-wife)'.
- 'Ananas marron (wild pineapple)' and a boiled onion were introduced into the cervix.

Women also reported the use of herbs, which were prepared in the following ways:

- Ingestion of a pineapple early in the morning on an empty stomach for two–three weeks until bleeding started.
- The ingestion of a boiled mixture of avocado leaves, ginger, tea leaves and the skin of a drumstick tree also taken in the morning on an empty stomach, to act as a dilator/irritant.
- Drinking boiled wine with cinnamon.
- Drinking epsom salts.
- Drinking 'eau de vie' (hard alcohol) and cinnamon.
- Drinking hot 'monis' (an iron supplement).

When women reported the use of pills they primarily referred to 'cytotec', a brand name for misoprostol, which is an analogue of the naturally occurring prostaglandin E1 manufactured by Searle and approved for use as a treatment for peptic ulcer. Cytotec protects the gastroduodenal mucosa by inhibiting basal, stimulated and nocturnal acid secretions and by reducing the volume of gastric secretions. This drug, which is available from private doctors or pharmacies without prescription in Mauritius, is contraindicated in pregnant women and in women who are planning a pregnancy, because it increases uterine tone and stimulates contractions that may cause partial or complete expulsion of the products of conception. The use of cytotec as an abortifacient is an example of how Mauritian women will quickly adapt a new method that promises to be safer and/or more effective than other self-induced abortion methods. Some women also administered a form of injectable abortifacient called 'prodiol forte'.

Another 7.1 per cent of the women reported having obtained an abortion by aspiration, which is done mainly by private doctors and therefore it was only accessible to those who could afford to pay for the procedure. The costs varied between Rs 1,000 and Rs 4,000 (US$ 65 to 260), depending on the expertise and qualifications of the practitioner. Most of these cases in our study, however, involved either incomplete abortion or complications due to infections.

From the data, it is not hard to understand why this group of women had complications resulting from their abortions that require hospitalization. Almost all the women (92.9 per cent) had used a crude and/or self-induced method to abort. Obviously, they were not using the safer procedures available in the medical setting, access to which requires knowledge, contacts, networks and a significant financial expenditure.

Reasons for the Abortion

As for the reasons for the abortion, women were asked to rate (on a five-point scale with 'very important' = 1 and 'not important' = 5) the relative importance for them personally of a number of reasons for abortion. The leading reasons for an abortion were: 'for the health of the woman' (1.8); 'the pregnancy was the result of an extramarital affair' (1.9); and 'the woman is too young' (2.1).

Other reasons included: 'marital problems' (2.4), 'no one to look after the child' (2.7), 'fear of the contraceptive method' (2.7), and 'couple not ready for a baby' (2.8). Rated of lesser importance were the reasons: 'completion of family size' (3.0) and 'husband wants the abortion' (3.6).

Information from the qualitative interviews also revealed the varied reasons women had for resorting to abortion. The age of the woman was an important factor, with women in the older age group feeling that they would not be able to bear and raise a child. A related reason among these older women was that they had adult children who would be embarrassed to have another sibling. The unmarried women were especially afraid of making their pregnancy known and so had resorted to abortion. Some women reported that they could not bear the financial costs of rearing another child. Others cited chronic health problems, such as high blood pressure and asthma, as reasons for aborting.

It is interesting to note that in quite a few cases, women had to resort to abortion because of their husbands' refusal to use a family planning method. While the great majority (78.7 per cent) of the women in the study sample had their abortion in the first trimester (at less than 12 weeks gestation), a significant minority had their abortion in the second trimester. The crude methods employed by this latter group and the relatively late timing of their abortions may have accounted for the complications that resulted in hospital admission.

Family Life Course

While the sociodemographic factors of education, ethnicity, and rural/urban residence were hypothesized to be important in accounting for the variation in behaviour and attitudes regarding abortion, it was found by looking at both the qualitative and quantitative data that the most important determinant was the stage in the 'family life course'. We have used this term to define the status of women according to their marital condition, their age, actual family size, desired family size and contraceptive use patterns. As a result, and for the purposes of our analysis, we have adopted the following categories: 'unmarried'; and for married women, 'delayers', 'spacers', and 'stoppers'.

In general, the family life course showed a clear gradation in terms of the age of the woman, her actual family size, and whether she had a desire for another pregnancy. For example, older, married women, with three or four children, would be more likely to use effective contraception to avoid another pregnancy than younger, unmarried ones. More detailed illustration of this finding is illustrated in the data that follows.

Unmarried group: Of the 25 women in the unmarried group, only two had children and another two had previous abortions. The majority, 23 women, were Creole—this being the only 'category' to show a relationship with ethnicity. The age range of this group was from 13 to 33 years, with a little more than half of them, 52 per cent, below the age of 19. Most women in this category were very young. The two women who had previous abortions were 18 and 33 years of age, respectively; and the two women with children were 23 and 33 years of age, respectively.

Delayers: The age range for this group was 16 to 33 years, with nearly two-thirds, 70 per cent, between the ages of 19 and 24. Their marriage at a relatively young age, even by Mauritian standards, may be associated with their desire to delay their first child.

Spacers: The women in this group ranged in age from 17 to 33 years, with 57 per cent over the age of 23. More than two-thirds, 78.1 per cent, had only one child (78.1 per cent); less than one-fourth, 17.3 per cent, had two children; and only 4.5 per cent had more than two children. Spacers showed a mean period of 32.5 months between the birth of their last child and their current abortion. The emphasis in this group on delaying the birth of their second child reflects the declining fertility rate in response to the increasing social and economic costs of raising additional children in the current conditions prevailing in Mauritius.

Stoppers: Women in this group showed the broadest range of age, from 17 to 50 years, and the widest distribution (standard deviation of 6.25). For the most part, this was the group that had more children than the random sample drawn in the CPS survey. In particular, about one-fourth of the women in this group, 26.2 per cent, had four or more children; a proportion one-and-a-half times as great as the 16.3 per cent of women in the CPS survey. Similarly, the mean number of children in this group was 2.8, which is well over the national mean of 2.3. We found that stoppers had also been involved in the process of limiting family size for a long period of time. The mean period between the birth of the last child and this abortion was 63.2 months. The lack of access to sterilization may have created the need for these women to use abortion as a last resort to control fertility.

Antecedent Factors

It was important and crucial to examine the antecedent factors of abortion. Two determinants were examined: behaviour and attitudes, both with respect to family planning use and abortion. Women's attitudes with regard to future use of family planning and abortion following the current abortion were also explored.

By definition, the study sample comprised women who did not desire a child at the time they became pregnant. Interestingly, when the study sample (eliminating unmarried women and those over 44 years of age) was compared with the CPS sample, it was observed that they matched the larger population in terms of the use of more reliable methods, but showed a much higher use of unreliable methods. For example, withdrawal was used by a third of the study sample, 32.5 per cent, compared to 21.1 per cent in the CPS sample. Similarly, 9.0 per cent of the study sample women were using natural family planning compared to 6.6 per cent in the CPS sample.

In short, among a group of women who should have been much more active contraceptors than the overall population, there was a significantly higher use of the less reliable methods of withdrawal and natural family planning. Also, despite their apparent lack of desire for a pregnancy, approximately 17 per cent were not using any method, which demonstrates a sizeable unmet need for family planning.

We found that the use of different methods of contraception could be linked to a woman's family life stage. For instance, unmarried women were either not using any method (60 per cent) or using the only method available to them at the moment, which in many instances was withdrawal (28 per cent). Of the three unmarried women who were taking pills, two were 20 years of age and one was 13 years old; in each case, either the method failed or it was being used inappropriately.

The high use of withdrawal and the high level of non-use among unmarried women could be attributed to the fact that this group is traditionally not included in family planning programme efforts; and consequently, they do not perceive family planning as necessary and do not have access to the service delivery points (MFPA, 1993). Currently, the family planning service delivery system caters only to the contraceptive needs of the married in Mauritius, despite growing evidence of increasing premarital sexuality among adolescents.

Delayers showed a very low use of reliable family planning methods with a pattern very similar to the unmarried group. While women who were using a supplied method and condoms represented 25 per cent, the other 75 per cent were using withdrawal or no method at all despite their strong desire not to have children at the moment. Delayers, therefore, showed a higher prevalence of family planning than unmarried women, but they also used withdrawal, a method that is not reliable. Possibly, delayers included newly married women who, when they were unmarried, had no access to family planning information, education and services. Therefore they relied on ineffective methods or used no method at all.

Spacers showed an increased use of supplied methods compared to delayers (36.3 per cent), but 63.7 per cent continued to use unreliable methods or no method at all. One would normally hypothesize that having at least one child would connect spacers to effective family planning methods. For this group of women, however, this does not seem to have happened.

Stoppers were the oldest age group and, as noted earlier, had a mean of over six years since the birth of their youngest child. It was to be expected that they would have the most experience in family planning. Their use of supplied methods, was the highest of any of the groups, at 47 per cent. Their pill-use was also the highest among all the groups, at 34.8 per cent. Their use of the condom, however, showed no increase over that of the delayers and spacers. Moreover, they continued to show an extraordinarily high use of unreliable methods and non-use (53 per cent), despite their intention not to have any more children.

The relatively low use of reliable methods among the women in the entire study sample reflected their lack of confidence in all family planning methods. When women in the study sample were asked to rate the effectiveness of the pill, condom, withdrawal and natural family planning on a five-point scale, ranging from to 'not good' (5) to 'very good' (1), the mean score was 3.3 for the pill, 3.8 for condom and withdrawal and 4.5 for natural family planning. It can be seen that none of the major methods was rated on the positive side of the five-point scale. The pill was rated relatively more positively, but it was still rated on the negative side while natural family planning method received the most negative rating.

We also found a considerable amount of method switching and discontinuation. At particular risk were those who discontinued the use of Depo-Provera injections without a back-up method; 93.2 per cent of the Depo-Provera users in our sample had stopped using the method for more than a month. The rates of discontinuation for all reversible methods of contraception for our sample was high, with the exception of women using IUDs, probably because it is the most passive method of some longevity that can only be removed in a health or family planning centre.

These findings make a strong case for strengthening family planning education programmes to promote the use of effective methods, which requires ongoing monitoring, information and counselling.

Behaviour and Attitudes Toward Abortion

Behaviour regarding abortion was assessed by the sample's previous abortion history. Of the 475 women interviewed, 112 or 24 per cent, had a previous abortion history. For the most part, these women were the 'stoppers', which is not surprising given that the mean period between the birth of their last child and this abortion was 63.2 months. This long period associated with the use of unreliable methods could account for their previous abortion history.

Earlier we explained the overall reasons for abortion in our study sample. Here, the attitudes toward abortion and reasons for it are described according to the various family life course categories.

Stoppers ranked as more important than the other groups the factor of having 'completed family size'; that is, they did not want any more children (X = 1.8). This was followed by 'contraceptive method failed' (X = 1.9) and 'fear of contraceptive side effects' (X = 2.0), as they were the main users of supplied methods.

Spacers considered their 'husbands desiring the abortion' (X = 2.4) as more of a factor than the other types, but in general these women were less positive about the other reasons for having an abortion.

Delayers' attitudes were also consistent with their life situation in that they ranked 'women too young to have a child' (X = 1.7), 'couple not ready for a baby yet' (X = 1.9), and 'couple cannot afford a baby' (X = 1.9) highest compared to women in the other categories. They also ranked 'fear of contraceptive side effects' highest of the groups, which was consistent with their lack of family planning information.

Unmarried women tended to rank the reasons for their abortion lower than the other groups, with the exception of 'women too young' (X = 2.1).

The reasons cited above all showed differences along the family life course stage of p < .02. The reasons of 'woman has a health problem', 'pregnancy was the result of an extra-marital affair', 'women who have marital problems' and 'no one to look after the child' all showed high rankings, but no significant differences in the rankings across groups. In general, each of the groups was more sensitive to their own situations than those of the other groups.

Additionally, when respondents were asked the circumstances under which a woman should be allowed to have an abortion, their rankings (mean score) indicate that women were generally positive about abortion for almost all valid reasons, including: 'if the woman has AIDS' (1.1); 'if the woman has been raped' (1.2); 'if the pregnancy endangers her life' (1.5); 'it's the woman's right not to have the baby' (1.6); 'if pregnancy is the result of extra/pre-marital affair' (2.0); 'if method used failed' (2.0); 'if the woman is too young to have a child' (2.2); and 'if the baby will affect marital relationship' (2.2). It is important, however, to bear in mind that these questions were asked after the women had an abortion. So it cannot be ascertained to what degree this represents their view prior to their decision and the abortion itself.

Is abortion considered taboo? Of the total sample of 475 women, 192 (40.4 per cent), reportedly said yes. The distribution of this attitude along our family life course categories indicated that both unmarried women (48 per cent) and spacers (48.2 per cent) seem to feel that abortion is taboo, while a significantly fewer number of the delayers (25 per cent) and stoppers (39.3 per cent) felt this way.

Given the impact of religion on attitudes towards abortion, we hypothesized that it would be a powerful predictor of views regarding abortion. The results substantiated our hypothesis. As expected, the Creole/Christian segment of the population (49.6 per cent) considered abortion a taboo, followed closely by the Muslims (40 per cent); while fewer Hindu women (28.7 per cent) felt this way.

Moreover, the timing of the abortion was found to be significantly related to the belief that abortion is taboo. Among women who had sought abortion before eight weeks of gestation, 60.4 per cent considered it taboo; while among women whose abortion took place after eight weeks of gestation, 76 per cent did not think of it as taboo. This suggests that those women who considered abortion taboo for religious reasons were significantly more likely to abort earlier in their pregnancy than those who did not consider abortion as taboo.

Post-Abortion Family Planning

The data that emerged show that these women are committed to improving their ability to regulate their fertility after an abortion. The projected scenario is an increase in the use of the IUD and Depo-Provera and a decrease in both the use of withdrawal and non-use. Sterilization (being illegal) took a second place, after the pill, in the method of choice for the study sample. The preference for reliable methods (the pill, IUD, Depo-Provera and sterilization) increased from 28 per cent before the abortion to 63 per cent afterward. The challenge still remains, however, to give women access to the information and services that are necessary to facilitate the use of these methods.

The different needs of the four groups along the family life course were explored in terms of their choices for family planning methods in the future. Results indicate that more women would prefer to use effective methods of fertility control in the future.

Among the unmarried women, preference was for the pill, followed by the condom. There was still a large segment of the unmarried women, however, who would use no method or who were undecided. As these findings indicate, an important challenge is to extend family planning and counselling services to sexually active unmarried women. In particular, their choice of the pill will be hazardous if it is done without effective counselling, education and monitoring, which can be provided only by family planning service centres.

Delayers showed the least positive pattern of future use, with only 24 per cent selecting reliable methods. While the pill was the most preferred method among these women, there was also a high preference for the use of withdrawal and the condom. It appears that delayers are entering marriage with little or no family planning information. They therefore represent a group with a high risk of repeat abortion.

Spacers showed a high preference for the pill (40 per cent). These women, in combination with those who chose Depo-Provera, the IUD and sterilization, comprised the 65 per cent of the women in this group who were intending to use reliable methods.

Stoppers showed an improvement in their approach to family planning, with 71 per cent opting for one of the reliable methods. As would be expected of women in more advanced stages of the family life course, sterilization was the most preferred method, selected by 27 per cent, followed closely by the pill (25 per cent). The question for this group is whether they can effectively access the medical services that provide sterilization, even though it is illegal. If they cannot have access to this permanent method, they may well fall back on unreliable methods and thus again be exposed to the risk of unwanted pregnancy.

Use of Abortion in the Future

Despite the complications and problems of this abortion, one-fourth (24.8 per cent or 118 women) of the total sample of 475 women would consider having another abortion in the future. There were significant differences across the family life course in the views regarding future use of abortion. Out of the 118 women who would consider an abortion in the future, the great majority, 101 women, are stoppers. For the most part, the women in the other stages of the family life course would not consider having another abortion.

The reason for this may be that the stoppers are most set against having a child, as this group contains the older women as well as those who have the most children. Or, based on their experience of contraception, these women may be the most pessimistic about their ability to gain access to effective family planning. In any case, these data demonstrate that if family planning fails for the stoppers, many will consider abortion for a second time and some for a third and more.

Summary and Conclusions

The women in the study sample were younger, had less children, were less well-educated, and with a higher percentage of Creoles than the general population represented by the CPS data. They combined a high desire for not having a child with a relatively poor utilization of reliable family planning methods. These women used a safe, medical means of abortion in only a small number of cases, indicating poor knowledge of appropriate abortion methods and inadequate finances to pay the doctors' fees. Consequently, the abortion process was a horrendous experience that involved the use of the crudest methods, hospitalization, and perhaps long-term negative consequences.

Because the study sample was not a random one, it cannot be said that the data is representative. But it is highly illustrative and the composition and patterns observed are not that dissimilar from national surveys. What our study has done is to provide a better understanding of this elusive group of women with unmet family planning needs. The sample identified different categories of women, at different stages of the family cycle, each of whom has different needs, attitudes and behaviours that must be addressed. Therefore, it is pertinent to emphasize that the need for fertility regulation can change in different ways throughout a woman's reproductive life.

The women in the study sample were significantly higher users for family planning services of the MOH clinics and the pharmacies for self-prescription, and were significantly lower users of the MFPA clinics, the hospitals, Action Familiale and the private clinics. Both the pharmacies and the MOH clinics were associated with having stopped using a method for over a month prior to conception. These results provided some evidence for the need to re-examine the services and counselling provided to those who suggest they are about to go off a method and who utilize these services. It was disturbing to see how generally negative all the women were about family planning methods. This negative feeling may be the best indicator of their lack of connection with the service system, regardless of what reproductive stage they are in.

In a country noted for its fertility control and family planning services, is it surprising that so many women have unwanted pregnancies and those in this study sample had to go to such lengths to terminate their pregnancies?

The answer to this question can be found, in part, in the broader socioeconomic structure of Mauritian society itself, which has been changing rapidly. The increasing cost of educating and raising children, housing and land shortages, and the rising costs of food and necessary consumer goods have all increased the need for multiple incomes in a family, thus putting increased importance on women working outside the home.

The answer can also be found in the nature of family planning services in Mauritius, which, despite successes, still has many shortcomings.

For example, family planning in Mauritius is seen as a service for married women. As a result, unmarried women are unlikely to access services despite their increasing sexual activity. Similarly, women who are recently married and want to delay their first child are unlikely to be knowledgeable because they had little or no access to information or services prior to marriage.

The Ministry of Health is now responsible for the bulk of family planning services in the country at the MOH clinics. These clinics are providing a wide range of services and may not have the time, personnel and resources to educate, counsel, monitor and follow-up family planning clients. This heavy responsibility is made more acute as families reduce their concept of the ideal number of children and require methods that more subtly adjust both number and timing of births.

Sterilizations are not legally sanctioned, putting those who feel they have completed their family size into a constant state of stress, method switching, and side effects that may have to last 20 years. Abortion is illegal and consequently performed at great risk to a woman's health and life if she cannot pay the high fees that physicians require because they are breaking the law.

Women's lives are changing more rapidly in Mauritius than services can keep pace. Women work in greater numbers and therefore may have less access to the standard service time periods and less tolerance of method side effects. They are more sexually active and more independent of the domination of their husbands, fathers and boyfriends.

In short, the great majority of families in Mauritius now accept the small family norm. Rising industrialization, education, and increasing felt needs are demanding that more resources go to a smaller number of children. The pressure to prevent the birth of the child of an unwanted pregnancy is so great that many women are willing to risk the dangers described in this chapter.

What role does abortion play in population control and fertility regulation in Mauritius? One answer to this question is provided by Mumford and Kessel (1986) who state that it is precisely because there is both high contraceptive prevalence and high abortion that there is a low fertility rate. If it were possible to eliminate all backstreet and self-induced abortions, these authors would argue that the fertility rate would become out of control.

According to this perspective, abortion is ultimately serving the needs of the country. However, as long as abortion is illegal and women are resorting to unsafe, self-induced and backstreet procedures, these needs are being met by putting a significant proportion of our women in danger. If this is the case, one could further argue that the danger is disproportionately distributed, because middle and upper class women have a better chance of accessing medically provided methods such as vacuum aspiration, while lower socio-economic groups of women must depend on the more dangerous methods.

To conclude, some women will continue to prefer abortion over contraception, under some circumstances, and at least at some point in their lives because of conflicting social norms and sexual relationships. These circumstances are derived from their social and personal situation and from the inadequacy of methods and/or delivery systems. Moreover, there is no perfect fertility regulation method or service delivery system, nor is there likely to be such a system. While some elements can be altered through programmatic intervention, others are embedded in social structures and gender relations that will require broader and deeper social transformations.

Recommendations for Future Action

1. Develop a full-scale, national survey of abortion behaviour and attitudes utilizing a randomly drawn, representative sample.

2. Initiate a study of the MOH clinics and pharmacies to identify problems in the structure of services to specific high-risk groups.

3. Legalize and provide governmental support for sterilization as part of the regular services of the public health care system.

4. Develop family planning education, counselling and service programmes for adolescents, unmarried women and newly married women.

5. Identify and provide follow-up of women at greater risk for conception due to method stoppage, method switching and failure to effectively use family planning services.

6. Legalize and provide governmental support for medically safe abortion for those individuals who can demonstrate method failure despite effective linkages with family planning services. Abortion could also be legalized in cases of rape, threats to health and other reasons that would avoid its use as a family planning method.

7. Improve the quality of contraceptive and reproductive health service delivery, which could be a significant step towards altering the reliance on abortion as a primary method of fertility regulation.

Dissemination

The results of the abortion study have been widely disseminated among policy makers, planners, health and other professionals. The MFPA hosted a round table discussion where the research report was made public and formed the basis of discussions. IPPF and WHO were invited to make key contributions to the dissemination effort of the MFPA. MFPA continues to act as a pressure group for sensitization of the issue.

Policy Impact

The results of this study have already generated a national discussion. Religious groups (mainly the Catholic Church) and women's groups have reacted against and in favour of decriminalizing abortion. The discussions included a motion that was tabled at the National Assembly to decriminalize abortion but there has been no debate on the motion as yet.

Because the FPA had taken the lead in stimulating a national debate, IPPF chose Mauritius as the regional venue for its Regional Conference on Unsafe Abortion and Post-Abortion Family Planning in Africa in 1994. But the opening of the conference started off with controversy. The Mauritian Minister of Health, a Roman Catholic, vehemently opposed abortion at the inaugural session, while his cabinet colleague, the Minister for Women's Rights, Child Development and Family Welfare disagreed and argued in favour of decriminalizing abortion. The conference led to the 'Mauritius Declaration on Abortion', which became a powerful lobbying tool at the 1994 International Conference on Population and Development (ICPD) in Cairo.

Moreover, based on the research effort, the White Paper on Women and Development by the Ministry of Women's Rights, Child Development and Family Welfare (1995), which spells out new policies and guidelines for promoting the advancement of women, calls for the legalization of abortion as a life-saving measure. In addition, the research report has been a most valuable document in the preparation of the National Development Plan and the National Report on Population for the International Conference on Population and Development.

✟ References

Mauritius Family Planning Association (MFPA). 1993. *Women, work and AIDS-related risk behaviour.* Port Louis, Mauritius: Mauritius Family Planning Association.

Ministry of Women's Rights, Child Development and Family Welfare. 1995. White paper on women and development. Port Louis, Mauritius: Ministry of Women's Rights, Child Development and Family Welfare, Mauritius.

Mumford, S.D. and **E. Kessel.** 1986. Role of abortion in control of global population growth. *Clinics in Obstetrics and Gynaecology* 13 (1): 19–31.

8

Determinants of Induced Abortion and Subsequent Reproductive Behaviour Among Women in Three Urban Districts of Nepal

A.K. Tamang, Neera Shrestha and Kabita Sharma

Introduction

Unwanted pregnancy and induced abortion occur in every society. Inevitably, therefore, all governments and health care systems face the challenge of providing some elements of abortion care, ranging from life-saving treatment of complications to safe, legal procedures. The way in which this challenge is responded to depends on the degree to which governments and their societies acknowledge the existence of unwanted pregnancy and abortion, which, in turn, directly influences the quality of care a woman receives with direct impact on her health.

Legal restrictions and bureaucratic or other barriers often force women with an unwanted pregnancy to seek abortion from unqualified providers, which poses a great risk to their lives. As is now often quoted, in addition to approximately 70,000 women throughout the world who die each year from unsafe abortion, many more suffer serious, often permanent physical impairment, chronic morbidity, and infertility from complications such as sepsis, haemorrhage, uterine perforation and cervical trauma.

In Nepal, as in many developing countries, abortion is a highly sensitive and divisive issue. Drawing upon the strict condemnation of abortion in Hindu and Buddhist teachings, a cultural ethos with respect to abortion in Nepal has resulted in making it a criminal act under all circumstances, punishable by law. Both the woman who undergoes the procedure and the service provider can be imprisoned.

In spite of the strong legal sanctions and general societal disapproval of abortion, community attitudes towards abortion seem to be increasingly tolerant towards women who seek abortion. The 1985 and 1986 studies by the Institute for Integrated Development Studies (IIDS) and a recently conducted study in two districts of Dhankuta and Dhanusha (Tamang, 1994) found a high degree of approval for abortions performed under specific circumstances; for example, pregnancy due to rape or incest, or not advisable for health reasons. The paradoxical situation in Nepal of very restrictive legal sanctions against abortion and at the same time an increase in its incidence, with only a few selected women having access to a safe procedure, has become a matter of concern for many policy makers, health professionals and women's health advocates.

There has been very little analytical research work done on the determinants and consequences of abortion in Nepal. Moreover, none of the existing studies of abortion in this country have attempted to explore the effect of abortion on a woman's subsequent reproductive and contraceptive behaviour, or to determine if abortion has medium-term health complications associated with the various techniques used for it.

The present study, which began in January 1992 and ended in July 1994, attempts to fill in some of these important data gaps. It also hopes to serve as a significant benchmark for government and reproductive health advocates in Nepal in their efforts to reduce the incidence of unsafe abortion and its complications, and to improve the accessibility of effective contraceptive methods to women who resort to abortion, or repeat abortion, to regulate their fertility.

Study Objectives

The study set out to ascertain the social, economic and health service factors that influence a woman's decision to have an induced abortion and repeat abortion(s), with a major focus on fertility regulation behaviour, particularly post-abortion contraceptive decisions.

Research Design and Methodology

This was a prospective study of women who resided in urban areas of three districts of the Kathmandu valley; namely, Kathmandu, Lalitpur and Bhaktapur. All women who visited the four government hospitals there[1] and one of the leading private clinics for the management of abortion complications or for medical termination of pregnancy during a six-month period constituted the study sample.

---

[1] These were: the Maternity Hospital and the Teaching Hospital, both in Kathmandu district; Patan Hospital, in Lalitpur district; and Bhaktapur Hospital, in Bhaktapur district.

A Medical Advisory Committee (MAC) was formed to assist the IIDS study team in identifying abortion cases, obtaining consent from the women for participation in the study, deciding on all technical matters regarding abortion classification, etc. Members of MAC were senior gynaecologists, most of whom had worked in various capacities in the four government hospitals of the valley.

The study design had four main elements: (*a*) recruitment of abortion cases; (*b*) two follow-up studies, at four-month and 15-month intervals after admission to the hospital/clinic; (*c*) case studies; and (*d*) focus group discussions.

Recruitment of Abortion Cases

Altogether, 1,241 women were interviewed during the six-month case recruitment period: 1,092 women from the four government hospitals; and 149 from the one private clinic. Of the total, 234 reported that they had an induced abortion, 814 reported a spontaneous abortion, 90 reported taking some drug—knowingly or unknowingly—and 103 had symptoms of a possible spontaneous abortion (Table 8.1).

Table 8.1: Study Population, by Type of Abortion and Place of Recruitment

Type of Abortion	Maternity Hospital		Teaching Hospital		Patan Hospital		Bhaktapur Hospital		Private Clinic		Total	
	(N)	%	(N)	%	(N)	%	(N)	%	(N)	%	(N)	%
Spontaneous abortion	587	75.4	60	74.1	136	70.5	21	52.5	10	6.7	814	65.6
Induced by untrained personnel & registered at hospital with complication	56	7.2	4	4.9	23	11.9	4	10.0	2	1.3	89	7.2
Induced by trained medical professionals	3	0.4	4	4.9	2	1.0			136	91.3	145	11.7
Induced by administration of drugs (knowingly/ unknowingly*)	66	8.5	6	7.4	13	6.7	5	12.5			90	7.2
Threatened abortion with continued pregnancy	66	8.5	7	8.6	19	9.8	10	25.0	1	0.7	103	8.3
Total (N)	778	62.7	81	6.5	193	15.6	40	3.2	149	12.0	1,241	100.0

* Considered as spontaneous abortion, because medicines were taken for health reasons, not for the purpose of inducing an abortion.

At each hospital/clinic, the women were registered on a 'case record card', which was designed for the purpose of the study, and then interviewed before leaving. The task of filling out the card was entrusted to the doctor or the clinician attending the abortion case, who was also required to explain the nature of the research to each woman and to obtain her consent to participate in the study.

The complaint(s) described by the woman, the clinician's diagnosis, any type of abortion-related complications, and date of admission were recorded on the card. The card also listed detailed information about the patients' marital status, number of previous pregnancies, gestational age at the time of abortion and consent given. All this information served as a useful tool in cross-checking and validating the abortion classification made during the initial and follow-up interviews.

A 'Code Manual for Case Record Card' had been prepared and was given to the clinicians to guide them in completing the card. To help them with abortion identification and classification, a guideline called 'Clinical Criteria for Diagnosis of Abortion' was developed and standardized by IIDS in consultation with MAC.

The initial interview questionnaire was administered by the IIDS research team after the women had agreed to participate in the study. (All but four women were willing to be interviewed.) The questionnaire solicited the following information on abortion determinants: (a) socioeconomic and demographic characteristics; (b) whether pregnancy was planned, a result of contraceptive failure or risk-taking behaviour; (c) knowledge, accessibility and availability of contraceptive methods, use and perceived/actual side effects; (d) factors impeding the use of contraception; (e) desired family size; (f) previous incidence of abortion, and perceptions about abortion; (g) reasons for the current abortion; and (h) past contraceptive use, future intentions, feelings about another pregnancy after the abortion, etc.

Case Classification

Women who had an induced abortion were divided into two groups: (a) those who attempted to self-induce an abortion or who were helped by untrained personnel to induce an abortion and then sought medical services at the hospital/clinic for the treatment of complications/incomplete abortion (89 women); and (b) women who sought the help of a qualified medical professional for medical termination of pregnancy (MTP) or for menstrual regulation (MR) (145 women).

Similarly, women who had a spontaneous abortion were classified into two groups: (a) those who experienced miscarriage in normal circumstances; that is, without any health complications at the time of the pregnancy (814 women); and (b) women who had knowingly or unknowingly consumed medicine on health grounds, which then resulted in abortion (90 women).

Women in the third category, those who had symptoms of a possible spontaneous abortion, had been admitted to the hospital/clinic with minor complications of pregnancy, such as bleeding and/or abdominal pain, but then were subsequently discharged once their pregnancy was considered stable. During the six-month case recruitment period, a total of 293 of these cases were admitted for treatment and kept under observation for some days. At the time of their discharge, only 123 of them were still pregnant. Another 20 women subsequently miscarried after being discharged. The women in this category were followed-up at home whenever possible, until the gestation period exceeded 28 weeks. Any foetal loss after this gestation period was not considered an abortion, but rather a pre-timed birth, irrespective of the outcome of the conception; and these women automatically fell out of the follow-up group.

Follow-Up I

The first follow-up interview was designed to collect information about the post-abortion reproductive behaviour of the women in the sample during the four-month interval that followed their admission to the clinic, either for abortion complications, pregnancy problems, or medical termination of pregnancy. The following issues were addressed: (*a*) reasons for the abortion; (*b*) reasons for non-use of any contraception prior to conception; (*c*) any regrets or guilt feelings about the abortion; (*d*) post-abortion contraceptive use and intentions; (*e*) reasons for not using contraception following the abortion, if applicable; (*f*) attitudes towards becoming pregnant again, and; (*g*) the existence, if any, of post-abortion health complications.

Several factors influenced the way these data were collected: the sensitive nature of the study in general; women's reluctance to be followed-up at their homes; and distance factors, such as the residential location of the women, accessibility and correctness of residential addresses, etc. It was finally decided to attempt home visitation of all the women who resided within the urban and semi-urban areas of Kathmandu valley. The original target for this first phase of follow-up was fixed at 550 women, so that during the second phase of follow-up, another 500 women could be successfully covered.

Fieldwork was conducted from June to December 1992. Each member of the IIDS field survey team visited the homes of the same group of women whom they had each interviewed initially. This approach ensured the confidentiality of the interviews and made it easier to re-establish a trusting, open dialogue with the respondent.

By the end of this first phase of follow-up, 632 women of the total sample of 1,241 initially interviewed had been contacted. This exceeded our target of 550 women, but we anticipated some possible interview refusals. Of this total, 501 were spontaneous abortion cases and 131 were induced abortion cases. These two categories of abortion are reported separately when the follow-up results are discussed.

Follow-Up II

The second follow-up interview was aimed at providing a more detailed picture of the fertility regulation behaviour of the women during the 15-month period following the date of admission to the clinic. A 15-month interval was chosen to allow sufficient time for actual behavioural changes to take place. We were particularly interested in the possible occurrence of another pregnancy, and repeat abortion. Attitudes towards unintended pregnancy in general and reasons for non-use of contraception even when it was easily available were also of specific interest. This phase of the study also aimed to identify any longer-term health consequences of women who had a repeat abortion.

We intended to visit all 632 women who were interviewed in the first phase of follow-up to get their permission to administer another questionnaire, with a target of reaching 500 women. Eventually, a total of 538 women were successfully interviewed from May to November 1993: 408 were original spontaneous abortion cases and 130 were induced abortion cases. Thus, almost all the induced abortion cases interviewed in the first phase of follow-up were successfully re-interviewed during the second phase.

Reasons for Follow-up Losses

Altogether, 609 women (49 per cent) in the first follow-up group and 65 women (12 per cent) in the second follow-up group could not be contacted. This was mostly because the women lived in difficult to reach or remote areas that were inaccessible by motorable road. Not surprisingly, women from across the Kathmandu valley or from remote areas visit the capital city for treatment of abortion complications or for termination of pregnancy because major hospitals (including the only maternity hospital in the country) and private clinics are concentrated there.

Follow-up of 48 women who were discharged from the clinic with their pregnancy intact, after experiencing symptoms of a possible spontaneous abortion four months earlier, revealed the following: 15 women had delivered a baby; another 22 women had carried their pregnancy beyond the 28-week allowable period at the time of the follow-up visit to their homes; and of the 11 remaining women with a possible spontaneous abortion, 10 women had experienced spontaneous foetal loss and one woman had subsequently terminated her pregnancy deliberately. These 11 women were included in the second phase of follow-up. The 22 women who continued their pregnancy to term, however, were dropped from the follow-up study.

Case Studies

An important element of the study design was to conduct in-depth interviews with 40 women selected from the total number of cases contacted for the first phase of the follow-up study. The purpose was to get an understanding of the dynamics of the women's behaviour prior to conception, their reproductive decision-making process, and their subsequent fertility regulation behaviour. The case studies were useful in explaining the linkages between various determinants as well as in describing the socio-psychological status of the women who underwent abortion.

The following criteria was used to select the women: (*a*) women who used either untrained or trained personnel for induced abortion; (*b*) women with bad obstetric history who had spontaneous abortions; (*c*) nulliparous women who had repeat spontaneous abortions; and (*d*) high parity women who had spontaneous abortions, possibly due to drug use.

From the 44 case studies collected, 34 were included in our analysis and discussion: 22 of them had induced abortion and 12 had spontaneous abortion. The cases of 10 women were dropped, because their histories appeared to repeat others in the group.

Focus Group Discussions

The purpose of the focus group discussions (FGDs) was to capture relevant 'qualitative' information regarding socio-psychological aspects of abortion, abortion-seeking behaviour, and contraceptive preferences and use, which would supplement the quantitative information gathered during the follow-up studies.

Two rounds of focus group discussions were conducted; seven sessions in the first round and six sessions in the second round. Round 1 was arranged after completion of the first phase of follow-up (March to April 1993); and Round 2, after completion of the second phase of follow-up (December 1993 to January 1994).

Participants for the FGDs were randomly selected from the abortion cases who had been successfully followed-up. However, to maintain both homogeneity and 'representiveness' of the participants, we selected women who had an induced abortion (either by untrained or trained personnel) and women who had a spontaneous abortion with the following characteristics: nulliparous women who had repeat spontaneous abortion, high parity women, and women who may have had a spontaneous abortion due to unintended use of drugs.

Study Results

The results of our study are presented here in three main sections. The first one presents the general context in which abortion occurs and the characteristics of the women in our sample, particularly contraceptive use and future contraceptive intentions. Some comparative data on women who have safe versus unsafe procedures are also offered. The second section discusses follow-up findings about the women who had induced abortion; and the third section discusses follow-up findings about the women who had spontaneous abortion.

The Determinants of Abortion

This section discusses the social and cultural context within which abortion occurs and the characteristics of the women who experienced it, particularly their contraceptive behaviour, and impediments, if any, to contraceptive use prior to conception.

About 95 per cent of all the induced abortion cases were the result of unplanned pregnancy. Spontaneous abortion also occurred among women whose pregnancies were unplanned: over 25 per cent of spontaneous abortion cases and one-sixth of the women who had symptoms of possible spontaneous abortion (Table 8.2).

Table 8.2: Pregnancy Status, by Type of Abortion

Pregnancy Status	Type of Abortion							
	Spontaneous		Induced		Threatened		Total	
	(N)	%	(N)	%	(N)	%	(N)	%
Planned	658	72.9	11	4.7	86	83.5	755	60.9
Unplanned	245	27.1	223	95.3	17	16.5	485	39.1
Total	903	72.8	234	18.9	103	8.3	1,240*	100.0

* Information on one case is missing.

Generally speaking, the women who had an unplanned pregnancy that resulted in termination of pregnancy were mostly young, between 20 to 29 years of age; had two or more sons; were more educated; and the majority of them demonstrated the risk-taking behaviour of not using any contraceptive method prior to conception. Unlike other situations described in this book, the case of Nepal indicates that abortion is not an adolescent problem, but rather one that is related to poor or no birthspacing practices.

Reasons for Induced Abortion: Unsafe Versus Safe

Given the social and political context of abortion in Nepal, many induced abortions are performed by untrained providers or initially self-induced.

Although the identification of abortion providers was difficult, given its illegal status, we were able to ascertain that a significant number of untrained providers were *sudenis* (traditional birth attendants). Some women also sought the help of a *vaidya*, or an endogenous ayurvedic practitioner, and others obtained abortifacients and other herbal remedies from faith healers and pharmacists. The actual procedures used by these untrained providers were dangerous and often barbaric; for example, involving the insertion of sticks pasted with cow-dung or herbal mixtures, the injection of unknown medicines or herbal mixtures into the uterus, the insertion of a rubber catheter dipped in unidentified substances, etc. Some women had tried to self-induce abortion by consuming honey, chemical powders (*sindur* and *nir*), anti-worm medicines, oral pills, and so on.[2]

Of the 234 women who had induced abortion, only 10 were unmarried and seven women were either widowed or separated; the large majority were married and living with their spouse.

We found the expected differences in characteristics between women who had unsafe procedures and women who sought abortion from trained providers. To begin with, there is a strong indication that for many of the women who had a clandestine procedure, abortion was their only available method of family planning; they had the procedure to limit births, rather than to space births. For example, 8 per cent of women who had an unsafe abortion did so after having only one surviving child. This compares with one out of every four women who sought safe abortion services. Moreover, among women who had an unsafe abortion, more than half of them already had two or more surviving sons. By contrast, among the women who had a safe abortion, 30 per cent had no surviving male offspring. Particularly because there is a strong preference for male children throughout Asia, especially at the start of family formation, these data would support the conclusion that women who had a safe abortion were using it as a spacing method or as back-up for contraceptive failure (Table 8.3).

Table 8.3: Women Who Had Induced Abortion, by Number of Living Sons and Type of Provider

No. of Living Sons	Induced by Untrained Personnel %	Induced by Trained Personnel %
None	19.8	29.8
1	29.1	49.6
2	41.9	16.3
≥ 3	9.3	4.2
Total (N)	86	141
Mean no. of living sons*	1.4	1.0
SD	(1.02)	(0.8)

* Respondents with no living children, or no living sons, are assigned zero values.

Women who generally resorted to clandestine abortion services were from the rural areas surrounding the cities of Kathmandu, Lalitpur and Bhaktapur. The majority of them were illiterate (51 per cent) or had completed primary

[2] For more information about the various types of practices, refer to Case Studies of Women Experiencing Abortions (IIDS, 1994).

level education only (15 per cent). In contrast, women who sought the abortion services of medical professionals at private clinics and nursing homes were urban-based and better educated: 83 per cent of them had completed over 10 years of secondary level education and above.

We also found that the more educated women sought abortion services within the first trimester, which is the safest period: About 82 per cent of the women had an abortion or menstrual regulation (MR) at a private clinic before eight weeks of gestation; and another 14 per cent, within 12 weeks. Only the remaining less than 5 per cent had an abortion after 12 weeks of gestation. In contrast, a substantial proportion of the women who had a clandestine abortion, 38 per cent (the majority of them illiterate) did so during the second trimester (13–24 weeks of gestation); another 8 per cent sought unsafe abortion at an even later stage of pregnancy, after 25 weeks.

We also found that there was a positive relationship between the educational level of the male partner and the use of safe abortion services: 83 per cent of the men living with women who had a safe abortion at a private clinic had completed secondary level education or above; while women who sought abortion from untrained providers were living with men of much lower educational level (Table 8.4).

A high proportion of service holders, women who are working for wages, and businesswomen preferred to visit private clinics for abortion than to seek an unsafe procedure. The occupation of the male partner of the women who sought safe abortion services was also notable: 59.7 per cent were service holders and 29.5 per cent were businessmen, which means they could at least afford the higher fees charged by a private clinic.

Reasons for Spontaneous Abortion

A large majority of the women who reported that they experienced a spontaneous abortion were young (below 25 years), had few previous pregnancies and not more than one surviving child. Moreover, a considerable proportion of them (35 per cent) were nulliparous women for whom this had been their first pregnancy. Three-fourths of them still wanted additional children. A substantial proportion of them, however, had no desire for more children (24 per cent). In fact, for 27 per cent of these women, the pregnancy that had just ended spontaneously was unplanned. Twelve per cent of these women were pregnant due to failure of contraceptive methods.

The reasons for spontaneous abortion as perceived by the women themselves, especially those who mentioned that their pregnancy was unplanned (245 women), are noteworthy. Over one-fourth, 29 per cent, mentioned that they had taken medicine for minor illness during pregnancy. Another 11 per cent cited long journey travel, lifting of heavy loads, etc. The rest, a substantial majority at 60 per cent, were unable or did not want to give any reasons for their miscarriage.

Table 8.4: Women Who Had Induced Abortion: Socioeconomic Characteristics and Type of Provider

Characteristics	Untrained Personnel %	Trained Medical Professional %
Marital status		
Never married	3.4	2.8
Married	92.1	95.9
Widow	3.4	0.7
Divorced/separated	1.1	0.7
Education		
Illiterate	51.2	14.2
Primary level	15.1	8.5
Secondary level (SLC)	15.1	12.0
SLC and above	18.6	65.2
Husband's education		
Illiterate	9.3	2.8
Primary level	19.8	3.5
Secondary level (SLC)	32.2	10.6
SLC and above	46.5	83.0
Occupation		
Housewife	55.1	61.4
Farmer	13.5	4.1
Service worker	11.2	19.3
Factory worker	–	2.1
Business	9.0	9.7
Casual labourer	4.5	0.7
Student	4.5	2.8
Other	2.2	–
Husband's occupation		
Farmer	11.0	3.6
Service worker	47.6	59.7
Factory worker	2.4	–
Business	23.2	29.5
Casual labourer	7.3	1.4
Student	–	2.9
Unemployed	3.7	2.2
Other	4.9	0.7
Sample size (N)	(80)	(145)

Whether or not women in this group had actually attempted to end their unintended pregnancy was difficult to determine. Only 12 women admitted during the follow-up study that they had tried to interrupt it. The probability in any study sample of abortion that more than 15 per cent of the women will have had a spontaneous abortion, however, is very unlikely. The reasons given by the women for this outcome, such as the lifting of heavy loads and taking medicines, also hint at the likelihood that most of the so-called 'spontaneous' abortions were actually self-induced.

We hoped that looking at the pattern of contraceptive use prior to conception and in the 15-month interval following termination of pregnancy would provide more insight regarding this possibility and also explain more clearly the distinctions between induced and spontaneous abortion cases in this study population.

Contraceptive Use Prior to Conception

We define ever-use of contraception as contraceptive practice at any time prior to the last conception that was aborted or miscarried. This use was high among the women who had induced abortion: 76 per cent among women who used trained providers and 58 per cent among those who used untrained ones.

In comparison, women who reported spontaneous abortion, or miscarriage, had a much lower level of contraceptive use, 33 per cent. This is not surprising, because the women who had miscarriages were younger in age, had fewer children and wanted more children than those women who had induced abortion. Moreover, access to methods of contraception is seriously hampered by their residence in remote locations and by their unmarried status. All this points to the possibility that these spontaneous abortion cases may include a high proportion of women who are trying to self-induce abortion to limit family size.

Among those who had contracepted prior to pregnancy, the majority were using pills and condoms on a temporary basis to space their pregnancies, followed by natural methods and injectables.

Negligence, fear of a method's side effects, the presence of a breast-feeding baby, and opposition from the husband were the major reasons for non-use of contraception among women who had no desire for additional children. The majority of these women had four or more children; and some of them had intended to undergo sterilization at some point, but had in the meantime failed to prevent the unintended pregnancy. Such women felt they had no alternative but to undergo abortion.

It is important to note that we found fear of side effects of most of the hormonal contraceptives, such as Depo-Provera, Norplant, and the pill as well as the IUD, had discouraged most of the women from accepting these methods. They either preferred to be 'exposed' to unwanted pregnancy or to wait for a convenient time to undergo sterilization.

Future Contraceptive Intentions

Roughly, nine-tenths of the induced abortion cases (89 per cent) said they intended to use contraception in the future. Again, this was expected, because this group of women had either completed their family size or did not wish to have the next conception immediately. Women who had spontaneous abortion were somewhat equally divided on the question of contraceptive use in the future: 51 per cent intended to use it in the future, compared to 48 per cent who had no intention to contracept (Table 8.5).

Table 8.5: Women's Contraceptive Intentions, by Type of Abortion

Plans to Use Contraception	Spontaneous		Induced		Threatened		Total	
	(N)	%	(N)	%	(N)	%	(N)	%
Yes	461	51.2	202	89.0	55	53.4	718	58.3
No	431	47.8	21	9.2	48	46.6	500	40.6
Undecided	9	1.0	4	1.8	–	–	13	1.1
Total	901	100.0	227	100.0	103	100.0	1,231	100.0

Female sterilization (26 per cent) followed by Depo-Provera injection (15 per cent) were the two most preferred methods for future use among all women in the sample. To some extent, male sterilization (12 per cent) and IUDs (10 per cent) were the preferred contraceptive methods among women who had induced abortion; and Norplant (13 per cent), among the women who had symptoms of spontaneous abortion. However, over 25 per cent of the women in this latter group were not certain as to which method they would choose in the future. In comparison, only 14 per cent of the women who had induced abortion were uncertain about their preferred future method (Table 8.6).

Table 8.6: Contraceptive Choices among Women Planning to Contracept, by Abortion Status

Method of Choice	Spontaneous %	Induced %	Threatened %	Total %
Pills	5.6	5.4	1.8	5.3
IUD	2.6	9.9	3.6	4.7
Condom	5.8	5.4	–	5.3
Injectable	16.2	12.4	12.7	14.9
Norplant	8.8	8.9	12.7	9.2
Female sterilization	25.2	27.7	33.3	26.3
Male sterilization	6.1	12.4	8.3	8.1
Others	3.7	3.5	3.6	3.6
Undecided	25.8	14.3	25.5	22.6
Total (N)	(461)	(202)	(55)	(718)

Repeat Abortion: Induced and Spontaneous

We found that previous abortion experience increased the chance of repeat abortion. Of the 188 women who had a spontaneous abortion and who reported that they had previous abortion experience, 92 per cent reported that the previous abortion had also been spontaneous. Similarly, of the 63 women who had an induced abortion and reported previous abortion experience, 68 per cent said their previous abortion had also been induced; the remaining 32 per cent said their previous pregnancy had ended in spontaneous foetal loss.

It is a significant finding that a considerable proportion of these women have been exposed to two or more previous abortions and some, to as many as four or more abortions (Table 8.7). The credibility of the finding is under-scored by the consistency between the women's declarations concerning the nature of their present and past abortion experiences.

Table 8.7: Prior Abortion Experience, by Current Abortion Status

Prior Experience	Type of Abortion			
	Spontaneous %	Induced %	Threatened %	Total %
Yes	20.8	27.3	22.3	22.2
No	79.1	72.7	77.7	77.8
Sample size (N)	(901)	(227)	(103)	(1,231)
Women with previous abortion experience				
At least one previous induced abortion	9.6	68.2	8.7	23.1
At least one spontaneous abortion	91.9	39.7	100.0	80.6
Women with previous spontaneous abortion				
0	8.5	60.3	–	19.7
1	70.7	30.2	69.6	61.3
2	13.3	6.3	21.7	12.4
≥ 3	7.4	3.2	8.7	6.6
Women with previous induced abortion				
0	90.4	31.8	91.3	76.6
1	8.5	58.7	8.7	20.1
2	1.1	7.9	–	2.6
≥ 3	–	1.6	–	0.4
Sample size (N)	(188)	(63)	(23)	(274)

Note: The totals and percentage figures exceed (N) and 100% because of the possibility of double counting a respondent who had undergone both induced and spontaneous abortions.

Awareness of Possible Risks of Abortion

Awareness about the possible side effects of abortion was low (37 per cent) among all the women in the sample. Those side effects that were mentioned were restricted to general problems, such as excessive bleeding, weakness, abdominal pain, etc. Other more serious risks, such as secondary infertility, repeat abortion or miscarriage were not considered abortion-related risks, probably due to lack of appropriate education and information.

None of the 1,241 women interviewed at the hospitals/clinics were aware that they were at risk of conception and that they needed to take precautions against unwanted pregnancy at the time they were discharged. Few amongst them knew that they would be safe from becoming pregnant, without contra-ception, only until their menstruation resumed.

Induced Abortion Cases: Post-Abortion Health Status and Reproductive Behaviour

This section reports on a total of 234 women recruited for follow-up: 131 were covered in the first follow-up, four months after admission; and 130 were contacted during the second follow-up, 15 months after initial contact. The follow-up process was helpful in detecting misreporting and previous misclassification; accordingly, 12 cases that were previously categorized as spontaneous abortion were reclassified as induced abortion.

Health Status

The majority of women who had an induced abortion did not experience any prolonged health complications; they said they were feeling physically fine. Only 17 per cent declared minor health problems at the time of the second follow-up interview, especially those who had used clandestine abortion services. Most of these problems, however, were non-specific complaints; except one woman who reported having a vaginal or uterine infection. Among women who had non-specific complaints, 45 per cent had suffered from back-pain, chest pain followed by lower abdominal pain during menses, menstrual irregularity, and headache and weakness. Every second woman who reported such problems associated them with their experience of induced abortion (Table 8.8).

Contraceptive Use

Immediate post-abortion contraceptive use among women who had an induced abortion was extremely high, 88 per cent. Moreover, the contraceptive

Table 8.8: Induced Abortion Cases: Post-Abortion Health Status at the Time of Second Follow-up

Complication	By Untrained Personnel		By Trained Personnel		Total	
	(N)	%	(N)	%	(N)	%
Yes	8	22.2	14	14.9	22	16.9
No	28	77.8	80	85.1	108	83.1
Type of complaint/complication						
Pain: backpain, chest pain, pain in limbs, muscle/bone, etc.	4	50.0	6	43.0	10	45.5
Headache, giddiness, weakness	1	12.5	1	7.1	2	9.1
Lower abdominal pain, pain during menses	2	25.0	4	28.6	6	27.3
Cough, cold, fever	–	–	1	7.1	1	4.5
Vaginal/uterine infection	–	–	1	7.1	1	4.5
Irregular menses/heavy bleeding	–	–	1	7.1	1	4.5
Other (amenorrhoea due to Depo. use)	1	12.5	–	–	1	4.5

prevalence rate had remained at 80 per cent, the same rate found during the first follow-up survey. Their choice of method, however, leaned towards low efficacy options, such as rhythm and withdrawal (Table 8.9). This was surprising, as most of these women were literate and had used a private clinic for their abortion, where family planning information was provided.

Table 8.9: Induced Abortion Cases: Post-Abortion Ever-Use of Contraception, by Method

Ever-Use	(N)*	%
Yes	113	87.7
No	16	12.3
Total	129	100.0
If yes, first method used		
Pills	23	20.4
IUD	3	2.6
Condom	23	20.4
Depo-Provera	9	8.0
Foaming tablets	1	0.9
Norplant	2	1.8
Female sterilization	11	9.7
Male sterilization	4	3.5
Calendar	30	26.5
Withdrawal	6	5.3
Other (traditional method)	1	0.9
Total	113	100.0

* (N) excludes one unmarried case.

This contact with the clinic still had some protective effect, in that the use rate for these methods declined from 36 per cent to 26 per cent in the 11-month period between the first and second follow-ups. At the time of the second follow-up study, condoms (18 per cent) and pills and female sterilization (12 per cent, each) had become the most popular methods, followed by Depo-Provera. Moreover, a higher proportion of the women were using permanent or semi-permanent contraceptive methods to avoid an accidental or unwanted pregnancy (Table 8.10).

Some of the proportion of women who were not using contraception at the time of the second follow-up interview were doing so for the reasons shown in Table 8.11. Although 31 of the 130 induced abortion cases were not using any contraception, nearly three-fourths of them said they intended to use contraception in the near future. For the majority of them, this meant as soon as they resumed their period or after the delivery of a current pregnancy. The method preference was for female sterilization, followed by Depo-Provera, pills and the condom. Unfortunately, one-third of the women who intended to use contraception in the future were not sure about which method they would use.

Table 8.10: Induced Abortion Cases: Current Use of Contraception at the Time of Second Follow-Up

Current Use	(N)	%
Yes	98	79.7
No	25	20.3
Total	123	100.0
If yes, which method?		
Pills	12	12.3
IUD	6	6.1
Condom	18	18.4
Depo-Provera	11	11.2
Foaming tablets	1	1.0
Norplant	3	3.1
Female sterilization	12	12.2
Male sterilization	8	8.2
Calendar	20	20.4
Withdrawal	6	6.1
Other (traditional method)	1	1.0
Total	98	100.0

Table 8.11: Induced Abortion Cases: Reasons for Non-Use of Post-Abortion Contraception

Reasons for Non-Use	(N)*	%
Carelessness	2	12.5
Infertile/amenorrhoea since last abortion	1	6.3
Husband is away	2	12.5
Husband opposed	2	12.5
Want to have a baby	2	12.5
Not necessary (on marital status basis)	3	18.7
Currently pregnant	1	6.3
Postpartum amenorrhoea	3	18.7
Total	16	100.0

* (N) excludes one unmarried case.

Reproductive Behaviour

One out of every six women had conceived at least once during the 15-month period following their abortion and the majority of these pregnancies were unplanned ones. Four of those who got pregnant a second time resorted to abortion again.

This demonstrates clearly that a lack of contraceptive protection and of post-abortion services leads to high-risk behaviour, for which induced abortion is then needed to regulate fertility, particularly among urban women of the Kathmandu valley. However, some of these unplanned pregnancies were also the result of incorrect or irregular contraceptive behaviour, as evidenced by the use of methods of low efficacy by most of the women who used contraception. Still other unplanned pregnancies were due to either carelessness or opposition by the spouse/family member to contraceptive use.

The antenatal care sought by the women who subsequently got pregnant was noteworthy. All pregnant women consulted medical doctors either at a private clinic or at the public hospitals for pregnancy confirmation and other necessary precautions. As the women in the follow-up represented mostly urban dwellers who are conscious of safe abortion practices (they were recruited from a private clinic), it is natural to find the health care-seeking behaviour of these women to be much better than expected. It also means that this finding should not be generalized.

The majority of the women, 60 per cent, said they would opt for pregnancy termination in case of another accidental or unintended pregnancy. This position reflects an increasing awareness among urban women of their reproductive rights and a high demand for ways to regulate fertility, including abortion. Thus, it points to the need for the provision of safe abortion services, at least in places where safe facilities and trained providers would be feasible.

The post-abortion fertility behaviour of these women, measured in terms of the differences in desired family size at the time of initial case recruitment stage and at the time of the second round of follow-up visits, shows that the desire for another child can change with the passage of time and depends on the existing household situation, the health of the mother and child, the woman's socioeconomic situation, and her degree of involvement in non-domestic activities, particularly paid work activities. However, the effects of these external factors on the fertility decision-making power of the women need more in-depth research and analysis.

Spontaneous Abortion Cases: Post-Abortion Health and Reproductive Behaviour

In contrast to the women who terminated their pregnancy, this section analyzes the post-abortion health status and subsequent reproductive and contraceptive behaviour of women who reported that they had a spontaneous abortion and could be followed-up in the study: 501 cases in the first follow-up and 408 in the second follow-up; these represent 61.5 per cent and 50.1 per cent, respectively, of the total sample of reported spontaneous cases.

Health Status

Every fifth woman (22 per cent) who had a spontaneous abortion had experienced some type of health problem following the miscarriage. However, most of these complaints were non-specific in nature. Over one-third of these women experienced health problems for the previous 12 months or more and most associated these problems with their spontaneous abortion (Table 8.12).

Table 8.12: Spontaneous Abortion Cases: Post-Abortion Health Status at the Time of Second Follow-Up

Complication	(N)	%
Yes	92	22.5
No	316	77.5
Total	408	100.0
Type of complaint/complication		
Pain: backpain, chest pain, pain in limbs, muscles/bone, etc.	36	39.1
Headache, giddiness, weakness	15	16.3
Lower abd. pain, pain during menses	14	15.2
Cough/cold/fever	10	10.9
Irregular menses/heavy bleeding	8	8.6
Other	9	9.9
Total	92	100.0

It is difficult to correlate these complaints with a miscarriage suffered some 15 months ago in the absence of any medical or clinical examination, however. Yet, from the perception and experiences related by the women themselves and presented here, there is no doubt that further investigation and research is needed to ascertain the long-term health consequences of spontaneous abortion; and more especially, of repeat spontaneous abortion.

Contraceptive Use

Over half the women who had a spontaneous abortion, 54 per cent, had not used any contraceptive method since the last miscarriage. Among the 46 per cent who had used a method, condoms and Depo-Provera had been the most popular choices, followed by the less effective traditional methods (Table 8.13). It was encouraging to find that the contraceptive prevalence rate had increased from 26 per cent to 40 per cent since the first follow-up, an increase of 14 per cent within an 11-month period (Table 8.14).

The method-mix among these acceptors was dominated by modern, spacing methods (66.7 per cent). Depo-Provera had become the most popular method (29 per cent); the use of traditional methods had dropped to second place (20 per cent), followed by condom use (14 per cent) and oral pills (12 per cent). The adoption of sterilization had doubled since the first follow-up, from 6 per cent to 13 per cent.

Among the 219 women not using any method, the major reasons given for non-use were postpartum amenorrhoea following the delivery of subsequent pregnancy, desire for additional children, negligence, fear of side effects, contraindication to health, and opposition by spouse or family member (Table 8.15).

It was encouraging to find that about two-thirds of the women who were not using any contraception at the time of the second follow-up said they

Table 8.13: Spontaneous Abortion Cases: Post-Abortion Ever-Use of Contraception, by Method

Ever-Use	(N)	%
Yes	189	46.1
No	219	53.9
Total	408	100.0
If yes, first method used		
Temporary methods		
Pills	29	15.4
IUD	9	4.8
Condom	38	20.2
Depo-Provera	43	22.9
Foaming tablets	6	3.2
Norplant	3	1.6
Permanent methods		
Female sterilization	9	4.8
Male sterilization	5	2.7
Natural methods		
Calendar	29	15.4
Withdrawal	18	9.0
Other (traditional method)	–	–
Total	189	100.0

Table 8.14: Spontaneous Abortion Cases: Current Use of Contraception at the Time of Second Follow-up

Current Use	(N)	%
Yes	129	39.9
No	194	60.1
Total	323	100.0
If yes, which method?		
Temporary methods		
Pills	16	12.4
IUD	10	7.8
Condom	18	14.0
Depo-Provera	37	28.7
Foaming tablets	2	1.6
Norplant	3	2.3
Permanent methods		
Female sterilization	10	7.7
Male sterilization	7	5.4
Natural methods		
Calendar	17	13.2
Withdrawal	7	5.4
Other (traditional method)	2	1.5
Total	129	100.0

Table 8.15: Spontaneous Abortion Cases: Reasons for Non-Use of Post-Abortion Contraception

Reasons for Non-Use	(N)	%
Fear of side effects	5	2.3
Carelessness	8	3.6
Thinking to undergo sterilization	4	1.8
Health does not allow	5	2.3
Husband is away	5	2.3
Husband opposed	6	2.7
Want to have a baby	62	28.3
Currently pregnant	44	20.1
Postpartum amenorrhoea	75	34.3
Infrequent coitus	4	1.8
Mother-in-law opposed	1	0.5
Total	219	100.0

intended to use a method in the near future. It was also interesting to note that the majority of these women preferred to use Depo-Provera injection. However, over one-fourth of non-users did not intend to practice contraception; most of them were willing to have an additional child but others were afraid of method side effects. Some of these women were undecided on future method use and the specific method they would like to choose.

Reproductive Behaviour

The majority of the women who miscarried were young, nulliparous and desired another child. It was therefore not surprising to find that two-thirds of them had conceived again during the 15-month observation period. A few women had even experienced two or more subsequent pregnancies within the study interval, indicating a possibility of at least one repeat miscarriage.

The majority of the women who had subsequent pregnancies had planned them. But a few of them (31 women) had a second unintended pregnancy, due either to irregularity or ineffectiveness in method use or to carelessness or negligence in method adoption.

Almost all the women who were pregnant at 15 months after their spontaneous abortion, had consulted medical professionals from either the hospitals or private clinics for pregnancy confirmation and necessary medical services. The women explained that the clinicians confirmed their pregnancy by physical examination, urine test and by taking a pregnancy history. However, these women represent a special group, as they had been forced by their miscarriage to seek modern health care. This is not true for the majority of women in rural areas or in most of Nepal, where less than 20 per cent of pregnant women receive antenatal care services from medical professionals and about 90 per cent deliver at home.

The women's lack of decision-making power regarding fertility regulation and the pressure from their spouses/in-laws to immediately get pregnant again were evident from the present analysis. For example, many nulliparous women during the case study discussion said their marital relationship was insecure and that their husband would bring a second wife to the household if they were not able to produce a child. This kind of threat had compelled these women to have a subsequent pregnancy, with the risk, in a few cases, of repeat miscarriage (Tamang, 1994; Tamang et al., 1994).

Discussion and Recommendations

The study has illustrated that women in Nepal, especially those who are less educated, economically disadvantaged, and living in rural areas, are prepared to take considerable risks to terminate unwanted pregnancy, by using unsafe, clandestine services. Because of the fear of legal action and societal disapproval, they subject themselves to a high risk of serious bodily injury, sterility, chronic disability or even death. As most unsafe procedures result in incomplete abortions and are associated with severe complications including sepsis and haemorrhage, these women are left with no choice but to spend considerable amounts of money for medical treatment and hospitalization once complications arise.

The number of spontaneous abortions experienced by the women in our sample reflect the poor state of women's health in general in Nepal and the complete absence of concern for their reproductive health within the family. Many may be actual cases of self-induced abortion or abortions performed by untrained providers that women are not willing to reveal. Still other women in this group are under pressure from husbands and in-laws to bear a child too quickly in order to ensure the stability of their marriage, with negative consequences for pregnancy outcome and their own health.

The study has also revealed the various factors influencing a woman's decision to either accept or avoid early conception following an abortion and the consequences of such decisions. The majority of the women who had experienced an abortion felt the need for post-abortion contraception, as indicated by the increase in their contraceptive prevalence rate and the proportion of women willing to contracept in the near future. However, a number of these same women continued to expose themselves to the risk of unwanted or mistimed pregnancy by not using contraception. The primary reason for not using contraception among women who wanted either to delay subsequent conception or to avoid conception altogether was a fear of side effects of modern methods; these women were left feeling like they had few contraceptive alternatives.

In general, abortion can be linked to the failure of family planning efforts that have either not reached women or have not provided them with safe and effective ways to regulate their fertility. Moreover, during the case recruitment period, the study team noticed that the clinicians made no effort to provide post-abortion family planning counselling. Consequently, most women, especially those who miscarried their intended pregnancy, had either conceived again within four months following their abortion or were anxious to conceive as soon as possible. They had no knowledge of the adverse consequences of closely spaced pregnancies, especially if the previous pregnancy had spontaneously miscarried or been aborted by unsafe abortion.

These findings emphasize the need for introducing post-abortion family planning counselling services at private clinics and hospitals. From the reproductive health point of view, it is suggested that women who experience abortion postpone subsequent pregnancy for at least a year or so to minimize the risks of repeat foetal loss/miscarriage, low birth weight babies, and other pregnancy-related complications. Women who have had spontaneous abortion and still wish to conceive should receive special prenatal care to minimize pregnancy complications and maternal risks, including another miscarriage.

Also, women who intend to use contraception in the future but who are unsure about which method is most suitable for them should be targeted for family planning counselling and motivation for contraceptive acceptance. Moreover, women who cannot use modern methods because of contraindications to their health should be encouraged either to use natural family planning methods or to persuade their male partners to use contraception.

Other strategies suggested by the participants of a dissemination workshop organized by IIDS to discuss these study findings include: educating TBAs and non-qualified health care providers about the dangers of unsafe procedures; creating public information campaigns for the masses with street dramas, radio and TV about the danger of illegal abortion practices; and encouraging and conducting further research on abortion.

These workshop participants also urged the government to make the existing abortion laws more flexible to minimize clandestine abortion and to reduce the strain on hospital resources from treatment of complications of unsafe procedures. Women's health advocates have also proposed a more liberal legal code for abortion. A more moderate abortion policy that would recognize wider grounds on which a woman could seek abortion services is a good idea. However, a more liberal abortion policy will not ensure the availability of safe abortion services throughout the country, especially in the rural areas where it is most urgent. Some restructuring in health service delivery and additional resources, such as necessary equipment and medical back-up services are needed to provide women with greater accessibility to safe abortion procedures.

✝ References

Institute for Integrated Development Studies (IIDS). 1985. Study on hospital-based abortion in Nepal. Project report, Kathmandu, Nepal.
————. 1986. Study on rural-based abortion in Nepal. Project Report, Kathmandu, Nepal.
————. 1994. Case studies of women experiencing abortions. Report No. 3, Sussex, UK.
Tamang, A. 1994. Baseline knowledge, attitude, and practice survey on community-based family planning project in Dhankuta and Dhanusha districts. Kathmandu, Nepal: Centre for Research on Environment, Health and Population Activities (CREHPA): Final Report.
Tamang, A., N. Shrestha, K. Sharma and **S. Khatri.** 1994. Case studies of women with abortion experiences. An IIDS prospective study on determinants of abortion and subsequent reproductive behaviour among women of three urban districts of Nepal: Report No. 3, June 1994.

9

Cultural and Psychosocial Factors Affecting Contraceptive Use and Abortion in Two Provinces of Turkey

Ayse Akin

Introduction

Unwanted pregnancy continues to be a major health problem in Turkey today, despite the fact that there has been a steady increase in contraceptive prevalence over the last three decades, from 22 per cent in 1963 to 63 per cent in 1993 (DHS, 1994). Moreover, contraception has been legally available for more than 20 years now in both public and private sector facilities and nation-wide population and health surveys demonstrate that the majority of couples of reproductive age are motivated to limit their family size.

This situation has inspired many studies on fertility behaviour in Turkey, most of which have classified the causes of unwanted pregnancy into the common and general categories of insufficient access to contraception, a lack of contraceptive use, and/or contraceptive failure (Tezcan and Omran, 1981). This classification has merit, and has brought to light important information about fertility behaviour in Turkey. Generally, it seems that couples still lack basic information about modern family planning methods and the necessary services, particularly in the more rural areas. More significantly, information about method preference has been revealed; for example, the traditional method of withdrawal has remained the most widely used method among currently married women, representing 41 per cent of total contraceptive prevalence today. It is widely believed that the use of this method is the primary reason for the country's high contraceptive failure rate and therefore a major contributing factor to unwanted pregnancy and subsequently, to the increasing abortion rate (Akin and Kisnisci, 1973; 1983; Turkish Population and Health Survey, 1989).

Further evidence to support this relationship between the practice of withdrawal and the abortion rate is the fact that abortion has remained an important component of fertility regulation for women in Turkey, ever since it was legalized in 1983. In fact, the rate and ratio of induced abortion have continued to increase over the years. Currently, the level is 35 per 100 pregnancies or 5 per 100 women of reproductive age (UNICEF, 1991).

While legalization has not reduced the abortion rate, it has reduced considerably the maternal morbidity and mortality associated with unsafe procedures. When abortion was illegal in Turkey, a safe procedure was almost exclusively available only to women in urban areas with high incomes. Poor, rural women either gave birth to unwanted children, suffered serious illness, or died from self-induced or unsafe abortion. Now abortion is available on request up to 10 weeks gestation and performed through safe and modern facilities by general practitioners in both public service and private.

Unfortunately, most studies about fertility regulation in Turkey have not provided insight into the 'real' behaviour and attitude of couples who use, or want to use, a method of fertility regulation (Eren et al., 1983; Fisek et al., 1978; Ministry of Health, 1985). For example, why does the use of withdrawal, with its relatively high failure rate, prevail, despite widespread knowledge and availability of more effective methods? How does the fact that Turkish men appear to play a dominant role in decisions about family size affect contraceptive choice? These and related questions about fertility behaviour need to be addressed using both qualitative and quantitative research methods (IPPF, 1984; Handy, 1982)

We were inspired to explore the specific role of abortion in fertility regulation, given its widespread and increasing use in a country where contraceptive prevalence has reached a relatively high level compared to many other developing countries (Cohen et al., 1984). We also thought that the patriarchal nature of Turkish society provided us with an opportunity to gain important insight into the role of men in fertility regulation, which could have significant implications for family planning and reproductive health policy.

Objectives

The general objective of our research was to understand the cultural and psychosocial determinants of abortion in Turkey and the relationship of abortion to other methods of fertility regulation.

The specific objectives were: (a) to find out the knowledge, attitude and practice of fertility regulation, including abortion, among couples; (b) to examine the cultural, psychosocial and environmental factors, particularly husbands' behaviour and attitudes, that influence a woman's decision regarding fertility regulation, including the use of less reliable methods (withdrawal); and (c) to use this knowledge to develop strategies that would better meet the obvious, but unfulfilled desire by couples to regulate fertility, and thus reduce the adverse effects of unwanted pregnancy on women's health and wellbeing. Ultimately, we were motivated by the hope that our research could influence reproductive health policies in Turkey.

Research Methodology

We conducted the research in two very demographically different provinces in Turkey, one largely urban and the other more rural. Ankara province, where the capital city is located, is 83 per cent urban; Van province is only 35 per cent urban and very different in regional and economic terms. Ankara province is the second most populated in Turkey and is in the central part of the country. It has a main metropolitan centre with large squatter settlements, as well as semi-urban and rural areas. Conversely, Van province, which is in the eastern Anatolia region, has the largest rural area in Turkey; it also has semi-urban and urban areas, but fewer squatter settlements.

These structural differences are reflected in very different characteristics of the populations in the two provinces. For example, demographic and health trends such as total fertility and crude birth rates have remained high in Van compared to Ankara. In fact, fertility rates are nearly twice as high in the eastern region (4.1 children per woman) compared to the central one (2.4 children per woman) (TDHS, 1994). There is also the predictable trend in the more urban areas towards modification of long-held traditional beliefs and values that still remain very strong in the more rural areas.

It was precisely these regional differences within Turkey that led us to design a study encompassing both these areas so that we could identify the common as well as the different factors responsible for fertility behaviour, particularly the practice of abortion.

Sample Size

A sample of 553 households was estimated as representative for each province, based on a sampling frame prepared by Hacettepe University in 1988. The total sample size was divided proportionally by type of community (urban, semi-urban, etc.) for each province. Equal probability was given to each eligible member of the communities selected. The sampling procedure was done by the State Institute of Statistics in Turkey. In each household both men and women were to be interviewed. As abortion is legal in Turkey, we felt it would be possible to interview men, which is rarely done in abortion studies.

Variables

We examined the following independent variables: type of community; family structure (i.e., nuclear, extended, etc.); socioeconomic status of the family; personal characteristics (age, education, occupation, economic status, duration of marriage, etc.). The intervening variables were: general view of women by men and by the women themselves (women's self-esteem); communication between couples; information, education and counselling on abortion; availability, accessibility and acceptability of the health care services. We also examined the attitudes of the couples towards hypothetical conditions related to abortion. We examined the following dependent variables: reproductive history; fertility regulating behaviour and attitudes; induced abortion. Past experience with induced abortion included information received from the provider, services received (availability and quality), contraceptive use before and after an abortion, feelings afterwards, and cost.

Focus Group Discussions

In the first phase of research, 13 focus group sessions were conducted in Ankara and 12 focus group sessions were conducted in Van with married women aged 25–50 in groups in each of the settlement units. Women were not together with men; a total of six focus group discussions were held with the men only, with three group discussions in each province. In addition, 15 semi-structured key informant interviews in Van and 12 interviews in Ankara were conducted at the professional level. Using information obtained from these focus group discussions, the questionnaires for the women and their husbands were developed.

Questionnaires

In this second phase of research, community-based data were collected by the use of pilot-tested questionnaires. Trained female interviewers interviewed 547 women and trained male interviewers interviewed 547 men in Ankara province. These figures were 544 and 541, respectively, for Van province.

In-Depth Personal Interviews

In this third phase of research, in-depth interviews with married women and their husbands were planned. The women chosen were to have had at least three induced abortions or a difficult abortion experience. This criteria was modified later, however, and 20 women in Van and 15 women in Ankara who were pregnant during the survey and wanted to end the pregnancy were interviewed in depth.

The Study Population

Sociodemographic Characteristics of the Sample

Sociodemographic characteristics of the women in both study provinces are summarized in Table 9.1. We found the usual differences between the urban and rural populations.

Table 9.1: Some Sociodemographic Characteristics of Women in Ankara and Van Provinces (in percentage)

	Ankara N = 547	Van N = 544
Type of community (present)		
Urban/metropol	24.9	25.2
Semi-urban	8.8	17.6
Rural	14.3	57.2
Squatter	52.0	–
Age (years)		
<19	1.1	12.2
20–29	39.7	44.2
30–39	38.5	33.3
40+	20.7	10.3
Education		
No formal education	17.9	71.1
Primary school	51.2	21.7
Secondary school	30.9	7.2
Pregnancies		
Average (number)	4.1	5.4
Abortions		
Spontaneous	22.1	22.4
Induced	41.0	13.7
Number of induced abortions		
0	59.0	85.5
1–2	30.3	12.6
3+	10.7	0.9

Most of the women in both provinces were between 20–39 years of age. The educational level of women was higher in Ankara; 40 per cent of the women had secondary school education or more compared to the women in Van, where 72 per cent had no formal education.

The pattern of fertility was also different in the two provinces, as expected. Multiparity (five pregnancies or more), average number of pregnancies, and average number of children were all higher in the more rural province of Van than in Ankara. The fertility pattern in Van is nearly the same as derived from national surveys; in Ankara, however, it is much higher than the provincial figure, reflecting the lower socioeconomic status of the families in our study population. Similarly, in Ankara, 41 per cent of the women had one or more induced abortions. This figure was significantly lower in Van, at 14 per cent. Repeat abortion (more than 3) was also much higher in Ankara than in Van; 11 per cent and 1 per cent, respectively.

The average age of first marriage is 18.9 years in Ankara and 17.4 in Van; both figures are close to the national average. Civil marriage has been compulsory since 1926 and polygamy is prohibited by law. However, it is not uncommon for some people to have only a religious marriage, which is not legal, and at the same time practise polygamy. Unfortunately, this kind of arrangement impairs the status of women, who in either situation have no legal rights. As expected, many more women in Van than in Ankara had only a religious marriage, 26.5 per cent compared to 3.5 per cent. The opinion regarding polygamous relationships followed this same pattern, with an even wider margin of difference: in Van, 82 per cent of the women accepted the idea of polygamy compared to only 11.5 per cent in Ankara. Obviously, urban life in Turkey has had a tendency to alter long-standing, more traditional cultural views.

In the Ankara region, the proportion of women living in squatter settlements was high (52 per cent), although the proportion living in such settlements for a long period was low (12 per cent), which reflects the rapid migration and unstable characteristics of such neighbourhoods. By contrast, in the Van region, the proportion of women living in squatter settlements was negligible, indicating that the squatter phenomenon is one that tends to develop mostly in large urban centres. Women in Van tended to be of rural origin and of rural residence, with a much smaller proportion living for most of their lives in an urban area.

Fertility Behaviour

Unwanted Pregnancy

In our sample, 6 per cent of the women in Ankara, and 18.1 per cent in Van were currently pregnant. Eighteen per cent of these current pregnancies were unwanted in Ankara; and 43 per cent were unwanted in Van. So while there were fewer pregnancies in the more urban areas, a much greater percentage of them were wanted or planned compared to the situation in the more rural areas, where nearly half of the women were experiencing an unwanted pregnancy. Again, the urban versus rural variation is an expected one.

Of all the currently pregnant women, 70 per cent were not using any contraceptive method before this pregnancy. Seventy-eight per cent of the pregnant women in Ankara and 69 per cent in Van, however, said they planned to use contraception after this current pregnancy. Obviously, the desire to limit family size is high in both these communities; and it is equally high in both urban and rural areas.

The Unmet Need for Family Planning

The proportions of men and women who wanted to limit their family size was remarkably high and similar, despite regional and urban/rural differences in characteristics of the families in the two study areas. Also remarkable was the degree of consensus between men and women. Eighty per cent of both men and women in Ankara and 70 per cent of both men and women in Van did not want any more children.

Similarly, 37 per cent of women in Ankara and 53 per cent in Van said that they had more children than they wanted. The most frequent reason given for this situation was lack of information on contraceptive methods; this was stated by 52 per cent of the women in Ankara and 58 per cent in Van. Other reasons given included: son preference (12 per cent in Ankara and 4 per cent in Van); and God's will (17 per cent in Van and 1.4 per cent in Ankara). These responses clearly indicate that there is an unmet need for family planning in these communities, or at least a need to improve the quality of the services being offered.

Main Results

We concentrate now on the main issue of our research: the determinants of induced abortion. In Turkey, it is clear that the primary determinant of abortion practice is the high rate of withdrawal, which surpasses the use of modern contraceptive methods. Uncovering the factors responsible for this very specific fertility behaviour became the main focus of our research and a discussion of our findings follows.

Contraceptive Knowledge and Use

To get a better grasp of the reasons why in a country with a fairly high level of contraceptive knowledge and presumably good access to contraception, prevalence of the more traditional and less effective method of withdrawal is so high, we began by taking a closer look at actual contraceptive knowledge and use. We found that the general level of contraceptive knowledge in both provinces was fairly high, averaging over 80 per cent for both oral contraceptives and IUDs in Ankara, and over 60 per cent in Van. However, when we probed into the quality of this knowledge, we found that both men and women had a much lower understanding of how modern methods of contraception actually work. (See Table 9.2.)

As expected, contraceptive knowledge was lower in the more rural Van province than in metropolitan Ankara. It was interesting, however, to discover that knowledge of existing male methods was significantly lower than knowledge of female methods. For example, 34 per cent of the men in Ankara and 53 per cent of the men in Van did not know anything about tubal ligation. Similarly, vasectomy is not known by 45 per cent of men and 54 per cent of women in Ankara and 75 per cent of men and 68 per cent of women in Van. Oral contraceptives were the best known in both provinces.

In both provinces the majority of women learned about contraceptive methods from friends and relatives; health personnel were the next source of

Table 9.2: Contraceptive Knowledge by Province and Gender

Method/Province	Knowledge					
	Spontaneous		After Probing		None	
	Male	Female	Male	Female	...ale	Female
Ankara						
Pill	64.2	82.6	31.8	15.4	4.0	2.0
IUD	62.3	86.6	34.2	12.6	3.5	0.7
Condom	50.6	50.2	37.1	39.6	12.2	10.3
Withdrawal	27.4	51.3	58.3	42.5	14.3	6.2
Rhythm	9.7	15.2	44.6	36.4	45.7	48.4
Sterilization						
Female	10.2	17.4	55.9	71.1	33.8	11.6
Male	7.7	3.3	47.2	42.5	45.2	54.2
Van						
Pill	43.6	63.1	47.5	30.0	8.9	3.9
IUD	36.9	60.4	37.5	30.4	25.6	9.3
Condom	18.6	23.9	41.2	45.0	40.3	31.1
Withdrawal	14.1	37.0	47.1	40.7	38.8	22.2
Rhythm	2.6	3.1	36.0	19.8	61.4	77.1
Sterilization						
Female	6.7	10.4	40.3	54.6	53.1	35.0
Male	0.9	3.1	23.9	29.3	75.1	67.6

information. This could explain some of the difference between general knowledge of a method and more precise knowledge of how it works. We also found that surgical contraception, especially vasectomy, was not learned from health personnel, which again shows the need to improve the quality of the information, particularly about male methods. The mass media was a source of information about contraceptive methods for less than 20 per cent of the women. Similarly, men learn about contraceptives in Turkey not from the formal health system but through peer discussions and from what they pick up in magazines and the media. Most of this information is inaccurate and therefore often of little value when they need to contribute to making critical decisions about fertility regulation.

Current contraceptive use of women in Ankara and Van provinces is summarized in Table 9.3. Not surprisingly, overall contraceptive prevalence was almost twice as high in the more urban province of Ankara as in Van (79 per cent compared to 44 per cent). The same was true of prevalence of modern methods (43 per cent and 22 per cent, respectively). These overall rates in Ankara were somewhat higher than the national average; and in Van they were somewhat lower. These patterns fit the urban/rural profile of our study group. The IUD was the most common modern method in both provinces, but used by only 30 per cent of the couples in Ankara and 15 per cent in Van. The prevalence of surgical contraception was very low in both provinces, as

Table 9.3: Contraceptive Use Among Women in Ankara and
Van Provinces (in percentage)

Use/Method	Ankara N = 546	Van N = 540
Currently Using	79.1	44.3
Method		
Pill	3.8	3.0
IUD	29.5	15.0
Condom	6.4	3.0
Withdrawal	32.6	20.6
Sterilization		
Female	3.5	0.9
Male	0.0	0.4
Other	3.3	1.4

was the prevalence of oral contraception, which was only 4 per cent in Ankara and 3 per cent in Van.

Withdrawal was the most common traditional method in both provinces (33 per cent in Ankara and 21 per cent in Van), again, a pattern consistent with the national trend of withdrawal being the most widely used method in Turkey today. What was significant, however, was that the prevalence of less effective methods was higher in the more urban province of Ankara than in Van (36 per cent compared to 22 per cent), which gave us our first evidence that the use of withdrawal may not be merely a function of knowledge and/or access to modern methods, especially in the face of such a strong desire on the part of couples in Turkey to limit family size.

The Role of Turkish Men in Fertility Regulation

We found that a very important key to the use of withdrawal among couples related to the role of men in reproductive decision-making, which in our study, remained fundamentally unaffected by urban/rural variations.

To begin with, we found that a high proportion of women in both provinces thought that the man should choose the contraceptive method. Only 39 per cent of women in Ankara and 35 per cent of women in Van said that the contraceptive method should be chosen by the woman herself.

In keeping with this cultural view, the choice of contraceptive method was made by the couple together, according to the responses of 86 per cent of the women from Ankara; however, according to the men from this province, this joint selection was made by a somewhat smaller number of couples, 68 per cent. Similarly, 87 per cent of the women from Van said that the choice of contraceptive method was made by the couple together; but the men claimed that this was true to a much lesser extent, 38 per cent. The percentages of both men and women who said that the woman chooses the method herself were higher in the more urban province of Ankara than in Van, as expected. It seems that women in the study may be exaggerating the role that men play in decisions about contraceptive use.

Similarly, a large number of both men (51 per cent) and women (56 per cent) from Van province said that the man should make the decision of whether the woman should have an abortion. The women who thought that this was their own decision were from Ankara only and were relatively few: less than one in five; there were some men in Ankara who also shared this opinion.

These stated opinions, whether exaggerated or not, do confirm that in this society men may have a significant influence over the selection of fertility regulation options. Moreover, their influence is clearly stronger in the more rural region. This is further supported by the finding that contraceptive prevalence of more effective methods and the rate of induced abortion was highest in the total study group among women who did not want any more children in the metropolitan area of Ankara, where the cultural traditions related to men's influence and the use of withdrawal would predictably lose some of their influence. As is the case in other developing countries, women living in these squatter settlements, although usually of rural origin, must adopt different strategies in order to survive in this new and wholly different environment, where they are frequently without a male partner for long periods of time. Conversely, only 13 per cent of the women in Van who did not want any more children used effective contraceptive methods; and among them the rate of induced abortion also appeared to be very low.

If men do influence contraceptive decisions within the family in Turkey, then it was not surprising to find that their knowledge of contraception is lower than women's, particularly of modern methods. For example, although nationwide studies show that the IUD is a well-known method in Turkey, 26 per cent of men in Van province, even when probed, did not know about the method; in Ankara, the proportion was an even lower, 4 per cent. Such influence shows itself in the low use of modern methods and the high prevalence of withdrawal. (See Tables 9.2 and 9.3.)

We began to see the choice of withdrawal as the best solution for couples who have misinformation and strong fears about the side effects of more modern methods, but who also have a strong desire to limit their family size. (The chapter by Bulut and Toubia in this same volume provides more detail about the negative opinion many Turkish couples have about modern methods.)

The choice of withdrawal also seemed to provide a solution to fertility regulation that was most in harmony with long-held traditional cultural views in Turkey. For example, during our discussions about family size, we discovered a somewhat contradictory societal force, which expressed itself as a stigma against childless women. This was a strong view, despite the general opinion of our study population that many families have more children than they want. We were told in both provinces that childless women were pitied or treated negatively by other women and members of their larger household. Moreover, nearly half the men in both provinces felt that a large progeny was important. Among the women, however, this feeling was much lower: only 17.6 per cent of the women in Ankara and even in rural Van, 41 per cent, felt that women with large families were more respected by their neighbours.

Here again, the choice of withdrawal seems to be more an expression of the men's preference and influence; the method has some effectiveness against pregnancy, but is male-controlled and in no way impairs a couple's ability to have children, offering the greatest degree of flexibility and freedom to conceive whenever they should decide to do so.

The Effect of a Couple's Education on Fertility Regulation

We wanted to see if the growing evidence for a strong relationship between the use of withdrawal and men's preferences held up against the more accepted influences on fertility regulation, such as education. We examined the relationship between the educational level of both men and women and their fertility regulation behaviour. (The results are summarized in Table 9.4.) There was a clear inverse relationship in both provinces between educational

Table 9.4: Education of Men and Women and Contraceptive Practice, Ankara and Van (in percentage)

	Non-User	Effective Method	Ineffective Method
Men			
Ankara			
Illiterate	66.6	–	33.4
Literate	28.6	28.5	42.9
Primary school	25.2	40.4	33.4
Secondary school+	16.5	50.9	31.6
Van			
Illiterate	83.9	3.6	12.5
Literate	71.0	12.9	16.1
Primary school	60.8	24.6	13.6
Secondary school+	33.3	32.7	34.0
Women			
Ankara			
Illiterate	40.3	19.4	40.3
Literate	26.1	17.4	56.5
Primary school	23.6	42.1	34.3
Secondary school+	16.1	56.5	27.4
Van			
Illiterate	68.2	17.4	14.4
Literate	44.3	16.4	39.3
Primary school	40.7	34.8	24.5
Secondary school+	28.2	51.3	20.5

level and use of contraception, with non-use highest among the least educated men and women. This was expected. The significant finding was that the use of effective contraceptive methods was higher when the educational level of the man was higher, in both provinces. The same relationship held true for women in both contexts. However, the relationship between education and use of ineffective methods was less clear. Men in Ankara use withdrawal fairly consistently across all educational levels; in Van men with higher education tended to use ineffective methods more than those with less education—possibly again indicating that in rural areas even the use of methods such as withdrawal requires education and motivation. These findings point to the possibility that the education of the man is a stronger factor than access or availability of modern methods in fertility regulation.

Woman's Work Status

We also examined the effect of women's work status on fertility regulation, including abortion. The results showed that if a woman has a paid job, she practises effective contraception more and has a fewer number of pregnancies than women who are not working for wages. This was particularly the case in Ankara. But working women in Van and in Ankara had more abortions on an average than non-working women, probably because of a fear of losing their jobs. Even in the higher fertility Van province, working women had fewer pregnancies and more abortions than those who stayed at home. (These results are summarized in Table 9.5.)

Table 9.5: **Women's Work Status by Contraceptive Use and Abortion, Ankara and Van**

Work Status	Using Effective Methods (%)	Had an Abortion (%)	Average No. of Abortions per Woman	Average No. of Pregnancies per Woman
Ankara				
Not working (170)	31.8	42.0	0.8	4.2
Working (440)	56.3	38.5	1.1	3.2
Van				
Not working (30)	55.9	28.6	0.2	5.1
Working (510)	36.7	43.3	0.5	3.3

Obviously, women working for wages, outside their home, are living under a different set of circumstances, and are exposed to different influences, than women who stay home and continue with their traditional household duties. Moreover, these influences seem to outweigh the influence of traditional cultural values that place men in a more dominant decision-making role, because these women can be seen to be relying less on their husbands' opinion and on the method of withdrawal. Contraceptive failure is a major threat to the improved status of these women as independent wage earners.

What Influences These Particular Gender Relations?

We wanted to go at least one step further in understanding the cultural view among both the women and men in our study that men should influence, and at times even dominate, decisions about fertility regulation.

We designed a series of broad questions whose answers would tell us more about how men perceive women and how women see themselves. For example, we asked: 'Can women explain their views and thoughts to men?' The answer was positive from only a third of both men and women in both provinces: 30 per cent of the men and 35 per cent of the women in Ankara; and 37 per cent of the men and 27 per cent of the women in Van. Another question was: 'Is it true that men are generally more intelligent than women?' In Ankara, 30 per cent of the men and 25 per cent of the women said yes. In Van, the numbers were even higher; a clear majority of both men and women (62 per cent and 52 per cent, respectively) thought that men were more intelligent than women. Another question was: 'If a women does not obey her husband, does the husband have a right to beat her?' In Ankara, more than a third of both men and women said yes (32 per cent and 35 per cent, respectively). Once again, in Van, the numbers were much higher; two-thirds of both the men and women answered affirmatively (63 per cent and 60 per cent, respectively).

It was obvious that the overall status of women, as evaluated by various questions in the study, was very poor, particularly among the low-income women in both provinces. The situation was the worst for the women in Van province, where the traditional cultural values continue to have a strong influence on the daily lives of people.

The next step was to compare these results to fertility regulation behaviour (Table 9.6). Predictably, women in both provinces who thought that men are generally more intelligent than women, that men have a right to beat their wives, and other views that indicated low self-esteem, tended to use effective contraception less, have fewer induced abortions, and have a higher average fertility than women who did not agree with these statements. In short, these women were more influenced by their husbands in their choice of contraceptive method and in their patterns of fertility behaviour. This relationship between degree of self-esteem and the influence of the husband was predictably stronger among the women in Van province.

Cultural Preferences in Contraceptive Service Delivery

Although gender relations clearly seemed to be a very important factor in explaining the high rate of withdrawal, and subsequently abortion, in our study population, we continued to explore other possible sociocultural factors. We discovered another factor that seemed to be contributing to the high prevalence of withdrawal. The existing locations where other contraceptive

Table 9.6: Women's Self-Esteem by Contraceptive Use and Abortion, Ankara and Van

Probing Question	Using Effective Methods (%)	Had an Induced Abortion (%)
As a Rule, Men are More Intelligent than Women?		
Ankara		
Agrees (139)	35.3	35.3
Does not agree (380)	50.3	42.6
Van		
Agrees (278)	18.0	10.1
Does not agree (236)	31.4	17.4
A Man Has the Right to Beat His Wife if She Does Not Obey?		
Ankara		
Agrees (187)	46.5	39.6
Does not agree (351)	44.7	42.2
Van		
Agrees (319)	17.9	9.4
Does not agree (212)	32.1	20.3

options are offered did not always coincide with the preferences of the Turkish couples in our study. In Ankara, for example, most women preferred to go to the pharmacy to get oral contraceptives and the condom; hospitals were preferred as sources for the IUD. In Van also, the pharmacy was preferred for oral contraceptives; health centres were used more often for the condom and the IUD.

Moreover, the providers for specific methods are not often what women in both provinces would wish either. They prefer female physicians or nurse/midwives over male physicians, especially for IUD insertion. In both provinces, hospital services were preferred for IUD insertion and for induced abortion, particularly if they knew that the physician or midwife in charge was a female. Unfortunately, there are not many female physicians in public hospitals available to perform an abortion; however, nurse/midwives in Turkey are allowed to insert IUDs following a special training programme.

Sociocultural Views About Induced Abortion

While most Turkish couples wish to limit family size, there is also a strong emphasis in Turkish society on bearing healthy children. The solution of couples to this 'dilemma', the method of withdrawal, generally requires abortion as a back-up method. Did the sociocultural view of abortion support or conflict with this solution?

We discovered that some men and women in both provinces thought of abortion as a fertility regulation method: 21 per cent of men and 3 per cent of women in Ankara; and 26 per cent of men and 18 per cent of women in Van.

It is noteworthy that the men were significantly more in favour of abortion for this purpose than the women in both provinces. It is also important to note that the women in Ankara were much less in favour of this than the women in Van, which illustrates that a man's influence over his wife's view of abortion, as well as its actual practice, is stronger in the rural province, as we have been finding all along.

Even though some couples accepted abortion as a method of fertility regulation, however, most couples in both provinces still thought of abortion as sinful. Predictably, this conservative view was stronger in Van province. It is interesting to note that women in both provinces were more conservative than their spouses on this issue. The general conservative attitude of both men and women towards induced abortion, in the face of a high rate of use of withdrawal, which requires abortion as a back-up method, points again to a strong desire to limit family size and the large unmet need for family planning in Turkey.

Contrary to their views on abortion, the large majority of the study population in both provinces did not think of contraceptive use as a sin. This is not surprising, given the fact that 98 per cent of the population of Turkey is Muslim, a religion that is more receptive to the idea of fertility regulation than many other religions.

Quality of Abortion Services: Public and Private

We were perplexed that the relatively easy access to safe abortion services in Turkey would not be contributing to higher use rates of modern contraceptive methods, in keeping with the general trend found in most developing countries with a similar profile. Were sociocultural factors a stronger influence than service delivery issues? Without it being a main focus of our study, we tried to get some sense of the quality of abortion services, particularly in terms of postpartum contraceptive counselling.

In Turkey, abortion services are provided both by public hospitals, where only a little money is charged, and by the private sector, where the cost is naturally higher. In the study population, almost half the women paid a significant amount of money for their last induced abortion. This would indicate that even in Ankara, where hospital abortion services are more easily available than in the more rural province of Van, women are using the private sector more. Although our research did not clearly indicate why this was happening, it is generally known that doctors prefer to provide abortions in private practice rather than in hospitals. Given the tendency of men to dominate decisions about fertility practice, the more significant difference between private and public services is that women do not need to provide a consent form from the husband for a private procedure.

Although family planning counselling should be an integral part of abortion services, only one-third of the abortion clients in our study received counselling or information about family planning methods. This appeared to be true, irrespective of whether the abortion service was performed in a public hospital or by a private doctor. (This is consistent with the results found in the study on the quality of abortion services in Istanbul by Bulut and Toubia in this same volume. The reader is referred to this article for additional, important detail about this aspect of the abortion experience in Turkey.)

We also found that after the experience of abortion, women began to use contraception more, but not as much as would be expected. About 8 per cent of the women had an unwanted pregnancy after their last induced abortion. Further analysis would be required to see which factor had the strongest influence here, poor service quality or gender relations.

Summary

Unwanted pregnancy continues to be a major health problem in Turkey today, despite the fact that there has been a steady increase in contraceptive prevalence over the last three decades. Moreover, this study has provided evidence to show that Turkey has a serious unmet need for family planning. The proportions of men and women in the communities we studied who wanted to limit their family size was remarkably high, and similar, despite regional and urban/rural differences in characteristics of the families. Also remarkable was the degree of consensus between men and women.

Although most couples want to limit their family size, and there are effective contraceptive methods available in the country, couples are not using them. The traditional method of withdrawal has remained the most widely used method among currently married women, and therefore is widely believed to be the primary determinant of abortion practice in Turkey.

The principal finding emerging from this study is that a very important key to the use of withdrawal among couples relates to the active role of men in reproductive decision-making, which in our study remained fundamentally unaffected by urban/rural variations. On this more general theme, some points in particular should be summarized.

To begin with, we found that a high proportion of women in both provinces thought that the man should choose the contraceptive method; only a third of the women thought that the woman should choose the method herself. Similarly, a large number of both men and women, although mostly from the more rural province, said that the man should make the decision of whether the woman should have an abortion. The women who thought that this was their own decision were from the more urban area only and were relatively few in number.

Further evidence to support these opinions that in this society men have a significant influence over the selection of fertility regulation options, particularly in rural areas where cultural traditions remain unaltered, was the finding that men's knowledge of contraception was significantly lower than women's, particularly of modern methods. We clearly saw this reflected by the fact that contraceptive prevalence of more effective methods and the rate of induced abortion was highest in the total study group among women who did not want any more children in the metropolitan area of Ankara, where women's empowerment increases under the modernizing effects of a stronger urban culture. Conversely, in the rural area, a much smaller number of women who did not want any more children used effective contraceptive methods or had induced abortions.

The choice of withdrawal, in addition to offering the best solution to couples who want to limit their family size but who have strong fears about the side effects of more modern methods, also seemed to provide a solution to fertility regulation that was most in harmony with a long-held traditional value in Turkey of large families. Nearly half the men in both provinces felt that a large progeny was important, although a far smaller proportion of women felt this way.

Moreover, the evidence for a strong relationship between the use of withdrawal and men's preferences held up against the more accepted influence of education on fertility regulation. That is, the use of effective contraceptive methods was higher when the educational level of the man was higher, in both provinces.

Even though the influence of gender relations continued to be such a strong factor, we managed to find a possible counter-influence. We found that if a woman had a paid job, she practised effective contraception more and had fewer pregnancies than women who were not working for wages and stayed at home. This relationship also held up in the more rural province. The new influences found outside the household, in a wage-earning environment, seem to outweigh the influence of traditional cultural values that place men in a more dominant decision-making role.

Indeed, when we evaluated the overall status of women, we found that it was very poor, particularly among the low-income women in both provinces. The situation was the worst for the women living in the more rural area. When we analyzed the relationship between these results to fertility regulation behaviour, predictably, women in both provinces who had views that indicated low self-esteem, tended to use effective contraception less, have fewer induced abortions, and have a higher average fertility than women who had more self-esteem.

Other sociocultural factors that possibly have a degree of influence on couples' choice of withdrawal were related to service delivery. Women had clear preferences for locations where contraceptives should be provided, which did not coincide with existing arrangements. And there was a clear preference for female providers, particularly for IUD insertion and for abortion.

The sociocultural view of abortion both supported and conflicted with its practice, and was related again to the character of gender relations among couples. Men were significantly more in favour of abortion as a fertility regulation method than the women and this influence over the women's view, as well as her practise of the method, was stronger in the rural province. The general attitude of men and women towards abortion, however, was conservative, which, in the face of such a high rate of withdrawal which requires abortion as a back-up method, points again to a strong desire to limit family size and the large unmet need for family planning in Turkey.

It is significant that contraceptive use is not thought of as a sin by the large majority of the couples, so that there is no religious obstacle to programme efforts. The greater obstacles seem to be on the side of service providers in that only one-third of the abortion clients in our study received counselling or information about family planning methods. This appeared to be true, irrespective of whether the abortion service was performed in a public hospital or by a private doctor.

Recommendations and Policy Impact

The principal investigator of this study became the General Director of MCH/Family Planning in the Ministry of Health in Turkey. This provided an immediate opportunity to disseminate some of the more significant results of this study in a way that would help to implement changes in the national family planning programme of Turkey. Indeed, the results of our study have already had an impact on policy in the country, by providing key information to implement several new strategies and new approaches in family planning programmes, including abortion care. Important new policies were adopted to improve reproductive health through reassessing and strengthening existing interventions or developing new ones.

Institutional Changes

A 'National Advisory Board on Population Planning' was formed in Turkey in early 1993 to report to the government's State Planning Organization, the highest body in charge of setting national planning and development policies. This Board consisted of high-level representatives from the Ministries of Education and Defense, the State Planning Organization, Turkish radio and television, the Higher Educational Council, the Turkish Medical Association, the Turkish Midwifery Association, religious authorities, some NGOs, and five scientists who have experience with the population planning issue. This Board is chaired by the Minister of Health and its Secretariat is the General Directorate of MCH/FP. The main objectives of the Board are to strengthen intersectoral collaboration to improve the status of women and to improve IEC on reproductive health, especially information on effective contraceptive methods.

At the first meeting of the Board, relevant strategies were formulated and a plan of action was prepared. Some examples of the planned activities include:

(*a*) The Ministry of Education will integrate the subject of reproductive health into the secondary education curriculum. The Ministry also decided to integrate the subject of family planning into in-service training of schoolteachers.

(*b*) The Ministry of Defense will provide educational programmes on reproductive health, especially family planning methods, to male soldiers between the ages of 20–21, who are recruited from different parts of the country into military station posts for one-and-a-half years. This approach is an attempt to address the problem of low contraceptive knowledge among men generally.

(*c*) Information on family planning as well as on effective contraceptive methods will be disseminated through religious leaders (Imams). In Turkey, each village has three community leaders, which are the head of the village, the Imam and the school principal or main teacher. Usually, people come to them for advice on various issues, health being one of them. The religious authorities decided to provide more information on health to the Imams during their training in order that they can provide correct information to the community.

Another intervention the Board agreed to was to collaborate with Turkish Radio Television Association to disseminate correct information on reproductive health and FP methods. The TV programmes utilized study results in preparation of the broadcasts; for example, special attention was given to TV spots for men.

A General Directorate on the Status of Women was established in 1990 to assist in the improvement of women's legal rights and in the monitoring of discrimination against women in Turkey. Our study results have helped to inform this Directorate about how existing cultural and psychosocial problems impair women's health and ability to undertake action leading to improved reproductive health.

Undoubtedly, an important policy impact was the strengthening at the national government planning level, of the integration and relationship between population and development policy. In Turkey, every five years since 1960, a five-year socioeconomic plan is prepared and implemented by the government's State Planning Organization. In 1993, preparation of the next plan of 1995–2000 was started, with the help of several expert committees. For the first time in the State Planning Organization's history, population and family planning were considered as an integral aspects of the country's development. They were given their due significance by incorporating them under independent sections in the draft of the new plan. Recommendations, based on the research findings of our study in Ankara and Van provinces, were included and specific intervention strategies were adopted to reach national targets to improve women's reproductive health.

Family Planning Information and Counselling Programme Impact

An important policy area that requires improvement and where this study was particularly important in detecting flaws, was in the information and counselling aspects of family planning services. Because our study showed that information and counselling was poor or insufficient, particularly for abortion clients, a new policy was adopted by the national family planning programme to make it an integral part of in-service training programmes of the health personnel working in family planning. The importance of providing good counselling on contraception to abortion clients before the procedure was emphasized.

The IEC programmes in Turkey should also concentrate on providing more information about how methods actually work, especially to men, and they should treat both male and female methods equally, since we found that there had been a distinct bias in our IEC programmes towards female methods only. The highest priority for these efforts should be the rural settlements.

Assessments performed in a few health centres where information and education activities had been improved, including the provision to women during the antenatal period of materials on effective contraceptive methods, and improved information to postpartum and post-abortion clients, showed a marked increase in the practice of effective contraception.

Additional strategies related to service delivery could also be considered based on the results of this study. For example, increasing pill availability in commercial outlets and teaching pharmacists how to screen potential clients might lead to an increase in oral contraceptive use, especially if counselling could be incorporated in the training given to these providers. More generally, in areas where female health personnel are preferred, improving the training of nurse-midwives could be given priority.

✝ References

Akin, A. 1983. Sociomedical aspects of abortion. In: A. Akin. *Family planning handbook for physicians*. Ankara, Turkey: Tanit Publishers.

Akin, A. and H. Kisnisci. 1973. *An epidemiological study on induced abortion in Turkey*. Ankara, Turkey: Hacettepe University publication D.25.

Cohen, L. et al. 1984. Coping with abortion. *Journal of Human Stress* 10 (3): 140–45.

Demographic and Health Survey (DHS). 1994. *Turkish Demographic and Health Survey—1993*, Ankara, Turkey: Hacettepe University and Ministry of Health.

Eren, N. et al. 1983. Physicians versus auxiliary midwives as providers of IUD services: A study in Turkey and the Philippines. *Studies in Family Planning* 14: 34–37.

Fisek, N.H. et al. 1978. The effects of husband and wife education on family planning in rural areas in Turkey. *Studies in Family Planning* 9 (10–11): 280–85.

Handy, J.A. 1982. Psychological and social aspects of induced abortion. *British Journal of Clinical Psychology* 21 (1): 29–41.

International Planned Parenthood Federation (IPPF). 1984. Male involvement in family planning: Trends and directions. *IPPF Male Involvement in Family Planning: Programme Initiatives.* London: IPPF.

Ministry of Health, Turkey. 1985. *Report on the baseline study in nine provinces in Turkey.* Ankara, Turkey: Ministry of Health.

Turkish Demographic and Health Survey (TDHS). 1993, 1994. Ankara, Turkey: Ministry of Health and Institute of Population Studies, Hacettepe University. January 1994.

Tezcan, S. and A.R. Omran. 1981. Prevalence and reporting of induced abortion in Turkey: Two survey techniques. *Studies in Family Planning* 12 (6/7): 262–71.

Turkish Population and Health Survey, 1988. 1989. Ankara, Turkey: Institute of Population Studies publication, Hacettepe University.

UNICEF. 1991. The Situation Analysis of Mothers and Children in Turkey. Series No. 2, UNICEF Turkey Office, April 1991.

PART II

Quality of Abortion Care

SECTION A

Women's Perspectives

10

Determinants and Medical Characteristics of Induced Abortion Among Poor Urban Women in North-East Brazil

Chizuru Misago and Walter Fonseca

Introduction

Designing an effective intervention programme to address the problem of induced abortion requires an understanding of the characteristics of women who seek it. Moreover, because the abortion situation varies from country to country, and even from region to region, any intervention programme has to be country or region specific. In this chapter, we present our findings on the determinants and medical characteristics of induced abortion in Fortaleza, north-east Brazil from a one-year prospective study of women admitted to hospitals with complications associated with pregnancy loss.

Study Context

In Brazil, induced abortion is a criminal offense except when the pregnancy seriously endangers the life of the pregnant woman, or when the pregnancy has occurred following rape. (So far, only one public hospital will perform an abortion for a rape victim, but several other public hospitals in Brazil are also trying to set up this 'legal abortion programme'.) The penalty for a woman who has an illegal abortion is imprisonment for one to 10 years, with twice that sentence for someone who practises or assists with the procedure (Penal Code Ats. 126–129, Decree Law No. 2848, 7 December, as amended in 1941 and 1969). Efforts to ease restrictions on abortion began in 1975 and to date have been unsuccessful.

Despite legal restrictions, and the fact that Brazil can be characterized as a mainly Catholic country where abortion is considered a sin, abortion is widely practised here. It is estimated that between 300,000 and 3.3 million illegal abortions are performed every year (Singh and Wulf, 1991). According to a more recent estimate calculated from data on the number of women hospitalized for treatment of abortion complications, after correcting for under-reporting and misreporting and adjusting to eliminate spontaneous abortions, the absolute number could be about 1.4 million per year (Singh and Wulf, 1994).

Fortaleza, our study site, is situated in the north-east of Brazil, in a tropical zone. It is the capital city of Ceará state, with a rapidly growing population of around two million people, over half of whom live in urban slums, or 'favelas'. This state is one of the poorest in the country, with an infant mortality rate that ranked among the highest in Brazil at 95 infant deaths per 1,000 live births in 1987, although there has been some improvement since then. Information on maternal health is quite scarce. A retrospective study at the Assis Chateaubriand Teaching Maternity Hospital of the Federal University of Ceará (MEAC/UFC), the largest public maternity hospital in Fortaleza, showed a maternal mortality ratio of 119 maternal deaths per 100,000 live births during the period of 1983–90 (Sa and Maia, 1990). In MEAC/UFC, abortions contributed 10 per cent of maternal deaths during the same period (Sa and Maia, 1990).

Local data suggest that induced abortion has increased in Fortaleza. In 1991, MEAC/UFC admitted a mean of 200 cases of abortion per month, an increase of about 55 per cent over 1990. These abortion admissions represent around 20 per cent of the hospital's total admissions, and were not accompanied by any significant increase in the hospital's operative capacity. The César Cals General Hospital of the State of Ceará Health Secretariat (HGCC/SSEC), another large public maternity hospital, admitted an average of 129 abortion cases per month from September to November 1991, representing 23 per cent of obstetric admissions.

One possible reason for the observed increase in the number of hospital admissions due to illegal abortion in Fortaleza is the widespread use of abortifacients obtained from private pharmacies. According to the results of a recent study on the use of abortifacients sold over the counter in pharmacies in Fortaleza, an abortifacient was offered during 121 of 190 visits for unwanted pregnancy (64 per cent), with misoprostol ('Cytotec') offered most frequently, in 82 per cent of the cases (Coelho et al., 1991). Misoprostol is a synthetic analogue of prostaglandin E_1, which is licensed in Brazil for the treatment of gastric and duodenal ulcers. The drug has some uterotonic effects, however, and so its use is medically contraindicated for pregnant women (Downie, 1991). Clearly, information about this side effect has spread rapidly among pharmacy personnel and among women in the general population who are seeking to end an unwanted pregnancy.

A deleterious effect of misoprostol on the development of the foetus cannot be ruled out. Congenital malformations have been reported in babies born to women exposed to misoprostol early in pregnancy in unsuccessful abortion attempts in Fortaleza as well as in other parts of Brazil (Fonseca et al., 1992; Gonzales et al., 1993). Studies of the determinants of induced abortion in the State of Ceará have therefore become a priority for the State Health Secretariat.

Objectives and Research Methodology

This study was originally designed to assess the extent of morbidity due to illegal abortion at the hospital level. It was conducted at the two main public maternity hospitals, MEAC/UFC and HGCC/SSEC, which serve primarily the urban poor population in Fortaleza. All women admitted to the two hospitals with a diagnosis of pregnancy loss from 1 October 1992 through 30 September 1993 were included in the sample.

Data were collected by trained interviewers using a structured questionnaire based on the core questionnaire prepared by the World Health Organization. There were four major parts: status at hospital admission; interview of subject; hospital discharge information; and additional country-specific questions, which examined the induced abortion procedures in detail. Data were collected from hospital record excerpts and by interviewing cases. Before the interview, the nature of the study was explained to each woman and her consent to participate in the study was obtained. Each participant was also assured of the confidentiality of her report and, whenever possible, anonymity. Interviews were conducted as privately as possible, and at a time convenient to the woman during her hospital stay. Interview topics included sociodemographic characteristics, reproductive history, contraceptive practices, and type of abortion, including a detailed description of the abortion method used. Detailed information was also recorded about each woman's hospital experience, including any medical complications, treatment, and duration of hospital stay.

A total of 2,094 and 2,322 cases were recruited from MEAC and HGCC, respectively. Women were classified into the following four categories, according to the WHO re-classification scheme (WHO, 1987):

1. 'Certainly' induced abortion: A case is classified as 'certainly' an induced abortion when the woman herself provides this information, when such information is provided by a health worker or a relative (in the case of a deceased woman), or when there is evidence of trauma or of a foreign body in the genital tract.
2. 'Probably' induced abortion: A case is classified as 'probably' an induced abortion when the woman: (a) has signs of an abortion accompanied by sepsis or peritonitis; and (b) states that the pregnancy was unplanned (either she was using a contraceptive method during the cycle of

conception or she was not using a contraceptive method because of reasons other than desired pregnancy).

3. *'Possibly' induced abortion:* A case is classified as 'possibly' an induced abortion if only one of the conditions listed under (2) above is present.

4. *'Spontaneous' abortion:* All other cases are classified as 'spontaneous' abortions.

Those cases that presented signs or a history of abortion, but with pregnancy still continuing, were classified as *'pregnancy continued'*.

Study Results

In interpreting the study results, it is important to keep in mind that it is not known what proportion of all induced abortions among poor women in Fortaleza result in complications that require admission to a hospital. Both total failures and total successes with an abortion attempt might be under-reported in our study population, because such women are less likely to seek hospital care. Therefore, these data may not be representative of all poor women who have induced abortion in the study area.

It is also important to note that our study was conducted in an urban population with relatively good access to health care services. Some findings, therefore, may not be applicable to other settings in Brazil, especially in rural areas. However, another study carried out in Rio de Janeiro in 1991 shows similar characteristics of women (Costa and Vessey, 1993). Although the economic situation in Brazil is very different between the impoverished northeast and the wealthier south-east, urban poor characteristics in both regions appear to be the same. Thus, the characteristics of the women in this study might be representative of the more general urban poor population of Brazil.

'Induced Abortion': Case Definition

A total of 4,359 abortion cases were recruited during the study period. Following the WHO classification method, 48 per cent of the total sample (2,084 women) had an abortion that was 'certainly' induced; 40 per cent (1,760 women) had a 'possibly' induced abortion; and 12 per cent (515 women) had a spontaneous abortion. In our discussion, we will use the term 'induced abortion' to mean a 'certainly' induced abortion. All but 10 of the women who had an induced abortion admitted that they had attempted to terminate their pregnancy (2,074).

Inevitably, misclassification of women's abortion status may have occurred, particularly among the cases identified as 'spontaneous'. This would be due to limitations of the methodology and the complex, sensitive nature of the study. An attempt was made to minimize misclassification bias by using a uniform criteria to identify abortion cases. Also important was ensuring good quality interviews by recruiting sympathetic, skillful and trained interviewers to collect the sensitive information required. A prospective hospital-based study in Rio de Janeiro interviewed 1,603 women admitted with abortion-related complications; and it is encouraging that their findings on the proportion of women classified as having an induced abortion (50 per cent) is similar to our study results (48 per cent) (Costa and Vessey, 1993). In contrast, a lower proportion of induced abortion cases (31 per cent) was found in a study carried out in Fortaleza that reviewed the records of women who underwent uterine evacuation in 1991 (Coelho et al., 1993).

Sociodemographic Characteristics

Table 10.1 shows the distribution of induced abortion cases according to selected sociodemographic characteristics. More than half the women (59.7 per cent) were 20–29 years of age and almost one-fourth (22.6 per cent) were less than 20 years of age. Only a small proportion of women were illiterate (4.3 per cent), and 73.2 per cent had some primary schooling. The majority

Table 10.1: Sociodemographic Characteristics of Women Admitted for Induced Abortion Complications

Characteristics	(N)	%
Age (years)		
< 19	471	22.6
20–24	750	36.0
25–29	493	23.7
30–34	242	11.6
35+	127	6.1
Marital status		
Single	1,094	52.5
Married/stable union	801	38.5
Separated/divorced/widow	188	9.0
Education (years)		
No schooling	90	4.3
1–4	577	27.7
5–8	947	45.5
8+	469	22.5
Occupation		
Housewife	708	34.0
Housemaid	315	15.1
Other service	263	12.6
Student	216	10.4
Business	184	8.8
Dress maker	154	7.4
Agriculture/industry	64	3.1
Unemployed/dependent	179	8.6
Total	2,083	100.0

(91.6 per cent) identified themselves as Catholic. Most women lived alone or were not in a stable union (61.5 per cent). The most commonly reported occupation was housewife (34.0 per cent); and about 10 per cent listed their occupation as 'student'.

Prior Pregnancy Outcome

The distribution of women admitted for induced abortion by prior pregnancy outcome is shown in Table 10.2. About 34 per cent had not experienced a previous live birth, while approximately 26 per cent had one live birth. Slightly over one-third (33.1 per cent) had two to four prior live births, and only 7.7 per cent were found to have five or more live births.

Table 10.2: Prior Pregnancy Outcomes of Women Admitted for Induced Abortion Complications

Prior Pregnancy Outcome	(N)	%
Live birth		
0	700	33.6
1–4	1,223	58.7
5+	160	7.7
Induced abortion		
0	1,621	77.8
1+	462	22.2
Spontaneous abortion		
0	1,836	88.1
1+	247	11.9

Approximately one-fourth of the women (22.2 per cent) reported a history of previous induced abortion, while 11.8 per cent had experienced a previous spontaneous abortion.

Medical Characteristics of Induced Abortion Cases

The mean gestational age at the time of abortion was 11.4 weeks, and the mean length of hospital stay was 1.7 days, as shown in Table 10.3. The majority of women (90.7 per cent) had no clinical signs of infection at admission. Antibiotics were used on a prophylactic or therapeutic basis for less than one-fourth of the women (20.6 per cent), and the mean duration of antibiotic therapy was 4.4 days. A small proportion of women (8.3 per cent) reported heavy vaginal bleeding at admission and only 2.9 per cent required a blood transfusion. The majority of cases (91.7 per cent) reported vaginal bleeding less than or similar to menstrual blood flow.

Table 10.3: Distribution of Women Admitted for Induced Abortion Complications, by Medical Characteristics

Characteristics	(N)	%
Mean gestational age (weeks)		11.4
Mean length of hospital stay (days)		1.7
Infection		
Yes	193	9.3
No	1,891	90.7
Use of antibiotics		
Yes	429	20.6
No	1,655	79.4
Mean length of antibiotic treatment (days)		4.4
Heavy bleeding at admission		
Yes	172	8.3
No	1,912	91.7
Use of blood transfusion		
Yes	60	2.9
No	2,024	97.1
Surgical procedure		
Curettage	1,965	94.3
Laparotomy	7	0.3
Other*	21	1.0
None	91	4.4
Total	2,084	100.0

* Most of these were manual removal of retained product of conception. There was no hysterectomy.

For most women (94.3 per cent), curettage was the only surgical procedure required; seven women received a laparotomy and no one had a hysterectomy. A few women did not require any surgical procedure at all (4.4 per cent).

Contraceptive Use

Table 10.4 shows the distribution of women according to contraceptive use when they became pregnant. Nearly two-thirds (61.1 per cent) were not using any contraceptive method at the time. Oral contraception was used by 12.3 per cent of women, and 1.7 per cent had been using an injectable. Condom use was reported by only 5.3 per cent; rhythm and withdrawal were reported by 11.2 per cent and 6.4 per cent, respectively. Other methods, including the diaphragm, spermicides and breastfeeding, were reported by 2.0 per cent of the women.

The most frequent reasons cited for not using any contraceptive method were: 'careless' (18.3 per cent); 'did not expect to have sexual intercourse' (18.3 per cent); 'thought not at risk of pregnancy' (13.8 per cent); and 'fear of side effects' (22.2 per cent). Lack of availability of contraceptive methods was reported by only 8 per cent.

Table 10.4: Distribution of 2,083 Induced Abortion Cases,
by Contraceptive Method Use at Month of Conception

Contraceptive Method	(N)	%
None	1,272	61.1
Oral contraceptive	256	12.3
Injectable	36	1.7
Condom	111	5.3
Rhythm	233	11.2
Withdrawal	134	6.4
Other*	41	2.0

* Including IUD, diaphragm, spermicide.

Methods Used by the Women to Induce Abortion

The procedures used by the 2,074 women who admitted they attempted to terminate their pregnancy are presented in Table 10.5. Most women tried more than one method to induce abortion. A full two-thirds (66 per cent) reported using misoprostol alone or in combination with another method. Mean cost per case of misoprostol was US $21 at the time of our study, which is cheaper than the mean cost women usually pay for an abortionist (US $41) or in a clinic under medical supervision (US $500–$1,000).

Table 10.5: Distribution of 2,074 Induced Abortion Cases,
by Women's Own Statement of Method

Method	(N)	%
Misoprostol		
Alone	607	29.3
With other methods	762	36.7
Other methods*	705	34.0

* Including herbal medication, other drugs, injections, etc.

The other frequently used medicines were: 'Cocktail', an injectable mixture of several hormonal preparations, such as oxytocin and prostigmine (240 women); 'Dicolantyl', or disopyramid, used by 82 women; and 'Ginacoside', a combination of normethandrone and methyloestradiol, used by 25 women. Another 14 per cent of the women in the sample drank only herbal tea as an abortifacient, to start bleeding. The remaining women said they used other methods, such as insertion of objects, catheter instillation and manual vacuum aspiration.

About half the women (49.5 per cent) had not sought anyone's advice before attempting self-induced abortion. Family members and friends were consulted by 40 per cent of the women. Only a small proportion of women, less than 3 per cent, consulted medical professionals; and only 7 per cent consulted non-medical practitioners to induce their abortions.

The most frequent reasons cited for inducing abortion were: 'cannot afford to have a child' (51.2 per cent); 'partner does not want a child' (21.7 per cent); and 'parent does not know about her pregnancy' (10.4 per cent). Only 2 per cent of the women reported the reason as contraceptive failure.

Discussion

Most significantly, our study results suggest that the use of misoprostol as an abortifacient, either alone or in combination with another method, is widespread among the poor urban women of Brazil, which confirm findings from two other recent studies (Costa and Vessey, 1993; Coelho et al., 1993). In fact, to our knowledge, Brazil is the first country where misoprostol is used so extensively as a means to circumvent the tight restriction on legal abortion. This situation continues, even though sales of the drug were suspended in 1991 in Ceará State and restricted in other states by the Brazilian federal regulatory agency.

With regard to determinants of abortion in our study, both women's marital status and age emerge as important characteristics in the induced abortion group, with two-thirds living alone or without a stable partner and nearly one-fourth teenagers. These results confirm findings of another study carried out in Rio de Janeiro (Costa and Vessey, 1993).

Our findings on the medical characteristics of the women in our study group differ substantially from those of Latin American women hospitalized with induced abortion complications (Baily et al., 1988, Fortney, 1981). Our respondents tended to induce abortion earlier, with about half the sample inducing at 10 weeks; and the mean number of days in the hospital was shorter, at 1.7 days, because less than 10 per cent of the women had some sign of infection on admission and very few reported heavy bleeding (8.3 per cent). Our finding of a relatively small proportion of women with severe complications of induced abortion might be related to the high number of women reporting the use of misoprostol alone or in combination with another method and very few reporting invasive methods, such as insertion of a foreign body or instillation of a catheter at clandestine clinics. It also suggests that most women may have sought hospital treatment soon after bleeding started and thus before severe infection developed.

Most women (61.1 per cent) were not using any contraceptive method at the time of conception. Worryingly, a very small proportion (5.3 per cent) of single women or those without a stable partner reported using condoms. Thus, if condoms prove to be an acceptable contraceptive method in this population, their use should be promoted particularly among these women, to help prevent the transmission of sexually transmitted diseases, including HIV/AIDS.

A recent study in north-east Brazil concluded that 35.7 per cent of reproductive-aged women reportedly use a modern contraceptive method, with tubal ligation the most prevalent (68.9 per cent). The majority of sterilized women are between 25 to 44 years of age (81.4 per cent) and have three or more live children (77.7 per cent) (BEMFAM, 1992). Thus, it is probable that a significant proportion of women older than 25 years and with high parity are not included in our study population.

In summary, our findings indicate that in our study population, self-administration of medicines (mainly misoprostol) plays an important role in pregnancy termination. Most women seeking hospital care for complications of induced abortion tend to be young, single (or living without a stable partner), of low parity, with limited formal education, and were not using an effective contraceptive method at the time of conception. Reports of previously induced abortion among the women in our study is not uncommon. Their medical characteristics tend to indicate much less complications than those found among women in previous studies. This is because a large proportion of the women in our study are seeking hospital care after self-administration of misoprostol, which means soon after bleeding starts and long before any sign of infection has occurred.

How the repeated practice of induced abortion affects women's health requires further study. Particularly necessary is information regarding cultural perceptions and concepts of abortion, and reasons poor women fail to adopt available family planning methods.

These study results reflect only the tip of the iceberg regarding complications of induced abortion admitted to hospital in an urban area where health service coverage is high. In countries like Brazil, where abortion is illegal, it is not possible to have accurate estimates of the magnitude of the problem of induced abortion.

The effect of misoprostol use in reducing complications of induced abortion should be treated with caution. Misoprostol is a weak abortifacient and has been available only on the black market, so that proper information on its effects will not be available (Fonseca et al., 1991). In many areas of Brazil, women with unwanted pregnancies face not only the illegality of abortion, but also poor access to medical care. In such circumstances, an increase in the number of severe complications with use of misoprostol would be expected. Furthermore, safety needs to be assured. Congenital malformations have been reported in foetuses exposed to misoprostol in utero (Fonseca et al., 1993; Gonzales et al., 1993).

The central issue regarding induced abortion in Brazil is the right of women to an affordable, safe and legal procedure. Improved access to family planning and health care, including surgical abortion by vacuum aspiration as well as a more efficient oral abortifacient regimen, would be expected to have a great impact on reducing morbidity and mortality associated with induced abortion.

✝ References

Baily, E.P., L.L. Saavedra, L. Kusbner, M. Welsh and B. Janowitz. 1988. A hospital study of illegal abortion in Bolivia. *PAHO Bulletin* 11 (1): 27–41.

BEMFAM. 1992. *Pesquisa Sobre a Saúde Familiar no Nordeste, Brasil—1991*, Rio de Janeiro: Sociedade Civil Bem-Estar Familiar no Brasil.

Coelho, L.L.H., C. Misago, W.V.C. Fonseca, D.S.C. Sousa and J.M.L. Araujo. 1991. Selling abortifacients over the counter in pharmacies in Fortaleza, Brazil. *Lancet* 338: 247.

Coelho, H.L.L., A.C. Teixeira, A.P. Santos, E.B. Forte, S.M. Morais, G. La Vechia, G. Tognoni and A. Herxheimer. 1993. Misoprostol and illegal abortion in Fortaleza, Brazil. *Lancet* 341: 1261–63.

Costa, S. and M.P. Vessey. 1993. Misoprostol and illegal abortion in Rio de Janeiro, Brazil. *Lancet* 341: 1258–61.

Downie, W.W. 1991. Misuse of misoprostol. *Lancet* 338: 247.

Fortney, J.A. 1981. The use of hospital resources to treat incomplete abortions: Examples from Latin America. *Public Health Reports* 96 (6): 574–79.

Fonseca, W., C. Misago and N. Kanji. 1991. Misoprostol and mifepristone. *Lancet* 338: 1594.

Fonseca, W., A.J.C. Alencar, R.M.M. Pereira and C. Misago. 1992. Congenital malformation of the scalp and cranium after failed first trimester abortion attempt with misoprostol. *Clinical Dysmorphology* 2: 76–80.

Gonzales, C.H., F.R. Vargas, A.B.A. Peres, C.A. Kim, D. Brunori, J. Marques-Dias, C.R. Leone, J. Correa Neto, J.C. Llereja and J.C.C. Almeida. 1993. Limb deficiency with or without Möbius sequence in seven Brazilian children associated with misoprostol use in the first trimester of pregnancy. *American Journal of Medical Genetics* 47: 59–64.

Sa, H.L. and N.C. Maia. 1990. Morte Materna e Aborto: Estudo Retrospectivo (1981–90) na MEAC-UFC. Unpublished dissertation. Fortaleza, Brazil: Federal University of Ceara.

Singh, S. and D. Wulf. 1991. Estimating abortions levels in Brazil, Colombia and Peru, using hospitals admissions and fertility survey data. *International Family Planning Perspectives* 17 (1): 8–13.

World Health Organization. 1987. *Protocol for hospital-based descriptive studies of mortality and morbidity related to induced abortion.* Geneva, Switzerland: WHO.

11

Induced Abortion and the Outcome of Subsequent Pregnancy in China: Client and Provider Perspectives

Zhou Wei-jin, Gao Er-sheng, Yang Yao-ying, Qin Fei and Tang Wei

Introduction

Induced abortion has been legal in China since 1953.[1] Abortions are available on request, up to six months of gestation with the consent of the family and spouse, and allowed on all grounds, including economic or social reasons. According to available national data, the number of reported induced abortions in 1989 was 10,566,911 and the abortion ratio was 63.2 per 100 live births. The corresponding abortion rate at that time was 37.5 per 1,000 women aged 15–44, which is similar to Hungary, but twice as high as Japan (Population Information Center of China, 1991).

Despite the large numbers of induced abortion performed in China today, and the generally safe, modern methods used for the procedure, there has always been widespread concern about its possible health consequences, especially long-term ones. More specifically, there is a common belief among Chinese doctors of obstetrics and gynaecology as well as among women themselves that the experience of induced abortion may adversely affect the outcome of subsequent pregnancy, with increased risks of spontaneous abortion, premature delivery (or low birth weight) and maternal morbidity (Sun Xio-ming, 1993; Hu Ting-yi, 1994). Doctors with this opinion routinely try to

---

[1] For a brief historical account of the development of family planning policy and abortion law in China, see the chapter by Luo Lin et al., *First-Trimester Induced Abortion Patients: A Study of Sichuan Province*, in this same volume.

persuade pregnant women, especially those who have never had a live birth or been pregnant before marriage, not to have an induced abortion.

Study Objective

In this chapter we explore the widely held belief among doctors and women in China that prior induced abortion adversely affects subsequent pregnancy outcome, particularly in the form of spontaneous abortion, low birth weight or premature delivery, and maternal morbidity. We were especially interested to know to what degree, if any, the belief actually influences a woman's decision to continue or to terminate a pregnancy. (The possible effect of China's one-child policy on this possible relationship was beyond the scope of this study, although some influence can be detected from the personal comments offered by many of the women we interviewed.)

Research Design and Methodology

Shanghai city was chosen as our study site, where the incidence of induced abortion is higher than the national average. It is estimated that 76,817 abortions took place in 1990, of which the majority, 73,809, were performed using vacuum aspiration, indicating that they were first-trimester pregnancies (Population Information Center of China, 1990). We gathered our sample from a total of 13 locations; the doctors were recruited from six hospitals and the women were recruited from seven other sites.[2]

This study relies on the methodology of the focus group discussion(FGD), which is an integral part of any research aimed at a better understanding of contraceptive behaviour, opinions and attitudes among the general population (Fern, 1982; Folch-Lyon et al., 1981; Khan and Manderson, 1992).

For our study, we conducted 20 FGDs with a total of 200 voluntary participants who were classified into three different groups: women who had never experienced an induced abortion (69) (group A); women who had experienced at least one induced abortion (71) (group B); and ob-gyn doctors (60) (group C).

Each discussion group was limited to 10 participants so that many different opinions could be expressed and the group could be easily monitored (Fern, 1982). The participants were organized so that each discussion group was

---

[2] 1) The Shanghai First Maternal and Infant Hospital; 2) The International Peace Hospital of Women and Children, The Chinese Welfare Committee; 3) Gynecology and Obstetric Hospital, The Shanghai Medical University; 4) Rui-Jin Hospital, The Shanghai Second Medical University; 5) Maternal and Infant Hospital, Pu-Tuo district; 6) Gynecology and Obstetrics Hospital, Chang-Ning district; 7) The Shanghai No. 1 Textile Mill; 8) Jiao-Tong University; 9) Institute of Chemical Research; 10) The Shanghai No. 4 Radio Factory; 11) Communication Installations Factory; 12) Shanghai Timepiece Element Factory; 13) The Shanghai First Television Factory.

relatively homogeneous, with similar experiences among members so that the discussion could have a greater depth than might have been possible if members had very different experiences. We controlled participant characteristics according to sex (except in the case of ob-gyn doctors, who could be either male or female), age, socioeconomic status, employment status, education and area of residence.

The moderator, or discussion leader, in each group session was trained to help the participants feel comfortable and encourage them to discuss the topics in a way that was lively and natural (Dawson et al., 1992). She/he introduced the general ground rules for the session, explained the aim of the FGD generally, without giving away the exact nature of the research questions, and gave each person a questionnaire to collect her/his basic demographic information such as name, age, sex, education, occupation, family structure (e.g., co-residence with parents) and area of residence.

One observer and one assistant were present for each discussion. The observer monitored the session and took notes, paying particular attention to body language and other nonverbal signs. The main task of the assistant was to operate the tape recorder and to prepare refreshments. Name cards or seating plans were used to help the moderator and observer remember the name of each participant. All focus group discussions were recorded using three wireless dynamic microphones and one cassette recorder. This equipment is essential for accurate interpretation and analysis of the information.

The discussions usually lasted from one-and-a-half to two hours for each group, so that all participants could express themselves and talk to each other; and the general topics came before the more specific ones, to allow the discussion to develop naturally. The general discussion focused on the participants' perception of the nature and scope of the association between a prior induced abortion and the outcome of subsequent pregnancy, and their attitudes and opinions towards induced abortion itself. The moderator raised the study topic and kept the discussion focused on it, without making any judgement about what was acceptable and what was not.

After all the topics had been discussed and no new opinion offered, the main points of each session were reiterated. Time was left to answer any questions raised by participants themselves about the general topic of human reproduction and contraception. These questions and opinions are important; they show what participants are interested in, particularly the medical questions that require answers. A sample list of questions used for the group discussions is included at the end of this chapter.

Study Findings: Client Perspectives

This section presents views expressed during the focus group discussions with the participants in the first two groups—women who had a history of abortion, and those who did not—about the experience of abortion and its possible association with adverse outcomes of subsequent pregnancy. Seven focus group discussions were held with each of the two groups.

The Discovery of An Unwanted Pregnancy

In all sessions, there were women who thought they would be very apprehensive, nervous and anxious if they discovered they had an unwanted pregnancy. A very significant finding is that there was a tremendous fear—indeed terror—of the pain of the procedure, which had been unbearable for most of the women who had an abortion. Many mentioned subsequent psychological anxiety towards coitus.

The attitudes and feelings of the focus group participants are presented below, almost verbatim, to portray as realistically as possible their perspective. In the next section, we summarize the significant findings.

When someone said that her menstruation was late, the whole group of workers in the textile shop would be alarmed. Induced abortions, like a delivery, may be one of the most agonizing experiences in a woman's life. Colleagues usually say that to go to the operating room for an induced abortion is just like to go to an execution ground. When I went to the hospital for an IUD insertion, I met a woman who told me she had come here twice accompanied by her husband to terminate an unwanted pregnancy, but she was so afraid that she went back home. Then she told me that she just had an induced abortion and the pain of the operation had made her feel that her heart was being cut out. (Textile worker, 35 years old, with one child and no experience of induced abortion.)

When I realized I could be pregnant, I was very nervous and afraid about having an induced abortion. I had been told by my friends and others that it was a very painful operation, much more so than delivery. So when I knew in the hospital that my urine test was positive for pregnancy, I was crying. Childbirth had been an experience of great suffering for me. (Accountant, 28 years old, who had one child before having an induced abortion.)

I was very angry when I found out that I was pregnant, because I had been using an IUD. [Other participants had the same feeling of anger because their unwanted pregnancy was also the result of contraceptive failure of methods such as the condom, the pills, and rhythm.] So after the first induced abortion, I changed my contraceptive method to condoms. It was a great horror when I discovered that I was unwillingly pregnant a second time, because my first abortion had been extremely painful. Both induced abortions have been so agonizing psychologically and physically, that now I feel very nervous when we have coitus. [Other participants nodded and said that they thought the impression of pain from prior induced abortion often affected their manner of coitus.] (Librarian, 34 years old, who had one child before undertaking two induced abortions.)

Reasons for Having an Abortion

Some participants said they would select, or had selected, an induced abortion to terminate their unwanted pregnancy. Still others said they would have preferred to carry their pregnancy to term, but finally had to terminate it for certain reasons, more commonly the one-child family policy.

> If I found out that I had an unwanted pregnancy, I would go to the hospital for diagnosis as soon as possible. Someone told me that the earlier you have the induced abortion, the easier the operation is and the less harm it has for women's health. Now I have a baby and do not have enough time and energy to raise another one. My husband and I are full-time employees, so I do not want to have a second baby. Of course, the Chinese family planning policy and our economic condition affect our reproductive behaviour. (Teacher, 31 years old, with one child and no experience of induced abortion.)

> If I had an unwanted pregnancy, I would go to see an ob-gyn doctor in a high level hospital with good care as early as possible to receive quality service. I would arrange the house work of my family so that I would have enough time to recuperate after the induced abortion. It would also be very important to take good nutrition during the rest period. I am very worried about suffering from possible complications of induced abortion, particularly not to be able to have an additional child. So that if I had an unwanted pregnancy, I would consider first whether or not my health, work, family and child would be affected by any side effects of an induced abortion. (Labour union chief, 31 years old, who has never been pregnant.)

> Originally, I had wanted to carry the second pregnancy to term so that my son could play with a younger brother/sister, but the family planning programme does not encourage me to have a second living baby. [Some participants had the same opinion and thought that it is a very heavy duty for one couple to take care of two sets of parents in the future, as they will not have brothers or sisters to share the burden of responsibility.] In fact, the 'one family, one baby' family planning policy is not very perfect because it causes the child to feel lonely, without the benefits of extended family. (Technician, 33 years old, with one child and the experience of two induced abortions.)

We thought it important to note that some participants preferred to use RU486 to terminate their pregnancy, mostly because they felt it would be less painful.

> When I found out that I had a second unwanted pregnancy, I wanted very much to find a different method of pregnancy termination to avoid the same pain I had with the first induced abortion. I very much hoped to be given an anaesthetic to reduce my agony. Now we know that RU486 can replace the induced abortion operation. [Other participants agreed that they had been forced to accept the method of surgical induced abortion, but now RU486 will be the best way to terminate another unwanted pregnancy.] (Machine repairer, 37 years old, who had one child before having two induced abortions.)

Is Abortion Harmful to a Woman's Subsequent Reproductive Life and Health?

In all sites, the topic of whether or not a prior induced abortion is hazardous for women's reproductive health arose spontaneously during the discussions. This clearly indicated the existence of widespread opinion about such a relationship. It was not a unanimous view, but a majority of women thought that induced abortion could negatively affect subsequent pregnancy outcome, and that this effect grew worse with the experience of multiple abortions.

> I think that induced abortion is not harmful to women's health, because some of my relatives and friends who have had induced abortions are very well after taking rest; although they felt very nervous before the operation. (Chemical researcher, 26 years old, with one child and no experience of induced abortion.)

> I had an unwanted pregnancy after already giving birth to a living child, so I wanted to have an induced abortion. The operator's skill and manner were fine and I took rest after the operation. I think the induced abortion was not harmful for me. (Administrator, 29 years old, with a child and one induced abortion.)

> It is not easy for me to evaluate whether or not induced abortion is hazardous to women's health, which depends on three factors. The first one is the cleanliness of the medical instruments used for the procedure, the next one is the patient's constitution, and the third one is proper rest and nourishment after the operation. [Some participants said that the operator's skill was also very important. In fact, the issue of the provider's experience and skill was often raised by the women in the groups.] If these factors are noted, I think an induced abortion is not harmful to women's health. In fact, I have had three induced abortions. The first time I took rest for 14 days, the next time I took rest for 21 days and the last time I took one month to recuperate. I have not discovered any difference in my health since the first induced abortion. (Welder, 37 years old, who had three induced abortions after giving birth to one child.)

> An induced abortion involves surgery on the human body. It will disturb a woman's normal internal functions and possibly injure her uterus, especially if she has more than one. It can result in secondary infertility, irregular menses and spontaneous abortion. My sister-in-law was ill with secondary infertility after her induced abortion. Since then, she has not had a pregnancy. [Some participants agreed with her view and gave other examples of complications from induced abortion.] So I think a woman should, if possible, keep her first pregnancy. The baby from the first pregnancy is the best baby. [Assembly line worker, 30 years old, with one child and no experience of abortion.]

> I was ill with a headache and lumbago after my induced abortion. [Other participants who had one or more induced abortions said they also had this experience.] (Administrator, 31 years old, who already had a child before undertaking an induced abortion.)

After having an induced abortion, I got secondary endometriosis. So I think that prior induced abortion can result in this disease. [Participants in the same or other focus group discussions also said that induced abortion could cause the disease easily]. (Textile worker, 31 years old, who had one child before having an induced abortion.)

I became pregnant while I was lactating, so I wanted to have an induced abortion. The procedure was very painful. I am not willing to use an IUD as my contraceptive method. I think the IUD should be removed from my uterus when the device is no longer effective. The removal of an IUD must be like an induced abortion and also very painful. (Administrator, 29 years old, who had one child before having an induced abortion.)

It was very interesting that some participants, both those who had previous abortion experience and those who did not, believed that both a pregnancy and an induced abortion could cure disease suffered during a prior pregnancy period, although no ob-gyn doctors talked about it.

The rest period after an induced abortion is very important. People usually say that if the woman takes good rest after having an induced abortion, some diseases suffered from prior gestation and delivery will be cured. [Women in other sessions who had a child and no induced abortion history also expressed this opinion.]

In fact, two participants wanted to get pregnant with the intention of having an abortion in order to cure pre-existing health problems such as headaches and lumbago. Women who had acted on this belief described different consequences.

After delivering my first baby, I was ill with lumbago and headache. My mother-in-law and other people told me that these disorders were a result of the pregnancy experience and could be cured by my next pregnancy or induced abortion. With this in mind, I became pregnant and then had an induced abortion. My health problems worsened, even though I had been careful to recuperate properly after the abortion. (Salesperson, 30 years old, who had one child before having an induced abortion.)

After having three induced abortions, my headache problem was cured naturally. (Welder, 37 years old, with one child and the experience of three induced abortions.)

Views about the relationship between prior induced abortion(s) and adverse outcomes of subsequent pregnancy were not unanimous.

I do not think that an induced abortion will cause adverse outcomes of subsequent pregnancy. (Nursery schoolteacher, 28 years old, who had a child and no experience of abortion.) [The same view was also expressed in other focus group discussions among women who had a child and one or more induced abortions.]

I think that premature delivery must not be a result of prior induced abortion(s), because premature delivery can take place in women who have not had an induced abortion. (Mess hall cook, 33 years old, with no history of induced abortion.)

I have been told that an induced abortion operation can cause secondary infertility and other diseases, but I do not believe that premature delivery can result from prior induced abortion history. (TV factory worker, 37 years old, with one child and the experience of one induced abortion.)

When I discovered I was unintentionally pregnant, and for the first time, I wanted to go to the hospital to terminate the pregnancy. But our neighbour advised me that an induced abortion operation would increase my risk of habitual abortion. [Participants in this and other sessions thought that the prior induced abortion caused not only habitual abortion but also spontaneous abortion]. I accepted her advice and delivered a baby from this unwanted pregnancy. (Mechanical engineer, 26 years old, with one child and no history of induced abortion.)

The infant delivered from the first pregnancy is the healthiest baby of all, because induced abortion is a surgery that injures women's reproductive health. If a woman becomes pregnant after having an induced abortion operation, it must be harmful to the baby's health. (Assembly worker, 30 years old, with one child and the experience of one induced abortion.)

There are a lot of elements that contribute to a premature delivery. For instance, the length of time between a previous induced abortion and the pregnancy may be very important for subsequent pregnancy outcome. Despite repeated attempts to become pregnant, my colleague, who had an induced abortion to end her first pregnancy, was sterile for six years. Finally, she delivered a premature infant at only 34 weeks gestation. So I think it is better not to terminate the first pregnancy. (Electron engineer, 30 years old, with one child and no history of induced abortion.)

Provider Perspectives

This section presents views expressed during the FGDs with the obstetricians and gynaecologists. In addition to addressing the central question of our study about possible adverse outcomes of abortion, most of them offered their opinions about why women have induced abortion, which added another important dimension to the results of our research. We held a total of six FGDs with these providers.

Is Abortion Harmful to a Woman's Subsequent Reproductive Life and Health?

As with the women clients, the general topic of whether or not induced abortion causes adverse outcomes of subsequent pregnancy was introduced by the participants themselves during the course of the overall study discussions. To answer this question, the women doctors drew from their own personal experience of abortion as well as from their medical experience with women whom they treated for abortion.

In general, this group did not believe that abortion was dangerous or harmful to women and only a few were actually opposed to it. Factors such as gestation period, number of previous abortions, and time interval since last pregnancy were mentioned as risk factors for a negative outcome of subsequent pregnancy. They also emphasized the importance of provider skill and proper disinfection procedures to ensure a safe abortion experience.

Pain management during the abortion procedure was raised often as a serious issue to be addressed with appropriate anaesthetic technique. Almost all emphasized the need for improvements in contraceptive information and services to reduce the incidence of abortion.

> After giving birth to my first baby, I was pregnant again due to contraceptive failure. As a gynaecologist, I did not feel nervous about terminating the pregnancy, because I knew the procedure of induced abortion. I received an injection of an anaesthetic to reduce pain and the operation was very successful. I have treated a lot of women with complications resulting from prior induced abortion, such as secondary pelvic inflammation and secondary infertility. To reduce the incidence of induced abortion, adolescent sex education and contraceptive knowledge should be promoted and existing public information programmes should be expanded. Routine disinfection of all materials for the procedure of abortion is mandatory for a safe experience. If these conditions exist, I think one induced abortion after having a child is not very harmful to women's reproductive health. (A female visiting gynaecologist, 31 years old.)

> It is not easy to say induced abortion is harmful or not harmful to women's health. It will depend on the patient's constitution, nutrition condition and medical skill of the provider. The rest period needed for most women is only about one to two weeks, so that they do not continue to have headaches, lumbago and other problems that they may suffer immediately after the operation. One patient I treated for abortion was ill with endometriosis and could not have a pregnancy afterward. But other women who have had three induced abortions are still very healthy and fertile. For us women, the most important thing to do is to use effective contraception to avoid an unwanted pregnancy. If I had an unwanted pregnancy, I would, sadly, prefer to have a painless induced abortion; that is, a drug abortion, although for most women induced abortion is a safe, effective and necessary method for early pregnancy termination. (Junior birth attendant, 26 years old, with one child and no history of induced abortion.)

> For most women, induced abortion is a safe, simple and effective surgical procedure. For other women, the operation can result in several complications. If I had an unwanted pregnancy, I would be afraid to have an abortion because of its possible negative sequelae. The post-abortion problems of secondary amenorrhoea, secondary infection, intrauterine adhesions and secondary infertility are very unfortunate for women who are very eager to have a pregnancy after having an induced abortion. Induced abortion causes placenta previa and then causes threatened abortion, spontaneous abortion and premature birth or low birth weight. These casualties are common in gynaecology. The fewer the number of induced

abortions, the less risk there is to women's reproductive health. The best way to prevent problems is to use very effective contraception so as to avoid unwanted pregnancy. (A female visiting doctor in obstetrics, 38 years old, with a child and no history of induced abortion.)

Induced abortion is very necessary for family planning. During a woman's reproductive life, she can experience at least one or two unwanted pregnancies even while using a very effective contraceptive method. For personal reasons and as a result of the Chinese family planning policy, many pregnant women have an induced abortion to terminate an unplanned pregnancy. There is not a very positive or negative answer for evaluating the relationship between prior induced abortion and subsequent sequelae. Induced abortion in the second trimester is much more harmful for a woman than in the first trimester. The length of time between prior abortion and the present unwanted pregnancy can also affect a woman's health. I think the actual technique used for induced abortion could be improved; for example, by improving the provider's skill and by using an anaesthetic to reduce pain. As a senior obstetrician, I have treated a lot of patients and seen that surgical induced abortion can result in several complications. Secondary infertility, spontaneous abortion, habitual abortion, habitual premature labour and endometriosis are more significantly common in women with prior induced abortion than in women with no induced abortion experience. Although the incidence of these complications is not very high, women who suffer from these diseases, particularly secondary infertility, will be very sad. So I think that women should deliver their first pregnancy. (A male professor of obstetrics, 56 years old.)

Women should avoid induced abortion by preventing unwanted pregnancy. Induced abortion is not a contraceptive method. Women who are breastfeeding usually ignore the need for contraception and therefore frequently have an unwanted pregnancy. If I ever have an unwanted pregnancy, I will go to the hospital for confirmation and have an induced abortion as soon as possible, although I will feel very nervous. The technique of uterine curettage in the second trimester has a much higher risk of complications than the method of uterine aspiration in the first trimester. Generally, complications from induced abortion are rare in childbearing women. It is a safe, effective operation for terminating unwanted pregnancy, if women go to the hospital for the procedure in early gestation, maintain personal hygiene, refrain from coitus for a time after the operation, and the doctor performs the procedure skillfully. Of course, it is wisest to deliver a baby before having an induced abortion so as to reduce unnecessary risk to maternal and infant health. One induced abortion may not be hazardous to women's health; but several induced abortions will increase the risk of habitual abortion. In outpatient treatment, I have seen several kinds of sequelae from prior induced abortion, particularly endometriosis. So I advise your family planning institute to study the relationship between induced abortion and endometriosis. These associations have been confirmed by clinical experience and by aetiology of gynaecology. (A female professor of gynaecology, 49 years old, with one child and no history of induced abortion.)

I oppose induced abortion strongly, except when needed for medical reasons. If a married woman is pregnant, I hope the woman can deliver the baby. In the outpatient family planning clinic, there are many reasons women give for having an induced abortion: 1) to work, study, or travel abroad; or 2) concern for possible genetic weakness in the foetus. In Shanghai city proper, pregnant women will terminate their pregnancy for eugenic reasons if they are ill with some minor diseases or if they take some medicine for these diseases during the early gestational period that they think will affect the foetus. Our ob-gyn doctors try to persuade them not to have induced abortion, because, in fact, most of these induced abortions for so-called eugenics are not necessary. The risk of complications following induced abortion have been discussed in detail and several examples of harmful sequelae have been described in this focus group discussion. The possibility of complication from prior induced abortion is not high for most women, but it is really sad for the women who do experience them. So our ob-gyn doctors and family planning staff should prevent excessive pregnancy terminations for eugenic reasons. (A female professor in family planning research, 55 years old, with one child and the experience of one induced abortion.)

Views About How to Reduce the Pain of the Procedure and the Risk of Complications

As providers of abortion services, the participants offered advice about how to ensure a safe, comfortable abortion procedure and reduce the risk of harmful sequelae. The role of RU486 was raised often during the FGDs, particularly whether or not it was a method that could offer fewer risks than those associated with surgical abortion procedures.

If a woman finds out she has an unwanted pregnancy, she will be very sad. She will be nervous, both during and after the induced abortion procedure. The experience often has psychological effects, such as a change in her interest and approach to coitus. The procedure can also result in any of the physical sequelae that almost everybody has mentioned. Although the incidence of these risks is not high, one child-bearing woman with any of these problems will meet with misfortune. To reduce the rate of complications, four approaches should be followed: (1) use anaesthesia to relieve the patient's pain, although providers may feel tense because they cannot then watch patient's reaction; (2) improve dilatation of the uterine neck to reduce the risk of cervical laceration; (3) control the intensity of xyster rugine to protect endometrial function, so that the risks of placenta previa, abruptio placentae, premature labour, adherent placenta, placenta implantation and antepartum haemorrhage are reduced; and (4) consider the use of RU486, especially in very early pregnancy. Drug abortion could reduce or prevent complications such as uterine perforation and endometriosis. You see, uterine aspiration causes a vacuum in the uterus, and as a result, residues could go through the fallopian tube and cause endometriosis. [Other ob-gyn doctors in this session and other sessions had this view.] RU486 is an advanced method for induced abortion: women with an unwanted pregnancy should take tablets of RU486 at home for two days and then go to the hospital/medical centre to have PG5. After about six hours observation, the embryo can be expelled and patients do not feel terror. This technique must be made more widely available for its use to be more effective.

(A senior female gynaecologist, 49 years old, with one child and no induced abortion history).

I have had two induced abortions, even though I have conscientiously used contraception. Before the first induced abortion I was very nervous, because I had seen patients in agony and sweating during the surgery. The procedure of cervical dilatation was so painful for me that I still keep it in mind. Some women have said that they were not nervous about having a second abortion, because they had already been through the experience before. But I was more nervous the second time, already thinking about the pain of cervical dilatation as soon as I discovered I had a second unplanned pregnancy. [The participant shook her head and spoke incoherently as she tried to describe her experience]. RU486 is a very meaningful intervention for child-bearing women. (A female visiting obstetrician, 49 years old, who had a child and two induced abortions.)

Abortion by the drug method should be more widely available, although the effectiveness of this procedure should also be improved. (A male professor of obstetrics, 56 years old.)

Opinion about the use of RU486 was not completely positive among the doctors in our study. The following comments illustrate the concerns of some of the participants.

Last year, I had an unwanted pregnancy. For personal reasons and to comply with the national family planning policy, I decided to have an induced abortion, but not by using RU486. This drug is 95 per cent effective, but I did not want to be in the 5 per cent ineffective group. Because if the drug were to fail, I would have metrorrhagia and would have to have an induced abortion. This method also carries a higher risk of secondary infection than surgical abortion, because the period of uterine haemorrhage afterwards can be longer. So I prefer the surgical method of induced abortion rather than the drug method. As an ob-gyn doctor, I asked my colleague with operation experience to do my surgery. Induced abortion is a useful technique for family planning and medical treatment. (A female visiting obstetrician, 35 years old, who had an induced abortion before having a child.)

I participated in the multicentre study on RU486 a couple of years ago. We found that some pregnant women suffered from petechial haemorrhage for two or three months after using the drug for abortion. By examination with hysteroscope and histopathology, only a few remains of villi and decidua were found in the uterine cavity. When treated by uterine curettage, the petechial haemorrhage immediately stopped and the menses became regular. A petechial haemorrhage for two or three months can cause secondary infection, such as pelvic inflammation and salpingitis. I recommend the use of RU486 only for women in early pregnancy (less than 49 days since the last menstruation) who do not have any contraindications to the use of the drug abortion and who could return to the hospital for follow-up. (Woman chief physician of family planning department, 55 years old, who had one child before having an induced abortion.)

In all the focus group discussions, all doctors believed that the earlier the gestational age at the time of induced abortion, the easier the procedure and the less risk of harmful sequelae. Only one female obstetrician did not agree with this view:

> If I had an unplanned pregnancy, I would prefer to have a second-trimester abortion induced by injection of a plant-derived substance called radix trichosanthis. I had participated in a study about induction of labour by trichosanthis for one year; subjects in this research were 12 to 16 weeks pregnant. Patients said that the advantages of this procedure were less pain, shorter convalescence and less vagus reflex compared to previous surgical abortion that they had during first-trimester pregnancy. If a patient is not allergic to radix trichosanthis, we put this and dexamethasone into the amniotic cavity to induce labour. We had not found any pernicious effects from this technique when the research was completed. (A female visiting obstetrician, 40 years old, with a child and no history of induced abortion.)

Summary

Most of the women in the study expressed feelings of great fear when they discovered they had an unwanted pregnancy, regardless of whether or not they already had abortion experience. Women with no experience of induced abortion more easily chose to have the procedure, while women with a history of one or more induced abortions were more resentful of contraceptive failure and more nervous about the discovery of another unwanted pregnancy.

While there were different concerns about the procedure, they all thought of it as a very painful experience. The reactions of dread and agony were much greater among the women who had already had at least one induced abortion than among the women with no abortion history. The experience of strong physical pain during the intervention had a significant psychological effect on several women who described subsequent anxiety toward coitus.

They also wanted the provider's skill to be good, and they worried about the risk of possible harmful complications. There was also anxiety related to how to arrange regular daily schedules, study or job, so that they could have rest and good nutrition after the procedure.

Some participants, both women and doctors, stated that the earlier the induced abortion was performed, the less the risk of complications and pain. Generally, women with higher education and employment status were more knowledgeable and objective about induced abortion, whether or not they had personal experience of it.

The majority of the participants in the study said they chose or would choose to have an abortion because of limited finances, to comply with the Chinese family planning policy, or if their health was not good. There was also a folkloric view, never mentioned among the doctors, that a new pregnancy could cure health problems resulting from a previous pregnancy. As described earlier, at least two participants had become pregnant to cure headaches and lumbago problems, with different consequences.

Health Problems Experienced After Induced Abortion

Women doctors who had an induced abortion suffered much less from abnormal menses and leucorrhoea than the other women with abortion experience we interviewed. By analyzing the data, we found that the length of rest taken after the procedure and the kind of work the women performed were key elements affecting women's menstruation. For example, women who were ill with abnormal menses were working in the Shanghai No. 1 textile mill and in the assembly line of the Shanghai No. 4 radio factory; they usually took about two weeks rest and would immediately resume their normal workload when they returned to work. One woman who had three induced abortions said that she took two, three, four weeks of rest for the first, second, third induced abortion, respectively. After the first induced abortion, for which she rested the least amount of time, she was very weak. But the third time, after taking the longest rest period, she felt the most comfortable afterwards. Almost all the doctors emphasized personal hygiene and abstention from sexual intercourse one month following induced abortion to prevent secondary infection. So it is possible that leucorrhea might be a result of women neglecting these important precautions.

Psychological harm from surgical induced abortion was self-evident from moving descriptions of personal psychic trauma experienced by some women in the focus group sessions. Most often this took the form of fear of sexual intercourse, so as not to experience again the agonizing pain of induced abortion to end another unwanted pregnancy. The fear can be so strong, for example, that one woman who had a child and one prior induced abortion chose to carry a second unwanted pregnancy to term to avoid the pain of another induced abortion procedure.

Views About Different Abortion Techniques

The choice of abortion method among the women was mixed, with some preferring a surgical procedure and others, the use of RU486. Only one woman, a doctor, said she would choose induction of labour by injection of a plant-derived substance to avoid the pain of surgery. Women with no experience of abortion tended to select RU486 as their first method of pregnancy termination.

The participants who suggested using RU486 to terminate unwanted pregnancy thought it was a safe method that should be more accessible in the future. The great advantage of the drug was thought to be freedom from the psychological harm of too much pain, and therefore anxiety-free sexual intercourse after the procedure. A few women doctors said that they would choose a surgical abortion method over RU486, however, because the drug carried a greater risk of secondary infection than a surgical procedure. Although it was generally thought that RU486 could be a very useful method of pregnancy termination in very early pregnancy and especially if improvements were made in its administration.

Opinion of Abortion as 'Unharmful'

Women who had one or more induced abortions were more preoccupied with the risk of complications than women with no abortion history, although most also believed that induced abortion was 'unharmful' to women's health. This belief among the women with a history of abortion was related to their personal experience of the procedure. It was also conditional, with the women saying that it depended on good provider skill and disinfection, good health of the woman, adequate rest and nutrition afterwards, and if it is the first abortion.

In contrast, only a minority of the doctors also felt that abortion was 'unharmful'; and these were the doctors who had a personal history of induced abortion rather than those who did not.

Opinion of Abortion as 'Harmful'

The opinion of induced abortion as harmful was formed differently by each group of participants. Women who had never had an abortion received this information through friends, relatives, colleagues, newspapers and magazines, and medical journals. Women with a history of abortion developed their views from their personal experience of the procedure, as well as from discussions with friends, relatives and colleagues. The third group, the doctors, formed their opinion of abortion as harmful from their experiences of clinical treatment of abortion patients.

The women with this opinion believed that abortion was a surgery that could cause irregular menses, habitual and spontaneous abortion, lumbago and other problems such as secondary infertility, premature delivery and low birth weight. They gave many examples of these problems, especially spontaneous abortion and low birth weight, although none of them had experienced them personally. Naturally, they also believed that the first pregnancy would result in the healthiest baby.

Among the doctors, several health problems associated with induced abortion were cited. Some noted that although uterine perforation rarely took place, the procedure damages the endometrium, especially when performed several times. Even if the endometrium is injured only lightly, problems such as placenta previa, placenta adherent and placenta abruptio could occur and cause premature delivery, low birth weight and prolonged labour. More serious injury to the endometrium could lead to worse consequences, including complete hysterectomy. Some mentioned that the procedure could also damage the cervix if the provider was not competent, resulting in cervical laceration and cervical incompetence, so that natural and habitual abortion would result. If the operation is not performed under strictly sanitary conditions and women do not pay proper attention to personal hygiene afterwards, the operation could also cause problems such as pelvic infection, which in turn could result in tubal obstruction, secondary infertility and ectopic pregnancy.

The doctors who talked about these complications added that although these adverse outcomes are not occurring for every woman who has had a history of abortion, the women who do suffer from these problems and complications have a history of induced abortion. Moreover, among these doctors there was an impression that the prevalence of endometriosis was increasing, bringing with it more secondary infertility.

The senior doctors seemed to be more objective than the junior ones in evaluating the risks of induced abortion. They indicated that induced abortion is a safe operation and that complications are rare if the skill of the operator is good, the conditions are sanitary, and women take good care of their personal hygiene and nourishment afterwards.

Conclusions and Recommendations

Generally, it was agreed that induced abortion is a safe, effective back-up procedure for contraceptive failure and for medical treatment that could not be replaced completely by other methods, even RU486. There was consensus that it must not be used as a contraceptive method. All the women, especially those with a history of abortion, very much longed for safe, effective, convenient and comfortable contraceptive methods.

Although the incidence of some complications/adverse outcomes of subsequent pregnancy associated with prior induced abortion experience is not very high, the procedure can still be harmful to women's health. Some may suffer from secondary infertility, spontaneous and habitual abortion, endometriosis, premature delivery and other diseases. Psychological harm is also possible: The experience of tremendous pain from the operation was common among the participants in the study and often affected women's interest and approach to subsequent coitus.

The results of this study clearly indicate the need to introduce changes in abortion routines. Specific recommendations to ensure a safe and comfortable procedure and to reduce the possible adverse consequences of induced abortion are: Improve availability and use of anaesthesia to reduce pain; provide more rigorous technical training to improve provider skill in applying available techniques; and, ensure strict adherence to disinfection procedures. Doctors should also be sure to remind patients to maintain good personal hygiene and to avoid coitus for at least a month following the procedure.

A recommendation specific to the context of Chinese culture was made by several doctors: Pregnant women who are ill with slight disorders should be persuaded to avoid unnecessary abortion because of concern for genetic weakness in the foetus. Appropriate information in this regard should also be disseminated in the media, which will have substantial influence as most of the people living in Shanghai have secondary level or higher education.

Finally, the majority of the doctors in this study indicated that it is necessary to study the actual association between prior induced abortion and adverse outcomes of subsequent pregnancy, to determine if such a relationship exists and, if so, whether adverse outcomes differ between women with and without induced abortion history.

✝ References

Dawson, S., L. Manderson and V.L. Tallo. 1992. *The Focus Group Discussion Manual.* Methods for Social Research in Tropical Diseases, No. 1. Geneva, Switzerland: The World Health Organization.

Fern, E.F. 1982. The use of focus groups for idea generation: The effects of group size, acquaintanceship and moderator on response quantity and quality. *Journal of Marketing Research* 19: 1–13.

Folch-Lyon, E. and J.F. Trost. 1981. Conducting focus group sessions. *Studies in Family Planning* 12: 443–49.

Hu Ting-yi. 1994. Cause of women's sexual hypoesthesia. *Popular Medicine* 7: 28.

Khan, M. and L. Manderson. 1992. Focus groups in rapid assessment procedures for tropical diseases research. *Health Policy and Planning* 7 (1): 56–66.

Population Information Center of China. 1991. Data of Chinese Population (1990), Vol. 1. Beijing: Beijing Economic Institute, pp. 123; 156.

Sun Xio-ming. 1993. Make a good choice of when they have an induced abortion. *Popular Medicine* 3: 27.

✝

12

Between Political Debate and Women's Suffering: Abortion in Mexico

Maria del Carmen Elu

Introduction

Mexico's population and fertility patterns have been significantly influenced by national policy over the years. The government's population policy was essentially pronatalist until 1974, in keeping with the prevailing values of a traditional, patriarchal society. During this time, government officials displayed the rapid increase in population as an indicator of the success of their political and economic policies. The result of encouraging high fertility levels during a period when child mortality was being reduced was a doubling of the population over the period 1950–70. During this time, contraception was not easily available; in fact, the sale of contraceptives was illegal until 1973.

Just before the 1974 Bucharest World Population Conference, the awareness that the rapid population growth would have long-term negative consequences for the country brought about an abrupt change in official thinking. In 1973, the President of Mexico, Luis Echeverria, decided to reverse the official position of the government on population and sent to the Mexican Congress a legislative proposal that would set the country on a path to reduce its very high level of fertility. The proposal was approved and officially published by the government in January 1974. Known as the 1974 Law, it set a new precedent for Latin America, because it showed that one of the most reluctant countries in the region had officially taken a position to lower its rapid population growth and had linked this new policy to its general development strategy.

However, a liberal abortion policy never became part of the new population policy or family planning strategy. It was expected that comprehensive access to family planning would reduce abortion. Unfortunately, this has not been the case. It is estimated that at least 850,000 abortions are performed annually in Mexico and that the number is increasing (López García, 1994). An indicator of this situation is the number of women who seek help in public hospitals from complications of unsafe procedures. Complications from unsafe abortion is the third or fourth cause of maternal death, with experts estimating that this cause of maternal mortality is under-reported by as much as 50–70 per cent (Chambers, 1994).

Legal abortion in Mexico, in general, is restricted to the following conditions: danger to the mother's life; the possibility of congenital defects; or to terminate a pregnancy that is the result of rape. Additionally, seven of the 31 states within the country permit abortion if the pregnancy will adversely affect the mother's health. In the state of Yucatán, the law is more liberal, allowing abortion if a pregnant woman has a difficult economic situation.

Objectives of the Study

This study has attempted to identify factors that contribute to a woman's decision, particularly poor women, to interrupt a pregnancy under unsafe, dangerous conditions. It was also designed to find out more about the perceptions, attitudes, and knowledge of the factors that affect the decision to abort from health care providers, particularly hospital staff. An important aspect of the study was to learn about the quality of care women receive when they arrive at hospitals with abortion complications.

Research Methodology

The research was conducted at the Hospital de la Mujer (Women's Hospital) in Mexico City. It is one of the oldest public health institutions in the country, dating back to the sixteenth century, when it was a place where the destitute would come for health care. In 1864, it turned its attention to women, most of whom were prostitutes, for the treatment of venereal diseases. Since 1941, its policy has been to help any woman who needed health care, particularly gynaecological and obstetric services.

It has 400 beds and attends some 13,000 deliveries annually; it also handles about 2,500 cases of abortion complications each year. The hospital also offers family planning services, but only one out of 10 women seeking obstetrical and gynaecological care come for these services.

The study population consisted of a purposive sample of 300 women admitted to the Hospital de la Mujer for abortion complications (either spontaneous or induced) between 15 August 1990 and 15 January 1991. Of the 300 women, 134 cases (44.7 per cent) were classified as induced abortion.

The study included quantitative and qualitative techniques. Structured interviews were carried out in the hospital with the 300 women and with 142 hospital staff, including 48 physicians, 65 nurses, and 29 social workers. A sub-sample of 10 women classified as abortion providers were interviewed in-depth at their homes. Lastly, there were four focus group discussions with the hospital staff.

Characteristics of the Study Sample

Most of the women in our study started their sexual life at a fairly young age. Thirty-eight per cent became sexually active before they were 17 years old and 80 per cent were sexually active by the time they reached the age of 20. For five of these women, their first sexual experience was a rape. The other women had their first sexual relations voluntarily, usually with their boyfriends.

The majority of the women, 71 per cent, lived in metropolitan Mexico City, which is officially known as the Federal District. The remaining women lived in the neighbouring State of Mexico, adjacent to the Federal District. Only slightly more than half of the women were born in Mexico City, the rest being of migrant origin from neighbouring states or other regions of the country.

Nearly 60 per cent of the respondents were below the age of 30; and one-third were not yet 20 years old. Another 12 per cent were near the end of their reproductive life cycle, which meant that their pregnancy was a real risk to their health. One out of every five women had not completed primary school; another 30 per cent said that they had.

Nearly 70 per cent were single or lived in consensual (free) unions. Among the 46 per cent in this marital situation, more than half said that their relationship lacked stability. Most women appeared to be in unstable unions of short duration, a situation that makes pregnancy undesirable for both social and economic reasons. In more than half of the cases, the male partner made the minimum legal salary or less, which is poverty level. Under these circumstances, a first or a new pregnancy puts additional financial pressure on the couple, which in some cases leads to the departure of the male partner. The situation is even more precarious for those women living with a man who is married to another woman, a not uncommon scenario.

In short, the data showed that women who were accepted at the hospital with complications of induced abortion had lower levels of education, income and marital stability than women who arrived at the hospital because of spontaneous abortions.

Study Findings

Although there were common sets of factors, such as those related to economic conditions, social situation, marital status and family size, we found that for each woman the way the factors interrelated could be different. It was not possible, from an analytical perspective, to say with some degree of exactness, which factors are the more powerful in influencing the decision to end a pregnancy when the overall picture is created by a complex and often seemingly contradictory interplay of, for example, rejection of contraception, an unstable union and expectations about the partner that do not materialize. Nonetheless, in the following sections, an attempt is made to sort out the more common influences that come into play when a woman faces an unwanted pregnancy.

The data gathered by our structured questionnaires are illustrated through the presentation of portions of our in-depth interviews. We have chosen this way to explain our findings in order to provide a better understanding of the reality of unwanted pregnancy; the way it impacts on the day-to-day lives of the women who must confront it.[1]

Poverty and Abortion

For all the women we interviewed, economic circumstances were an ever-present factor in the decision-making process of whether or not to have an abortion. In some cases, extreme poverty was the primary reason to choose abortion; in others, it reinforced the role of social and psychological factors in their lives, such as an unstable relationship, or an already large number of children, or a partner's broken promise to marry.

In the following case, we see how poverty can be the main influence on the decision to interrupt a pregnancy.

> Doña Esperanza was born in a small town, a journey of two hours from the capital city. At the age of 14, she came to Mexico City to work as a housemaid. Now she lives with her husband, and her two children, a 19-year-old daughter and a 17-year-old son, from a previous relationship that ended when that husband died in an accident. She had her first abortion just after she arrived in Mexico City. She had a second one after the birth of her eldest daughter. In both cases, the reason for the abortion was her unstable economic situation, which made it difficult even to get proper nourishment.

As we offer more details of individual women's lives, it will become clear that the economic dimension comes up in every situation. But it is inescapably linked not only to the decision to abort, but also to the sequelae of abortion complications, to quality of care, such as inadequate or delayed treatment, and to a host of other problems that surround abortion in a society where it is illegal.

Gender Relations and Abortion

Male attitudes have an important influence on a woman's fertility behaviour, particularly in societies where 'machismo' prevails. In Mexico, it is not

---

[1] The case presentations are descriptions given by the women themselves and have not been altered. None of the names used are real.

uncommon for a man to demand that a woman get pregnant in order to 'reinforce the relationship', although it does not mean that he is willing to assume the related responsibilities. Similarly, it is often a man's refusal to support and raise a child that leads a woman to end a pregnancy, often an advanced one.

Men in Mexico also frequently oppose the use of contraception, which is a major reason for non-use among the women in our study. Unfortunately, when an unintended pregnancy results, and abortion follows, some men will disclaim responsibility and act in ways that are detrimental to the stability of the relationship and to the woman, particularly to her physical and emotional wellbeing.

The situation of women such as Doña Esperanza provide us with an example of these influences and behaviours found repeatedly in many interviews.

During the last eight years, Doña Esperanza had maintained sexual relations with a man who was 16 years younger than her own age of 44 years. At the beginning of their relationship, she took oral contraceptives. But then he insisted that she stop taking them so that they could have a child of their own. Her other children got angry when she got pregnant, because it was risky to give birth at her age and because both her economic situation and the relationship with this man were unstable. After a great deal of reflection, she decided to end her pregnancy. She took a 'tea' and a few hours later she began to bleed and to feel very bad. At the clinic (Centro de Salud) five blocks from her house, they suggested that she go immediately to the Hospital de la Mujer, where they managed to save her life. Before leaving the hospital, Doña Esperanza did not accept the contraceptive injection offered, because her partner had already disappeared when he found out that she had an abortion. But her children predicted that he would return because she supported him financially.

In the complex and contradictory Mexican society, where unions tend to be unstable, a woman's own tendency to use her fertility to establish or strengthen a marital arrangement is also common. The possibility of giving birth to a son, in particular, is often seen as a way to create a more harmonious and stable relationship. Unfortunately, many times this aspiration is not achieved and the pregnancy ends in an abortion. The situation of Doña Clara illustrates how desperate hopes can turn into suffering and loneliness.

Doña Clara was born in Mexico City. After primary school, she began to work in a factory. Her dream was to get married as soon as possible. At 17, she became the girlfriend of a man with whom she lived for 10 years. She got pregnant three times in the hope of getting married. But each time, the pregnancy ended in abortion because he refused to marry her. Someone would give her an injection and afterwards, she would go to a clinic where someone performed a surgical curettage (D&C). Shortly after the third abortion, she broke up with her boyfriend. Some years later, she began a relationship with a married man who promised to get a divorce and marry her when they had a child. But when she got pregnant, he 'did not keep his word'. Clara decided to go ahead with her pregnancy and a son was born. Sometime later, at the beginning of a new pregnancy, she learned that the man had never begun divorce proceedings. He threatened to abandon her if she insisted on marriage, so she had another abortion. Not even after this fourth abortion did she agree to use a contraceptive method offered at the hospital. Although she is afraid that she might die during an abortion procedure, she thinks getting pregnant is the only way to get a man to marry her.

Married Women and Abortion

Women in unstable relationships are not the only ones who resort to abortion. Many married women in harmonious and stable relationships also choose to have one. We found that poverty was often the overriding reason these women, too, sought induced abortion. Like their unmarried counterparts, they did not have the means to raise another child. And when poverty defines the economic circumstances of the household, safe abortion is not an option. In desperation, despite the risk of serious health complications or death, these women also usually seek a clandestine abortion or try to self-induce one.

> Doña Minerva and her husband were both born in a village, but they moved to the capital city 16 years ago. They have both worked very hard to survive. With great sacrifice they saved enough money to make a down payment on a small house, which will be paid for in four years. After having their first son, Minerva had to abort a second pregnancy because they could not support themselves financially. Since then, they have used the 'rhythm method', but it has failed repeatedly and four more children have been born.

> When she was 40 years old, Minerva became pregnant again. She and her husband did not know what to do. She was four months pregnant when she decided to terminate the pregnancy. She threw herself down a set of soapy steps. A few hours later, the haemorrhage began, accompanied by a strong pain in the abdomen. Much to her disgrace, it was a Friday. Her husband took her to two clinics where she was not attended. As time went by, her pain and anguish grew. Doña Minerva's major worry was about what would happen to her children. She was finally attended to early on Monday and later that same day went home from the hospital. Although she remembers those hours with horror, and thinks that only a miracle saved her, she decided not to be sterilized at the hospital. But she says she is determined to avoid a new pregnancy.

As the case of Doña Minerva just illustrated, family size can be an important determinant of induced abortion. The trend towards smaller families in Mexico is a result of economic pressures, particularly escalating food costs and a growing awareness that educational costs for children must be met to break the cycle of poverty. When couples have exceeded their reproductive goals and have already more children than they planned, an unexpected pregnancy can bring an enormous pressure to bear.

For mothers of large families in particular, the threat of their own death or serious illness arising from a botched up abortion summons a scenario of drama containing devastating consequences. We found that for many of these women, the nightmare of having to cope with the pressures of life with an additional family member outweighed even a possible confrontation with their own death.

Doña Amalia lives in a village with her husband, a peasant who also works as a bricklayer. At 37, she already has six children, even though they wanted to have no more than five. When she was pregnant with her sixth child, they decided to keep him, but they were firmly agreed that he would be the last one. This son was three when she became pregnant again. A midwife induced an abortion. On the following day Doña Amalia woke up with fever and a growing haemorrhage. Her husband took her to two health centres, but they were closed. Finally they went to a social security health centre where she was not accepted, because she was not 'derechohabiente' (a member). While she was waiting, the haemorrhage increased and she lost her sight. In an ambulance they took her to the Hospital de la Mujer. During the journey of more than an hour, in the midst of great pain, she thought only of what would happen to her husband and children if she died. At the hospital a hysterectomy was performed and the seriousness of her condition kept her in the hospital for 14 days. Doña Amalia has never taken contraceptives because she thinks they are bad for a woman's health. 'Thank God,' she says. 'I was saved and now we can live in peace without the fear of another pregnancy.'

Adolescents and Abortion

Among the women in the study, 80 per cent had become sexually active by age 20. The majority began their sexual life with their boyfriend, but deferred to him the responsibility to protect them against pregnancy. In many cases, however, a boyfriend's promise 'to take care of the situation' doesn't work and the young girl becomes pregnant. The cultural, economic and social circumstances of the girl's family usually make it impossible for her to carry such a pregnancy to term and the 'solution' is an unsafe abortion.

Rape is not uncommon among young girls in this country. Although the law permits an abortion after such an experience, many are often not aware of this right and others ignore it because of the long and emotionally difficult process it requires. As described in earlier cases, the attitude of other family members influences the way a woman resolves this difficult situation.

Lucía was 17 years old. She lived with her mother and six brothers in a small apartment. She was attending preparatory school and had never had a boyfriend. One day, in the middle of the afternoon, two young boys, apparently on drugs, beat and raped her half a block from her house. They threatened to kill her mother or a brother if she talked about what had happened. Lucía did not say anything, but she dropped out of school because she was afraid to go out in the street. She could not sleep at night. She lost her appetite and became thin. When her mother suggested going to the doctor she strongly refused. When she realized she had missed her period, she locked herself in her room and began shouting that she wanted to die. Her mother insisted on knowing what had happened and Lucia told her. Lucía's mother persuaded her to report the rape. Lucía did not want to do it, but finally agreed. On the road to the deposition Lucía did not stop crying. At the Delegation they gave her a pregnancy test that confirmed what they thought. They told her that she had a legal right to an abortion and sent her to Hospital de la Mujer. She had to wait three weeks full of anguish before they could perform the abortion. Before leaving the hospital, she was invited to attend some therapy sessions to discuss what had happened to her, but she did not go because she wanted 'to forget everything'. She has stopped her studies and she cannot go out on the street by herself anymore. Her neighbours reproach her for having accused people of the neighbourhood as rapists. The police never found one of the rapists; the other spent eight months in jail.

Lucía had the legal support that the great majority of women lack when they have an abortion. Nonetheless, the experience caused her great personal anguish and changed her life forever. Her long wait to receive the abortion illustrates the lack of understanding and compassion of health personnel toward women faced with an unwanted pregnancy (Elu, 1992).

Contraceptive Behaviour and Abortion

For many women, young and old, one important variable to consider when trying to understand their motivation to seek an abortion is contraceptive behaviour. In nearly every case, contraceptives had not been used, or even considered, even when it was apparent that an unintended pregnancy would place their emotional well being or economic situation in jeopardy.

Such conduct is the result of fear of contraceptive services and methods, or simply a lack of motivation to use them. It often has at its roots in a desperate hope for greater love and stability with a partner, or simply more companionship, no matter how unrealistic or illusionary such aspirations may be.

Even women who had experienced numerous abortions were not using contraception. Some complained that the methods available do not 'easily adapt to their needs'. Others said that their male partners will not permit the use of contraception. Still others were simply reluctant to consider family planning as an option.

Gloria is 20 years old. She lives in a poor neighbourhood with her parents, brothers, husband and a two-year-old son. Her husband is a driver, but without a steady job. They have lived together since she was 17 and never used any contraceptive method. After a first son was born, she found it was easier to inject herself each time she skipped her period rather than to use a contraceptive method. This always worked; she never had 'major problems' due to the injections, although she spent some days 'like dizzy'. The last time she missed her period, however, the injection she gave herself did not work. She became desperate because her husband was jobless. Her sister gave her an injection with a triple dose of medication. Four days later, she began bleeding. After another three days, the haemorrhage increased as well as the headaches. Finally, she went to the Hospital de la Mujer, where she had a surgical curettage.

The Quality of Abortion Services

Complications from self-induced or poorly performed procedures were characteristic of nearly all the abortion experiences described by the women in our study. The problems associated with getting timely treatment for life-threatening symptoms, even in an urban context, were also distressingly commonplace. Many times, health centres were either closed or unprepared to deal with these complications. At some hospitals where appropriate facilities did exist, these women were not accepted. Many were referred, without receiving any treatment, to other hospitals at a great distance away, such as Hospital de la Mujer, thus increasing their risk of more serious complications or even death.

It seemed evident that the women could have received better care if the health providers were more compassionate and well-trained and the facilities had appropriate equipment so that emergency services for treatment of abortion complications could be offered regardless of whether or not a woman had 'institutional rights' to them.

We conducted structured interviews and focus group discussions with health providers to see more clearly how their values and attitudes affected the quality abortion care received by the women in our study. Nearly three-quarters of the providers we interviewed were women. One-third had worked in the hospital 15 years or more; a similar proportion had worked there for five years or less. The nursing staff had the longest employment history, with 20 per cent of them working in the hospital for 20 years or more. Hospital salaries are very low, and were a major complaint among the nurses and auxiliaries; even the physicians received a low salary of under US $300 per month.

All of them saw complications from unsafe abortion as a major health problem, which they said is increasing yearly. What makes this increase in patient load so difficult for them to handle is the severity of the complications and the lack of trained personnel. They cited examples of women arriving at the hospital with haemorrhages caused by metal and other objects inserted into the uterus or by injections that have severe side effects, others with cases of severe septic shock, and other internal damage, such as perforated uterus. The staff were also aware of the psychological implications of the sequelae of clandestine abortion, and described examples of young girls who end up being sterilized and the long recuperation of others in shock from their confrontation with death.

They expressed the opinion that the medical services are not properly set up to deal with the cases of abortion complications that arrive daily at the hospital. For example, no maternity hospital (or general hospital) has a special unit for such emergencies. So that women suffering from unsafe abortion who arrive at the Hospital de la Mujer compete for already scarce medical resources with women coming for obstetric or gynaecological services.

Many of these providers are fully aware of the need for safe abortion services, because they themselves are often requested by women to terminate a pregnancy. This was the experience of 88 per cent of the physicians and 35 per cent of the nurses. None of these providers said they had agreed to perform an abortion, however; they had simply tried to convince the woman to continue with the pregnancy. In some very special cases, they had let the woman know 'who can help her'.

Few of the medical personnel had a clear knowledge of the Mexican laws regarding abortion and the circumstances under which it is legal. But they generally agreed that a more liberal abortion law is needed. They were particularly sympathetic to women who, for example, became pregnant because their contraceptive method failed. They also expressed concern, however, about some negative effects that a more liberal law could have. Many worried about a possible increase in unnecessary abortions, because 'women would find it very easy to get one'; and others anticipated more of a work burden if more women were allowed to come to the hospital for abortions.

Commentary and Conclusions

Each day more and more people agree that induced abortion in Mexico, performed under the current restrictive conditions in the country, constitutes a serious and major public health problem, particularly because of its association with maternal morbidity and mortality (MSR, 1993).

The case histories offer a glimpse into the personal anguish and risks that women living in poor neigbourhoods in Mexico face during the experience of unsafe induced abortion. Significant factors that explain the determinants of abortion practice have emerged from the profiles of these women, although precise relationships cannot be deduced. The inability of the health care system to treat complications of unsafe abortion has been revealed, and is shown to contribute to the continued suffering of many of these women.

But what is the solution? To prevent induced abortion and its consequences in Mexican society is not easy. It requires not only a modification of many aspects of the maternal health care system but also an understanding of the complex cultural values that support its existence.

The Concept of Unwanted Pregnancy

The practice of abortion is logically associated with unwanted pregnancy. But the concept of 'unwanted pregnancy' is not as simple as it would appear. The 'desire' for a pregnancy is not necessarily conscious or rational; and it is rarely contemplated 'in advance'. Moreover, any 'desire' is usually fleeting or unstable, a feeling that appears and disappears according to circumstance or mood. A woman may want another child but be prevented from having it by the couple's current situation. There is often an ambivalence with respect to the 'longing for children', which varies by age, marital situation, economic condition and the contexts in which fertility decisions are being made (Elu, 1993). In short, a woman or couple's 'wanted' pregnancy can become 'unwanted' when the fact of it meets with reality.

The Decision to Abort

The decision to have an abortion is the final outcome of a process; and one that is almost always difficult. An unwanted pregnancy creates great internal and external conflicts. A recurring misconception about women who seek abortion, often expressed by some providers, is that if abortion were legal, women would 'easily' make use of it and abuse its practice. This opinion reflects a lack of information and ability to perceive how desperate and difficult this decision is for most women, even those who have rights to a legal procedure.

Self-induced Abortion

The evidence for and information about the way in which women try to induce abortion themselves must be confronted, and not ignored, as grisly or horrifying as it may be. The majority of women who seek abortion resort to dangerous methods at great risk to their life and health. Of course, not all women who seek an induced abortion suffer the dangerous physical and emotional trauma of the women presented in the case studies in this chapter. There are women in every society who are wealthy enough to afford an abortion performed by medical personnel in safe and clean conditions. But in Mexico these women constitute a privileged minority. The great majority of the women who opt for an unsafe, self-induced abortion are of low socioeconomic status and more than a few of them live in situations of extreme poverty (Gonzalez, 1990). Under these conditions, the health risks associated with the practice of self-induced abortion are greatly multiplied.

The Unmet Need for Family Planning

Of all the women we interviewed, 72 per cent said that they did not want any more children. The remaining 28 per cent want to have one or two more children, but not for another two years or more. This points to a potential danger of repeat abortions. Forty-six per cent of these women have never used contraception, although 81 per cent know of at least one method. Among the population in the study, the use of effective contraception was very low and many of the abortions and suffering these women inflicted on themselves could have been avoided with appropriate access to and use of effective contraception.

The Concept of Access to Services

A simple answer to the issue of unsafe abortions would be to guarantee universal access to family planning. Theoretically, the relationship is unquestionable: If contraception can prevent unwanted pregnancy, and if a wide choice of methods is made available to more and more women, then induced abortions to end unwanted pregnancy would be less and less necessary. Unfortunately, reality does not correspond so simply with theory.

As described earlier, Mexico has had a national family planning programme for several years. And women who went to the Hospital de la Mujer for complications of self-induced abortion do not live in geographically isolated areas, where there are no health facilities. On the contrary, a high proportion, 86 per cent, had a health centre less than half an hour away by foot or bus. A similar proportion stated that they usually go to these centres for their children's health needs, but not for their own general or reproductive health care, or family planning.

This evidence forces us to argue strongly for a re-examination of the concept of access. Health service planners reduce the problem of access and its solution to physical proximity. However, for the women themselves, the issue of access is much more complex. It must answer their own perceived needs, in a way that is consistent with their values and way of life. This also means an approach that respects a woman's right to reproductive health services that offer quality, personalized care. If programmes and services do not take these two aspects of women's reproductive health care into account, then it cannot be said that 'access' exists.

The Controversy Over the Legalization of Abortion

There is a group of people who consider that to reduce maternal morbidity and mortality caused by unsafe induced abortion it is necessary to legalize the practice so that it can always be performed by qualified personnel in appropriate conditions. As the Pan American Health Organization points out, legalizing abortion may not necessarily reduce its use, but it would sensibly decrease its negative consequences for women's health (PAHO, 1986).

In Mexico, the issue of the depenalization of abortion radicalizes opposing forces within sectors of the society. On the one hand, there are the so-called 'feminist' movements and women's groups who for decades, especially since 1976, have been fighting to legalize abortion or to at least extend its allowable clauses. The rationale for this position is to protect women's health and provide for maternity without risks. There are doctors who support this view because they have been witness to the suffering and needless illness and death that results from unsafe abortion. But their voices have not been heard openly, mostly because they would have to face contradictions in which personal values conflict with medical, legal and institutional norms (Elu, 1992). Among the providers, there are also strongly divided opinions based on gender, with women providers more in favour of a more liberal legislation on abortion than their male counterparts.

On the other hand, irreconcilable in their opposition, there are the conservative sectors, with the Pro-Vida movement at its head and supported by the hierarchy of the Catholic Church and the Acción Nacional Party (PAN). The establishment of diplomatic relations with the Vatican, which had been interrupted a century ago, along with the official acknowledgement of these religious organizations, have given these conservative sectors the chance to strengthen their public leadership and their participation in national policies. They not only are opposed to more liberal abortion laws, but also they are fighting to make them more restrictive, as recently occurred in the state of Chihuahua. Bishops have accused the government of not prosecuting abortion sternly enough, and they recommend a stronger, more organized campaign against participating doctors and women. While these conservative groups recognize abortion as a major public health problem, they think the solution to unwanted pregnancy lies in the re-affirmation of the laws against abortion and in the promotion of total abstinence or periodic sexual relations.

Government officials responsible for national population policies have kept themselves 'apparently' in the margin of the abortion debate, even while expressing concern for the high fertility rate in the rural areas of the country.

By the end of 1990, in Chiapas, a state whose fertility and birth rates are some of the highest in the country and where family planning programmes have had little success, the local congress approved a law that provided a more liberal access to abortion, under some circumstances, up to 90 days gestation. The conservative sectors were so strongly opposed, however, that the law was subsequently suspended.

If the government could not endorse a more liberal abortion law at the end of 1990, it is unlikely that it will do it under the currently more difficult political circumstances. The legislative bodies and social forces of the country are dealing now with the fundamental national priorities of maintaining democracy and peace. In this political climate, there is no place or will to introduce controversial issues.

But the discussions will continue. It is expected that the programme of Action on Population and Development approved at the Cairo Conference will help direct more attention to the need for safe abortion, and to its necessary place within the context of women's reproductive health and rights. Hopefully, at the very least, greater effort will be made to guarantee better and more compassionate services for women suffering the complications of unsafe abortion.

✝ References

Chambers, V. 1994. Abordando la calidad de atencion del aborto y la planificacion familiar post-aborto. (Considering the quality of care of abortion and post-abortion family planning.) In: M.C. Elu and A. Langer (eds), *Maternidad Sin Riesgos en Mexico*. Mexico: MES.

Elu, M.C. 1992. El aborto visto por el personal de salud. (Abortion as seen by health care personnel.) In: M.C. Elu and L. Leñero, *De Carne y Hueso*, México: IMES.

————. 1993. *La Luz Enterrada: Estudio Antropológico Sobre la Mortalidad Materna en Tlaxcala. (The Hidden Light: Anthropological Study on Maternal Mortality in Tlaxcala.)* México: FCE.

Gonzalez, R. 1990. El aborto: Un analisis de factores psicosociales. (Abortion: An analysis of psychosocial factors.) In: *Boletin del Instituto de Ingenieria*, UNAM, cited by M. Belausteguigoitia in 'El aborto en Mexico', in *Debate Feminista*, Vol. 3.

López García, R. 1994. El aborto como problema de salud pública. (The public health problem of abortion.) In: M.C. Elu and A. Langer (eds), *Maternidad Sin Riesgos en México (Maternity Without Risk)*. Mexico: MES.

Maternidad Sin Riesgos (MSR) (Maternity Without Risk). 1993. Declaración de la Conferencia Nacional, Cocoyoc, Morelos, 8–11 April 1993.

Panamerican Health Organization (PAHO). 1986. *La Salud de la Mujer en las Américas. (Women's Health in the Americas.)* Washington, D.C.: PAHO.

13

Abortion Services in Two Public Sector Hospitals in Istanbul, Turkey: How Well Do They Meet Women's Needs?

Aysen Bulut and Nahid Toubia

Introduction

The government has been responsible for family planning education and service provision in Turkey since 1965. Consequently, contraceptive prevalence among currently married women has increased from 22 per cent in 1963 to 63 per cent in 1993 (UNICEF, 1991; DHS, 1994).

The method mix, however, has changed very little. Among the users, only 35 per cent have adopted modern methods, with the majority using the IUD (19 per cent). The condom is the second most popular method (7 per cent). The traditional method of withdrawal remains the most widely used method among currently married women; the rate of use is 26 per cent, which represents 41 per cent of total contraceptive prevalence in Turkey (DHS, 1994). (See Table 13.1.)

There is clearly a need for family planning services in Turkey. More than two-thirds of married women (70 per cent) indicated that they did not want a(nother) child or were surgically sterilized. An additional 14 per cent of women wanted to wait at least two years before the birth of the next child. Thus, more than four out of five married women in Turkey can be considered to be potentially in need of family planning services.

This large need for family planning services, combined with the majority of couples using the unreliable method of withdrawal, has put the estimated number of abortions per year at 450,000. The abortion ratio is 35 per 100 live births (Omran and Roudi, 1993; Hacettepe University Institute of Population Studies, 1989). Moreover, National Demographic Surveys show that there

Table 13.1: Percentage Distribution of Currently Married Women by Contraceptive Methods Currently Used, Turkey, 1988 and 1993

	1988	1993
Any method	63.4	62.6
Any modern method	31.0	34.5
Pill	6.2	4.9
IUD	14.0	18.8
Injection	0.1	0.1
Diaphragm/foam/jelly	1.8	1.2
Condom	7.2	6.6
Female sterilization	1.7	2.9
Male sterilization	0.1	0.0
Any traditional method	32.3	28.1
Periodic abstinence	3.5	1.0
Withdrawal	25.7	26.2
Vaginal douche	2.5	0.6
Abstinence	0.1	0.1
Other methods	0.5	0.2
Not currently using	36.6	37.4

Source: Hacettepe University Institute of Population Studies, 1994.

has been a systematic increase in the incidence of reported abortions over the years, from 16.8 to 23.6 per cent in the period 1978 through 1988 (Hacettepe University Institute of Population Studies, 1989).

Since 1983, Turkish law has allowed abortion up to 10 weeks gestation, with the husband's consent. This has considerably reduced the mortality and morbidity associated with unsafe abortion. The procedure is now more accessible to poor women through public sector hospitals, whose fees are minimal. In fact, low cost is the most important reason why women choose public hospitals for abortion, although many women also think that they provide better services than some private facilities and they tend to be more conveniently located. However, only four of the more than 20 general public hospitals in the city provide abortion services on demand, mainly for pregnancies of less than eight weeks.

Because of the difficulty in obtaining data on private sector services, we decided to limit our study to two public hospitals with a fairly good reputation for public abortion services. The latest figure of reported abortions done in public hospitals was 100,000 in 1990 (MOH, 1991).

Objectives

Our study was designed to explore the experience and subsequent behaviour of women who had abortions in two public hospitals in Istanbul with fundamentally different approaches to abortion service delivery. We wanted a

profile of these women in terms of their general attitude towards the procedure and their knowledge and use of contraception to gain a better understanding of the determinants of abortion practice.

The main objective, however, was to compare the quality and efficiency of
two different approaches to service delivery. Quality was to be measured by
the women's reports of post-abortion complications, particularly bleeding
and pain; women's expressed satisfaction with the services; and their pattern
of post-abortion contraceptive use. Efficiency was to be measured by financial costs, both to the patient and to the health care system.

Research Methodology

Sample Size

The total sample size was calculated as 500 (250 cases from each hospital).
This size was expected to demonstrate differences of 15 per cent with a power
of 95 per cent ($p < .05$). Allowing for possible drop-outs, 300 cases were
planned to be recruited from each hospital.

Selection of the Two Different Hospitals

A sample consisting of clinic clients from two different hospitals in Istanbul,
the largest city in Turkey, was considered appropriate. Both hospitals provide
free or very low-cost services that are usually used by working or
lower-middle-class women. However, they were chosen for a comparative
study because of their distinct differences in service delivery.

The Bakirkoy Hospital

The Bakirkoy Maternal and Child Health Hospital (BSSK) is a social security
('national insurance') hospital open only to those who have social security
coverage. When a woman applies for an abortion, a pregnancy test is
required and then an appointment is given for the procedure. Required documents on the day of the abortion are marriage certificate and a signed paper
showing husband's consent. The husband must be present to sign his consent
at that time.

The abortion clinic is part of the outpatient obstetric and gynaecology services. Abortions are performed by rotating resident doctors as part of their
training, under the supervision of a specialist in obstetrics and gynaecology.
The clinic is open from 10 a.m. to 12 noon, Monday through Friday.

The technique used is a combination of dilatation and curettage (D&C)
with electric suction, without paracervical local anaesthesia. All women are

given intramuscular methergine towards the end of the procedure to minimize blood loss and help contract the uterus. Six beds are allocated for patients to rest after the procedure and resting time varies from 10 minutes to 45 minutes. Upon discharge, women are given antibiotics and painkillers, and occasionally tablets to contract the uterus. No follow-up visit is scheduled.

Doctors who perform the abortions have no responsibilities or connection to the family planning clinic, which is located next door and run by a trained nurse/midwife. There is very little communication or cross-referral between the two services. The family planning services and counselling are limited; pills, condoms and IUDs are offered.

The Sisli Eftal Hospital

The Sisli Eftal Hospital is a Ministry of Health, or 'government' hospital, open to everyone. Women who come for an abortion are examined and given a pregnancy test for confirmation and then given an appointment. Required documents on the day of the procedure are marriage certificate and a signed paper showing husband's consent. (This initial step is very similar in both hospitals.)

The abortion service is part of an independent family planning unit within the hospital that includes contraceptive services. The unit has its own manager, two specialists in obstetrics and gynaecology, and three or four general practitioners working under the supervision of the specialists. The department also trains other physicians from other parts of the country.

The technique most often used is the simpler method of menstrual regulation by manual vacuum aspiration, using the Karman syringe, without anaesthesia. Eight beds are available for post-operative resting, with two or three additional beds if necessary. When the patient feels well, she is told to see the doctor before leaving for drug prescription. She is also given a package to take home after the operation that contains sanitary towels, antiseptic solutions for perineal cleaning, antibiotic tablets, pain killers and tablets to contract the uterus. The doctor explains how to use the medicine and gives information on possible complications following the abortion.

The family planning clinic is run by the same staff who provide abortion services; the two services are inseparable. Abortions are performed three mornings a week from 10 a.m. to 12 noon. The remaining time is spent for follow-up of abortion patients, examinations and family planning service provision. Doctors who perform abortions are trained in family planning counselling and provision. The women discuss their contraceptive practices with the doctor before the abortion. If appropriate, an IUD is inserted immediately after the procedure. Patients are requested to come 10 days later for follow-up, at which time their plans for contraception will be discussed again.

Initial Questionnaires

An initial questionnaire was given in each hospital between 17 September 1990 and 31 January 1991. A total of 550 women were interviewed immediately before and after their abortion. First, the interviewers explained the aim of the study to the women. Then they told them that if they wanted to participate in the study, they would also have to participate in a second interview six months later, either at the clinic or at home.

This initial contact, identification of the cases and completion of the 'case' part of the questionnaire was done before the operation. Interviews took place shortly after the procedure, while the patient was resting in the recovery room. The women were also asked to fill out diaries later at home for two weeks to record any post-operative complications and fertility behaviour.

A traditional 'get-well' gift in Turkish society of two bars of scented soap and a small bottle of cologne, worth about US $1, was given to each woman after the interview so as not to bias her decision to enter the study. Women were told they would be paid approximately US $2.50 to cover transportation costs when they came back for the follow-up interview.

Follow-up

A follow-up questionnaire for the study group was started six months later on 18 March 1991 after a testing period. All women were sent reminder letters confirming their follow-up dates at the clinic. The letter included a telephone number where they could call and change their appointments if they wished to and also a note reminding them of the reimbursement for transportation costs.

Women who did not wish to be interviewed at the clinic were invited to be interviewed at the Institute. Some clients opted to conduct the interview over the phone rather than at the clinic or at home. Therefore a decision was made to allow a third category of interviews by telephone.

At the follow-up interview many women refused to take the offered transportation money and expressed their happiness and gratitude for participating in a study that would help women's health and improve the services.

During the follow-up, 460 women out of 550 were interviewed. Of these, 53.5 per cent of the interviews took place at the clinics, 15.6 per cent during home visits and 30.8 per cent by telephone. The total follow-up rate was 83.6 per cent, which is a high rate considering that these are women who live on the periphery of the city where transportation is difficult. Many also have children and job responsibilities.

Although the use of personal diaries seemed like an excellent way to obtain more detailed information, it proved to be an ineffective approach. Only 51 per cent of the women who participated in the follow-up returned their diaries. (There were no significant differences in educational status of the women who returned or failed to return the diaries.) Nineteen per cent of the returned diaries were completely empty and only 6 per cent of them contained relevant information. We therefore decided not to include diary information in the analysis.

Focus Group Discussions

To obtain in-depth knowledge on women's views and attitudes towards services, the research team conducted a series of focus group discussions with questionnaire respondents. Two groups were planned for each hospital, one with women who had primary school education (5 years or less) and one with women who had more than primary school education. Selection for the groups was not random; based on their initial questionnaires, women with different types of post-abortion experiences were chosen. The discussions took place from 30 May–8 July 1991, in the presence of two moderators using a prepared guide.

Additional Data Collection

Information on services was also collected by on-site observation of the family planning clinic and the abortion service clinic of the two hospitals.

The information on institutional cost was collected by developing specific questions for the hospital staff and for the hospital administration. The estimate of institutional cost was based on staff time and cost of disposable materials. Cost to the patient was calculated by adding transport expense for the appointment visits and the operation expenses. Actual payment to the hospital for the operation and medicines was also recorded.

Main Results

Characteristics of the Study Sample

No significant or remarkable differences were observed in the personal background between women who used the abortion services of the two hospitals during the data collection period. They were split evenly above and below age 30, with only a very small proportion (3 per cent) less than 20 years of age. The majority had completed primary education; 20 per cent had secondary education or higher. Most were housewives, with an average of 2.5 living children. More than half the women had already had at least one abortion. All were married, reflecting the legal requirement that the husband give his consent. (See Table 13.2.)

The average number of pregnancies, deliveries and pregnancy wastage of women who used both hospitals were essentially similar. Except that there was a relatively higher number of lifetime induced abortions among women

Table 13.2: Summary of the Main Characteristics of the Women in Our Study

Characteristics	Women	
	Number (N)	%
Age (years)		
15–24	(129)	23.5
25–34	(324)	58.9
35+	(97)	17.6
Education		
None	(119)	21.6
Primary	(327)	59.5
Secondary	(104)	18.9
Occupation		
Housewife	(445)	81.4
Working	(102)	18.6
Living in Istanbul (years)		
0–5	(181)	33.0
6–15	(203)	37.1
16+	(164)	29.9
Abortion experience		
No	(270)	49.1
Yes	(280)	50.9
Live children		
1	(99)	18.7
2	(229)	41.6
3–4	(180)	32.7
5	(39)	7.0

in Bakirkoy than in Sisli. The number of abortions did not differ by educational level.

The findings showed that three out of four women who applied for abortion to Sisli hospital had unplanned pregnancies of less than seven weeks gestation. Women who applied to the Bakirkoy hospital had pregnancies of relatively more advanced gestational age. The statistical difference between hospitals was significant. Half of the women at Bakirkoy had never visited the hospital before for an abortion or for any other reason. Conversely, 95 per cent of the clients at Sisli had used its facilities previously. Possibly this previous contact with the hospital was the reason why women came to Sisli at an earlier gestational age.

Attitudes Toward Induced Abortion

Most of the women in the groups had experienced at least one unwanted pregnancy during their married life. How and why these pregnancies occurred was a major topic of discussion in the focus groups. There were no differences in the frequency of or reasons for unwanted pregnancy by education or by hospital.

All the pregnancies were unplanned, except for six (1 per cent), which were terminated for medical reasons. When all the other women were asked the reason for this unwanted pregnancy, in their own words, the majority said either 'faulty use of method' or 'pregnant accidentally'. In fact, the striking finding was that by far the majority of unwanted pregnancies occurred while the women were trying to use a method of family planning. Only a few cases of unwanted pregnancy while using no method were reported.

The most common solution to an unwanted pregnancy was induced abortion. The most frequently stated reason for abortion was that desired family size had already been attained (52 per cent). The second reason was lack of sufficient means. 'No time for more children' was the next reason following these two. It was rare that health or age were given as reasons.

Nearly all the women (94 per cent) decided on induced abortion together with their husbands. For 4 per cent of the women, the husbands had made the decision. Only 2 per cent of the husbands had opposed the induced abortion. In addition to the husband, neighbours and friends were usually informed of the woman's abortion (66 per cent). Mothers and/or sisters were the next people to be informed (50 per cent). Male relatives were the last people to be informed (4.2 per cent).

All women in the focus groups affirmed that they did not look upon induced abortion as a method of contraception. They did not find comfort in the possibility of abortion; they did not have the feeling of 'anyhow I can abort'. They had tried to prevent this unwanted pregnancy, and when they had not been able to find another solution, they had chosen to have an induced abortion. A common phrase in the focus groups was 'Mecbur Kaldim', meaning 'I had to do it; I had no other choice'.

Women in the focus groups pointed out that abortion is still generally regarded as a sin in Turkey, and some stated that they felt ashamed about their abortion. However, they believed that it would be a greater sin to have a child that could not be taken care of.

Unwanted pregnancies after the initial abortion (11 per cent) were found more in the Bakirkoy groups than in the Sisli groups. Since group participants were not randomly selected, we cannot draw any conclusions based on this finding. However, it could be related to the fact that many women who have abortions at Sisli have an IUD inserted immediately postpartum. Most of the women who had another abortion after the initial interview went to a private clinic for the second abortion. One woman said she felt sure that they would refuse to do another abortion at Bakirkoy for health reasons. Women in all groups agreed that repeated abortions are dangerous to a woman's mental and physical health. However, if they are unable to find and effectively use a family planning method, they see abortion as the only available solution.

Contraceptive Knowledge and Practice

Nearly all the women in the study (99 per cent) stated that using contraception is always a better way to regulate fertility than induced abortion.

For all the women in the study, regardless of which hospital they attended, withdrawal (WD) was the method most widely known (94 per cent), and most extensively used in the past (81 per cent). IUD and oral contraceptives also had been widely used in the past (30 per cent each), and another 14 per cent of the women in the study had used condoms. These percentages reflect the use of one or two methods, in sequence or in combination (Table 13.3).

Table 13.3: Contraceptive Knowledge and Use Among the Women
Attending Both Hospitals*

Methods	Hospitals (%)		Total (%)
	Bakirkoy	Sisli	
Knowledge			
Withdrawal	95	92	94
Pill	98	88	94
IUD	99	86	94
Injectables	11	22	16
Condoms	85	58	73
Spermicide	67	32	51
Ever-use			
Withdrawal	83	80	81
Pill	24	37	30
IUD	23	34	28
Injectables	0.4	5	2
Condoms	5	25	14
Spermicides	4	12	8

* Percentages reflect knowledge or ever-use of more than one method.

The majority of the women (72 per cent) declared that they had been using a method at the time of conception of this present pregnancy (Table 13.4). However, three out of every four women who said they had been using contraception identified the method as 'my husband protecting himself', meaning simply, withdrawal. Even some women who used modern methods (11 per cent) experienced failures (Table 13.5). Several women who got pregnant

Table 13.4: Use of Contraception Before Last Pregnancy

Before Pregnancy	BSSK (N)	%	Sisli (N)	%	Total (N)	(%)
Used	(223)	73.6	(171)	69.5	(394)	71.8
Not used	(80)	26.4	(75)	30.5	(155)	28.2
Total	(303)	100.0	(246)	100.0	(549)	100.0

Table 13.5: **Method in Use When the Last Pregnancy Occurred Among Users***

Method	BSSK (N)	(%)	Sisli (N)	(%)	Total	(%)
Withdrawal	(209)	82.6	(142)	66.4	(351)	75.2
Pill/IUD	(19)	7.5	(30)	14.0	(49)	10.5
Condom/spermicide	(20)	7.9	(25)	11.7	(45)	9.6
Other	(5)	2.0	(17)	7.9	(22)	4.7
Total	(253)	100.0	(214)	100.0	(467)	100.0

* Percentages reflect use of more than one method.

while using a modern method were then afraid that having the baby would be dangerous for their health or for the health of their baby. It appears that the majority of the women in the groups were really trying to prevent pregnancy. This was equally true regardless of education level.

When women were asked the reason for not using a medical method, the majority of women (135 women) said it was their husband's disapproval. The second reason given (by 72 women) for not using a medical method was fear of health risks. The other main reasons given were not knowing how to use a more reliable method (46 women) and their doctor's advice against medical methods (41 women).

Wide use of withdrawal is basically the husband's preference. Yet, women did not express any complaints about withdrawal, possibly based on their belief that other methods produce negative side effects.

Given that IUD is the most widely used modern method in Turkey, we felt it was important to examine how the women in our study who were using IUDs experienced an unwanted pregnancy. Some women in the groups got pregnant after their IUDs were expelled. Others got pregnant after a health provider advised them to have their IUDs removed for a while so that their bodies could have a 'rest'. Still others reported pregnancies occurring while the IUD was in place. In the groups, we noted that many women worried about pregnancy while using the IUD and mistrusted the method in general.

An interesting subgroup difference was found on the topic of dialogue with husbands about fertility regulation. Women in the high education groups were much more likely to discuss the problem of unwanted pregnancy with their husbands, and then to decide what to do together, than those in the low education groups. Several women in the low education groups said that their husbands did not show much interest in problems related to unwanted pregnancy. A few women were even using contraception without their husband's knowledge.

Quality of Care

Quality of care is an issue that has become increasingly important to understanding whether or not reproductive health services are acceptable and respectful to the women receiving them. The issue is therefore an important key to whether or not services are effective. In this study, the following indicators are used to assess the quality of abortion services at the two hospitals: reports of post-abortion complications, the pattern of contraceptive use six months after the abortion, and women's expressed satisfaction with the services. (The results are summarized in Table 13.6.)

Table 13.6: Quality of Care

Elements Used to Define Quality of Care	Hospitals	
	Bakirkoy	Sisli
Post-abortion complications*		
Pain duration (in days)	3.60 (±11.86)	4.83 (±11.35)
Bleeding duration (in days)	4.37 (±10.36)	7.25 (±11.35)
Contraceptive use after six months (%)		
Modern methods	36	79
Non-medical	64	21
Satisfaction with services (%)		
– Appointment given within three days	29	42
– Technical competency of provider judged by whether operation for woman was:		
painful	94	77
difficult	80	51
– Interpersonal relations with the providers judged by woman as 'very good':		
with the physician	6	37
with the nurses	6	34
– Additional services:		
postpartum care judged by woman as 'very good'	2	13
family planning care judged by woman as 'very good'	9	11
Overall quality of care index (%)		
Women receiving high quality care	10	37

* In Sisli, a higher number of IUD insertions were done immediately postpartum, a procedure that increases bleeding and pain duration. Therefore the data on these factors do not necessarily reflect lower quality of care.

Women's Reports of Post-Abortion Complications

Women's reports about bleeding, pain, fever, etc., which they may have experienced after their abortion, were used to measure service acceptability. Since very few women complained of discomfort other than pain and bleeding, only these two criteria were used as indicators.

Pain

Pain was a very important aspect of the abortion experience for these women. In each focus group, there were a few women who said they felt a lot of pain during the abortion. Women in one group spent time hypothesizing about the reason for pain; some thought it could be related to the number of previous pregnancies or births a woman had had or to the gestational age of the foetus. Some women felt that general anaesthesia is necessary to avoid a painful abortion.

Reported duration of pain in the post-operative period was different between the two hospitals. This period was longer in Sisli, 4.83 ± 11.35 days, compared to 3.60 ± 11.86 days in Bakirkoy ($t = 1.94$, $p < 0.05$). When the whole group was analyzed, post-abortion IUD insertion, which was more frequent in Sisli, was found to significantly increase pain duration: Mean duration of reported pain in IUD-inserted women was 9.50 ± 21.38 days; the time period was 5.17 ± 16.39 days in the remaining women ($t = 1.92$, $p > 0.05$).

Bleeding

Mean duration of bleeding was 5.63 ± 10.89 days in the total group. Reported duration of post-abortion bleeding was significantly different in the two hospitals, however. In Sisli, again, where more IUD insertions were done immediately postpartum, mean bleeding time was longer, 7.25 ± 11.35 days. In Bakirkoy, this period was 4.37 ± 10.36 days ($t = 2.80$, $p < 0.05$).

When the total group was included in the analysis, the duration of bleeding, as with pain, was found to be severely affected by IUD insertion. Mean number of reported bleeding days was longer, 7.87 ± 12.51 days, in the 123 IUD-inserted cases. This figure was 4.38 ± 10.14 days in the non-IUD inserted cases ($t = 2.38$, $p < 0.05$).

Discussion

When reported post-abortion pain and bleeding are used to measure the quality of service provision, Bakirkoy appeared to give a much more acceptable service than Sisli (32 per cent compared to 11 per cent, respectively). Pain and bleeding that normally occur as a result of IUD insertion, however, need to be taken into account in any conclusions about the quality of the services being offered. We also analyzed women's reports of pain and bleeding according to their educational and occupational characteristics. Their reports did not vary by these characteristics.

Patterns of Post-Abortion Contraceptive Use at Six Months

One significant change in fertility behaviour noted six months after the abortion was an increased use of modern methods. Thirty-six per cent of the women who had an abortion at Bakirkoy were using a modern method of contraception compared to nearly 80 per cent at Sisli. This confirms that the quality of services at Sisli, when defined as an increased use of modern methods, is much higher than at Bakirkoy.

The use of the IUD had significantly increased. Sisli had a much higher post-abortion rate of IUD insertions (65 per cent) compared to Bakirkoy (25 per cent). Withdrawal was still the most popular method, however; although its prevalence had decreased slightly to 36 per cent.

Women's Expressed Satisfaction with the Services

Women were asked to express their opinion about their satisfaction with services received at the two hospitals on a scale ranging from very good to poor. The different aspects of service delivery that were evaluated are discussed next and summarized in Table 13.6.

The Application Process

In both hospitals women were satisfied with the application process. Mean time until appointment given for the procedure was 4.62±2.45 days after applying. Appointments given sooner, within three days, were significantly higher in Sisli. Forty-two per cent of the women applying to Sisli got an appointment within three days, compared to 29 per cent at Bakirkoy. Only three women had the abortion on the day of the first outpatient visit.

Technical Competence of the Provider

The technical competence of the provider stands out as one of the most important criteria of satisfaction for the women. They judged the competence of the provider according to the duration of the procedure and the amount of pain they experienced. So that if the abortion was quick and painless, women considered the doctor to be competent. In both hospitals, a very high percentage of women experienced pain: 94 per cent of the women at Bakirkoy found the operation painful, compared to 77 per cent at Sisli. The proportion of women who found the operation 'difficult' was 80 per cent and 51 per cent, respectively, for each hospital. Overall technical competence was rated significantly higher in Sisli (17 per cent) than in Bakirkoy (3 per cent), although generally both hospitals received a low rating.

The focus group participants said that they did not have much information about the different abortion techniques and most of the women were unsure about which method had been used for their abortions. Many women said they felt the suction pulling on their womb and heard the sound of a machine. A few women from Sisli said they saw a large injector and felt as if they had been stuck with a needle. Some women said that the 'new' abortion techniques are less painful and therefore much better than the 'old' techniques.

Interpersonal Relations

Women were also asked their opinion about the quality of interpersonal relations with both the doctors and the nurses, which was much higher again in Sisli than in Bakirkoy. The proportion of women declaring that the care given by the doctors was 'very good' was 6 per cent at Bakirkoy and 37 per cent at Sisli; similarly, women who said that the nurses gave 'very good' care was 6 per cent at Bakirkoy and 34 per cent at Sisli.

Women in the focus groups from both hospitals, however, complained about a lack of individual attention from abortion providers. This complaint extended to follow-up services at Sisli; women felt rushed and wanted more individual attention from providers. The focus group discussions revealed that education could be a factor here: it seems that women with higher education were more outgoing and assertive than the women with less education, and thus were able to extract more information from their providers.

At the Bakirkoy hospital, which is a teaching hospital for obstetricians/gynaecologists, 97 per cent of the abortions are performed by male residents. At Sisli, where general practitioners are trained, 83 per cent of the abortions are performed by trainees or trained general practitioners, who are mainly female. In general, however, it seems that women did not think the sex of the provider was important. This finding was surprising, given the well-documented preference for female health providers among women in Turkey. The likely explanation is that abortion is an immensely stressful experience that women want to get through as rapidly and painlessly as possible; this could easily mask an existing concern about the sex of the provider.

Postpartum Care and Family Planning Care

Postpartum care also received a higher rating in Sisli where routine follow-up was more often advised than in Bakirkoy. Although, overall, the rating of 'very good' was very low for both hospitals: only 2 per cent at Bakirkoy and 13 per cent at Sisli.

The quality of family planning care was also generally low for both hospitals; only one out of 10 women expressed a high degree of satisfaction with the care received. It was clear from the interviews that both hospitals failed in this respect: neither usually gives family planning counselling and information at the time of an abortion.

Moreover, several women in the focus groups pointed out the need for pre-abortion counselling services, such as screening for health problems, discussion of how and why the pregnancy occurred, and information on what to expect during the abortion procedure, including information about the type of method being used.

In all the focus groups, women expressed their strong desire to learn more about family planning methods. Women with more education were able to get some information and counselling from the abortion clinic staff through assertiveness and personal contacts.

It appears that to get information and/or counselling in these clinics, a woman has to ask for it and keep insisting. This takes a certain amount of self-confidence, which often comes with education.

In short, in both hospitals, the choice of methods and the quality of family planning information and counselling offered to women before and after their abortions appeared to be very poor.

The Hospital Environment

In focus group discussions, differences in opinion emerged about the physical set-up of the hospitals, indicating problems of maintaining cleanliness and order. For example, women who undertook the abortion at earlier hours were more satisfied with the physical conditions. In general, women in the higher education groups had some complaints, while women with less education tended to be satisfied with the clinic settings.

Overall Satisfaction with the Services

To evaluate women's overall satisfaction with the services received, regardless of the hospital attended, they were asked the following question: 'If you needed another pregnancy termination, would you use this hospital even if you had access to all other options and services?' The answer 'Yes' was considered to express satisfaction. When asked this question immediately after the operation, 273 women (50 per cent) said 'Yes'. When the same question was asked of them six months later, 58 per cent still gave an affirmative answer. Only 34 per cent of the women maintained a negative opinion. The remaining were ambivalent. First impressions right after the operation are probably more indicative of a true perception of service satisfaction. Overall satisfaction did not differ according to educational level.

When only three of the measures of expressed satisfaction—technical competence, interpersonal relations, and postpartum care (excluding pain and bleeding concerns)—are combined to measure overall quality of care, the result shows that 37 per cent of the women at Sisli and 10 per cent of the women at Bakirkoy received high quality care. The difference was significant.

Multivariate Analysis

Even though there was a clear expression of overall satisfaction with the services, a logistics regression analysis was performed to determine which factors were associated with a satisfied perception. (The results are summarized in Table 13.7.) The following factors showed an association with satisfaction:

quality of care (defined as an index of the three factors related to women's expressed satisfaction just described), completion of the operation (effectiveness), family planning services, provision of IUDs, gestational age at the time of pregnancy termination, physician's gender and physician's qualifications.

Table 13.7: Factors Relating to Satisfaction (Logistic Regression Analysis)

	R	p	Odds
Quality	.2025	.0000	4.6157
Effectiveness	.0572	.0490	2.8066
FP services	.0829	.0104	2.8583
IUD insertion	.0000	.8386	.9532
Gestational week	.0000	.4665	.8034
Provider's gender	.0100	.1514	1.8207
Provider's qualifications	.0000	.3562	1.4509

Other factors that were found not to affect client satisfaction to any significant degree included the woman's education, her age, her occupation, her family's acceptance of abortion, her own consent, previous abortion experience (including whether the provider was a private doctor), and whether or not there was any post-abortion bleeding and pain.

The results of the multivariate analysis also showed that the strongest associations with client satisfaction were quality of care, completion of the operation and family planning services. For example, the women who ranked highest in their appreciation of quality of care were four times more satisfied with the services than those who ranked low. Similarly, women who were satisfied with the outcome of the operation and those who received family planning services were three times more satisfied with the overall services than those who did not. Advanced gestational age was not a significant negative factor to explain satisfaction. There were no significant differences between the two hospitals regarding effectiveness of the procedure or the provision of family planning services.

It is interesting to note that in this analysis of the factors related to client satisfaction, the physician's gender was not statistically significant although the ratio of male/female doctors were different in the two hospitals. Overall, 54 per cent of the women who were attended by male providers and 70 per cent of those attended by female providers expressed satisfaction. Whether he/she was a hospital trainee or a specialist was not found to be an important factor relating to satisfaction in Bakirkoy, where the majority of providers were residents in training. Yet, differences in technical competence, performance of pregnancy termination, postpartum care, experience of bleeding and pain, service provision of family planning and IUD insertion were significant when trainee or trained general practitioners were compared with ob/gyn specialists in Sisli.

Service Efficiency

All cases in the Bakirkoy hospital were covered by social security, because it is a social security hospital. In Sisli, social security coverage was 45 per cent.

Eighty-seven per cent of all women interviewed agreed that the abortion services in public hospitals were inexpensive relative to the present cost of living. This view was expressed particularly by the Bakirkoy clients, the majority of whom had insurance coverage and consequently did not have to pay much for the procedure.

From the perspective of financial cost to clients, it can be concluded that the services are cost-effective. In fact, the cost of transportation constituted the biggest portion of the cost for the Bakirkoy clients; while for the Sisli patients, the largest expense was to buy medicines. For the women who attended Bakirkoy, the total expense of the abortion was fairly modest (TL18,473 or US$4.62); while the cost at Sisli hospital was somewhat higher (TL41,227 or US$10.31). (The exchange rate was US $1.00 = TL4000 during the research period.)

Table 13.8: Total Cost Distribution of Pregnancy Termination Services in Both Hospitals

	Bakirkoy		*Sisli*	
	TL	*%*	*TL*	*%*
According to clients				
Transport	14.038	76.0	6.126	14.9
Hospital	2.947	16.0	14.134	34.3
Medication	1.488	8.0	20.967	50.8
Total	18.473	100.0	41.227	100.0
Institutional				
Staff	30.800	93.0	67.388	96.8
Supplies	2.354	7.0	2.250	3.2
Total	33.154	100.0	69.638	100.0
Total sum	51.627	–	110.865	–

Note: The exchange rate at the time of the study was US$1 = TL4000.

Most of the women who discussed the issue of cost during the focus group sessions, however, felt that the costs of abortion in terms of mental and physical health were much harder to bear than the monetary costs. They agreed that using a family planning method to prevent pregnancy is less expensive than undergoing an abortion. Nevertheless, they felt that the more expensive alternative would have been going ahead with the pregnancy.

From an institutional perspective, the highest cost was for hospital staff salaries. In Sisli, the hospital cost was twice as high as at Bakirkoy; but it should be kept in mind that in Sisli, the intervention more often included an IUD insertion, or in a few cases, tubal ligation. However, cost-per-case at Sisli would decrease if client load were to increase. At Bakirkoy, where more changes are needed, cost-per-intervention could increase. Overall, the costs at both hospitals seem reasonable, even at Sisli where they are still below US$20 per case.

Conclusions

Some important conclusions emerge from this study. Abortion among the women is undertaken largely as a result of contraceptive failure: About three out of four women were using some form of contraception when they became pregnant. The use of modern methods, however, is relatively low; the most commonly used method at the time of unplanned pregnancy was withdrawal. Women prefer to rely on withdrawal for reasons that have important programme and policy implications: Husbands object to modern contraceptive use; there is considerable fear of side effects of modern methods; and doctors themselves often advise against modern methods.

These constraints are powerful; only about one-quarter of the women who had become pregnant while using withdrawal have switched to a more reliable method. But these obstacles have not led women to abandon contraception altogether, but to rely on less effective methods, like withdrawal; in some cases, women even secretly continued to use modern methods of contraception, despite their husbands opposition. This shows a real desire to use contraception rather than to resort to abortion (McLaurin et al., 1993).

Women at Sisli hospital, where family planning and abortion services were more integrated, expressed greater satisfaction with their experience than women who attended Bakirkoy hospital. However, we found that only a few women overall had received any counselling and information on fertility regulation methods either before or after their abortion. It was clear that women desperately wanted more information on contraception and abortion; some women in the focus group discussions went so far as to suggest techniques for information delivery. Counselling that explains the details of the abortion procedure and offers information about subsequent family planning options is a critical factor in the women's overall satisfaction. Some women had even expressed the desire to have a choice of abortion technique. Our findings further support the need for post-abortion contraceptive counselling as recommended in previous studies (Bulut, 1984). For example, while it is true that IUD insertion immediately postpartum is the easiest method to provide, we observed that if this service is not accompanied by appropriate counselling, continuation of use will be low.

In general, women were evenly split with respect to the quality of the abortion services they had received. Only half said that they would apply to the same institution for another abortion if needed. This assessment was not derived from the subjective opinions of the women but from their direct perceptions of the quality of the service received. What is lacking in quality, in general terms, is a more individualized response that deals with the informational and personal needs of these women. This is particularly important at the time they request abortion services and later when they need individual post-operative counselling. In fact, we found that the quality of interpersonal relations improved when the individual provider attitude was friendlier and more receptive (Finger and Hardee, 1993).

The issue of pain management emerged as an important factor in women's satisfaction and comfort with abortion services. Providers should do whatever is possible to minimize the level of pain during an abortion procedure (Kizza and Rogo, 1990).

This study also supports women's greater satisfaction with menstrual regulation as a safe and efficient method of fertility regulation. Not only can it be provided by non-medical personnel (Dixon-Mueller, 1988; Freedman et al., 1986), but also it has the important advantage of not requiring anaesthesia.

Recommendations

Based on the conclusions of our study, the following general recommendations can be made:

1. In Turkey, public sector women's health services should be reorganized to integrate family planning services with abortion services. For example, when first applying for an induced abortion, women should be given counselling on contraceptive choices and needs. Post-abortion follow-up on contraceptive use should also be part of the services.
2. Good quality abortion services need to have an individualized, personal approach. Also, women should be told what the procedure is about and what to expect from it, including possible post-abortion sequelae; a choice of techniques should be offered whenever possible. Providers should make a special effort perform the procedure without unnecessary delay.
3. The issue of pain management should be addressed in service delivery. For example, anaesthesia should be made available to women who want it and they should have the right to choose the type of anaesthesia as general or local.

We believe that any added expense resulting from implementing these recommendations to improve the quality of services will, in the long run, be cost-effective.

Policy Impact

This study is notable for having had an immediate impact in the way the services are delivered in a major hospital in Istanbul. It is worth noting that following the end of the study, some of these recommendations were immediately implemented in Bakirkoy hospital, where an additional direct observation of services was undertaken to verify the results. The changes made included moving the Family Planning and Abortion Clinic to a separate building away from the main maternity wards and where the physical conditions were much better. Appointments are now given for the next day, avoiding the delays that existed before. The application for termination of pregnancy is filled out in the family planning clinic, where a pregnancy test and a physical examination is first done. At the time women apply for an abortion, counselling on family planning is immediately provided, emphasizing available options for post-abortion contraceptive use. If the woman wishes to undergo tubal ligation, there is another evaluation of her case by the abortion clinic staff. Then the abortion and sterilization are performed simultaneously. Women are also given an option to choose what type of anaesthesia they would prefer, local or general, and the resting period for abortion patients has been increased. Those who provide abortion services are now the same staff of the family planning clinic, further integrating these services. All women are asked to return 15 days after the abortion procedure, whether they received family planning services or not, and all now receive additional counselling on contraception. The quality of the services at Bakirkoy hospital has greatly improved following the introduction of these changes.

✝ References

Bulut, A. 1984. Acceptance of effective contraceptive methods after induced abortion. *Studies in Family Planning* 15 (6): 281–84.

Demographic and Health Survey (DHS). 1994. *Turkish Demographic and Health Survey—1993*. Ankara, Turkey: Hacettepe University and Ministry of Health.

Dixon-Mueller, R. 1988. Innovations in reproductive health care: Menstrual regulation policies and programs in Bangladesh. *Studies in Family Planning* 19 (3): 129–40.

Finger, W.R. and K. Hardee. 1993. What is quality of care *Network. Family Health International* 14 (1): 4.

Freedman, M.A., D.A. Jillson, R.R. Coffin and L.F. Novick. 1986. Comparison of complication rates in first trimester abortions performed by physician assistants and physicians. *American Journal of Public Health* 76 (5): 550–54.

Hacettepe University Institute of Population Studies. 1989. *Turkish Population and Health Survey, 1988*. Ankara: Hacettepe University Institute of Population Studies.

Kizza, A.P.M. and K.O. Rogo. 1990. Assessment of manual vacuum aspiration equipment in the management of incomplete abortion. *East African Medical Journal* 67 (11): 812–21.

McLaurin, K.E., P. Senanayake, N. Toubia and N. Ladipo. 1993. Post abortion family planning: Reversing a legacy of neglect. *Lancet* 342: 1099–1100.

Ministry of Health (MOH). 1991. Ankara, Turkey.

Omran, A.P. and F. Roudi. 1993. The Middle East Population Puzzle. *Population Bulletin* 48: 1–40.

UNICEF. 1991. The situation analysis of mothers and children in Turkey. Series 2. Ankara: UNICEF-Turkey.

✝

SECTION B

Provider Perspectives

14

The Attitudes of Health Care Providers Towards Abortion in Indonesia

E. Djohan, R. Indrawasih, M. Adenan,
H. Yudomustopo and M.G. Tan

Introduction

In recent years in Indonesia, newspapers and magazines have been reporting incidents of newborn babies found dead in garbage dumps or among shrubs along the road, or left behind in hospitals by mothers who have disappeared. Attention has also been drawn to the alarmingly high rate of maternal mortality in the country, estimated at about 450 per 100,000 live births in 1980–88, including deaths resulting from clandestine abortions (UNICEF, 1991).

Unwanted pregnancy and its surrounding events are not new, but the increasing media attention to reproductive health issues has been concurrent with growing public concern. It is also evident that there is an increasingly more open dialogue regarding sexuality and contraception in Indonesian society. Two particular trends have emerged to encourage this greater openness. The first is that with greater freedom in social interaction among teenagers and young people, accidental pregnancy has become more common. Interviews with girls who have had these 'accidents' reveal a complete lack of knowledge and unpreparedness to handle their new 'freedom'. Through no fault of their own, as sexual topics are largely taboo, they know next to nothing about the changes happening in their bodies, especially their reproductive functions, or how pregnancy comes about (Widyantoro, 1989). More than half the women in this particular study were between 15 and 20 years of age and 78 per cent were still in school or university. It showed that girls who have an unexpected pregnancy often face resistance when seeking services from maternity clinics and gynaecologists because they are unmarried, and often they are asked to pay three times more for an abortion than married women. Consequently, and usually in a panic, they do whatever they can to have the pregnancy terminated, which means they frequently resort to unqualified practitioners, often a traditional birth attendant (TBA). The second contributing factor is that there is an increasing number of women using contraceptives, which increases the probability of contraceptive failure in a context of increased expectations of being able to control fertility and keep family size small.

While these trends may affect the incidence of abortion, its practice has traditionally been performed among the peoples of Indonesia. The most common method is abdominal massage, usually performed by a traditional healer with a specialized technique. Another method, best known in Java, is to drink *jamu peluntur*, made by boiling certain leaves and roots and then drinking the liquid or by pounding the ingredients into a powder and boiling it in water (Rahardjo, 1990). A more 'modern' way to take this medicine, in pill or capsule form, has been developed. Ingestion of quinine and the insertion of instruments into the uterus are also widely used traditional methods. Unfortunately, the serious health risks of such techniques are usually inevitable. Massage of the abdomen by traditional means can cause bleeding and damage to internal organs. Quinine can cause poisoning, kidney disorders, and vomiting followed by dehydration, and even death. Haemorrhage, shock, fever, sepsis, tetanus, perforation of the uterus and laceration of the cervix are the most common complications that need treatment (Utomo et al., 1982). Women who take these actions to terminate an unwanted pregnancy are under tremendous physical and emotional strain, especially if they have to make the decision entirely on their own, placing not only their health but even their life at great risk.

Conscious efforts to expose the problems associated with unwanted pregnancy and abortion, and to discuss them openly, started as far back as the mid-1960s. In 1964, the Indonesian Medical Association and the Indonesian Association of Obstetrics & Gynaecology held a symposium on abortion, where the need to formulate laws allowing abortion for therapeutic reasons was discussed. The existing law, found in the Penal Code of Indonesia, originates from the Criminal Law of the Netherlands Indies (1918) during the colonial period. It makes abortion for the sole purpose of terminating a pregnancy a criminal act (Utomo et al., 1982). Anyone who advertises, encourages, performs or has an abortion is liable to prosecution. Moreover, any physician, midwife or pharmacist convicted of being an abortionist will have his/her license revoked.

The failed coup in 1965 that led to the government of President Suharto delayed the publication of the 1964 symposium results for two years. Five recommendations addressed to the Minister of Health were finally made public in 1966: (*a*) increase the research on the determinants of induced abortion; (*b*) reform the laws on induced abortion to allow for medically indicated pregnancy terminations; (c) include the Medical Code of Ethics in the required course work of all medical schools, which states that abortion is illegal except when done for medical reasons; (d) promote the distribution of information on family planning; and (e) eliminate illegally induced abortions (Tjiong, 1966). While some of these recommendations began to be implemented, no change in the law was forthcoming.

The incidence of women admitted for treatment of complications following clandestine abortion was already increasing by the mid-1970s. A study in 18 general hospitals and 22 maternity clinics and hospitals in Jakarta covering the period 1972–75 showed that there were 18 abortion cases per 100 deliveries in hospitals in 1972, rising to almost 40 in 1975. In the maternity hospitals, the number of cases per 100 deliveries rose from four to seven in the same period. These women were, on average, 28–30 years old and 98 per cent were married. About half were pregnant for the fifth time and 20 per cent had already had six or more previous births. Generally, women were brought to the hospital in an already critical condition. Studies in other Indonesian hospitals showed similar patterns (Jatipura et al., 1978).

In 1973, a symposium in Indonesia of the Second Congress of Obstetrics & Gynaecology agreed to support an initiative by the government to propose the formulation of laws on abortion on medical grounds (Samil, 1989). That same year, the teaching hospital of the University of Indonesia started to provide menstrual regulation with the tacit approval of the legal authorities in Jakarta, even though no formal protection for providers had been instituted. Since then, more clinics have made menstrual regulation services available.

In subsequent years, symposiums organized by legal associations and others also advocated amendment of the abortion laws, to which the government responded positively. In January 1977, by decision of the Minister of Health, an inter-departmental committee was set up to formulate a bill legalizing abortion on medical grounds. More than a year later, this committee produced a set of draft laws. These were discussed at a seminar organized by the Ministry of Health in October 1978. However, the government did not bring this bill before the Parliament; not all groups in society accepted the use of menstrual regulation, especially religious groups and some ethnic groups.

Nonetheless, by 1982, three main methods of menstrual regulation were being used in Indonesia: vacuum aspiration, suction curettage and injection of hypertonic saline solution (Utomo et al., 1982). (More recently, vacuum aspiration appears to have become the most widely used of these, especially in the big cities, and reported problems are minimal.) During the 1980s it was shown that where menstrual regulation services were available, the rate of septic abortions had decreased. Where no hospital or clinic was providing menstrual regulation services, septic abortion cases continued to increase (Moeloek et al., 1988). In spite of the clear evidence in support of providing safe abortion services, the law remained the same until 1992.

At present, a woman who needs an abortion may be referred from any of several hundred health care clinics and health posts staffed by community volunteers to a facility offering abortion care, if the staff are sympathetic. To have her pregnancy terminated at a recognized facility, she must have a referral letter from her doctor confirming that the pregnancy poses a threat to her health, the results of a pregnancy test, her husband's approval if she is married or the consent of her parents if she is not, and a statement indicating her willingness to use contraception afterwards. In mid-1991, clinics were reported to be charging Rp 50,000–150,000 (US$ 30–80 approximately) for an abortion. Nonetheless, the majority of women continue to attend illegal and surreptitiously-known clinics, or traditional practitioners, who operate clandestinely.

Study Objectives

The literature on abortion in Indonesia includes a significant number of studies on its medical aspects, mostly conducted in hospitals. The lack of non-medical studies is due, no doubt, to the sensitivity of the topic in a country where abortion continues to be very restricted and socially condemned.

After consulting with a number of well-informed people in medical, family planning and policy fields, we decided to conduct a study on the attitudes of health care providers towards abortion, including their involvement in its actual practice, which we considered to be the easiest approach to the issue. We hoped the results would contribute to the improvement of service norms that would enhance the ability of health care providers to treat women with unwanted pregnancy in a safe and caring way, and help reduce the risk of maternal death due to abortion. We also hoped to encourage further studies that would address themselves to the social and behavioural context of unwanted pregnancy and abortion.

Research Design and Methodology

We interviewed a selected group of men and women general practitioners (GPs) and gynaecologists, women midwives (*bidan*) and traditional birth attendants (TBAs) (*dukun bayi*), and men and women family planning field workers (PLKB), all of whom were working in the municipality of Jakarta and all of whom were Muslim.[1] The total of 76 respondents came from five different ethnic groups but most were Javanese. Of the total of 12 women gynaecologists in Jakarta in 1990, we spoke to seven.[2] (See Table 14.1.)

In addition, we consulted two Muslim religious leaders, three lawyers from legal aid institutions, one high official from the National Family Planning

---

[1] About 85 per cent of the population of Jakarta is Muslim.

[2] These were taken from a list of 200 gynaecologists obtained from the Jakarta chapter of the Indonesian Association of Obstetricians and Gynaecologists, 1990.

Table 14.1: Type and Distribution of Respondents

Occupation	Female	Male	Total
General practitioners	7	7	14
Gynaecologists	7	7	14
Midwives	16	0	16
Traditional midwives	16	0	16
Family planning field workers	8	8	16
Total	54	22	76

Coordinating Board, two psychologists, one member of Parliament, one editor of a well-known women's magazine, one high official from the Central Bureau of Statistics, a staff member of the Indonesian Planned Parenthood Association, and a staff member of another non-government organization—also because they are considered knowledgeable on this topic.

The respondents were either known to us personally or identified through physicians and gynaecologists we contacted in Jakarta. They were not a representative sample, but rather a purposive one. They were selected because they were in positions where they could potentially help or advise women who had had or were seeking abortions, and because they were knowledgeable on abortion, and would therefore give an indication of attitudes among those with influence in this area.

One-to-one interviews conducted by four women researchers took place over a period of six months from October 1990, with some follow-up continuing into April 1991, at the general and maternity hospitals, public health centres and clinics where the providers worked, and in a few cases, in their private offices or homes. An interview guide with a specific list of topics was used, based on a conceptual framework that identified our key issues and variables, but the wording of the actual questions asked during the interviews was not always the same depending on the exchange between the interviewer and each interviewee. Note-taking was as comprehensive as possible and a tape recorder was used only with the explicit consent of the respondent.

Responsibilities and Characteristics of the Different Providers

In this study we define the formal health providers as general practitioners (GPs), gynaecologists and midwives. Nonformal health providers include *dukun bayi* or the traditional birth attendants (TBAs) and family planning field workers (*Petugas Lapangan Keluarga Berencana*) (PLKB), who work in close collaboration with each other.

There are two kinds of family planning clinics in Jakarta: ordinary and fully equipped. The ordinary ones provide pills, condoms, foam tablets and jelly; and give advice on natural methods. The fully equipped ones provide IUD and other medical methods, such as implants and injections. Each clinic has a staff consisting of a physician, a midwife, an assistant midwife and administrative people. However, not all clinics have a full-time physician. These clinics are part of maternity clinics, MCH clinics and health centres, while others are located on separate premises. The family planning clinics located in the health centres are managed by midwives, sometimes with the assistance of TBAs and PLKB.

As is usually true for all physicians, general practitioners and gynaecologists have a highly respectable position in society. They are considered to have a higher status than other health providers, because of their more specialized and formal education. In Indonesia, becoming a gynaecologist takes another four years after finishing medical school.

Midwives in Indonesia are qualified nurses with two extra years of midwifery training, and they work mainly in maternity clinics, health centres, general hospitals, or from home. Patients come to these facilities for antenatal care, uncomplicated delivery, family planning services and sometimes for pregnancy termination.

TBAs attend more than 80 per cent of births in Indonesia, especially in the villages, and they are highly regarded by their communities. Most of the TBAs in our study were 50–60 years old, with the youngest aged 40 and the oldest aged 83. They lived on the outskirts of Jakarta or in the densely populated poorer sections, the same neighbourhoods as most of their patients. Five of them had had a TBA training course. Some of them appeared hesitant to discuss abortion, probably because they were older and uneducated and are popularly viewed as willing to perform abortions.

PLKB are the front-line workers for the family planning programme. They follow a three-week training course; sometimes they receive additional training and some of them follow training for midwives. They act as family planning motivators and counsellors. As motivators, they visit the homes of eligible couples, hold meetings with community leaders and participate in social and religious activities, where they give information on family planning. Their task is to advocate use of the IUD, implants and injectables as the methods considered more reliable. People obtain the methods themselves from clinics or health posts.

As counsellors, the PLKB monitor contraceptive users and motivate them to have regular checkups. During these home visits, they listen to any complaints about side effects and about pregnancies due to contraceptive failure. They are expected to be able to solve these problems, especially if there is contraceptive failure. If a woman does not want a pregnancy, the PLKB is the first person she would turn to. The PLKB send women with problems of contraceptive side effects or contraceptive failure to a health centre where they are examined and treated or referred to a hospital if necessary. Fourteen of the PLKB respondents had completed secondary education and nursing school. The other two had nine years of schooling.

Study Results: The Views of the Health Care Providers

In this section we review and compare the various perspectives of the different sets of providers. Because the views did not vary significantly by formal versus nonformal provider characteristics, our presentation is organized according to the most salient issues that emerged during the interviews.

The Influence of Religious Belief

Religion appeared to be the strongest determining factor influencing the views of these health care providers on abortion. While this was especially true of the TBAs and PLKB, many of the trained midwives, GPs and gynaecologists shared the view that abortion was a sin.

Most of the GPs, gynaecologists and midwives pointed out that according to Islam, *roh* (life, spirit or soul) is infused in a foetus after 120 days of pregnancy, even if there is life in the biological sense before that. On this basis, most of the respondents did not consider menstrual regulation as abortion, and this probably helped to overcome any ambivalence they may otherwise have felt.

A prominent Muslim leader confirmed their understanding of Islam on this point, but explained that there are different schools of thought in Islam. For the Hanafi school, termination of pregnancy can be tolerated when done before 120 days. The Sjafii school, on the other hand, which is predominant in Indonesia, rejects this view. Therefore, most religious leaders in Indonesia consider abortion a deadly sin regardless of the gestation period.

However, some of the health care providers who expressed anti-abortion views for religious reasons still indicated a willingness to tolerate and support women who wanted early abortion; and in some cases, to refer women for or perform abortions. In this, the reasons given by formal sector providers sometimes differed from those given by PLKB and TBAs.

Acceptable Reasons for Abortion

Almost all the gynaecologists, GPs and trained midwives approved of abortion for medical reasons if done by a gynaecologist. Many of them thought that at least two gynaecologists should validate the reasons. In cases of rape, the gynaecologists believed a psychologist should be involved. The GPs believed that most of their colleagues had these same opinions and some of the midwives said the same about their colleagues, adding that it was better if the pregnancy was no more than two weeks along.

Three of the gynaecologists approved of abortion without any qualification. Only one gynaecologist expressed disapproval, but she was more ambivalent than completely rejecting. Another said that when she first became a gynaecologist, she was strongly against abortion. But experience and the many problems faced by her patients had completely changed her attitude. She was now willing to do an abortion if the patient's menstrual period was no more than two weeks late, especially when it was for a teenager who had become pregnant out of wedlock, but only after consultation with a psychologist. She would try to persuade the girl to marry, but if the girl insisted, she would usually comply and do menstrual regulation.

In addition to medical grounds for abortion, only two GPs said they would refer a woman in the case of contraceptive failure, while most of the gynaecologists, midwives and PLKB considered contraceptive failure a valid reason for abortion. The PLKB in particular felt responsible for women who experienced contraceptive failure and were all tolerant of abortion on these grounds. Apparently, in the case of contraceptive failure, the National Family Planning Coordinating Board will take care of the expenses. However, it is the task of the PLKB in the first instance to try to persuade the woman to continue her pregnancy if she has a positive pregnancy test.

Most of the midwives, PLKB and TBAs mentioned other reasons for abortion that they thought were valid. These included when a woman was poor and could not afford to have more children, to protect her existing children if another child would cause hardship, and also if she was in poor health or had had too many pregnancies spaced too closely together. One PLKB expressed concern that the infant might be neglected if the pregnancy had been unwanted.

Their Role as Abortion Providers

Only six of the gynaecologists said they were prepared to perform abortions, provided the pregnancy was no more than two weeks along and the method used was menstrual regulation, mainly vacuum aspiration. Four others said they would refer women to someone else; and one of these said she would make an exception and do the procedure herself if there were health reasons and no one else was available. The remaining three said they were not willing to give a referral even though they approved of abortion on medical grounds.

None of the GPs or midwives considered themselves qualified to perform an abortion, and some of the midwives said they would not be willing to take the risks. Other midwives assisted gynaecologists who did abortions, even if they were against it, mainly to earn additional income. PLKB sometimes accompanied women to a clinic for an abortion, but some of them felt uneasy about this.

Many of the GPs, midwives and PLKB said they usually tried to dissuade any woman requesting an abortion from having it, but if she insisted they would refer her to a gynaecologist or a clinic. Six of the PLKB had apparently told women that their efforts to abort might fail and thereby convinced them to continue the pregnancy. Only one GP said she would not even consider giving a referral. Those midwives who were against abortion altogether said they did not even want to give a referral, because that made them accomplices in an act prohibited by their religion.

Half the TBAs said they would do an abortion, as long as menstruation was no more than two weeks late. This included three who accepted it, one who was against it and four whose views were ambivalent. Five others, who held very strict religious views, said they would not perform an abortion. Four of these said that they even refused to help if women came to them with a botched abortion.

Although most TBAs did not comment on the practice of their colleagues, three said that their fellow TBAs approved of abortion, one mentioned that some practised it and another said that they practised it surreptitiously.

Opinions About Reform of the Abortion Law

The formal sector health providers indicated that the law and Medical Code of Ethics had an important influence on their thinking. Most of the gynaecologists were in favour of reform of the existing laws on abortion, in line with the position of the Indonesian Association of Obstetricians & Gynaecologists. Some of the GPs were of the opinion that the laws and regulations should be formulated by a group of specialists in health, social science, religion and related fields. One midwife stressed the necessity for the law to protect physicians who do abortions for medical reasons.

Most of the PLKB were not sure what the law was, but thought it prohibited abortion. Others said that if there was a law, then it should be respected. Only a few of the TBAs knew that abortion was illegal.

Conclusions

We expected to find differences in responses by sex, age and ethnicity within each of the four categories of service providers. This turned out not to be the case, most probably because of the similarities in professional training, except for the TBAs, and because of the big city environment.

The majority of the respondents' acceptance, if not approval, of menstrual regulation was based on their experience of unsafe abortion and the situations and needs of women, their families and their existing children. For example, many of these health care providers, especially the TBAs, described the social stigma assigned to young women who are not married, but become pregnant. Several of the gynaecologists and GPs felt that families did not care about the law in such cases, as their only concern was to protect the reputation of the girl and the family itself. In such cases, when money was not a consideration, they thought families could usually find someone to perform an abortion. But GPs also said that some parents would rather use the money for the abortion, which they consider expensive, to marry their daughters off instead.

The willingness of many providers to assist a woman who requests termination of pregnancy was ultimately practical—that it is better to help a woman than to have her go to an unqualified person. Otherwise, she will come after she has had an unsafe abortion, usually in a critical condition and possibly with fatal consequences.

Thus our study suggests that, at least among many of the health care providers who are involved in abortion-related services, the use of menstrual regulation early in pregnancy appears to be increasingly accepted, though not by everyone and not without some provisos and ambiguities. Given these limitations, the roles of TBAs and PLKB remain central in taking care of the women that the formal sector does not help, with many negative consequences. Thus they should be given training in 'safe motherhood' to reduce unwanted pregnancy and make appropriate referrals for requests for pregnancy termination.

On the one hand, as the psychologist for the menstrual regulation services at the Wisma Pancawarga clinic in Jakarta observed in 1990: '...the medical profession has been able to ensure the provision of safe pregnancy termination services in a manner accepted by the government and society, even though the literal statement of the law would imply that such practices are illegal' (Widyantoro et al., 1990).

Yet on the other hand, abortion remains in a legal vacuum, which the limited provision of menstrual regulation cannot overcome. It therefore continues to be imperative to make it possible in Indonesia to provide safe abortion services to all women who need a pregnancy termination, and at the same time protect service providers from potential legal consequences. Given the importance of the law in supporting safe practice, and in order to achieve 'safe motherhood' and 'safe womanhood' (Hull, 1990), further revision in the law and further direction from the government and the medical and legal profession will be needed to clarify how any legal reform should be implemented.

Meanwhile, the numbers of 'accidents' and unwanted pregnancies are increasing. No doubt, one of the immediate steps that needs to be taken is to increase efforts to provide young men and women with sex education and awareness of the possible consequences of sexual behaviour, including HIV infection and AIDS.

The society at large should also be made aware of the realities of the health risks faced by women as they fulfill the social role demanded of them to bear children and, at the same time, limit their family size. The various media as well as nongovernmental organizations, especially those concerned with the reproductive health of women, would be the most appropriate agencies for these efforts.

APPENDIX

Recent Events in Legal Reform

Towards the end of 1991, a Bill on Health that included an Article on abortion was submitted to Parliament and debate continued well into 1992. Religious leaders made strong statements against abortion, while the official from the National Family Planning Coordinating Board thought that it was something positive for the phenomenon of induced abortion to be recognized and debated rather than ignored. Discussions and pronouncements were made by health people, especially gynaecologists, legal people and women's groups. Then in September 1992, the President of Indonesia officially enacted the new Health Law, in which Article 15 about abortion did not contain the term 'abortion' at all, an indication of the continuing sensitivity of the topic (Indonesian Law No. 23, on Health, 1992). Instead, the term *tindakan medis tertentu*, meaning 'a certain medical procedure', is used. The procedure was approved if it was needed to save the life of the woman. However, some ambiguity in the wording led to immediate debates, with some politicians, certain religious leaders and lawyers arguing that the new article did not automatically change the legal status of abortion, because it did not explicitly revoke the existing law. They even argued that 'certain medical procedure' could mean anything except abortion. A seminar organized by the Institute for Law Development in November 1992 could not reach agreement on this matter either. Then in early December 1992, a statement was issued by the Department of Health, though not directly by the Minister of Health, saying that this Article was specifically intended to regulate the practice of abortion in the country, even though it could also cover other medical procedures (Mohamad, 1993).

As indicated by the reactions, especially from health care providers, this new law, which has been awaited since the early 1960s, has not resolved the problem, especially from a legal point of view. The ambiguity in the wording, the inconsistencies within the Article itself and the differing explanations of it, have given rise to heated debates, adding to controversy rather than clarifying the issue, at least in the short term.[3] It still remains to be seen what the improvements for women will be.

✝ References

Hull, Terence H. 1990. Safe womanhood: a critique of the safe motherhood initiative in public health. In: *Materi Sidang Pleno* (plenary papers), 3rd Annual Meeting, National Epidemiological Network, Bandung, 26–30 November.

Hull, Terence H., S.W. Sarwono and N. Widyantoro. 1993. Induced abortion in Indonesia. *Studies in Family Planning* 24 (4): 241–51.

Jatipura, S. et al. 1978. *Abortion in hospitals and maternity hospitals in Jakarta 1972–1975.* Jakarta: Faculty of Public Health, University of Indonesia. Quoted in R.S. Samil. 1989. Commentary on menstrual regulation as a health service: Challenges in Indonesia. *International Journal of Gynecology and Obstetrics* (Supplement 3): 29–33.

[3] For an analysis of Article 15, see also: Hull et al., 1993.

Moeloek, F.A. et al. 1988. The relationship between menstrual regulation services and the incidence of septic abortions in Indonesia. Paper presented at Christopher Tietze International Symposium on Women's Health in the Third World: The Impact of Unwanted Pregnancy, Rio de Janeiro, 29–30 October.

Mohamad, Kartono. 1993. Taking risks to save lives and health. *Planned Parenthood Challenges* 1: 34–35.

Rahardjo, Julfita. 1990. Jamu peluntur: Traditional medicine for menstruation regulation and abortion in Indonesia. Paper presented to the Third International Congress in Traditional Asian Medical Systems, Bombay, India, 4–7 January.

Samil, R.S. 1989. Commentary on menstrual regulation as a health service: Challenges in Indonesia. *International Journal of Gynecology and Obstetrics* (Supplement 3): 29–33.

Tjiong, Hoo Swie (ed.). 1966. *Laporan Lengkap Symposium Abortus 1964* (Final Report of the 1964 Symposium on Abortion). Jakarta: Department of Health. Quoted in Widyantoro et al. 1990. Induced abortion: The Indonesian experience. Paper presented to Population Association of America Annual Meeting, Toronto, Canada, 3–5 May 1990.

UNICEF. 1991. *The state of the world's children.* New York: UNICEF.

Utomo, B., S. Jatipura and **A. Tjokronegoro.** 1982. *Abortion in Indonesia: A review of the literature.* Jakarta: Faculty of Public Health, University of Indonesia. pp. 28–31.

Widyantoro, N. 1989. Enhancing the quality of women's reproductive health care: An experimental approach in Indonesia. Paper presented at the Population Association of America Annual Meeting, Baltimore, USA, 30 March–1 April.

Widyantoro, N. et al. 1990. Induced abortion: The Indonesian experience. Paper presented to Population Association of America Annual Meeting, Toronto, Canada, 3–5 May 1990.

15

Pharmacists and Market Herb Vendors: Abortifacient Providers in Mexico City

Susan Pick, Martha Givaudan, Suzanne Cohen, Marsela Alvarez and Maria Elena Collado

Introduction

Abortion in Mexico is illegal in most cases, with restrictions varying from state to state. The state of Yucatán has the most liberal law, which allows abortion for socioeconomic reasons, including to limit family size. Several states allow abortion in the case of foetal defects. But most states, including Mexico City, allow abortion only to save the mother's life or when the pregnancy is the result of rape.

As in most countries where abortion is illegal, the law does not stop women from having abortions; it only endangers their life and health because it forces them to have an unsafe, clandestine procedure. Moreover, these illegal abortions are very rarely prosecuted, even though the clandestine conditions breed corruption and blackmail by the police and other sectors.

The Mexican law is doubly unrelated to reality—it rarely prosecutes illegal abortions and at the same time makes legal abortion very difficult to obtain. For example, until very recently, a woman who was pregnant as a result of rape had to wait until the rapist was convicted to have a legal abortion. Since a trial can take a year to complete, the woman was forced to either give birth to the child or to risk her life and health by having an illegal abortion.

Even in states where the law is more liberal, both women and doctors are unlikely to be aware of the conditions under which abortion is permitted. This means that a woman who does know her rights and is entitled to a legal abortion may have trouble finding a qualified doctor who will perform a safe procedure, because the impression persists among doctors that abortion is always an illegal practice and can only be carried out by disreputable practitioners.

In short, the restrictive abortion law in Mexico has created a major public health problem. Naturally, the problem is hard to quantify, but research has estimated that at least 850,000 induced abortions occur annually (López García, 1993). Complications from unsafe induced abortion are registered as the third or fourth cause of maternal mortality in Mexico, with experts estimating that this cause of death is under-registered by 50 to 75 per cent (Chambers, 1993).

Study Objectives

Although a more quantitative profile of unsafe abortion has been emerging over the last few years, the more qualitative aspects of the problem have remained largely unexplored. As in most countries with restrictive abortion laws, wealthier women in Mexico can afford to pay for a safer procedure by a qualified provider, even at clandestine clinics, or can travel to a country where the procedure is legal. How women of lower socioeconomic status have abortions is less well-known. Why are the illegal procedures so unsafe, so life-threatening? One important area that needs study is on the ways in which these poorer women obtain abortions.

We know already that pharmacies are a principal source of general medical care for the poor in Latin America. In fact, studies have shown that a large percentage of contraceptives and remedies for sexually transmitted diseases are obtained from pharmacies without a doctor's prescription (Lande and Blackburn, 1989). One study found that 52 per cent of adolescents using some form of contraceptive had obtained the method in a pharmacy (Pick de Weiss, et al., 1988). Two recent studies have shown that as many as 250,000 Brazilian women abort annually using the over-the-counter ulcer drug misoprostol (brand name Cytotec), which they purchase in pharmacies (Brooke, 1993).

Market herb vendors (MHVs) are another common source of information and medication for reproductive health problems, particularly in Mexico. A study of women who had entered the Hospital General de México for abortion complications showed that 36 per cent had aborted using herbal remedies or teas and 22 per cent had used pharmaceutical injections. These were the two methods of aborting that women cited most frequently (Rivera, 1990). According to another study of Mexican women who had recently had an abortion, 75 per cent had attempted to self-induce an abortion using herbs, injections or some combination of these methods before turning to someone else (either a doctor or another type of practitioner) to perform the abortion (Pick de Weiss and David, 1990).

As the information available pointed to pharmacies and herb vendors as common sources of self-induced abortion methods, we decided to conduct a qualitative study with the following goals:

1. To assess the knowledge and attitudes of pharmacists and herb vendors regarding abortion and contraceptives;

2. To determine what information and which medications are distributed to clients;
3. To measure these providers' perceptions of and attitudes toward clients who request contraceptives and abortifacients.

Even though the project goals included gathering information about contraceptive methods prescribed by pharmacists and herb vendors, this chapter concentrates on the results obtained regarding the practice of abortion.

Research Methodology

The study sample was chosen randomly from the total number of pharmacies and markets identified through a census and by direct physical observation in three Mexico City 'delegaciones' (districts). Because abortion is illegal, we anticipated that the collection of accurate data would be difficult, at best. We therefore decided to use two different methods.

The Questionnaire

The first method used to collect data in Mexico City pharmacies and markets was a cross-sectional survey questionnaire comprising structured field interviews for which special guides were prepared, which was developed as a part of a project supported by the Social Science Research Unit of the Special Programme of Human Reproduction of the World Health Organization. In the pharmacies and markets chosen, a total of 181 pharmacy workers and 41 market herb vendors were interviewed.

The socioeconomic classification of the pharmacies and markets chosen was determined according to the Marketing Plan for Mexico City, prepared by Wilsa, a specialized marketing group, in 1988. The pharmacies were distributed almost evenly between low, middle and high socioeconomic rankings, while most of the markets belonged to a predominantly low socioeconomic level. As can be seen in Table 15.1, the pharmacy worker and market herb vendor samples differed substantially in sex, age and educational level.

The sample of pharmacy workers is representative for this group in Mexico City, and by extension, other large cities in Mexico. The sample of market herb vendors is less representative. Originally, 82 herb vendors were to have been included in the study, which would have been a representative sample. However, some markets in the areas of Mexico City selected for interviews did not have herb vendors at all or had very few. In addition, some market herb vendors refused to participate, demonstrating that they are more concerned about discussing sensitive issues than pharmacy workers. All the pharmacy workers contacted agreed to participate.

The pharmacy workers and herb vendors were interviewed in their work places by a team of five interviewers who had been trained in interviewing on

Table 15.1: Summary Characteristics of the Study Group

	Pharmacy Workers		Market Herb Vendors	
	%	No.	%	No.
Sex				
Male	70.2	127	41	16
Female	29.8	54	59	23
Total	100.0	181	100	39*

* 2 persons did not answer.

Education				
Did not study	0.6	1	3.6	1
Elementary	17.7	32	53.5	15
Secondary	33.1	60	28.6	8
Vocational	6.6	12	–	–
High School	23.2	42	10.7	3
Professional	18.8	34	3.6	1
Total	100.0	181	100.0	28**

** 13 persons did not answer.

Average age (years)	33.7		42.6	

sensitive subjects. The interviewees agreed voluntarily to answer the questions. Data referring to the locations of pharmacies and markets where the interviews were performed were destroyed after the questionnaire was applied, to assure anonymity.

Role-Playing Visits

To obtain a more in-depth picture of the way pharmacists and market herb vendors interact with clients, a second methodology was implemented independently by IMIFAP. Young, female interviewers visited each of the pharmacies and markets where the questionnaire had been applied and requested assistance from the same individual who had completed the questionnaire. The interviewer claimed that her period was three weeks late, and that she wanted something to bring on menstruation. This is a common euphemism for abortion and the woman made it clear during further questioning that she believed herself to be pregnant. If the provider said he/she knew of a method, the woman requested details, such as how the method is used, what it is called, possible side effects or symptoms it could cause, what to do if menstruation didn't occur after taking the medicine, and how much it would cost. In addition, if the method prescribed was herbal, the interviewer requested the names of the specific herbs 'for a cousin in another city' with the same problem.

At the end of the conversation, the interviewer asked about contraception; which method the provider would recommend and how it is used. Afterward, the interviewer wrote down as much as possible regarding the answers given, including notes on provider attitudes.

Some Methodological Problems

The problem of missing responses occurred with both methods of data collection. Refusal to answer the questionnaire items was more common among the market herb vendors. Some of these individuals were reluctant to discuss both contraception and abortion with interviewers. Therefore, the role-playing visits were generally a more effective way of obtaining information from market herb vendors than the formal questionnaire. Although during the role-playing visits, it was not always possible for the interviewer to portray the situation realistically and obtain all the information that could have ideally been collected, nonetheless, while the information presented here is not completely consistent or uniform, it remains a valuable contribution to knowledge regarding how women abort in Mexico.

Some Comments About the Data Analysis and Presentation

After the results had been gathered, they were subject to descriptive statistical analyses, including the crossing of some variables. In a few cases, the person interviewed for the questionnaire was different from the person who participated in the role-playing visit. These cases were eliminated when variables were crossed between the two methods.

Since we felt that the richness of the material gathered in the role-playing visits could not be portrayed entirely through frequencies and statistical analysis, we have included direct quotes from the subjects to illustrate the more qualitative aspects of the study.

The group of subjects interviewed in pharmacies are described as 'pharmacy workers' (PWs) and the group interviewed in markets are described as 'market herb vendors' (MHVs). These two terms encompass a wide variety of provider experiences and qualifications. A pharmacy worker could be anyone from a professionally trained pharmacist to a clerk. Likewise, a market herb vendor could be someone who only sells the herbs or someone who is more a herbalist; that is, a person who collects herbs and has knowledge of their properties.

For several questionnaire items, more than one mention was recorded. Therefore, in the presentation of the results of certain questions, the percentages exceed 100 per cent when combined. This is because more than one mention is included in the percentage.

Results of the Study

Provider Knowledge About Abortion

Subjects had a low level of general knowledge about abortion and pregnancy. One third of pharmacy workers and over half the market herb vendors did not know that the safest time to induce an abortion is during the first trimester.

Almost equal percentages of pharmacy workers (62.8 per cent) and herb vendors (64.3 per cent) said that there are methods that will induce an abortion. However, the two groups mentioned different methods when asked to specify. Almost all pharmacy workers (88.7 per cent) mentioned injections, 23.6 per cent mentioned pills and 4.7 per cent mentioned herbs or surgical abortion (a method that would require surgical intervention like curettage or suction). Among the herb vendors, a large majority named herbs (94.1 per cent), followed by injections and surgical abortion.

It is interesting that so few in either group mentioned surgical abortion as an option. It seems that this was due not to ignorance that such methods exist, but to a tendency to mention only methods accessible to themselves, since many of them mentioned surgical methods during the role-playing visits as an option if the primary method of an injection or a herbal preparation did not work. For example, one provider who prescribed quinine said, 'If you don't get your period, you have to go so they remove it with a sound at a hospital that's in the Merced [market district of Mexico City]. A year ago it cost half a million pesos [about US.$160].'

A substantial majority of the pharmacy workers and herb vendors said they had obtained their knowledge about abortion through work experience or written materials. Fewer than 20 per cent of either group had acquired the information in school or from formal courses.

Information and Medications Given to Clients

Substantial majorities of both pharmacy workers (87.2 per cent) and market herb vendors (76.9 per cent) reported on the questionnaire that clients have asked them for help in inducing an abortion. When asked what methods clients have requested, a majority of pharmacy employees answered injectable drugs; and most herb vendors said their clients have asked for herbal preparations. Almost 20 per cent of both groups said that clients ask for 'whatever I provide', indicating that these individuals do not only supply what clients request, but take an active role in actually choosing and prescribing specific abortifacients.

On the questionnaire, subjects were not directly asked whether they provide abortive methods to clients, due to the issue's sensitivity. However, in the role-playing visits, 39.8 per cent of the pharmacy workers recommended some method for aborting, 42 per cent recommended nothing and 18.2 per cent said that abortive methods do not exist. Among the market herb vendors, 65.9 per cent recommended a method for aborting and 34.1 per cent did not.

Among the pharmacy workers who recommended an abortion method, most recommended injections (86.1 per cent), followed by pills (20.8 per cent), curettage and herbs (about 10 per cent each). In the markets, all the vendors who recommended a method recommended herbs, and some also recommended pills. (See Table 15.2.)

Table 15.2: Substances Recommended as Abortifacients in Role-Playing Visits

	Pharmacy Workers		Market Herb Vendors	
	%*	No.	%*	No.
Substances				
Injections	86.1	62	–	–
Pills	20.8	15	22.2	6
Herbs	8.3	6	100.0	27
Curettage	9.7	7	–	–
Total subjects (No.)	72**		27***	
Total mentions (No.)	90		33	

* The percentage is calculated based on the number of subjects mentioning each of the possible responses.
** 109 pharmacy workers did not recommend substances.
*** 14 market herb vendors did not recommend substances.

Medications Recommended by Pharmacy Workers

The medication most prescribed by the pharmacy workers was metrigen (56.3 per cent). Other substances included quinine, benzoginestril, lutoginestril, prostigmine, syntocinon and calgluquina. (See Table 15.3.)

Table 15.3: Medications Recommended as Abortifacients in Role-Playing Visits*

	Pharmacy Workers		Market Herb Vendors	
	%	No.	%	No.
Medication				
Metrigen	56.3	63	–	–
Quinine	11.6	13	66.7	4
Benzoginestril	10.7	12	–	–
Lutoginestril	7.1	8	–	–
Prostigmine	4.5	5	–	–
Syntocinon	3.6	4	–	–
Calgluquina	1.8	2	–	–
Other (perlutal, apiol, peletier, primtest)	4.5	5	33.3	2
Total subjects (No.)	112**		6***	
Total mentions (No.)	112		6	

* Only the principal medication prescribed is listed here. Any other pharmaceuticals mentioned are not included. A total of 104 providers did not mention medications.
** 69 pharmacy workers did not recommend medications.
*** 35 market herb vendors did not recommend medications.

Metrigen, an injection containing estrogen and progesterone, is normally used by doctors to restore the menstrual cycle in women who lack one of these hormones. Pharmaceutical literature indicates that it has a long list of contraindications, including possible adverse effects on blood pressure and circulation; it should not be given to women with diabetes, hypertension, epilepsy, liver problems or migraines (PLM, 1981: 621). In addition, one source mentioned that if taken during the early stages of pregnancy, metrigen can cause virilism in a female foetus (Rodriguez, 1994, personal communication). Moreover, metrigen in any dose cannot cause an abortion. Lutoginestryl F contains the same formula as metrigen.

Because almost half the pharmacy workers recommended the use of metrigen, we wanted to further analyze the uses that these providers attached to it.[1] We found that this medicine was given for two different purposes—as a pregnancy test and as a method for aborting. (A pharmacy worker was only counted as recommending a method for aborting if she/he recommended metrigen as an abortifacient.) Although the women in the study were implicitly asking for a method to abort, over two-thirds of the pharmacy workers who mentioned metrigen recommended it as a pregnancy test. The following comment demonstrates this use of the medication: '...there's an injection called metrigen but it's just a pregnancy test, many [people] who are trying to sell tell you that it works [for aborting], but it's not true, it costs $1.00 (USD) and if in a week you don't get your period it means you're pregnant and for that it's better to take a test, go to a doctor and if you're pregnant it's your decision...'.

It is interesting that metrigen was so frequently prescribed as a pregnancy test, when its use for this is specifically contraindicated in pharmaceutical literature (PLM, 1981: 621). A pharmacist we consulted said that metrigen is considerably cheaper than regular pregnancy tests, which do not sell well in pharmacies due to their high cost. We take all of this as evidence that some pharmacy workers recognize the role of economic concerns in a woman's approach to dealing with unwanted pregnancy.

One-fourth of the pharmacy workers who prescribed metrigen recommended it as a method of abortion and five providers recommended it while expressing uncertainty about its effects. Even discounting those who recommended metrigen as a pregnancy test, more pharmacy workers recommended metrigen as an abortifacient than any other medication. It is interesting that there is a consensus about using a medication that is not effective. It is possible that this false knowledge is encouraged by the clients themselves. For example, if a woman suspects she is pregnant and takes metrigen, and then gets her period, she may begin to see it as an abortion method rather than as a way to solve the problem of menstrual irregularity, which is what it is meant for.

---

[1] To examine the uses of metrigen, we registered every time it was mentioned, even when another medication was given as the primary method.

The second most commonly mentioned method was quinine, a medication primarily taken for malaria that can, however, provoke an abortion. According to one of our sources, however, the amount of quinine necessary to provoke an abortion could also cause death. The toxic side effects of quinine include disturbances in hearing and sight, nausea, vomiting, abdominal pain, delirium and fainting spells (PLM, 1981: 799). Unlike metrigen, quinine was prescribed consistently as an effective method for aborting. The following quote shows the extent to which pharmacy workers felt confident of this medication's effectiveness: 'Quinine is the most effective thing, take four before going to bed and you'll have a slight headache, maybe a fever, but tomorrow you'll be fine…. I promise you you'll get your period, I'm one hundred per cent sure.'

Calgluquina, which contains gluconate of quinine, is important to mention here. Only two pharmacy workers actually prescribed this medication, but it was mentioned by several others as highly effective; apparently so effective that it was taken off the market a few years ago. As one provider said, '…there is no medicine for aborting. Before, there was calgluquina that was used for aborting, but the health authorities realized and they took it off the market.' Unfortunately, calgluquina was implicated as a cause of death in some women as well. As one pharmacy worker explained, 'Before, there was a medicine called calgluqina, but since it was very effective, they discontinued it, because many women even bled to death.'

Three other medications were prescribed as abortifacients by the pharmacy workers. One was a hormonal injection, called benzoginestryl, that some doctors use to correct irregular menstrual cycles, and to treat frequent miscarriages. Side effects can include swelling of the breasts, edemas and haemorrhages when the medication is stopped. It cannot cause abortions. Another one mentioned was prostigmine, which is normally indicated for treating muscle spasms. It provokes smooth muscle activity and therefore can cause uterine contractions and, potentially, abortion. Side effects include intestinal blockage, slowing of the heart's action, nausea and vomiting (PLM, 1981: 786, personal conversations). Finally, the substance syntocinon was suggested; it contains a synthetic version of the hormone that stimulates uterine activity during labour. According to one physician, it would only cause abortion in the early stages of pregnancy and only if combined with other medications such as a prostaglandin. Unfortunately, little information was registered regarding the dosages of these medications prescribed by the pharmacy workers.

It is interesting that cytotec was not mentioned by any of the pharmacists surveyed. In other countries, notably Brazil (Brooke, 1993), this drug has become one of the most common methods used by women to abort illegally. This medication is widely available in Mexican pharmacies as an ulcer drug, but apparently its potential as an abortifacient is still unknown here.

Medications Recommended by Market Herb Vendors

One-third of market herb vendors gave the actual names of the herbs they prescribed as abortifacients; while 35.9 per cent did not provide names, only the herbs themselves. The reasons most commonly given for not providing the names were a fear of punishment and the desire to keep the herbal combination secret to protect the business. As one vendor said: 'I can't tell you the name of the herbs, it's my business. How can you think I would tell you? No one will tell you that.'

Among the providers who prescribed herbs, six combined the herbal preparation with a medication and the rest prescribed exclusively herbs. The medications prescribed in combination with herbs were not manufactured pharmaceuticals but drugs extracted from natural sources. The most frequently prescribed drug was quinine, recommended by 66.7 per cent of the MHVs. (See Table 15.3.)

It was not practical or useful to quantify how many vendors mentioned each type of herb, because the numbers are too small. Also, as many as 10 or 12 herbs were often prescribed in combination, and we know too little about most of the herbs to reach a conclusion about the combination's effectiveness. Herbal remedies often consisted of, in part, common kitchen herbs such as basil, clove, marjoram and parsley; apparently some of these can have abortive or menstruation-inducing properties in sufficient concentrations (Martínez, 1991: 464, 476).

Two herbs—zoapatle (*Montanoa tomentosa*) and ruda (*Ruta graveolens*)— were more commonly mentioned and are known to have abortive properties. Among the 13 herb vendors who gave the names of the herbs or preparations they prescribed, over 50 per cent prescribed both zoapatle and ruda, 23.1 per cent prescribed zoapatle only, and the same number prescribed ruda only. In some of these cases, ruda and/or zoapatle were the only herbs prescribed; in others, they were combined with as many as nine or 10 other herbs.

Zoapatle has been used both to cause abortions and to facilitate labour at least since the sixteenth century (Lozoya and Lozoya, 1982: 193). The Mexican name for this herb was Cihuapatli, or women's medicine, and it was widely enough used for colonial Spanish scholars to comment on it extensively. The exact way in which this herb works has not been determined. Apparently, it works like an oxytocin to cause contractions and also changes the hormonal balance in the uterus. In addition, the herb has been shown to have potential characteristics that prevent embryo implant, which suggests that it could potentially work as a contraceptive as well as an abortifacient and labour inducer (Lozoya, 1976: 164–65). This study's results demonstrate that it is still widely known and used in Mexico as an abortifacient. If excessive doses are given, tetanization of the uterus can occur.

Ruda, or rue, is also an effective abortifacient according to Martínez (1991: 283). This same source mentions that excessive doses of the herb can cause gastroenteritis and even poisoning. In addition, very high doses can cause uterine haemorrhaging (Guerin, et al., 1985: 28). We do not have information on the potential effects of combining ruda and zoapatle, which was the most common situation found in this study. Nor do we know whether the two herbs are seen to complement each other or if they are prescribed together to insure that if one herb is not effective for a certain woman, the other will be.

Knowledge of Potential Side Effects

When providers were asked what side effects could be caused by the methods prescribed, the responses were not very detailed. Moreover, not one subject mentioned any pre-existing conditions that could contraindicate the medication or herbal preparations prescribed. Three-quarters of the pharmacy workers who mentioned the possibility of side effects at all said that cramps and bleeding would be the principal ones and a few mentioned vomiting and dizziness. One pharmacy worker, however, did mention death as a potential risk of taking the medication prescribed; which, in this case, was syntocinon.

The responses to this question show a certain level of either ignorance or negligence among pharmacy workers regarding the side effects that could be caused by the medications they prescribe. This situation is particularly disturbing in the case of quinine. As mentioned earlier, the dose needed to cause an abortion can be fatal; however, not one of the pharmacy workers who prescribed quinine mentioned the possibility that it could cause the woman's death. This dangerous attitude is also reflected in the dialogue these providers have with clients: 'When I asked him what side effects I would have with the injection, he told me that I would get my period—what else did I want to happen.'

Similarly, among the market herb vendors, little information was given regarding the possible side effects of the herbal preparations prescribed. Of those who did mention side effects, 83.3 per cent described bleeding and cramps, and the rest mentioned vomiting, dizziness or nervous ailments. Again, not one of the vendors asked the client about pre-existing conditions or mentioned more serious side effects like tetanization of the uterus, poisoning or death, all of which can be caused by high doses of the herbs prescribed.

Prices of Pharmaceuticals and Herbs Prescribed

The majority of the medications prescribed by pharmacy workers cost between $0.30 and $3.00 (all prices are in US dollars). The price exceeded $3.00 in less than 20 per cent of the cases. The prices given by market vendors for herbal preparations were considerably higher. Over half the vendors who quoted a price for their preparation asked for between $13.00 and $23.00. The substantial price differences between pharmaceuticals and herbal preparations is probably due to price controls on pharmaceuticals. Herbs are not subject to this kind of regulation.

Two years ago when this study was done, the minimum wage in Mexico was approximately $4.00 per day. So the cost of a $20.00 herbal preparation would be substantially difficult for a woman earning minimum wage. However, the cost of herbal preparations are still much less expensive than surgical methods of abortion. For example, one herb vendor referred her client to a 'hospital' where she could have an abortion done at a cost of approximately $160.00. A safe abortion would cost at least twice as much.

Provider Beliefs and Opinions About Abortion

The pharmacy workers and market herb vendors were asked several questions about the Church's role with regard to abortion. A majority of both types of providers said that a woman who aborts can be considered a 'good Christian'. However, opinions were divided in both groups on whether women should consider the Church's stance when deciding to abort and whether the Church should continue to condemn the practice of abortion. In general, the pharmacy workers saw the Church's position as less relevant in the question of abortion than did the market herb vendors.

The opinions of the two groups were more similar on the question of what role the government should play with regard to abortion than regarding the role of the Church. Approximately one-fourth of pharmacy workers and vendors said the government should continue to condemn abortion; 10 per cent of pharmacy workers and 7.1 per cent of vendors said abortion should be completely legal; and 22.8 per cent of pharmacy workers and 10.7 per cent of vendors said abortion should be legal only in some cases, such as rape or danger to the mother's health.

These opinions are considerably more conservative than those found in the general population. In the 1992 national Gallup poll on abortion, 67.5 per cent of Mexicans surveyed said that abortion should be legal when the pregnancy endangers the woman's health (Pick de Weiss, 1993: 4). One possible explanation for the less favourable views of our study group towards legalizing abortion is that clandestine abortion creates a demand for the products of these pharmacy workers and market herb vendors.

When asked to describe their perceptions of a woman who aborts, approximately half of both pharmacy employees and market herb vendors gave a neutral response, saying they do not judge women or that the women 'must have their reasons'. Half gave a negative opinion, calling women who abort evil, murderers, ignorant and/or not conscious of their actions; very few expressed a positive judgement. A slightly more negative general attitude towards a woman who has an abortion was observed in herb vendors than in pharmacy workers. The most negative attitude towards a woman who aborts was found among the vendors and pharmacy workers with the least education.

Attitudes Versus Behaviour

It is important to note that the beliefs expressed by the providers on the questionnaire were not necessarily consistent with their actions during the role-playing visits. For example, the belief that a woman who aborts is 'bad' did not prevent either pharmacy workers or market herb vendors from prescribing an abortifacient. In fact, almost half the PWs who had a negative image of a woman who aborts recommended an abortifacient during the role-playing visits as did over 50 per cent of MHVs.

It was difficult to classify the attitudes of the subjects during the role-playing visit as 'negative', 'positive' or 'neutral', because the reactions were so diverse and complex. Instead, we attempted to organize the responses into categories that reflected the dominant modes of interaction with clients. We identified five different types of interactions:

1) Popular: This refers to a provider with magical or traditional beliefs. In one example, an MHV commented on the side effects a woman could have if she took the recommended 'preparation': 'It can give you a fever and chills or the bleeding can be normal, as if you had a very heavy period, [it varies] according to your temperament, if you're calm you'll only bleed a little bit, if you're more impetuous, well, your period will be heavier...'

2) Legal: This means a provider with a demonstrated awareness of abortion as a prohibited, clandestine procedure that implies a risk of punishment for those who practice it. For example, 'I'm sorry but if someone finds out about this, I could go to jail because they're going to think I'm helping you, although who knows, that might not be true, but you'd better go away.'

3) Emotional: This defined some type of provider involvement, which might support or reject the act of abortion, but always included an expression of concern for what was happening to the woman: 'I recommend that you buy the quinine and let me know what day you come for the tea, and I can prepare it for you and give it to you here, you can also stay here all day with me to see how you feel and so I can give you something depending on what side effects you present. Being so young, what can you do with a baby? And if you're in school, it's worse, for the baby and for you.'

4) Instructions: This referred to recommendations that merely offer a list of herbs or medications and instructions on how to take them, without any emotional involvement or opinion regarding abortion.

5) Economic: This means the provider interest is primarily directed towards selling the product, without offering another type of assistance. As one interviewer reported regarding a herb vendor: 'He said if I brought all the money, $33.00, he would give it to me but that I should come another day when I had money, he refused to give names of the herbs and only told me that it was a preparation and that it was very good. Because of the money, he couldn't sell it to me, I gave him $23.00 and he refused.'

These different types of interactions show that PWs and MHVs take on a wide variety of functions with respect to abortion. Some see the transaction in principally commercial terms of buying and selling; while others get more emotionally involved, which results in their assuming some responsibility for the problem in conjunction with the woman who is asking them for help.

More MHVs than PWs expressed 'popular' beliefs. This is logical, because the work of herb vendors involves magical or 'non-scientific' beliefs and practices, whereas pharmacy workers are more closely tied to mainstream medical practices. In addition, more MHVs than PWs were primarily concerned with the economic aspect of the transaction. This finding is supported by the high prices that MHVs charged, which lead one to believe that some MHVs make a healthy profit out of women's desperate situations.

The presence or lack of 'emotional involvement' is an important element for a woman who faces an unwanted pregnancy in a society where abortion is a criminal act. The significance of this type of involvement stems from the fact that the damage of illegal abortion to a woman's health is not limited to physical scars; it can also include mental and emotional effects. Approximately the same proportion of PWs and MHVs showed emotional involvement.

Summary and Conclusions

The Role of Pharmacy Workers and Herb Vendors

Pharmacy workers and market herb vendors are providers of abortive (or pseudo-abortive) methods for women. A majority of them said they knew of methods sold in their workplace that would cause abortions, said that clients ask them for abortifacients, and recommended methods during role-playing visits. Many of these individuals not only provide the herbs and pharmaceuticals women request, but also take an active role in recommending methods to their clients. In this sense, pharmacy workers and market herb vendors fulfill the role of a medical provider, except that their knowledge is inadequate for such assumed responsibility. This lack of knowledge is reflected in the fact that fewer than 20 per cent of either group had learned what they know about abortion and contraception in formal courses. Instead, the majority learned through their 'work experience'.

The implications of 'learning through work experience' may be different for the two groups studied, however. On the one hand, the fact that the information of pharmacy workers regarding abortion comes from 'experience' rather than formal courses seems to have resulted in a common pool of false knowledge shared by the majority of this group. We do not know whether this knowledge originates with clients or with the pharmacists themselves. Perhaps it is a combination of the two processes. On the other hand, the market herb vendors' knowledge of herbal abortive methods seemed more accurate overall, because they prescribed herbs that could potentially cause an abortion, whereas the pharmacy workers prescribed injections that were clearly ineffective. This is in spite of the fact that market herb vendors have a lower general level of formal education. Therefore, it seems that herb vendors' knowledge of abortive methods should not be discounted merely because they learned through empirical experience.

The kind of interaction the providers had with the clients who requested abortive methods ranged from exclusively commercial to genuine emotional and practical support. This range reflects a wide variety of provider experiences and motivations.

The Type of Abortifacients Provided

Most medications recommended in pharmacies are not effective. Pharmacy workers seem to share a common pool of false knowledge, in which menstruation-inducing hormonal injections are confused with medications that could actually cause an abortion. Quinine was the one effective medication recommended by a significant number of pharmacy workers, even though it is extremely toxic and the dose required to induce an abortion can cause death.

In contrast, the herbal preparations recommended by the vendors have the potential to be effective, although we do not have enough information to determine whether the exact preparations prescribed would have caused an abortion or to calculate what other effects these preparations could have.

In terms of economic cost, the pharmaceuticals recommended were very inexpensive. The herbs, however, had prices that were high enough to represent an economic difficulty for the majority of Mexicans. However, all medications prescribed were still far less expensive than a surgical method of abortion.

Belief Versus Action Regarding Abortion

This study showed that individuals' beliefs regarding abortion do not have a predictable impact on their actions. We found, for example, that a provider's negative opinion of women who abort did not have any significant impact on whether or not they provided abortive methods. In fact, the herb vendors had more negative attitudes towards women who wanted an abortion but they were also more likely to provide an abortifacient than pharmacy workers.

The issue of abortion in Mexico is surrounded by a tremendous amount of guilt, which causes a lot of ambiguity in speech and action. It is possible that because of the general guilt attached to abortion, the market herb vendors, who are more deeply involved in practising abortions, express less open views. Herb vendors may also be a more religious population than pharmacy workers, as their work involves mystical elements based on religious beliefs. Again, it seems contradictory that the more religious population would be more willing to provide abortive methods. However, it is a well-known phenomenon that the Catholic Church's prohibition of such practices as premarital sex, contraception and abortion are often ignored by even those Catholics who consider themselves devout.

It is important to note that the religious and societal guilt about abortion manifested in contradictory beliefs and actions may have a negative impact on the way market herb vendors treat women seeking the solution to an unwanted pregnancy. While we were not able to measure this effect, it seems logical that someone who believes that women who abort are sinners would not treat these women well, even if he/she is willing to sell abortive herbs for economic or other reasons.

Recommendations for Action

Recommendations for policy changes, for training programmes and for further research can be derived from this study.

Policy

The principal policy recommendation that has evolved from this study is that abortion should be legalized and regulated so that women can receive safe, inexpensive procedures from qualified personnel in clinics and hospitals. We hope that the results presented here will help achieve abortion law reform. They will be presented to groups working toward reproductive rights in Mexico with this goal. In addition, findings will be brought to the attention of the media and other groups likely to influence policy changes.

Training Programmes

While the long process of legislative change takes place, training programmes for women and providers could improve the situation. Women are going to have abortions, regardless of what the law allows; this has been proven in all societies where abortion is illegal. Therefore, punishing providers of clandestine methods (no matter how incompetent) without providing a better option is not necessarily helpful. However, the following topics could be covered in an educational programme for providers such as pharmacy workers and market herb vendors, preferably as part of wider courses on reproductive health and family planning:

1) Courses could give some perspective on the abortion issue in Mexico, including an explanation of the factors that can result in an unwanted pregnancy, statistics that show the extent of illegal abortion in Mexico, and exploration of the beliefs that women who abort must be 'bad' or 'prostitutes'. This type of information could encourage pharmacy workers and market herb vendors to treat clients seeking abortions more humanely.

2) For pharmacy workers, in particular, courses could cover the ineffectiveness of metrigen and other injections prescribed in this study as abortifacients and the specific dangers of prescribing quinine as an abortifacient due to its toxicity.

3) The case of the herb vendors is more difficult to address, since we do not know how effective or how dangerous the herbal methods can be. Some thought should be given to how to approach this group, with appreciation of the fact that they are trusted providers of health remedies to women.

4) Finally, in training programmes with both groups, the importance of family planning for clients who request abortifacients should be stressed in an attempt to prevent repeat abortions. Pharmacy workers and market herb vendors should learn to automatically discuss contraceptive methods with women who want to abort.

Further Research

This study's relatively small sample (especially of market herb vendors) and the rate of missing responses make it only a preliminary research inquiry into this important subject, rather than a definitive examination. More systematic research using a wider sample is essential. It would also be useful to expand this type of study to other kinds of abortion providers in Mexico, including, if possible, those who perform 'surgical' methods (curettage, catheter insertion, etc.). However, these practitioners would probably be much more difficult to locate and approach.

It would also be useful to compare results from Mexico City with other parts of the country as well as with Latin America as a whole to try to determine why certain methods are common in specific countries or regions. For example, it is fascinating that the drug cytotec, which is so widely sold in pharmacies in Brazil for abortion, is not mentioned by a single pharmacist surveyed here, even though the substance is widely available in Mexico as an over-the-counter treatment for ulcers. Comparative studies might also provide some information about variations in mortality rates from illegal abortion.

We recommend use of the two methodologies employed in this study, because comparison of the two sets of results allowed us to examine contradictions between what people say are their beliefs and how they actually behave. The role-playing visits were particularly valuable, because the complexity of the abortion issue and particularly the guilt and mixed feelings involved in discussing it, limit a formal questionnaire's ability to determine people's true attitudes and behaviour patterns.

✝ References

Brooke, J. 1993. Ulcer drug tied to numerous abortions in Brazil. *New York Times*, 19 May.

Chambers, V. 1993. Abordando la calidad de atención del aborto y la planificación familiar post-aborto. Paper presented at the Safe Motherhood Conference, Cocoyoc, Morelos, Mexico.

Frejka, T., L. Atkin, O. Toro and **J. Paxman.** 1990. A conceptual framework for the study of induced abortion. Unpublished document, The Population Council.

Guerin, H.P., A. Guyot, S. Rastein and **P. Thiebaut.** 1985. *Plantas Medicinales.* Barcelona, Spain: Ediciones Daimon.

Lande, R.E. and **R. Blackburn.** 1989. Pharmacists and family planning. *Population Reports*, Series J, No. 37: 1–31.

López García, R. 1993. El aborto como problema de salud pública. Paper presented at the Safe Motherhood Conference, Cocoyoc, Morelos, Mexico.

Lozoya, X. (ed.) 1976. *Estado actual del conocimiento en plantas medicinales mexicanas.* Mexico: Instituto Mexicano para el Estudio de las Plantas Medicinales.

Lozoya, X. and **M. Lozoya.** 1982. *Flora medicinal de México*, Mexico: Instituto Mexicano del Seguro Social.

Martínez, M. 1991. *Las plantas medicinales de México, sexta edición.* Mexico: Ediciones Botas.

Pick de Weiss, S. 1993. Development of support for national sex education in Mexico. Report presented to The Moriah Fund, The Prospect Hill Foundation and the John Merck Fund.

Pick de Weiss, S., R. Díaz Loving, P. Andrade Palos and **L. Atkin.** 1988. Adolescents in Mexico city: A psychosocial study of contraceptive methods and unintended pregnancy. Report pre-· sented to the Pan American Health Organization.

Pick de Weiss, S. and **H. David.** 1990. Illegal abortion in Mexico: Client perceptions, *American Journal of Public Health* 80: 715–16.

PLM: 1981. *Diccionario de especialidades farmacéuticas.* Mexico: Ediciones PLM.

Rivera, A. 1990. Abortos inducidos en México. *Doblejornada*, July 2, p. 5 (article based on a study by Dr Armando Valle Gay, President of the Medical Society of the Hospital General de México).

Rodriguez, M. 1994. Personal communication. Mexico City, Mexico.

16

Induced Abortion in a Province in the Philippines: The Opinion, Role, and Experience of Traditional Birth Attendants and Government Midwives

Fred V. Cadelina

Introduction

Abortion in the Philippines is both illegal and socially condemned. It is allowed only if it can be medically proven that it is the only recourse to save a woman's life. Moreover, Article II, section 12, of the 1986 Philippine Constitution promises that the state will 'protect the life of the mother and the life of the unborn from the moment of conception'. Despite legal and social sanctions, and the Church's strong conviction to respect and preserve life however, it is estimated that half-a-million women each year choose to terminate their unwanted pregnancy by abortion (Department of Health, 1993).

Women obtain illicit, induced abortion services from various sources. The most popular and accepted ones are the traditional practitioners who can be found in most cities and municipalities. These may include traditional birth attendants, or Hilots, and formally trained government health workers, known as midwives. Other sources, who are also working illegally, include licensed government and private medical doctors. It is estimated that complications from unsafe, illegal abortions cause one-third of the country's total maternal deaths (NEDA, 1990).

Although the number of married women using any modern method of contraception is above average for a developing country—about 70 per cent in 1991 (United Nations, 1994)—information on family planning and access to contraception is still governed by the existing social norms and the position of the influential Catholic Church, which generally oppose the government's family planning programme. Information and services are generally available only to married persons. Similarly, they are available to those who are going to be formally married; family planning counselling is routinely given to all couples when they apply for a marriage license. This policy and the prevailing social values concerning sexuality that support it neglect all other women—adolescents, single women and women in more informal unions—who generally have an insufficient understanding of their reproductive capabilities as well as limited or no access to other sources of family planning services.

Objectives

This chapter focuses on the opinions and experiences of induced abortion among birth attendants in the province of Negros Oriental, the Philippines. Interviewing providers in contexts where the practice is illegal is fraught with difficulties. Yet the opinions and information collected, regardless of their somewhat tentative nature, do contribute to a better understanding of the issue and point to the existence of a real problem.

It is hoped that the information presented in this chapter will contribute to the ultimate goal of reducing unsafe abortion and its related problems, both locally and nationally.

Research Methodology

Our study was an exploratory, descriptive survey begun in 1991 that examined knowledge of induced abortion practices and views on induced abortion among government midwives and Hilots (traditional birth attendants) in Negros Oriental, the Philippines.

We conducted the research in two stages, over a time period of 16 months. First, an in-depth study was carried out for four months to identify specific variables for a more intensive investigation. In the second phase, a survey was conducted over a 12-month period. Although a number of variables were included in the study, this report will concentrate solely on the subjects' opinions, experiences and involvement in abortion, their knowledge and practice of abortion methods, and their knowledge of abortion providers in the province.

The term 'birth attendant' will henceforth be used to refer to both midwives and Hilots. Of the approximately 560 birth attendants in the province of Negros Oriental identified through records at municipal and city health centres, 13 midwives and 13 Hilots were randomly chosen for in-depth interviews as part of the first stage of the research. It was originally planned that all 560 of the identified birth attendants would be involved in the second stage of the study, but due to field obstacles we could only contact 458 of them: 229 midwives and an equal number of Hilots.

We selected birth attendants for this study because they have direct, day-to-day contact with people in the community who need assistance with matters related to pregnancy. Given the nature of their work, they have access to relevant information, they may have offered assistance to women seeking abortions, and they are the major representatives of the reproductive health care community. Their attitudes and opinions are therefore useful in identifying the determinants of induced abortion, and their cooperation is essential to the future development and implementation of family planning policies and programmes, including abortion services.

Profile of the Birth Attendants

The characteristics of the midwives and Hilots in our study are summarized in Table 16.1. Midwives of Negros Oriental are all women, who are, on average, 37 years old; about 80 per cent are married or have been married; and they have an average of two children each. Hilots are usually women but they can also be men, as were 3 per cent in our study. They are generally 20 years older than the midwives; all are married or have been married; and they have an average of seven children each. Hilots are usually in service longer than

Table 16.1: Profile of the Birth Attendants in Our Study

(Number)	Hilots (229)	Midwives (229)	Total (458)
Average age (years)	58.8	37.4	48.0
Live children	7.1	2.4	4.7
Years in practice	25.3	12.7	19.0
Mothers delivered per month	5.3	8.1	6.5
Marital status (%)			
Married	91.7	76.9	84.3
Single	1.3	16.6	9.0
Had been married	7.0	6.6	6.7
Religion (%)			
Catholic	77.8	88.2	83.0
Non-Catholic	22.2	11.8	17.0
Contraceptive use among married birth attendants: 131 Hilots; 115 midwives (%)			
Using	75.0	100.0	86.6
Not using	25.0	0.0	13.4
Education (%)			
Illiterate	34.1	0.0	17.0
Elementary level	58.1	0.0	29.1
High school level	6.1	0.0	3.1
College level	0.8	100.0	50.4
No information	0.9	0.0	0.4

midwives. The differences in average age and in length of service are because midwives, as government workers, are required to retire at the age of 65 years.

Midwives generally deliver eight mothers per month compared to the average of five mothers per month delivered by Hilots. This could possibly be an indicator of women's preference for more 'modern' health services. However, many women still seek the services of Hilots, because they are established members of the community and relationships with them are generally more relaxed and informal.

Although most birth attendants are members of the Catholic Church, they actively show their support and belief in the government's programme of family planning for married couples. Many also use contraceptive methods themselves.

More than half of the Hilots have received an elementary school education, although approximately one-third are illiterate; less than 1 per cent have a college education. Midwives have more education; all of them have attended college.

Results and Discussion

Knowledge of Abortion Methods and Procedures

A range of mostly 'traditional' methods for inducing an abortion are known to most of the birth attendants interviewed. (These are presented in Table 16.2.) The most frequently known and used techniques include abdominal massage, herbal preparations administered orally, or a combination of the two. More sophisticated methods usually performed clandestinely by medical doctors include dilatation and curettage, intra-amniotic injection, or menstrual regulation.

Women are also known to consume large quantities of substances believed to have abortifacient properties such as alcohol, paracetamol, or other pharmaceutical products of questionable efficacy. Birth attendants also reported that they have heard of women who have attempted abortion by having their husbands jump on their uterus, by inserting sharp objects into the uterus, intentionally falling down stairs, or doing excessive exercise for several hours. They feel that women choose these self-induced methods, in spite of their ineffectiveness and harmful results, because they are inexpensive and can be used secretly. Such women are very desperate; usually they cannot afford a safe abortion or fear that family and friends will find out about their pregnancy if they go to an abortionist. Many consequently arrive in hospitals suffering serious complications from incomplete or unsafe abortions that cause permanent damage or death.

About one-third of the birth attendants in our study had knowledge of people in the community who had induced abortion during the 12-month period

Table 16.2: Knowledge of Induced Abortion Methods and Methods Known (%)

Knowledge of Methods (Number)	Hilots (171)	Midwives (187)	Total (358)
Have knowledge	74.7	81.7	78.2
1. Herbal preparation	38.0	45.5	41.9
2. Abdominal massage	44.0	59.4	52.0
3. Chemical abortifacient	0.0	5.3	2.8
4. Very high dose of pregnancy-testing pills	1.2	17.1	9.5
5. Abortion performed by a medical doctor	0.0	2.7	1.4
6. Use of catheter	1.8	12.8	7.5
Combination of 1 & 2	17.5	0.0	8.4
Combination of 2 & 4	1.2	2.1	1.7
Combination of 1, 2, very high dose of paracetamol & wine	1.8	1.1	1.4
Combination of 1 & 4	1.2	3.2	2.2
Combination of 1 & very high dose of paracetamol	2.4	2.7	2.5
Combination of very high dose of paracetamol & wine	0.6	4.3	2.5
Other	1.8	0.5	1.1
Total*	111.3	156.3	134.9
No knowledge	23.1	17.0	20.1
No information	2.2	1.3	1.7

* Total is more than 100% due to multiple response.

prior to the survey. Most of the reported cases had abortion performed by traditional practitioners using the methods just described. More than 50 per cent of these reported cases had complications, such as abdominal pains during coitus, continuous spotting, severe bleeding, hospitalization, near death, and even the actual death of several women.

Opinions About Induced Abortion

The great majority of birth attendants do not approve of abortion: 93 per cent of midwives and 98 per cent of Hilots. The two reasons most often cited for their disapproval is that abortion is not allowed by society and it is not in keeping with the fundamental beliefs and principles of the Catholic religion (Table 16.3). Although the majority of birth attendants do not approve of abortion, a significant number find it acceptable under certain circumstances (Table 16.4). About 50 per cent of midwives and 20 per cent of Hilots said they thought induced abortion was permissible in cases where the mother's health is in question, the pregnancy has occurred out of wedlock or is due to rape, or if there are social and economic reasons for not wanting the child.

Most birth attendants are against legalizing abortion, saying that it would only lead to other immoral acts. They believe that it would mean an increase in induced abortion and abortion complications, even with the use of modern

Table 16.3: Opinion on Induced Abortion and Reasons (%)

Opinion (Number)	Hilots (229)	Midwives (229)	Total (458)
Reason women should not have an abortion	97.8	93.0	94.5
(Number)	(224)	(213)	(437)
Not allowed by society/immoral	37.5	36.6	37.0
Illegal	6.3	2.4	4.4
Religious and medical reasons	1.8	1.9	1.8
Other	0.0	0.9	0.5
Women can have abortion	2.2	7.0	5.5

Table 16.4: Opinion on When Induced Abortion May Be Allowed (%)

Opinion (Number)	Hilots (229)	Midwives (229)	Total (458)
May be allowed in some circumstances	20.2	48.5	34.3
(Number)	(46)	(111)	(157)
If mother's life is endangered	65.2	84.7	79.0
If pregnancy/child is unwanted because of too many children	4.4	5.4	5.1
If woman has no husband	8.7	1.8	3.9
If child's father refuses to marry the woman	6.5	0.9	2.5
If pregnancy is due to rape or immorality	4.4	1.8	2.5
Economic reason	4.4	0.0	1.3
Other	2.2	2.7	2.5
No answer	4.4	2.7	3.2
Should not be allowed in any circumstances	80.0	51.5	65.7

methods. Some felt that it would destroy the dignity of women. They cited common problems such as the very high incidence of complications and the marital problems created by couples being faced with the decision of whether or not to abort. Some even advocated prosecution and imprisonment for both abortion providers and abortion seekers. Many Hilots are vocally opposed to abortion because of their growing reputation for being abortionists, which diminishes their standing in the community.

Those who favour legalizing abortion believe that it would allow abortions to be performed more safely by trained practitioners, thus reducing the incidence of complications and the number of maternal deaths. They believe that abortion is a personal decision to be made by the woman, involving and affecting only the mother and the abortion provider. They also hope that legalizing abortion would help to reduce the country's high birth rate.

Experiences and Involvement with Induced Abortion

In the year prior to this study, 641 women wanting information on how to terminate their pregnancies asked the birth attendants in our study for help or advice. (The number of women actually seeking abortions could have been greater, however, because some may have consulted friends or family.) The different ways the birth attendants responded are presented in Table 16.5.

Table 16.5: Response of Birth Attendants to Women Asking for Assistance to Terminate an Unwanted Pregnancy (%)*

Experience and Form of Assistance Given (Number)	Hilots (229)	Midwives (229)	Total (458)
Was never asked for assistance	53.7	56.4	55.0
Was asked for assistance	46.3	43.2	44.8
(Number)	(106)	(99)	(205)
Did not give assistance	70.8	51.5	61.5
Gave assistance	29.2	48.5	38.5
Advised the person not to have induced abortion	58.0	75.0	68.4
Gave the person information on abortion methods and source of services	9.7	6.3	7.6
Administered abortion through abdominal massage and gave herbal concoction for drinking	19.4	0.0	7.6
Told them to seek medical advise	0.0	10.4	4.3
Administered abortion through abdominal massage	12.9	0.0	5.0
Gave them very high dose of pregnancy-testing pills	0.0	6.3	3.8
No answer/information	0.0	2.0	1.3

* Total number of women seeking help: 641.

About 40 per cent of the birth attendants interviewed said that they offered assistance, mostly by advising the woman to reconsider her decision to have an abortion. The birth attendants emphasized that their responsibility as health workers is to encourage women not to commit illegal and immoral acts, but rather to consider family planning methods for the future.

Despite the overwhelmingly negative attitude towards induced abortion, a significant number of birth attendants admitted that they gave patients information on abortion methods and on how to locate abortion practitioners. Moreover, there was some direct involvement with abortion practice. Ten Hilots admitted that they performed abortions using abdominal massage and herbal preparations. Even more surprising, because of their affiliation with the government, was the admission by three midwives that they had performed abortions by administering high doses of pharmaceutical products. The midwives gave humanitarian reasons, such as extreme poverty and therefore a woman's inability to care for another child, to explain why they had performed an abortion.

A comparison of these findings to the data on opinions about abortion shows that approximately 50 per cent of birth attendants who said they disapproved of induced abortion have been at some point either indirectly or actively supportive of it.

Table 16.6: The Experience of Abortion Among the Birth Attendants Themselves

Experience (Number)	Hilots (229)	Midwives (229)	Total (458)
Have abortion experience	38.0	15.3	26.6
(Number)	(87)	(35)	(122)
Induced	5.8	11.4	7.4
(Number)	(5)	(4)	(9)
Reasons			
Too many children	80.0	25.0	55.6
Economic problems	20.0	0.0	11.1
Pregnancy unintentional/child unwanted	0.0	50.0	22.2
Afraid that boyfriend will not marry her	0.0	25.0	11.1
No abortion experience	59.0	68.1	63.5
Not applicable	3.1	16.6	9.8

A total of 122 birth attendants have had abortions themselves, nine of which were reported as induced. Given the usual under-reporting of induced abortion, particularly in face-to-face interviews, the total can be assumed to be substantially higher, however. The rather high proportions of 'spontaneous' abortions clearly hide a substantial number of induced cases. Most of the induced abortions occurred in situations where the women were already married, yet chose to terminate the pregnancy because either their contraceptive method had failed or they already had too many children to support. One midwife became pregnant before she was married and had an induced abortion for fear that her boyfriend would not marry her. She emphasized how different the situation would have been if contraceptives were made available to all women of reproductive age regardless of civil status, a view shared by several of her colleagues.

Knowledge of Abortion Providers in Negros Oriental

Twenty-three per cent of the birth attendants can identify at least one abortion provider in the province. The data indicate that more than 150 abortion providers exist in Negros Oriental, with an average of seven per city or municipality. Only five of the abortionists known by the birth attendants are licensed medical doctors, however. All the others practise traditional methods, such as abdominal massage or the use of herbal formulas (Table 16.7).

Table 16.7: **Knowledge of Abortion Providers by Birth Attendants**

Knowledge (Number)	Hilots (229)	Midwives (229)	Total (458)
Have knowledge (%)	32.8	12.7	22.7
Number of abortionists known:			
Traditional (herbs or massage)	124	37	161
Licensed medical doctor	1	4	5
Total (frequency)	125	41	166
No knowledge (%)	60.7	47.2	53.9
No answer/information	6.6	40.2	23.4

Despite their use of unsafe methods, traditional practitioners are more popular than medical doctors throughout the Philippines, mostly because they are less expensive and women are assured of complete confidentiality. They typically perform abortions wherever it is convenient for the woman, and no one else is involved in the procedure. This shows that confidentiality is more important to many women seeking abortions than their own safety.

Conclusions and Recommendations

Complications due to unsafe induced abortion constitute one of the most serious health problems facing Philippine communities today. In keeping with the law and with social and religious pressures and beliefs, all birth attendants should oppose abortion. When they are confronted with the reality of unnecessary suffering and complications of self-induced abortion in their own communities, however, they frequently offer information, and occasionally, services. Their increasingly active role should be recognized by established health authorities, keeping in mind that they would not be actively involved in the practice of abortion unless there was a substantial demand.

It is evident from the collected data and from their own reported use of contraceptive methods that birth attendants support their country's family planning programme. In fact, all the midwives and 86 per cent of Hilots in our study said that they supported family planning and routinely discussed it with their clients. Because they are obviously respected as a source of reproductive health care in their communities where they have daily contact with women and their families, training them to improve their skills in counselling women about sexuality and contraception, as well as other matters related to women's reproductive health, could effectively reduce the number of abortions as well as the complications from unsafe abortion.

Improving the national family planning programme should also include filling the unmet need for family planning for all women of reproductive age, not just soon-to-be-married or married women. There are some efforts by legislators to extend service provision to the entire population. The considerable human suffering and escalating health costs of hospitals struggling to treat the complications of unsafe abortion are strong arguments in favour of improved legislation. A comprehensive programme of family planning is, in the case of the Philippines, an urgent and necessary measure for lowering the abortion rate.

Such a programme should also include adolescents. The large proportion of the country's population that is now entering their reproductive life cycle is uneducated on matters relating to sexuality; this makes them vulnerable to all the potential and preventable problems related to sexuality, such as unwanted pregnancy, abortion, and sexually transmitted diseases. It is important that sex education and sexuality be emphasized in the schools' curricula as early as elementary school, so that young people are informed before they reach reproductive age.

This study is illustrative of the difficulties inherent in abortion research, particularly when the objective is to study the source of abortion services in contexts where the practice is illegal. It clearly shows the problems and limitations of this kind of effort. However, it also provides important insight into the conflicts of health service personnel who, when confronted with the 'other side' of unwanted pregnancy—the side of desperate struggle and unnecessary suffering—choose to act in what has become a much more humane way than the law allows.

† References

Department of Health. 1993. Report. Region 7, the Philippines. Colombo, Sri Lanka.

National Economic and Development Authority (NEDA). 1990. Region 7, Central Visayas, Philippines. Colombo, Sri Lanka.

United Nations. 1994. *Abortion policies: A global review.* New York: United Nations, Department for Economic and Social Information and Policy Analysis, Population Division.

17

Induced Abortion in Sri Lanka: Opinions of Reproductive Health Care Providers

P. Hewage

Introduction

Despite increased contraceptive use and a highly restrictive abortion law, indirect evidence confirms the widespread practice of induced abortion in Sri Lanka. The Family Health Bureau of Sri Lanka reported 4,279 abortions among 2.4 million women of reproductive age in 1991. According to the medical statistician of the Ministry of Health, however, 25,000 to 30,000 abortions were reported annually throughout the island in the late 1970s and early 1980s. At present, there are no national level data on the incidence of induced abortion.

The existing abortion law, which was enacted in 1883, prohibits the 'causing of a miscarriage', except under conditions where the mother's life is in danger. Although it is a criminal offense, services for induced abortion of varying quality exist all over the island. Perhaps this is because the law is not rigorously enforced or because service providers are willing to risk prosecution.

Legal abortions, under special conditions, are usually done in the government sector, while most illegal abortions obviously must be performed in the informal or private sector. The government sector is composed of doctors, specialists, nurses and midwives, and public health care is available to the whole population at no cost. The private sector has similar kind of personnel, but fees are required for services. Private physicians, if they perform an abortion in their own clinic, will charge a high fee. Naturally, clandestine abortion providers are less expensive. Unfortunately this kind of procedure is usually unsafe, being performed in unhygienic conditions, using primitive techniques, and without any medical supervision. In fact, the techniques used by providers of clandestine abortions are often the same ones used by women themselves for self-induced abortions. Among such techniques are the introduction into the vagina of, boiled cotton, taro leaves, or bamboo shoots; or the consumption of unripe pineapples, large doses of oral contraceptives or drugs commonly prescribed for malaria.

The negative health, psychological, social and economic consequences of illegal and self-induced abortion have been well-documented worldwide. As in many developing countries, an analysis of the data on the causes of maternal mortality indicate that abortion is a leading cause of maternal death in Sri Lanka.

Moreover, the proper medical attention required by women who suffer complications due to improperly performed abortion represents an enormous drain on the limited resources allocated to the health sector, particularly for obstetric and gynaecological services. A hospital-based study conducted at a gynaecological unit in a government hospital reported that of a total of 1,638 admissions over a period of six months, approximately 25–30 per cent were cases of abortion complications. It is clear that the cost of providing emergency medical care to a woman with complications from induced abortion vastly exceeds the cost of regular obstetric and gynaecological care, including child delivery (Ministry of Plan Implementation, 1983).

In short, there is considerable potential for both the reduction of maternal mortality and the reallocation of financial resources to other important reproductive health needs of the population of Sri Lanka, such as family planning, treatment of sexually transmitted diseases, and prenatal, delivery and postpartum care. This can be achieved, at least in part, by reducing the incidence of unsafe and self-induced abortion.

Objectives

There is an urgent need, particularly in countries where abortion laws are restrictive, to understand the multiplicity of factors that lead women to the point of induced abortion, even when it threatens their very life.

Our approach was designed to understand the reality of abortion through the perceptions and attitudes of health care providers, a relatively new perspective in abortion research. Such an approach follows from the general hypothesis that the attitudes of health care personnel towards the practice of induced abortion, including their perceptions of the women who seek abortion or come for emergency care services, profoundly affect the practice of abortion, particularly the way these services are delivered and their overall quality (David, 1992). This has important implications for the effectiveness of existing family planning services as well as for any new strategy that aims to reduce unsafe abortion.

This study design was also thought to be a good one for Sri Lanka, where the highly restrictive abortion law makes the collection of reliable information, such as that obtained from direct survey interviews, very difficult. We thought a study of health care providers with direct knowledge and experience of abortion practices would help us to get a more accurate picture of the determinants of abortion in Sri Lanka.

With these hypothetical assumptions in mind, we then decided on the following working objectives:

(1) To examine the attitudes of health personnel towards the practice of both contraception and abortion as a means for fertility regulation;
(2) To examine the perceptions that health providers have of the psychosocial and demographic characteristics of the women who seek these services;
(3) To suggest strategies, based on the profiles that emerge from the information collected in (1) and (2) above, that could be used to improve the quality and scope of reproductive health services in Sri Lanka. Ultimately, the aim to be kept in mind is the reduction of the incidence and consequences of unsafe abortion.

Research Methodology

The providers selected as the main study population for this research included health care personnel involved in reproductive health services. Among them were doctors, nurses, midwives and family health workers, all of whom had either direct or indirect experience with induced abortion, and were known to have significant knowledge about the subject.

Fieldwork was carried out in 1991–92 in 17 government and local government hospitals and 10 Medical Officer of Health (MOH) Divisions, which are designated field areas under the supervision of a Medical Health Officer, in the Colombo district. We chose this district because it is the most populous in the country, has the greatest availability of government health services and family planning services, and is also the district where the highest number of abortions are performed.

The sampling approach with this kind of study population requires maximum flexibility, because full representation is impossible. A purposive strategy works best, with a quota in mind in order to be able to perform statistical analyses. The quota we estimated as necessary was 500 providers working in government health services with a high probability of servicing abortion cases, particularly complications. In the end, we were able to interview 502 respondents.

Interviewers were asked to conduct the interviews with personnel who were available on the day they visited the health institution selected, and to make contacts for further interviews with respondents who would be willing to participate in the study voluntarily. Only physicians, nurses and midwives employed at obstetric and gynaecological wards were invited to participate in the interviews. Those who refused to participate in the study were excluded and no further information is available on them. If a bias exists as a result of this approach, its relative importance cannot be ascertained.

We would like to stress that the results are not representative of the attitudes of all health care providers; the results obtained permit only a broad view of what remains a challenging research issue, given the legal and social status of abortion in Sri Lanka.

Questionnaire and Interview

The questionnaire was carefully designed after holding a series of separate focus group discussions (FGDs) with small groups of doctors, nurses, midwives, family health workers and public health inspectors about the various issues related to induced abortion. These people were selected from health institutions in another area of Sri Lanka, known as the Matara district. On the basis of these discussions, the critical health issues, linguistic codes and other aspects of induced abortion as perceived by providers could then be worked into the main interview questionnaire.

The final questionnaire was administered during a personal direct interview, by five well-trained and highly qualified research assistants. Interviews with the health providers lasted an average of 30–40 minutes. Respondents were asked to answer questions about their personal background, express opinions about their personal feelings and perceptions concerning abortion, and to provide views on what they felt were the main reasons women seek abortion as well as what were the consequences of induced abortion. They were also asked to suggest possible strategies for its reduction.

We should note that, from a methodological point of view, conducting the interviews with health providers on such a complex topic was not easy. It was made more difficult because often respondents had to talk with the interviewers while they were on duty.

Characteristics of the Study Sample

Of the 502 respondents, 76 (15 per cent) were physicians, principally obstetricians and gynaecologists as well as other specialists relevant to reproductive health services. Other respondents included 167 female nurses (33 per cent), and 259 midwives, family health workers and public health inspectors (52 per cent). Table 17.1 shows the distribution of respondents according to their age and profession.

As expected, the majority (97 per cent) of respondents were Sinhalese, and their religion was mainly Buddhist (92 per cent); only 6 per cent were Catholic or Christian, 1 per cent Hindu, and 0.6 per cent Islamic. In Sri Lanka,

Table 17.1: **Study Sample by Age and Profession**

Age (years)	Doctors		Nurses		Midwives & Others		Total	
	(N)	%	(N)	%	(N)	%	(N)	%
20–29	22	28.9	32	19.2	62	23.9	116	23.1
30–39	29	38.1	31	18.6	112	43.2	172	34.2
40–49	13	17.1	40	24.0	61	23.5	114	22.8
Over 50	12	15.9	64	38.2	24	9.4	100	19.9
Total	76	100	167	100	259	100	502	100
		(15.1)		(33.3)		(51.6)		(100)

there is a well-known correlation between ethnicity and religion, which is naturally reflected in the study group.

Over 80 per cent of the respondents were women, which was anticipated because the support staff at hospitals is made up mostly of nurses, midwives and family health workers. These women providers are the ones, who, on a daily basis, are in contact with the people who come to the hospitals for health services and attend to them when they become patients.

The length of employment is often an indication of a health worker's level of experience. The largest proportion of our respondents (43 per cent) had been employed for over 10 years; 31 per cent had four–10 years of work experience.

The Determinants of Induced Abortion

In our interviews with respondents on the topic of induced abortion, we were guided by the principle that the decision-making process leading to an abortion, and the characteristics of the women relying on abortion, are shaped by the social, economic, legal, cultural and political climate that surrounds both the abortion provider and the abortion seeker (David, 1992). In other words, the context within which induced abortion is sought and obtained is defined by particular sets of circumstances. For example, poor women commonly induce an abortion themselves using primitive techniques or seek cheap, poorly performed, clandestine services; while a middle-income housewife is more likely to try to obtain an abortion from a private physician whom she can trust, because she can afford the higher fee.

What are the Causes of Unwanted Pregnancy?

We thought it essential to try to understand provider perceptions about the circumstances surrounding unwanted pregnancy. Ninety-two per cent of the respondents in our sample recognized 'unwanted pregnancy' as a serious problem in Sri Lanka.

Our respondents identified three main causes of unwanted pregnancy that often lead to abortion. The first reason was thought to be economic hardship, a common situation for many families in Sri Lanka (35 per cent). A second reason was thought to be insufficient attention to spacing pregnancies, which leads to too short an interval since the last birth (20 per cent). A third reason given was unstable sexual relationships either outside of marriage or before marriage (18 per cent). Contraceptive failure (6 per cent) and involuntary sexual intercourse, including rape (6 per cent) were also thought to be reasons leading to unwanted pregnancy.

A very significant finding was that nearly 90 per cent of the health personnel did not believe contraceptive failure was a sufficiently strong reason for the practice of induced abortion. To support this opinion, they remarked that actual contraceptive failure rates were low and that many women can be convinced to continue their 'unwanted' pregnancy to term.

Why do Women Seek Abortion?

Our respondents gave three main reasons why they thought women would seek an abortion (Table 17.2). Nearly two-thirds said that psychosocial pressures force a woman to resort to abortion, despite the fact that it conflicts with religious beliefs and the high value placed on family life. This pressure can be seen most clearly in cases where the pregnant woman is not married; the social stigma is so great that she will usually choose to have an abortion. The second reason was a family's lack of financial resources for childrearing and education of a new child. Third, it was thought that women felt that abortion was a better alternative to some contraceptives in terms of perceived cost, confidentiality, safety and availability.

Table 17.2: Provider Perceptions of Why Women Seek Abortion

Reason	(N)	%
Psychosocial pressure	330	65.7
Limited economic resources	76	15.1
Perceived cost, availability, confidentiality and safety of abortion are better than contraception	57	11.4
Other	39	7.8
Total	502	100.0

Over 80 per cent of the health care workers felt that abortion was on the increase and gave their reasons (Table 17.3). Interestingly, the main reason for this increase was attributed to women's negligence of social values, by 41 per cent of the respondents. Twenty-nine per cent maintained that the increase in abortion was due to the same reasons for resorting to abortion; that is, lack of financial resources, particularly among poor families, and the desire for smaller families.

Table 17.3: Provider Perceptions of the Increase in Abortion Practice

Reason	(N)	%
Women's neglect of societal values	204	40.6
Scarce economic resources and preference for smaller families	144	28.7
Poor knowledge about sexuality and reproduction	43	8.6
Easy access to abortion services	28	5.6
Other	83	16.5
Total	502	100.0

What is the Availability of 'Safe' Versus 'Unsafe' Abortion?

The legal context, the skill of the provider, and the stage of gestation are all factors that help determine the 'safety' of an induced abortion. At the present time in Sri Lanka, the number of ways women can obtain safe services is very limited, largely because most abortions are illegal and thought to conflict with the prevailing cultural and religious norms pertaining to marriage and the family. When women need an abortion, they have to go outside the normal health care system, which means they use the more accessible, clandestine services that are more dangerous. So it can be said that abortions in Sri Lanka are generally 'unsafe'.

Indeed, as shown in Table 17.4, the opinion of health care workers reflected the legal reality in Sri Lanka, where the highly restrictive law allows abortion only to save the life of the mother: 95 per cent felt that the prevalence of legal abortion is very low in Sri Lanka.

Table 17.4: Provider Perceptions of the Prevalence of Legal, Self-Induced, Unsafe, Safe and Late Abortions

Level of Prevalence	Legal		Self-Induced		Unsafe		Safe		Early	
	(N)	%	(N)	%	(N)	%	(N)	%	(N)	%
High	19	3.8	93	18.5	363	72.3	264	52.6	74	78.3
Low	478	95.2	385	76.7	129	15.7	213	42.4	393	14.7
Other	5	1.0	24	4.8	10	2.0	25	5.0	35	7.0
Total	502	100.0	502	100.0	502	100.0	502	100.0	502	100.0

A context in which most abortions must be performed illegally limits the willingness of many potentially qualified providers to perform them. Indeed, 72 per cent of respondents felt that most abortions are performed by unskilled providers under unsafe conditions. They think that most women who seek abortion are willing to take great health risks with unqualified practitioners if that is their only solution. Another 19 per cent of the respondents felt that the prevalence of self-induced abortions is high because the chance of having a safe medical procedure is so low.

Over 50 per cent of the respondents felt that the prevalence of safe abortion was high among economically well-off women, because they could afford quality private services that are too expensive for the average family. At first, this finding seemed to contradict the earlier opinion that safe abortion was rare in Sri Lanka. A closer look at the responses showed that provider perception of abortion incidence may vary according to socioeconomic characteristics of the women. This requires further investigation for a more precise profile of when abortion is safe and for whom.

A majority of the respondents, 78 per cent, thought that women prefer to obtain abortions as soon as they are aware that an unwanted pregnancy has occurred, that is, in the early stages of gestation. Our respondents believed that most Sri Lankan women are often able to detect a pregnancy at an early stage of gestation, and prefer to obtain an abortion as quickly as possible if the pregnancy is not desired.

The Consequences of Unsafe Abortion

Since most induced abortions are performed under unsafe conditions, it was generally thought that a large proportion of women who undergo abortion suffer adverse physical and psychological consequences.

Moreover, according to the majority of the respondents, most women suffering from complications of unsafe abortion come to government hospitals for treatment, rather than returning to private sector providers. Over 58 per cent of respondents felt that treating these complications was very costly for the government, and also depleted the health care resources needed to treat other important reproductive health care problems.

The respondents cited three main reasons why they thought women preferred to go to government facilities for treatment of abortion complications: women felt more confident of proper medical attention (42 per cent); the cost was lower (20 per cent); and private facilities did not have the necessary equipment (15 per cent).

An important finding related to the reasons why women prefer to go to government hospitals for abortion sequelae was that many respondents thought that abortion providers in the private sector often refuse to treat abortion complications. The respondents gave two reasons for their refusal: a lack of proper training or facilities to deal with the complications (58 per cent); and fear of legal prosecution (35 per cent).

Another important factor in the scenario of abortion complications is the refusal or delay on the part of the woman herself to get treatment. The majority of respondents (80 per cent) felt that the reasons for this are shame and fear of legal prosecution.

Reasons for Repeat Abortions

Some women continue to be exposed to the risk of having repeat abortions. We asked our respondents why they thought a woman would do this. Equal proportions of respondents answered that they thought these women are either unaware of effective methods of contraception or they are at high risk for abortion because they practice prostitution. A substantial number also felt that women who have repeat abortions are unaware of the health risks, particularly of unsafe procedures.

Respondents also had a clear opinion about which contraceptive methods were most unpopular, which they thought could also be a factor for repeat abortions. Condoms and pills are particularly thought of as being disliked by couples (Table 17.5).

Table 17.5: Provider Perceptions of How People Feel About Available Contraceptives

Least Preferred Method	(N)	%
Condom	229	45.6
Pills	103	20.5
IUD	61	12.2
Other methods	109	21.7
Total	502	100.0

Personal Opinions About Contraception Versus Induced Abortion

A significant finding with important significance for family planning efforts was that 61 per cent of the health care workers believed that the use of contraception was not an acceptable way for unmarried women to regulate their fertility. They felt that such use would be in conflict with the prevailing social values concerning marriage and the family. Younger, unmarried women are not supposed to engage in sex before a formal marriage has taken place. Doctors, nurses and midwives continually emphasized their feeling of being caught between the conflicting pressures of providing contraception to unmarried women and upholding the strong social values of their society.

Moreover, over 60 per cent of our respondents also rejected the practice of abortion as a means of fertility regulation, and they did so for all women, not just for unmarried women. They oppose induced abortion largely because of the potential it had for adverse effects on women's health.

Provider Opinions and Recommendations about Various Strategies to Reduce Unsafe Abortion in Sri Lanka

This study attempted to evaluate, from the point of view of the health care providers, the effectiveness and efficiency of various strategies that are presently being used or could be implemented in the future to reduce the incidence of unsafe abortion and its adverse consequences in Sri Lanka (Table 17.6). Again, the point to be underscored and kept in mind while reviewing this information is that every health care strategy requires the fundamental acceptance and support of the providers themselves for an enduring success.

Table 17.6: Provider Opinions on Strategies to Reduce Unsafe Abortion

Opinion	Liberalize Abortion Law		Train Abortion Providers		Improve Sex & Health Education Programmes		Improve Family Planning Programmes	
	(N)	%	(N)	%	(N)	%	(N)	%
Acceptable	240	47.8	73	14.5	462	92.0	484	96.4
Unacceptable	255	50.8	419	83.5	35	7.0	14	2.8
Others	7	1.4	10	2.0	5	1.0	4	0.8
Total	502	100.0	502	100.0	502	100.0	502	100.0

Improve the Quality of Clandestine Abortion Services

Even where abortion legislation is highly restrictive, some attempts have been made to improve the quality of clandestine services in order to reduce the high morbidity and mortality with which they are associated (Frejka et al., 1989). However, the idea of a training programme designed to improve the technical skill of untrained abortion providers for the medical management of abortion complications was rejected by over 83 per cent of our respondents. They indicated that such a programme might further increase the incidence of induced abortion. A referral system to safe services under certain well-defined circumstances, however, could be an acceptable step in this direction.

Improve Family Planning Programmes

In the area of reproductive health, there is an increased emphasis on improving access to family planning as a way to reduce unsafe abortion. The view is that as contraceptive practice improves with a greater choice of a steady supply of modern methods, the incidence of abortion and repeat abortion can be expected to decrease. However, actual experience worldwide is indicating that contraception can reduce, but not eliminate, the need for abortion. Frejka estimates that seven out of 10 women using a 95 per cent-effective method will still require at least one abortion in their lifetime in order to achieve a two-child family (David, 1992).

Because of the relationship of abortion to contraception, we asked our respondents for their views about the impact of family planning programmes on the practice of unsafe abortion. Over 96 per cent of them agreed that improving family planning programmes should be part of an overall strategy to reduce its incidence. As 45 per cent of respondents pointed out, the government's contribution was more significant in the area of family planning services than its success in reducing abortion. A further 50 per cent stressed that additional support from both the government and private sector was necessary to implement even more effective measures within the context of family planning programmes.

One specific recommendation to increase women's use of contraception, suggested by 88 per cent of our respondents, was to educate their husbands or male partners, who have a much more significant influence on decisions about contraceptive use than on the decision to have an abortion. Over 76 per cent of our respondents pointed out that both partners should have adequate information about contraception in order to achieve satisfactory and sustained prevalence.

Together with improved family planning information and advice, abortion counselling should also be provided so that women are aware of the risks of unsafe abortion, a suggestion that was made by over 80 per cent of our respondents.

Improve Health and Sex Education Programmes

The large majority of respondents, 92 per cent, agreed that improvements in existing health and sex education programmes, at both the primary and secondary school levels, would help to reduce unwanted pregnancy and consequently the need for abortion. The feeling is that teachers have not had a substantial impact on adolescents' sexuality, perhaps because they are not specifically trained to teach about sexual and health issues. Therefore, special teacher training programmes were recommended.

We asked our respondents to identify the best person to effectively handle the sex and health education programme for women and 78 per cent of them recommended the family health worker (FHW), who is a female health worker and who visits households regularly. She would need, of course, to be adequately supported by both teachers and health administrators.

An additional recommendation, supported by 97 per cent of respondents, was to establish a sex and health education clinic for men at government hospitals. The idea was that such a programme would be useful to husbands who come to the hospitals with their wives, but who always wait idly outside the antenatal and gynaecological clinics.

Change the Abortion Law

The opinion of respondents regarding the liberalization of the abortion law is given in Table 17.7. Surprisingly, for a group of providers who often give care to women with abortion complications, over half of the respondents would not favour changing the existing abortion law. About a third would approve of a modification in the law that would protect both the physical and mental health of the pregnant woman, thus opening the door somewhat for greater access to legal abortion.

Table 17.7: Provider Opinions on Best Abortion Law for Sri Lanka

Opinion	Doctors		Nurses		Midwives & Others		Total	
	(N)	%	(N)	%	(N)	%	(N)	%
Complete prohibition	1	1.3	2	1.2	5	1.9	8	1.6
Should be allowed upon request	6	7.9	6	3.6	7	2.7	19	3.8
Only to save mother's life (no change in law)	32	42.1	96	57.5	130	50.2	258	51.4
To protect physical and mental health of mother	27	35.5	57	34.1	109	42.1	193	38.4
For defined social reasons	10	13.2	6	3.6	8	3.1	24	4.8
Total	76	100.0	167	100.0	259	100.0	502	100.0

Interestingly, a proposed amendment to the abortion law that would allow only a specially qualified doctor to perform an induced abortion was approved by over 72 per cent of the respondents. This reflects the genuine concern of the providers to improve the safety of the abortion procedure.

Even if abortion were to become legal, 54 per cent of the health personnel in our study would disapprove of the idea of providing safe abortion services at government hospitals. Undoubtedly, there is a fear that the limited budgets and already overcrowded conditions in public hospitals would be worsened by an increased case load of abortion patients. Despite this conservative position, the majority of the respondents still admitted that government hospitals would be the best provider of these services under such changed circumstances.

Imposing legal and administrative restrictions on private sector facilities that provide safe as well as unsafe abortion services was rated as an effective way to reduce unsafe abortion by 70 per cent of our respondents, again reflecting a conservative approach to the abortion issue among these health care workers.

These data confirm that the challenge to policy makers involved in efforts at changing the abortion law in Sri Lanka is complex. While the health personnel in our study clearly recognize that unsafe abortion is a serious health problem and would like to make the procedure safe, there is also a real fear among them that easier access to safe abortion may lead to its increase. The situation is made more complicated by their view that abortion, as well as family planning, are social and religious issues over which the law should have primary jurisdiction.

Summary and Conclusions

This study of the attitudes and opinions of health personnel who play a key role in advising and providing services to women seeking methods of fertility regulation and care for abortion complications has contributed some important information which undoubtedly should be considered by policy makers, health planners, educational authorities and family planning programme administrators involved in efforts to reduce the practice and consequences of unsafe abortion and to improve family planning access and choice.

The finding that almost all respondents recognized unwanted pregnancy and unsafe abortion as major public health problems in Sri Lanka should be generally helpful to any effort to reduce unsafe abortion in this country.

We have also obtained a reasonably reliable profile of women who seek abortion on the basis of our respondents' knowledge. Not surprisingly, urban women who are unmarried and employed are more likely to seek induced abortion than other categories of women. Adolescents less than 18 years of age, as well as married women who use contraception are least likely to seek abortion services.

Regarding the practice of abortion itself, the prevalence of illegal, unsafe abortion performed early in pregnancy is much higher than self-induced abortion, abortion in late stages of gestation, and legal abortion, which is not surprising given the country's restrictive law. Moreover, the majority opinion is that clandestine abortion services offer mostly unsafe procedures and are widely available. It is not clear, however, to what extent safe abortion is available.

In spite of the clear majority opinion that the prevalence of unsafe abortion is very high, and the genuine concern for its adverse effects on women's health and wellbeing, most respondents do not favour a substantial change in the existing abortion law. Some of them, however, wish for an amendment to the law that would better protect the physical and mental health of women.

The most significant finding for policy makers involved in the implementation of strategies designed to reduce unsafe abortion is that for some health providers a more humane approach to the abortion issue may present an ethical and moral conflict between their personal beliefs and their clients' rights and wishes. A very critical finding, for example, was that the large majority of our respondents did not approve of contraception for unmarried women. This attitude could, in fact, be contributing to the higher rate of abortion among unmarried women compared to married women.

It is, therefore, essential to find ways to ensure that the general attitude of health personnel be sensitive to women's needs and empowerment, regardless of the personal preferences of the providers themselves.

It is also important to consider for implementation some of the specific recommendations suggested by the respondents, who are in daily contact with families in need of reproductive health care services. For example, one important suggestion for future programmes in Sri Lanka is to create sex and health education classes for men and to provide them with family planning information, because they have considerable influence over a woman's decision regarding contraceptive use. Another useful recommendation is to improve sex and health education programmes at the primary and secondary school levels through teacher training programmes. Similarly, the suggestion was made to provide more family planning education to women, including abortion counselling, through the already established network of family health workers.

It cannot be overemphasized that the attitudes and fundamental support of health personnel are central to the implementation of strategies aimed at reducing abortion, because they are the ones who carry out the daily routines required for effective service delivery. Hopefully, this study has contributed to a better understanding of the perceptions of health care providers regarding the practice of abortion and contraception, which will help to improve efforts to reduce the needless and avoidable suffering that results from unsafe abortion.

✝ References

David, H.P. 1992. Abortion in Europe, 1920–91: A public health perspective. *Studies in Family Planning* 23 (1): 1–22

Frejka, T., L. Atkin and **D.L. Toro.** 1989. Research program for the prevention of unsafe induced abortion. Working Papers 23, Mexico: The Population Council.

Ministry of Plan Implementation. 1983. *Perspectives on Abortion in Sri Lanka*. Sri Lanka: Ministry of Plan Implementation.

PART III

Adolescent Sexuality and Abortion

18

Induced Abortion Among Unmarried Women in Sichuan Province, China: A Survey

Luo Lin, Wu Shi-zhong, Chen Xiao-qing
and Li Min-xiang

Introduction

In China, sexual relations among unmarried people have always been taboo. Even today, such activity carries strong societal disapproval. To reduce the possibility of such behaviour and the even worse consequence of premarital fertility, for centuries women were married soon after menarche, especially in the remote rural areas of the country. Then in 1950, the Chinese government passed a law that set the ages for marriage at 18 for women and 20 for men, primarily to end this custom of early marriage, particularly the betrothing of children in or before their teens.

Then again in 1980, this time as part of the major effort to sharply limit fertility throughout the country, the Chinese government delayed marriage further by setting the legal age minimums even later, at 20 years for women and 22 years for men. This was in conjunction with the national birth control campaign that succeeded in bringing the country's fertility rate to below replacement level in a very short period of time. (For a brief history and discussion of this fertility reduction effort, see the longer article, Chapter 4, in this book by the same authors.) The law did effectively stop the centuries-old custom of early marriage and many young people accepted the new marriage laws, in part because of the government's new emphasis on the wellbeing of parents and infants, although the law itself was intended to reduce population growth. Today, the age of marriage for most women and men is determined primarily by their education, income and status, including the administrative level of the place in which they live.

Unfortunately, while the national family planning effort focused its fertility reduction programmes on married couples, providing them with easier access to contraception, broadening the grounds for legal, safe abortion, and providing material incentives for limiting family size, unmarried adolescents were virtually ignored. Indeed, the government continued to assume that they would have no sexual life at all until the later age at marriage called for by the new 1980 policy.

So despite all the attention and controversy surrounding the fertility behaviour of couples in China since the 1970s, still very little is known about the fertility behaviour and patterns among unmarried women in China, especially in rural areas, who have been excluded from national family planning efforts that provide information about and easy access to modern contraception.

Not surprisingly, the few studies about unmarried adolescents in China reveal that these young people, too, have sexual lives. They also must confront the same experience of unwanted pregnancy as their married counterparts. And for them, the pressures and risks of unwanted pregnancy are far greater, because they are younger and unmarried. Their unmarried status usually implies a lack of economic support as well as a great potential for social dishonour, which leads them to seek abortion (United Nations, 1992). And as numerous studies worldwide have reported, younger women who undergo abortion, particularly unsafe procedures, face a much greater risk to their life and health than older women.

Objectives

What can be said about induced abortion among unmarried women in China, especially in rural areas? This chapter is based on the findings from a survey designed to explore the sociodemographic characteristics of unmarried women who underwent first-trimester induced abortion in hospitals and family planning clinics in six rural counties of Sichuan province and the quality of abortion services they received.

Research Methodology

Sichuan is China's most populous province, where approximately 9.6 per cent of the country's estimated 1.1 billion people live. Our study was conducted in six rural counties of this province to ensure that abortion was observed in different contexts, including areas with different geographic characteristics, income profiles and abortion facilities. The counties are geographically different and cover a wide area: Changxi and Jiang-go are in remote mountainous regions far away from Chengdu, the capital of Sichuan province; Guanxin and Pengxin are in distant hilly and plain areas; and Guanghan and Xinngdu are in the rice-growing plain areas much closer to Chengdu City.

Gathering the sample of women for this prospective clinical follow-up study required access to family planning clinic and hospital records as well as interviews with clinic patients. After initial screening of all women seeking abortion during the first trimester of their pregnancy, 457 unmarried women were selected from among those women aged 18–40 years who had volunteered to participate in the study.

The field procedure was conducted locally in the six rural counties between July 1990 and June 1991. More than 100 gynaecologists and psychologists from county or regional hospitals and family planning clinics joined in the discussions of the fieldwork or participated in the study.

Local doctors were recruited as interviewers in an attempt to obtain more accurate answers from the unmarried women, because pregnancy among them is such a sensitive issue in China. These doctors participated in a pre-survey training course for one week, which was held in the Sichuan Family Planning Research Institute in Chengdu.

Unmarried women scheduled to undergo first-trimester abortion by vacuum aspiration, by aspiration and curettage, or by curettage only were first seen by trained gynaecologists and psychologists for a pre-abortion assessment and baseline interview. Then our interviewer met each woman on the day of the intervention, explained the procedure as well as the requirements of the research, obtained their consent, and introduced and explained the follow-up questionnaire. All the women in the study voluntarily agreed to participate in the research. These women were then followed-up for a period of six months, during which periodic interviews took place.

Study Findings

Sociodemographic Characteristics of the Women

Table 18.1 shows that most of the unmarried women in the sample (93 per cent) were less than 24 years of age; and 28 per cent were less than 20 years of age. For the majority of the women (64 per cent), gestation at the time of the abortion was between 41 and 60 days; for another one-third of the women, it was between 61 and 90 days. A third of these women had some primary school education and more than half had completed middle school. Most of the girls were farmers living in low-income households in rural areas.

Contraceptive Behaviour

The data in Table 18.2 indicate that 92.6 per cent of the 457 unmarried women who were requesting abortion were not using any method of contraception when their pregnancy started. Even though any married woman or man in China who requests contraception can obtain it easily, either free-of-charge or inexpensively without prescription in the nearby pharmacy, unmarried women are generally ashamed to go to the pharmacy given the

Table 18.1: Percentage Distribution of Sample by Age, Gestation Period, Education, Occupation, Income and Residency

Variable	Number	%
Age group		
< 20	129	28.2
20–24	296	64.8
25–29	18	3.9
30–34	9	2.0
35–39	5	1.1
Total	457	100.0
Days of gestation		
=< 40	12	2.6
41–60	292	63.9
61–90	153	33.5
Total	457	100.0
Education		
Illiterate	8	1.8
Primary	152	33.3
Middle	258	56.4
High+	39	8.5
Total	457	100.0
Occupation		
Housewife	10	2.2
Farmer	350	76.6
Worker	58	12.7
Teacher	3	0.7
Cadre	5	1.1
Other	31	6.7
Total	457	100.0
Income (Chinese yuan/person/month)		
0–50	201	44.0
51–100	190	41.6
101–200	58	12.7
201+	8	1.7
Total	457	100.0
Residence		
Rural	383	83.8
Urban	74	16.2
Total	457	100.0

social stigma against premarital relations. Going to the local family planning staff to request free contraception presents the same kind of potential embarrassment, especially in small rural towns and villages, where everyone has known each other since birth. To support this finding, we compared the low price of contraception with the earnings of the women in our study, which were relatively adequate. We found that non-use of contraception seemed to be the result of inexperience or shame concerning their sexual behaviour rather than their economic situation.

Table 18.2: **Percentage Distribution of Sample by Contraceptive Use**

Contraceptive Use	Number	%
None	423	92.6
Pill	5	1.1
IUD	15	3.3
Condom	2	0.4
Other	12	2.6
Total	457	100.0

Reasons for Abortion

The overriding reason given by these young women (92.5 per cent) for ending their pregnancy by induced abortion was simply the fact that they were unmarried. Societal disapproval of premarital sexual relations clearly forced them to end the pregnancy. The social stigma against such behaviour is so strong that it also prevents them from securing a method of contraception, so that if they do have premarital sexual relations and get pregnant, abortion becomes their only way out. In effect, it becomes their only contraceptive option.

Previous Abortion Experience

As shown in Table 18.3, nearly 40 per cent of the unmarried women in this study had one or more previous pregnancies before this abortion. Furthermore, 35 per cent had one or more previous induced abortions before this abortion. Only 3.2 per cent of the 457 women had gone on to complete their previous pregnancy before this abortion.

Table 18.3: **Percentage Distribution of Sample by Number of Previous Pregnancies and Abortions**

Variable	Number	%
No. of pregnancies		
0	278	60.8
1	142	31.1
2	22	4.8
3 or more	15	3.3
Total	457	100.0
No. of abortions		
0	297	65.0
1	132	28.9
2	22	4.8
3	6	1.3
Total	457	100.0

The results appear to indicate that at least in rural areas, some young people cohabit while they wait to reach the legal age for marriage. Or some may claim cohabitation to get a marriage certificate before they reach the legal age, which is still possible in some rural areas. In short, early sexual unions and cohabitation still appear to be a reality in present-day Chinese rural life. The greater flexibility in marriage arrangements reflects the different character of poor, remote rural regions, where the availability of labour, economic conditions and ethnicity are still strongly associated with family formation. These factors allow for cohabitation of young people, who are then expected to formally marry at some point in the future.

Quality and Safety of Abortion Services

Provider Skill

An important measure of the quality of abortion services available is the professional capacity of the health providers. The training levels and experience of the health personnel that performed the abortions on the 457 women interviewed are shown in Table 18.4. Most providers were trained by the Sichuan Family Planning Programme and had more than three years of experience. Ten per cent received their training at a medical college and one-third attended specialized vocational facilities, such as nursing schools.

Table 18.4: **Percentage Distribution of Sample by Training and Experience of the Operator**

Variable	Number	%
Training of the operator		
Medical college	43	9.4
Vocational school	139	30.4
FP. programme	270	59.1
None	5	1.1
Total	457	100.0
Experience of operator		
< 6 months	9	2.0
6–12 months	14	3.0
1–2 years	22	4.8
> 3 years	412	90.2
Total	457	100.0

Since the 1970s, a major effort has been underway to provide the services required by the national family planning programme, which include, in addition to safe abortion, a wide choice of contraception, including voluntary methods of sterilization. To this end, the skills of providers have been improved through numerous training programmes organized at provincial and county levels. As noted before, there are no impediments to legal abortion in China. If a woman seeks a legal first-trimester induced abortion for economic or social reasons, she can obtain it in a hospital or clinic, where services will be performed by well-trained family planning personnel.

Complication Rate

Another way of looking at the quality of the services is to assess the complications resulting from an induced abortion performed in a young adult population, such as the one included in our study. Table 18.5 indicates that most of these induced abortions produced low blood loss. Moreover, there were no complications of retained tissue, cervical or uterine trauma, or uterine perforation in any of the 457 cases studied.

Table 18.5: Blood Loss During Operation

Volume (ml)	No. of Cases	%
< 50	348	76.1
50–100	94	20.6
101–200	14	3.1
201–300	1	0.2
Total	457	100.0

Results of the physical examination 15 days after the induced abortion are shown in Table 18.6. They demonstrate that in virtually all cases there was no vaginal purulent discharge or genital bleeding at this time. Moreover, none of the women ever experienced fever. These data suggest that induced abortion was performed under very safe medical conditions.

Table 18.6: Physical Examination 15 Days Post-Operation

Variable	No. of Cases	%
Vaginal purulent discharge		
No	452	98.9
Yes	5	1.1
Bleeding		
No	437	95.6
Yes	20	4.4
Fever		
No	457	100.0

Summary and Discussion

When considering the results of this study, it is important to remember that this survey was conducted in several rural counties in Sichuan province, in the south-west region of China, and that some of our study sites were in remote and difficult-to-reach areas.

Also, this research is not about the issue of whether or not abortion should be employed in China. There has been a wide awareness and acceptance of abortion in China since antiquity (H. Yuan Tien, 1991) and the government's official position on abortion is that it should not be used as a primary means of contraception; it should be used only when contraception fails.

In general, these findings are meant to contribute to a better understanding of the fertility behaviour of unmarried women living in rural areas in China, particularly whether and why they seek abortion.

We found that even though many young people in China have broken away from the tradition of early marriage, largely as a result of the government's new marriage laws, 'early marriage' in the form of cohabitation is still practised in the more remote rural regions. Couples live together while they wait to reach the legal age for formal marriage.

Moreover, our study provides evidence that unwanted pregnancy and induced abortion exist among these young farming women. Their pregnancies are the result of the social disapproval of premarital sex, which leaves them either too embarrassed to obtain contraception or completely ignorant of sexual reproduction and modern methods of contraception, or both.

The social stigma against premarital sex does not prevent some of these young rural couples from living together, but it still seems to be a factor that prevents them from carrying a pregnancy to term. Almost all the girls in our study said they had abortions because they were not married. From these findings, we conclude that the taboo against sex may be less strong now, but that a child out-of-wedlock is still totally unacceptable. It was not clear what effect the one-child policy may also have on their decision to have an abortion, however.

All the unmarried women in our sample had easy access to abortion by qualified providers under safe conditions. As a result, the complications of the procedure were very low, in stark contrast to countries where abortion is illegal. In these areas of the world, as many of the other chapters in this book point out, mortality and morbidity from unsafe abortion are still major public health problems.

These findings point to the need for national family planning officials to recognize, rather than ignore, the existence of premarital sexuality among young people, especially in rural areas of the country. Reproductive education should be improved and a greater effort is needed to promote acceptance of the later age for marriage among the rural, unmarried population. Information on family planning and related issues should also be made available to younger, unmarried women as well.

It is our hope that this study will be useful to the further development of population policy in China to benefit the young unmarried people.

✝ References

H. Yuan Tien. 1991. *China's strategic demographic initiative*, New York: Praeger, pp. 175–96.
United Nations, Department of Economic and Social Development. 1992. *Abortion policies: A global review, Vol. I.* New York: Department of Economic and Social Development (DOEASD), United Nations.

19

Sexuality, Contraception and Abortion Among Unmarried Adolescents and Young Adults: The Case of Korea

Kwon Tai-hwan, Jun Kwang Hee and Cho Sung-nam

Introduction

Korea was successful in joining the ranks of so-called newly industrialized countries, or 'middle-income countries', early in the 1980s. The homogeneity of Korean society in terms of culture, language, values and tradition probably facilitated this transition from a rural-agricultural economy to an urban-industrial one. This shift in its position in the world economy, together with modernization and urbanization, has had a tremendous impact on the internal distribution of the population as well as on the pattern of population growth.

Korea has now completed its fertility transition, from a total fertility rate of six children per woman in 1960 to a below-replacement level of 1.6 in 1990, nearly three decades after the initiation of the national family planning programme in 1962 (Kwon and Jun, 1994). The rapid fall may be attributed, directly, to the implementation of vigorous family planning activities. Indirectly, during the initial period of the fertility transition, roughly around 1960–65, delayed marriage and induced abortion were the two main factors underlying fertility change. During the next five years, contraception use and induced abortion became more important in explaining the continuing fertility decline. As the fertility transition advanced during the 1980s, the effect of delayed marriage again became important, in addition to the combined role of contraception and abortion. Contraceptive prevalence increased from 9 per cent in 1964 to 79 per cent in 1991, while the incidence of induced abortion has continued to decrease during the last three decades.

To more precisely understand how the shift to an industrialized economy has influenced reproductive behaviour in Korea, we should try to briefly characterize the growing labour force. Young single women are particularly preponderant in the stream of rural–urban migration and therefore in the newly industrialized cities of Korea. The system of patriarchy that assigns preferential treatment to male offsprings seems to produce the consistent pattern of female dominance among young rural–urban migrants. According to the results from the 1983 Korean National Migration Survey, the primary reason for urban migration of women aged 15–19 was to get to work, while for men the same age, it was to achieve a higher education (Jun, 1987; Kwon and Jun, 1994). These studies also demonstrated that education-related migration was higher for men than for women in all age groups, with the difference being particularly great for the 15–24-year-old age group. Often, young women have to spend a substantial amount of time helping defray the educational costs of their brothers, which can be understood by the prevalence of familism and strong preference for male offspring in the Korean society as a whole.

Contributing to the predominance of young single women in the industrial workforce is an employment structure that favours their participation. Korean businessmen and labour management prefer to employ them because they seem more willing and able to adapt to routine assembly operations than young male workers, especially the tasks that require finger dexterity. Moreover, single female factory workers are generally more productive, and more likely to accept low wages and poor working conditions.

Another identifiable group of young working women prefer to keep away from the difficult and dirty work conditions found in the manufacturing firms of the secondary sectors and instead choose jobs in the entertainment sector. In Korea, sexuality can often be treated as a commodity to be bought and sold in a well-defined marketplace that includes bars and other entertainment enterprises. For example, in 1990, more than half of 340,000 entertainment establishments offered commercial sex services to their male clients.

Naturally, these work patterns have influenced the age at first marriage in Korea, which has steadily increased. The proportion of women remaining single in their early 20s has more than doubled during the last 30 years. The delay in first marriage has been accompanied by a sustained increase in premarital sexual activity. One earlier survey in Korea revealed that about 80 per cent of unmarried women aged 20–29 had experienced routine sexual intercourse; and of them, about half were sexually active at the survey date (Shim, 1991). The rise found in premarital sexual activity, particularly in urban areas, shows that young women are seeking sexual gratification that they would otherwise find within a marital union. It also reflects feelings of greater financial and emotional independence and thus a shift away from equating marriage and a husband with economic and moral support.

The increase in premarital sexual activity, in turn, has led to a rise in unwanted, out-of-wedlock pregnancies, which are now an important component in the maternity history of women in Korea. In this country, however, there are still strong social biases against unmarried mothers and their illegitimate offspring; institutional support for both of them are extremely meagre. Counselling services and professionals working with welfare agencies for single mothers have noticed that even though premarital pregnancies appear to be increasing, the number of single mothers has decreased over the last five years. This leads to the inevitable conclusion that induced abortion is increasing and playing an important role in fertility regulation among unmarried adolescents and young adults in Korea. In fact, several studies support this conclusion (Hong, 1979; Min, 1978; Park, 1976).

The Korean government adopts the clause of abortion 'on causes', in which abortion can be obtained for medical and genetic causes, and in the case of rape or incest. It is not available for social or economic reasons, or simply on request. Two articles of the Penal Code of Korea define abortion as criminal behaviour, but the Infant and Maternal Health Law provides the legal foundation for the provision of abortion services, depending on the condition of the pregnant woman as well as her unborn foetus. But the law has rarely been enforced and abortion has been freely practised in most obstetric and gynaecological clinics. Unfortunately, a safe procedure performed by a physician is very expensive. Thus, economically disadvantaged women, particularly unmarried adolescents, often have no choice but to seek the services of less skilled providers who practise dangerous procedures. The backyard abortion markets in South Korea, in particular, make it very easy for pregnant adolescents and other women to get an abortion. In addition to the increased risks to their physical wellbeing, younger women are also more vulnerable to the possible psychological effects of induced abortion.

Even though policy makers and health professionals recognize this disturbing trend, unfortunately they do not consider themselves primarily responsible for the situation. Nor do they see the provision of contraceptive education or improved reproductive health services as part of their mission. They believe that most adolescents and young adults today are aware of family planning: 'What is absent among this portion of society is the will to take responsibility for reproduction.' (Ahn, 1984).

Objectives

Sexual, contraceptive and abortion behaviour among unmarried female adolescents and young adults has clearly emerged as a growing and serious health and social problem in Korea. This is a study of the determinants of this behaviour, which requires an exploration of attitudes towards premarital intercourse, marriage and abortion; a better understanding of the circumstances of first sexual experience; and information about contraceptive practice and experience of abortion.

Research Methodology

This study was organized according to a decision-making model that outlines the path to induced abortion proposed by Frejka et al. (1989). The model integrates the factors influencing the causes and consequences of induced abortion, and requires an interpretation of abortion behaviour within the context of the general social and economic conditions and the cultural patterns and norms in which these elements interact.

We chose to study reproductive behaviour among unmarried female adolescents and young adults in three export industrial zones of Korea: Kuro (Seoul), Kumi (Kyongbuk) and Masan-Changwon (Kyongnam). An export industrial zone refers to an industrial park that contains plants and other enterprises engaged in manufacturing. The designation of certain medium-sized cities as export industrial zones has been one of the most popular strategies of the Korean government for implementing an export-led industrialization to affect rapid economic development. The three particular zones we chose have been industrial complexes with residential communities occupied mostly by unmarried female industrial workers since the early 1960s.

Data were obtained from a survey using a structured questionnaire as well as from in-depth interviews and focus group discussions, because although abortion is common in Korea, it is still very difficult to assess its socio-behavioural aspects in a structured interview, particularly among a population of young, single women. Identified sociocultural perceptions of induced abortion would then be related to the demographic configuration of the sample in terms of age, residence, education, etc.

A little more than 500 single female adolescents and young adults in three sectors comprised our study sample: (a) women working in manufacturing sectors and living in factory-affiliated dormitories or housing, and who participated in a public information programme set up by the project; (b) female commercial sex workers serving at bars and other entertainment service enterprises, whom we interviewed during their mandatory physical check-ups at the local health centre; and (c) a small group of unmarried adolescents and young adults seeking pregnancy tests or abortion services who were interviewed at the hospital ob-gyn service or at the health centre in an export industrial zone and, therefore, we assumed to be sexually active. To simplify the presentation of these data, we will refer to each group as follows: 'programme participants', 'commercial sex workers', and 'ob-gyn clinic patients'. Adolescents in this study are broadly defined as 'those in their late teens and early 20s; that is, the state of life between childhood and adulthood, the latter being a symbol of maturity and responsibility'. Young adults are defined as 24–29-year-old unmarried women.

The sampling was designed to ensure the participation of sufficient numbers of unmarried adolescent women with abortion experience. These three groups were selected as a 'purposive' sample: a population that would, in general, be unmarried, living independently from their families, and likely to be sexually active. Obviously, they are not representative of all unmarried female adolescents and young adults in Korea. Moreover, the nature of the sample makes it difficult to test a specific research hypothesis or to estimate the value of generalizable parameters. The study can, however, provide a description of young women at high risk of unwanted pregnancy, abortion, and STDs, which is information needed by any effort to improve women's reproductive health in Korea.

The study had the cooperation of the Ministry of Labour, the Ministry of Health and Social Affairs, and the export manufacturing enterprises. Local health centres, general hospitals, and private clinics were also part of the local network system used to obtain information for our study. During the fieldwork, we provided small wrapping cloths and a set of sex education pamphlets to the women we interviewed.

Selected Socioeconomic Characteristics of the Women

A sociodemographic profile of the three study groups is presented in Table 19.1.

Age

The mean age of respondents was lowest for the programme participants (22 years), followed by the commercial sex workers (22.5 years), and then by the ob-gyn clinic patients (23.8 years). Respondents were heavily concentrated in the age group 20–24 years: 64 per cent for the ob-gyn clinic patients; 78 per cent for the commercial sex workers; and 82 per cent for the programme participants. Discussions with medical personnel we interviewed revealed rough estimates of the proportion of their abortion patients who were under 20 years of age ranging between 25 to 50 per cent, confirming a high level of abortion among teenagers.

Residential Background

The birthplace of one-third, or 34 per cent, of the respondents was an urban one. The proportion was highest among the commercial sex workers (60 per cent); followed by the ob-gyn patients (45 per cent) and the programme participants (17 per cent).

About two-thirds of the women, or 65 per cent, spent their childhood in rural areas. The remaining third who spent their childhood in urban areas are highest among the commercial workers (64 per cent), followed by the ob-gyn patients (40 per cent) and the programme participants (17 per cent).

Table 19.1: Sociodemographic Profile of the Women in Our Study

Sociodemographic Variables	Survey Groups			Total
	Programme Participants	Commercial Sex Workers	Ob-Gyn Clinic Patients	
Age (years)				
> 19	8.6	9.4	4.8	8.6
20–24	81.9	76.7	64.2	78.7
25–29	9.5	13.4	21.5	11.8
30–34	0.0	0.5	9.5	0.9
Proportion with Urban Background				
Birth community	16.6	59.5	44.7	33.9
Childhood community	16.6	64.0	39.5	35.1
Previous community	34.2	70.8	44.8	48.0
Duration of Current Residence				
0–1 years	15.1	28.0	12.8	19.5
2–4 years	58.8	35.8	30.8	48.6
5+	26.1	36.2	56.4	31.9
Schooling (years)				
0–9	5.8	11.4	0.0	7.4
10–12	90.5	70.8	76.2	82.4
13+	3.7	17.8	23.8	10.2
Job Changes				
1	40.9	20.9	34.3	33.3
2	35.4	28.6	42.9	33.5
3+	23.7	50.5	22.8	33.2
Age at First Job (years)				
15–17	28.6	10.0	4.0	20.2
18–19	42.2	29.3	34.6	37.1
20–21	27.4	43.0	34.6	33.5
22+	1.8	17.7	26.8	9.2
Religion				
Buddhist	15.1	23.0	21.4	18.4
Protestant	16.0	10.0	16.7	13.9
Catholic	7.4	12.0	4.8	7.8
No affiliation	61.5	55.0	57.1	59.9
Income (Korean won)*				
> 300	20.3	7.6	11.4	15.1
310–400	40.9	23.7	31.4	34.1
410–500	26.2	22.2	20.0	24.3
510+	12.6	46.5	37.2	26.5
Sample Size (N)	(326)	(203)	(42)	(571)

* 1,000 Korean won is equivalent to about US$ 1.25

About half of the women, or 48 per cent, spent their time in metropolitan or medium/small-sized cities before moving to their current urban location. Again, the proportion of those whose previous residence was urban was highest among the commercial sex workers (71 per cent); followed by the ob-gyn patients (45 per cent), and the programme participants (34 per cent).

In our study, it is important to note that between 80–90 per cent of the programme participants moved from rural farms to newly industrialized areas in order to make money to support their families and generally improve their standard of living.

Education

The level of educational attainment was relatively high, with 93 per cent of the women having more than 10 years of schooling. Educational levels were somewhat lower than average for commercial sex workers, with most girls reaching middle school only (up to nine years).

Religion

Religious affiliation was not very notable among these women. More than half of them answered that they had none. The commercial sex workers and the ob-gyn clinic patients were more likely to be Buddhists.

Income and Job Experience

As we pointed out in the introduction, the labour of young female industrial workers is interpreted as the household response to the family members' pressing needs to satisfy their requirements for basic necessities such as food, shelter, clothing, electricity, education and health. Single women, being part of the social system, are viewed as a significant element assisting the family household to meet its survival goal. 'Working for money', however minimal, is being used as a strategy for coping with the demands of the present-day economic pressures on rural households.

Most respondents started working in their late teens or early 20s. About 90 per cent of the programme participants and 80 per cent of the commercial sex workers had their first job between the ages of 15–21; and almost 70 per cent of the ob-gyn patients had their first job between the ages of 18–21.

About eight-tenths of the respondents had a monthly income higher than 310,000 won (400 US dollars). The mean monthly income for the commercial sex workers was nearly twice as high as for the programme participants and the ob-gyn patients. It is significant that about two-thirds of the programme participants were dissatisfied with their meagre wage, which was supposed to include basic salary, over-time allowances, and other fringe benefits. Similarly, they described their working conditions at the factory as dirty, unsafe, and presenting extreme hardship.

Commercial sex workers tended to have less stable jobs than the female manufacturing workers in export industries. The number of total job switches was highest in the commercial sex sector (2.8 times), followed by the ob-gyn patients (2.1 times) and the programme participants (1.9 times). Similarly, the mean duration of employment at the current job was highest, 3.5 years, for both the programme participants and the ob-gyn patients; and 1.9 years for the commercial sex workers.

The programme participants are viewed as working hard to support their families of origin, particularly their brothers and sisters; but most commercial sex workers are seen as working in order to pursue an extravagant, vain lifestyle of personal, unrestrained enjoyment and to improve their general standard of living. In conjunction with these views it is interesting to note that most programme participants come from lower-income families, while a majority of the commercial sex workers come from middle-income families.

Study Results

A series of multiple regression analysis techniques were used for identifying the determinants and consequences of induced abortion. In interpreting the findings from the quantitative survey data, in-depth interview materials as well as focus group data were utilized extensively.

KAP Findings: Premarital Sex, Marriage, Contraception and STDs

In this section, we summarize the knowledge, attitude and practice (KAP) variables of our sample of single women, with regard to premarital sexual activities, marriage, contraception, including knowledge and use of methods, and sexually transmitted diseases (STDs).

Premarital Sexual Relations and Marriage

Korea is no longer a traditional society, at least in regard to the norms governing sexual activities among adolescents and other young, single people. As touched upon earlier, the most significant change is that premarital sexual relations are less frequently tied to entry into formal marriage and the beginning of family formation. Indeed, living together, or cohabitation, has been gaining wide popularity as an alternative lifestyle to traditional marriage.

About 50 per cent of the young women in all three categories said that marriage is not a necessity in life. A much lower proportion of the total sample, about 19 per cent, said that everyone must get married. It is interesting, however, that only a very small number of respondents in all three groups answered that living alone is best, implying that unmarried women may still feel pressure to get married.

The general consensus on ideal age at marriage was 28–29 years for men and 25 years for women. During in-depth interviews and focus group discussions, various reasons emerged for these ideal ages. Half of the respondents linked increased age to increased physical and financial maturity. Similarly, others thought later age at marriage allowed more time to accumulate savings and an advanced level of schooling.

Quantitative data about premarital sexual activity is largely of poor quality, because of its clandestine nature in this society. Traditionally, the patriarchal family system in Korea arranged for young girls to be married before age 16 and premarital sexual activity was strongly controlled by social norms. About half of the single respondents reported that they had sexual experience. As seen in Table 19.2, however, the degree of exposure was very different among the three sub-samples. The programme participants in export industrial zones reveal a rather low level of sexual exposure: only 30 per cent had ever experienced sexual intercourse. By comparison, 70 per cent of the girls working in the commercial entertainment sector had sexual experience. Although the highest level, 83 per cent, was found among the ob-gyn respondents, which is logical as most of them were there to take a pregnancy test or to have an induced abortion.

Table 19.2: First Sexual Experience

	Survey Groups			
	Programme Participants	Commercial Sex Workers	Ob-Gyn Clinic Patients	Total
Proportion with sexual experience	30.4	70.4	83.3	48.5
Age at first sex (years)				
> 14	8.3	2.1	0.1	4.1
15–17	10.4	17.4	3.1	13.4
18–20	37.5	64.3	49.9	53.0
21–23	37.5	14.2	28.1	24.2
24+	6.3	2.0	18.8	5.3
Partner at first sex				
Fiance	7.0	2.2	8.8	4.7
Lover or friend	65.4	73.7	76.5	71.1
Colleague	8.2	7.8	11.8	8.5
Others	19.4	16.3	2.9	15.7
Sample size (N)	(98)	(143)	(35)	(276)

In all three categories of respondents, among those with sexual experience, about 75 per cent had their first intercourse between the ages of 18–23. The proportion of those whose age at first intercourse was less than 18 reached about 20 per cent for both the programme participants and the commercial sex workers, which was a much higher proportion then among ob-gyn patients (3 per cent). This first sexual experience was with either a lover or friend for the majority of the respondents. Many explained that they had first sexual intercourse with their boyfriends because formal wedding was promised in the near future or simply because they loved each other. However, some women indicated that their first sexual experience had been rape or had been forced on them by company colleagues or supervisors, indicating the harsh and dangerous work environment of many of the female factory workers, or programme participants. It appears that the first sexual experience was attended by uneasiness for most of the respondents. A great majority said that they were uncomfortable about possibly getting pregnant; and about one-third feared contracting STDs.

Not surprisingly, we found contrasting attitudes towards premarital sexual activities among our respondents. About one-third of our sample, or 33 per cent, had the opinion that talking about premarital virginity is old-fashioned and unacceptable. Predictably, this opinion was more prevalent among the commercial sex workers than among the programme participants and ob-gyn patients. Nearly half of the sample felt that premarital sex should be forbidden, while one-third said that it was acceptable. This latter attitude was much more popular among the commercial sex workers. The attitude of the women towards premarital sex appeared to be substantially influenced by parental values. It appears that those adolescents and young adults who frequently visited and talked with their parents, many of whom lived in rural villages, were more restrained in their sexual behaviour. The family institution, at least in Korea, seems to still have a strong influence on adolescent sexual behaviour.

Contraceptive Knowledge and Use

It appears that most of the respondents had reasonable knowledge about when the ovulation period begins, especially in relation to menstruation, and when they are at the highest risk of becoming pregnant. Similarly, about 79 per cent said they knew generally about methods of contraception (Table 19.3). The most commonly known methods included oral contraceptives (31 per cent), rhythm (24 per cent), and condoms (19 per cent).

Nevertheless, more than 80 per cent of the young women in our study did not use any contraception during their first sexual experience. A large majority of these women said that they had worried about getting pregnant, but many explained that they had hesitated to use any contraception at the time because they feared that male partners might label them as a 'bad-quality girl'.

Of the respondents who used contraception at the time of their first sexual experience, about 20 per cent used one or more contraceptive methods. As expected, the commercial sex workers obtained the highest level of contraceptive protection (29 per cent), followed by the ob-gyn patients (15 per cent), and the programme participants (8 per cent).

Current use of a contraceptive method was highest among the commercial sex workers at 53 per cent, compared to 21 per cent for the programme

Table 19.3: Contraceptive Knowledge and Use at First Intercourse

Family Planning Knowledge and Use	Survey Groups			
	Programme Participants	Commercial Sex Workers	Ob-Gyn Clinic Patients	Total
Knew FP at first sex?				
No	22.4	24.1	22.9	20.8
Yes, but not in detail	55.2	58.2	56.6	57.2
Yes	22.4	17.7	20.5	22.0
Sample size (N)	(98)	(143)	(35)	(276)
Methods known				
Oral pills	26.3	35.4	24.1	30.6
Rhythm	23.4	23.4	24.1	23.5
Foam, jelly, tablet	9.2	9.2	13.8	9.8
Condom	20.0	20.0	13.8	19.2
Withdrawal	3.4	3.4	1.8	3.0
None	17.7	8.6	22.4	13.9
Sample size (N)	(76)	(109)	(27)	(212)
Percentage using contraception at first intercourse	8.3	28.7	14.8	19.6
	(76)	(109)	(27)	(212)

participants and 20 per cent for the ob-gyn patients (Table 19.4). As expected, pill use was highest among the commercial sex workers at 49 per cent and much lower for programme participants (13 per cent) and ob-gyn patients (6 per cent). The in-depth interviews revealed, however, that the majority of these women were not regular pill users and often took them after intercourse with the hope that they would induce menstruation. Some women took 'pills' without knowing what they were, having asked the pharmacist to provide something to bring on menstruation. Also, as expected, the highest use of the least effective methods of rhythm and withdrawal was found among the ob-gyn patients.

The highest contraceptive failure rate (18 per cent) was also found among the commercial sex workers. The ob-gyn patients had a failure rate of 14 per cent and the programme participants, 9 per cent (Table 19.5). The pattern of method failure was different for each group; most notably, 45 per cent of the commercial sex workers who experienced failure of their method were pill users. As just described, this was largely due to inappropriate use.

Pregnancy History and Contraceptive Use

The proportion of women with sexual experience who had ever been pregnant was nearly 60 per cent for the group as a whole, but differed greatly for the sub-samples (Table 19.6). It was naturally much higher, at 91 per cent, for the ob-gyn patients; 66 per cent for the commercial sex workers; and 37 per cent for the programme participants. Although the commercial sex workers

Table 19.4: Past and Current Contraception Use, by Method

Past and Current Use	Survey Groups			
	Programme Participants	Commercial Sex Workers	Ob-Gyn Clinic Patients	Total
Past use	10.2	62.3	50.0	42.2
Methods*				
Oral pills	6.5	62.3	27.3	8.0
Rhythm	10.1	32.1	50.0	26.6
Foam, jelly, tablet	4.2	32.0	22.6	20.9
Condom	6.8	51.9	25.7	32.5
Withdrawal	10.2	28.0	31.4	18.7
Current use	21.2	52.6	20.0	37.3
Methods*				
Oral pills	13.3	48.6	6.3	38.5
Rhythm	31.4	12.7	31.2	17.8
Foam, jelly, tablet	6.7	10.6	12.5	9.9
Condom	24.3	20.4	18.8	21.1
Withdrawal	24.3	4.9	31.2	10.6
Others	0.0	2.8	0.0	2.1
Sample size (N)	(98)	(143)	(35)	(276)

* Reflects all methods ever used; percentages do not add up to 100 as one person could have used several methods.

Table 19.5: Contraceptive Failure

	Survey Groups			
	Programme Participants	Commercial Sex Workers	Ob-Gyn Clinic Patients	Total
Contraceptive failure	9.1	18.1	14.3	14.5
Sample size (N)	(98)	(143)	(35)	(276)
No. of failures				
1	71.4	85.7	81.4	82.0
2+	28.6	14.3	28.6	18.0
Sample size (N)	(9)	(26)	(5)	(40)

were the highest risk group for unwanted pregnancy: 60 per cent had had two or more pregnancies; compared to 35 per cent for the programme participants and 38 per cent for the ob-gyn clinic patients. All premarital pregnancies had ended in induced abortion. And most of the respondents who were pregnant at the time of our interview wanted to have an abortion, performed under extremely private conditions at local medical institutions. This indicates the strength of societal disapproval in Korea of single mothers and their illegitimate offspring.

Table 19.6: Pregnancy History and Contraceptive Use Among the Sexually Active Women

Pregnancy and Contraceptive Use	Survey Groups			
	Programme Participants	Commercial Sex Workers	Ob-Gyn Patients	Total
Proportion ever pregnant	37.1	65.6	91.4	58.7
Pregnancies				
1	64.7	39.6	62.5	49.7
2	20.6	30.8	18.8	26.1
3+	14.3	29.6	18.7	24.2
Used contraception before first pregnancy	14.3	16.0	8.8	14.5
Used a modern method before first pregnancy	50.8	30.0	38.9	37.9
Sample size (N)	(98)	(143)	(35)	(276)

About 85 per cent of the sexually active women had not been using contraception when they experienced their first pregnancy. The general behaviour of these respondents was one of risk-taking; not only were they relying on low-efficacy methods, but also about three-fourths answered that they were not practising contraception during the period they knew they could easily become pregnant.

Sexually Transmitted Diseases (STDs)

In a world threatened by an increasing incidence of sexually transmitted disease, it was important to learn about the experience of the women in our study. The presence of STDs was significant: 14 per cent said that they had STDs as a result of their first sexual experience. As expected, commercial sex workers had a higher incidence of STDs (20 per cent) than the other two groups.

After contracting STDs, about 80 per cent visited a local health centre or private clinic, while the rest bought medicines at the pharmacy. Programme participants visited private clinics more frequently than the commercial sex workers and were better informed about STDs. A routine checkup (basically, STD checkup) takes place monthly at the local health centre.

The Determinants of Induced Abortion

In this section, we identify key risk factors for induced abortion in our study population of young single women and summarize our main findings from descriptive statistics and multiple regression results.

Characteristics of the First Abortion

About 80 per cent of the respondents with abortion experience had their first abortion performed during the first-trimester (Table 19.7). Many consulted with their male partners (37 per cent) and girlfriends (24 per cent) before-hand. Women were more frequently accompanied by their male partners, sisters, or female friends than by their parents. Those who relied most heavily on their male partners were the programme participants (54 per cent), while those who relied most heavily on their girlfriends were the commercial sex workers (32 per cent). Some of them mentioned that they bought some medicine to try to induce an abortion themselves, before seeking an abortion

Table 19.7: First Abortion Experience

Abortion Attributes and Sequelae	Survey Groups			
	Programme Participants	Commercial Sex Workers	Ob-Gyn Clinic Patients	Total
No. of abortions				
1	62.9	39.1	62.5	49.0
2	20.0	30.4	21.9	26.5
3	11.4	19.6	10.6	17.0
4	5.7	6.5	5.0	6.0
5+	0.0	4.4	0.0	4.0
Average no. per woman	1.59	2.26	1.94	21.5
Age at first abortion (years)				
> 19	0.0	14.3	3.6	9.0
20–21	10.0	45.3	25.0	33.4
22–23	53.0	27.4	28.6	33.3
24–25	30.0	13.0	25.0	19.2
26+	7.0	0.0	17.8	5.1
Contraceptive failure	9.7	11.5	13.8	11.6
Gestational age (months)				
1–3	90.4	82.4	80.4	83.8
4+	9.6	17.6	19.6	16.2
With whom consulted?				
No consultation	17.4	6.0	21.4	14.6
Family member	6.5	14.2	17.9	13.2
Male partner	54.4	32.8	42.9	36.6
Girlfriend	17.4	31.5	7.1	23.5
Doctor/FP worker	4.3	15.5	10.7	12.1
Considered the health risks?	85.7	60.4	76.7	69.2
Abortion method				
Surgical	93.9	90.6	96.9	92.6
Medication	6.1	6.3	0.0	5.0
Other	0.0	3.1	3.1	2.4
Proportion with sequelae	39.4	22.2	21.9	25.9
Treatment for sequelae				
Visited hospital	30.4	57.8	37.5	45.0
Took medicine	8.7	12.5	25.0	13.3
No particular treatment	60.9	29.7	37.5	41.7
Sample size (N)	(35)	(92)	(32)	(159)

provider. Physicians who performed the abortions seemed to do it regardless of whether the clients were single or not.

Over 90 per cent of the respondents relied on a surgical method for their first abortion and about one-fourth said they had experienced complications immediately after their procedure. The proportions of women with complications was highest among the programme participants (39 per cent); it was lower for the commercial sex workers and the ob-gyn clinic patients (20 per cent). About 45 per cent of those with complications visited a hospital or took medicine to treat the problems. About three-fourths of these respondents said that they had considered the health effect of induced abortion before having it.

Lifetime Abortion Experience

Among the single respondents who were sexually active, 58 per cent had abortion experience. Two-thirds of the first abortions took place between the ages of 20 and 23. Of these women, half had had two or more abortions. Table 19.8 presents the results of our regression analysis. Abortion experience was taken as the dependent variable, while age, type of subgroup, current as well as childhood residence, educational level, and religion were used as explanatory variables.

The result reveals that the higher the age of the respondent, the more likely she was to experience both first and repeat abortions. Urban childhood

Table 19.8: Logistic Regression of All Abortion Experiences

Variables	Coefficients (1) N = 276	Coefficients (2) N = 159
Age (years)		
> 19	−1.217*	−0.345*
20–24	0.226**	0.134*
25–29	0.437**	0.213
30–34		
Survey group		
Programme participants	−1.518**	−1.634*
Commercial sex workers	1.313**	1.214**
Ob-gyn patients		
Current residence		
Kuro (Seoul)	0.043	0.027
Kumi (Kyongbuk)	−0.031	−0.009
Masan-Ch'angwon (Kyongnam)		
Childhood residence		
Urban	0.214*	0.007
Rural		

Table 19.8 continued

Education (years)		
> 9	0.286**	0.183*
10–12	0.001	0.000
13+		
Religion		
No religion	−0.104	−0.001
Buddhist	0.101	0.100
Catholic	−0.204**	−0.104**
Protestant	0.107	0.003
Other		
	dependent: 1 = abortion experience 0 = no experience	1 = two or more abortions 0 = one abortion

* Significant at 0.05 level.

** Significant at 0.01 level.

Note: Estimates of the coefficients are not displayed for the last category of each variable, but the coefficients will be summed to zero for all categories of a particular variable.

residence also increased exposure to an abortion, but not to repeat abortion. Conversely, Catholic religious affiliation decreased the risk of abortion and repeat abortion. It is also evident from the analysis that the risk of an abortion before marriage is lowest among the programme participants and highest among the commercial sex workers. This profile fits our earlier descriptions of the differences in premarital sexual activity and contraceptive use between these two groups, with the programme participants considerably more conservative in their behaviour than the commercial sex workers.

The logistic regression analysis of post-abortion complications after first and most recent abortion is shown in Table 19.9. The results indicate that commercial sex workers were more prone to post-abortion complications than the other two groups. Complications also tended to increase with age. The respondents with less than nine years of schooling were more likely to experience post-abortion complications than those with a high school diploma.

Repeat Abortion

Among the women who said they were sexually active, abortions were remarkably high; they had an average of 2.1 abortions. The highest average was among the commercial sex workers, at 2.3 abortions, followed by the ob-gyn patients at 1.9, and the programme participants at 1.6. The share of repeat abortions was also largest among the commercial sex workers (61 per cent), followed by the ob-gyn patients (38 per cent) and the programme participants (37 per cent).

Table 19.9: Logistic Regression of Post-Abortion Complications

Variables	Coefficients
Survey group	
Programme participants	−0.016
Commercial sex workers	0.317**
Ob-gyn patients	
Age (years)	
> 19	0.000
20–24	0.121
25–29	0.213**
30–34	
Current residence	
Kuro (Seoul)	−0.019
Kumi (Kyongbuk)	0.002
Masan-Ch'angwon (Kyongnam)	
Childhood residence	
Urban	−0.050
Rural	
Education (years)	
> 9	0.018**
10–12	−0.013
13+	

Dependent: 1 = complication
0 = no complication

* Significant at 0.05 level.

** Significant at 0.01 level.

Note: Coefficients are not displayed for the last category of each variable, but the coefficients will be summed to zero for all categories of a particular variable.

Knowledge and Attitudes Regarding Abortion

Most respondents possessed a fair amount of knowledge, much of it correct, regarding methods of abortion. Menstrual regulation, defined as uterine evacuation in a woman at risk of being pregnant before she can be declared as 'obviously pregnant', was thought to be an acceptable means of ending an unwanted pregnancy by a little more than half of the ob-gyn patients. More than a third of the commercial sex workers and nearly half of the programme participants did not know precisely about the procedure. But most of the respondents said that a surgical procedure would be safe and acceptable within four months gestation.

About 77 per cent of the total number of women in our study agreed to the use of induced abortion in general, for all women with an unwanted pregnancy. Similarly, 89 per cent approved of the use of abortion for single women. A lower proportion, 75 per cent, agreed to the use of induced abortion for married women. The proportion of respondents who were against abortion for married women was highest among the programme participants, whose views throughout the results have been found to be the most conservative (Table 19.10). The proportion of approval of abortion increased with the age of the respondent, the level of education, and the number of induced abortions experienced. The reasons to approve abortion were highest when teenagers and other adolescents were experiencing an unwanted pregnancy (85 per cent), followed by abortion performed for the purpose of birth spacing (70 per cent) and lastly for economic difficulties (41 per cent). The lowest rates of abortion approval were found for couples with marriage plans (9 per cent) and for childless couples (8 per cent). The general trend in attitude of more acceptance for unmarried women than for married women is in keeping with Korean proverbs, such as 'fellow sufferers sympathize most emphatically with each other', and 'grief is best consoled with grief's company'.

Table 19.10: Approval of Abortion (Full Study Sample)

Abortion Approval	Survey Groups			
	Programme Participants	*Commercial Sex Workers*	*Ob-Gyn Clinic Patients*	*Total*
In general	71.5	83.6	82.9	76.6
For single women	88.0	90.4	88.1	88.5
For married women	68.2	83.5	80.4	74.6
Sample Size (N)	(326)	(203)	(42)	(571)

One of the most important conclusions emerging from the in-depth interviews is the apparent reliance on induced abortion as a strategy for dealing with unwanted, out-of-wedlock births among adolescents and younger women. In virtually every in-depth interview and focus group session, unsafe or unhygienic abortions were reported to be widespread.

Discussion and Policy Recommendations

The rapid pace of industrialization in Korea has caused growing numbers of young women to postpone marriage in pursuit of employment opportunities and training to support their families, to enhance their professional careers, or to improve their standard of living. The result of the overall increase in the age at marriage has been a naturally corresponding increase in premarital sexual activity and informal, often temporary, sexual unions.

These rapid changes in fertility behaviour, along with a very strong traditional social stigma against out-of-wedlock pregnancy, have brought about a substantial increase in the number of induced abortions among adolescents and young adults. Existing reproductive health services, because they generally have continued to ignore this growing population of sexually active couples, have aggravated the situation.

Our study has shed more light on the dynamics of adolescent sexuality in Korea. For example, the young single Korean women who regard themselves as virtuous, 'good-quality' girls in the traditional sense of the word are those least likely to use contraception, not because they are ignorant of methods, but because to do so would contradict their moral self-image. And once an unwanted pregnancy occurs, it is likely to create the greatest difficulties for the young woman who is trying hardest to be respectable. This is a kind of vicious circle that cannot be broken merely by improving sex education.

While our sample of women is not representative of the whole population of Korean adolescents and young women, we would like to suggest a number of policy and programme recommendations based on the more significant findings of our study.

In Korea, counselling services for young girls who may feel regretful about having had careless sexual intercourse are of extremely poor quality. Incest relations are not uncommon and the social practice of viewing sexuality as a commodity to be bought and sold entraps many young girls in a world of sexual impulses rather than allowing them to mature sexually in a compassionate and psychologically supportive way. Such an atmosphere almost encourages the practice of induced abortion. The most obvious and important recommendation therefore, is to establish 'good-quality' counselling and family planning services, particularly for adolescents and single women, under the auspices of both national and local governments. Such services should also extend to abortion services at both public hospitals and private clinics, where providers often fail to provide contraceptive information and services, so that repeat abortions are not avoided. This is of critical importance as a means of reducing unsafe abortion among adolescents.

Government policy makers and family planning professionals should create public information and education campaigns about family planning methods, particularly for commercial sex workers and young women working in the various textile, electronic, manufacturing and other industrial sectors. Emphasis should be placed on the adverse health consequences of abortion, particularly when performed by incompetent or untrained providers.

As an example, during our focus group sessions, we held a series of education programmes using pamphlets with contraceptive information based on United Nations publications. Many participants at first hesitated to be involved, but then began to appreciate the field staff for providing them with the reproductive health materials. Many of them had come from remote rural villages and so recommended that such information be given to rural adolescents, rather than to themselves. Local doctors and educators generally agree that rural adolescents are more exposed to dangerous unprotected intercourse than their urban counterparts. Therefore, we recommend that contraceptive information be provided to adolescents in rural areas as well as in the export zones described in this study.

Programmes designed only to extend contraceptive distribution are not sufficient to reduce risk-taking behaviour and the need for induced abortion among the younger population. High school and college education programmes need to offer courses on human sexual behaviour, particularly premarital sexual activity, to encourage women and men to take thoughtful and premeditated responsibility for their sexual activity, and to repeal the sexual double standard for men and women. Sexual behaviour should be regarded as a natural, positive phenomenon in the curriculum. Again, since many of our participants had originally come from rural villages, we recommend such a curriculum for adolescents in both rural and urban areas. Additionally, our research has shown us that these kinds of programmes are especially needed for male adolescents. In our in-depth interviews, many girls mentioned that teachers should 'give advice to girls to stop friendships with "bad quality" boys' and that these boys are not likely to accept responsibility for their roles in the pregnancy of their girlfriend. It was also implied that many of the girls, who are under strong social pressure to avoid sexual intercourse until they are formally married, may have acquiesced to their partner's demand for sexual relations because of strong pressure or threat of violence.

Our study also showed that young single women in Korea are at significant risk of contracting STDs, particularly the young women who work in the entertainment sector. We believe that this threat posed by STDs should be addressed by working towards three important goals: (*a*) the establishment of comprehensive, integrated reproductive health services; (*b*) the development of a better understanding of the process through which communities can lower the risk of STDs; and (*c*) the rapid mobilization of a concerted effort to identify a safe and effective method for preventing STDs, which is within the control of women.

Feminist and religious organizations should be encouraged to develop and reinforce informal information networks to aid women who are eligible under law to obtain legal abortions and to provide other women with knowledge needed to implement their decision to have an abortion in the safest way available. Because even under the restrictive abortion law, the conditions surrounding the process of securing an abortion vary greatly in Korea. Open competition for quality services can reduce the fees charged and further facilitate access to safer services. This would be particularly helpful to female industrial workers and commercial sex workers, whom we found to be at greater risk of falling into the hands of incompetent practitioners because this kind of information is shrouded in far more secrecy and therefore more difficult for them to obtain.

Moreover, despite its potential dangers, the purchase of induced abortion for small fees represents a time-honoured tradition among the commercial sex workers and unmarried industrial workers, because they are strongly motivated to control their fertility. This implies that the practice of early menstrual regulation should play a unique role as a method of family planning in Korean society, particularly among adolescents and unmarried adults. We believe that expanded menstrual regulation programmes, together with contraceptive information campaigns, could offer significant new opportunities for young, single women to regulate their fertility with the highest degree of safety and greatest efficacy.

Complete legalization of abortion in Korea should also be considered. The high prevalence of abortion among young people attests to the existing contradiction between the ideals of written law and actual medical practice as health providers attempt to cope with a growing demand for abortion services. Moreover, providers who perform unsafe abortions are not punished unless clients report them. The 'full' legalization of abortion, with special provision for adolescents and young single women, would contribute to the reduction of unsafe abortions performed by incompetent providers.

Although our study did not specifically address the issue of treatment of post-abortion complications, the mere existence of a restrictive law implies their existence. As in other countries where unsafe abortion procedures are common, women who suffer from badly performed procedures do not always receive appropriate care and attention until their condition is considerably worsened or too late to treat. This is, in part, because the people to whom they turn, such as doctors, friends, and nurses, do not recognize the symptoms or simply do not want to be involved for fear of legal punishment. Adolescents and young women are especially at risk for complications of unwanted pregnancy. We therefore recommend that there be support for the training of abortion providers and local health centre personnel for early detection and treatment of post-abortion complications.

Our research has also revealed a paucity of information on all aspects of sexuality, contraception and induced abortions among Korean adolescents and young adults. The consequences for adolescents' health, the social and cultural context within which their abortions are performed, and even the characteristics of those who resort to abortion are unknown or only roughly estimated. Therefore, the need to identify adolescents who have induced abortions exists, regardless of any particular study objectives and the source of data. One particularly important issue, for example, is the influence of peers and parents. Are adolescents influenced in their decision to abort by their peer groups, particularly company colleagues? To what extent does living together with their parents influence adolescent sexual behaviour? Many of these issues should be urgent priorities for future study.

Lastly, but not least importantly, researchers should always keep in mind that the important index of the incidence of induced abortion is plagued by reporting errors—both intentional and unintentional—despite the apparent simplicity of the definition of abortion. This complicates case identification. For example, self-induced abortion is often misclassified as spontaneous abortion in cases that are ambivalent, such as when a woman attempts to abort using herbal medicines or other folk methods, a common practice among teenagers and single women. A woman may also 'terminate' a suspected pregnancy when, in fact, she is not pregnant at all. One of the participating physicians mentioned that, depending on the study site and the days of amenorrhoea, 16–83 per cent of women using menstrual regulation are not pregnant, although they believe that they have had an induced abortion. Most physicians, however, say that the main source of classification error is likely to be intentional; that is, clients are not always willing to disclose that they have had an induced abortion. These physicians say: 'Women presenting themselves at private clinics or other health facilities with vaginal bleeding may not be able to disguise an abortion; while women interviewed in a survey have the opportunity to deny an abortion of any type.' Moreover, the distinction should be made clearly between abortions arising from lack of knowledge and abortions due to contraceptive failure.

✝ References

Ahn, S.D. 1984. *Korean single mothers: Paths and welfare strategies.* (in Korean) Seoul: Korea Institute of Woman and Development.

Frejka, T., L.C. Atkin and **O.L. Toro.** 1989. Research program for the prevention of unsafe abortion and its adverse consequences in Latin America and the Carribean. Program Division Working Paper No. 23. New York: The Population Council.

Hong, S.B. 1979. Recent changes in patterns of induced abortion in Seoul: Based on changing patterns of age structure of abortees. *Korea Journal of Obstetrics and Gynaecology* 22.

Jun, K.H. 1987. Reproductive behavior of rural-urban migrants in Korea: An analysis of the proximate determinants. Ph.D dissertation, Department of Sociology, Seoul National University.

Kwon, T.H. and **K.H. Jun.** 1994. Demographic change and urbanization. An unpublished manuscript. Department of Sociology, Seoul National University.

Min, B.K. 1978. *The attitudes and behaviors of Korean adolescents.* Seoul: The Korean Adolescent Research Institute, Chungang University.

Park, I.S. 1976. Clinical study for medical aspects of pregnancy and abortion in Korea. *Korea Journal of Obstetrics and Gynecology* 19.

Shim, Y.H. 1991. An empirical study of induced abortion in Korea. Research monograph. Seoul: Korean Institute of Criminology.

✝

20

Female Adolescents at the Crossroads: Sexuality, Contraception and Abortion in Mexico

N. Ehrenfeld

Introduction

Mexican society is generally very conservative in the values that define family life and family formation, particularly sexuality, including the norms that relate to sexual practices, patterns of sexual behaviour, the rights of sexual minorities, and even in its approach to sex education. Naturally, these values apply equally to the issue of induced abortion. Many groups in today's Mexican society, among them a large number of physicians, still remain opposed to its practice.

While certain studies suggest that 'public opinion regarding abortion has become more liberal' in Mexico (Pick de Weiss and Givaudan, 1991), it seems that there is still a considerable gap between an emerging liberal opinion and effective action. The most obvious example of this gap is that induced abortion is still very much illegal in Mexico; the only exceptions are when the pregnancy endangers the health or the life of the mother. Otherwise its practice is punishable by a jail sentence. This legal framework leaves the practice of abortion very much in the hands of individual physicians, who are free to perform procedures using methods and under conditions wholly outside of any medical or legal jurisdiction.

As a result, access to safe abortion is strictly confined to wealthier women who can pay the high cost of a confidential, safe procedure. For thousands of lower-income women, however, induced abortion is a very different reality. The experience is defined by a series of risky alternatives, the outcome of which is almost always some form of illness, and not uncommonly, death. The personal experiences of individual women who undergo clandestine abortion, especially the emotional impact of such an experience, are not adequately recorded in surveys or statistics. Similarly, the extent to which the sequelae of unsafe abortion affect sexual and reproductive health are very poorly understood. This is despite the fact that most people find it hard to believe that any woman could undergo an abortion, even under favourable conditions, without experiencing emotional stress.

Undoubtedly, family planning is the best solution for avoiding unplanned and unwanted pregnancy, but there is always some possibility of failure even when contraceptives are properly used. Moreover, official family planning programmes do not always reach the target population because of frequent cultural, familial, medical or service obstacles. In this type of situation, abortion becomes the only alternative to interrupting an unplanned or unwanted pregnancy.

A largely ignored aspect of abortion research worldwide is the health and emotional risks for adolescents of unsafe abortion, even though such risks can be greater for them than for older women, generally because young girls tend to be much farther along in their pregnancy when they finally contact an abortion provider. This is usually out of basic ignorance of their body's reproductive functioning or due to emotional denial of a situation that is far too overwhelming for them to confront. Evidence suggests that this is also because the procedure may be more technically difficult, as a nulliparous cervix can be difficult to dilate and there is more risk of perforation and cervical tears. The two most obvious examples of more serious health risks for adolescents are the possible sequelae of infertility and death; although the emotional and psychological impact of an unsafe abortion also can present a much greater and long-lasting trauma to a young girl 12 or 14 years of age than for a woman of 35. Adolescent sexuality should also be regarded as a significant component of general abortion research, because it is the starting point for the patterns of sexual behaviour and fertility regulation that will continue for the rest of a woman's reproductive life.

Studies of adolescent sexuality, however, must do more than describe the general background characteristics of pregnant girls who request abortion services, for example. We must try to understand the circumstances and conditions underlying such a request, by studying adolescents' own views and perceptions about their sexuality, contraception, partner relationships and goals for their future.

Objectives

This study sought to identify the determinants of the decision to continue or interrupt an unplanned pregnancy among adolescents aged 12 to 19, by examining the circumstances and sociocultural conditions underlying such a decision. This included looking at factors such as the girl's sexual and reproductive behaviour, her partner's and mother's response to the pregnancy, the partner relationship, her education and employment characteristics, and so forth.

Research Methodology

The study sample, gathered using the quota system, included 72 adolescent girls who requested services related to their pregnancies at the Obstetrics and Gynaecology Clinic of the Hospital General Dr Manuel Gea González, in Mexico City. One half of the girls were pregnant and the other half had recently had an abortion. All of them were under the age of 20.

The hospital is a public, second-level, general care, Ministry of Health hospital, located in the south of the city, which provides care for low-income people. During 1993, 2,208 deliveries were assisted and 822 caesarean sections were performed. It also provided 4,155 scheduled obstetrics consultations, in addition to 11,190 obstetric emergencies. It should be noted that for almost nine years now, the hospital has been running a comprehensive programme for adolescents, including a service that provides special attention to high-risk obstetric cases. In 1992, the hospital was named 'Friend of the Mother and Child Hospital', which is a special official recognition.

The research included two phases, each with different objectives. The first phase consisted of two separate series of focus group discussions: one with the currently pregnant adolescents and the other with the girls who had had an abortion. The objective here was to obtain a useful and accurate description of abortion from the adolescents' own reproductive and sexual health perspective.

The second phase consisted of in-depth interviews with each of the women who met the requirement to continue in the study. The main objective was to identify the different factors that influence the decision to either carry the pregnancy to term or to abort, including who else besides the girl herself may have taken part in that process. The in-depth interviews also served as a way to discover which methods are commonly used for abortion and to describe the conditions under which the procedure took place.

Gathering the Sample

Gathering the proposed sample presented a challenge that was eventually met. We offer an account of our experience here, because the study of clandestine abortion among young girls in any society will be problematic and other researchers may therefore find it helpful to know how we overcame the various obstacles that arose. Also, this experience revealed some hidden issues with important significance for our study.

First Contact

The pregnant girls were contacted when they attended the outpatient clinic or the hospital emergency service. The girls with abortion experience were contacted when they were admitted to the hospital for abortion complications, but they were interviewed two weeks later.

At this first contact, all the girls were informed about the objectives of the study and the goal of the future improvement of adolescent reproductive health care in Mexico. They were also told that their participation was voluntary and would be completely confidential. The methodology of the focus group discussion was also explained in detail.

Pregnancy Cases

To carry out the first phase of the research successfully, we decided to have four sessions with each of the pregnancy focus groups, because more time would be needed to become familiar with the terminology adolescents use to discuss topics such as sexuality, contraception and abortion. It was apparent once the sessions started, however, that more sessions for each group would be needed. In the end, a total of 11, three-hour sessions were held.

Initially, all 36 girls in each of the four discussion groups attended the first sessions. As the process continued, however, 21 of the 36 girls initially selected were either excluded from the sample or did not go to subsequent sessions for the following reasons:

1. They had incorrect information as to the month of their pregnancy, which turned out to be a more advanced second-trimester pregnancy than the criteria of first-trimester pregnancy required for inclusion in this study. It is significant that this group represented 43 per cent of the total number of girls who had to be later excluded.
2. Their partner, who was notified after the first session, opposed their return to the next session. The girls openly said that their partner did not like 'those things' being discussed in his absence and that he would not allow them to continue attending. This group represented 19 per cent of those who discontinued.
3. Unknown reason; never returned.

The second phase, the in-depth personal interview, was much less problematic than the focus group discussions. All of the girls agreed to be recorded, irrespective of their participation in the group discussions.

Abortion Cases

It was much easier to form a group of nine pregnant girls for the focus group discussions than to achieve the same with the abortion group. It required twice as much time and effort to establish a rapport with a group of girls with abortion experience as it did with the girls who were pregnant.

There was frequent dropping out after the abortion, because the girls were reluctant to attend interviews, medical follow-ups or respond to surveys after such an experience. We were obliged to decrease the number of girls in each focus group to five and the number of groups to three. Finally, a total of 14 girls participated in the abortion focus groups.

The reasons for the high drop-out rate among these girls were distinctly different from those who were in the pregnant focus groups. Four women were forbidden to return by their partner, and the rest did not return for unstated reasons. It was clear to us, however, that many did not return after the first session because they were uncomfortable relating their experience in front of their peers. This reflects the much more personal nature of the abortion experience and also a more conscious decision not to continue; while most of the pregnant girls did not return because they no longer met the study criteria. Further research confirmed that the number of adolescents not wanting to discuss their abortion experience afterwards is similar to that found by other studies.

All 14 girls remaining in the abortion focus groups were very willing to participate in the second phase of the research, the in-depth interview. To compensate for the 22 girls in the focus groups who never came back, we contacted, sensitized and invited 60 more girls to be personally interviewed. Of this second group, 70 per cent did not return, leaving us with an additional 18 girls, for a total of 32. These 18 girls will be referred to throughout our discussion as those who did not participate in a focus group. This will be discussed later, because it relates to the importance of the discussion groups and to the use of qualitative methods in research on abortion.

General Profile of the Study Group

Age

The ages of all the girls in our sample ranged from 12 to 19 years, and were lower, on average, for the pregnant girls than for the girls who had abortions (Table 20.1).

Education

None of the girls could be classified as illiterate. We did, however, confront some comprehension and language problems, especially in the discussion groups, among girls with only partial or complete primary school education. The girls in the abortion group had more secondary education and seemed to concentrate on nonformal studies, which in present Mexican society may generate a comparatively higher income. These data need further evaluation, however, because most of the pregnant girls stop working or studying, and

Table 20.1: **Summary Characteristics of the Study Group**

Characteristics	Pregnancy Group	Abortion Group
Average age (years)	17	18
Education		
Primary level		
Incomplete	17	13
Complete	6	16
Secondary level (1–3 yrs)		
Incomplete	22	11
Complete	28	38
Advanced secondary level (4–6 yrs)		
Incomplete	19	16
Complete	8	3
University (some)	–	3
Marital status		
Single	36	53
Free union	42	25
Married	22	22
Average age at first intercourse (years)	15	16
Average length of time between first sexual contact and establishment of the union (months)	5	12
Average duration of gestation (weeks)	23*	9

* This was for the initial sample. It should be noted that a large proportion of these girls (72%) had attempted abortion but had not succeeded.

apparently do not resume their studies; while the girls who undergo abortion are more assertive and persistent in reaching their educational goals.

Comparison of the mother and daughter educational levels is important, because it yields information about the transmission of general cultural values. We found that the daughters in our study had more secondary education (more than twice as long) as their mothers. But almost one-third of the girls had a lower level of education than their mothers.

Employment

Adolescents, generally speaking, usually cannot find jobs. While most of the pregnant girls were neither working nor studying, 53 per cent of the girls in the abortion group were working at the time of the interview. Among the girls who were working, 50 per cent were in domestic services, 11 per cent were textile industry workers, and the rest worked in various service areas.

Marital Status

Although one-fifth of both the pregnant girls and the girls with abortion experience were married, the number of single girls was higher in the abortion group. Moreover, when the girls who are either formally married or in a free union are defined as the married group, pregnant girls predominate. (In Mexico, a 'free union' is a common and socially acceptable form of co-habitation for couples, although there is no fixed pattern of duration, or other characteristics.)

Urban Migration

Almost all the girls participating in this research project were from Mexico City, but only 45 per cent of their parents were born there. Surprisingly, a large portion of girls in both the pregnancy and abortion groups did not know where their father or mother came from (41 per cent and 31 per cent, respectively). This points to a lack of family communication and/or cohesion; it also indicates the common situation of an absent or unknown father.

Sexual and Reproductive Behaviour

Important data were obtained on this topic during both the in-depth interviews and the focus group discussions. All the girls, with one exception, said they initially had intercourse at their boyfriends' request. Not only was first intercourse usually the boy's wish, but it was also the boy who said: 'I want you to give me a son.' Only three girls mentioned the expression that showed the pregnancy to be a joint wish: 'I want us to have a child.'

The pregnant girls interviewed began their active sexual life around age 15, and those in the abortion group, at age 16. The moment was usually spontaneous, and often unplanned, the result of taking advantage of a favourable moment and place. Most said they had intercourse for the first time at the boy's home, while his family was out, and a smaller proportion (three girls) went to a home lent to them by a friend. Seven girls went with their boyfriends to a motel.

The average time interval between first intercourse and the decision to live together was 5.3 months in the pregnancy group and 11.6 months in the abortion group. An understanding of why the couples agreed to form a union so soon after the onset of first sexual activity requires further examination. Do the girls have sexual intercourse to establish a reason for getting married or forming a free union? Do they have intercourse for fear of losing their boyfriend's love? Or do they have intercourse without premeditation, and simply out of a natural sexual desire that later brings pressure from a partner, family or society to enter into a union?

Although the time interval between first sexual activity and the decision to establish a union was more than twice as long among the girls who have had an abortion than among the pregnant girls, both time intervals are extremely short for establishing a formal relationship, especially since the girls are still very young. In other research with pregnant adolescents in Mexico (Ehrenfeld, 1992; 1994), it has been found that there is an average time span of five months, at the most, between first sexual intercourse and pregnancy, meaning that a pregnancy is likely to result from first sexual intercourse. This would support the conclusion that formal unions seem to result more as a consequence of becoming pregnant than from a desire to establish a relationship or to become sexually active.

Reproductive Characteristics

First sexual relationships, as noted before, generally occur without advance planning, so that not surprisingly, 98 per cent of these girls did not use any contraception at the time of first intercourse. As one girl explained: 'When you're in that boat, you don't think.... We'll worry later.'

Because the mother plays an important role in the transmission of sexual values to her daughter and serves as a point of reference for maternity and other related matters, we also analyzed certain reproductive characteristics of the mothers of the girls. The average age at first union for the mothers was only slightly higher than that of their daughters. The eventual profile of these women describes a very young group of mothers, averaging 42 years in age, with an average of 5.2 children. This high fertility coincides with the 'demographic phase' of the cohort to which these mothers belong, so that one could not expect the pattern to be repeated in the offspring.

Predictably then, with just one exception, all the girls stated that two children was the ideal family size. However, the number of total pregnancies per girl was 1.3, which could be considered inconsistent with this reproductive ideal, because they are all under 20 and have at least 20 to 25 reproductive years ahead of them.

Study Findings

The following sections are based on the results of the qualitative information obtained through the focus group discussions and the in-depth interviews, and offer a more comprehensive view of the experience of unwanted pregnancy among young girls in Mexico.

Results from the Focus Groups

One of the aims of the focus group discussions was to obtain information on the linguistic codes adolescents use to refer to induced abortion, including its meaning and significance within this particular sub-culture of lower income, urban adolescents. We developed a glossary of specific linguistic codes and idiomatic expressions with which they refer to themselves, to their body, their partner, their sexual life and sexuality, and in particular to the subjects of pregnancy and abortion.

Another objective was to be able to generate and sustain an active exchange of views among adolescents on a comprehensive range of personal subjects normally considered 'taboo', such as their bodies, sexuality, sexual practices and feelings about abortion. It was also hoped that such a participatory experience with a group of their own peers for the first time would facilitate and enhance the next phase of the study, the in-depth interviews.

The discussion groups revealed a remarkable ignorance of the anatomy and physiology of the female body. The vagina seemed not to exist for many of them; this is not metaphor, but an unfortunate finding. Sexual intercourse was referred to as 'the relationship' or, in most cases, the linguistic code was 'doing it'. Another girl explained: 'It is not something you think about, for who can think at that moment? Love is what counts.' This ignorance, however, did not hinder their understanding of other subjects that were discussed, such as their present circumstances or previous pregnancies.

The discussion of abortion revealed particular nuances between the different terms used to refer this matter. The word 'abortion' has strong negative connotations, as well as implications of clandestine and illegal activity. The word also refers to a deliberate act; to clearly not wanting a child, which is still thought to be a woman's greatest achievement in most of Mexican society. Alternatively, the expression 'dilatation and curettage (D&C)' is a cleaner term, more 'proper', and its medical connotation implies that it was not the woman's wish to interrupt her pregnancy. When we suggested the use of the term 'voluntary interruption of pregnancy', the girls felt that this was the best way to refer to abortion; so much so, that they later on repeated this phrase during their in-depth interviews. (It is important to note that at the time of this study, no other abortion technique was available at the hospital clinic. Today abortions are performed using vacuum aspiration.)

We found it surprising that the law was never mentioned, even though voluntary induced abortion is illegal and the penalty is a jail sentence. A strong feeling of guilt, the fear of the physical consequences of abortion such as sterility, the body getting used to miscarrying, and death were all the punishments the girls seemed to fear. Four of the girls who underwent a medical termination of pregnancy under adequate health standards felt more guilty about having had to resort to abortion as their only option than about the abortion itself. Guilt is verbalized in a number of different ways, but it is always there as part of their mental make-up. They felt guilty for having had intercourse, for failing to fulfill the requirements of becoming a 'real' woman by aborting the child, for killing, or for having been forced by their partners to have the abortion. Much of this guilt is probably due to the perceptions of abortion in popular culture and by the increasing influence of the anti-abortion propaganda over the past few years.

Pregnancy Cases

The discussion dynamics in the pregnancy groups were different among the girls who were over·16 years of age in comparison to those who were under 16. In the group of younger girls, the ways of talking about their body or about their own development of a feminine identity, especially experiences relating to sex or gender roles, often assumed the character of a children's game. Similarly, their discussion and view of the impact of pregnancy and abortion on a woman's life also had a childlike character. For example, one girl said when referring to her pregnancy: 'I won't be able to ride around on my bicycle, or play basketball with my brother anymore.' Aged 13, 'B' was still 12 when she came to the first group session. She explained that she had become pregnant through external genital contact with her 16-year-old boyfriend. When her mother suggested that she have an abortion, she refused, because she was afraid that the abortionist would stick metal tools and knives into her.

Abortion Cases

The same topics discussed in the pregnancy groups were also covered in the abortion groups, except that there was naturally more of a focus on abortion-related issues. Those who participated in the group sessions were also better prepared for the in-depth interview that followed. Within the groups it was frequently said: 'How I wish we had the opportunity of being here or of finding someone like you before, then we wouldn't be in such a mess.'

Even with a good rapport among the participants and an acceptance of the group activity, we had great difficulty in gathering a larger group of girls who had had an abortion. As soon as the number participating in the sessions increased, those who had been attending for longer periods dropped out.

There were also some unforeseen events that led to the exclusion of several candidates for the group sessions. Several girls came with their girlfriends, pretending to have had a recent abortion at the hospital; yet after the first group session, they turned to the discussion leader and requested an abortion. The same happened with three other girls who were told by peers that research was being conducted at the hospital and that they might get an abortion over there.

Another situation we had not foreseen was the inclusion in one of the abortion groups of a girl who had been raped. During the group discussions she resisted discussion of topics related to the body, sexuality, and/or partner relationships, which would be expected had we known her situation. Nevertheless, this girl attended each session punctually. Suddenly, during the third session she opened the discussion by saying: 'I was raped. I did not choose that and I certainly feel no remorse whatsoever for having had an abortion. Nobody could possibly want a child that way.' Needless to say, her statement had a strong impact on the group discussion, which turned out to be particularly helpful to her. She later commented in her private interview that she had learned that rape victims are not the only ones who seek abortion, that there are other reasons as well, a fact she had not understood before. Obviously her experience of abortion was a secondary problem; her experience of rape was the main problem to address.

Results from the In-Depth Interviews

The Decision-Making Process

Generally, mothers and boyfriends were the two most influential figures when a girl was faced with deciding whether to continue with the pregnancy or to have an abortion. The first person to be informed about the probable pregnancy was the boyfriend; then the mother or an equivalent authority figure was told.

Four girls who had not participated in the focus group discussions talked about the ways in which they had been pressured into either continuing with their pregnancy or having an abortion. One was forced by her mother to use injections to try to abort. Another was forced by her partner to take pills to try to abort. Two others were forbidden by a mother and by a partner to have an abortion and forced to continue their pregnancy against their will.

Friends of either sex are notably absent from the decision-making process. Apparently this subject is not discussed with friends, although it is important to keep in mind that most girls were not attending school at the time they became pregnant and therefore they lacked a peer or reference group. Their life had been confined to domestic activities and their boyfriend had become the main object of their attention.

A very significant factor in the decision-making process for these low-income girls was the economic aspect. The price of abortion varies according to the type and quality of the services being offered. For a safe abortion, usually a D&C performed by a qualified physician, the cost varies between US $340 and $1000. A 'sonda' (introducing a catheter, rubber tube or other such instrument) costs about US $300; the commonly used infusion of xoapactle costs about US $130.

Moreover, the decision-making process had two clear phases: the first was actually making the decision; and the second was acting on the decision and looking for an abortion practitioner.

We found that a high proportion of girls who decided to have an abortion never reached the second stage of carrying it out, because they didn't have the money or anyone who would help them. These girls may make several unsuccessful self-induced attempts at abortion before realizing that their pregnancy is there to stay. This is typical of many girls with an unwanted pregnancy that we interviewed. Every girl was asked what price they would consider reasonable for an abortion, since so many pregnant girls said that lack of money was the reason for not having had an abortion. One girl answered: 'I wouldn't request any free services. I don't trust free services, nobody does anything for free.' The preference was to pay a modest fee for a reliable service under good conditions.

For those who actually move on to the second phase and actively start seeking an abortion, what follows entails a great deal of anguish and misery as they confront their poverty and realize their lack of sufficient means to deal safely with their situation.

Without exception, all of the girls interviewed said that 'had I known...', meaning they all regretted their ignorance, including their lack of awareness of their bodies and of the risks they were taking when they had sexual relations.

Pregnancy Cases

Even when their mothers scolded and challenged them, most girls said they wanted to keep the pregnancy rather than have an abortion. The girl's fathers were not informed until it was no longer possible to hide the pregnancy. In most cases, there was also an additional female figure—an aunt, a neighbour, the godmother, an employer—who supported the girl in her decision not to abort.

Abortion Cases

For these girls, in addition to their mother's opinion, their partner's wish not to have the child or a situation where their partner already had children by another woman or was in another union clearly influenced a girl's decision to have an abortion. The more educated girls were more assertive in facing their partners; two girls were left by their boyfriends when they informed them that they were pregnant. Many girls expressed the clear desire to become pregnant at another and better time in their lives.

The girl who had become pregnant as a result of being raped, said: 'I would not take anybody's life, but who could want to have a child that way? I had never even had a sexual relationship with my real boyfriend.' (This boyfriend was later murdered by the rapist.) Another girl explained: 'No, I don't feel guilty. It is not a good thing to do, but it isn't that monstrous either. I was scared, but what was I to do? I had a good job and didn't want to leave it. My sister had already left with her baby to the farm; it would have been more shame for my mother. I was angry, I hated being pregnant, I thought I was going to loose my boyfriend.' This girl did not tell her mother or her boyfriend, but consulted the lady of the house where she worked. The woman gave her advice, told her to think about it and decide what she wanted, and said that she would support whatever decision the girl made. She finally ended up having an abortion by a qualified physician, arranged by her employer, with no complications.

Attempts at Self-Induced Abortion

Methods mentioned by the girls and used in combination, alternately, or repeatedly included the following: (*a*) 'strong' injections, with no specific name mentioned (they claim not to remember); (*b*) injections of Metrigen, a drug often used for inducing abortion, although its actual purpose is to act as a menstrual regulator; (*c*) tea infusions of spices such as oregano, cinnamon, 'estafiate', 'rumina', or oregano mixed with chocolate; (*d*) infusions of xoapactle.

This last infusion is exclusively administered in one of the most sophisticated herb markets in Mexico. Apparently there are only two providers, both old women, who prepare it on the premises and the infusion must be taken in their presence. The two-litre dose of the infusion is divided in four equal amounts and taken over a period of one hour. All women described the procedure in the same way; they said the taste is horrible, bitter and disgusting. The cost is equal to about US $130. If it is vomited, more doses must be prepared at an additional cost of US $20 each. This infusion most probably contains some kind of oxytocic drug or other abortifacient. After 24 to 48 hours, the girls started bleeding and were eventually brought to the emergency room, complaining of very acute abdominal pain and severe bleeding, but without fever.

Other methods mentioned include: taking quinine tablets in high dosages; swallowing syrups of different types; violent physical activity; carrying water in heavy containers for long distances; taking high dosages of aspirin with lemon juice; intentionally falling down steps or other surfaces. This last method is not simply falling, without knowing how. One of the girls interviewed put it this way: 'I'm not stupid, I was not going to break my neck.... The point is, you have to fall down several steps, abruptly, so that you land on the little bone, with open legs. It should be a fall of more than four steps, of course'.

Pregnancy Cases

Among the group of pregnant girls participating in the discussion groups, 72.2 per cent (13 out of 18 women), had sought an abortion or had unsuccessfully attempted abortion. The average number of such attempts was 2.28 per woman, with three girls saying that they had had a previous abortion. In the group of pregnant girls who did not participate in discussion groups, a much lower number of girls, one-third, said they had made various unsuccessful attempts, with an average of two attempts per woman. (This seems to indicate that the discussion groups facilitate the expression of facts and feeling that had been hidden either through self-condemnation or precaution.)

The conclusion we drew from this group was that pregnancy was clearly undesired and unplanned, particularly because most of the girls had just initiated their sexual life. It seems that they had initially been unable to realize that they were pregnant or were unwilling to believe it. The first skipped period is always considered a delay, the second one an irregularity. They refused to believe that they might be pregnant and this may be why so many girls originally selected for our study were later found to be too far along in their pregnancy to meet the study criteria. They attempted abortions, following a number of approaches, none of them very effective and their pregnancy, though unwanted, continued.

Abortion Cases

In the abortion group we found three types of abortion: those clearly induced; those probably induced; and spontaneous.

Abortions defined as probably induced were those where there were signs of external manipulation, heavy physical effort, or the intake or injection of a drug or other substance. It is impossible to establish whether without these factors, the pregnancy would have continued anyway. The girls who succeeded in their efforts at self-induced abortion made between one and four separate attempts each, before achieving their purpose.

Spontaneous abortion, without complications, was more easily identified, especially in the individual interviews. It was sadly regretted by the patient, she was often depressed for 'not being woman enough to carry the pregnancy and keep it', and she feared that 'now he will abandon me'. In these situations we also saw the family giving moral support to the girl. While the family is not supportive of the decision to have an induced abortion, it is supportive when the girl has lost the pregnancy naturally, which is associated with sentiments of being sick, and needing compassion.

Abortions among the girls who did not participate in the group discussions were distributed as follows: five clearly induced (four septic); four probable; and nine spontaneous. Among the girls in the discussion groups, four were clearly induced, three were probably induced, and seven were spontaneous.

Among girls who had not attended a focus group, evidence of septic abortions was found during the in-depth interviews. Two of them had uterine ruptures (perforation), one with a major purulent abscess and the other requiring a colostomy for multiple perforations. Both required a hysterectomy and hospitalization of three and four weeks in the intensive care unit, then a further two months at the obstetrics ward. A third septic abortion resulted from the use of a non-professional rubber device (sonda). A fourth one was from a poorly performed surgical procedure and a fifth was a result of a xoapactle infusion and multiple injections.

It is impossible in this study to estimate the cost for the two girls who had to be hospitalized. Such costs should obviously be estimated in emotional costs as well as financial ones. One of these girls already had a daughter, the other had only had intercourse for the first time with her first boyfriend. The latter had asked in her last interview: 'Doctor, when is my next period going to start?' even though she had already been told that she would not be able to have children. Her case was particularly pathetic. She had gone to see a doctor, had paid US $340 that was difficult for her to borrow, and did not tell anyone about her intentions. She lives with her grandparents under poor conditions and had just recently found a paid job. When asked about sequelae, guilt, and the general impact this event had on her health and life, she answered: 'In the end it was not the physician's fault. It's my fault for having decided to have an abortion. But what could I do? I couldn't take the child to my grandfather. He has enough problems supporting us all.' When it was pointed out to her that the skill of the physician was obviously poor, she reflected, 'Well, maybe he was barely learning to do it, I don't know.'

Except for the unfortunate cases of septic abortions, those performed under safe conditions apparently left no major damage. Our attempts at 'guilt estimation' found that many girls did not refer to guilt, but to 'relief now that it is all over'.

All agreed that they would have sought safe abortions if safe induced abortion services had been available to them. They also wished they could have received adequate counselling to help them in their predicament. The majority would have preferred women doctors, but 35 per cent expressed no preference, as long as the procedure was safe and reliable.

Contraceptive use is not a useful issue here, because only 2 per cent of the girls claimed to have used contraception at the time of first intercourse, and the 6 per cent who said they were using contraception at the time of our interview were using withdrawal. As one girl explained: 'He looks after me', although looking after her resulted in making her pregnant.

Research Design: Lessons Learned

The research design had two important advantages. First, it provided sociocultural information about the abortion experience among adolescents, including very young ones under the age of 15, that is rarely found in the literature. And second, through the participation in a study that gave them a chance to share their experience with their peers, the adolescents themselves could gain new insight and understanding about their sexual lives, reproductive health, current situation and life circumstances.

The focus group approach had special advantages in terms of successfully meeting the objectives of the study itself. It allowed us to discover the language and vocabulary that the girls use so that we could later use this glossary for the in-depth interviews and for future survey instruments. The approach was also useful in guaranteeing success in the second phase of research: All the girls participating in the discussion groups later attended their in-depth interviews. It is especially noteworthy that the rate of return of the girls who had abortions was 100 per cent.

The focus group discussions also provided an opportunity for these young girls to learn about the subjects of sexuality and abortion in a way that they would not be able to find in any other environment, because their contacts normally are restricted to the immediate family members living in the same household, a few friends, and a boyfriend with whom there is often just the start of a love relationship. In fact, many of the girls could not, at first, grasp the meaning of a 'group', due to their often unstructured household conditions. At the start, each girl felt alone and isolated in a unique and tragic drama. As the peer group discussions went on, this impression vanished and a more realistic assessment of their situation emerged. Looking at each other as into a mirror at a time of crisis in their adolescent lives led to a better understanding and respect for themselves as human beings and gave them a better hold on their situation. Additionally, concepts related to their body, abortion, pregnancy, sexuality, machismo and relationships between men and women assumed a more realistic dimension. In the end, all of the girls were feeling fortunate to have been able to participate in these discussions.

Another important lesson learned relates to the selection of girls who were carrying their pregnancy to term, as a control group for the abortion cases. In our study, we later discovered that many of these pregnancy cases had to be rejected because they were second-trimester; moreover, most were unwanted and many of these girls had unsuccessfully attempted induced abortion. We therefore suggest for future studies of this kind that pregnant girls in the control group are carefully probed to determine with certainty the actual duration of their current pregnancy and that it is indeed wanted.

Our difficulty forming discussion groups with the same girls with abortion experience over a period of time taught us that for future studies of this kind with adolescents of the same age group, the group size for discussions about abortion experiences be limited to a maximum of five girls. After our unexpected experience with a rape victim, we also now recommend that rape victims who have had abortions not be put in the same group with girls or women who have had abortions for other reasons (including spontaneous abortions), unless specific measures are taken to explain that there are different motives that lead to an abortion.

Conclusions and Recommendations

The voluntary interruption of pregnancy among young adolescents seems to be a particularly dangerous and traumatic experience, especially when it is performed under clandestine, unsafe conditions. These women are young, have little or no knowledge of contraception, often get pregnant after just becoming sexually active, and few have a stable partner. The men are generally two to three years older and do not use contraceptive methods, except withdrawal in very few cases. Only half of the girls work and when they do, it is usually in domestic services earning very low salaries.

Because these young girls are usually without the knowledge, support and resources needed to obtain qualified care in an illegal setting, they face life-threatening risks of which they are not even vaguely aware. For such adolescents, the wish to end their pregnancy is very clear and overrides all other considerations.

In their attempts to make a decision as to whether to abort or to keep the pregnancy, adolescents are often torn between the diverging opinions of people who have the greatest influence in their lives. In half of the cases, the mother will persuade their daughters to have an abortion; in the other half, the mother will force them to continue with the unwanted pregnancy in order to pay for their sins, such as having had sex before marriage. Equally powerful is the boyfriend's influence, which can range from support for the pregnancy to taking the pregnant girl to have a 'sonda' (catheter) inserted to induce abortion, without telling her what is going on.

The most critical element in deciding whether and how to have an abortion is always economic: Is there money to pay for it? Abortions are expensive, even when there is no guarantee that they will work. Money is an important determining factor in all the stories of the adolescents who participated in the study. If they had had the economic means to pay for it, there would have been many more abortions than pregnancies in the study group.

Abortion Policy

The present law on abortion in Mexico makes induced abortion illegal, except to save the woman's life, or in cases of rape and incest. This legal situation penalizes the large majority of induced abortions and makes the search for safe abortion services very difficult. Moreover, very few adolescents are aware of their rights in the case of rape.

Most qualified physicians are not willing to provide abortion services privately, because they are afraid of criminal prosecution. The few who do, charge very high fees. As a result, it is a daily occurrence in Mexico to find women arriving at hospitals with abortion complications, after unsuccessfully attempting to end their pregnancy using a panoply of ineffective and unsafe methods. Hospital statistics are meaningless in determining actual morbidity and mortality from these complications, because the procedure is illegal and hospitals fear that health authorities might associate them with such a clandestine activity. There is no question in anyone's mind that each death due to induced abortion complications is totally preventable; each death is a mark of shame that weighs heavily on society as a whole.

One important step towards a more liberal and healthy approach to the abortion issue would be to remove the abortion law from the penal code and place it under the sanitary code. Another measure would be to eliminate the jail sentence as the penalty for performing an induced abortion. Though the law is not often enforced, the threat of a jail sentence frightens women, doctors and hospital administrators and reduces the already limited abortion services available, even in cases where they are legally justified, such as in the case of rape. Positioning the issue of abortion within the context of health policy is a measure that brings it to the field where the most can be done to effectively bring about its reduction.

Sexual and Reproductive Health Education

The absence of sufficient information on sexual and reproductive health provided at an early age, by educational systems, is responsible for the outrageous ignorance we found during this research. Providing education at an early age through public schools, beginning with primary education, should be a priority. Although there have been a few attempts in Mexico, schools are far from providing the comprehensive information necessary for creating a basis to develop more responsible sexual behaviour. At present, sex and reproductive health education is limited to textbooks about reproductive organs. Teachers are ill-prepared to face this new educational challenge and teacher training programmes are badly needed.

Family Planning Programmes

One-fourth of the population of Mexico is under 24 years of age, and adolescents between the ages of 12–19 number almost 20 million. After nearly 25 years of public policies offering free family planning services, young people still do not use modern contraceptive methods, especially when they become sexually active. Few programmes are designed to meet the needs of this age group. The adequate use of modern contraceptive methods when young people become sexually active may reduce induced abortions by preventing unwanted pregnancies. It is urgent to design service and information strategies adapted to adolescent needs and in line with the requirements of their lifestyle.

Medical Training and Hospital Services

In medical schools, it is necessary to educate physicians specializing in the gynaecology and obstetrics fields about the realities of the abortion situation in Mexico and to train them in the application of modern abortion techniques, such as vacuum aspiration, which would lower the risk to women of the traditional surgical method of dilatation and curettage, and anaesthesia. At the Gea González Hospital this has already been achieved.

Creating a centre for abortion counselling and data collection in hospitals would allow women to be offered adequate counselling when arriving in the emergency room, in addition to establishing a real national registry system that would reveal the magnitude of the problems created by unwanted pregnancy. A permanent research programme would allow follow-up of patients as well as permit the evaluation of counselling services, to monitor and assess the quality of care being provided. Post-abortion family planning should be an essential part of such programmes.

✝ References

Pick de Weiss, S. and **M. Givaudan.** 1991. Del aborto inducido y su despenalización en cuatro localidades. *Este Pais* 8, Noviembre: 25–27.

Ehrenfeld, L. Noemi. 1992. La adolescente embarazada, su perfil y un programa hospitalario para su atencion. Mexico: Publicación del Hospital General Dr. Manuel Gea González, SSA.

———. 1994. Evaluación de un programa hospitalario de educación para la salud reproductiva y sexual de la adolescente embarazada. *Salud Publica de México* 36 (2): 1–8.

21

Induced Abortion in Dar es Salaam, Tanzania: The Plight of Adolescents

G.S. Mpangile, M.T. Leshabari and D.J. Kihwele

Introduction

Abortion is the oldest known measure to end an unwanted pregnancy and has been practised in almost all societies worldwide and throughout history, with various traditional methods (IPPF, 1978). For example, the ancient Greeks advocated abortion to regulate population size and maintain stable social and economic conditions. In 400 B.C., Plato recommended abortion for pregnant women over 40 years of age, possibly for health reasons, and Aristotle suggested using abortion to limit family size (Farr, 1980). Cultural, social and other constraints to abortion are mostly the result of relatively recent developments generated by religious ideology and social elites.

Given the high prevalence of unintended pregnancy, induced abortion is frequently performed worldwide; but it has serious consequences for individuals and health systems when it is done in countries where there is no legal access to safe procedures (Sai, 1984). In developing countries where maternal mortality rates are high, the risk of death following complications of unsafe abortion procedures is between 100 and 500 times higher than that of an abortion performed under hygienic conditions.

The problem of unsafe abortion is a very serious issue for African populations. Moreover, the problem is likely to worsen, because of significant changing trends in the region: increased modernization and urbanization; the earlier start of sexual relations by young people; and limited access to effective contraception, especially for adolescents.

Although abortion is widespread and there is evidence of a definite increase in the number of unsafe procedures and their complications in Africa (Rogo, 1989), the situation is not yet recognized as a significant health and social problem. It is mistakenly placed within a context of controversial and complex political, moral and religious issues (IPPF, 1991). Abortion should be seen essentially as a health issue, however, and not as an ideological one. Moreover, it must be recognized that while contraceptive information and services are an important remedial strategy to help reduce the high incidence of unwanted pregnancy, these efforts are not, on their own, a sufficient remedy for the magnitude and character of the problem of unsafe abortion.

The incidence of abortion in countries where the law remains restrictive continues to be difficult to assess. Hospital-based information is the most reliable, although it usually represents just a small portion of what may be going on in a community. Hospital records in one consulting hospital in Dar es Salaam show that the number of abortion-related admissions to gynaecological wards rose from 38 per cent in 1974 to 61 per cent in 1976 (Mtimavalye et al., 1980). Although no distinction is made between spontaneous and induced abortions, there is every reason to believe that the increase represents an increase in the proportion of illegal, unsafe abortions. Similarly, a Kenyan study reported in 1982 that up to 60 per cent of gynaecological admissions at the Kenyatta National Hospital in Nairobi were abortion cases, and of these, 62 per cent were illegally, and unsafely induced (Aggarwal and Mati, 1982). In Sudan, a prospective study of patients with incomplete abortion in Khartoum hospitals in 1975 showed that there was one abortion admission for every maternity admission (IPPF, 1978).

According to the World Health Organization, the proportion of maternal deaths in Africa attributable to abortion varies from below 10 per cent to as high as 60 per cent (WHO, 1990). However, one study found that abortion caused up to 80 per cent of maternal deaths at Kenyatta National Hospital and of these, 65 per cent were induced (Wanjala et al., 1985). A review of maternal deaths over a 13-year period in one hospital in Nigeria showed that abortion was one of three major causes of death (Unuigbe et al., 1988). Among those who died from abortion, 91 per cent were confirmed cases of induced procedures.

Adolescent sexuality is of great concern in this context. In the Nairobi study cited above, of the illegally induced cases, 43 per cent were adolescents, 79 per cent were single women and 60 per cent were either schoolgirls or unemployed women. Another study at the University Teaching Hospital in Enugu, Nigeria, showed that 71 per cent of women suffering from complications of unsafe induced abortion were 20 years old or younger (IPPF, 1991).

Study Objectives

This study was undertaken in four public hospitals in Dar es Salaam, which are used primarily by women of low income. First, the study aimed to describe the socioeconomic and demographic profile of these women as well as their fertility regulation behaviour. Second, it intended to explore the circumstances surrounding the abortion experience; to trace the events leading up to hospital admission, including the informal referral network. Because a lot of secrecy exists behind the process of procuring an illegal abortion, social networks are involved from the moment a woman tells someone else about the pregnancy. The decision to abort, the search for an abortionist, payment for the procedure, and referral to a hospital for management of complications occur within this context. The identification of key people in this social network is important, because they could then be targeted in efforts aimed at preventing unsafe abortions as well as unwanted pregnancy, particularly in the promotion of effective contraceptive practices. Third, the study wanted to describe the actual experience of clandestine abortion, particularly health complications, costs, and perspectives of the women and providers. This was to help inform discussions of how to reduce the incidence of unsafe abortion.

Study Design and Methodology

This was an exploratory study—perhaps the first of its kind in Tanzania—to gather personal information on a highly sensitive topic and therefore could not follow strict random sample selection procedures. Women who had no complications could not be covered, and private hospitals were also not covered, where it is presumed that middle- and upper-class women attend because they can afford the cost. Contact with the abortionists themselves was not attempted, because this would have violated the requirements of confidentiality promised to the patients of the study.

All women admitted to four public hospitals in Dar es Salaam with a diagnosis of incomplete, threatened or septic abortion were first interviewed by nurses who had considerable experience in dealing with abortion patients and who were additionally trained for this research. The nurses were recruited in consultation with hospital authorities, to ensure that they could cover all shifts day and night during the study. Attending physicians were told about the study and trained to provide more detailed information about the patients after the required routine examination. The study instrument was pre-tested in one of the hospitals and the experience gained was used in training the interviewers from other hospitals.

A total of 965 women were screened over a six-week period, of which 455 were found to have had an induced abortion. All the 455 women agreed to participate in the study after they were informed of its purpose and assured of confidentiality. Among this group, 418 initially volunteered the information that they had tried to terminate their pregnancy. The remaining 37 who did not initially admit to an induced abortion were identified during medical examination, because of genital/cervical trauma or the presence of a foreign body. (A further 82 women were excluded from the analysis because the attending physicians were uncertain about their diagnosis and the women themselves did not admit to an induced abortion.) Interviews with the women were conducted in private in a room on the hospital premises.

Study Results

Profile of the Women

Sociodemographic Characteristics

The sociodemographic characteristics of the women in the sample are presented in Table 21.1. The most significant finding was that one-third of the

Table 21.1: Demographic Characteristics of the Women (%)

Age (years)	
14–17	14
18–19	19
20–29	50
> 30	17
Marital status	
Single	66
Cohabiting with a man	1
Married	23
Separated/divorced/widowed	10
Level of education	
Non/low literate	7
Primary school	56
Secondary or higher education	6
Currently students, all levels	20–24
Perceived lack of basic needs	
Food/clothing/accommodation	10
Entertainment	< 5
Religion	
Muslim	49
Catholic	26
Other Christian	24
(reflects composition of population sub-group)	
Religion in their daily lives considered	
Very important	50
Moderately important	45
Lived in the city	
1 year or less	12
1–5 years	28
6 years or more	60
N = 455	

respondents were teenagers, and nearly half of them were 17 years of age or younger. Less than 17 per cent of the women were 30 years or older. This striking finding, which was also a surprising one, in a sense forced us to shift our attention to adolescent women and to focus on the reasons for the high incidence of abortion among this age group.

Not surprisingly, about two-thirds of the group were single; and 23 per cent were married. The majority had dropped out of primary school; and only about 16 per cent reported secondary or higher education. Although half the women said religion was very important in their lives and daily activities, actual participation in religious activities was minimal or nonexistent. Almost 60 per cent had lived in the city for six or more years.

Sexual and Reproductive Histories

Nearly one in five of the teenagers less than 17 years old had had boyfriends for six years or more, suggestive of commencement of early sexual relationships. The youngest age at which sexual intercourse was reported was 11 years. By age 17, more than half the women had had sexual intercourse at least once.

Almost half the women said they had never been pregnant before. Of these, 76 per cent said they were sexually active, while the other 24 per cent said they had become pregnant the first time they had sexual intercourse.

For 20 per cent of the women, this was their second pregnancy; for 11 per cent, their third pregnancy; and for the remaining 23 per cent, their fourth or higher pregnancy. Fourteen per cent of the women (65 women) said they had had an induced abortion in the past. Among these, 53 had done so once and nine had done so twice. Two women had had three abortions, and one woman had had six.

Contraceptive Knowledge and Use by Selected Socioeconomic Variables

In general, contraceptive knowledge was low among this group; and 45 per cent did not know of any method of contraception. There was an inverse relationship between level of contraceptive knowledge and age: 89 per cent of the women aged 17 years or less knew nothing about either modern or traditional methods of contraception; conversely, at least 60 per cent of the women aged 30 and above had medium to high knowledge of contraception. Only one teenager out of 150 in the study sample knew six or more methods of family planning.

Similarly, the women with little or no formal education formed the highest proportion of those who did not know about any method (65 per cent). This proportion declined as education level increased, to 20 per cent with no knowledge among women with secondary level or higher education. Most noteworthy is that almost half the current students had no knowledge of contraceptive methods, despite their high level of sexual activity. Considering that these young women were urban residents, this low level of contraceptive awareness is quite revealing in that it suggests a real unmet need for family planning.

The single women generally, both current students and others, had less contraceptive knowledge than the married or previously married women. Perhaps the low level of contraceptive knowledge is related to the fact that contraceptive use by students is prohibited by school regulations and single women and adolescents are not welcome clients in family planning clinics. Family planning policy in Tanzania has had a long history of providing information and services only to married couples, although in 1989 the Ministry of Health re-defined eligibility for family planning services to include any adult, irrespective of marital status and parity.

Religious background revealed different levels of contraceptive knowledge. Those women who were Muslim had the highest proportion who did not know any method of contraception, almost half; followed by 40 per cent of the Catholic women and a third of the other Christian women. Only 11 per cent of the Muslim women knew of six or more methods compared to 23 per cent of the Catholic women and 14 per cent of the other Christian women. Neither extent of active participation in religious activities nor perceived importance of religion, however, were significantly related to contraceptive knowledge.

The pill was the most widely known and used method, which was not surprising because this is also true of the general population (Tanzania DHS, 1992). However, it is interesting to note that 4 per cent of the women claimed to be using the pill at the time of conception. Incorrect use may account for this; for instance, some respondents, especially students, said they borrowed their supplies from friends. Similarly, some of the teenagers bought their supplies from shops and may not have received proper instructions on correct use. Indeed, some of the teenagers reported that they used the pill during or after coitus only.

The condom was the second most commonly used method. Given the extensive campaign and distribution of condoms for AIDS prevention purposes since 1988, it is quite possible that the high rate of awareness and use of condoms at least one time was more for prevention of HIV infection than for contraception. As with the pill, more than 4 per cent of condom users claimed to have become pregnant while using the method. Some of the young girls said they suspected their male partners had deliberately cut off the tip of the condom in order to get them pregnant.

The proportion of women who knew about and had used contraception is summarized in Table 21.2.

Table 21.2: Contraceptive Knowledge and Use, by Method (%)

Method	Aware of Method	Ever-Used Method	Using at Time of Conception
Pills	63	30	4
Condom	42	10	4
IUD	32	3	1
Calendar	26	10	6
Injectables	24	1	< 1
Withdrawal	18	4	1
Cap	12	< 1	0
Spermicides	12	1	< 1
Traditional	6	2	< 1

Partner Characteristics

This information about the men with whom they had sexual relations resulting in unwanted pregnancy was given by the women as informed estimates. The ages of the men ranged from 16 to 52 years, with less than 4 per cent of them under age 20. Almost a third of the adolescent girls reported male partners aged 45 or over. Similarly, almost a quarter of the students reported partners of 45 years or older, and less than 9 per cent had partners of their own age group.

These findings reflect the widespread 'sugar-daddy' phenomenon in African cities (Leshabari, 1988). With the increase in HIV/AIDS awareness, older men are shunning prostitutes and luring younger, 'safer' girls into sexual relations by promising them some degree of protection and financial security. The Family Planning Association of Tanzania (UMATI), which has a programme to rehabilitate school girls who are normally 14 years of age or less when they are expelled from primary school because of pregnancy, reveals that most of them engage in sex with old working class men who give them some money for school lunches and small gifts. Similarly, recent newspaper articles show that a number of commercial sex workers have resorted to putting on school uniforms to hide their true identities.

The kind of relationship that existed between the women and their sexual partner with whom the pregnancy occurred is shown in Table 21.3. Looking at the total sample of women, almost 30 per cent of them had a relationship of

Table 21.3: Marital Status of the Women and Type of Relationship (%)

Relationship	Single	Formerly Married	Married	Total
Husband	0	23	88	23
Boyfriend	63	40	4	47
Casual partner	29	27	7	24
Stranger	7	7	1	5
Other	1	3	0	1
Total	67	10	23	100

less than one year with their partner. Among the women more than 30 years of age, 64 per cent had been in the relationship for over five years. In contrast, among the teenagers, about half had been in the relationship less than a year. Teenagers as a group had a high tendency towards short-lived relationships, with men who were casual partners or strangers.

The Social Network Behind Induced Abortion in Dar es Salaam

Although precise information is lacking about what goes on from the time pregnancy is suspected until the point when women report to health institutions with abortion complications, anecdotal information suggests that a social network provides support at various key points in the process. In this section of the report, an attempt is made to describe the characteristics of this informal referral system.

The Decision to Abort

The majority of women, nearly 48 per cent, decided to terminate their pregnancy the first time they suspected they were pregnant. About 7 per cent of the women initially decided to carry their pregnancies to term, but later changed their minds. Some 13 per cent made no immediate decision. Before deciding what to do, a further 16 per cent informed their partner, while another 9 per cent told a close girlfriend or relative.

The main reasons behind the decision to abort were: economic inability to take care of another child; the pregnancy was accidental; the previous child was still too young; the woman was still a student. It was found that no student had decided to carry the pregnancy to term; and indeed, the majority of them, 43 per cent, decided on their own to abort while the rest aborted on the advice of their first confidants.

In at least some cases, however, the general reasons for abortion hide as much as they reveal. For example, two of the schoolgirls in this group reported the following experiences when asked why they had decided to have an abortion. The first girl was in a secondary-level boarding school. She was ordered by the head of her school to report to a room where a visiting school inspector was staying. Not suspecting any foul play, she went and was made to sleep with him. During the school holidays, she told her mother what had happened. Rather than raise an alarm, they decided to get her an abortion. This young girl was very bitter about what she described as the moral decadence of adults and she detested those adults who condemned young girls for engaging in sex. The second girl was in her last year of primary school and was living with her married sister. When her sister was away, her brother-in-law asked for and then demanded sex from her. She had no option but to succumb. She did not realize she was pregnant until her aunt noticed it and told her what it meant. When she told her brother-in-law that she was in trouble, he threw her out of the house and accused her of being a prostitute. She never told her sister what had happened, but went to live with her aunt who helped her to arrange for an abortion. She felt very bitter about her brother-in-law's behaviour.

The First Confidant

More than half the women, 53 per cent, first told the responsible male partner about the pregnancy, while 24 per cent told a mother, sister or aunt, and 15 per cent told a close girlfriend. Adolescents were most likely to inform their mothers, sisters or aunts; women over 30 were least likely to do so. Male relatives were never mentioned as confidants by the women in this group.

As level of education increased, the tendency to inform the male partner also increased; this was highest among the students. The tendency to inform relatives decreased with increasing level of education, and here again, students were most likely to report their pregnancy to relatives.

The reaction and advice of the women's first confidants is shown in Table 21.4. The data obtained tend to suggest that in most cases the male partner (56 per cent) and a substantial proportion of close relatives are behind the decision to procure illegal abortion. Half the friends also advised pregnancy termination. Very few confidants reacted to the news about the pregnancy positively: only 8 per cent of relatives and 6 per cent of girlfriends advised the women to carry the pregnancy to term in spite of negative social, economic, and perhaps emotional consequences.

Table 21.4: Reaction/Advice of First Confidant (%)

Reaction/Advice	Male Partner	Relative	Friend	Other	Total
Good news	5	1	3	0	3
Carry to term	19	8	6	23	14
Abort	56	43	51	23	51
Not interested	15	18	18	15	16
Other	5	30	22	39	16

Finding and Paying the Abortionist

There was a close connection between who the women's first confidants were and who advised them to go to a particular abortionist to have the pregnancy terminated. For example, almost 60 per cent of the women who first told a close relative about the problem also had a close relative connecting them to abortionists. In contrast, only 7 per cent of close relatives were involved in securing an abortionist when the pregnancy was first reported to friends and about 13 per cent of those that were first reported to the responsible male partner.

Interestingly, only 37 per cent of pregnancies first reported to the men responsible were connected to an abortionist recommended by the same men. It appears that the men who helped bring about the unwanted pregnancy do not share the burden of arranging for the abortion with the same vigour as other confidants who provide social support.

Generally, girlfriends facilitated the link to abortionists for almost 30 per cent of the women. Although close female relatives arranged only 20 per cent of abortions overall, nearly half of the teenage girls aged less than 17 and 26 per cent of those aged 18–19 said they were taken to abortionists by mothers, sisters or aunts.

Although the men responsible for the pregnancies were less likely to arrange an abortionist than other confidants, 44 per cent of them paid for the cost of the abortion itself once a provider was found. About 34 per cent of the women themselves paid for their own abortion, and close female relatives paid for another 19 per cent of the women.

Characteristics of the Abortion Experience

The Abortion Itself

Of the 384 abortionists described by the women, 22 per cent were identified as 'doctors', 65 per cent as 'other health workers' and 13 per cent as 'quacks'. Whether or not the 'doctors' were actually skilled professionals is difficult to determine, because most lay people refer to any hospital worker, especially those who wear white uniforms, as doctors. Past experience shows that even low-level hospital personnel, such as ward attendants in some places, perform abortions, and they are known as 'doctors' in the neighbourhoods where they operate.

The cost of the abortions ranged from 60 Tanzanian shillings (TSH) to 20,000, with a mean of 4,424 TSH. The majority of providers, 60 to 70 per cent of the 'doctors' and 'other health workers', charged 2,000 TSH or more for an abortion. The 'quacks' charged significantly less. At the time of the study, the minimum government salary per month was 2,500 TSH (12.50 US$), which means that the procedure cost nearly the equivalent of two months salary for the low-income girls.

Most of the abortions were performed in some sort of health facility: either a hospital, health centre or dispensary. It was not clear from the women's descriptions whether these places were government or private facilities. All the others were done in an ordinary bedroom, with a few done in rooms of lodgings or guest houses (Table 21.5).

Table 21.5: Where and By Whom Abortions Are Done (%)

Type of Facility	Doctor	Health Worker	Quack	Total
Health facility	71	62	6	56
Bedroom	29	37	88	42
Other	0	1	6	2

An attempt was made to determine the level of provider skill by asking the women what kind of advice they were given after the abortion (Table 21.6). The fact that the majority of the 'doctors', 56 per cent, gave medication suggests that they had some idea of how to treat women with abortion-related problems. However, the fact that the remaining 'doctors' did not give appropriate medication raises doubts about whether they were indeed doctors, because any physician can handle such cases and give appropriate medication without the need for further referral. Moreover, most of the women who were attended by other types of health care workers were advised to go to the hospital following the abortion.

Table 21.6: Advice/Treatment by the Abortionist (%)

Advice/Treatment	Doctor	Other Health Worker	Quack	Total
Go to hospital	31	60	32	51
Given medication	56	32	10	35
Other	13	8	58	14

Post-Abortion Complications and Care

Among 421 identified confidants of the women, close female relatives were most likely to advise going to a hospital (40 per cent) when this was necessary, followed by the responsible male partner (27 per cent); while 23 per cent of the women took the decision to attend hospital on their own.

Abortion was the most common single reason for admission to the gynaecological wards in all four hospitals. Incomplete abortion was diagnosed for 72 per cent of the women in the study group and post-abortion sepsis was the most common complication.

The most frequent single gestational age at which the abortions were obtained was 8 weeks (41 per cent), with 11 per cent between 9–10 weeks of gestation, 37 per cent between 10–16 weeks, and 11 per cent between 16–20 weeks.

According to information recorded during admission, 84 per cent of the women arrived in fair or bad condition and only 8 per cent were in good condition. About 15 per cent had a history of fever, and temperatures taken indicated that nearly 85 per cent actually had fevers.

About a third of the study group were described as having heavy vaginal bleeding at the time of admission (500 mls of blood or more resulting in clinical conditions related to anaemia). About 20 per cent were considered to be in need of blood transfusion, but only seven women were transfused due blood shortage. Shock due to either haemorrhage or trauma was recorded in 0.7 per cent of the cases.

Almost 53 per cent of all the women in the study group had signs of trauma to their genitals, most commonly the cervix. Of these, 8 per cent had cervical bruises, oedema, inflammation and forceps bites. The remaining 45 per cent had cervical tears and lacerations. Foreign bodies, including leaves, roots and intrauterine devices in women using this method for contraception, were found in about 3 per cent of cases. Foul-smelling discharge was recorded in 16 per cent and evidence of septicaemia in about 15 per cent of cases.

During the study, three laparotomies were performed. The first was for an adolescent of 17 years whose uterus had been perforated from improper instrumentation by a quack; a sub-total hysterectomy had to be performed. A second young woman with septic abortion developed pelvic abscess and a laparotomy was done to drain off the accumulated pus. The third woman was admitted first to a medical ward with diagnosis of anaemia and abdominal pains, and found to be pale with marked abdominal tenderness. She admitted to attempting to self-induce an abortion and then was transferred to the gynaecological ward with a diagnosis of ruptured uterus. When laparotomy was done, she was found to have an ectopic pregnancy.

Only three patients were treated and discharged on the same day. Twenty-seven per cent spent one night in the hospital, 46 per cent spent two nights, 23 per cent spent 3–5 nights, and the remaining 4 per cent spent six nights or more.

Abortion Deaths

No death was recorded in this group, although hospital sources indicate that this is unusual. Indeed, one study done some years earlier in one of the four hospitals gave a case-fatality rate of 26 per cent among 23 induced abortion patients admitted over a nine-month period, of whom six died due to sepsis (Mtimavalye, 1980).

Cost to Health Services

The national policy in Tanzania is to provide free health and medical services to all citizens. Therefore an attempt was made to estimate what it costs the government to treat cases of induced abortion complications. Items included in the calculation were drugs, meals, hospital stay and surgical procedures, but not the time spent by health workers on these cases. When the estimated costs were divided by the number of patients, the amount was 1,500 TSH per day per case of induced abortion. This must be placed within the context of the Ministry of Health budget, which at the time of the study was a much lower 210 TSH per capita per year.

Views of the Health Care Providers

Health care workers in wards where women are admitted with induced abortion complications generally sympathized with their patients and were almost universally of the following opinions:

1. A lot of their precious time and public funds were being unnecessarily wasted on this increasing and yet preventable, serious problem.
2. It would be much better if they were able to do the abortions themselves.
3. Given the inability to control the decisions of the women who experience unwanted pregnancy, it is wrong to deny them the benefits of safe, modern abortion methods.

Views of the Women in the Study

The women we interviewed thought that existing laws were discriminatory, because they denied women the right to choose in the case of unwanted pregnancy, while the men who got them pregnant did not have to bear the hardships involved. They also felt that poor women were being denied access to safe abortion services because they could not pay the high prices in private clinics where safe abortions were being performed despite the legal restrictions.

Discussion

Unwanted pregnancy and abortion are often discussed in the abstract, from the point of view of moral, social or political perspectives, which are unrelated to the real life experience of the women who suffer the consequences of unwanted pregnancy.

The study results indicate that there is a public health problem in Tanzanian society associated with unsafe abortion practices that merits serious scrutiny and a clear plan to reduce it. More specifically, the most signficant finding of our study was that nearly a third of the victims of unsafe abortion practices were teenagers, of whom almost half were 17 years of age or younger. About one in every four were students in primary or secondary school. This finding is in agreement with several other study findings that indicate that adolescent pregnancy is a serious problem in Dar es Salaam (Leshabari, 1988; Senderowitz and Paxman, 1985; Mbunda, 1988). Between 40 and 60 per cent of school children are sexually active and pregnancy is the leading cause of the school drop-out rate among the girls.

For some people, it is tempting to condemn these girls as social misfits, badly behaved and atypical. This would be highly incorrect, because the behaviour of young people is to a great extent the result of the way society is fostering its future generations. The high rate of adolescent sexual relations seems to be associated with the high level of permissiveness in society, combined with a lack of sex education in the schools.

In fact, the findings of this study support the reality that it is Tanzanian society that is 'corrupting' young girls. Of the total of 62 girls aged 14–17 in the study, only 13 of them said they had become pregnant by partners who were teenagers. The remainder said that their male partners were older than themselves. Indeed, 19 of them said their partners were men of 45 years of age or older; and among the students, more than one out of five said they had a male partner of 45 years of age or more. It is the behaviour of these adult men that ought to be addressed, along with proper sex education programmes developed for young people.

The study also exposed the lack of knowledge about contraceptives among the young women. For example, as stated earlier, only one teenage girl out of 150 had a high level of knowledge about contraception. As a result of this near total ignorance, the use rate was also very low. It is thus a mistake to think that our youth are not a priority group for contraceptive information and education. Where contraceptives are scarce, as was true in the Soviet Union for many years, for example, the abortion rate is high. Popov reported in 1991 that Soviet women were believed to undergo six or more abortions on average during their reproductive years (Popov, 1991). Conversely, where contraceptive information, education and services have deliberately been made more accessible and available to a broader section of eligible population groups, abortion rates have gone down.

The high degree of casual sex revealed by our study is also a concern, particularly because of the attendant risks of sexually transmitted diseases (STDs), particularly HIV and AIDS. Six per cent of the respondents claimed to have been made pregnant by strangers and over half of these were teenagers, while close to a quarter of respondents described their partners as casual friends. Similarly, 12 per cent of the married women became pregnant by men who were not their husbands; 75 per cent of these male partners were either casual friends or strangers. Of equal interest is that 20 per cent of the male partners of these women were themselves married to other women, but had extramarital sexual relations.

Various reports and statements made in the public media in Tanzania indicate that a substantial number of adults, including parents, politicians and other public leaders, are strongly opposed to including contraceptive information in sex education for youth. They argue that doing so is tantamount to giving a licence to practise illicit sex.

The government has introduced on a pilot basis a Family Life Education (FLE) programme for in-school youth which does not include contraceptive information, for the same reasons. The Ministry of Education in the Tanzania Islands (Zanzibar) is about to launch an FLE programme, but in a newspaper report in September 1992, the Zanzibar Minister of Education is quoted as saying that 'there would be no loophole to introduce the students to the modern methods of birth control to such an extent that students could be tempted to indulge in illicit sex without fear'. Further, 'the teachers will be restricted on the lessons related to the human anatomy and in no way would they be allowed to introduce the subject of love affairs to the students' (*Sunday News*, 1992).

This type of thinking seems to be outside the realities of life in Tanzania. Such statements are made without any supporting information data and often in total disregard of the evidence of the extent of adolescent sexuality, with all its negative consequences of school drop-outs due to pregnancy, teenage motherhood, abortion complications, STDs and HIV infection.

This study suggests that adults who have had to confront problems related to adolescent sexuality in their own families may be more likely to view this problem realistically. Indeed, 59 per cent of the respondents, most of whom were teenagers and students, who first confided in a close female relative were advised by them to terminate their pregnancies. A majority of such relatives went even further and looked for someone to perform the abortion.

Cost is another major public health issue. There is no doubt that the financial implications for the individual woman are immense, and especially when she is poor, a teenager, single, a student, or abandoned by the responsible male partner. Such girls have been known to commit suicide or to resort to fatal practices such as taking large doses of chloroquine, incidents that are repeatedly reported in the local press.

The cost to the Ministry of Health is also high. For a woman spending one day in hospital, the cost is seven times higher than the Ministry's annual health budget per person; and for a woman with more severe complications who stays six days, the amount is 42 times higher. And this does not even include the cost of health workers' time. A report of one of the four study hospitals shows that in one year, the department of obstetrics and gynaecology performed a total of 4,897 operations, of which 3,547 were evacuations due to incomplete abortions, a substantial number of which would have been induced abortions (Muhimbili Medical Centre, 1981).

Lastly, in terms of medical complications, although there were no deaths recorded in this study, deaths are not uncommon. Often, women collapse and die on the way to hospitals or in the emergency wards, and are sent straight to mortuaries, where post-mortems are not routinely done. This study found potentially serious complications among the vast majority of patients from incomplete abortions. The longer-term complications of unsafe abortion practices—such as gynaecological disorders, sterility, spontaneous abortions, cervical incompetence and premature births—were beyond the scope of this study, but their effects on society must be borne in mind.

Conclusions and Recommendations

Unwanted pregnancy and unsafe abortion is a serious public health problem in Tanzania. It is costly to the individuals concerned and to the country's health system as a whole, in terms of human and financial resources.

One solution is increased accessibility and availability of family planning information, education and services for all eligible couples and individuals, including sexually active adolescents. Effective sex education programmes must be instituted for the in- and out-of-school teenagers, and must include correct information about reproduction and contraception. There is a need to develop a degree of openness about sexuality that takes into consideration the reality of current lifestyles, modernization and generational behavioural changes.

Further, there is a strong need to review and amend our current abortion laws. By maintaining the current restrictive laws, we are actually denying a substantial number of poor women in our society access to the safe services that modern science and technology make possible. This amounts to denying equal treatment to the poor and the rich. At the moment, it is the latter who can easily afford high prices for illegal pregnancy termination in the safe hands of private medical practice.

The law as an instrument of justice should aim to improve the quality of life of the people and not compel people to undergo dangerous practices when safer ones are available. The law should make safe abortion more available and accessible on a wider scope of indications that address the social, economic and psychological needs of women with unwanted pregnancy.

If these suggestions are implemented with the determination that is required, they are likely to reduce this public health problem significantly, and consequently reduce maternal morbidity and mortality.

✝ References

Aggarwal, V.P. and J.K. Mati. 1982. Epidemiology of induced abortion in Nairobi, Kenya. *Journal of Obstetrics & Gynaecology East Central Africa* 1: 54.

Farr, A.D. 1980. The Marquis de Sade and induced abortion. *Journal of Medical Ethics* 6 (1): 7–10.

IPPF. 1978. *The human problem of abortion—medical and legal dimensions*. London, UK: IPPF.

———. 1991. Meeting of the IPPF/Western Hemisphere Regional Council, San José, Costa Rica, 3–4 October 1991. Agenda Item 21.

Leshabari, M.T. 1988. Factors influencing school adolescent fertility behaviour in Dar es Salaam, Tanzania. Doctoral of Science Thesis in Public Health, submitted to Johns Hopkins University, Baltimore, USA.

Mbunda, W.M. 1988. *Adolescent fertility in Tanzania, knowledge, perceptions and practices*. Dar es Salaam: Family Planning Association of Tanzania (UMATI).

Mtimavalye, L.A. 1980. *Induced abortion and its consequences*. Proceedings of the Scientific Conference, Association of Gynaecologists and Obstetricians of Tanzania, Dar es Salaam, Tanzania, Volume 2.

Mtimavalye, L.A. et al. 1980. Maternal mortality in Dar es Salaam, Tanzania 1974–1977. *East African Medical Journal*. 57: 111–18.

Muhimbili Medical Centre, Dar es Salaam. 1981. *A report of activities for the period 1 July 1979 to 30 June 1980.* Dar es Salaam: MMC.

Popov, A. 1991. Family planning and induced abortion in the USSR: Basic health and demographic characteristics. *Studies in Family Planning* 22 (6): 368–77.

Rogo, K.O. 1989. Legal termination of pregnancy at Kenyatta National Hospital using prostaglandins and in mid-trimester. *East African Medical Journal* 66: 333.

Sai, F. 1984. Adolescent sexuality and reproductive health. In J.K.E. Mate, O.A. Ladipo, R.T. Borkman, R.H. Magarick and D. Huber (eds). *Reproductive Health in Africa*. Baltimore, Maryland: John Hopkins University, pp. 16–31.

Senderowitz, J. and J.M. Paxman. 1985. Adolescent fertility: Worldwide concerns. *Population Bulletin* 40 (2): 1–51.

Sunday News. 1992. Zanzibar to introduce family life education curriculum. 13 September, No. 6.

Tanzania Demographic and Health Survey. 1992. Preliminary results. Tanzania: Tanzania Bureau of Statistics.

Unuigbe, J.A., A.U. Oronsoje and A.A. Orhue. 1988. Abortion-related morbidity and mortality in Benin City, Nigeria 1973–1985. *International Journal of Gynecology and Obstetrics* 26 (3): 435–39.

Wanjala, S.H., N. Murugu and J.K.E. Mate. 1985. Mortality due to abortion at the Kenyatta National Hospital 1974–1983. *Abortion: Medical Progress and Social Implications*. Proceedings of CIBA Foundation Symposium 115, London. 41.

WHO. 1990. *Abortion—A tabulation of available data on the frequency and mortality of unsafe abortion*. Geneva, Switzerland: World Health Organization, Maternal Health and Safe Motherhood Programme.

PART IV

Research and its Implications for Policy: Conclusions

22

The Incidence and Social and Demographic Characteristics of Abortion in Colombia

Lucero Zamudio, Norma Rubiano
and Lucy Wartenberg

Introduction

The practice of induced abortion is mostly illegal in Latin America, where the Catholic Church, for whom the issue is particularly sensitive, is a relatively solid presence in the political scene and in the daily life of ordinary people. In such a context, it is not surprising that there have been very few population-based surveys on abortion in the region, because the atmosphere makes such an undertaking methodologically and ethically challenging, not to mention full of serious, practical problems.

During public debate on the issue, of which there has been much in recent years, estimates of incidence are often unverifiable, incomplete, and either exaggerated or understated. There has been for some time an obvious need to provide reliable estimates based on scientifically sound research, not merely on information from public sector hospital discharge records. Such data suffer from problems such as under-reporting, misclassification, incompleteness and lack of recency. Furthermore, because most of this information comes from state hospitals, which are used by more or less homogeneous populations of low socioeconomic status, it offers only a limited opportunity to analyze social differences. As a result, there are no baseline population studies on induced abortion that could serve as a reference to estimate levels of induced abortion among large segments of the population in Latin America.

Objectives

The first objective of our project was to obtain new and reliable knowledge on induced abortion incidence in Colombia, including its magnitude, social impact and time trends, and to that effect design a methodology that would make it possible to obtain accurate information, recognizing the practical issues involved when dealing with such a sensitive subject. The second objective was to attempt to understand the circumstances leading to unwanted pregnancy and the decision to abort, including the health conditions or practices used to perform the abortion, for which we would use a different research approach.

To achieve our objectives, we developed a research programme on induced abortion focused on the urban population of Colombia, because most of the country's population, 73 per cent, today lives in cities. The project counted on the strong political backing of the Special Advisory Office for Youth, Women and Family of the Presidency of Colombia.

Since our objectives required different types of data, both quantitative and qualitative, it was necessary to combine methods, techniques and strategies for data collection in order to obtain reliable results, and to make sure that the two types of information were fully consistent with each other.

Research Methodology

To meet our first objective, we had to design a representative population-based survey. In theory, the technical problem of obtaining a statistically significant representative sample is a simple one. If a sample is to be representative, the parameters of the base population must be known, and this in turn requires that the characteristics of the participants must be identified. However, for our purposes, there was no national sampling frame for women by age, or for women who had abortions, to use as a reference point. Moreover, we needed to maintain representative validity, to be sure that the information gathered would be reliable while at the same time fully protecting the identity of the women who were to be interviewed.

In short, we had to design an instrument that was sensitive to the objectives of the methodology and technical requirements, and sensitive to the nature of the subject of abortion. The form would contain the required items to calculate abortion indicators, and yet it had to be clear to the participant and short enough to be completed in no more than 5–10 minutes. We also decided on a strategy for gathering the needed information that respected the women's anonymity and also permitted them to respond in a secluded environment, their own homes. The women were to complete the confidential questionnaire, which was self-administered, and then place it in a blank envelope and drop it into a sealed urn. To ensure the technical validity of the form we tested it against other types of instruments, and we also tested the strategy for gathering information. Since the questionnaire had to be filled out by the participant herself, illiterate women were excluded. Our premise was that urban women in Colombia are, for the most part, literate. In fact, this proved to be the case.

The 16 items in the questionnaire were designed to obtain the critical information required to quantify abortion and estimate its incidence. Another purpose was to trace the evolution and current character of abortion in Colombia. For this, we needed to classify the quantitative information by respondent's social strata, region, education, age, number of births, number of pregnancies, marital situation, age group and employment at the time of abortion, pressure on the decision to abort exerted by the male partner, the relative use of abortion as a means of reducing family size up to the time of the interview, and use of contraceptives at the time of the last pregnancy.

The objectives of the research also required qualitative information in order to gain a clearer understanding of the many complex factors that enter into the decision to abort. Material of this kind could not be included in the survey questionnaire. We had to use other techniques of information-gathering, different methods of selecting respondents, and different ways of analyzing the results. Finally, this information was drawn from 100 in-depth interviews focused on the women's life histories and from 180 thematic narratives. The selection of this sub-sample was based on the results of the statistical analysis and the trends that emerged, in order to obtain a group of socially significant cases.

Life histories provided detailed information on the conditions and circumstances in which the abortion decision was made, describing any dilemma or conflicts that emerged, and the process to obtain services. We were also interested in learning about how women found out about the service options available, their quality and the support networks they had during that time. Similarly, the prevailing attitudes, perceptions and value-judgements with regard to abortion among these women were explored, including how they dealt with the threat of legal punishment and opposing religious ideology.

Representativity

In an abortion survey, a series of questions arise concerning the representativity of the sample, as well as its reliability. In our case, we had to obtain a sample size which was representative by region and by social strata, and which would include sufficient numbers of women with induced abortion experience. We had to work without having access to a sampling frame of women by age, or much less women with experience of induced abortion. The only available sampling frame was that of the government's statistical office (DANE), which is based on a housing count of census tracks and is stratified by sectors and by blocks.

Utilizing this information we designed a sampling strategy that included 22 cities and their surrounding metropolitan areas, and within each, a representative sample of all households. A basic census listing of all households was prepared. A simple census-type questionnaire was then applied to each household in order to find out the number of women who lived in each, including the number of women aged 15–55 years. This allowed us to obtain a sampling frame of women of reproductive age.

No nationwide reference data existed on the abortion experience of urban women. Therefore we used estimates from hospital studies to develop an initial neutral hypothesis which assumed that three out of 10 women of reproductive age would have abortion experience. On that basis, in order to guarantee widespread coverage, the sample was divided into quotas. In each cluster (a city block including 30 households), 10 women with experience of abortion had to be found. In order to keep sample error at a level that would still validate differences between regions, social strata and other variables, we could not set a fixed sample size for the number of households. We therefore kept the quota of 10 women with abortion experience, but allowed for a flexible increase in the number of households.

All women aged 15–55 in the selected households were required to complete the survey form. This established the proportion of women with abortion experience among all women aged 15–55 for each cluster. This also allowed us to establish the universe that each woman with experience of abortion represented. We could then expand the results of the sample survey to the total urban female population.

The fixed quota of 10 women with experience of abortion, with a maximum of 40 households surveyed, meant that the clusters obtained were unequal. As a result, we had to work with estimated ratios rather than simple proportions, because proportions assume that clusters are all the same size. To establish statistical significance for the comparison of simple proportions, a hypothesis of differential ratios was tested. Similarly, sample errors had to be calculated for each cluster. For this calculation we used the CLUSTERS programme, which was used in the World Fertility Survey.

For each urban area we obtained a representative sample that reflected the universe of women aged 15–55 years for that area. We used a specially stratified random sample procedure, with fixed proportions, including clusters of unequal size and quotas. Following this procedure we arrived at a total sample size of 33,275 urban women, aged 15–55, which was a sufficiently large number for the purposes of our study. The study was conducted over a period of nine months, from April to December 1992.

Reliability

With respect to reliability, we encountered three problems. The first was how to de-emphasize the presence of survey field staff while the survey form was being completed, and at the same time, allow their presence to explain the project objectives. Second, we had to guarantee that replies would be anonymous and that the identity of the women would be fully protected. Third, there was the problem of how to control the quotas of women with experience of abortion by cluster, without examining the replies of each individual woman as soon as she completed the survey form.

These challenges had to be dealt with during the design of the survey questionnaire and the strategy for information-gathering and analysis. Because the survey questionnaire had to be short and easy to complete, we did not include pre-coded or numbered skip sequences. As described earlier, for each woman to complete the answers in total privacy, they were given the questionnaire with an envelope and instructed to place their replies in it, then seal and deposit it in an urn held by survey staff.

The survey field staff was composed of women graduates, or those about to graduate, from social sciences or health programmes. The brevity of the survey instrument allowed them to explain its purposes quickly. There was no need for them to enter the house, unless the respondent found it helpful. In most cases, interviewers waited outside while the form was being completed. This reduced the possibility of rejection and eliminated bias in the interpretation of answers by the survey team.

Lastly, the verification of responses was done independently, by supervisors, and rapidly entered into computers to ascertain that the quotas were met.

Validity

The survey instrument was validated by comparing it with another instrument. We conducted a test in Villavicencio, a medium-sized city, where the two questionnaires were applied to two similar samples containing 60 clusters each. Since the characteristics of both samples were similar to those of the sample as a whole, we used the same methodological procedure. We used the CLUSTERS package to calculate the sample error. In order to establish the significance of differences of frequency, a hypothesis of differences of ratios was tested on the proportion of women with experience of abortion and the proportion of induced abortions. The results validated the survey instrument.

Significance

The issue of significance applies only to the methodology of life histories and thematic narratives. One way we ensured significance was to draw the cases to be interviewed from a sub-sample of women who most closely matched characteristics or profiles emerging from the main survey trends. These women were contacted and asked whether they would voluntarily describe their life history on tape, changing (if they wished) some details concerning their own identity and of the people involved in their history. This guaranteed the coherence of quantitative and qualitative information. The sub-sample had no statistical representativity. The fact that the women interviewed reflected the profile of trends emerging from the basic sample was a guarantee of the sociological significance of their life histories.

The structure of a life history may be guided or open, depending on the objectives being pursued. In this case, the women interviewed were told why their information was important, but were left to construct and verbalize their own life histories. The resulting structure thus became an additional element of information for the organization and hierarchical ordering of data. The same procedure was followed with the thematic narratives. As required by our ethical procedures, each woman was asked to state at the beginning of her life history that she was aware of the purpose of the research and of the intended use of the information. She also said that she was making her contribution to the research out of her own free will. Since the quality of the life history depends on the empathy established between the researcher and the interviewee, each woman was asked to choose for herself one of the three researchers with whom she had initial contact to tell her life history to.

In the life histories and thematic narratives there is reconstruction, brought about by the passage of time and by subsequent experiences; but this, too, is an important part of the information concerning the life of these women.

Field Issues

There was no advance publicity for the survey. No local authority was informed, nor asked permission to conduct it, but senior members of government were aware that the survey was taking place. Only in some sections of the north-eastern neighbourhoods of Colombia's second largest city, Medellin, where there was a strong presence of popular militia ('organizacion popular armada'), were field staff asked by militiamen what they were doing in the area. In two cases, the militiamen insisted on accompanying the interviewers. We did complete that cluster, but because of this unusual circumstance, it was subsequently replaced by another where no such pressure existed.

No form of indirect explanation or subterfuge was used to approach the women in the sample. The objective of the study and the purpose of the questionnaire was clearly explained to them in simple but direct language. The structure of the questionnaire also reflects this same approach.

In each city, information-gathering was organized to be as quick and as unobtrusive as possible. Acceptance by the women in the sample was surprising; we experienced minimal rejection, with only 2 per cent refusing to cooperate. The careful selection of days and times to make the visits proved an important factor. For housewives, it had to be on days and at times when the husband and the children were out. For working women, it was in the late afternoon or on Saturday morning. Saturday afternoon and Sunday were the least appropriate for interviews.

Completion of quotas was checked by a supervisor at the end of each day's work. If the quota of women with abortions was not completed for a given segment, the maximum size of the cluster was increased to 40 households. The check on collection of data was made with two simple questions: Had the survey team been to the house? How many women lived there?

Data Analysis

We analyzed induced abortion from two perspectives: using the individual woman as a unit of observation; and shifting the unit of analysis to induced abortion itself. By shifting the unit of observation to abortion, the analysis could be made from three points of view: first, as the ratio of abortions to all pregnancies occurring at a point in time; second, as the ratio of abortions per woman; and third, as the distribution of abortions in various sets or groups. Adding the average number of abortions to the average number of children per woman gives us an average total number of potential children the woman would have had if she had not had an induced abortion. The pattern of abortion by cohort and by year of abortion, and changes in specific abortion rates and ratios, are indicators that trace its evolution. Utilizing the qualitative data, particularly the reconstruction of life histories that focused on fertility and abortion, allowed us to delineate even better the determinants of trends and their evolution in Colombia.

The Extent of Induced Abortion

The proportion of women who said that they had one or more abortions, the proportion of pregnancies reported as ending in abortion, and the average number of abortions per woman, all suggest that abortion is a common practice in Colombia.

Of all women aged 15–55 years who were surveyed, 22.9 per cent reported that they had at least one induced abortion (Figure 22.1). This proportion represents about 1,127,485 women of reproductive age who are residents in cities of over 100,000 inhabitants (based on the 1985 Census) and who have had at least one experience of induced abortion. Perhaps a more accurate universe would be the 1,213,899 urban women projected to 1993. As this denominator includes women who have not yet started their sexual life or who have never been pregnant, this indicator should be considered a gross measure. On the other hand, it reveals that at least one-fifth of all urban women in Colombia have had abortion experience.

Induced Abortion Differentials

When we examined differences between regions for the gross indicators, we found some variation. For example, the Andean area and Antioquia have abortion levels substantially below the urban average. When looking at social

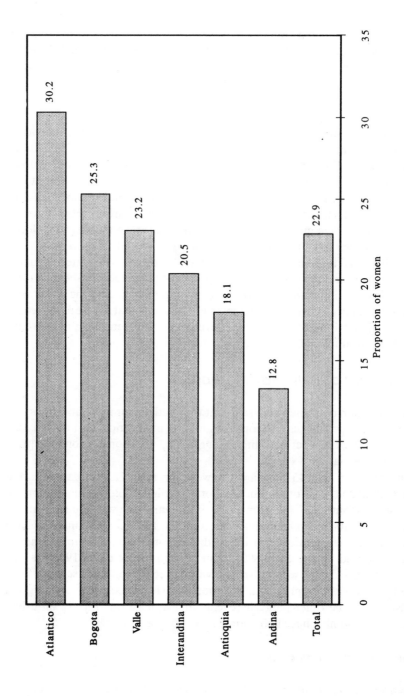

Figure 22.1: Proportion of Women, 15–55 Years, With Abortion Experience, by Region, Urban Colombia, 1992

class, we found that the higher proportion of abortions were at both extremes of the social pyramid. Differences by education are even more marked: 28.7 per cent of the women with incomplete primary education have at least one experience of abortion as compared with 18.1 per cent of women with incomplete high school education. Surprisingly, the proportion among university educated women is similar to that of women with no education (Figure 22.2).

Age also shows important differences with respect to abortion behaviour. For example, 12 per cent of the women under 20 years of age said that they had experience of induced abortion, but this proportion rises to 20.6 per cent for the 20–24 age group and to 27–28 per cent for the next three age groups (Figure 22.3). The largest proportion of abortion occurs for women in their late 20s and 30s, falling rapidly thereafter as women become less fertile. This shows that women at opposite ends of their reproductive life cycle have different reasons for choosing abortion, a point we will discuss in greater detail later.

Employment is also a differential factor. Working women have substantially more abortions (27.1 per cent) than women who do not work (20 per cent). The latter include students, unemployed workers, housewives and others who do not work. High abortion levels are also found among women who are employed in commercial activities, in services or who are small business owners.

The proportion of women with abortion experience who have children hovers around 25 per cent; but it is much lower among women who have no children, 17.4 per cent. This is because the latter group includes those who have not yet started their sexual life or who have never been pregnant; and they represent a much higher proportion of their age group than women in the older age groups where marriage predominates (Figure 22.4).

Women at Risk

Women at risk of abortion are defined as those who have been pregnant at least once and who are sexually active. They represent 75.4 per cent of the universe of women aged 15–55 years.

When we recalculated the abortion rate and included in the denominator only women exposed to the risk of pregnancy (ever-pregnant and sexually active women), the result indicates that nearly one-third of these women (30.3 per cent) at one time or another had experienced an induced abortion (Table 22.1). This is a very significant figure since it shows the true magnitude of the abortion problem in Colombia.

Both these figures are based on abortion reported by women and thus are reliable. We can also safely say these are minimum estimates, considering that, as in all abortion studies, there is some under-reporting. It should also be noted that this proportion is for all abortions ever experienced and does not represent the abortion rate for the year of the survey. The rate calculated for all urban women for the year 1992 would be 24.6 per 1,000 women.

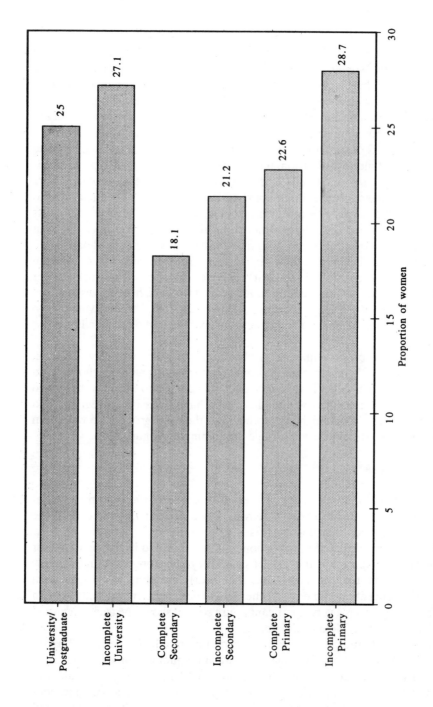

Figure 22.2: Proportion of Women, 15–55 Years, With Abortion Experience, by Education, Urban Colombia, 1992

Age

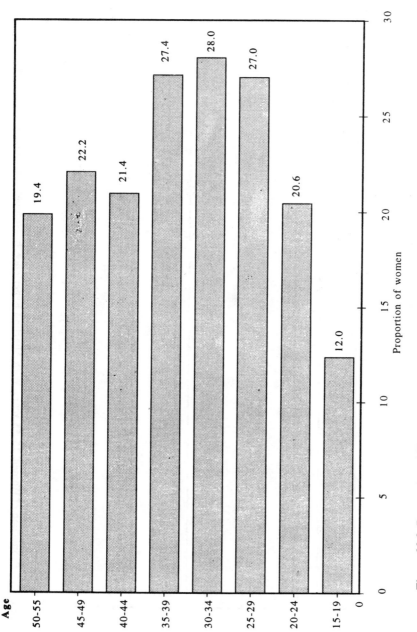

Proportion of women

Figure 22.3: Proportion of Women, 15–55 Years, With Abortion Experience, by Age, Urban Colombia, 1992

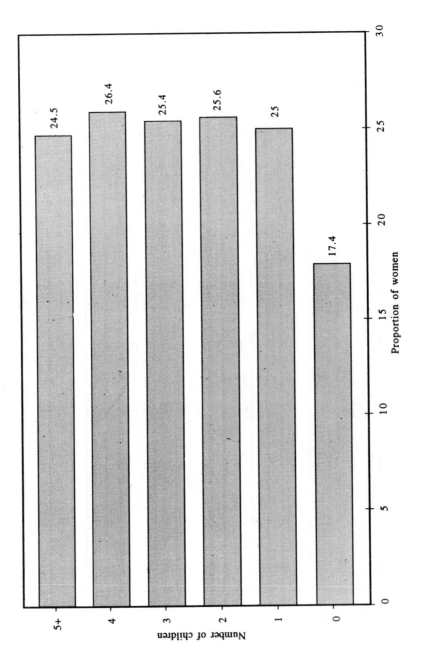

Figure 22.4: Proportion of Women, 15–55 Years, With Abortion Experience, by Number of Children, Urban Colombia, 1992

Table 22.1: Women, Aged 15–55 With Abortion Experience, as a Proportion of All Women Pregnant at Least Once, by Order of Abortion

Category	All Women Aged 15–55	Percent Pregnant At Least Once	Percent Who Aborted— All Orders	Women Who Pass From One Abortion to the Next*			
				1 Abortion	2 Abortions	3 Abortions	4+ Abortions
Total	3,733,323	75.4	30.3	23.9 '	20.3	22.5	33.5
Region							
Bogota	1,213,056	74.5	33.9	26.2	22.3	22.7	37.4
Antioquia	811,880	74.2	24.4	19.3	20.5	20.1	38.9
Atlantico	676,833	80.5	37.3	30.1	19.2	20.2	14.5
Andina	300,811	71.1	18.8	19.7	13.5	28.8	10.8
Valle	417,742	75.4	30.9	35.2	19.2	29.1	41.7
Interandina	313,001	76.0	27.0	21.0	21.1	22.5	48.9
Social class							
Lower-lower	274,387	84.1	32.9	25.5	22.5	22.5	21.7
Lower	998,938	78.1	31.1	24.0	23.8	18.8	29.6
Lower-middle	1,685,925	75.8	24.9	23.2	17.2	23.6	23.4
Middle	538,173	69.7	36.9	24.0	22.9	23.7	52.6
Upper-middle	197,305	68.1	37.3	28.8	20.6	34.0	25.7
Upper	38,595	63.9	30.3	19.9	10.9	–	–
Education							
Primary-incomplete	713,822	88.9	32.4	34.6	28.6	23.5	44.5
Primary-complete	679,021	87.1	25.7	27.0	23.4	17.6	21.6
Secondary-incomplete	1,120,328	70.5	30.3	35.6	17.8	15.8	31.5
Secondary-complete	701,240	70.3	25.4	27.8	16.8	22.2	52.7
University-incomplete	214,424	58.1	47.2	38.6	11.5	80.6	14.2
University complete	225,802	72.6	34.8	41.0	25.4	9.1	48.6
Unknown education	78,686	–	–	–	–	–	–

Table 22.1 continued

Table 22.1 continued

Category	All Women Aged 15–55	Percent Pregnant At Least Once	Percent Who Aborted—All Orders	Women Who Pass From One Abortion to the Next*			
				1 Abortion	2 Abortions	3 Abortions	4+ Abortions
Total	3,733,323	75.4	30.3	23.9	20.3	22.5	33.5
Number of pregnancies							
1	905,106	NA	25.4	25.4	–	–	–
2	908,072	NA	22.9	20.4	12.4	–	–
3	710,322	NA	31.7	26.3	17.0	20.3	–
4	482,784	NA	38.1	25.7	40.4	14.9	25.8
5	277,246	NA	40.3	26.3	41.0	22.2	35.9
6	161,375	NA	40.9	26.8	37.5	25.4	58.1
7+	288,418	NA	37.1	18.1	59.4	53.0	43.0
Age (years)							
15–19	223,458	26.8	44.5	42.6	3.9	10.9	–
20–24	520,291	63.7	32.4	27.1	11.8	14.4	8.5
25–29	700,916	81.9	32.9	39.7	18.8	19.8	19.0
30–34	672,976	90.9	30.7	34.8	21.3	20.6	44.6
35–39	567,750	94.2	29.1	31.3	23.1	21.4	52.1
40–44	403,868	95.1	28.1	28.3	29.9	18.4	54.9
45–49	298,639	94.8	25.2	18.9	42.2	22.8	19.9
50–55**	263,585	94.6	–	–	–	–	–
Unknown age	81,840	–	–	–	–	–	–

* Women with (N+1) abortions as proportions of women with (N) abortions.

** No rates were calculated for this group due to some inconsistencies, probably due to memory loss.

The risk of abortion is high for all age groups. Among the youngest women we found: 26.8 per cent of women aged 20 or less had been pregnant at least once; and by their late 20s, a large majority (82 per cent) had experienced pregnancy. Women under 25 years of age are the group at highest risk of abortion. A girl of 19 years has double the risk of abortion of a woman of 40 years. Almost half of the girls under 20 who had been pregnant (44.5 per cent) had a history of abortion. Among women 20–24 years of age, 32.4 per cent had abortion experience. Although the proportion falls to 22.5 per cent for older women, between the ages 45 and 50, it still remains high. It should be noted that this refers to abortions women had at any time in the past and not to abortions in the past 12 months (Figure 22.5).

Abortion Risk Differentials

From a social structure point of view, the comparison between the risk of pregnancy and the risk of abortion is highly suggestive. While the risk of pregnancy increases as we move down the social scale (since fewer precautions against pregnancy are taken), the risk of abortion appears to be somewhat lower, since more pregnancies end in childbirth (Table 22.1). Our results indicate that while there is a lower risk of abortion among the lower social strata, it is higher among the middle and upper-middle social class groups (Figure 22.6). Since the latter groups use contraceptive methods more extensively, their greater risk of abortion expresses a lower degree of tolerance of unwanted pregnancies.

Similar patterns can be observed in terms of educational level. Uneducated women as well as university educated women have the highest risk of abortion. For the less educated women, this reflects lower use of contraception or higher tolerance for unplanned pregnancy, while among the more educated, this shows a commitment to smaller families and to professional goals. Contraceptive failure, among these women, is more easily remedied by abortion given their high motivation to control family size (Table 22.1).

The relationship between the number of pregnancies and women who abort is particularly interesting. Women with two pregnancies or less (22.9 per cent) have less abortion experience than women with five or six pregnancies, who also have more repeat abortions (Figure 22.7). The drop in abortion experience in women with more than six pregnancies occurs among women of the older generation, for whom abortion was probably less common, and infant and child mortality higher.

The relationship between the number of pregnancies and of abortions was confirmed by means of a regression analysis; the regression coefficient was 74.9 per cent. On average, each additional pregnancy increases the proportion of women who abort by 1.5 per cent. It seems that as women reach higher pregnancy levels, the use of abortion becomes an alternative form of fertility regulation. Therefore, while the proportion of women who resort to abortion

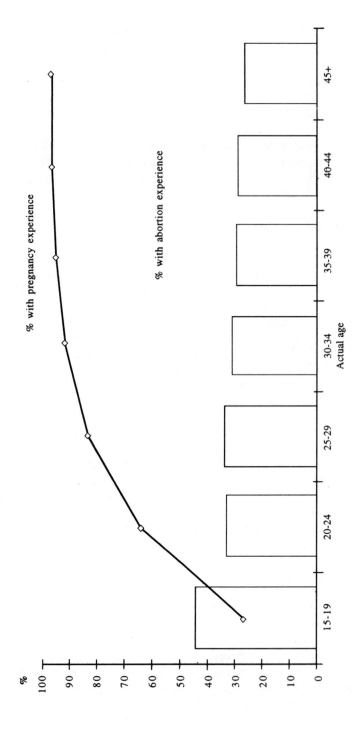

Figure 22.5: Women, 15–55 Years, Proportions Ever Pregnant and Who Aborted, Urban Colombia, 1992

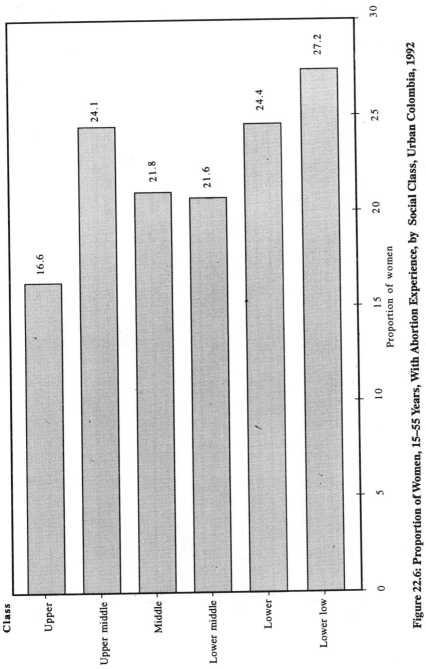

Figure 22.6: Proportion of Women, 15–55 Years, With Abortion Experience, by Social Class, Urban Colombia, 1992

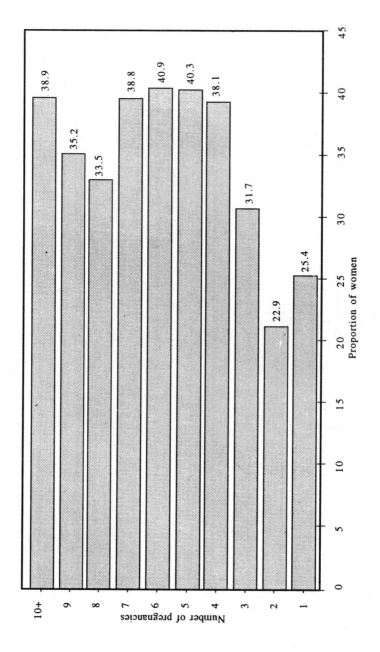

Figure 22.7: Women, 15–55 Years, With Abortion Experience, by Number of Pregnancies, Urban Colombia, 1992

does not vary significantly by number of children, it does vary significantly by number of pregnancies.

Pregnancy Order and Abortion

As the variable that mainly affects the risk of abortion is the number of pregnancies, it is illuminating to analyze the proportion of women with experience of abortion and number of pregnancies, by region, social stratum, education and work.

In all major regions of Colombia and at all levels, the proportion of women with experience of abortion increases with higher pregnancy orders. However, in the more traditional regions, where stronger social controls prevail, the pattern is different. In the high Andes (Andina Region), where induced abortion is least common, a very large proportion of abortions occur to put an end to a first unwanted pregnancy, especially among single women who would be socially stigmatized. This pattern is also to be found in Antioquia, where control of the first pregnancy is much stronger. Half the women who have aborted there have had one or two pregnancies only (Figure 22.8).

The other extreme is Bogota, where greater numbers of women resort to abortion, and where services are more easily available. In Bogota, women with experience of abortion show a much more even pattern by order of pregnancy. One woman in five ended her first pregnancy with abortion, and the same is true for the second, third and fourth pregnancies. In the region of Valle, the pattern is somewhat similar to that of Bogota, but on the Atlantic coast, abortions tend to rise with the number of pregnancies.

In the valleys between the Andean ranges, a more traditional family formation pattern emerges. Families in these valleys are large, there is less control of early pregnancies among single women, and more family support (especially from the women's mothers) in bringing up young children. The strongest motivation to limit family size appears somewhat later, 38 per cent of the women who aborted were in their third or fourth pregnancy.

Generally speaking, women in the higher socioeconomic levels have more abortions at the time of their first pregnancy (early unwanted pregnancies), or later, after their fourth pregnancy, which suggests a strong commitment to maintain a pre-determined family size. This suggests both a desire to have two or three children, and to have the first child later (Figure 22.9).

The middle classes also seem to want fewer children, and the largest proportion of these women who abort do so in their third pregnancy. Among the lower classes, abortion takes place later in the reproductive cycle, being more common in the sixth or seventh pregnancy (32.4 per cent of the women at the higher pregnancy levels had abortion experience).

The analysis by educational level repeats the pattern observed by social strata. The less-educated women resort to abortion to control family size; as more pregnancies occur, more abortions take place. While women with

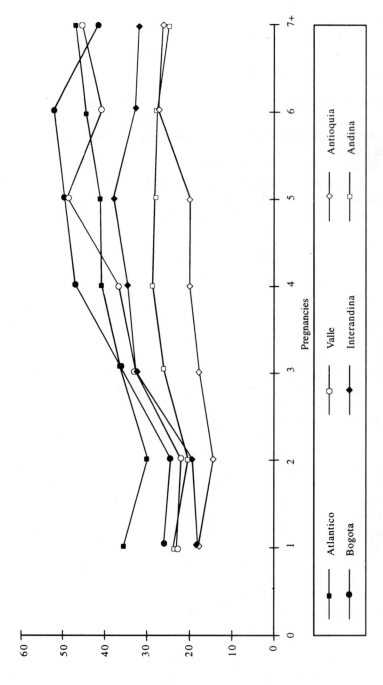

Figure 22.8: Women, 15–55 Years, With Abortion Experience by Number of Pregnancies and Region, Urban Colombia, 1992

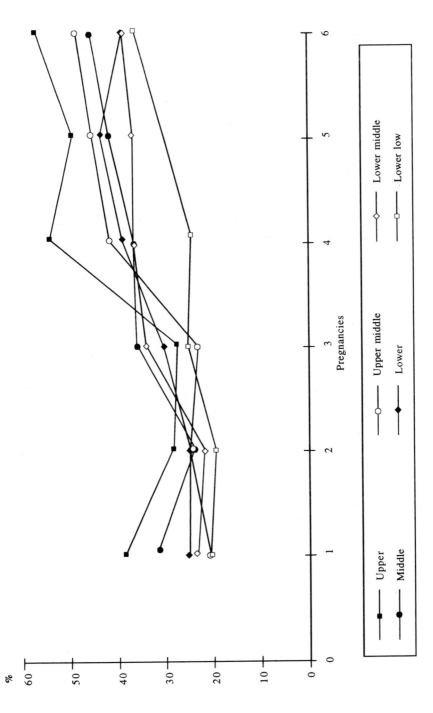

Figure 22.9: Women, 15–55 Years, With Abortion Experience by Number of Pregnancies and Social Class, Urban Colombia, 1992

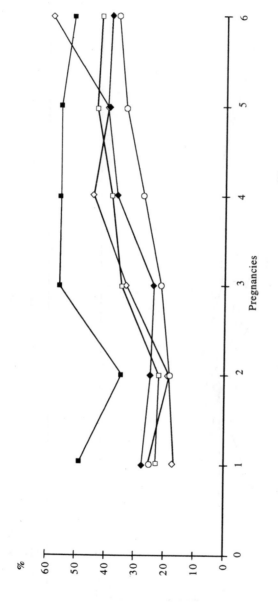

Figure 22.10: Women, 15–55 Years, With Abortion Experience by Number of Pregnancies and Education, Urban Colombia, 1992

higher levels of education are more likely to terminate a first pregnancy (42.4 per cent). Women who have completed university education are more likely to resort to abortion to interrupt a first or a second pregnancy (53.6 per cent) (Figure 22.10).

Our analysis of employment patterns contains some marked differentials. Among working women who had abortion experience, 40 per cent of the abortions were to end a first or second pregnancy; fewer occur at the higher pregnancy levels. For students who work, the pattern is quite different; nearly 90 per cent of all abortions occur as a result of a first or second pregnancy. Housewives not only have the smallest experience of abortion overall, but also resort to it most commonly during their third or fourth pregnancy. Only 7 per cent of housewives abort their first pregnancy, while the rate among working women is nearly three times as high (20 per cent). Students, indicative of the age differential, have very high first pregnancy abortions, nearly 70 per cent (Figure 22.11).

Abortion Ratios

Pregnancies ending in abortion, the average number of abortions per woman with abortion experience, and the ratio of abortions per 100 pregnancies are important indicators of the evolution of induced abortion in Colombia. The abortion ratio is a particularly accurate indicator, because there is no bias introduced by greater or lesser risk of pregnancy; this happens in other measures where the denominator includes all women regardless of abortion risk.

Women with abortion experience had 33 per cent more pregnancies than the general average. The average number of pregnancies in the total sample of women was 2.3; but among women pregnant at least once, with abortion experience, the average was higher, at 3.1. Among ever-pregnant women, the average number of abortions was 0.3 per woman; but among women with abortion experience, this average rose to 1.3, being highest for women in Bogota (Table 22.2). In Bogota, the abortion ratio, 14.7 per hundred pregnancies, was also higher than the national average of 12.4. The Andina region, as noted before, had the lowest abortion level.

Abortion ratios increase by social class, and also by educational level. But in both cases, there is a dip at the upper end of these categories, indicating that at the very top of the socioeconomic scale fertility control is much more effective (Table 22.2). A similar pattern can be observed in the average number of abortions per woman.

Pregnancies are higher among lower socioeconomic and educational groups. Women with incomplete primary education have the highest average number of pregnancies (4.3) and children, and therefore their induced abortion ratio is relatively low (10.3 per 100 pregnancies). Middle and upper-middle-class women with abortion experience have an average of 2.8

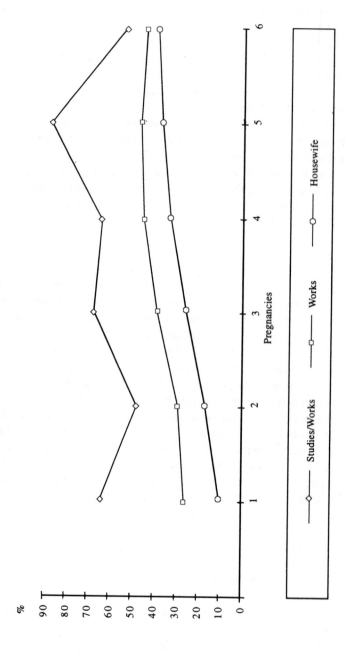

Figure 22.11: Women, 15–55 Years, With Abortion Experience by Number of Pregnancies and Work Status, Urban Colombia, 1992

Table 22.2: Average Number of Pregnancies and Abortions for Women With Abortion Experience and Abortion Ratios, by Main Differentials, Urban Colombia, 1992

Category	Ever Pregnant Women	Average Pregnancies of Women with Abortion Experience	Abortion Ratio*	Average Number of Abortions of Women with Abortion Experience
Total	3,733,323	3.1	12.4	1.3
Region				
Bogota	1,213,056	3.0	14.7	1.3
Antioquia	811,880	3.0	10.4	1.3
Atlantico	676,833	3.5	13.2	1.2
Andina	300,811	3.1	7.2	1.2
Valle	417,742	3.1	13.1	1.3
Interandina	313,001	3.2	10.8	1.3
Social class				
Lower-lower	274,387	3.8	11.1	1.3
Lower	998,938	3.3	12.0	1.3
Lower-middle	1,685,925	3.0	11.7	1.2
Middle	538,173	2.8	14.7	1.3
Upper-middle	197,305	2.8	17.4	1.3
Upper	38,595	2.9	8.5	1.1
Education				
Primary-incomplete	713,822	4.3	10.3	1.4
Primary-complete	679,021	3.7	8.9	1.3
Secondary-incomplete	1,120,328	2.8	12.9	1.3
Secondary-complete	701,240	2.4	13.5	1.2
University-incomplete	214,424	2.2	27.5	1.3
University complete	225,802	2.3	19.6	1.3
Unknown education	78,686	–	–	–
Employment**				
Studies and/or works	159,827	1.4	49.0	1.1
Works	1,541,413	2.9	15.3	1.3
Stays at home	477,255	3.4	9.0	1.3
Occupation**				
Professional	188,678	2.3	19.9	1.3
Non-prof. worker	113,358	2.4	19.4	1.3
Manual work/crafts	132,764	3.3	10.7	1.8
Commercial employees	253,355	3.2	15.6	1.4
Service workers	159,692	3.2	14.7	1.4
Small enterprises	39,028	2.9	20.6	1.4
Workers (general)	104,493	2.6	12.9	1.2
Domestic workers	282,571	3.6	12.3	1.3
Others	75,348	2.7	17.2	1.3

Table 22.2 continued

Table 22.2 continued

Category	Ever Pregnant Women	Average Pregnancies of Women with Abortion Experience	Abortion Ratio*	Average Number of Abortions of Women with Abortion Experience
Number of pregnancies				
1	905,106	–	25.4	1.0
2	908,072	–	12.7	1.1
3	710,322	–	12.7	1.2
4	482,784	–	13.2	1.3
5	277,246	–	11.6	1.3
6	161,375	–	10.1	1.4
7+	288,418	–	7.7	1.4
Age (years)				
15–19	223,458	1.3	36.6	1.1
20–24	520,291	1.7	21.6	1.2
25–29	700,916	2.3	17.6	1.2
30–34	672,976	2.9	13.8	1.2
35–39	567,750	3.4	11.3	1.0
40–44	403,868	4.1	9.3	1.6
45–49	298,639	4.7	6.9	–
50–55	263,585	5.5	6.4	–
Unknown age	81,840	–	–	–

* Abortion per 100 pregnancies.

** For employment and occupation only selected categories are shown, therefore numbers do not add up to the total sample.

pregnancies, but their abortion ratios are much higher, 17.4 abortions per 100 pregnancies (Table 22.2).

Working women have higher abortion ratios than housewives. By age, the abortion ratio was highest among the youngest group; for women 15–19 years old it was 36.6 per cent. The ratio falls among older women aged 45–50, to 6.9 per cent. For all adolescent women, aged 15–19 years, the average number of pregnancies is 0.3, but this rises to 1.3 among those who have aborted; and for this group the average number of abortions per woman with abortion experience was 1.1. In short, as age increases, the average number of abortions for women with abortion experience increases, reaching 1.2 abortions for ages 30–34 and decreasing somewhat afterwards (Table 22.2).

Repeat Abortion

Not only did we find the incidence of induced abortion high among the sample we studied, but also we found that a considerable proportion of women had experienced more than one abortion. In fact, one out of every five women had repeat abortions: 16.2 per cent had two; 3.4 per cent had three;

and 1.2 per cent had four or more. If applied to the universe these women represent, this would mean that 956,668 urban women had one abortion; 195,682 had two; 41,069 had three; and 14,495 had four or more (based on the 1993 urban census population estimates). In addition, we believe that repeat abortions may be somewhat under-reported, because the life histories conducted following the main survey indicated that women were often ashamed of admitting to a repeat abortion, especially after a second abortion.

There are no important variations between regions or strata in repetition. Repeat abortions are somewhat higher in Bogota and mostly among the lower socioeconomic strata, and among women with either no education or with very high levels of education.

Once again, it is the number of pregnancies that plays a stronger role in explaining repeat abortion patterns. Women with seven or more pregnancies have five times as many repeat abortions (51.1 per cent) as those with two pregnancies (11.1 per cent) (Figure 22.12). We found that in general, the greater the number of pregnancies, the greater the number of first abortions and repetitions. This relationship is so strong that it even shows up by number of living children (Figure 22.13). For example, repeat abortion among women with five or more children rises to 32.6 per cent; and among these women the proportion with three or more abortions is the highest of all (9.8 per cent). Repetition increases quickly with the number of children.

The highest levels of repeat abortion are to be found among the least educated women (27 per cent) and the most educated women (23.1 per cent), a further confirmation that the pattern at the top of the social scale is similar to that at the bottom (Figure 22.14). In terms of employment, working women have slightly higher repeat abortions, 22.6 per cent of the cases, compared to 19 per cent for housewives.

Age is also a factor in repeat abortions. Among women of 40–45 years, 27.5 per cent had repeat abortions, rising to 38.4 per cent among women aged 50–55. This must be considered as a sort of maximum level, as women at that age have already finished their reproductive life (Figure 22.15).

The Risk of Repeat Abortion

About a quarter of women who have been pregnant (23.9 per cent) have had one abortion; and a fifth of them have had a second abortion. Of these, about a quarter (22.5 per cent) have had a third abortion; and a third of this last group have had four or more abortions (Table 22.1).

We find here again, a close correlation between the number of pregnancies and the risk of repeat abortion. The risk of the first abortion varies little as a function of the number of pregnancies, but the risk of repeat abortion increases. For example, among women with five pregnancies, the risk of a second abortion is 41 per cent; the risk of a third, 22.2 per cent; and the risk of a fourth, 35.9 per cent. Women who have been pregnant six times and have

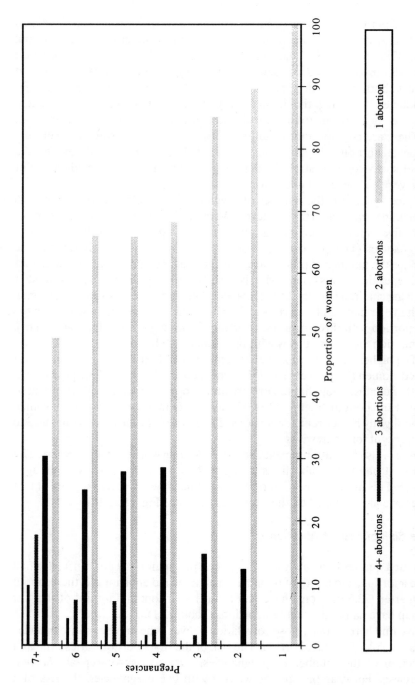

Figure 22.12: Women, 15–55 Years, With Abortion Experience by Number of Pregnancies and Abortions, Urban Colombia, 1992

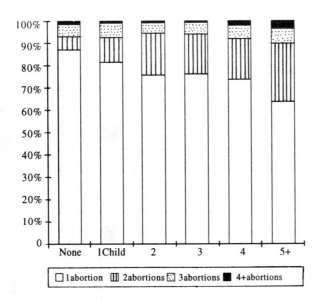

100% 90% 80% 70% 60% 50% 40% 30% 20% 10% 0

None 1Child 2 3 4 5+

□ 1abortion ▥ 2abortions ▧ 3abortions ■ 4+abortions

Figure 22.13: Women, 15–55 Years, With Abortion Experience by Number of Abortions and Children Ever-Born, Urban Colombia, 1992

had one abortion have a 37.5 per cent probability of a second abortion; a 25.4 per cent probability of a third; and 58.1 per cent probability of a fourth (Figure 22.16).

The risk of repeat abortion, especially a second or third one, is high in the middle and upper middle classes. The risk of repetition is also high among women 30–45 years of age. It can be hypothesized that if these women abort less often than younger women, but reach a higher level of repetition, girls aged 19 whose abortion rates are already double those of the older generation will have reached higher levels of repetition than their mothers by the end of their reproductive cycle.

The Impact of Abortion on Family Size

The information obtained from our survey makes it possible to calculate the relative influence of induced abortion on the reduction in family size. For urban women, the average number of children is 1.9, and the average number of abortions is 0.29. Therefore, the total potential fertility of these women would be 2.19 children on average, from which we can deduce that induced abortion has reduced family size by 13.3 per cent. If we make the same

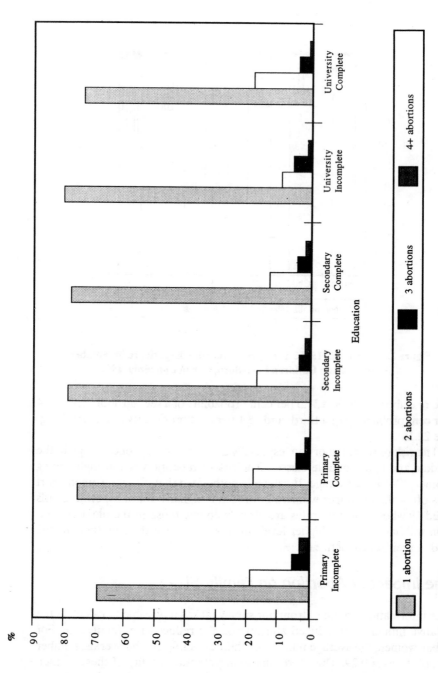

Figure 22.14: Women, 15–55 Years, With Abortion Experience by Number of Abortions and Education, Urban Colombia, 1992

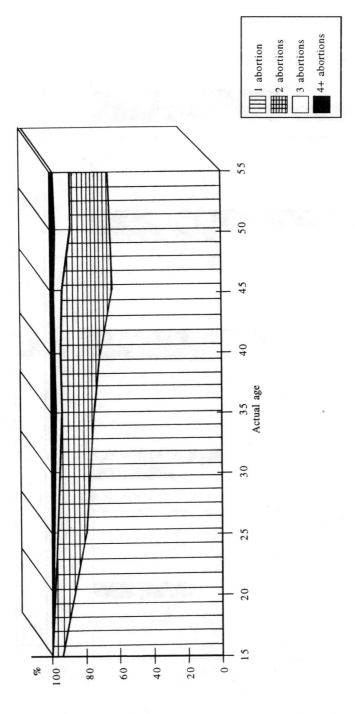

Figure 22.15: Women, 15–55 Years, With Abortion Experience, by Number of Abortions and Age, Urban Colombia, 1992

Legend:
- 1 abortion
- 2 abortions
- 3 abortions
- 4+ abortions

Actual age

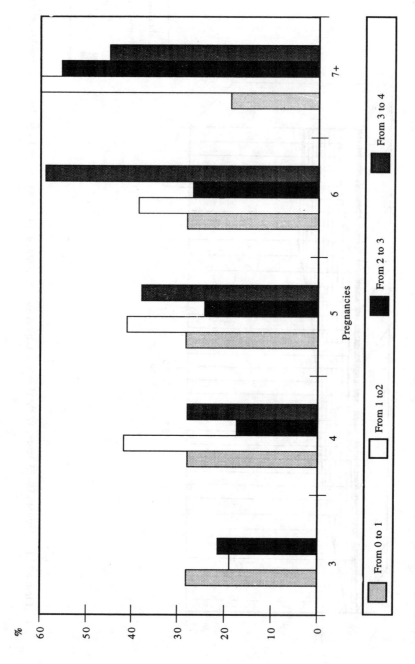

Figure 22.16: Women, 15–55 Years, With Abortion Experience and Three or More Pregnancies, According to the Risk of Moving From One Abortion Level to the Next, Urban Colombia, 1992

From 0 to 1　　From 1 to2　　From 2 to 3　　From 3 to 4

Pregnancies

%

calculation for women who have had abortion experience, and whose average number of children is 2.2, they would have had 3.4 children instead; therefore, abortion contributed to reducing their potential fertility by 37.7 per cent.

The impact of abortion in reducing fertility levels was strongest in Bogota (15.4 per cent); followed by Valle (13.7 per cent) and the Caribbean coast (13.8 per cent). It was less marked in Antioquia (10.8 per cent) and the high Andes (7.8 per cent). The data also show that the higher the social stratum, the more common the use of abortion. At lower levels, abortion explains an 11.3 per cent reduction in the average number of children, compared with 19.2 per cent for the upper-middle-class group. The same pattern is observed by educational level: women with incomplete primary education reduced their fertility with abortion by 10.7 per cent, while women with incomplete university education reduced theirs by 30.5 per cent. Within this group, repeat abortion (three or more abortions) reduced fertility by 75.4 per cent, with the average fertility for this group being a very low 1.2 children. Although university educated women marry later than others and have a longer period of premarital sexual activity, they plan their families more carefully and are more committed to their fertility aspirations.

Generational Effects

Two groups significant to the evolution of abortion in Colombia are women aged 15–17 and 18–19 years. Among women aged 15–17, abortion rates for the cohort born in the years 1968–72 are double those of cohorts born prior to 19⁻³. The rates increase from 2.22 per cent to 4.18 per cent for these very young women. For women aged 18–19, the rate is four times greater, rising from 2.04 per cent to 8.16 per cent between the same cohorts (Figure 22.17).

The cohort analysis shows that the practice of abortion as a means of reducing fertility seems to be an old one, judging by the experience of abortion among the older generations. The abortion rate is around 20 per 1,000 among women aged 40 today, most of whom have completed their reproductive cycle. The abortion rate peaks around age 23, when it reaches close to 40 per 1,000 women (Figure 22.18).

Regional differences are illustrative of differences in social change occurring in the country. The region with the highest abortion rates at almost all ages is Bogota, which has systematically higher rates for all age groups after 25 years. This suggests that the practice of abortion is older and more stable among the women of Bogota (Figure 22.19).

Time Trends

Turning next to time trends, we tried to estimate retrospective induced abortion rates for the urban population for the period 1952–56, for which the rate was 1.7 per cent. For the period 1988–91, the abortion rate had increased six

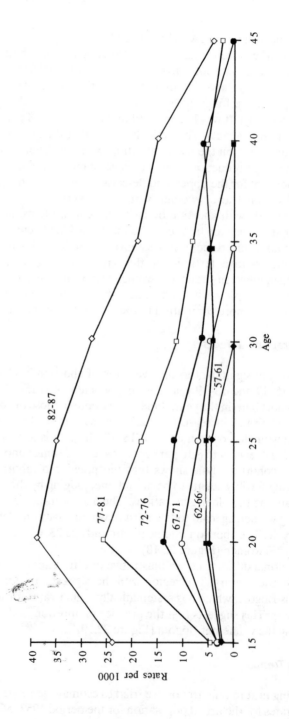

Figure 22.17: Age-Specific Abortion Rates by Year of the Abortion

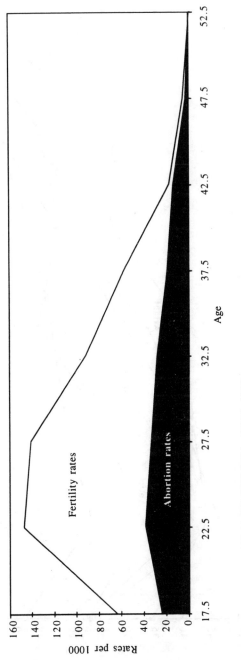

Fertility rates 1987-90: PROFAMILIA, EPDS, 1990
Abortion rates (1987-92): Abortion study

Figure 22.18: Age-Specific Fertility and Abortion Rates, Urban Colombia, 1992

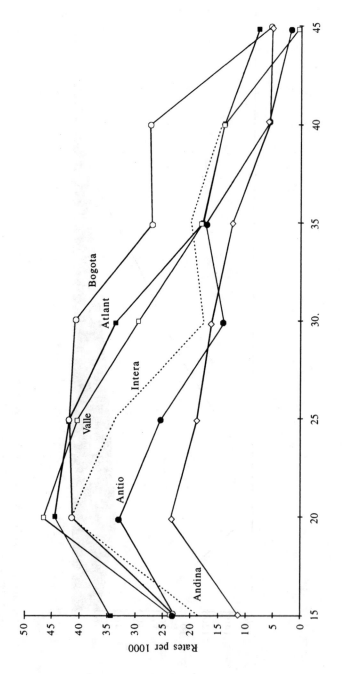

Figure 22.19: Age-Specific Abortion Rates by Regions, Urban Colombia, 1992

times, to 12.3 per cent (Table 22.3). The proportion of women experiencing their first abortion increased 6.5 times, from 1.6 per cent to 9.7 per cent during the same period. Second abortions were almost nonexistent in 1952–56, but were 2 per cent in 1987–91.

Table 22.3: Annual Abortion Rates per 100 Women: Total and by Order of Abortion

Year of Abortion	Women at Risk	Abortions of All Order	By Order of Abortion			
			1	2	3	4
1952–1956	342,336	1.70	1.63	0.07	–	–
1957–1961	657,263	2.23	1.72	0.43	0.1	0.00
1962–1966	1,081,810	4.30	3.23	0.74	0.26	0.10
1967–1971	1,684,817	4.30	3.26	0.76	0.18	0.08
1972–1976	2,426,383	4.50	3.84	0.58	0.06	0.00
1977–1981	3,282,223	5.00	3.95	0.86	0.16	0.03
1982–1986	4,100,259	6.82	5.48	1.07	0.22	0.05
1987–1991	4,934,002	12.30	9.65	2.01	0.50	0.14

Overall, abortion rates in the last five years seem to reflect an increase in induced abortion among younger women, which, added to the total experience of the older generations, contributes to high annual rates. If prevention were more efficient, these rates should fall.

Age-Specific Rates

Lastly, we calculated age-specific rates prior to the survey in order to assess the increase in abortion in recent times. We assume that women report their recent abortions more accurately than their past ones, either due to memory loss or intentional forgetfulness. The analysis shows that specific rates increase yearly for all age groups. Women in the 20–24 age group, for example, had rates for 1988–91 eight times higher than the level for 1967–71, indicating an increase in abortion over the past 20 years.

Contexts and Circumstances

We have approached the study of induced abortion by analyzing social and demographic background characteristics of our respondents, such as age, employment, marital status, number of children, number of pregnancies and associated contraceptive and reproductive behaviour, which are the key determinants contributing to an understanding of why women have abortion.

In our study of urban women in Colombia, the average age of women who had abortion experience was 24.8 years, substantially younger than the average age for all women in Colombia (34.2 years). This shows that induced abortion is increasingly experienced by younger women. Of all abortions reported, 14.8 per cent were among adolescents aged 15–17 years, and a third had taken place among women under 20 years of age.

The relationship between marital status and induced abortion offers another view of the situation, with single women accounting for 42.1 per cent of all abortions. Moreover, single women account for 46.3 per cent of all first abortions. And the proportion is still significant for second abortions, at 26.3 per cent; third abortions, at 23.6 per cent; and fourth abortions, at 17.1 per cent. Looking next at the distribution of single women by social strata, we found that 31.1 per cent of all abortions that occurred in the lower socioeconomic level were by single women; but among the upper classes, the proportion was substantially higher (54.6 per cent). As noted earlier, women in the latter group are more highly motivated to control family size; in part due to their stronger commitment to professional goals. By contrast, married women accounted for 28.1 per cent of all abortions; and unmarried women living in stable unions, for 26.4 per cent of all abortions. The general explanation for these differences in abortion experience by marital status is that single women are generally more exposed to unwanted pregnancy; and in the absence of support from a male companion, they opt for abortion more frequently than their married counterparts.

One group that faces special risks is that in which the husband or the wife, or both, already have children from other relationships or marriages. If one partner already has children, he or she is likely not to want any more, and there will be pressure for abortion when a pregnancy is suspected. Still another group where there is great pressure to terminate an unplanned pregnancy is that of separated women not in a stable relationship. We found a high prevalence of abortion among these women.

Our study sample revealed that in 42.7 per cent of the cases, the woman was working at the time of the abortion, a proportion 13 per cent higher than the average for all working women in Colombia. There may be some distortion in these proportions, because repeat abortion is included; nonetheless, this is an indicator of the high level of working women who have induced abortion.

As we have already mentioned, the proportion of women experiencing induced abortion does not vary much by number of living children, but it is strongly affected by number of previous pregnancies. Abortion is therefore used as a means by which women adjust the number of children conceived to meet family size aspirations. For example, among women with two pregnancies, 22.9 per cent had abortion experience, while in women who have had six pregnancies, this proportion more than doubles, to 40.1 per cent.

The lack of contraceptive use to avoid unwanted pregnancy is a major finding of our study: 78.4 per cent of all abortions were the result of unintended pregnancy due to non-use of contraception. The absence of contraception explains over two-thirds of the problem. For the rest, 21.6 per cent, the pregnancy was the result of contraceptive failure or misuse.

Conclusions

Our study has, for the first time in Latin America, attempted to survey a large sample, over 30,000 women, on their abortion experience. Although there is a serious risk of failure involved in this type of research in a part of the world where the issue is sensitive both from an ideological as well as a religious point of view, we believe we succeeded in meeting the objective of our study. To discover that nearly a one-third of all urban women who are sexually active in Colombia have had one abortion, and that repeat abortion is also quite common, sends a strong message to health authorities in charge of improving reproductive health policy in the country.

We also believe that the methodology we developed and then applied to a large sample of urban women has provided a general model for resolving the various obstacles that affect studies of induced abortion, especially in contexts where its practice is illegal. We were able to ensure the representativeness, reliability and validity of the information collected on a topic of high social sensitivity. Applying qualitative techniques in another phase of the study made it possible to obtain more detailed information and a better understanding of abortion determinants. We believe that the same approaches, with appropriate adjustments, could be applied in other countries of the region, especially where hospital registers are deficient and literacy is high.

Our study has revealed the magnitude and determinants of the problem of induced abortion and provided a profile of high-risk groups. Among the key reasons why women have abortion, are the low level and inconsistency of preventive behaviours, and the failure or misuse of contraceptive methods. In the high-risk category, single women under age 20 are clearly an important group, followed by any woman, regardless of marital status, who has had four or more pregnancies. Women who become pregnant in the short postpartum period (first six months), as well as those who become pregnant in the postabortion period, are also at high risk of abortion. Lastly, women who discontinue use of contraception or women who tend to shift from one method to another also have clear abortion risks.

Despite the fact that Colombia is known for its large network of family planning clinics and that private programmes, such as PROFAMILIA, have been very successful in making contraception available to Colombian women, our study results show that information on contraceptive methods, or access to them, is not a guarantee to their being used properly or used at all. The behaviour of women with regard to contraception often contains elements of mistrust of the methods and inconsistency in their use.

Our findings suggest that one-fifth of all abortions in urban Colombia could be avoided by improving access, use-effectiveness and the quality of services. And the rest, the large majority, could be reduced by intensifying prevention campaigns. Aside from knowledge of contraceptive methods and access to them, prevention involves highly complex social and cultural issues which have not so far been discussed in-depth in Colombia.

Lastly, the fact that induced abortion is illegal in Colombia results in a situation characterized by profound social discrimination. It is the poorer women, as well as the younger ones, who confront the highest risks or morbidity and mortality, the worse consequences of abortion. We hope that our findings contribute to delineate policy actions and preventive strategies that will lower induced abortion in Colombia.

23

Abortion in Ljubljana, Slovenia: A Method of Contraception or an Emergency Procedure?

Dunja Obersnel Kveder

Introduction

The continuing high prevalence of abortion has become a challenge to the experts and a topic of debate among the general public, both worldwide and in Slovenia. Increasingly, the question is asked: Why can't abortion be eradicated, or at least substantially contained? Many expected that the availability of effective contraceptives would eliminate abortion completely. With greater access to modern contraception in Slovenia, the number of abortions has indeed diminished, but it has not happened to the extent that was predicted.

An important reason for this continuing situation is that currently available modern contraceptive methods are not acceptable to everyone. Studies show that while contraceptive information may improve knowledge, it does not necessarily ensure the acceptance or use of contraception (Marshall, 1977; David, 1978; Zeidenstein, 1980). While it is unrealistic to expect that biomedical research will produce a single method with universal appeal, a higher acceptance could be achieved by providing women with a wider choice of methods suited to their varying needs. In fact, Snowden (1985) argues that contraceptive acceptance depends on the characteristics and needs of individual women. Similarly, effective contraceptive use depends on a host of motivational, attitudinal, psychological and interpersonal factors (Sachdev, 1981). Within this context, abortion remains a necessary and unavoidable solution to unwanted pregnancy when contraception fails.

From a family planning perspective, an important issue is whether women use abortion as a means of regulating fertility or as an emergency procedure to be used when contraception fails. The fear that women may replace contraception by abortion and that the availability of abortion could result in decreased motivation to use contraception has been expressed by a number of researchers (Klinger and Szabady, 1978; Steinhoff et al., 1979) as well as by the opponents of more liberal abortion laws. This fear has been reinforced by Tietze's estimations that the use of abortion as a regular means of regulating fertility can generate a very large number of abortions during a woman's fertile years (Tietze, 1983; Tietze and Henshaw, 1986). However, a number of studies have not been able to confirm Tietze's hypothesis (Kapor-Stanulovic and Friedman, 1978; Klinger and Szabady, 1978; Peled, 1978; Schneider and Tompson, 1979; Shepard and Bracken, 1979; Steinhoff et al., 1979). Moreover, Klinger and Szabady (1978), as well as Steinhoff et al. (1979), found that the reason women seek abortion is not their preference for abortion over contraception, but rather the shortage of contraceptives and contraceptive failure.

More interestingly, Aguirre (1980) does not agree with the abortion determinant researchers, most of whom have focused their research on contraceptive failure as a major indicator of abortion-seeking behaviour. He believes that the attitude towards abortion is to a larger extent determined by cultural values and social norms regulating man–woman relations in a society (e.g., marital status) than by contraceptive use. A similar opinion has been expressed by Luker (1977), who argues that some women decide to use abortion as a fertility regulating method, having made a 'cost-benefit' choice between risking pregnancy or preventing it by using less efficient contraception. In this context, contraceptive use means that a woman admits to sexual activity and renounces spontaneity in sexual intercourse. The woman's decision is made after a self-evaluation of aspirations and possibilities concerning the number of children wanted, her position in the family and in the society, and the advantages and disadvantages of available contraceptive methods.

Nevertheless, the evidence of the influence of sociodemographic characteristics and contraceptive practice on abortion seeking behaviour differs perhaps because the social contexts are different in the studies undertaken (David, 1978; Leach, 1977; Peled, 1978; Steinhoff et al., 1979).

In Slovenia, the only survey on the attitudes of women with abortion experience towards contraception, fertility regulation and abortion was carried out by Andolsek (1961). In the survey, 28 per cent of the women used abortion to regulate fertility and rejected all contraceptive devices and methods. The author recommended that more work be done to educate women, men and health professionals about contraception. She called for efforts to develop contraceptive counselling programmes and to provide greater access to modern contraceptives.

During the past decade, the family planning policy in Slovenia has, in fact, been developed along those lines, with relatively satisfying results. Following world trends on family planning legislation and organization of health services, a widely available health care network now exists that delivers fertility regulating methods to women in Slovenia at the primary health care level.

These measures have significantly contributed to a decrease in infant and maternal mortality and maternal morbidity rates (Simoneti-Kranjc, 1982).

After liberalization of the legislation on abortion in Slovenia in 1977, the number of recorded induced abortions doubled from 11,108 in 1976 to 21,185 in 1982. (The abortion rate was 23.8 per 1,000 women aged 15 to 49 years in 1976; and 41.3, in 1982). Since 1983, however, the number of abortions has been steadily decreasing by approximately 500 a year and the abortion rate decreased to 31.2 per 1,000 women aged 15 to 49 years in 1989.

The increase in the incidence of abortion occurred at a time when the number of live births had dropped below replacement level. In 1982, the average number of children per woman of reproductive age was 1.9 (total fertility rate), which was insufficient for population replacement, which is estimated at 2.1 children (Malacic, 1989). In 1989, the total fertility rate decreased even further, to 1.5 children per woman of reproductive age.

By the end of the 1980s, the use of effective methods of contraception (hormonal, IUD and barrier) was estimated at 35 per cent for women aged 15 to 49 years (Institute of Public Health of the Republic of Slovenia, 1990). Approximately 30 per cent of women of reproductive age either intended to get pregnant or already were pregnant, infertile or sexually inactive. The remaining 35 per cent were women who were engaged in regular sexual intercourse, used less effective contraceptive methods or none at all, and consequently were at a higher risk of unwanted pregnancy and abortion. It is not possible to determine whether women used abortion routinely as a contraceptive method, or only as an emergency measure when their contraceptive method had failed. This dilemma can only be resolved by getting a better insight into women's reproductive motivation and behaviour and a more detailed understanding of the factors shaping their attitude towards abortion in a specific environment (University Institute of Public Health, 1990).

Objectives of the Study

A number of studies have suggested that there is a correlation between contraceptive use and abortion in a population where both are legally accessible (Shepard and Bracken, 1979; Grady et al., 1988). This recognized correlation was the starting point for the present study, which is based on a broadened definition of the use of abortion as a fertility regulation method following Snowden (1985), who showed that the use of methods depends on users' behavioural characteristics, individual method attributes (e.g., safety, effectiveness, accessibility) and quality of services. Moreover, we assumed that a woman perceives abortion as a fertility regulating method when she is not using contraception as well as when she consciously uses a less effective contraceptive method.

To assess women's perception of abortion use, we planned to analyze data on the use of either effective contraceptive methods or less effective ones during a two-year period prior to conception and also at the time of conception. Our primary concern was to determine whether women perceive abortion as a fertility regulating method or as an emergency procedure. Our second objective was to identify the determinants that explain these two different perceptions, including associated behaviour patterns, and to measure the degree of influence, or correlation, of selected individual and psychosocial factors on them. We also wanted to verify the suitability of the use of either more or less effective contraceptive methods as a criterion for differentiating between these perceptions and associated behaviours.

Research Design and Methodology

The study was designed as a cross-sectional survey, with a simultaneous collection of current and retrospective data. In order to understand determinants of abortion perceptions and subsequent behaviour, we decided to concentrate our study on women who sought abortion for a second time or more.

All women who were pregnant up to 10 weeks and who sought abortion at the University Department of Gynaecology and Obstetrics (UDGO) in Ljubljana during the period between March and August 1988, and who were also willing to participate, were included in the study. UDGO performed 6,197 abortions in 1988, and the total abortions reported for Slovenia that year were 17,355. UDGO performs approximately 35 per cent of all abortions in Slovenia (Table 23.1).

Interviewing lasted until approximately 100 women with previous abortion experience within the last two years (recent repeat abortion) were recruited. This meant that we had to interview a much larger number of women seeking abortion in order to obtain this particular group. In the end, our survey included a total of 473 women: 102 of whom had a previous abortion within the past two years, representing 21.6 per cent of our study sample; 147 women whose last abortion had taken place more than two years before, 31.1 per cent of the study sample; and 224 women without previous abortion experience, 47.5 per cent of the study sample.

Data Collection

Before the abortion was performed, the women were interviewed by our study's social worker, who used a questionnaire designed to collect data on the personal and psychosocial characteristics that we hoped would identify one of the two behaviour patterns under observation. It contained nominal variables regarding personal attributes, religion, socioeconomic status, contraceptive knowledge and use, abortion experience, reasons for not using contraceptives and for seeking abortion and contraceptive advice seeking.

Ordinal and numeric variables were used because they are suitable for analysis of variance, and also for discriminant and multiple regression analysis.

The following variables were included: age, education, educational aspiration, career aspirations, estimated level of income, number of children, reproductive aspirations, abortion experience, attitudes towards abortion and perception of contraceptive counselling provided.

Definition of Outcome

Since all the women in our study were soliciting an induced abortion, and more than half had previous abortion experience, the outcome was defined as women's perception of abortion use. The development of specific perceptions concerning abortion use is part of a process involving well-defined behaviour patterns; that is, using less effective contraception, frequent method switching or discontinuing method use. We therefore felt it necessary to analyze contraceptive use not only at the time of the last conception that led to this particular abortion, but also during a specific reference period prior to it. This allowed us, for example, to include women who got pregnant because of method switching, a behaviour pattern that in subsequent analysis turned out to be risky.

We created two different categories of this perception:

1. Use of abortion as a fertility regulating method was defined in the study as the woman's sole reliance on abortion to regulate her fertility without any use of condoms or medically prescribed contraception (hormonal, intrauterine, diaphragm) within the previous 24 months despite regular sexual intercourse (once or more per week);
2. Use of abortion as an emergency procedure, defined in the study as the woman seeking abortion because her regular and usual use of medically prescribed contraception (including condoms) had been interrupted or had failed, leading to an unplanned and unwanted pregnancy.

We defined the more effective contraceptive methods as hormonal, IUD, and barrier (diaphragm and condom), all characterized by a very low pregnancy rate (between 0.7 per cent and 5 per cent). All the other methods were categorized as less effective. The term abortion was used for a legal, medical termination of pregnancy. As noted before, abortion is legal in Slovenia and, therefore, easily accessible.

Data Analysis

The statistical analysis was done after first organizing the set of explanatory variables into two groups: The nominal variables were analyzed by means of contingency tables, using the Chi-square test; and the ordinal variables were examined using analysis of variance, discriminant analysis and multiple regression analysis (Nachmias and Nachmias, 1981; Kosmelj, 1983).

In our analysis, these different types of multivariate methods were used to allow for a simultaneous measurement of independent effects of users' characteristics on their specific perception of abortion use. Unfortunately, these statistical methods have some shortcomings. They can only be applied to ordinal variables and not to nominal variables such as religion, socioeconomic status and contraceptive advice seeking. Were it possible to include the latter group in the analysis, it might have had a significant effect on the power of some of the determinants as well as on the perception of abortion use itself.

Demographic and Reproductive Characteristics of the Sample

The average age of the women participating in the study was 28 years, the youngest being 14 years and the oldest, 44 years. Six per cent of the sample were teenagers. Nearly 70 per cent of the women were married and 85.9 per cent were employed. Nearly half of the women (46 per cent) had 12 or more years of education. A great majority earned their own income (86.3 per cent) and lived in a family (90.9 per cent), with a relatively good atmosphere (96.7 per cent). However, their income level was less satisfying: 23.6 per cent of the women said it was insufficient, and an additional 16 per cent said they had to restrict their purchases if they wanted to make ends meet. Living conditions were perceived as inadequate by 35.7 per cent of these women. One-fifth of the women had no children; 27.2 per cent had one child; 41 per cent had two children; and 11.3 per cent had three or more children (Table 23.1).

The 102 women, whose last abortion had taken place within the last two years, represented 41.0 per cent of the total of 249 women with previous

Table 23.1: Characteristics of the Women in the Study Sample Compared to Women Having Abortion at the UDGO in Ljubljana and in Slovenia, 1988

Characteristic	Study Group		All Women, UDGO		All Women, Slovenia	
	(N)	%	(N)	%	(N)	%
Age (years)						
< 19	29	6.1	428	6.9	1,165	6.7
20–24	126	26.6	1,430	23.1	3,871	22.3
25–29	130	27.5	1,534	24.8	4,383	25.3
30–34	111	23.4	1,365	22.0	3,941	22.7
35–39	58	12.2	983	15.9	2,761	15.9
> 40	20	4.2	457	7.3	1,234	7.1
Marital status						
Single	96	30.4	1,865	30.1	4,554	26.2
Married	366	67.3	4,166	67.2	12,368	71.3
Divorced	10	2.1	142	2.3	364	2.1
Widowed	1	0.2	24	0.4	69	0.4

Table 23.1 continued

Education (years)						
< 8	29	6.1	122	2.0	415	2.3
8	125	26.4	2,120	34.2	7,318	42.2
10	102	21.5	1,089	17.6	3,359	19.4
12	155	32.8	2,200	35.5	4,942	28.5
> 14	62	13.2	666	10.7	1,321	7.6
Employment						
Employed	406	85.9	5,484	88.5	15,231	87.8
Unemployed	67	14.1	713	11.5	2,124	12.2
No. of children						
0	97	20.5	1,585	25.6	3,304	19.0
1	129	27.2	1,582	25.5	4,429	25.5
2	193	41.0	2,458	39.6	7,671	44.2
> 3	54	11.3	572	9.3	1,951	11.3
Total (N)	473		6,197		17,355	

Note: UDGO stands for the University Department of Gynaecology and Obstetrics.

abortion experience. For half of them, the interval since the last abortion was less than a year; and for the other half, less than two years (Table 23.2).

A comparison of certain characteristics of our study sample, such as the proportions of adolescent, employed, single and childless women, with those

Table 23.2: Contraceptive Use Before the Conception, by Education, Number of Children, Perception of the Method Used and Abortion Experience

Variable	More Effective Method*		Less Effective Method		Non-User		Total Study Sample	
	(N)	%	(N)	%	(N)	%	(N)	%
Education (years)								
< 8	62	25.4	87	40.8	5	31.3	154	32.6
8+	182	74.6	126	59.2	11	68.7	319	67.4
Number of children								
0	61	25.0	30	14.1	6	37.5	97	20.5
> 1	183	75.0	183	85.9	10	62.5	376	79.5
Perception of contraceptive method								
More effective	210	86.1	108	50.7	2	12.5	320	67.5
Less effective	34	13.9	105	49.3	14	87.5	153	32.5
Previous abortion								
No abortion	81	33.2	131	61.5	12	75.0	224	47.4
Within 2 years	82	33.6	20	9.4	–	–	102	21.5
Earlier	81	33.2	62	29.1	4	25.0	147	31.1

* Hormonal, intrauterine and barrier (diaphragm and condom).
+ All other methods.

of the total population of women who had an abortion in the whole of Slovenia in 1988 did not show significant differences. However, the proportion of women under 30 years of age and the average level of education were higher in the study group than in the total population.

Results of the Study

Contraceptive Use Before Conception

In the two years prior to the current unwanted pregnancy, most women had been using a contraceptive method to regulate their fertility. The sample was divided almost evenly between women who used a more effective method (45.9 per cent) and those who used a less effective method (50 per cent). Only 4.2 per cent did nothing to prevent pregnancy.

There was no statistically significant effect of age on the use of either more or less effective methods. Educational level did have an association, however: Users of more effective contraception and non-users had substantially more education than users of less effective contraception. Three out of every four users of effective methods had more than eight years of schooling compared to 60 per cent among users of less effective methods.

We were surprised by the relationship between levels of contraceptive use and fertility. Higher fertility women, with more than one child, were using less effective methods, which indicates some degree of unmet need for family planning. One-fourth of the users of effective contraception had no children, but the highest proportion of women with no children was found among the non-users (Table 23.2).

Only half of the women had consulted their gynaecologists during the last two years regarding the most appropriate contraceptive method to use. Among the women who had sought contraceptive advice during the period before conception, a significantly higher proportion used more effective contraceptive methods (66.4 per cent compared to 39 per cent of the users of less effective methods).

When women were asked how they perceived the effectiveness of the method they had been using, 13.9 per cent of the users of effective contraception perceived their method as less effective. Even more surprising and significant is that half of the women who were using less effective contraception (50.7 per cent) perceived their method as more effective than it actually was. Non-users were generally aware of the risk they had been taking. The differences between these three groups were statistically significant.

Users of more effective methods had significantly more abortion experience than users of less effective methods and non-users. Among the women with previous abortion experience, who were users of effective methods, half got pregnant again less than two years after the last abortion, but there was no statistically significant difference in contraceptive use between this group and the rest of the women with abortion experience (Table 23.2). Multivariate analysis of variance of the number of abortions showed that, on average, women who had used more effective methods in the two years before the last conception had had more abortions than non-users of contraception (1.1 compared to 0.5).

Multiple regression analysis was used to determine the joint influence of the variables under investigation on contraceptive use before conception. Simultaneous inclusion of the selected variables into the model (the Enter method) showed that contraceptive use before conception was most strongly affected by perception of effectiveness of the method used and number of previous abortions. Educational level and educational aspirations had a statistically significant effect as well. The model explained 25 per cent of the variance in contraceptive use before conception (Table 23.3).

Table 23.3: **Multiple Regression of Contraceptive Use Before Conception°**

Independent Variable	Contraceptive Use (β coefficients)
Perception of contraceptive effectiveness	0.41**
Number of children	−0.05
Attitude towards abortion	0.05
Number of abortions	0.14**
Educational level	0.11*
Educational aspirations	0.11*
Reproductive aspirations	0.02
R square	0.248

° Use in the two years prior to conception.
* Significant at 0.05 level.
** Significant at 0.001 level.

Contraceptive Use at the Time of Conception

At the time of conception, overall contraceptive use was still high at 90.9 per cent, which was only 5 per cent lower than during the two-year interval prior to conception. However, three-quarters of the women (75.1 per cent) were using less effective contraceptive methods, a proportion 50 per cent higher than during the two-year period prior to conception. We also found that the use of more effective methods had decreased by 65 per cent (Table 23.4). Moreover, of the only 15.8 per cent of the women who were using more effective methods at the time of conception, 55 per cent who were users of hormonal contraceptives had used their method inconsistently or improperly, as did 78 per cent of diaphragm users and 50 per cent of women whose partners used a condom. Thus, probably only 33 women, or 7 per cent of the study/ sample, were properly and reliably protected against pregnancy at the time of conception.

**Table 23.4: Contraceptive Use Before Conception and at Conception,
by Type of Contraception**

Type of Contraception	Before Conception*		At Conception	
	(N)	%	(N)	%
More effective	217	45.9	75	15.8
Less effective	236	49.9	355	75.1
None	20	4.2	43	9.1
Total	473	100.0	473	100.0

* Use in the two years prior to conception.

A total of 43 women (9.1 per cent) used no contraception, which is twice the number of non-users in the two years prior to conception. Almost half of these women could not or would not give a reason for this; 28 per cent said that they had wanted to have a child, but changed their mind after getting pregnant; 16.3 per cent had been relying on breastfeeding; 7 per cent had discontinued for health reasons; and one woman had run out of pills.

Discontinuation and Method Switching

In our discussion, the concept of 'discontinuation' is used to mean that a woman has stopped using any kind of contraception. 'Method switching' is used to describe a woman who changed her method, but continued to use contraception.

A high continuation rate was found for users of less effective methods in the two-year period prior to conception: 96.6 per cent had continued using the same method until the time of conception. Only eight out of the 236 women (3.4 per cent) had discontinued a method use, and none had switched to a more effective method. At the time of conception, the number of users of less effective contraceptive methods had increased by 45.8 per cent, as women using more effective methods switched to less effective ones.

Surprisingly, the lowest continuation rate was found for users of more effective methods during the two-year interval prior to conception: only one-third continued to use a more effective method. Thus, at the time of conception, the percentage of users of more effective methods had dropped by almost 70 per cent; only 73 women (15.4 per cent of the total sample) were still using a more effective method.

As expected, the most stable behaviour was found among the original non-users, who by the end of the interval, had increased in number by 56 per cent (from 20 to 45 women), because they were joined by eight women who had discontinued the use of less effective methods and by 17 women who had discontinued the use of more effective methods.

Using Pearson's correlation coefficient (the more exact Spearman's correlation coefficient could not be computed due to a specific data distribution), the statistically significant positive correlation between contraceptive use at the time of conception and contraceptive use during the two-year period prior to conception was confirmed ($R = 0.43$, $p < 0.001$). In short, this means that women who had been using contraception before conception were also using it at the time of conception, although the methods used were mostly the less effective ones.

We also found some statistically significant differences between non-users and users of more effective methods at the time of conception, analyzing the two-year interval prior to conception. Non-users had the smallest number of children and of abortions, desired the largest number of children in the future, and had a lower level of education than the users of more effective methods. It should be noted also that this group is made up of very small numbers (Table 23.2). Conversely, users of more effective methods had more abortions and more children, did not want any more children, and were better educated. Users of less effective methods before the conception fell somewhere in-between these other two groups with regard to the examined variables. It would seem that the influence of education on effective use of contraception is clearly at work here and that it is also an indication of a commitment to maintaining a specific family size, which in any case is very small in this low fertility country.

The simultaneous inclusion of all the variables in a regression model showed that the factor with the greatest effect on contraceptive use at the time of conception was contraceptive use before conception. Another statistically significant factor was the number of living children. The variables included in the model explained 20.4 per cent of the total variance in contraceptive use at the time of conception (Table 23.5).

Table 23.5: Multiple Regression of Contraceptive Use at the Time of Conception

Independent Variable	Contraception at Conception (β coefficients)
Attitude towards abortion	−0.027
Number of abortions	0.023
Educational aspirations	−0.017
Contraceptive use before conception	0.433**
Educational level	0.070
Reproductive aspirations	0.000
Number of children	0.118*
R square	0.204

* Significant at 0.05 level.
** Significant at 0.001 level.

Behaviour Patterns of Contraceptive Users

It is generally known that the best indicators of effective fertility regulation are the contraceptive effectiveness rate and the contraceptive failure rate.

We used these criteria to classify the women in our study into three groups and consequently compared their characteristics and behaviour patterns.

Group 1 consisted of highly motivated women who were continuous users of more effective contraception during most of the two-year interval prior to conception and at the time of conception.

Group 2 also included highly motivated women, but they were less consistent in their use of more effective contraception during most of the two-year period before conception. They then either switched to a less effective method or discontinued altogether.

Group 3 consisted of women who used less effective contraception or none at all, during the two-year period prior to conception and at the time of conception. They may be regarded as the least motivated group.

Comparison of Characteristics

Group 1 had the fewest number of women (73 women, 15.5 per cent of the sample); and group 2 contained almost one-third of the sample (144 women, 30.6 per cent). Interestingly, it was the less motivated group 3 who comprised more than half of the total sample (254 women, 53.9 per cent), while the youngest women were in group 1. Most of these women in group 3 were married (82 per cent), although there was a high number of married women in the other two groups as well (72 per cent).

The more educated women were concentrated, as expected, in groups 1 and 2. Only 59 per cent of the women in group 3 had completed more than eight years of education, compared with 80.8 per cent and 75 per cent, in groups 1 and 2, respectively. This difference was statistically significant. Similarly, higher educational aspirations were expressed by one-fourth of the women in groups 1 and 2, compared to only 10.6 per cent in group 3. In short, the data clearly showed that higher educated women were using more effective contraception and were more motivated to regulate their fertility.

Group 3 was also different from the other two in occupational activity, with a significantly higher proportion of employed women in comparison to the other two groups.

Women's socioeconomic status was determined on the basis of estimated income level, number of income earners in the household, and the quality of interpersonal relations within the household. Statistically significant differences among the groups were found only in the number of income earners in the household.

Regarding fertility levels, group 2 had the lowest average number of living children, while group 3 had the highest average number (1.6); the proportion of women with no children was highest in group 1 (28.8 per cent). Over half of the women in groups 1 and 3 (57.2 per cent and 58.5 per cent, respectively) had two or more children. The differences among the groups were statistically significant at the 5 per cent level. Group 1 contained both the highest number of women who wanted no more children (54.8 per cent) and the highest number of those who still wanted to have them (38.4 per cent). This made sense, as one-third of the women in this group had not yet had a child.

Regarding previous abortion experience, groups 1 and 2 were nearly the same (61.6 per cent and 63.9 per cent, respectively) and group 3, the women who were using less effective methods or no method at all, had significantly less abortion experience than the other two groups (47.9 per cent). On average, women in groups 1 and 2 had 1.1 previous abortions, and women in group 3 had 0.7 abortions. The most frequent reason given for abortion in all three groups was the decision to have no more children. In groups 1 and 3, half of the women gave this reason. A lack of adequate resources to raise a child was the second reason, and the most frequent in group 2 (29.9 per cent). Childbirth spacing was an important reason in groups 1 and 3 (21.9 per cent and 15.4 per cent, respectively).

Discriminant analysis (with one statistically significant discriminating variable) showed the greatest difference between groups 2 and 3 in educational level, educational aspiration, number of living children and number of abortions (Table 23.6). Group 1 and group 2 behaved similarly. But group 3 remained apart: these women were the least educated, the most satisfied with their level of education, and had the highest levels of fertility and abortion. Conversely, group 2 had the highest educational level, with the highest aspiration to improve it further, and the lowest number of children and of abortions.

We also examined women's attitudes towards abortion. The discriminant analysis again revealed similar patterns between groups 1 and 2 and major differences in group 3. More specifically, women in group 3 did not agree for certain that abortion was a shameful practice and they seemed more willing

Table 23.6: Discriminant Analysis of Individual Variables in the Three Groups of Contraceptive Users

Variable	Standard Discriminant Weights
Age	0.00
Educational level	0.63
Educational aspirations	0.50
Career aspirations	−0.11
Estimated income	0.04
Number of children	−0.39
Reproductive aspirations	−0.18
Number of abortions	0.56
Group centroids	
Group 1	0.36
Group 2	0.40
Group 3	−0.33
Canonical discriminant function coefficient	0.34
Chi square	68.18

than the other two groups to accept abortion when contraception had failed. Therefore, their indecision concerning abortion changed to a more acceptable attitude when faced with contraceptive failure. Women in group 3 also tended to agree with the statement that abortion was not better than other contraceptive options, but they were not sure whether or not it was an effective fertility regulating method.

The greatest difference in attitudes toward abortion was observed between groups 2 and 3. Women in group 2 did not consider abortion to be a shameful practice, but they were not certain if it was acceptable when there were no other contraceptive methods available (Table 23.7). They also felt uncertain about whether or not abortion was better than other contraceptive methods and whether or not it was an effective fertility regulation method. In short, as noted earlier, women in group 3, who were users of less effective methods or not users at all, tended to be somewhat more inclined to accept abortion when faced with unwanted pregnancy than women in the other two groups whose contraceptive behaviour was more effective.

Discussion and Conclusions

The question of whether women tend to use abortion as an emergency procedure to complement contraception when it fails or to rely exclusively on contraception or abortion to regulate their fertility has not been answered. In practice women do use abortion when contraception fails but it is less clear that they rely on abortion as their only method of fertility regulation.

Our results show that most women did use contraception either permanently or only during a limited period of time prior to conception (95.8 per cent) and at conception (90.9 per cent). The high proportions indicate that easy accessibility of abortion did not reduce motivation to use contraception. These findings agree with those of some other investigators (Klinger and Szabady, 1978; Steinhoff et al., 1979). In the two-year period prior to conception, half of the women studied used more effective contraception and half used less effective methods. However, at the time of their last conception, only 15.8 per cent were still using effective contraception, while as many as 75 per cent were using less effective methods. The change is the result of beliefs among women, often users of more effective methods, that they may be protected after discontinuing use. Also, a substantial proportion of women, 30.6 per cent, switched from more effective methods to less effective ones.

A similar behaviour pattern was found by Grady et al. (1988), who analyzed reproductive behaviour of married American women: During the course of one year, 28 per cent of the women changed their contraceptive behaviour (15 per cent switched to another method and 13 per cent discontinued), for a number of personal reasons besides planned or unplanned pregnancy and divorce. In the same study, users of more effective contraceptive methods (hormonal, intrauterine, barrier) rarely decided to discontinue, and if they

Table 23.7: Discriminant Analysis of Attitudes Towards Abortion in the
Three Groups of Contraceptive Users

Attitude	Standard Discriminant Weights
Abortion is a very effective fertility regulation method	0.29
Abortion is not suitable for young women	0.24
Abortion is socially acceptable	−0.23
Abortion is an ideal fertility regulating method	−0.19
Abortion should be kept secret from the family	−0.40
Abortion should be used only if other contraceptive methods have failed to be effective	−0.22
Abortion is very harmful for woman's health	−0.12
Abortion is better than any other contraceptive method	0.44
Abortion is shameful	0.62
Man, too, should take responsibility for his partner's seeking abortion	0.20
Abortion should be kept secret from friends	0.03
Abortion may be used as a regular fertility regulating method	−0.31
Abortion is acceptable when other contraceptive methods are not available	0.62
Abortion should only be used when a woman cannot (is not allowed to) use any other contraceptive method	−0.12
Groups centroids	
Group 1	0.24
Group 2	0.48
Group 3	−0.34
Canonical discriminant function coefficient	0.35
Chi square	67.96

did, they more often switched to another method than discontinued contraceptive use altogether.

The same author also believes that switching from one contraceptive method to another is a very important indicator of contraceptive method acceptability and has a direct effect on use effectiveness. The most effective fertility regulating methods are those with a low pregnancy rate and a high continuation rate. But it is important to distinguish between method switching and discontinuation, a distinction that is often difficult to establish, especially when women get pregnant unintentionally and eventually have abortion. One explanation for this may be that women who report switching from a more effective method to a less effective one, actually did not use the latter, which was the case in our study. It may be assumed that in distress, women blame an unplanned pregnancy on the method they had been using occasionally and which was less effective. Naturally, these women exhibiting this pattern of switching and erratic use have a higher abortion risk.

We also suspect that use of more effective contraceptive methods does not prevent unplanned pregnancy to the extent it could, in view these methods' effects on physiology, particularly the woman's ability to withstand any side effects. The risk of method discontinuation when side effects are not tolerated, combined with an illusory feeling of prolonged protection against pregnancy after discontinuation, leads to unwanted pregnancy. This creates the same risk of unplanned pregnancy as when less effective methods are used. Under these circumstances, the question of which women may be said to perceive abortion as an emergency procedure and which may be said to perceive it as a fertility regulating method becomes important.

Abortion was undoubtedly an emergency procedure for the 15.5 per cent of the women in our sample who had continued to use a more effective contraceptive method up to the time of conception (irrespective of the fact that over half these women admitted they had used their method irregularly or inadequately in the past).

More difficult is the interpretation of perception of abortion use by the 30.6 per cent of the women who had switched from a more effective contraceptive method to a less effective one or were not using any method when the pregnancy occurred. However, if they did discontinue, it may be assumed that they consciously or, more likely, subconsciously perceived abortion as a fertility regulating alternative in case of unplanned pregnancy. Luker (1977) says that some women may decide to use abortion as a fertility regulating method, after having assessed their reproductive aspirations and possibilities for their realization, including advantages and disadvantages of available contraception.

It seems more likely that the women in our study who appeared to have discontinued use of an effective method, more often switched to a less effective one. This would allow us to conclude with a higher degree of confidence that they actually perceived abortion as an emergency procedure. Such a conclusion is supported by the fact that these women have similar personal and demographic characteristics to those women who continued using more effective contraceptive methods and chose abortion only as an emergency procedure. They are very similar at a statistically significant level in their educational level, educational aspirations, number of living children, number of previous abortions, perception of contraceptive counselling provision and in two of the attitudes towards abortion (i.e., 'abortion is shameful' and 'abortion is acceptable when other contraceptive methods are not available').

Also difficult to understand is the behaviour pattern of over half the remaining sample, 53.9 per cent of the women who had regular sexual relations and yet continued to use a less effective method or no method at all. (Twenty-four women, or 9.4 per cent, were not using a method at the time of conception.) Although the risk of getting pregnant was very high, it seemed that many of them were not consciously aware of this risk. This is supported by the fact that this group had above-average contraceptive use and half of them reported they had thought the method they were using was an effective protection against pregnancy. It may therefore be concluded that they also perceived abortion as an emergency procedure, at least at a conscious level.

However, this conclusion is much more tentative and more easily contested than for the other groups.

In summary, the factors with the strongest effect on contraceptive use before conception were a woman's perception of the effectiveness of the method used and the number of previous abortions; and to a lesser extent, the woman's educational level and educational aspirations. These four variables could explain only 24.4 per cent of the variance in contraceptive behaviour before conception, however. At conception, the strongest determinants were contraceptive use before conception and number of children. Yet, only 19.9 per cent of the variance was explained by these variables. It may be assumed, therefore, that the mechanisms controlling the motivation to use contraception and the decision to continue its use are very complex, difficult to account for and, above all, extremely subjective.

Perhaps the chosen approach to explaining women's perception of abortion use through the analysis of contraceptive use, although a logical one, is not the best one. In the Slovenian population, where abortion and contraception are universally accessible, it would probably be more fruitful to define the parameters of contraceptive behaviour in more detail and to observe them over a longer period of time. Still another possibility that should be considered is that contraceptive use is of no significant relevance for the perception of abortion use, as claimed by Aguirre (1980). A more important factor in the decision to terminate a pregnancy may be the commitment to a particular level of fertility that couples may have and their motivation for meeting that goal.

It is hoped that the present study will stimulate family planning researchers to pay increased attention to the complex determinants and factors that explain sexual and reproductive behaviour and specific contraceptive use patterns, including abortion. This information can be helpful to providers so they can take action to help women to prevent unplanned pregnancies. We hope our study contributes to demonstrating that proper and continuous use of effective contraceptive methods can prevent unplanned pregnancy and in this way protect women's reproductive health. Abortion under these circumstances would be less necessary, particularly as a method of contraception.

✝ References

Aguirre, B.E. 1980. Repeat induced abortion: Single, married and divorced women. *Journal of Biosocial Science* 12: 275.

Andolsek, L. 1961. Kako gledaju na kontracepciju zene, koje su imale dozvoljeni pobacaj (How abortion is perceived by women who have had abortion). *Ginek i opstetr* (3–4): 71–6.

David, H.P. 1978. Psychosocial studies of abortion in the United States. *In*: H.P. David, H.L. Friedman, J. Van Der Tak and M.J. Sevilla (eds). *Abortion in psychosocial perspective: Trends in transnational research*. New York: Springer Verlag, p. 77.

Grady, W.R., M.D. Hayward and F.A. Florey. 1988. Contraceptive discontinuation among married women in the United States. *Studies in Family Planning* 19 (4): 227.

Institute of Public Health of the Republic of Slovenia. 1990. *Health Statistical Annual, Slovenia, 1990.* Slovenia: Institute of Public Health of the Republic of Slovenia.

Kapor-Stanulovic, N. and **H.L. Friedman.** 1978. Studies in choice behaviour in Yugoslavia. *In:* H.P. David, H.L. Friedman, J. Van Der Tak and M.J. Sevilla (eds). *Abortion in psychosocial perspective: Trends in transnational research.* New York: Springer Verlag, p. 119.

Klinger, A. and **E. Szabady.** 1978. Patterns of abortion and contraceptive practice in Hungary. *In:* H.P. David, H.L. Friedman, J. Van Der Tak and M.J. Sevilla (eds). *Abortion in psychosocial perspective: Trends in transnational research.* New York: Springer Verlag, p. 168.

Kosmelj, B. 1983. *Uvod v Multivariatno Analizo (An introduction to multivariate analysis).* Ljubljana: Ekonomska Fakulteta.

Leach, J. 1977. The repeat abortion patient. *Family Planning Perspectives* 9: 37.

Luker, K. 1977. Contraceptive risk taking and abortion: Results and implementation of a San Francisco area study. *Studies in Family Planning* 8: 190.

Malacic, J. 1989. Prenizka rodnost in pretirano staranje prebivalstva ali kaksna je prihodnost pred razvitim delom sveta (in Slovenijo) (Excessively low fertility and excessive aging of population or what future is facing the developed world [and Slovenia]). *Srce in oko* (Jan): 26–34.

Marshall, J.F. 1977. Acceptability of fertility regulating methods: Designing technology to fit people. *Preventive Medicine* 6: 65–73.

Nachmias, D. and **C. Nachmias.** 1981. *Research methods in the social sciences.* New York: St. Martin's Press.

Peled, T. 1978. Psychosocial aspects of abortion in Israel. *In:* H.P. David, H.L. Friedman, J. Van Der Tak and M.J. Sevilla (eds). *Abortion in psychosocial perspective: Trends in transnational research.* New York: Springer Verlag, p. 57.

Sachdev, P. (ed.). 1981. *Abortion: Readings and research.* Scarborough, Canada: Butterworth.

Schneider, S.M. and **D.S. Tompson.** 1979. Repeat aborters. *American Journal of Obstetrics and Gynaecology* 126: 316.

Shepard, M.J. and **M.B. Bracken.** 1979. Contraceptive practice and repeat induced abortion: An epidemiological investigation. *Journal of Biosocial Science* 11: 289.

Simoneti-Kranjc, S. 1982. Nacrtovanje potomstva v aktivnem zdravstvenem varstvu v SR Sloveniji (Planning the progeny in active health care system in the Socialist Republic of Slovenia). *Medrazgl* 21: 229–38.

Snowden, R. 1985. *Consumer choices in family planning.* London: Family Planning Association.

Steinhoff, P.G., R.G. Smith, J.A. Palmore, M. Daimond and **C.S. Chung.** 1979. Women who obtain repeat abortions: A study based on record linkage. *Family Planning Perspectives* 11: 30.

Tietze, C. 1983. *Induced abortion: A world review 1983.* New York: The Population Council.

Tietze, C. and **S.K. Henshaw.** 1986. *Induced abortion: A world review 1986.* New York: The Alan Guttmacher Institute.

University Institute of Public Health. 1990. Zdravstveni statisticni letopis Slovenije 1989. (The 1989 health care statistical annals of Slovenia.) *Zdrav var* Suppl 1: 11–25.

Zeidenstein, G. 1980. The user perspective: An evolutionary step in contraceptive service programs. *Studies in Family Planning* 11 (1): 24–29.

✝

24

Research Methodology:
Lessons Learnt

Axel I. Mundigo

Introduction

The study of abortion behaviour, especially its determinants and consequences, requires the utilization of exploratory research methods, often inno-
vating or combining techniques derived from a variety of disciplines. The
authors of chapters in this book have drawn their research methods from
anthropology, demography, epidemiology, psychology, and health services
research. The book stresses the social and psychological dimensions of
induced abortion, therefore research designs are firmly anchored in the
methodology of the social sciences. Given the difficulties inherent in measuring the actual incidence of induced abortion in countries where this practice
is illegal, it was decided from the start not to give priority to estimating incidence levels, with one exception that seemed particularly promising, the
study conducted in Colombia by Zamudio and her colleagues. In recent times
major efforts to estimate incidence levels, utilizing hospital and other data
have been conducted by researchers associated with the Alan Guttmacher
Institute (see for example Alan Guttmacher Institute, 1994; Remez, 1995;
Singh and Wulf, 1991; 1994). As Henry David (1993) has remarked: 'one reason for the difficulty of estimating the incidence stems from the fact that in
many countries abortion has long been shrouded in secrecy, enmeshed in cultural taboos, and surrounded with personal value conflicts.' The same reasons apply when shifting the question from the how many to the why.

This book is mostly devoted to answering the question: why do women opt
for induced abortion even when contraception is available. Undoubtedly for
most women in the developing world where abortion is unsafe contraception
offers a better choice. In fact the great puzzle that the book findings bring to
light is the existence of considerable levels of induced abortion in countries
known to have excellent family planning programmes, such as Mauritius,

Mexico or Colombia. In these circumstances what was required was to go beyond the mere issue of large numbers and try to understand the root problem. A highly personal and private behaviour, stigmatized by society, condemned by community and neighbours, is not easily studied by applying structured questionnaires in large surveys (Huntington et al., 1993). While following a life history pattern to designing questionnaires would facilitate the organization of the data to be analyzed, this option may not give the researcher the answers he or she is looking for. To the contrary, induced abortion has to be approached as part of a larger more flexible conceptual framework, often relating it to other reproductive health issues for women to answer questions without embarrassment.

Several studies showed that for many women denial is a protective device to avoid dealing with the reality of their abortion experience, often expressed in terms of real or feigned memory loss of past events (Bleek, 1987). In other cases women did acknowledge their having had an abortion but declared it as being spontaneous. It was only when qualitative techniques were used that researchers could move women away from denial or alteration of events to the harsher reality of their abortion behaviour. In some cultures, where even simpler health issues are relegated to discussions among the most intimate family members, the mere idea of publicly relating episodes as potentially traumatic as an induced abortion added to the difficulties of studying this issue.

Recently a paper by several authors associated with the Department of Epidemiology of the London School of Hygiene bluntly stated: 'In most developing countries, the consequences for women's health, the social and cultural context within which induced abortions are performed, and even the levels and data characteristics of women resorting to abortion are unknown' (Barreto et al., 1992). They add: 'The neglect of induced abortion research extends to methodological issues.' Among the greatest challenges from a methodological viewpoint is to establish a clear relationship between induced abortion and contraception. In countries where abortion is legal and the practice is not socially stigmatized, this is possible and the studies in China and Turkey reported in this book are good illustrations of attempts to show the interaction between contraception and induced abortion. Abortion among adolescents, including the partner's role, is another urgent research priority that poses formidable methodological difficulties.

Qualitative Studies

Anthropological techniques such as direct observation, in-depth interviewing utilizing interview guides, focus group discussions (FGDs) and subject-focused one-on-one discussions are particularly well-suited to pursue difficult questions such as those that arise in abortion research, e.g., why did you choose to terminate your last pregnancy? While the strength of FGDs lies in the ability for the researcher to observe the nature of the interaction on a particular topic, they may present difficulties when the topic is very sensitive (Morgan, 1988). Among the panoply of qualitative methods, in-depth interviews are particularly well-suited when the population being studied is made up of adolescents or young adult women experiencing unwanted pregnancy and facing the dilemma of single motherhood or abortion. The interview process itself may help them to clarify the implications of their choices. FGDs can also be attempted in such cases but they may be less useful and more difficult to undertake when adolescents have already aborted and are traumatized by the experience. In these cases the one-on-one interview is the more appropriate approach. The researcher who wants to learn more than the descriptive variables outlining the personal background of the young woman will have to carefully assess various data collection options in order to delve into the psychological and emotional circumstances leading to the abortion. This includes the adolescent's understanding of her own reproductive physiology, knowledge of contraception and perceptions of her sexuality. The chapter by Ehrenfeld who conducted a study of adolescents in Mexico illustrates the problems encountered when trying to obtain volunteers for FGDs among post-abortion cases as opposed to a group experiencing unwanted pregnancy. In some cases girls were forbidden to return for an additional interview session by their partners and in others they were uncomfortable in relating their abortion experience in front of others. The various studies that used these techniques corroborate Helitzer-Allen et al.'s (1994) assertion that focus groups alone are insufficient 'as the sole data-gathering method in situations when sensitive information is needed'. As a whole, the WHO studies show that FGDs provide a broad overview of the cultural and situational underpinnings leading to unwanted pregnancy or abortion but that the more detailed information needed to understand the decision processes can only be derived from in-depth interviews conducted in privacy and in a supportive environment.

A major difficulty when undertaking abortion research is finding out who has had an abortion in order to then continue through the application of qualitative techniques probing into more difficult experiential terrain, such as determinants of the decision, partner involvement, expectations, and so forth. We found that the most common way to identify a population at risk of abortion or a population with proven abortion experience was by studying women with abortion complications in a hospital or clinic. Starting from populations of known cases or potential cases of induced abortion in clinic settings, several researchers then moved to investigate the underlying factors applying in-depth interviewing and other qualitative techniques.

Many of the studies reported in this book also mix qualitative and quantitative approaches and only a few can be called of a 'pure' type. Among the exceptions are the study of health providers conducted in Indonesia by Djohan et al. and the study of adolescents in Mexico, by Ehrenfeld. Similarly, the study by Zhou in China relied on qualitative methods for collecting data on people's beliefs about the effect of induced abortion on subsequent pregnancies and their outcomes.

When qualitative and quantitative approaches are combined, the mix can take diverse routes. In the Mexico study by Elu, the main objective was to identify the factors that affect a woman's decision to undergo an abortion under illegal circumstances. The study first surveyed women admitted with abortion complications to a large maternity hospital in Mexico City. The survey provided the demographic and socioeconomic profiles of these women but the antecedent factors, the process of decision-making, the personal experiences and the nature of the inter-partner relations leading to the abortion came from in-depth interviews with a sub-sample of these women. The study also included FGDs with hospital staff to obtain providers views concerning post-abortion care and the problems in servicing these cases.

In other cases, qualitative approaches were used as a basis to develop instruments for structured surveys. This was the approach taken by Akin in her study in two provinces of Turkey. As part of the preparatory phase for the main survey, 25 FGDs were conducted in both Ankara and Van province. The data obtained from the FGDs were supplemented by means of semi-structured interviews. On the basis of this information the final survey questionnaires were constructed. The exact wording and language used in this survey was important since the objective was to examine independently men's and women's views of themselves, particularly their self-esteem, their standing in the family, the community and the nation. The researchers then linked these self-assessments to the practice of withdrawal and abortion, both of which are common in Turkey. While the procedure followed here is an excellent way to ensure that the linguistic codes being used in the quantitative survey are fully validated, there seems to be no real need to conduct 25 FGDs to achieve this purpose. Since the study was conducted in a rural province and in and around a metropolitan area, the culture and linguistic nuances may be quite different yet it can be safely assumed that with a third of the FGDs the same objective can be achieved.

Despite our efforts to separate qualitative from quantitative studies, the fact is that most of the survey-based chapters also utilized the tools of qualitative methods, often in the preparation of questionnaires, or once analyses were completed, for validation purposes, particularly if findings seemed inconclusive. Similarly, those who used qualitative methods often relied in a mix of data collection approaches, which, as Khan and Manderson (1992) noted, is more reliable and likely to yield valid social data. Khan and others have also noted the importance of long periods of field observation to get a better understanding of the context in which perceptions, attitudes or behaviours evolved.

An important lesson that was learnt from the WHO research effort is that when focusing on extremely personal aspects of human behaviour, such as abortion, the cultural nuances and the circumstances involved could not have been faithfully documented without the fine-tuned information obtained through the application of qualitative methods. It is much easier, for example, for a young woman to omit details of her behaviour when responding to a set of structured questions than when she is involved in a one-on-one discussion with a skilled interviewer or when she finds herself in the supportive atmosphere of an FGD where other women are talking about similar experiences. It is therefore not surprising that so many studies utilized qualitative approaches, alone or in combination with quantitative ones. Yet, despite the advantages of the various data collections techniques offered by qualitative approaches, a major challenge remains, that is to improve the quality of information transcripts, especially from FGDs, and to develop better and more systematic methods for the analysis of these data.

Quantitative Studies

The studies that utilized quantitative approaches as their central technique for data collection are divided into hospital-based surveys, follow-up studies, community surveys, special group surveys and national surveys. A final category 'provider studies' is another example of the mix of approaches. It requires separate discussion because of the special problems in first identifying and then interviewing abortion providers in countries where abortion is illegal.

As previously noted, the studies that relied on quantitative methods, mostly surveys utilizing structured questionnaires, often include further data collection using FGDs or in-depth interviews to probe more deeply into the questions the authors are trying to answer. Most of the quantitative studies rely on hospital-based populations with the exception of the Turkey study already mentioned, the Chile study by Molina, the Cuba study by Alvarez and the Colombia study by Zamudio.

Hospital-based Studies

In countries where abortion is illegal and unsafe, maternity hospitals attend numerous cases of abortion complications. This is not to say that all women who have an unsafe abortion seek hospital post-abortion care. Some are also able to pay for a safe abortion or suffer no complications. Nonetheless, hospitals offer a safe and convenient place to study abortion and to interview women who are known to have had an abortion. In countries where abortion is legal, they offer the added advantage of providing access to a population of women seeking abortion services who can also be interviewed during regular pre-abortion admission protocols. Most hospital studies are based on a purposive sample design that includes either the universe of cases over a period or a quota sample which once reached ends the case recruitment. It should be noted that conditions for admission to hospital surveys may vary from country to country and that the environment under which the interviews take place depends on the institutional setting, including the tolerance toward abortion cases by hospital staff, especially where abortion is not legal. The stigmatization of women with abortion complications is a serious problem and affects the care that hospital staff provides to these cases. By extension it also affects the way in which the research is conducted. This is clearly demonstrated by the Dominican Republic study that is discussed below.

The Dominican Republic survey by Paiewonsky merits special discussion because it highlights some of the logistical problems involved in abortion research, even when conducted in the relative protection of a hospital setting. The study was conducted in two large maternity hospitals in Santo Domingo, was retrospective in nature, and included all cases seeking post-abortion complication care. The hospital survey was supplemented with in-depth interviews with women who had previously aborted. The researcher noted two problems: one was the respondents' reluctance to acknowledge the voluntary nature of their abortion, which is perfectly understandable in countries where the practice is illegal. Many women *pretended* that their abortion had been spontaneous. The second problem was the lack of facilities at the hospital to carry out the interviews, in particular the crowded, noisy, impersonal environment which was detrimental to building the trust necessary to conduct the interviews. As in many public hospitals, space was at a premium, privacy nonexistent, and the possibility of separate office space for the interviews was not available.

The Dominican study also highlights another problem that is common to many other hospital-based abortion studies: the negative attitude of the hospital staff towards women who arrive at what are largely maternity services with abortion complications, often of a very serious nature. The staff mocks these women, threatening them with calling the police, and reprimands them for their low moral standards. Subjected to this kind of stigma, women feel very insecure when an interviewer appears to ask questions about their decision to terminate their pregnancy. This, we feel, are important points to consider when planning studies in situations similar to those described by the Dominican study. In fact, this study points at another important research need, that is to understand better the attitudes of hospital personnel and other health care providers with respect to abortion. Here again the use of qualitative methods is perhaps the only possible approach.

Another hospital-based study by Misago and her colleagues was carried out in Fortaleza, the capital city of Ceara, one of the poorest states in Brazil. The researchers had detected an increase in abortion cases in the city and one possible explanation was the use of illegal abortifacients obtained from pharmacies. The study was designed as a retrospective survey to learn about the conditions leading to the abortion and the methods used to abort. It was conducted in two large public maternity hospitals and all women admitted with a diagnosis of pregnancy loss during a period of 12 months were screened and included in the sample which needed to be large. This highlights another problem in abortion research, the length of the data collection period in order to get significant numbers of women for a valid statistical analysis. This study was one of the few that was essentially quantitative in its approach. Women were classified according to the WHO abortion classification scheme into: 'certainly', 'probably' and 'possibly' having had an induced abortion and a fourth category 'spontaneous abortion'. The study detected a high proportion of use of misoprostol, a drug prescribed for ulcers but which also acts as an abortifacient.

The study in Tanzania by Mpangile and colleagues had a much shorter data collection period than the Brazilian, six weeks, although it was similar in its objective. However, the number of hospitals was larger, four, all in Dar es Salaam. They used the WHO classification scheme and found that almost half of the women screened fell into the category of 'certainly having had an induced abortion'. To their surprise, a high proportion of them were teenagers. The researchers decided to train nurses to conduct structured interviews. They were also supported by the hospital authorities which allowed for better conditions to interview than in the Dominican Republic study. A lesson from these experiences is the importance of involving and gaining support from hospital authorities when planning hospital studies of abortion. In most cases, hospital authorities stand to gain from better information about the situation.

Follow-up Studies

Prospective studies, or follow-up studies are difficult in abortion research and they are restricted to countries where abortion is legal. In China, Luo Lin and her colleagues conducted a hospital-based follow-up survey of women aged 18–40 years in six rural communities of Sichuan province to shed light on the sequelae of abortion. Women who came for first-trimester abortion were asked to participate in the study which involved visits at 15, 90 and 180 days following the procedure. Women were interviewed at the service for the initial interview and at home by trained medical staff for the subsequent interviews. The study also included the testing and validation of psychological scales applied to a Chinese population.

A different type of follow-up was included in the study by Bulut in Turkey, which compared services in two different types of hospitals in Istanbul. It included an initial survey of abortion cases at each hospital, plus a follow-up to obtain data on post-abortion complications and related problems. To obtain follow-up data a personal diary was designed, which the women would complete and then return to the researchers. While this was seen as a key component of the project's methodology when it was originally planned, the actual data collection experience was not very encouraging. Only half of the women returned the diaries and many entries were blank. The researchers then changed their original plan and gathered women in FGDs to obtain data on sequelae of abortion. This study represents a good example of how project designs are modified as a result of field problems and how qualitative methods come to the rescue when other options fail.

Community Surveys

The study by Molina in Chile is unusual and perhaps unique in abortion research. It was designed as a traditional experiment that included a service intervention and a 'before' and an 'after' community survey to measure changes in abortion rates. The objective of the intervention was to reduce abortion incidence in three lower-income urban communities. It was also a long and costly study that took nearly five years to complete. The study faced many methodological challenges and its design consisted of five phases. First, a retrospective survey of three lower-income communities in the periphery of Santiago was conducted. Second, a predictive instrument designed to detect a woman's risk of having an abortion (based on the characteristics of women with previous abortion histories) was constructed and then used to identify women with high risk of abortion. In the third phase, the communities were divided into three types of service intervention: full, medium or none (control). During the fourth phase the improved services (intervention) were put into effect for a period of 24 months. Lastly, the 'after' survey was conducted to assess the impact of the intervention. With any design as complicated as this one and of such long duration, the risk of external interference or contamination is very high. Although there was no special event that could have biased the results, the project was delayed by an earthquake. The researchers concluded that the support of community health authorities was a major factor in ensuring the success of the project. The development and application of the predictive instrument to detect women with high risk of abortion was considered a success. It is easily applicable by health staff with basic training in primary health care. However, a major problem with studies of such lengthy duration is unavoidable: people in low-income communities are not stable and many women interviewed in the original survey had moved out. The 'after' survey had to be restricted to those women who had stayed and who were interviewed in the 'before' survey, reducing substantially the sample size for the final analysis. Furthermore, these women have aged, or completed family size, or become more effective users of family planning, thus raising questions that projects like this cannot answer. This project points at the methodological pitfalls of experimental designs carried over very long periods of time.

Surveys of Special Groups

In some contexts, naturally exposed populations exist that facilitate the study of induced abortion, for example, areas that gather large numbers of young, unmarried women. The study by Kwon, in Korea, was conducted in industrial export zones where single young women work in a variety of skilled or semi-skilled factory occupations. Kwon also added a group of women working in the so called 'entertainment occupations' which included bar waitresses and commercial sex workers. Lastly, because the objective of the study was to understand abortion behaviour among women under 25 years of age, the research design included women attending obstetrics and gynaecological clinics where legal abortion services are offered. As we have noted before, the cultural context and policy situation does affect the research methods used. In Korea, legal abortion services are available but they are somewhat restricted. The Penal Code defines abortion as a criminal act, it permits abortion only for medical and genetic reasons, including rape and incest. But the Infant and Maternal Health Law provides a legal foundation for the provision of clinic-based abortion services. The study was designed according to a decision-making model to outline paths to induced abortion. The sample design was purposive including structured interviews and in-depth interviews of selected cases. As in other studies, FGDs were also held. The methodological interest of this project lies in the way the populations studied were selected. While these convenience samples lack representativity, they offer an effective alternative to the samples obtained from hospital cases.

National Surveys

As already noted, the only nationally representative, population-based survey included in this book is the study in Colombia by Zamudio. This massive survey is representative of all urban women of reproductive age living in cities of 100,000 inhabitants or more in Colombia. Over 30,000 women aged 15 to 55 were interviewed. Large-scale surveys on abortion have seldom been attempted because of the reluctance of women to answer questions on abortion. The abortion initiative considered this project as a unique possibility to open up a field thus far known for its problems and frustrations. The methodology used was a self-administered one page questionnaire that took less than 10 minutes to complete. The women were told the purpose of the study, given the form and an envelope. The interviewer waited while the woman, in total privacy, moved to another part of the house to complete the form, then placed it in the nameless envelope and brought it back to be deposited in the urn carried by the interviewer. No name was required and total anonymity was emphasized throughout. The questionnaire included only 16 items necessary for the estimation of abortion incidence. The role of the interviewer, a misnomer in this case, was to make sure the proper house was visited and that the respondent understood that there was total confidentiality. The study showed a high incidence of abortion and has been the object of discussions at the highest levels of policy making in Colombia. It also received a coveted scientific prize. It is hoped that this pioneer methodology is used elsewhere where abortion is illegal and unsafe. There is no more powerful tool to influence policy than hard data, collected by national researchers, that can show the extent of a problem such as that of unsafe abortion.

Provider Studies

Among the most difficult populations to study in abortion research are providers. There are legal, ethical and situational factors that need to be considered before embarking on this type of research. The problem is less difficult when studying abortion providers in clinical settings where the practice is legal. Where abortion is not legal, an option is to study opinions of hospital or clinical personnel. This can help to improve post-abortion care for women arriving with complications at hospitals or clinics. This is the approach followed by three researchers in this book: Djohan in Indonesia, Cadelina in the Philippines and Hewage in Sri Lanka. These studies are based on purposive samples, the interviews are conducted on a one-to-one basis by senior researchers, and in the case of Sri Lanka FGDs were also held. The studies relied largely on qualitative approaches, often simply following an interview guide.

The one study that attempted to go to the source of abortion provision was by Pick in Mexico. This study included two types of abortion providers: employees of pharmacies who prescribe and sell abortion drugs (whether effective or not), and market herb vendors who sell preparations to abort. The sample of pharmacies was chosen randomly from the total number of pharmacies in Mexico City. A similar approach was used for the markets. Both pharmacies and markets were drawn from a census of commercial establishments. The next phase was to select a representative sample of pharmacy employees for interviewing. The sample of herb vendors was not representative given the nature of traditional markets. Aware of the difficulties in obtaining accurate responses from providers, two approaches were used to obtain data. The first was a structured questionnaire with fairly flexible open items, and the second, role-playing visits during which specially trained women interviewers would actually go to the pharmacies or herb vendors seeking advice and drugs to abort, thus verifying the data obtained from the survey. These women stated that their period was late and that they needed something to induce menstruation. If the provider knew a drug or method, the next step was to ask how the method was used. Later these responses were checked against the earlier responses to the survey questionnaire as a validity check. A major problem encountered was refusal to answer the survey questions, especially by market vendors. Despite the many pitfalls and difficulties of undertaking this type of research the project did contribute valuable information to the paths and methods that women use to abort in Mexico.

Some Suggestions for Future Research

One important area that requires further work and for which this book provides an interesting test case is the study of abortion incidence utilizing the methodology devised by Zamudio. While the Colombian case is a first and it works only with literate populations there is a need to validate this methodology. It is well suited to urban populations and it is fairly easy to carry out despite the large sample needed to obtain sufficiently large abortion cases for the final analysis.

The ever increasing problem of teenage pregnancy, which is common nearly everywhere, requires further study, particularly when abortion is used to terminate unwanted pregnancies in contexts where the practice is unsafe. Here the application of qualitative techniques, the use of FGDs, supplemented with in-depth interviews appears to be particularly appropriate. What is needed are more precise data-gathering approaches as well as more rigorous analytic tools to deal with data collected in complex or unusual situational circumstances. Some FGDs can become emotionally charged with people either crying or upset and data recording under such circumstances may miss key points or exact opinions. Double data collection should be used, taping if there is no opposition as well as hand recording of the discussion. The use of computerized analysis is another step that helps in sorting out and interpreting these sets of data.

Another major area for which qualitative methods are recommended is the study of providers, both of care and of abortion. Again where abortion is not legal there are often insurmountable problems to reach the actual providers of abortion since they work outside the law, they operate in irregular settings, and would not welcome anyone asking questions. It is here that the biggest challenge exists. The study of pharmacies and herb vendors in this book suggests ways to proceed and also notes the difficulties. The study of abortion is never independent of ethical, legal and religious connotations and all of them affect the way in which this type of research can or cannot be designed.

A last suggestion for future efforts in the field of abortion research is the study and assessment of different methodologies, alone or in combination, including not only techniques of data collection but also an analysis of the conceptual basis on which indicators and key items for interviewing are formulated, thus improving the validity and quality upon which findings are built.

✝ References

Alan Guttmacher Institute. 1994. *Clandestine abortion: A Latin American reality*. New York and Washington: Alan Guttmacher Institute.

Barreto, T., O.M.R. Campbell, J.L. Davies, V. Fauveau, V. Filippi, W. Graham, M. Mamdami, C.I.F. Rooney and N. Toubia. 1992. Investigating induced abortion in developing countries: Methods and problems. *Studies in Family Planning* 23 (3): 159–70.

Bleek, W. 1987. Lying informants: A fieldwork experience from Ghana. *Population and Development Review* 13 (2): 314–17.

David, H. 1993. Realities in abortion research. Discussion Paper presented at the session on 'Health and Social Aspects of Induced Abortion', XXII Conference of the International Union for the Scientific Study of Population, Montreal, Canada.

Helitzer-Allen, D., M. Makhambera and A.M. Wangel. 1994. Obtaining sensitive information: The need for more than focus groups. *Reproductive Health Matters*, 3: 75–82.

Huntington, D., B. Mensch and N. Toubia. 1993. A new approach to eliciting information about induced abortion. *Studies in Family Planning* 24 (2): 120–24.

Khan, M.E. and L. Manderson. 1992. Focus groups in tropical diseases research. *Health Policy and Planning* 7 (1): 56–66.

Morgan, D.L. 1988. *Focus groups as qualitative research*. Thousand Oaks: Sage Publications.

Remez, L. 1995. Confronting the reality of abortion in Latin America. *International Family Planning Perspectives* 21 (1): 32–37.

Singh, S. and D. Wulf. 1991. Estimating abortion levels in Brazil, Colombia and Peru, using hospital admissions and fertility survey data. *International Family Planning Perspectives* 17 (1): 8–13.

———. 1994. Estimated levels of induced abortion in six Latin American countries. *International Family Planning Perspectives* 20 (1): 4–13.

✟

25

Policy Impact of Abortion Research

Axel I. Mundigo and Iqbal H. Shah

The collective research effort on induced abortion encompassed in this book represents a unique case of forward thinking and creative investment by one of the world's leading reproductive health research programmes—the Special Programme of Research, Development and Research Training in Human Reproduction—of the World Health Organization (WHO). When the Special Programme, in 1989, decided to announce the research initiative, open to developing country scientists, to explore one of the most sensitive issues in the field of reproductive health—induced abortion—the main objective was to fill the existing gap in knowledge about why abortion persists despite the enormous advances in contraceptive technology and the efforts to make family planning available to all individuals. The ultimate goal of the research initiative was to contribute to lowering abortion incidence by documenting its determinants and consequences, particularly where abortion practices are unsafe, and thus contribute to policy improvements in this area. As aptly stated in the Platform for Action on Women and Health issued at the World Conference on Women in Beijing (1995): 'Unsafe abortions threaten the lives of large numbers of women, representing a grave public health problem as it is primarily the poorest and youngest who take the highest risk. Most of the deaths, health problems and injuries are preventable....'

From its inception, the WHO initiative on induced abortion had both a scientific and a practical objective. From a scientific standpoint, it was important to generate reliable information that could be useful to improve the quality of services offered to women seeking care for abortion complications, to prevent repeat abortion by providing counselling and services for family planning, to simplify access to abortion services in contexts where they are legal, to increase the level of staff capacity, and to inform health professionals of the dimensions of the problem. These examples represent the applied objective. To achieve them, policies and service norms must change.

In general, applied objectives in any research activity are more difficult to achieve as researchers tend to focus on the scientific aspects of projects giving less emphasis to the more elusive policy analyses and their implications for real-life application. The reason for this neglect is that the transmission of scientific information to policy making officials and politicians is difficult and requires a series of intermediate steps that are radically different from routine scientific reporting. On the other hand, informed policy making should consider the available national information on the subject and, if the required analyses are not available, make efforts for the necessary studies to be carried out. As Nunes and Delph (1995), reporting on the recent change in the abortion law of Guyana, put it: 'A main weakness of public policy formation in many developing countries is the paucity of factual data and the lack of a tradition of using data to inform decision-making.' 'The subject of abortion law reform is perhaps the most vexed of all public policy issues and is prone to be in the absence of facts.' It is hoped that the new information contained in the case studies, which document the reality of induced abortion in developing countries, will help reverse the deficiency in knowledge on this topic so that better policies are formulated.

Obstacles to Policy Utilization of Research

Policy makers, programme managers and other public figures who influence policy may not understand the language of scientific research, or may not be inclined to read long technical reports and, even if they do, they may not be aware of the policy implications inherent in research findings. In order to reach a policy audience it becomes necessary to present relevant results in a style and with precision that can be useful to ongoing processes such as legislative proposals to create or improve legal statutes, or change the normative direction of major service programmes. This often requires presenting findings within a strategic framework for action, weighing or ranking each recommendation. Another consideration is the timing of political agendas. When a project is completed and its findings made public, the new information may not coincide with policy timetables or legislative processes. Timing is very important to ensure the utilization of research results for policy purposes.

In order to facilitate the utilization of research findings for policy purposes it is important to consider some of the potential obstacles. The very concept of policy utilization or impact is not always clear or well understood, e.g., impact on what exactly? Some research projects may in fact contribute, along with other information, to strengthen national debates on a critical issue but have only an indirect effect on policy. In fact, it may be impossible to assess a research project's exact contribution to, for example, the final parliamentary decision on a given change of an existing law. Conversely, when there is clear evidence that research findings have contributed directly to policy change, that impact may have to take a low profile in order to enhance the political dimension of the action approved.

It is obvious, therefore, that there are inherent tensions between the academic/scientific and the policy/political worlds with respect to the how, when and through what means scientific information is used for policy purposes. In the health field, both these worlds converge on the behaviour of individuals, the basic tenet being one where the wellbeing of men and women depends on changing attitudes, improving service utilization and other measures for people to act upon to prevent disease and to improve their lives. An important role of research, especially social science research, is to elucidate existing patterns that may stand in the way of increasing health-seeking behaviour, including actions related to fertility regulation and abortion. How people perceive services, their quality and what they would prefer as alternatives, is just one example. The role of policy makers, on the other hand, is to create or improve the service programmes to meet the real needs of men and women. It should also be pointed out that the avenues to improve existing programmes or services suggested by research may be correct but not always feasible from an economic standpoint.

In the field of family planning—where research evidence has accumulated in the past 30 years—it is not exactly clear what proportion of the research output, or what specific studies, have had a direct impact on policy formulation (Freedman, 1987). The argument is often made that development, socio-economic change, and making contraceptives widely available is what has changed people's reproductive behaviour (see, for example, Bongaarts et al., 1990). But there is no doubt that research has contributed to the strengthening of programmes and has made a major contribution to the development of population policies (Ross and Frankenberg, 1993). Simultaneously, the adoption of population policies and the growth of family planning programmes have called for research to assess service quality, document patterns of contraceptive use and develop approaches to estimate the existing demand for contraception. Along with these concerns, as more people use contraception and the risk of contraceptive failure becomes a possibility for more couples, the need to understand the determinants of induced abortion has emerged as a major theme in reproductive health research. There is, therefore, a symbiotic relationship between research and policy, whereby one feeds the other and this relationship works in both directions (Mundigo, 1992).

Political Climate and Research Receptivity

The political environment in which policy decisions are made is very important, particularly when we consider topics as sensitive as induced abortion. A pluralistic society, where democratic values allow open debate of controversial issues, is more able to discuss and debate publicly issues such as abortion legislation and abortion rights. The public debate often includes the mass media as well as advocacy groups favouring one position or the other. These groups introduce available research evidence to the debate in order to back their positions. It is often through these debates that policy makers' attention is drawn to available research evidence, which leads to its utilization for policy change. By contrast, in authoritarian societies, where policy options are not always subject to public debate, the role of the scientific community, and of research in particular, may be relegated to the narrow confines of professional associations.

The process through which scientific knowledge is made available to and used by policy makers is also an important consideration, especially the nature of the supply and demand for policy information in a particular situation or context. Some policy makers may demand information on particular issues yet others might prefer to ignore available data to achieve their own political agendas. For example, during the long public debate that preceded the approval of the 1993 Abortion Law in Poland, both those in favour of a more liberal abortion law as well as those opposed to abortion used polls and demographic data selectively, often misusing information. In the end, the efforts to pass a more liberal abortion law failed in the face of organized Catholic Church opposition (Kulczycki, 1995). Often, politically elected officials fear risking votes if they publicly advocate liberalization of abortion legislation, especially if confronted by organized forces in the society advancing moral and religious counter-arguments. In the case studies we discuss, this is often the case—the policy agenda moves forward but often stops short of its goals as the opposition grows. The political climate at any point in time is crucial for policy action. For the research community it is also difficult to gauge the shifts and currents in political and ideological circles and it is often necessary to use well-informed sources to facilitate the flow of information to policy makers. Even in the best of cases, it is not always clear that such efforts would succeed.

Illustrating Impact

The case studies in this book provide concrete examples where social science research, conducted on the very politically sensitive issue of induced abortion, has resulted in major impact for policy utilization. The examples discussed below emphasize the utilization or relevance of this research for policy purposes, providing also a summary outline of the studies and their key findings in order to place the policy aspect within a concrete reality (for more details please refer directly to the corresponding chapters). The utilization and impact of the research has been felt in three main areas: facilitating and expediting legislative processes, strengthening the public and political debate on national abortion policy, and improving the quality of care in family planning, abortion and post-abortion counselling and services.

Impact on Legislative Processes

One important measure of policy impact is the utilization of research findings in formal debates concerning projected or actual legislative action. The discussions leading to changes in the law can be long and, as already noted, the results are always subject to shifts in political environments. Changing abortion laws is particularly difficult as the legislative debate is easily fuelled by the arguments of pro- and anti-abortion groups who influence members of parliament with their views. Having scientifically valid information available to parliamentarians is one way to assist them to make decisions independent of external pressures. The studies in Mauritius, the Dominican Republic and the Republic of Korea are examples of the impact on legislative processes and labour union health policies.

Although contraceptive prevalence is high (76 per cent) in Mauritius, it is estimated that there are some 20,000 induced abortions each year. This figure was disconcerting for a country with an estimated population of two million in 1990 and of 300,000 women of reproductive ages. The study by Oodit and Bhowon revealed a considerable use of less effective methods (39 per cent of all users relying on withdrawal and abstinence) which were not used correctly and consistently by women who arrived at the study hospitals with abortion complications. These women also showed a high degree of switching from one contraceptive method to another without protection during the transitional periods. Among these women, one-fourth had already had a previous abortion. These findings came as a big surprise in a country that prides itself on its excellent family planning services. To discuss these findings, a National Symposium was held in July 1993, attended by government ministers, members of parliament, and international experts in the family planning field. As a result of the Symposium, discussions took place at the National Assembly, where a motion was tabled to decriminalize abortion. This was an important starting point for further legislative action on induced abortion. The study findings, and the ensuing discussions also helped to facilitate the approval of Norplant in Mauritius. The findings of the study provided basis for the Country Report prepared for the 1994 International Conference on Population and Development (ICPD) and for the plans for maternal and child health.

In the Dominican Republic, the study conducted by Paiewonsky in two Santo Domingo hospitals showed that the majority of the women with abortion complications were of low socioeconomic status, mostly under 30 years of age, and that adolescents represented 16 per cent of cases. Use of contraception among these women was low and unsystematic, with high discontinuation rates, resulting in many unwanted pregnancies and induced abortions. This information was used to argue for the need for changes in health legislation. In 1993, a revised Health Code was presented to the Dominican Congress for discussion and approval. The senator who introduced this legislation presented the results of the study and requested a modification of the law with respect to therapeutic abortions to include a clause to make abortions legal when the life of the mother is in danger, the pregnancy is unwanted due to rape, incest or potential emotional instability of the mother, or when there is malformation of the foetus. The motion also requested that the state provide safe abortion services to all entitled women under the proposed changes as part of its Maternal and Child Health Care Programme.

Despite the fact that abortion at demand is not legal in the Republic of Korea, recent health legislation makes it possible to obtain abortion in specialized clinics for the purposes of menstrual regulation. Authorities recognize that in a society where unwed motherhood has a strong negative connotation, induced abortion may be an inescapable reality for many young women. The study conducted by Kwon et al. of young unmarried women working in factories, within special export zones, showed that many of them were sexually active and that regular use of effective contraception was very low. Abortion was common and many reported having had a history of previous abortions. Only one in five of a group of women interviewed at a clinic that offered abortion services had used a method of contraception at the time they became pregnant. These results were discussed with labour unions and worker organizations and changes in union rules to allow for improved access and quality of family planning and women's health services, particularly at the work site were discussed.

Impact on Public Debates on National Abortion Policy

One important contribution of research is to feed into national public debates credible information that can contribute to changing the ways in which the society deals with certain issues, ideally bringing them to the attention of policy makers. Strengthening the public debate on reproductive health issues, including abortion, is a way to build a better basis upon which later decisions concerning the health and wellbeing of women can be formulated. The studies in Indonesia, Colombia, Nepal and Turkey have contributed to enhance the national debates on induced abortion, affecting policy at the highest level.

In Indonesia, the study by Djohan and colleagues focused on the attitudes of health providers, including general practitioners, gynaecologists, midwives and traditional birth attendants concerning abortion practices. It revealed that among the formal service sector personnel the use of menstrual regulation early in pregnancy was increasingly well accepted, though not by everyone and not without many provisos and ambiguities. Traditional birth attendants, on the other hand, were more favourable and readily willing to help women requesting abortion services. They seemed more aware of the social ostracism that younger unmarried women would experience if they continued with their pregnancy. This study coincided and contributed to a much

publicized national debate on health that included abortion. Towards the end
of 1991, a new Bill of Health was submitted to Parliament which included an
article on abortion. However, discussions on this Bill continued well into
1992. There was strong opposition from religious groups to the inclusion of
an abortion clause in the Bill. When the new health legislation was signed by
President Suharto in September 1992, the article dealing with pregnancy termination did not mention abortion directly but referred to it obliquely as 'a
certain procedure' (*tindakan medis tertentu*). This reference upset groups
opposed to abortion. Given the lack of clarity on the issue, the Department of
Health, in December 1992, issued a statement saying this article was in fact
intended to regulate the practice of abortion in the country (for additional
details, see Djohan et al., 1993). The study findings contributed to clarify the
Department of Health position and, as a result, the National Family Planning
Coordinating Board has given increased attention to the issue of abortion
provision in Indonesia.

In Colombia, a large-scale population-based survey to measure the incidence of induced abortion in urban areas showed that 23 per cent of all
women had experienced at least one abortion, and among ever-pregnant
women, the proportion reached 30 per cent. This information had a major
impact on the public as the media published it in detail. The project findings
were also made available to the staff of the Presidential Counsel for Youth,
Women and the Family, a unit of the Office of the President of Colombia,
headed by the President's wife. The Presidency took a strong interest in the
results of the project and used them for the development of improved reproductive health policies.

The Colombian researchers (see the chapter by Zamudio et al.), encouraged by the success of their project, decided to host the first ever meeting on
induced abortion in Latin America, which took place in November 1994 in
Bogota. The meeting, sponsored by the World Health Organization, the Ford
Foundation and the Alan Guttmacher Institute, gathered investigators from
the region to discuss abortion research findings and policy needs. To enhance
the policy dimension of the discussions, legislators from several Latin American countries were also invited. The meeting was opened by the President of
the Colombian Senate and concluded with a formal document signed by sen-
ators and legislators from Argentina, Brazil, Chile, Colombia, Cuba, Panama
and El Salvador, calling for the Latin American Parliament to discuss ways to
open up the debate that may lead to the modification of existing legislation in
the countries of the region. The Latin American Parliament functions as a
forum to discuss critical legislative issues of regional scope and to suggest
ways to proceed with changes in the law. Following the regional meeting in
Colombia, national meetings and discussions in other countries have also
taken place. A report on the conference issued by the Alan Guttmacher Institute states: 'It was the first time that researchers as a group had sat down with
politicians to deal with the issue of abortion. The conference gave substance

to what was apparent—how much both groups needed each other; as the conference organizers had stressed: research fuels the political debate.' (For a full discussion of this meeting and its impact, see Remez, 1995.) The findings of the Latin American case studies in this book were presented and discussed at this important event, thus contributing to the regional dialogue that followed.

The study in Nepal (by Tamang et al.) which examined the determinants of induced abortion and subsequent reproductive behaviour among women in three urban districts of Kathmandu valley provided a good example of how results can generate awareness of an important and sensitive issue and lead to a discussion in the national parliament. Yet, political events may overtake the momentum before changes in laws are passed. The study was conceptualized in 1990 when the country was in transition from monarchy to democracy. Abortion was a taboo under monarchy and officials were reluctant to discuss it or to provide abortion services. The reports describing the study findings were circulated periodically by the investigators to the health ministry, medical professionals and government and non-government agencies. These findings were taken up by reproductive health advocates, women advocacy groups, legal experts, and medical professionals for discussion and debate on the existing restrictive abortion laws in the country. The dissemination workshop, organized in 1994, was useful for exchanging and formulating opinions among the participants which included members of the parliament, members of the national planning commission, lawyers and senior gynaecologists. The participants urged the government to make the existing abortion laws to be' more flexible to minimize backstreet abortion and reduce strains of abortion complications on hospital resources. The proceedings of the workshop were covered extensively by the media. In the same year, an Abortion Bill was tabled in the parliament. This Bill, if passed, would have made abortion accessible to women under specific circumstances. However, before the Bill could be discussed, the parliament was dissolved to pay the way for the mid-term election. The study had, nevertheless, heightened the debate on the extent of unsafe abortion. National NGOs, such as Society of Obstetricians and Gynaecologists, Nepal Medical Association and Family Planning Association of Nepal have organized seminars and workshops to discuss abortion issues and reproductive health and rights in Nepal. In the current session of the parliament, a member of the Upper House (who is also the president of the Family Planning Association of Nepal) has tabled an Abortion Bill as a private bill. It is difficult to project whether the bill, that recommends legalizing abortion under certain conditions, will be passed in the current parliamentary session. However, public opinion as measured from media coverage is in support of legalization.

In addition to the above, several other studies have also been the subject of national policy discussions and have contributed to changes in long-term development policies, as is the case of the Turkish study conducted in Ankara and Van provinces by Akin. The National State Planning Organization of Turkey debated the results of the project during its discussions of the country's socioeconomic development plan for the period 1995–2000 and increased its commitment to reproductive health and family planning as a way to lower abortion incidence. It is expected that the documentation of the reality of induced abortion contained in the case studies in this book will continue to contribute to national debates on induced abortion.

Impact on Improving Quality of Care

The studies in Mexico, Chile, Cuba, Tanzania and Turkey provide clear evidence of the impact of abortion research on the improvement of services and quality of care. The results of each of these studies were used by national or municipal authorities to introduce important changes in the way services were delivered.

The study in Mexico by Elu, conducted at the Hospital de la Mujer, a large women's hospital in Mexico City, explored the reasons why women resort to induced abortion. Women hospitalized for abortion complications as well as the providers of post-abortion care were interviewed. From the outset, the project had the full cooperation of the hospital authorities as well as of the Ministry of Health. Abortion complications represent an important proportion of the case-load at the hospital, close to 20 per cent of the annual maternity ward admissions. Interviews with service personnel at the hospital shed light on the frustration they experienced having to attend abortion complications rather than deliveries—their main duty. The study concluded that urgent reforms, including improved family planning services and information, were needed in order to reduce the number of abortions. These recommendations were presented to the General Director of Maternal and Child Health Care of the Ministry of Health, who used them to implement changes to improve post-abortion care throughout the public hospital system of Mexico. Simultaneously, the Women's Hospital authorities agreed to take steps to improve general service quality.

The project in Chile shows the results of an intervention study conducted in three low-income urban communities of metropolitan Santiago. The study, by Molina et al., was carried out in three phases, including: a base line survey (phase I); followed by a period of 18 months when interventions (consisting of home visits and improved services in one community, improved services only, in the second, and no change in the third, the control area) were provided (phase II); and a post-survey (phase III) to evaluate the effect of the intervention on abortion rates. The study showed that the intervention had been successful in lowering abortion incidence where the full intervention was applied, and somewhat less where services had been improved but no home visits took place. In the control area the situation did not change, abortions in fact increased somewhat. These findings have been widely discussed with national and municipal health authorities in Chile. As a result, improvements in family planning services in low-income communities and in reproductive health services for adolescents in poor areas of Santiago have been implemented.

In Cuba—the only country in Latin America where abortion has been legal, since the 1960s (recently Guyana changed its former restrictive abortion law)—a study conducted by Alvarez and colleagues in a municipality of Havana showed that one out every 10 sexually active women aged 13–35 years of age, had had at least one induced abortion. The most important reason given for seeking an abortion was poor use and little knowledge of modern contraception. It concluded that services in the municipality should give special attention to the family planning needs of single women, particularly to young women who are not in stable unions. The results were discussed with municipal health authorities and also with the Ministry of Health. Improvements in family planning services outreach and post-abortion care were implemented following the study's recommendations.

In Tanzania, the study by Mpangile and colleagues, conducted in four public hospitals in Dar es Salaam, showed that less than one-fifth of the women who had an abortion had been using a contraceptive method at the time of conception. A substantial proportion of the women who arrived at these hospitals seeking care for abortion complications were adolescents. These findings alerted the hospital authorities to the problem which was severely draining hospital resources. The cost of treating abortion complications was very high, surpassing the annual budget for health care allocated by the Ministry of Health for each citizen. As a result of this study, a one-year post-abortion family planning counselling and services, including promotion of effective contraception, was implemented in all major hospitals of Tanzania. These efforts were considered to reduce the level of repeat abortion.

The study in Istanbul (Turkey), by Bulut and Toubia, was concerned with the efficiency and effectiveness of abortion services in two different types of public hospitals: a government hospital and a hospital run by the social security system. Abortion is legal in Turkey. Three out of every four women interviewed relied on withdrawal as their main contraceptive method, but used it with little success. This led to the high level of unwanted pregnancy and abortion among the users of withdrawal. The study showed that terminations of pregnancy were seen as an indispensable part of fertility regulation, in fact as a back up to withdrawal failure. The lower cost of abortion at the government hospital was the main reason to seek its services and women stated that other options, such as the services at the social security hospital, were not as good. The study found that family planning and abortion services should be re-organized to integrate their activities to improve their quality with more user friendly procedures for admission. As a result of these findings the Family Planning Clinic and the Abortion Clinic in the Social Security Hospital were divided and moved into separate buildings but their operations were functionally integrated through a new referral system. The application procedure for abortion was moved to the Family Planning Clinic, and appointments to the Abortion Clinic are now given for the following day, eliminating the delays previously experienced. Consequently, service quality has been greatly improved. These policy changes were considered for implementation in other hospitals in Turkey, once their longer term effectiveness had been confirmed.

Final Reflections

The findings generated by the many case studies included in this book tell a larger picture of the political and policy environment that defines the abortion situation in the developing world. Abortion continues to be a very controversial issue, many and diverse points of view about it are argued in heated public debates. Seldom in these debates does one find a concern about the women and families affected and the plight of women who experience unwanted pregnancies. Nor is there much consideration of the negative health impact that induced abortion has when it is practised under unsafe circumstances. In that sense, the evidence included in the chapters of this book will provide new light on what the reality of abortion means under different social, legal and political contexts. It represents an effort to legitimize a topic that for a long time has been a taboo among those that deal with the larger issues of reproductive health.

The fact that the WHO research initiative on induced abortion attracted so many researchers from every world region—many of whom had to overcome major methodological and cultural obstacles—is indicative of the commitment of the scientific community to shed light where darkness prevailed. Barriers to conduct research on induced abortion are many and range from institutional hostility to women's refusal to answer questions during fieldwork. However, the findings obtained by the case studies presented in this volume bring forward new information on the reality of induced abortion—both in contexts where it is illegal and there where it is legal—providing new information unknown to policy makers. Examples abound, as is clear from these studies, that induced abortion is not restricted to adolescents facing unwanted pregnancy but occurs equally within marriage to limit family size. It is also clear that induced abortion exists everywhere, both in contexts where family planning programmes are strong as well as where they are weak or nonexistent. Where family planning services are readily available and motivation to reduce family size is high, women use abortion when contraception fails. In other contexts, where contraceptive choices are more limited, abortion forms part of fertility regulation strategies that include a mix of traditional and modern methods, often used ineffectively. In general, women who had an abortion reported very low use of modern contraception, and this was particularly evident among younger women. It is also clear from these studies that unsafe clandestine abortions are more likely to be sought by poorer, less-educated women, and also by adolescents. The studies dealing with providers' perspectives point to the cost in both human and financial resources of treating abortion complications that drain hospital budgets unnecessarily.

Most of the many findings depicted throughout this book have important policy relevance not only for the country, city or community where the research took place but for institutions working worldwide to improve women's reproductive health. The case studies also teach a broader lesson to all those concerned with women's health advocacy and with the advancement of reproductive rights.

Finally, the success with which this WHO initiative was implemented and the interest with which its results have been followed, discussed and used for policy and programme changes confirm that the study of induced abortion has gained a new level of legitimacy, overcoming many political and religious barriers, and providing a formidable tool for the improvement of reproductive health policy.

✝ References

Bongaarts, J., W.P. Mauldin and J.F. Phillips. 1990. The demographic impact of family planning programmes. Working Papers, Research Division, No. 17. New York: The Population Council.

Djohan, E., R. Indrawasih, M. Adenan, H. Yudomustopo and M. Tan. 1993. The attitudes of health providers towards abortion in Indonesia. *Reproductive Health Matters* 2: 32–40.

Freedman, R. 1987. The contribution of social science research to population policy and family planning program effectiveness. *Studies in Family Planning* 18 (2): 57–82.

Kulczycki, A. 1995. Abortion policy in postcommunist Poland. *Population and Development Review* 21 (3): 471–506.

Mundigo, A. 1992. The determinants of impact and utilization of fertility research on public policy: China and Mexico. In: J.F. Phillips and J.A. Ross (eds). *Family Planning Programmes and Fertility*, Oxford: Clarendon Press.

Nunes, F. and Y.M. Delph. 1995. Making abortion law reform happen in Guyana: A success story. *Reproductive Health Matters* 6: 12–23.

Remez, L. 1995. Confronting the reality of abortion in Latin America. *International Family Planning Perspectives* 21 (1): 32–37.

Ross, J. and E. Frankenberg. 1993. *Findings from two decades of family planning research*. New York: The Population Council.

World Conference on Women, The Beijing Declaration and the Platform for Action on Women and Health. 1995. *Population and Development Review* 21 (4): 907–13.

✝

The Contributors

M. Adenan
Pusat Penelitian Dan, Pengembangan
Kemasyarakatan Dan
Kebudayaan (PMB-LIPI)
Centre for Social and Cultural Studies
P.O. Box 496 KBY
Jakarta
Indonesia

Marsela Alvarez
Instituto Mexicano de Investigacion de
Familia y Poblacion
Apartado Postal 41–595
Mexico, 11001 DF
Mexico

Maria Elena Benitez
Instituto Nacional de Endocrinologia
Zapata y D. Vedado
Habana
Cuba

Uma Bhowon
Family Planning Association of
Mauritius
30 SSR Street
Port Louis
Mauritius

Aysen Bulut
Institute of Child Health
University of Istanbul
Cocuk Hastanesi
Millet Cad. 34390 Capa
Istanbul
Turkey

Fred V. Cadelina
Department of Sociology-Anthropology

Silliman University
Dumaguete City
Philippines

Sonia Catasus
Instituto Nacional de Endocrinologia
Zapata y D. Vedado
Habana
Cuba

Chen Xiao-qing
Family Planning Research Institute of
Sichuan
No. 15, Section 4, South People's Road
Chengdu, Sichuan Province
China

Cho Sung-nam
Ewha Woman's University
Seoul
Korea

Suzanne Cohen
Instituto Mexicano de Investigacion de
Familia y Poblacion
Apartado Postal 41–595
Mexico 11001 DF
Mexico

Maria Elena Collado
Instituto Mexicano de Investigacion de
Familia y Poblacion
Apartado Postal 41–595
Mexico 11001 DF
Mexico

Francisco Cumsille
Department of Obstetrics and
Gynaecology, School of Medicine

Jose Joaquin Aquirre Hospital
Casilla 7001 1–7 Santiago
Chile

Ayse Akin
Department of Public Health
Hacettepe University
Ankara
Turkey

E. Djohan
Pusat Penelitian Dan, Pengembangan
Kemasyarakatan Dan
Kebudayaan (PMB-LIPI)
Centre for Social and Cultural Studies
P.O. Box 496 KBY
Jakarta
Indonesia

N. Ehrenfeld
Hospital General Dr Manuel Gea
Gonzalez
Calzada de Tlalpan
4800 Mexico
14000 DF
Mexico

Maria Del Carmen Elu
Instituto Mexicano de Estudios Sociales,
A.C.
Apartado Postal, 22–179
Mexico, 14000 DF
Mexico

Walter Fonseca
Department of Community Medicine
Ferderal University of Ceara
Brazil

Gao Er-sheng
Shanghai Institute of Planned
Parenthood Research
2140 Xie Tu Road
Shanghai 200032
China

Caridad Teresa Garcia
Instituto Nacional de Endocrinologia
Zapata y D. Vedado
Habana
Cuba

Martha Givaudan
Instituto Mexicano de Investigacion de
Familia y Poblacion
Apartado Postal 41–595
Mexico 11001 DF
Mexico

Gui Shi-xun
Institute of Population Research
East China Normal University
No 3663 Zhong Shan Road (North)
Shanghai 20062
China

P. Hewage
Department of Geography
University of Ruhuna
Matara
Sri Lanka

R. Indrawasih
Pusat Penelitian Dan, Pengembangan
Kemasyarakatan Dan
Kebudayaan (PMB-LIPI)
Centre for Social and Cultural Studies
P.O. Box 496 KBY
Jakarta
Indonesia

Cynthia Indriso
Via Augusta
76(3/1), 08006 Barcelona
Spain

Jun Kwang Hee
Chungman National University
Seoul, Korea

D.J. Kihwele
Family Planning Association of Tanzania
 — UMATI
Makao Makuu-Mtaa Samora/Zanaki
S.L.P. 1372 Dar es Salaam
Tanzania

Dunja Obersnel Kveder
Institute of Public Health
Trubarjeva 2
61000 Ljubljana
Slovenia

Kwon Tai-hwan
The Centre for Area Studies
Seoul National University
Seoul 151–742
Korea

M.T. Leshabari
Family Planning Association of Tanzania
 — UMATI
Makao Makuu-Mtaa Samora/Zanaki
S.L.P. 1372 Dar es Salaam
Tanzania

Li Min-xiang
Family Planning Research Institute of
 Sichuan
No. 15, Section 4, South People's Road
Chengdu, Sichuan Province
China

Luo Lin
Family Planning Research Institute of
 Sichuan
No. 15, Section 4, South People's Road
Chengdu, Sichuan Province
China

Maria Teresa Martinez
Instituto Nacional de Endocrinologia
Zapata y D. Vedado
Habana
Cuba

Eduardo Miranda
Department of Obstetrics and
 Gynaecology, School of Medicine
Jose Joaquin Aquirre Hospital
Casilla 7001 1–7 Santiago
Chile

Chizuru Misago
Institute of Woman and Child Health
Rua Barbosa de Freitas 60
Sala 402, 60170–020
Fortaleza, Ceara
Brazil

Ramiro Molina
Department of Obstetrics and
 Gynaecology, School of Medicine
Jose Joaquin Aquirre Hospital
Casilla 7001 1–7 Santiago
Chile

Temistocles Molina
Department of Obstetrics and
 Gynaecology, School of Medicine
Jose Joaquin Aquirre Hospital
Casilla 7001 1–7 Santiago
Chile

G.S. Mpangile
Family Planning Association of Tanzania
 — UMATI
Makao Makuu-Mtaa Samora/Zanaki
S.L.P. 1372 Dar es Salaam
Tanzania

Axel I. Mundigo
International Programs
Center for Health and Social Policy
P.O. Box 994
Manchester VT 05254
USA

Luis Martinez Oliva
Department of Obstetrics and
 Gynaecology, School of Medicine
Jose Joaquin Aquirre Hospital
Casilla 7001 1–7 Santiago
Chile

Geeta Oodit
Family Planning Association of
 Mauritius
30 SSR Street
Port Louis
Mauritius

Denise Paiewonsky
Instituto de Estudios de Poblacion y
 Desarrollo, IEPD-PROFAMILIA
Apartado Postal 1053
Santo Domingo
Dominican Republic

Cristian Pereda
School of Public Health, University of
 Chile
Santiago, Chile

Susan Pick
Instituto Mexicano de Investigacion de
 Familia y Poblacion

Apartado Postal 41–595
Mexico 11001 DF
Mexico

Qin Fei
Shanghai Institute of Planned
  Parenthood Research
2140 Xie Tu Road
Shanghai 200032
China

Norma Rubiano
Centre for Research on Social Dynamics
Universidad Esternado de Colombia
Apartado Aereo 034141
Santa Fe de Bogota
Colombia

Iqbal H. Shah
UNDP/UNFPA/WHO/World Bank
  Special Programme of Research
Development and Research Training in
  Human Reproduction
World Health Organization
1211 Geneva 27
Switzerland

Kabita Sharma
Institute for Integrated Development
Studies (IIDS)
P.O. Box 2254
Kathmandu
Nepal

Neera Shrestha
Institute for Integrated Development
Studies (IIDS)
P.O. Box 2254
Kathmandu
Nepal

A.K. Tamang
Centre for Research on Environment
  Health and Population Activities
P.O. Box 9626
Kathmandu,
Nepal

M.G. Tan
Pusat Penelitian Dan, Pengembangan
Kemasyarakatan Dan

Kebudayaan (PMB-LIPI)
Centre for Social and Cultural Studies
P.O. Box 496 KBY
Jakarta
Indonesia

Tang Wei
Shanghai Institute of Planned
Parenthood Research
2140 Xie Tu Road
Shanghai 200032
China

Nahid Toubia
The Population Council
New York, N.Y. 10017
USA

Luisa Alvarez Vasquez
Instituto Nacional de Endocrinologia
Zapata y D. Vedado
Habana
Cuba

Lucy Wartenberg
Centre for Research on Social Dynamics
Universidad Esternado de Colombia
Apartado Aereo 034141
Santa Fe de Bogota
Colombia

Wu Shi-zhong
Family Planning Research Institute of
  Sichuan
No. 15, Section 4, South People's Road
Chengdu, Sichuan Province,
China

Yang Yao-ying
Shanghai Institute of Planned
Parenthood Research
2140 Xie Tu Road
Shanghai 200032
China

H. Yudomustopo
Pusat Penelitian Dan, Pengembangan
Kemasyarakatan Dan
Kebudayaan (PMB-LIPI)
Centre for Social and Cultural Studies
P.O. Box 496 KBY
Jakarta
Indonesia

Lucero Zamudio
Centre for Research on Social
  Dynamics
Universidad Esternado de Colombia
Apartado Aereo 034141
Santa Fe de Bogota
Colombia

Zhou Wei-jin
Shanghai Institute of Planned
Parenthood Research
2140 Xie Tu Road
Shanghai 200032
China

Index

abdominal massage, as a traditional form of abortion, 155, 282, 314, 315, 317, 318, 319

abortifacients, 41, 155, 174, 218, 224, 225, 226, 295, 299, 300–309 *passim*, 314, 315, 380, 470

abortion, and age, 80, 104, 118–19, 120–21, 134, 135, 157, 195, 221, 225, 226, 251, 373, 374, 390–91, 415, 416, 432, 433, 443–44; and correlation with education, 80–81, 121, 122, 134–35, 175–76, 177, 221, 226, 247, 351–52, 372–73, 390, 415, 416, 429, 431–32, 433; and correlation with occupation, 81, 121–22, 136–38, 177, 202, 221, 222, 247, 373, 415, 429, 430–32, 433; and economic situation, 36–37, 124, 184, 248, 250, 288, 315, 316, 317–18, 325, 326; and education of partners, 37, 176, 177; and gender relations, 37, 176, 177, 248–50, 266; and guilt, 48, 376, 382; and impact on subsequent reproductive health, 37, 228–44, 233–38, 242–44, 376, 401, 435, 439; and marital status of women, 89–90, 104, 105, 106–107, 115, 122–23, 136, 157, 177, 221, 225, 226, 247, 250–51, 373–74, 390, 391, 444; and psychological distress, 100, 102, 103, 108–14, 231, 238–39, 240, 241, 243, 253, 348, 369; and rural women, 81, 123, 135, 175–76, 350–52; as a sin, 161, 287, 305, 308, 316, 384; attitude to, 33, 125, 128, 129, 160–61, 170, 205, 208, 231, 241–43, 308, 315, 318, 362–63, 376, 459–60, 462, 470; by aspiration and curettage, 102, 339; cost of services, 275, 304, 307, 378, 380, 384, 396, 401, 486; crude methods of, 43, 154–55, 156, 253; in urban areas, 81, 123, 135, 176, 350–52; incidence of, 57, 80, 98, 168, 170, 218, 245–46, 259–60,

282, 283, 294, 311, 321, 328, 330–31, 346, 366–67, 388, 407, 449, 465, 472, 473, 475, 483; induced. *See* induced abortion; legalization of, 24–25, 99, 228, 256–57, 283, 366; male attitude to, 208; more than one method of, 224, 225, 294, 380; to cure pre-existing health problems, 234, 240–41

abortion and contraceptive behavior, relationship between, 25, 26–33, 39, 72–74, 75, 82, 105, 118, 127–28, 137, 252–53, 330–31, 447, 449–50, 454–63, 465–66, 486–87

abortion as contraceptive method, 32–33, 100, 118, 151–66, 237, 266, 267, 276, 326, 329, 341, 344, 421, 425, 447–48, 449–50, 451, 459–60, 461, 462, 486, 487

abortion counselling, 37–38, 45, 331, 334, 382, 386

abortion history, 64, 82, 83, 104–105, 120, 160, 222, 226, 229, 230–31, 234, 235, 240, 242, 243, 341, 359, 360–61, 380–81, 391, 413, 419–20, 421

abortion laws, 51, 189, 289–91, 293–94, 308, 321, 322, 327, 331–32, 333, 365, 384–85, 399, 402, 478, 479–80, 481, 484, 486

abortion providers, attitudes of, 35, 40–45, 253, 277, 287–89, 305, 308, 309, 322, 323, 326–27, 329, 332, 470, 482; need for female, 204, 207, 272

abortion rates, 70–74, 79, 80, 106, 121, 123, 129, 131, 191, 192, 200, 207, 228, 400, 415, 439–43, 449, 472

abortion ratios, 70–74, 121, 123, 192, 228, 259, 429–32

abortion risk, 36–37, 58–60, 62, 64, 65–66, 68, 71, 72, 74, 97, 124, 129, 146, 147, 180, 183, 329, 361, 415, 421–25, 445, 461, 472